Praise for the Fourth Edition of *The College Finder*

"Dr. Antonoff often refers to himself as a 'student of colleges.' No one spends more time exploring, analyzing, and investigating colleges, from academic challenges, to social expression, to engagement with faculty. His work with thousands of students and thousands of college counselors and independent consultants make him uniquely qualified to present the lists in this book. For any student exploring college possibilities, *The College Finder* is a required resource. Its lists are fun, informative, and addicting."
- *Mark Sklarow, CEO, Independent Educational Consultants Association*

"I have been advising students on the process of applying to college for over 30 years, and I depend on *The College Finder* as my go-to source, as it is consistently reliable and serves as a wealth of information on great colleges and universities across the country."
- *Sarah Soule, Educational Consultant*

"*The College Finder* is the bible for college counselors. In an age where fit is the most important criterion for finding the right school, Dr. Antonoff has created lists for every possible academic field, athletic life, and student experience for which we are always searching. This is a 'must' book to keep on your desk when creating the proper school lists for all of your advisees to research. We have waited nine long years for the updated version, and my colleagues and I are thrilled."
- *Warren Zucker, College and Guidance Counselor, Gulliver Preparatory, Miami, Florida*

"Imagine my excitement when I learned that a new edition of *The College Finder* would soon be available. As an independent educational consultant who specializes in helping students and families find, apply to, and pay for the right-fit college, it is essential that I have the most up-to-date college search resources. As we all know, researching colleges on the Internet can be akin to drinking from a fire hose. *The College Finder* provides expert guidance to help me select colleges that are a sound match along multiple dimensions for individual students. It will be wonderful to have the brand new fourth edition to replace the trusty, well-worn copy that sits on my desk."
- *Francine Schwartz, Independent Educational Consultant, Founder and President, Pathfinder Counseling, LLC*

"*The College Finder* is the rare college guide that offers information in a way that helps every student create a truly individualized college plan. Its approachable tone and thoughtful attention to detail make it one of the first books I use in working with students, and one of only a handful I recommend to students and parents."
- *Dr. Patrick O'Connor, Associate Dean, College Counseling, Cranbrook Kingswood School; Former President of NACAC; Board of Directors, The Common Application*

"I have been using *The College Finder* for over six years to support my college counseling work. I wish I had discovered Steven Antonoff's book years earlier! It has become my go-to resource in helping students find their best fit. The book is well organized and easy to use, providing insight into colleges and universities across the United States while focusing on a wide spectrum of student preferences."
- *Karen Ekman-Baur, Certified Educational Planner, Independent Educational Consultant, StudyHorizons*

"*The College Finder* is the most reliable and excellent source for helping students find the best colleges. It is extremely well researched and well thought out."
- *Martha Black, Independent College Admissions Advisor*

"Reliable data is indispensible in guiding students and their families to make best-fit college decisions. In my work as a certified educational planner, there is not a day in my professional practice that I do not pour over the pages of *The College Finder* and cross-reference its extremely relevant lists to leave no stone unturned for my clients. The categories are varied and relevant to this generation of applicants who are discerning a good match through the lens of numerous fit attributes. Dr. Antonoff homes in on pertinent topics, including engagement and affordability, aggregating the top picks of experts in the field. His post-prestige approach to the college search delves beyond ratings and rankings to help all college admission stakeholders to access accurate and balanced information."
- *Dr. Erin Avery, Certified Educational Planner, Founder, Avery Educational Resources*

"*The College Finder* is a staple for any college counselor or independent consultant. Steve has visited and researched schools all across the country, and his accurate lists will help counselors identify the best match for any student. I have used this book for many years and find it to be one of the most valuable resources available."
- *Matt Baker, Riley Baker Educational Consulting*

"*The College Finder* is my go-to book for either locating or confirming college possibilities for my students. The lists are comprehensive and accurate. I don't know how I ever lived without it! Thank you, Steve, for your ongoing commitment to helping educational consultants always be students of colleges."
- *Rachel Sobel, PhD, Certified Educational Planner, College Possibilities, LLC*

"At last, the fourth edition of *The College Finder* is here. College counselors and parents have come to rely on Steven Antonoff's knowledge and research to assist them in finding colleges that will be a fit for each student. This easy-to-use resource is my first go-to book, whether searching for the academics, athletics, or ambiance of a college. There is even a category devoted to college trivia. *The College Finder* should be a part of every college search."
- *Tina Heiman, Certified Educational Planner, College Choice*

"*The College Finder* has been my go-to resource for students since I became a counselor 12 years ago. The variety of well-researched lists are the perfect starting point for college search, and I especially like the lists about student life and campus vibe things that are super important but usually not on a student's radar."
- *Steven Kohuth, College Counselor, East High School, Denver, Colorado*

"Every counselor who is responsible for college counseling should have a copy of *The College Finder*. The book is a must in accomplishing research on colleges!"
- *Dr. Mark Fisher, Educational Consultant, Fisher Educational Consultants*

"I have served as an educational consultant for over twenty years and *The College Finder* continues to be the most useful and popular resource book that I share with my clients. I highly recommend it for all students who are college-bound and want practical information presented in a user-friendly fashion."
- *Kathie Carnahan, Certified Educational Planner, Carnahan Lyndrup, LLC*

The
College
Finder

Steven R. Antonoff, Ph.D.

WINTERGREEN
ORCHARD HOUSE

Wintergreen Orchard House
A Division of Carnegie Communications

A Wintergreen Orchard House Book
Published by Wintergreen Orchard House.

Wintergreen Orchard House is a division of Carnegie Communications.

www.WintergreenOrchardHouse.com

Library of Congress Cataloging-in-Publication Data
Antonoff, Steven R.
The College Finder / Steven R. Antonoff – Rev. ed.
Includes indexes.

ISBN 978-1-936035-90-8

Cover design by Erik Ledder
Illustrations by Matt Bradshaw

Manufactured in the United States

First Edition: September 1993
Revised Editions: April 1999, 2008, 2017
Reprints: 2009

Wintergreen Orchard House
2 LAN Drive, Suite 100, Westford, MA 01886
Tel: 978-692-9708, Fax: 978-692-2304
info@wintergreenorchardhouse.com
www.WintergreenOrchardHouse.com

To my great nieces and nephews: Josh, Jake, Lauren, Rebekah, Katie, Liz, Rachel, and Ben.

This book honors Gary, still my brother and my friend.

Table Of Contents

Acknowledgments

From its inception, *The College Finder* has been a collaborative effort, but never more so than in the current edition.

I am very grateful to my editor, Maripat Murphy. Maripat read lists with intensity and care. Her skill with the language and clarity of thought make the book more readable and more coherent.

The members of my robust research team dedicated themselves to ferreting out information, assembling lists, and checking facts. They also helped me decide how best to organize the book to make it as user-friendly and accessible as possible. They provided invaluable support and perspective. Ekaterina Olson Shipyatsky and Caroline Nellis helped me in countless consistent, constructive ways. Kevin Ramos-Aguilar, Ben Papadopoulos, Robert Schwartz, and Natalie L. Rhodes completed their assignments with determination and zeal. Ann Chambers assisted me with final editing, organization, and continuity. These pages also reflect the efforts of Jane Stephens and Maya Waldstreicher. Beyond sharing a list of favorite traditions and researching many others, Jay McCann, a Colorado-based college counselor, worked with me on the content and organization of the Experts' Choice lists.

My consulting and counseling colleagues were generous with their time and know-how. Thanks also go to the hundreds of public and private high school counselors and independent educational consultants who responded to my online surveys with their impressions of colleges in almost 125 categories. Survey results are reported in the Experts' Choice lists throughout this book.

Much of what I know about colleges comes from sharing with my consulting colleagues. I am lucky to have found the profession of independent educational consulting. I am even luckier to have been able to interact throughout my career with a wonderful group of men and women who are dedicated students of colleges. Over the years, these colleagues not only discussed colleges with me but also encouraged me to revise this book.

Students I taught through the University of California, Irvine Independent Educational Consultant Certificate Program wittingly (and unwittingly) provided leads and ideas.

I am beholden to the following colleagues who were kind enough to research lists related to their specialized knowledge: Mark Fisher, Rachel Sobel, Sandy Aprahamian, Sandy Furth, Jay McCann, and Jennifer Tabbush.

I am fortunate that Wintergreen Orchard House again published this edition of *The College Finder*. Stephanie Farah was my primary contact and chief motivator.

College counselors and independent educational consultants from almost every state were asked to name colleges in their home state that provide an outstanding education and should to be better known. The names of these colleges appear in the State-by-State Hidden Gems list in Chapter 7. These are the counselors who contributed:

Matthew Baker; Sandy Bercu, MA, CEP; Judith Berg, CEP; Laura J. Blanche; Lisa Bleich; Laurie R. Bosin; Laurie Brandow; Joan Bress, CEP; Joan C. Britt, CEP; Andrew Bryan; Lisa Buchwalter, CEP; Jennifer Buyens; Kathie Carnahan, CEP; Vita Frances Cohen, CEP, MA, MAT.; Kim R. Crockard; Mark Cruver; Glenda Durano, CEP; Jean Flowers; Mark Gathercole, CEP; Deb Davis Groves, CEP; Tracy Gruenig; Maite Halley; Susan Hanflik, MEd, CEP; Sean Hawes, CEP; Jane C. Hoffman, MBA, CEP; Debi

Hudson, CEP; Terry Hurley-Maciulexicz; Calvin T. Ishii, CEP; Amy Jasper; Bill Kellerman; Donna Kelly; Charlotte Klaar, CEP; and Katelyn Gleason Klapper, CEP.

In addition: Jane Klemmer, CEP; Diane Lomonaco, CEP; Janet Loren, CEP; Rosalyn Lowenhaupt, CEP; Wendie Lubic; Catherine Marrs, CEP; Steven Mercer, EdD; Dori Middlebrook, CEP; Kathryn Miller; Betsy Morgan, CEP; William Morse, CEP; Carolyn P. Mulligan, CEP; Terrie Shipley; Jane Shropshire, CEP; Rachel Sobel, CEP; Brian Swan; Jennifer Tabbush; Jon W. Tarrant, CEP; Joni Towles, CEP; and Perry Youngblood, CEP.

Finally, I'd like to thank my consulting students in Colorado and all the young people I've met through my workshops and presentations around the country. Through them, I learned how information on colleges and the admission process is filtered and interpreted by high school students. They reinforced my thinking that reliable data can result in a great college match.

Steven R. Antonoff, PhD
Certified Educational Planner
Denver, Colorado
February 2017
collegefinder@comcast.net

Introduction

Planning for college should be an interesting, thoughtful, and energizing voyage of discovery—a time to consider your life, your goals, and your dreams. But for too many students and their families, choosing a college is a journey into a confusing territory mined with unforeseen obstacles and studded with conflicting signposts. In creating *The College Finder,* I hoped to ease some of this stress and help make the college selection process a positive and productive experience for you and your family.

Why Is the College Admission Process So Stressful?

It can be difficult to find information that is both accurate and helpful. Some of the stress surrounding college admission stems from the flood of information available, much of it sensationalizing the difficulty of getting accepted to and paying for college. Everywhere you turn, you find more books, promotion by colleges, promotion by the higher education industry (companies that work to move colleges higher on search lists and companies that want parents to borrow money from them, to name just two), websites, college fairs, and more press coverage of higher education issues.

The numerous thick college guides offer too many details and too little subjective content, leaving readers unable to differentiate among colleges. In contrast, many narrative-type guidebooks, with their "up close and personal" reviews of individual schools, are fun to read but only provide three- or four-page glimpses into fewer than 10% of colleges. Cost guides can be helpful, but again, deal with only a single aspect of choosing a college.

The annual "best colleges" or "best value colleges" rankings published by various magazines and websites highlight the academic and economic sides of college but don't address the social aspects of campus life. And for most college-bound students, fitting in on campus has a high correlation with retention and happiness. Moreover, colleges can't be rated like vacuum cleaners or toothpaste. There are too many variables, and the interaction between student and college is too complex to make these kinds of rankings valid for most individuals.

"What's a FAFSA?!"

Another stressor is the jargon that students and their families must learn in order to maneuver through the college process. Some examples are listed here.

ED (Early Decision): A binding agreement to attend an institution if you are admitted.

EA (Early Action): Students submit an application early in the fall and are notified of acceptance earlier than other applicants.

FAFSA (Free Application for Federal Student Aid): The primary form students and parents submit to demonstrate financial need.

Pell Grants: A federal subsidy for students with limited financial resources.

Subject Tests: Part of the SAT suite of tests, these are one-hour exams in specific areas.

Honors, AP (Advanced Placement), and IB (International Baccalaureate): Differing "levels" of high school instruction.

A "reach" school: A college that is most selective in terms of admission for a particular student.

A "backup" college: A college that is less selective in terms of admission for a particular student.

Deferred admission: The college delays making a decision on an application until a later date, e.g., after accepted students accept or decline their spots or, in some cases, after additional materials are submitted.

Rolling admission: The applicant is notified of admission status as soon as all admission documents—transcript, test scores, application, etc.—have been reviewed.

Open admission: All students who apply are admitted.

Wait list: Students are put on hold and are admitted if/when a space becomes available.

Demonstrated need: The difference between the cost of attending a college and the expected family contribution.

Merit-based aid: Money awarded to a student on the basis of grade point average (GPA) and/or other signs of academic excellence, community involvement, etc.

Need-based aid: Money awarded to a student on the basis of the family's ability or inability to pay the cost of college.

The Perils of Prestige
Focusing on name and prestige is a sure way to increase the stress surrounding college selection and application. Students (and their parents) can sometimes feel success depends on admission to a particular college—for example, an Ivy League or their state's flags school. With friends, fellow students, and the media all contributing to the frenzy for a "name brand" school, it can seem like future happiness, life accomplishments, and financial stability all come down to a fat or thin envelope.

Such thinking simply doesn't reflect the state of higher education today. There are more than just a handful of great colleges; in fact, there are literally hundreds of colleges that offer a first-rate education and an incredible experience. Students who believe "If I don't get into College X or College Y, my life is over" are setting themselves up for anxiety, disappointment, and, worse, an enduring sense that they are not good enough. And what if they do secure that coveted admission only to discover it's not what they wanted after all?

On the other hand, students who focus on fit and match (and not merely on the *perception* of quality) will not only find many choices that are right for them but also experience far less stress during the college planning process and far more satisfaction with the school they ultimately attend.

Behind Closed Doors: The Mysteries of the Admission Process
Beyond the information gap and misplaced focus on prestige, stress is embedded in the admission process itself. Which of the major tests should be taken—the SAT or the ACT? How many, if any, Subject Tests are required? Another factor contributing to confusion is the range of college applications available. Some colleges subscribe to the Common Application. Some schools are part of the Coalition for Access, Affordability, and Success, while others ask for a different application, such as the Common Black College Application. Some colleges use several of these applications, whereas others may require their own individual application.

Students and their parents also stress as they try to decipher what colleges want and what happens once the applications are submitted. A rite of passage that was once fairly straightforward and transparent has evolved into a process that is cloaked in secrecy and

Steven R. Antonoff

characterized by seemingly capricious, inexplicable results. College admission officers often seem to be sending mixed messages. They advise the applicant to take the most advanced classes, achieve the highest scores, pursue individual passions, demonstrate strong commitment to activities—and then they reject the student. Why? Part of the reason, especially at the most competitive colleges, is that there are simply too many applicants and a limited number of slots. Another part of the reason is that admission officers strive to achieve the holistic goal of "balancing the class." In other words, they blend academic, personal, and demographic variables to create an incoming class of diverse individuals who as a group meet the needs and character of the institution.

Paying for College

Perhaps the biggest stressor in college admission for most families is their confusion or even paralysis surrounding the question of how to pay for college. With tuition skyrocketing, it is tempting to strike viable college options off the list even before financial aid possibilities have been fully explored. Many students end up choosing schools to apply to on the basis of financial aid expectations, only to realize after they are accepted and receive their financial aid package that the college is out of their price range. In order to plan effectively for the costs of college, it is imperative that families sort through layers of need- and merit-based awards, even though these are often difficult to penetrate and always impossible to predict.

Fact vs. Fiction in the College Admission Process

While the stress associated with the college admission process is real and can't be entirely eliminated, it can be drastically reduced. The first step is to shoot down some of the college search myths, misperceptions, outdated opinions, and outright lies that ultimately hinder a full exploration of a student's options.

Myth: The only college worth attending is an Ivy League, top 10, or upper-tier school. I addressed this earlier, but it bears repeating: A name-brand education is not right for everyone not even every outstanding, high-achieving student. Although American higher education has only grown stronger in the past 30 years, the perception of quality hasn't kept pace with the reality. Colleges today enroll better-prepared and brighter students, and faculty quality, in both teaching and research, has taken great strides. Rather than just a handful of "good" colleges, there are 100—even 200—top-tier colleges in the United States, as well as hundreds more that provide extraordinary opportunities for their students. *The College Finder* lists numerous colleges that experts consider comparable in quality to better-known schools.

Myth: A degree From a "name" college is key to getting ahead in life. Collateral to the myth of the name-brand school is the fallacy that lifelong success correlates with the university seal on the diploma. In reality, employers want the best person they can find, and graduate schools want candidates who have demonstrated they can do the work and contribute to their department. A strong grade point average, good recommendations, commitment to campus life and community responsibility, and use of summers to build a résumé are the most important indicators of success after college.

Myth: Only a stellar student can get into a good college. In truth, gaining admittance to a terrific school does not require straight A's or even all B's. True, some 100 schools accept less than 40% of their applicants, but the vast majority of the more than 4,700 colleges and universities in the United States accept well over 70% of those who apply. The B student with average ACT or SAT scores can be admitted to literally thousands of schools (and good ones, too). In short, anyone motivated to attend college has choices.

Myth: Only the rich can afford college. College tuition in the 21st century is by no means cheap, but families don't need the wealth of Bill Gates to afford the cost of college.

Too often, parents believe that, because of cost, their student has no option but the local state school. This is not always true. Many schools provide a high-quality academic experience at a *relatively* reasonable price, and there are numerous types of financial aid available. Even at expensive private colleges, students rarely pay the full "sticker price" (the amount of tuition and room and board listed by the college). A related myth claims that only a handful of colleges in the country are worth the price. Given the quality of higher education in the United States today and the quality of resources, faculty, and facilities at many colleges and universities, numerous schools represent a worthwhile investment in a student's future.

Myth: To make an informed college choice, I need to know what I want to study. Career planning is important, and students should use their high school years to learn about career paths. Excellent free online resources are available to help young people discover unfamiliar job positions and potential vocational choices. High school students who have a fairly clear idea of their career path (and their college major) tend to be interested in specialized areas such as business, accounting, engineering, or nursing. But those who haven't decided on a career and either make a tentative decision as to a college major or remain undecided for a semester or two are not at a disadvantage at the end of their college years, provided they take classes in several fields, take full advantage of their college's career counseling office, seek advice from faculty and other adults, and use summers to gain experience.

Myth: The best colleges are the most selective ones. Selectivity doesn't always translate to higher quality; selectivity is driven by an array of factors, including perceived popularity, location, athletic success, and even the college's marketing budget. Moreover, "best" is a subjective term; in the end, the "best" schools are those that best match the needs and interests of the individual student.

There are more than 4,700 colleges and universities in the US alone, and even colleges with comparable reputations are neither equal nor identical. Besides the obvious differences in size, academic offerings, and location, each school has a unique ethic, culture, and feel—which can either stimulate a young person's growth or inhibit it, depending on the individual. Colleges differ in terms of their admission requirements, academic intensity, conventional versus alternative approaches to education, focus on careers, study abroad opportunities, cost and aid availability, character of the student body (from deeply academic to fun-loving, religious to outdoorsy, and homogeneous to diverse), campus safety, residence hall life, athletic strength (for both participant and spectator), and overall quality. These are just some of the topics covered in *The College Finder*.

What Makes The College Finder Different?

The College Finder evolved from my experiences with students and their parents and was created in response to their questions and concerns as they wrestled with college choices. Early in my career, first as dean of students at a private university and later as dean of admission and financial aid, I saw first-hand how admission offices operate, and I learned how families grapple with college costs. Eventually I left my administrative post to work as an independent educational consultant specializing in advising students during their college planning process. Since then, I have worked with more than 5,000 students. Some of my clients are top students; many are not. Some can afford any college; most cannot. Some attend public high schools; others are enrolled in private schools. Some will be first-generation college students; others have college-educated parents. Some will be entering college for the first time; others are transfers. Whatever their background, these students share the belief that taking the extra time to thoroughly explore their college options is worth it.

Steven R. Antonoff

In my work, I've listened as young people struggle to understand the distinctions among colleges. I am bothered by the high percentage of undergraduate students who transfer from one four-year college to another, not because they failed to research colleges but because they neglected to *identify* and then focus on the information that mattered most to them. Often in my travels, students tell me they have no idea why they chose their college! Clearly, there is a critical need to expose students to all the college options that suit their individual desires, interests, and personality. With *The College Finder,* I hope to fill that need.

Why Lists?

The College Finder has its roots in lists that I began compiling for my own reference and as an aid for my clients. The list format provides a straightforward way to group colleges by almost any characteristic. Chapter 2, for example, identifies hundreds of schools that rank highly in terms of various definitions of academic excellence. However, there is no single list of the "best" colleges academically because different features or aspects of academic quality will be better for some students than for others.

For some students, *The College Finder* may represent the first time in their college search that they are able to look at a range of colleges that send graduates on to medical school or have unusually accessible faculty or are surprisingly affordable. Armed with this information and their own self-knowledge, they can both widen their college search to include schools they might otherwise never have considered and focus their college search to encompass their individual interests, the social scene they are looking for, and the new ideas and unexpected activities they crave.

The primary goal of *The College Finder* is to expand the pool of schools that students consider, extend the possibilities they envision, and magnify their sense of power as they research colleges. No one factor—not overall prestige, academic program of interest, prowess of athletic teams, nor social environment—is all-important; college choice is best done when numerous aspects are considered. The unique format of this book should provide many ways to cross-reference and analyze multiple issues. If *The College Finder* helps a student identify even one new college for consideration, then it will have fulfilled its purpose.

But just as colleges are not perfect, neither are college-planning guidebooks—including this one. The lists found here are neither all-inclusive nor exhaustive. For example, students who are "lovers of ideas" can be found in the student body at most colleges, not just the ones included on the "lover of ideas" Experts' Choice list. By the same token, there are hundreds of colleges with strength in history or mathematics in addition to the ones listed here.

Many lists were compiled from objective data, such as longest football winning streak, college enrollment, and populations of college towns. Other lists, however, are more subjective, such as Colleges That Students Rave About or lists whose titles include such terms as "excellent," "highly ranked," "innovative," "strength in," "unique," "affordable," and "fun-loving." The schools on these lists should be considered excellent, highly ranked, or innovative in comparison with numerous other institutions that share these traits but to a lesser degree. Lists based on subjective data reflect my research and the other list-building strategies described in the next section.

Where do the Lists Come From?

As I compiled more and more lists over the years, I conducted additional research and began soliciting colleagues in higher education for their opinions. The lists continued to multiply and their range of content mushroomed. Data were confirmed or disproved; outdated information was jettisoned. Eventually these lists were compiled in the first edition of *The College Finder* published in 1993, followed by a second edition in 1999, a third edition in 2008, and now the fourth edition that you hold in your hands.

This new edition of *The College Finder* includes nearly 700 lists reflecting five primary sources.

1. Lists based on my experience, knowledge, and research (and that of *The College Finder* team). The names of the colleges on these lists were compiled using the following data collection techniques:

- **Personal visits to colleges.** Spending several weeks each year visiting colleges gives me an opportunity to compare and contrast. Over time, I have honed the questions I ask of students, faculty members, and administrators.
- **Personal research.** As a student of colleges, I'm always on the lookout for facts, interesting tidbits, and potential schools to explore. Media, both electronic and print, provide ideas. I follow up on credible leads and search my college counseling files for useful data. For example, information on admission selectivity reflects the actual decisions made by the colleges, not claims made by the schools.
- **Research conducted by others specifically for this book.** *The College Finder* team consists of a half-dozen individuals who worked with me for more than a year to develop and research many of the lists in this book. They tracked down information to create new lists, such as colleges in or near major US and Canadian cities, colleges for undocumented students, colleges with comprehensive course requirements, colleges with respected art museums, colleges with the largest libraries, colleges with golf courses, colleges offering a bachelor's degree in architecture, those with good e-business programs, and those with innovative academic programs. They also fact-checked lists to verify that colleges offered the major or the sport indicated.
- **Professional interaction.** I discuss my college impressions with colleagues and seek out their perceptions. I ask college personnel for additions, updates, and suggestions. For the academic section, faculty members and heads of departments often provided their assessment of the best programs in their field. The athletics section reflects input from coaches, sports information directors, and representatives of national sports organizations.
- **Discussion with my consulting students.** In more than three decades as a college consultant, I've worked with thousands of students who shared their perspectives as college applicants and, more significantly, their experiences as students. At the end of my students' freshman year, I send a survey asking for their perceptions of the academic and social aspects of their college. I repeat this polling after each academic year. The result is a vast, invaluable collection of opinions and insights that inform some of these lists.
- **Interaction with my graduate students.** Through the University of California, Irvine, Division of Continuing Education independent educational consulting program, I have taught hundreds of professional college counselors. As with my consulting clientele, these individuals generously shared their experiences of both their colleges and the students with whom they have worked.

2. Lists from associations, organizations, publications, websites, and others. I'm indebted to the many organizations/websites/groups whose findings—commonly posted on the web for all to see—are compiled here as a way to construct and deconstruct the landscape of higher education. This edition includes lists from such wide-ranging sources as the Association of Independent Colleges of Art and Design, Educate to Career (educatetocareer.com), the Association of Recovery in Higher Education, *Community College Week* magazine, *Hispanic Outlook in Higher Education* magazine, I'm First (supported by the Center for Student Opportunity), *Journal of Blacks in Higher Education*, the National Association of Schools of Dance, and the Society of American Foresters. Significantly, Wintergreen-Orchard House made its extensive database available to me.

3. Lists formed by tallying opinions of experts. These lists reflect the results of a survey of college admission professionals conducted in the fall and winter of 2015. An online survey was distributed to more than 200 counselors, most of them members of three counselor organizations: the National Association for College Admission Counseling, the Independent Educational Consultants Association, and the Higher Education Consultants Association. About 60% of survey respondents were independent educational consultants (private or independent college counselors), and the remaining respondents were counselors working in high schools, both private and public. Survey participants represented almost every state. In total, 145 questions were asked in five separate survey forms. Typical questions included: "Which colleges would you recommend for the lover of ideas?" "What colleges come to mind for the budding entrepreneur?" "Which colleges are great for a flip-flop wearer?" "Which are the best colleges for an undergraduate education?" The responses were used to create approximately 100 lists.

I believe that these Experts' Choice lists are among the more interesting and valid of the lists selected for inclusion in this fourth edition. After all, these are the people who know colleges best. The typical counselor responding to the survey has more than five years of experience helping students learn about colleges. As far as I am aware, *The College Finder* is the only guidebook with such a systematic, comprehensive polling of admission scholars.

4. Lists from invited counselors in each state. To create a subset of the general Experts' Choice lists, I invited 100 counselors nationwide—both independent educational consultants and school-based counselors—to participate in a special survey. In this survey, respondents were asked to list and describe schools in their state that offered great quality but may have been overlooked by students looking for colleges. The participating counselors responded with reviews, raves, and reports, now compiled in the section State-by-State Hidden Gems. Whether you are considering in-state or out-of-state colleges, you will likely find interesting possibilities in this section.

5. Lists from specialists in specific areas of college planning. I asked a small group of counselors to share their perspective about such topics as colleges with "direct entry" nursing programs, schools that are "autism friendly," colleges with kosher meal pans, great choices for students interested in advertising and public relations, and notable gap year programs.

A Final Caveat

As often as lists have been checked and rechecked, *The College Finder* will always be a work in progress. Higher education is inherently changeable, and researching the lists in this book was much like shooting at a moving target. Colleges regularly institute or eliminate majors and programs, revise admission requirements, open new facilities, change fees, become "hot" or "uncool" in the eyes of students, create or cut scholarship programs, add or drop athletic teams, or change directions in countless other ways. Indeed, the lists of "strong" colleges in both the academic and athletic areas are particularly vulnerable to change. Readers should be mindful of these developments and check directly with the school for the most current information.

What's in the New Edition?

The fourth edition of *The College Finder* is the most carefully researched and features a wider scope of lists that should appeal to more types of students. Although some of the topics are the same as in earlier editions, almost every list has been rewritten. Many new lists mirror the changes taking place on college campuses as well as the trends and issues I hear students and parents talk about as they seek to find a good match college.

Some groupings of colleges received more attention this time around. For example, this edition features more lists pertaining to college cost and financial aid. These lists are included not only because college costs have continued to rise, but also because colleges have made significant progress in helping students and families afford college. Several lists focus on community colleges, reflecting the many students who opt for a two-year education. Because of the increasing interest in globalization, there are also more lists of international colleges and study abroad programs.

This fourth edition also features more fields of study (more engineering lists, for example) and more vocational majors such as cabinet making, boat building, and cartooning. New lists also capture student interests, priorities, and personality traits. Chapter 1, for example, has lists for students who see themselves as fashion-forward, procrastinator, or indifferent to sports.

A revised organization sorts these hundreds of lists into ten primary topics: your identity and personality, the academic experience, campus athletics, campus location, campus enrollment and student life, finances and costs, expert opinions, admission, tidbits and trivia, and general resources for the college-planning process.

Chapter 1 focuses on who you are because the baseline of your college search should be you. At which colleges will your personality and interests have the most opportunity to grow and develop? The chapter begins with lists based on identity—everything from ethnicity/race, gender, and faith/religion to learning style and personality. Even categories that don't apply to you may be of interest. For example, the lists of schools with a high percentage of black students may be helpful in looking for a campus with a diverse student body. Everyone learns differently, and the lists of colleges with learning disability programs can be useful to a range of learners. A particularly interesting section is labeled "Personality/Interests/Priorities." Here you'll find a list of "Colleges for the Bookworm," "Hippy Colleges," "Colleges for the Flip-Flop Wearer," and "Colleges for the Socially Conservative."

Chapter 2 hones in on qualities defining the kind of academic experience you want in college. If you have your heart set on a particular major, this is the place to look. In addition to highlighting colleges with strength in an individual field, however, this chapter will help you understand different aspects that make up academic life on college campuses, such as research opportunities, green schools, and colleges where lots of student go off to the Peace Core. In addition, this chapter examines relationships with other colleges and universities, career preparation, community colleges, and different academic calendars. Some colleges give students free rein in choosing classes, and the list of colleges with no core requirements directs you to those schools. Colleges with a strong emphasis on internationalism and study abroad and schools that are particularly helpful in advising students on career options can also be found in this chapter. Other lists include "Colleges That Help Students Find Careers," "Honors Colleges at Public Universities," and "Colleges Offering a Cybersecurity Major."

Chapter 3 is about student life on campus and includes issues such as how enrollment and student activities may color your college experience. Participation in campus culture

Steven R. Antonoff

contributes to student satisfaction, so learning about places with dynamic debate teams or indie radio stations or intense sorority and fraternity life can be illuminating. Do you want to be surrounded by a lot of people all the time? Would you prefer to have fewer fellow students and smaller, more discussion-based classes? Lists of schools in or near more than 60 cities in the U.S. and Canada should prove helpful in myriad ways, including planning campus visits. How does weather affect your outlook? Would you be comfortable in a city that gets eight feet of snow per year or are you ready to bask in the sun? College facilities—libraries, dorms, workout areas, golf courses, rock-climbing walls—vary considerably; what's most important to you? Do you need a bike-friendly city that you can maneuver easily? What about a college with a great art museum? This chapter also includes information on campus safety and residence hall quality. Lists in this chapter include "Colleges in or Near Chicago," "Most Beautiful College Campuses," and "Cities with Clear Days."

Chapter 4 is your A-to-Z glimpse into college athletics. Aside from lists of top NCAA Division I schools, this is the place to look if you'd like to continue playing a sport you played in high school or pick up a new, perhaps uncommon, physical activity ("Quidditch, anyone?"). Maybe you want to spend your college years where lots of students are varsity athletes or intramural sports are popular. Lists include "Colleges With Badminton Clubs," "Colleges With Strength in Squash," and "Colleges That Are Members of Major Athletic Conferences."

Chapter 5 tackles cost considerations, a thorny topic for most college planners. The more than 50 lists in this chapter may make you think twice about eliminating a college merely because of its sticker price. Why? Because many colleges meet family financial need. Some colleges offer merit scholarships to students regardless of family income. In this chapter, you will find "States Offering Tuition Discounts to Students in Neighboring States," "Colleges Awarding Generous Merit Aid," "Colleges With No Tuition," and "Colleges Worth Every Penny."

Chapter 6 addresses selectivity and how to navigate colleges and universities by their admissions standards. Trying to figure out which the schools likely to accept you can be stressful, whether you are an ace test-taker or your class rank bumps around in the middle of the pack. This chapter is meant to help ease your anxiety about admission. Lists include "Colleges That Do Not Consider Standardized Test Scores," "Colleges That Accept Many Students Through Early Decision," "Drool Schools," and "Super colleges for the Poor Test-Taker." Information on gap year programs is also included, in case you opt for an entirely different learning experience prior to attending college.

While Experts' Choice lists can be found throughout The College Finder, Chapter 7 compiles the most significant of these lists. Particularly noteworthy is "State-by-State Hidden Gems," a list of college counselors' pick of the schools they feel offer a superior undergraduate education and vibrant social scene but are not particularly well-known. Other lists include "Colleges That Change Lives," "Colleges That Are Overrated," and "Colleges With the Best Undergraduate Education."

Chapter 8 highlights tidbits and trivia about colleges and universities, from their famous alumni to their quirkiest traditions. Here's where you'll discover that Lin-Manuel Miranda ("Hamilton") graduated from Wesleyan U (CT), Caitlin Jenner attended Graceland U (IA), and students Arizona State U in Tempe celebrate the end of classes with a Bra and Boxers Run. Other lists in this chapter cover college nicknames, schools with interesting mascots, and "Campuses Where Movies Were Filmed."

Chapter 9, recognizing that The College Finder serves as a starting place for college planning, names the best resources to help you continue to learn about schools. This chapter includes such lists as "Best Subjective Guidebooks" and "Best General Planning Websites" that will help you uncover more information about the colleges that pique your interest.

Student Guide To Using The College Finder

Responsible college planning begins by taking a good look at yourself: your aspirations, motivations, goals, friends, curiosity, and independence. In addition to an education, what do you hope to get out of college? Are you a self-starter or do you sometimes need a push to get going? Do you make friends easily or do you hang back in social settings? A self-analysis that goes beyond academic aspirations will place your college planning in an individual context and help you define what is most important to you and what you want in a college. Readers may find the Self-Survey in *College Match* (available free on my website, schoolbuff.com) helpful in clarifying college-going goals and preferences.

Above all else, *The College Finder* is a book of ideas to jumpstart your thinking. The lists in this book offer several hundred ways that colleges can be sorted and viewed. Before you begin, two features of the book deserve your attention: the Table of Contents and the List Index.

The Table of Contents is organized by topics that students often consider in their college selection. As you scan the chapter heads and section titles, think about those factors, issues, and needs that are most important to you. The more specific you are, the more direct your search will be. If you know you want to study engineering, for example, look at several engineering lists (including specific areas such as chemical and mechanical engineering) in the Academics chapter (under fields/subjects to study). On the other hand, if you have an interest in engineering but want to ensure that your education includes a good dose of liberal arts, the list "Great Engineering and Liberal Arts" deserves a look. And if you have no clue about what you want to study, the same section provides lists related to an undecided major.

The List Index can direct you to every topic covered in *The College Finder*. If you know the specific qualities you are seeking in a college, then the List Index will point you to appropriate lists. As you read through a section or examine the listings, you may think of additional college-planning factors or topics that concern you. You can review by specific topic (e.g., cost, athletics, international opportunities, career preparation) or by your particular interests (e.g., kosher kitchen, winning sports teams, conservative student body).

Now take a look at how three "typical" students—Abby, Bianca, and Josh—use *The College Finder* effectively in their college planning.

Abby starts by identifying her likes and dislikes, goals and aspirations, past experiences and future hopes. Her realizations include that she has had to work hard in high school for her B+ average, she gets homesick easily, and she really enjoys participating in class discussions. How do these conclusions factor into her college search?

- Abby hopes to be challenged in college but she also needs and wants time for extracurriculars. Aware that a high-pressure college is probably not right for her, she searches *The College Finder* for schools that have a balance of academics and social life.
- Abby's predisposition to homesickness prompts her to look at in-state options and colleges within driving distance or a short flight away from home. She searches the lists of colleges in and around nearby cities and the "State-by-State Hidden Gems" list for leads on great colleges in states bordering hers.
- Abby's desire to participate in class discussions prompts her to consider smaller colleges or schools that offer smaller classes, leading her to lists such as "Colleges With the Smallest Student–Faculty Ratios" and "The Experts' Choice: Large Universities, Small Feel." She also reviews the lists of colleges known for having teachers who are especially accessible to students.

To these factors, Abby adds others that reflect her specific resources and interests. Because she's considering several career paths, she'd like to have a solid liberal arts and sciences education so she checks for appropriate colleges in the fields of study/subjects to study lists. Although her parents can afford to pay for college, Abby realizes that with two younger siblings, it makes sense to look at colleges that offer merit scholarships (i.e., awards that are not based on financial need but are given to those who have high grades, an excellent record of leadership, or extensive community service). She finds these colleges listed in Chapter 6.

Bianca has clear ideas about what she wants and doesn't want. She's looking for a change after four years of typical high school classes, but she also values the familiar.

- Bianca craves some hands-on learning so she turns to the Career Preparation section (Chapter 2) and the lists of schools with cooperative education programs that combine academic work and job opportunities.
- Bianca prefers either a Catholic college or one that has many Catholic students so she browses the faith/religion section in Chapter 1. At the same time, she wants a school with racial and ethnic diversity, so she also scans lists of schools with diverse student bodies in Chapter 1 (in the ethnicity/race/nationality section) and also looks at the internationalism/study abroad section of Chapter 2. She notes which ones overlap with Catholic colleges.

Bianca then adds other factors to the mix. She takes a hard look at her transcript and searches for schools that fit her admission credentials. Using leads and realizations generated by *The College Finder*, Bianca follows up on colleges that could be possible matches. She reads more, talks to advisors, and reviews printed and online materials to narrow the list of colleges she'll apply to.

While Abby and Bianca know—at least to some extent—what they want in a college, Josh doesn't. He isn't sure what factors are important in his college search, so his approach to using *The College Finder* is different.

- First, Josh reads the list titles and looks at how the book is organized. This helps him identify some qualities he wants in a school and the factors that would make his college experience a success. The fields of study/subjects to study section in Chapter 2 opens his eyes to the many fields available and some intriguing areas he hadn't considered. He decides to learn more about archaeology and combining music and business.
- In Chapter 2, Josh finds colleges with unique calendars, innovative learning environments, and unusual majors. Browsing through this chapter piques his interest in colleges committed to the environment. Until *The College Finder*, Josh never realized that schools differed in so many ways. He discovers that big universities can seem smaller through participation in an honors college. He's interested in study abroad and in the internationalism/study abroad section, notes those colleges where a high percentage of students participate in an international experience. In Chapter 1, he carefully studies the list of schools for the bookworm.

For Josh, *The College Finder* is a guidance tool that prompts him to first identify and then focus on what matters most to him in his college search. Armed with this information, he can zero in on specific lists and then single out schools that best fit his needs.

How will you use *The College Finder*? If you are like most students, you'll try to combine the factors that matter to you with a list of appropriate colleges. You might merge a great business program with a reasonable price or a conservative student body with strength in journalism and hidden gems in New York State.

However, because the "perfect" college doesn't exist, college planning often involves trade-offs. *The College Finder* can help you sort out what is essential to you and prioritize your needs and wants. Is class size more important than being a spectator at football games? If you can't have both small classes and a popular, successful football team to cheer for each Saturday, which will you choose? You may be able to find both, but if you can't, then *The College Finder* may lead you to smaller colleges devoted to their sports teams.

Here's another example of trade-offs. What are you willing to give up to find a college that is less expensive? You want to go to a large college, but you realize you need financial aid to make college affordable. Under such circumstances, would you go to a small college if it provided a great deal of financial aid? Or if your preference is to stay in state, would you go out of state if you found a college that was a better match and wasn't much more expensive?

What if you come to *The College Finder* with a tentative list of colleges already in mind? You can use *The College Finder* to confirm a choice or cross it off the list. Search the College Index to locate schools on your draft list and then flip to any lists on which these colleges appear. Is your dream school less diverse than you expected? Do you have your heart set on international study only to discover that very few students at your first-choice college leave campus for a semester abroad? With *The College Finder*, you can uncover a wide range of characteristics about different schools. In addition to obtaining new information about the colleges on your list, you can use the indexes to help verify claims made by a particular school. Perhaps *The College Finder* will confirm for you that you've made good choices. Or maybe it will encourage you to look further and point you in new directions.

A final word. To end this user's guide, let me offer some specific recommendations to help you get the most out of *The College Finder*.

- Don't be too quick to dismiss a section as insignificant, even if it does not immediately appeal to you. For instance, religion may not be a particularly salient issue in your college search, but the fact is that a religious college has a particular "feel" that may or may not be significant. Similarly, you may not want to play a sport, but you may want to attend a school where you can cheer on a winning team.
- Pay particular attention to Chapter 1. The atmosphere of a college and the types of students who attend are essential considerations. What are the kids like at your ideal college? Are they scholars? Fun-loving? Diverse? Spirited? Activist? Some combination of these?
- Consider the college's focus on undergraduate education. Some schools—often liberal arts and sciences colleges—are devoted to the first four years. Other colleges cater to graduate or professional students. But most colleges have a mix of undergraduate and graduate students. The percentage of graduate students to undergraduates and the priority placed on undergraduate teaching can be a factor to consider in finding the right school for you. You will find these lists in Chapter 3 (enrollment section).
- Keep in mind that there are many ways to measure the academic quality and the social characteristics of a college. Only by looking carefully at the schools included on a wide range of lists in this book will you be able to determine the colleges that are best for you.
- Simply browsing through the book may open your eyes (and mind) to colleges you hadn't considered. You may discover schools where you take only one course at a time in Chapter 2 or an unfamiliar college that students rave about in Chapter 7 or intriguing collegiate traditions in Chapter 8. This information increases your understanding of the opportunities available to you.

- *The College Finder* is best used in combination with other college reference materials. Consider this book a source of options, and then follow up with websites and books for complete information about particular schools. Because specific facts about a college may change over time, you will want to check with the college website or the admissions office to determine degrees offered, recently added majors, tuition costs, and other up-to-the-minute details.
- *The College Finder* is a great place to start your college search, but don't forget to seek out other resources and people to round out the facts you need to make an informed choice. You may want to discuss your college selection and ideas from *The College Finder* with your college counselor, parents, and other knowledgeable advisors. These people can help you zero in on those colleges that will have the highest likelihood of meeting your academic and social needs.

As with any worthwhile endeavor, it takes time, commitment, and effort to find a college that fits the person you are and the person you hope to be. You will need to ask yourself hard questions, and you may have to give up long-held dreams to embrace new ones. But the result will be worth it, when you find yourself at a good-fit college—enthusiastic about learning, excited about relating to your new peers, professors, and environments, and reaching your true potential intellectually, socially, and emotionally.

Steven R. Antonoff

Chapter One
About Me

PERSONALITY/INTERESTS/PRIORITIES

The Experts' Choice: Colleges Where Life Is Balanced

Experts were asked to name colleges for the student who wants a balance of academics and social life.

Bates C (ME)
Boston C (MA)
Boston U (MA)
Bowdoin C (ME)
Bucknell U (PA)
Carleton C (MN)
Chicago State U (IL)
Clemson U (SC)
Colby C (ME)
Colgate U (NY)
Colorado C
Connecticut C
Dartmouth C (NH)
Davidson C (NC)
Denison U (OH)
Duke U (NC)
Emory U (GA)
Florida Southern C
Furman U (SC)
Georgetown U (DC)
Gettysburg C (PA)
Indiana U, Bloomington
James Madison U (VA)
Lehigh U (PA)
Loyola U (MD)
Miami U (OH)
Miami, U of (FL)
Michigan, U of, Ann Arbor

Middlebury C (VT)
New York U
North Carolina, U of, Chapel Hill
Northwestern U (IL)
Oklahoma State U
Pennsylvania State U
Pittsburgh, U of (PA)
Portland, U of (OR)
Puget Sound, U of (WA)
Rochester, U of (NY)
Santa Clara U (CA)
Southern California, U of
Southern Methodist U (TX)
St. Lawrence U (NY)
Stanford U (CA)
Syracuse U (NY)
Texas Christian U
Tufts U (MA)
Tulane (LA)
Union C (NY)
Vanderbilt U (TN)*
Villanova U (PA)
Virginia, U of
Wake Forest U (NC)
Washington U (MO)
Wisconsin, U of, Madison
Wooster, C of (OH)
* The Top Choice

The Experts' Choice: Colleges With a Sense of Community

Experts were asked for colleges with a strong sense of community, with "community" defined here as a sense of "we-ness." At these colleges, the focus is on campus life and particularly strong connections among students.

Austin Community C (TX)
Colorado C
Colorado, U of, Boulder
Creighton U (NE)
Dickinson C (PA)
Ft. Lewis C (CO)
Hastings C (NE)
Howard Payne U (TX)

Iowa State U
Juniata C (PA)
Nebraska, U of, Kearney
Nebraska, U of, Lincoln
St. Mary's C (CA)
Tarleton State U (TX)
Taylor U (IN)
William & Mary, C of (VA)

The Experts' Choice: Colleges That Are Especially Welcoming to Freshmen

Experts were asked to name schools that stand out in the way they welcome freshmen and integrate them into the college community.

Azusa Pacific U (CA)
California State U, San Diego
California, U of, Los Angeles
Chicago, U of (IL)
Colby C (ME)
Colorado C
Colorado State U, Ft. Collins
Dartmouth C (NH)
Davidson C (NC)
DePauw U (IN)
Duke U (NC)
Eckerd C (FL)
Elon U (NC)
High Point U (NC)
Indiana U, Bloomington
Johns Hopkins U (MD)
Kenyon C (OH)
Mercer U (GA)
Middlebury C (VT)
Missouri State U
Muhlenberg C (PA)

Notre Dame, U of (IN)
Ohio Wesleyan U
Pomona C (CA)
Puget Sound, U of (WA)*
Rensselaer Polytechnic Institute (NY)
Rice U (TX)
Stanford U (CA)
Syracuse U (NY)
Texas A&M U
Texas Christian U
Tufts U (MA)
Tulane U (LA)
Union C (NY)
Vanderbilt U (TN)
Villanova U (PA)
Washington U (MO)
Washington, U of, Seattle
Wellesley C (MA)
Wisconsin, U of, Madison
Whitman C (WA)
* The Top Choice

The Experts' Choice: Colleges for the Leader (or Soon-to-Be Leader)

Experts were asked to list colleges particularly suitable for a student leader.

Agnes Scott C (GA)
Alabama, U of, Tuscaloosa
American U (DC)
Arizona State U
Boston C (MA)
Bowdoin C (ME)
Bucknell U (PA)
Carleton C (MN)
Claremont McKenna C (CA)
Colgate U (NY)
Cornell U (NY)
Dartmouth C (NH)
Davidson C (NC)
Dickinson C (PA)
Duke U (NC)
Elon U (NC)
Emory U/Oxford C (GA)
Franklin & Marshall C (PA)
George Washington U (DC)
Georgetown U (DC)

Hamilton C (NY)
Harvard U (MA)
Haverford C (PA)
Lehigh U (PA)
Macalester C (MN)
Massachusetts, U of, Amherst
Norte Dame, U of (IN)
North Carolina, U of, Chapel Hill
Northwestern U (IL)
Oberlin C (OH)
Pennsylvania, U of
Pomona C (CA)
Princeton U (NJ)
Rhodes C (TN)
Richmond, U of (VA)
Stanford U (CA)
Syracuse U (NY)
Tulane U (LA)
Wellesley C (MA)
Wofford C (SC)

Steven R. Antonoff

The Experts' Choice: Tolerant Colleges

Experts were asked to identify colleges that are tolerant and accepting of differing student perspectives.

Bard C (NY)
Bates C (ME)
Beloit C (WI)
Boston U (MA)
Brown U (RI)
Bryn Mawr C (PA)
California State U, San Francisco
California, U of, Berkeley
California, U of, Los Angeles
Carleton C (MN)
Chicago, U of (IL)
Clark U (MA)
Colorado C
Columbia U (NY)
Earlham U (IN)
Evergreen State C (WA)
Goucher C (MD)
Grinnell C (IA)
Guilford C (NC)****
Hampshire C (MA)
Haverford C (PA)
Hendrix C (AR)
Kenyon C (OH)

Lewis & Clark C (OR)
Macalester C (MN)
Mt. Holyoke C (MA)
New C (FL)
New York U
Oberlin C (OH)*
Pitzer C (CA)
Reed C (OR)***
San Francisco, U of (CA)
Sarah Lawrence C (NY)
Skidmore C (NY)
Smith C (MA)
St. John's C (NM)
Swarthmore C (PA)
Tufts U (MA)
Vassar C (NY)
Warren Wilson C (NC)
Wesleyan U (CT)**

* The Top Choice
** The Second Choice
*** The Third Choice
**** The Fourth Choice

The Experts' Choice: Colleges Where Morals and Values Are Emphasized

Experts were asked to look beyond the traditional Christian and Bible colleges to consider other colleges that promote moral values.

Top Choices

Brandeis U (MA)
Davidson C (NC)**
Furman U (SC)
Haverford C (PA)*
Hope C (MI)
Notre Dame, U of (IN)
Pepperdine U (CA)
Santa Clara U (CA)
St. Olaf C (MN)
Swarthmore C (PA)
Villanova U (PA)
Whitman U (WA)

Second Choices

Bates C (ME)

Boston C (MA)
Bowdoin C (ME)
Brigham Young U (UT)
Chapman U (CA)
Earlham C (IN)
Elon U (NC)
Flagler C (FL)
Gonzaga U (WA)
Gordon C (MA)
Grove City C (PA)
Guilford C (NC)
High Point U (NC)
Hillsdale C (MI)
Holy Cross, C of the (MA)
Lawrence U (WI)
Moravian C (PA)
Muhlenberg C (PA)
Naropa U (CO)
Oberlin C (OH)

Pitzer C (CA)
Richmond, U of (VA)
Samford U (AL)
Seattle U (WA)
South, U of the, Sewanee (TN)
St. John Fisher C (NY)

Virginia, U of
Wake Forest U (NC)
Washington & Lee U (VA)
Wheaton C (IL)
William & Mary, C of (VA)
Wofford C (SC)

The Experts' Choice: Colleges for the Socially Conservative

Baylor U (TX)**
Brigham Young U (UT)
Colorado Christian U
Davidson C (NC)
Furman U (SC)
George Fox U (OR)
Grove City C (PA)
High Point U (NC)
Hillsdale C (MI)*
Holy Cross, C of the (MA)
Liberty U (VA)
Notre Dame, U of (IN)
Pepperdine U (CA)*
Richmond, U of (VA)

South, U of the (TN)
Southern Methodist U (TX)**
St. Thomas Aquinas C (NY)
Texas Christian U
Vanderbilt U (TN)
Villanova U (PA)
Wake Forest U (NC)
Washington & Lee U (VA)**
Wheaton C (IL)
Wofford C (SC)

* The Top Choice (tie)
** The Second Choice (tie)

Most Conservative Colleges

These colleges were named the most conservative by the Young America's Foundation.

Christendom C (VA)
Colorado Christian U
Franciscan U (OH)
Grove City C (PA)
Harding U (AR)
Hillsdale C (MI)
King's C, The (NY)
Liberty U (VA)

Ohio Christian U
Ozarks, C of the (MO)
Patrick Henry C (VA)
Regent U (VA)
St. Vincent C (PA)
Thomas Aquinas C (CA)
Thomas More C (NH)
Wisconsin Lutheran C

Source: Young America's Foundation (*yaf.org*)

Colleges That Are Conservative and Offer a "True Liberal Education"

These colleges were selected by the Intercollegiate Studies Institute (ISI) for inclusion in the college guidebook *Choosing the Right College*. ISI uses the tagline "Educating for Liberty" and declares it is "Inspiring college students to discover, embrace, and advance the principles and virtues that make American free and prosperous." Among the criteria considered were "the presence or absence of a core curriculum, the nature of student living arrangements, the strength of distribution requirements, the protection of free inquiry, and the state of campus safety."

Amherst C (MA)
Ave Maria U (FL)
Barnard C (NY)
Bates C (ME)
Baylor U (TX)
Belmont Abbey C (NC)
Berry C (GA)
Boston C (MA)
Boston U (MA)
Bowdoin C (ME)
Brandeis U (MA)
Brown U (RI)
Bryn Mawr C (PA)
Bucknell U (PA)
California Institute of Technology
Carnegie Mellon U (PA)
Catholic U (DC)
Centre C (KY)
Chicago, U of (IL)
Christendom C (VA)
Claremont Colleges Consortium (CA)
Columbia U (NY)
Cornell U (NY)
Dallas, U of (TX)
Dartmouth C (NH)
Duke U (NC)
Emory U (GA)
Fordham U (NY)
Georgetown U (DC)
Gordon C (MA)
Grinnell C (IA)
Grove City C (PA)
Hampden-Sydney C (VA)
Harvard U (MA)
Haverford U (PA)
Hillsdale C (MI)
Johns Hopkins U (MD)
Kenyon C (OH)
King's C, The (NY)

Massachusetts Institute of Technology
Middlebury C (VT)
Mt. Holyoke C (MA)
New York U
Northwestern U (IL)
Notre Dame, U of (IN)
Oberlin C (OH)
Patrick Henry C (VA)
Pennsylvania, U of
Pepperdine U (CA)
Princeton U (NJ)
Providence C (RI)
Rice U (TX)
Sarah Lawrence C (NY)
Seton Hall U (NJ)
Smith C (MA)
South, U of the (TN)
Southern California, U of
Southern Methodist U (TX)
St. John's C (MD)
Stanford U (CA)
Swarthmore C (PA)
Thomas Aquinas C (CA)
Tufts U (MA)
Tulane U (LA)
Vanderbilt U (TN)
Vassar C (NY)
Villanova U (PA)
Wabash C (IN)
Wake Forest U (NC)
Washington & Lee U (VA)
Washington U (MO)
Wellesley C (MA)
Wesleyan U (CT)
Wheaton C (IL)
Whitman C (WA)
Williams C (MA)
Yale U (CT)

Source: Zmirak, John. *Choosing the Right College 2014-15: The Inside Scoop on Elite Schools and Outstanding Lesser-Known Institutions*. Wilmington, Delaware: ISI, 2013. Print.

The Experts' Choice: Colleges for the Most Fun-Loving

Alabama State U
Arizona State U
Arizona, U of
Auburn U (AL)
Chicago State U (IL)
Clemson U (SC)
Colgate U (NY)
Colorado C
Colorado, U of, Boulder
Elon U (NC)
Florida Atlantic U
Florida State U
Florida, U of
Georgia, U of
Indiana U, Bloomington

Miami U (OH)
Miami, U of (FL)
Michigan, U of, Ann Arbor
Missouri, U of Columbia
North Carolina, U of
Ohio U
Rollins C (FL)
Southern California, U of
Southern Methodist U (TX)
Syracuse U (NY)
Texas, U of
Tulane U (LA)
Virginia, U of
Wisconsin, U of

The Experts' Choice: Colleges for the Student Who Wants to Work Hard and Play Hard

Boston C (MA)
Bucknell U (PA)
California, U of, Berkeley
California, U of, Los Angeles
Chicago, U of (IL)
Claremont McKenna C (CA)
Colgate U (NY)
Colorado C
Colorado, U of, Boulder
Dartmouth C (NH)
Davidson C (NC)
Duke U (NC)*
Emory U (GA)
Florida, U of
Furman U (SC)
Gettysburg C (PA)
Lehigh U (PA)*
Maryland, U of, College Park
Miami, U of (FL)
Michigan, U of, Ann Arbor
North Carolina, U of, Chapel Hill
Northwestern U (IL)
Ohio State U

Pennsylvania State U
Pennsylvania, U of
Pittsburgh, U of (PA)
Princeton U (NJ)
Rice U (TX)
Richmond, U of (VA)
Southern California, U of
Stanford U (CA)
Swarthmore C (PA)
Syracuse U (NY)
Tufts U (MA)
Tulane U (LA)
Vanderbilt U (TN)
Vermont, U of
Villanova U (PA)
Virginia, U of
Wake Forest U (NC)
Washington & Lee U (VA)
Washington U (MO)
Williams C (MA)
Wisconsin, U of, Madison

* The Top Choice (tie)

The Experts' Choice: Colleges for the Procrastinator

Experts were asked for colleges for the student who has, on occasion, put off study assignments and papers.

Alabama, U of, Tuscaloosa

Albright C (PA)

Steven R. Antonoff

Allegheny C (PA)
Arizona, U of
Atlantic, C of the (ME)
Azusa Pacific U (CA)
Baylor U (TX)
Beacon C (FL)
California State U, Humboldt
Champlain C (VT)
Colorado C
Colorado, U of, Boulder
Cornell C (IA)
Curry C (MA)
Dean C (MA)
Defiance C (OH)
Dillard U (LA)
Florida State U
Hampshire C (MA)
Knox C (IL)

Landmark C (VT)
Lawrence U
Lynn U (FL)
Marymount U (CA)
Michigan, U of, Ann Arbor
Northern Arizona U
Prescott C (AZ)
Quest U (Canada)
Reed C (OR)
Southwestern Community C (IA)
St. Michael's C (VT)
Texas A&M U
Transylvania U (KY)
Wabash C (IN)
Widener U (PA)
Wisconsin, U of, River Falls
Wisconsin, U of, Stout
Worcester Polytechnic Institute (MA)

The Experts' Choice: Colleges With Plenty of School Spirit

Alabama, U of, Tuscaloosa
Auburn U (AL)
Bowling Green State U (OH)
Clemson U (SC)
Duke U (NC)
Georgia, U of
Gonzaga U (WA)
Notre Dame, U of (IN)
Southern California, U of
Washington U (MO)

The Experts' Choice: Colleges for the Student With No Interest in Sports

American U (DC)
Babson C (MA)
Bard C (NY)
Brandeis U (MA)
California Institute of Technology
Carnegie Mellon U (PA)
Champlain C (VT)
Chicago, U of (IL)
Columbia U (NY)
Emory U (GA)
Hampshire C (MA)
Haverford C (PA)
Hendrix C (AR)

Johnson & Wales U (RI)
Lawrence U (WI)
Lewis & Clark C (OR)
New York U
Oberlin C (OH)
Quest U (Canada)
Reed C (OR)
St. John's C (NM) (MD)
Swarthmore C (PA)
Tufts U (MA)
Vassar C (NY)
Wesleyan U (CT)

The Experts' Choice: Colleges for the Free Spirit

Experts named these schools as places where the nonconformist or independent thinker who doesn't care about fitting in would fit right in.

Bard C (NY)
Bennington C (VT)
Brown U (RI)
California State U, Humboldt
California, U of, Berkeley
California, U of, Santa Cruz
Colorado C
Colorado, U of, Boulder
Earlham C (IN)
Eckerd C (FL)
Emerson C (MA)
Evergreen State C (WA)*
Goucher C (MD)
Hampshire C (MA)*
Lewis & Clark C (OR)
Macalester C (MN)
Marlboro C (VT)

New C (FL)
New Hampshire, U of
North Carolina, U of, Asheville
Oberlin C (OH)
Pitzer C (CA)
Prescott C (AZ)
Reed C (OR)*
Sarah Lawrence C (NY)
St. John's C (MD) (NM)
Vassar C (NY)
Vermont, U of
Warren Wilson C (NC)
Wesleyan U (CT)
Whitman U (WA)

* The Top Choice (tie)

Hippie Colleges

The colleges in this list are selected from cities across the United States known to be "hippie towns." Rock your tie-dye and flip-flops at these campuses!

Homer, AK: Home of Alaska, U of, Fairbanks
Santa Cruz, CA: Home of California, U of, Santa Cruz
Manitou Springs, CO: Home of Colorado, U of, Colorado Springs
New Haven, CT: Home of Yale U
Key West, FL: Home of Florida Keys Community C
Athens, GA: Home of Georgia, U of
Bloomington, IN: Home of Indiana U, Bloomington
Decorah, IA: Home of Luther C
Lawrence, KS: Home of Kansas, U of
Louisville, KY: Home of Louisville, U of; Bellarmine U
Unity, ME: Home of Unity C
Takoma Park, MD: Home of Washington Adventist U; Montgomery C
Northampton, MA: Home of Smith C
Ann Arbor, MI: Home of Michigan, U of
Duluth, MN: Home of C of St. Scholastica; Minnesota, U of, Duluth
Missoula, MT: Home of Montana, U of
Lincoln, NE: Home of Nebraska, U of, Lincoln
Reno, NV: Home of Nevada, U of, Reno
Keene, NH: Home of Keene State C
Ithaca, NY: Home of Cornell U; Ithaca C
Asheville, NC: Home of North Carolina, U of, Asheville
Fargo, ND: Home of North Dakota State U
Yellow Springs, OH: Home of Antioch C
Ashland, OR: Home of Southern Oregon U
Spearfish, SD: Home of Black Hills State U

San Marcos, TX: Home of Texas State U
Moab, UT: Home of Utah State U
Burlington, VT: Home of Vermont, U of; Champlain C; St. Michael's C
Olympia, WA: Home of Evergreen State C
Eau Claire, WI: Home of Wisconsin, U of, Eau Claire
Laramie, WY: Home of Wyoming, U of

The Experts' Choice: Colleges for the Quirky Student

Experts were asked to identify schools for the student who marches to a different
drummer and takes pride in doing so.

Bard C (NY)
Beloit C (WI)
Bennington C (VT)
Brown U (RI)
California, U of, Santa Cruz
Carleton C (MN)
Chicago, U of (IL)
Colorado C
Cornell C (IA)
Earlham C (IN)
Eckerd C (FL)
Eugene Lang C (NY)
Evergreen State C (WA)
Goucher C (MD)
Grinnell C (IA)
Guilford C (NC)
Hampshire C (MA)**
Hendrix C (AR)
Kalamazoo C (MI)
Knox C (IL)
Lawrence U (WI)
Lewis & Clark C (OR)

Marlboro C (VT)
Massachusetts Institute of Technology
Muhlenberg C (PA)
New C (FL)
New York U
Oberlin C (OH)
Occidental C (CA)
Pitzer C (CA)
Quest U (Canada)
Reed C (OR)*
Rice U (TX)
Sarah Lawrence C (NY)
Swarthmore C (PA)
Tufts U (MA)
Vassar C (NY)
Warren Wilson C (NC)
Wesleyan C (CT)
Yale U (CT)

* The Top Choice
** The Second Choice

Colleges Where Students Can Hit the Books and the Backcountry

Outside Magazine ranks the 40 top schools in this category on the basis of "top-notch
academic credentials, a healthy environmental ethos, and an A+ sense of adventure."

1. California, U of, Santa Cruz
2. Colorado, U of, Boulder
3. Middlebury C (VT)
4. Warren Wilson C (NC)
5. Montana State U
6. Simon Fraser U (Canada)
7. Dartmouth C (NH)
8. Virginia, U of
9. Northern Arizona U
10. Iowa, U of
11. Vermont, U of
12. California, State U of, Humboldt

13. Colorado C
14. Cornell U (NY)
15. Montana, U of
16. Bowdoin C (ME)
17. Stanford U (CA)
18. Wisconsin, U of, Madison
19. Hawaii, U of, Manoa
20. Southern Oregon U
21. Prescott C (AZ)
22. Williams C (MA)
23. Arkansas, U of, Fayetteville
24. Evergreen State C (WA)

25. St. John's C (MD)
26. Sheldon Jackson C (AK)
27. Brevard C (NC)
28. Oregon, U of
29. Idaho, U of
30. Ft. Lewis C (CO)
31. Alaska Pacific U
32. California, U of, San Diego
33. Arizona, U of

34. Wyoming, U of
35. Princeton U (NJ)
36. Minnesota, U of, Duluth
37. California Polytechnic State U, San Luis Obispo
38. Georgia, U of
39. Texas, U of, Austin
40. Miami, U of (FL)

Source: *Outside Magazine* (used with permission)

The Experts' Choice: Outdoors Lover

Boise State U (ID)
California, U of, Berkeley
Colorado State U, Ft. Collins
Colorado, U of, Boulder
Dartmouth C (NH)
Montana State U, Bozeman

Oregon State U
Southern California, U of
Utah, U of
Vermont, U of
Washington, U of
Westminster C (UT)

The Experts' Choice: Colleges for the Lover of Ideas

Top Choices

Chicago, U of (IL)
Reed C (OR)

St. John's C (NM) (MD)
Swarthmore C (PA)

Second Choices

Amherst C (MA)
Bard C (NY)
Brown U (RI)
Haverford C (PA)

Oberlin C (OH)
Pomona C (CA)
Vassar C (NY)
Wesleyan U (CT)

Third Choices

Beloit C (WI)
Bryn Mawr C (PA)
Carleton C (MN)
Colorado C
Grinnell C (IA)
Hampshire C (MA)
Kenyon C (OH)

Middlebury C (VT)
Pitzer C (CA)
Sarah Lawrence C (NY)
Wellesley C (MA)
Williams C (MA)
Yale U (CT)

Honorable Mention

Barnard C (NY)
Bates C (ME)
Bowdoin C (ME)
California Institute of Technology
California, U of, Berkeley
Colby C (ME)
Columbia U (NY)

Cornell C (IA)
Davidson C (NC)
Deep Springs C (CA)
Denison U (OH)
Earlham C (IN)
Georgetown U (DC)
Goucher C (MD)

ABOUT ME

Guilford C (NC)
Hamilton C (NY)
Harvard U (MA)
King's C, U of (Canada)
Knox C (IL)
Lafayette C (PA)
Lawrence U (WI)
Massachusetts Institute of Technology
New C (FL)
Occidental C (CA)

Pennsylvania, U of
Princeton U (NJ)
Quest U (Canada)
Rhodes C (TN)
Shimer C (IL)
Tufts U (MA)
Washington U (MO)
Whitman C (WA)
William & Mary, C of (VA
Wooster, C of (OH)

The Experts' Choice: Colleges for the Bookworm

Experts were asked to identify colleges for someone who loves reading and is happiest with a book (or two or three) close at hand.

Chicago, U of (IL)*
Reed C (OR)**
St. John's (NM) (MD)*
Swarthmore C (PA)**

* The Top Choice (tie)
** The Second Choice (tie)

Colleges Earning Praise

Barnard C (NY)
Bowdoin C (ME)
Brandeis U (MA)
Bryn Mawr C (PA)
California Institute of Technology
Carleton C (MN)

Carnegie Mellon U (PA)
Columbia U (NY)
Davidson C (NC)
Georgia Institute of Technology
Harvard U (MA)
Harvey Mudd C (CA)
Haverford C (PA)
Johns Hopkins U (MD)
Massachusetts Institute of Technology
Oberlin C (OH)
Princeton U (NJ)
Rhodes C (TN)
Sarah Lawrence C (NY)
William & Mary, C of (VA)
Yale U (CT)

The Experts' Choice: Literary-Friendly Colleges

Experts were asked to name universities that are literary friendly—colleges that have great environments for the well-read student.

Barnard C (NY)
Bennington C (VT)
Boston U (MA)
Brown U (RI)
Bryn Mawr C (PA)
Bucknell U (PA)
California, U of, Irvine
Carnegie Mellon U (PA)
Chicago, U of (IL)
Colorado C
Columbia U (NY)
Cornell U (NY)
Davidson C (NC)

Emerson C (MA)
Emory U (GA)
Hamilton C (NY)
Harvard U (MA)
Illinois, U of, Urbana
Iowa, U of
Johns Hopkins U (MD)
Kenyon U (OH)
Knox C (IL)
Miami, U of (FL)
Michigan, U of
Michigan, U of, Ann Arbor
Middlebury C (VT)

Mississippi, U of
New School (NY)
New York U
New York, City U of, Brooklyn
Notre Dame, U of (IN)
Oberlin C (OH)
Pennsylvania, U of
Pomona C (CA)
Princeton U (NJ)
Sarah Lawrence C (NY)
Skidmore C (NY)

Smith C (MA)
South, U of the (TN)
Stanford U (CA)
Texas, U of, Austin
Vanderbilt U (TN)
Vassar C (NY)
Virginia, U of
Washington U (MO)
Wesleyan U (CT)
Williams C (MA)
Yale U (CT)

The Experts' Choice: Colleges for the Foodie

Experts were asked to identify colleges with outstanding cuisine.

Bowdoin C (ME)
California, U of, Berkeley
California, U of, Los Angeles
Charleston, C of (SC)
Claremont McKenna C (CA)
Cornell U (NY)
Culinary Institute of America (NY)
Denison U (OH)
Fordham U (NY)
Franklin & Marshall C (PA)
Georgia, U of, Athens
High Point U (NC)

James Madison U (VA)
Johnson & Wales U (RI)
Middlebury C (VT)
New York U
Pitzer C (CA)
Richmond, U of (VA)
San Diego, U of (CA)
Scripps C (CA)
Tufts U (MA)
Tulane U (LA)
Villanova U (PA)
Wisconsin, U of, Madison

The Experts' Choice: Colleges for the Clothes Horse

Experts were asked to name colleges for the clothes horse (that is, for the student who is an aficionado of brand names).

American U (DC)
Brandeis U (MA)
Bucknell U (PA)
Colby C (ME)
Colgate U (NY)
Davidson C (NC)
DePauw U (IN)
Duke U (NC)
Elon U (NC)
Emory U (GA)
Furman U (SC)
Georgetown U (DC)
George Washington U (DC)
High Point U (NC)
Hofstra U (NY)
Miami U (OH)
Miami, U of (FL)

New York U
Richmond, U of (VA)
Rollins C (FL)***
Southern California, U of
Southern Methodist U (TX)*
Syracuse U (NY)
Texas Christian U
Tulane U (LA)
Vanderbilt U (TN)**
Virginia, U of
Wake Forest U (NC)***
Washington U (MO)

* The Top Choice
** The Second Choice
*** The Third Choice (tie)

The Experts' Choice: Colleges for the Person Who Hates Brand Names/Designer Clothing

Experts were asked for colleges for the student who is not interested in brand names or designer-label clothes.

Bard C (NY)
Beloit C (WI)
California Polytechnic State U, San Luis
   Obispo
California State U, Humboldt
Carleton C (MN)
Clark U (MA)
Colgate U (NY)
Earlham C (IN)
Evergreen State C (WA)
Guilford C (NC)
Hampshire C (MA)
Haverford C (PA)
Hendrix C (AR)

Lewis & Clark C (OR)
New C (FL)
Oberlin C (OH)
Puget Sound, U of (WA)
Reed C (OR)*
Sarah Lawrence C (NY)
Scripps C (CA)
Warren Wilson C (NC)
Wesleyan U (CT)
Western Washington U
Willamette U (OR)

* The Top Choice

The Experts' Choice: Colleges for the Flip-Flop Wearer

Experts were asked to name colleges where wearing flip-flops to class is common.

Arizona State U
California Polytechnic State U, San Luis
   Obispo
California, U of, Berkeley
California, U of, Los Angeles
California, U of, San Diego*
California, U of, Santa Barbara**
California, U of, Santa Cruz
Chapman U (CA)
Colorado, U of, Boulder
Eckerd C (FL)
Florida Gulf Coast U
Florida International U
Florida State U
Florida, U of

Hampshire C (MA)
Hawaii Pacific U
Hawaii, U of, Manoa
Miami, U of (FL)**
New C (FL)
Pepperdine U (CA)
Reed C (OR)
Rollins C (FL)
Southern California, U of
Tampa, U of (FL)
Vermont, U of
Washington, U of

* The Top Choice
** The Second Choice (tie)

The Experts' Choice: Colleges With Lots of Concerts, Speakers, and Events

Adrian C (MI)
Agnes Scott C (GA)
Augsburg C (MN)
Bard C (NY)
Baylor U (TX)
Birmingham-Southern C (AL)
Bucknell U (PA)
California State U, Humboldt

Calvin C (MI)
Carthage C (WI)
Centre C (KY)
Claremont McKenna C (CA)
Clarkson U (NY)
Clemson U (SC)
Coe C (IA)
Colby C (ME)

Connecticut C
Creighton U (NE)
Dayton, U of (OH)
Denison U (OH)
DePauw U (IN)
Dickinson C (PA)
Duke U (NC)
Elon U (NC)
Emerson C (MA)
Fairfield U (CT)
Gonzaga U (WA)
Gustavus Adolphus C (MN)
Hamilton C (NY)
Hillsdale C (MI)
Illinois Wesleyan U
Kenyon C (OH)
Millikin U (IL)
Mills C (CA)
Oberlin C (OH)

Ohio Wesleyan U
Pitzer C (CA)
Pt. Loma Nazarene C (CA)
Rhodes C (TN)
Scripps C (CA)
Southern Oregon U
St. Lawrence U (NY)
St. Michael's C (VT)
Towson U (MD)
Union C (NY)
Washington U (MO)
Wells C (NY)
Wheaton C (MA)
Whitman C (WA)
William Jewell C (MO)
Wisconsin, U of, Madison
Wisconsin, U of, Milwaukee
Wooster, C of (OH)

The Experts' Choice: Most Sexually Active Campuses

Experts were asked to identify colleges where numerous students are sexually active.

Arizona State U
Arizona, U of
Bennington C (VT)
Reed C (OR)
Wesleyan U (CT)

The Experts' Choice: Least Sexually Active Campuses

Experts were asked to identify colleges where fewer students are sexually active.

Baylor U (TX)
Biola U (CA)
Bob Jones U (SC)
Brigham Young U (UT)*
California Institute of Technology
Grand Canyon U (AZ)
Hope C (MI)
Liberty U (VA)
Oral Roberts U (OK)
Pepperdine U (CA)
Westmont C (CA)
Wheaton C (IL)

* The Top Choice

ETHNICITY/RACE

AMERICAN INDIAN/ALASKAN NATIVE STUDENTS

Members of the American Indian Tribal Colleges

Most of these colleges are situated on reservations in Western and Midwestern states. Many are two-year schools.

Bay Mills Community C (MI)
Blackfeet Community C (MT)
Chief Dull Knife C (MT)
Dine C (AZ)
Ft. Belknap Community C (MT)
Ft. Berthold C (ND)
Ft. Peck Community C (MT)
Haskell Indian Junior C (KS)
Institute for American Indian Arts (NM)
Lac Courte Oreilles Ojibwa Community C (WI)
Leech Lake Tribal C (MN)
Little Big Horn C (MT)
Little Priest Tribal C (NE)

Menominee Nation, C of the (WI)
Nebraska Indian Community C
Northwest Indian C (WA)
Oglala Lakota C (SD)
Salish Kootenai C (MT)
Sinte Gleska C (SD)
Sisseton-Wahpeton Community C (SD)
Southwest Indian Polytechnic Institute (NM)
Standing Rock C (ND)
Stone Child C (MT)
Tohono O'Odham Community C (AZ)
Turtle Mountain Community C (ND)
United Tribes Technical C (ND)

Colleges With the Largest Enrollment of American Indian or Alaska Native Students

These numbers show the total enrollment of American Indian and/or Alaska Native students at each school.

California State U, San Marcos: 3,913
Northeastern State U (OK): 1,709
Alaska, U of, Fairbanks: 1,202
Alaska Anchorage, U of: 1,064
South Carolina, U of, Columbia: 974
Oklahoma, U of: 899
Ft. Lewis C (CO): 880
Northern Arizona U: 707
Central Oklahoma, U of: 613
East Central U (OK): 595
Utah State U: 512
Alaska, U of, Southeast: 469
Portland State U (OR): 346
Arizona, U of: 337
Cameron U (OK): 325
Institute of American Indian Arts (NM): 323
American Public U System (WV): 299
Wisconsin, U of, Stout: 263
Washington, U of, Seattle: 257

Utah Valley U: 243
California State U, Sacramento: 240
Lake Superior State U (MI): 216
North Dakota, U of: 205
Montana State U, Billings: 199
Montana State U, Bozeman: 182
New Mexico Highlands U: 181
California, U of, Santa Barbara: 180
Northern Michigan U: 167
Washington State U: 163
Oregon State U: 160
Boise State U (ID): 155
North Texas, U of: 154
Auburn U (AL): 152
Idaho State U: 150
Eastern New Mexico U: 144
Eastern Washington U: 138
Tulsa, U of (OK): 133
Troy U (AL): 132
Utah, U of: 130

Source: Wintergreen Orchard House

Colleges With the Highest Percentage of American Indian or Alaska Native Students

Institute of American Indian Arts (NM): 78.02%
California State U, San Marcos: 36.46%
Northeastern State U (OK): 23.00%
Ft. Lewis C (CO): 21.85%
Alaska, U of, Southeast: 17.40%
East Central U (OK): 15.84%
Alaska, U of, Fairbanks: 14.88%
Science & Art, U of (OK): 14.07%
Lake Superior State U (MI): 8.88%
New Mexico Highlands U: 7.55%
Source: Wintergreen Orchard House

Alaska, U of, Anchorage: 6.42%
Cameron U (OK): 6.07%
Minnesota, U of, Morris: 5.91%
Southern Nazarene U (OK): 5.70%
Montana State U, Billings: 4.46%
Oklahoma, U of: 4.12%
Central Oklahoma, U of: 4.03%
South Carolina, U of, Columbia: 4.03%
Tulsa, U of (OK): 3.88%

Community Colleges Awarding the Most Associate Degrees to American Indian Students

Blackfeet Community C (MT)
Calhoun Community C (AL)
Carl Albert State C (OK)
Central New Mexico Community C
Central Texas C
Coconino Community C (AZ)
Connors State C (OK)
Eastern Oklahoma State C
Fayetteville Technical Community C (NC)
Ivy Tech Community C (IN)
Lac Courte Oreilles Ojibwa Community C (WI)
Little Big Horn C (MT)

Mesa Community C (AZ)
New Mexico, U of, Gallup
Northeastern Oklahoma C
Phoenix C (AZ)
Pima Community C (AZ)
Portland Community C (OR)
Robeson Community C (NC)
Rose State C (OK) San Juan C (NM)
Scottsdale Community C (AZ)
Southwestern Indian Polytechnic Institute (NM)
Tarrant County C District (TX)
Tulsa Community C (OK)
Universal Technical Institute (AZ)

Source: *Community College Week* magazine (used with permission)

ASIAN STUDENTS

Colleges With the Largest Enrollment of Asian Students

These numbers show the total enrollment of Asian students at each school.

California, U of, Berkeley: 9,066
Rutgers U, New Brunswick (NJ): 8,587
California State U, San Francisco: 7,549
California State U, Fullerton: 7,153
Texas, U of, Austin: 7,130
Washington, U of, Seattle: 7,119
California, U of, Riverside: 6,713
California State U, Sacramento: 6,445

Hawaii, U of, Manoa: 5,887
New York, City U of, Baruch C: 4,843
California, U of, Santa Barbara: 4,640
Illinois, U of, Urbana: 4,613
New York, City U of, Hunter C: 4,275
Southern California, U of: 4,179
Maryland, U of, College Park: 4,117
New York, City U of, Queens C: 4,108

New York U: 4,103
George Mason U (VA): 3,866
New York, State U of, Stony Brook: 3,856
California State U, San Marcos: 3,778
Nevada, U of, Las Vegas: 3,759
Illinois, U of, Chicago: 3,737
California State U, Northridge: 3,712
Texas, U of, Dallas: 3,456
Michigan, U of, Ann Arbor: 3,453
California State U, Los Angeles: 3,197
California State U, Fresno: 3,147
New York, City U of, City C: 3,041

Texas, U of, Arlington: 3,024
New York, City U of, C of Technology: 2,983
California State U, East Bay: 2,953
Minnesota, U of, Twin Cities: 2,920
Temple U (PA): 2,806
Georgia Institute of Technology: 2,603
St. John's U (NY): 2,576
New York, State U of, Buffalo: 2,535
Florida, U of: 2,486
Ohio State U, Columbus: 2,432
Cornell U (NY): 2,342

Source: Wintergreen Orchard House

Colleges With the Highest Percentage of Asian Students

Hawaii, U of, West Oahu: 40.66%
Hawaii, U of, Manoa: 40.60%
Honolulu, U of, Chaminade (HI): 37.48%
California, U of, Riverside: 36.05%
Philadelphia, U of the Sciences in (PA): 35.89%
California State U, San Marcos: 35.20%
California, U of, Berkeley: 34.94%
New York, City U of, Baruch C: 34.39%
Art Center C of Design (CA): 34.07%
Otis C of Art & Design (CA): 33.03%
California State U, San Francisco: 28.86%
New York, City U of, Queens C: 26.76%
Texas, U of, Dallas: 26.48%
New York, City U of, York C: 26.24%
New York, City U of, Hunter C: 25.62%
California, U of, Merced: 25.34%
Rutgers U, New Brunswick (NJ): 25.33%
Washington, U of, Seattle: 24.61%
California State U, East Bay: 24.49%
Washington, U of, Bothell: 24.44%

New York, State U of, Stony Brook: 24.11%
New York, City U of, City C: 24.08%
California, U of, Santa Barbara: 23.96%
Massachusetts Institute of Technology: 23.94%
Carnegie Mellon U (PA): 23.03%
Lawrence Technological U (MI): 22.98%
Southern California, U of: 22.66%
Illinois, U of, Chicago: 22.43%
California State U, Sacramento: 22.02%
Rutgers U, Newark (NJ): 21.88%
California State U, Fullerton: 21.60%
Harvey Mudd C (CA): 21.58%
Rice U (TX): 21.19%
Duke U (NC): 20.31%
Maryland, U of, Baltimore County: 19.87%
Wellesley C (MA): 19.81%
California State U, San Francisco: 19.43%
New Jersey Institute of Technology: 19.17%

Source: Wintergreen Orchard House

Community Colleges Awarding the Most Associate Degrees to Asian American Students

De Anza C (CA)
East Los Angeles C (CA)
El Camino Community C District (CA)
Honolulu Community C (HI)
Houston Community C (TX)

Kapiolani Community C (HI)
Leeward Community C (HI)
Mission C (CA)
Montgomery C (MD)

Mt. San Antonio C (CA)
New York, City C of, Borough of
  Manhattan Community C
New York, City C of, Kingsborough
  Community C
New York, City C of, LaGuardia
  Community C
New York, City C of, Queensborough
  Community C
Northern Virginia Community C

Orange Coast C (CA)
Pasadena City C (CA)
Portland Community C (OR)
Richland C (TX)
Sacramento City C (CA)
San Francisco, City C of (CA)
San Joaquin Delta C (CA)
Skyline C (CA)
Tarrant County C District (TX)

Source: *Community College Week* magazine (used with permission)

BLACK STUDENTS

Historically Black Colleges and Universities

Alabama A&M U
Alabama State U
Albany State U (GA)
Alcorn State U (MS)
Allen U (SC)
Arkansas Baptist C
Arkansas, U of, Pine Bluff
Benedict C (SC)
Bennett C (NC)
Bethune-Cookman U (FL)
Bishop State Community C (AL)
Bluefield State C (WV)
Bowie State U (MD)
Central State U (OH)
Cheyney U (PA)
Claflin U (SC)
Clark Atlanta U (GA)
Clinton Junior C (SC)
Coahoma Community C (MS)
Concordia C (AL)
Coppin State U (MD)
Delaware State U
Denmark Technical C (SC)
Dillard U (LA)
District of Columbia, U of the
Edward Waters C (FL)
Elizabeth City State U (NC)
Fayetteville State U (NC)
Fisk U (TN)
Florida Agricultural & Mechanical U
Florida Memorial U
Fort Valley State U (GA)
Gadsden State Community C (AL)
Grambling State U (LA)
Hampton U (VA)
Harris-Stowe State U (MO)

Howard U (DC)
Huston-Tillotson U (TX)
Interdenominational Theological Center
  (GA)
J.F. Drake State Community &
  Technical C (AL)
Jackson State U (MS)
Jarvis Christian C (TX)
Johnson C. Smith U (NC)
Kentucky State U
Lane C (TN)
Langston U (OK)
Lawson State Community C,
  Birmingham Campus (AL)
Le Moyne-Owen C (TN)
Lincoln U (MO)
Lincoln U (PA)
Livingstone C (NC)
Maryland Eastern Shore, U of
Meharry Medical C (TN)
Miles C (AL)
Mississippi Valley State U
Morehouse C (GA)
Morehouse School of Medicine (GA)
Morgan State U (MD)
Morris C (SC)
Norfolk State U (VA)
North Carolina A&T State U
North Carolina Central U
Oakwood U (AL)
Paine C (GA)
Paul Quinn C (TX)
Philander Smith C (AR)
Prairie View A&M U (TX)
Rust C (MS)
Savannah State U (GA)

Selma U (AL)
Shaw U (NC)
Shelton State Community C (AL)
Shorter C (AR)
South Carolina State U
Southern U and A&M C (LA)
Southern U at New Orleans (LA)
Southern U at Shreveport (LA)
Southwestern Christian C (TX)
Spelman C (GA)
St. Augustine's U (NC)
St. Philip's C (TX)
Stillman C (AL)
Talladega C (AL)
Tennessee State U

Texas C
Texas Southern U
Tougaloo C (MS)
Trenholm State Community C (AL)
Tuskegee U (AL)
Virgin Islands, U of the
Virginia State U
Virginia U of Lynchburg
Virginia Union U
Voorhees C (SC)
West Virginia State U
Wilberforce U (OH)
Wiley C (TX)
Winston-Salem State U (NC)
Xavier U (LA)

Source: *The College Finder* research, including White House Initiative on Historically Black Colleges and Universities School Directory

Colleges With the Largest Enrollment of Black, Non-Hispanic Students

These numbers show the total enrollment of African-American students at each school.

American Public U System (WV): 10,401
Florida A&M U: 8,358
Maryland, U of, University C: 7,775
North Carolina A&T State U: 7,581
Memphis, U of (TN): 6,578
Troy U (AL): 5,971
Prairie View A&M U (TX): 5,771
New York, City U of, C of Technology: 5,465
Southern U (LA): 5,415
Morgan State U (MD): 5,269
Texas Southern U: 5,263
North Carolina Central U: 5,143
Old Dominion U (VA): 5,108
Tennessee State U: 5,083
Norfolk State U (VA): 5,040
Alabama State U: 4,973
Bowie State U (MD): 4,747
Florida International U: 4,726
Georgia Southern U: 4,713

New York, City U of, Medgar Evers: 4,390
Middle Tennessee State U: 4,362
Southern Mississippi, U of: 3,951
Eastern Michigan U: 3,934
Wayne State U (MI): 3,918
North Texas, U of: 3,865
New York, City U of, York C: 3,788
Temple U (PA): 3,763
Texas, U of, Arlington: 3,763
North Carolina, U of, Greensboro: 3,617
North Carolina, U of, Charlotte: 3,596
Winston-Salem State U (NC): 3,552
Mississippi State U: 3,480
East Carolina U (NC): 3,467
Valdosta State U (GA): 3,445
South Florida, U of: 3,406
Houston, U of, Downtown (TX): 3,394
West Georgia, U of: 3,355
Bethune-Cookman U (FL): 3,340
Maryland, U of, College Park: 3,326

Source: Wintergreen Orchard House

Colleges With the Highest Percentage of Black, Non-Hispanic Students

Lane C (TN): 100.00%
Morris C (SC): 97.21%

St. Augustine's U (NC): 96.54%
Morehouse C (GA): 95.52%

Virginia Union U: 95.44%
Central State U (OH): 94.99%
South Carolina State U: 94.89%
Martin U (IN): 94.05%
Florida A&M U: 93.59%
Southern U (LA): 93.39%
Alcorn State U (MS): 93.28%
Alabama State U: 92.85%
Arkansas, U of, Pine Bluff: 92.62%
Paine C (GA): 90.80%
Bethune-Cookman U (FL): 89.69%
Paul Quinn C (TX): 89.64%
Philander Smith C (AR): 89.21%
Bennett C (NC): 88.68%
Cheyney U (PA): 88.30%
Prairie View A&M U (TX): 85.74%
North Carolina A&T State U: 85.45%

Bowie State U (MD): 85.36%
Oakwood U (AL): 84.85%
Morgan State U (MD): 84.28%
Norfolk State U (VA): 83.71%
Texas Southern U: 83.70%
North Carolina Central U: 82.68%
Fisk U (TN): 82.59%
Lincoln U (MO): 78.93%
Xavier U (LA): 76.72%
Tennessee State U: 75.31%
Johnson C. Smith U (NC): 74.91%
Elizabeth City State U (NC): 73.40%
Marygrove C (MI): 73.20%
Huston-Tillotson U (TX): 73.00%
Maryland, U of, Eastern Shore: 72.73%
Winston-Salem State U (NC): 71.93%
Delaware State U: 71.81%

Source: Wintergreen Orchard House

Great Historically Black Colleges

The following were chosen on the basis of reputation, admission statistics, and student experience.

Bethune-Cookman U (FL)
Bowie State U (MD)
Claflin U (SC)
Delaware State U
Dillard U (LA)
Elizabeth City State U (NC)
Fayetteville State U (NC)
Florida Agricultural & Mechanical U
Hampton U (VA)
Howard U (DC)
Jackson State U (MS)
Johnson C. Smith U (NC)
Lincoln U (PA)
Maryland Eastern Shore, U of
Morehouse C (GA)

Norfolk State U (VA)
North Carolina A&T State U (NC)
North Carolina Central U
Oakwood U (AL)
Philander Smith C (AR)
Prairie View A&M U (TX)
Risk U (TN)
Spelman C (GA)
Tougaloo C (MS)
Tuskegee U (AL)
Virginia State U
Virginia U, Lynchburg
Wilberforce U (OH)
Winston-Salem State U
Xavier U (LA)

Source: *The College Finder* research

United Negro College Fund Member Colleges and Universities

Allen U (SC)
Benedict C (SC)
Bennett C (NC)
Bethune-Cookman U (FL)
Claflin U (SC)
Clark Atlanta U (GA)
Dillard U (LA)

Edward Waters C (FL)
Fisk U (TN)
Florida Memorial U
Huston-Tillotson U (TX)
Interdenominational Theological Center (GA)
Jarvis Christian C (TX)

Johnson C. Smith U (NC)
Lane C (TN)
LeMoyne-Owen C (TN)
Livingstone C (NC)
Miles C (AL)
Morehouse C (GA)
Morris C (SC)
Oakwood U (AL)
Paine C (GA)
Philander Smith C (AR)
Rust C (MS)
Shaw U (NC)

Spelman C (GA)
St. Augustine's U (NC)
Stillman C (AL)
Talladega C (AL)
Texas C
Tougaloo C (MS)
Tuskegee U (AL)
Virginia Union U
Voorhees C (SC)
Wilberforce U (OH)
Wiley C (TX)
Xavier U (LA)

Source: United Negro College Fund (*uncf.org*)

Liberal Arts Colleges That Accept Many Black Freshmen

Amherst C (MA)
Barnard C (NY)
Bates C (ME)
Bryn Mawr C (PA)
Bucknell U (PA)
Claremont McKenna C (CA)
Colgate U (NY)
Davidson C (NC)
Grinnell C (IA)
Hamilton C (NY)
Harvey Mudd C (CA)
Haverford C (PA)

Lafayette C (PA)
Macalester C (MN)
Oberlin C (OH)
Pomona C (CA)
Smith C (MA)
Swarthmore C (PA)
Trinity C (CT)
Vassar C (NY)
Washington & Lee U (VA)
Wellesley C (MA)
Wesleyan U (CT)
Williams C (MA)

Source: *The College Finder* research, including the *Journal of Blacks in Higher Education*

The Experts' Choice: Colleges Welcoming to African-American Students

Experts identified predominately Caucasian colleges that are particularly welcoming to African-American students.

Agnes Scott C (GA)
Chicago, U of (IL)
Florida State U
Harvard U (MA)
New York U
Occidental C (CA)
Pennsylvania, U of
Tulane U (LA)

Community Colleges Awarding the Most Associate Degrees to Black Students

ASA C (NY)
Baltimore County, Community C of (MD)
Central Texas C
Cuyahoga Community C District (OH)
Essex County C (NJ)
Georgia Military C, Distance Learning
  Campuses
Georgia Perimeter C
Hillsborough Community C (FL)
Hinds Community C (MS)
Houston Community C (TX)
Ivy Tech Community C (IN)
Lone Star C System (TX)
Montgomery C (MD)
Nassau Community C (NY)

New York, City C of, Borough of
  Manhattan Community C
New York, City C of, Kingsborough
  Community C
Northern Virginia Community C
Philadelphia, Community C of (PA)
Prince George's Community C (MD)
St. Louis Community C (MO)
Southwest Tennessee Community C
Tallahassee Community C (FL)
Tarrant County C District (TX)
Tidewater Community C (VA)
Wayne County Community C District
  (MI)

Source: *The College Finder* research, including *Community College Week* magazine

HISPANIC STUDENTS

Colleges With the Largest Enrollment of Hispanic Students

Florida International U: 26,031
Texas, U of, Pan American: 15,806
California State U, Northridge: 13,502
California State U, Fullerton: 12,381
Texas, U of, San Antonio: 11,791
California State U, Los Angeles: 11,634
Texas State U, San Marcos: 9,748
Texas, U of, Austin: 8,679
Texas A&M U, College Station: 8,634
California State U, Fresno: 8,494
Arizona, U of: 7,714
Texas, U of, Brownsville: 6,686
California, U of, Riverside: 6,678
Texas, U of, Arlington: 6,536
California State U, Sacramento: 6,507
California State U, San Francisco: 6,341
Florida, U of: 6,273
South Florida, U of: 6,045
North Texas, U of: 6,036
Inter American U of Puerto Rico, Ponce:
  5,603
Houston, U of, Downtown (TX): 5,321

Nevada, U of, Las Vegas: 5,313
New York, City U of, John Jay C: 5,262
New York, City U of, C of Technology:
  5,175
Puerto Rico, U of, Bayamon: 5,069
New York, City U of, Lehman C: 4,864
California, U of, Santa Barbara: 4,689
American Public U System (WV): 4,399
Inter American U of Puerto Rico, San
  German: 4,375
Northern Arizona U: 4,323
Inter American U of Puerto Rico,
  Aguadilla: 4,275
Rutgers U, New Brunswick (NJ): 4,138
Illinois, U of, Chicago: 4,120
Texas A&M U, Kingsville: 4,111
Caribbean U (Puerto Rico): 3,931
New York, City U of, City C: 3,898
Polytechnic U of Puerto Rico: 3,855
Incarnate Word, U of the (TX): 3,852
Montclair State U (NJ): 3,565

Source: Wintergreen Orchard House

Colleges With the Highest Percentage of Hispanic Students

Puerto Rico, U of, Ponce: 100.00%
Puerto Rico, U of, Arecibo: 100.00%
Caribbean U (Puerto Rico): 100.00%
Puerto Rico, U of, Medical Sciences
    Campus: 100.00%
Inter American U of Puerto Rico, Ponce:
    100.00%
Inter American U of Puerto Rico,
    Aguadilla: 99.88%
Puerto Rico, U of, Bayamon: 99.88%
Polytechnic U of Puerto Rico: 99.84%
Inter American U of Puerto Rico, San
    German: 99.54%
Universidad Adventista de las Antillas
    (Puerto Rico): 95.26%
Texas, U of, Pan American: 89.80%
Florida National U: 89.25%
Texas, U of, Brownsville: 88.59%
St. Mary's U (TX): 73.42%
Texas A&M U, Kingsville: 67.16%
Florida International U: 66.67%
Pacific Oaks C (CA): 63.58%

California State U, Los Angeles: 59.44%
Incarnate Word, U of the (TX): 59.34%
New Mexico Highlands U: 55.88%
La Verne, U of (CA): 50.89%
New York, City U of, Lehman C: 49.20%
Texas, U of, San Antonio: 48.44%
DeVry U (FL): 47.62%
Sul Ross State U (TX): 47.56%
California State U, Stanislaus: 44.94%
California, U of, Merced: 43.86%
Texas, U of, Permian Basin: 42.82%
California State U, Fresno: 41.85%
La Sierra U (CA): 41.43%
Fresno Pacific U (CA): 40.75%
California State U, Northridge: 40.43%
Dominican U (IL): 39.83%
New York, City U of, C of Criminal
    Justice: 39.81%
Houston, U of, Downtown (TX): 39.46%
DeVry U (IL): 37.55%
California State U, Fullerton: 37.39%
St. Thomas, U of (MN): 37.02%

Source: Wintergreen Orchard House

Four-Year Colleges Awarding the Most Bachelor's Degrees to Hispanic Students

Colleges are listed in order of total number of degrees conferred on Hispanic students.
The second number is the percentage of Hispanic students among those receiving
degrees.

1. Florida International U: 5,007; 65%
2. Texas, U of, El Paso: 2,552; 80%
3. Texas, U of, Pan American: 2,446; 89%
4. Central Florida, U of: 2,232; 18%
5. California State U, Fullerton: 2,219; 30%
6. Texas, U of, San Antonio: 2,059; 47%
7. California State U, Northridge: 1,910; 28%
8. California State U, Long Beach: 1,850; 27%
9. Texas, U of, Austin: 1,583; 17%
10. San Diego State U (CA): 1,580; 27%
11. California State U, Los Angeles: 1,552; 43%
12. Houston, U of (TX): 1,496; 26%
13. Arizona State U: 1,479; 16%
14. Texas A&M U, College Station: 1,456; 15%
15. Florida, U of: 1,450; 18%
16. Texas State U, San Marcos: 1,428; 25%
17. California State U, San Bernardino: 1,360; 43%
18. California, U of, Riverside: 1,319; 30%
19. New Mexico, U of, Albuquerque: 1,286; 37%
20. South Florida, U of: 1,285; 17%

21. California State U, Fresno: 1,284; 35%
22. California Polytechnic State U, Pomona: 1,262; 30%
23. Florida Atlantic U: 1,208; 24%
24. New Mexico State U: 1,193; 46%
25. California, U of, Santa Barbara: 1,190; 23%
26. Texas A&M U, Kingsville: 1,187; 69%
27. Ashford U (IA): 1,182; 9%
28. California, U of, Los Angeles: 1,178; 16%
29. Arizona, U of: 1,163; 18%
30. California State U, San Francisco: 1,163; 18%
31. Texas, U of, Arlington: 1,156; 19%
32. Florida State U: 1,155; 15%
33. California State U, San Jose: 1,105; 21%
34. California State U, Dominquez Hills: 1,098; 44%
35. North Texas, U of: 1,000; 16%
36. California, U of, Davis: 986; 14%
37. California State U, Sacramento: 983; 18%
38. California, U of, Irvine: 958; 16%
39. California, U of, Berkeley: 937; 12%
40. Texas, U of, Brownsville: 928; 89%
41. Houston, U of, Downtown (TX): 855; 36%
42. California, U of, San Diego: 849; 13%
43. New York, City C of, John Jay C: 824; 35%
44. California, U of, Santa Cruz: 797; 20%
45. New York, City C of, Lehman C: 773; 43%
46. Texas Tech U: 767; 15%
47. Rutgers U, New Brunswick (NJ): 743; 11%
48. Texas A&M U, International: 739; 94%
49. Northern Arizona U: 727; 16%
50. Illinois, U of, Chicago: 725; 19%

Source: *The Hispanic Outlook in Higher Education* magazine (used with permission)

HACU Member Hispanic-Serving Institutions

The Hispanic Association of Colleges and Universities recognizes the following colleges and universities as "Hispanic-Serving Institutions," or institutions where total Hispanic enrollment constitutes a minimum of 25% of the total enrollment.

Adams State U (CO)	Bergen Community C (NJ)
Aims Community C (CO)	Boricua C (NY)
Alamo C (TX)	California Lutheran U
Allan Hancock C (CA)	California Polytechnic State U, Pomona
Antelope Valley C (CA)	California State U, Bakersfield
Antioch U, Santa Barbara (CA)	California State U, Channel Islands
Arizona, U of, South	California State U, Chico
Arkansas, U of, Cossatot	California State U, Dominguez Hills
Atenas C (Puerto Rico)	California State U, East Bay
Atlantic University C (Puerto Rico)	California State U, Fresno
Austin Community C (TX)	California State U, Fullerton
Azusa Pacific U (CA)	California State U, Humboldt
Bakersfield C (CA)	California State U, Long Beach
Barry U (FL)	California State U, Los Angeles

California State U, Monterey Bay
California State U, Northridge
California State U, Sacramento
California State U, San Bernardino
California State U, San Diego
California State U, San Diego, Imperial
  Valley
California State U, San Francisco
California State U, San Jose
California State U, San Marcos
California State U, Sonoma
California State U, Stanislaus
California State U, System Office
California, U of, Irvine
California, U of, Merced
California, U of, Riverside
California, U of, Santa Barbara
California, U of, Santa Cruz
Capital Community C (CT)
Caribbean U (Puerto Rico)
Central New Mexico Community C
Cerritos C (CA)
Cerro Coso Community C (CA)
Chaffey C (CA)
Chicago, City C of (IL)
Citrus C (CA)
Clovis Community C (NM)
Coastal Bend C (TX)
Cochise C (AZ)
Colorado State U, Pueblo
Columbia Basin C (WA)
Crafton Hills C (CA)
Cypress C (CA)
Dallas County Community C (TX)
Del Mar C (TX)
Denver, Community C of (CO)
Desert, C of the (CA)
Dewey U (Puerto Rico)
Dodge City Community C (KS)
Dominican C (NY)
Donnelly C (KS)
East Los Angeles C (CA)
Eastern New Mexico U
Eastern New Mexico U, Roswell
Eastfield C (TX)
El Camino C (CA)
El Centro C (TX)
El Paso Community C (TX)
Emily Griffith Technical C (CO)
Esperanza C of Eastern U (PA)
Estrella Mountain Community C (AZ)
Evergreen Community C (CA)
Felician U (NJ)
Florida Atlantic U
Florida International U

Fresno Pacific U (CA)
Fullerton C (CA)
Galveston C (TX)
GateWay Community C (AZ)
Glendale Community C (AZ)
Golden West C (CA)
Grossmont C (CA)
Hartnell C (CA)
Heritage U (WA)
Hillsborough Community C (FL)
Hodges U (FL)
Houston, U of (TX)
Houston, U of, Clear Lake (TX)
Houston, U of, Downtown (TX)
Houston, U of, Victoria (TX)
Hudson County Community C (NJ)
Illinois, U of, Chicago
Imperial Valley C (CA)
Incarnate Word, U of the (TX)
John F. Kennedy U (CA)
Kern Community C (CA)
La Sierra U (CA)
La Verne, U of (CA)
Laredo Community C (TX)
Las Positas C (CA)
Life Pacific C (CA)
Lone Star C (TX)
Long Beach City C (CA)
Los Angeles City C (CA)
Los Angeles Harbor C (CA)
Los Angeles Mission C (CA)
Los Angeles Pierce C (CA)
Los Angeles Trade-Technical C (CA)
Los Angeles Valley C (CA)
Loyola Marymount U (CA)
Mainland, C of the (TX)
Maricopa Country Community C (AZ)
Marymount California U
Mendocino C (CA)
Merced C (CA)
Mercy C (NY)
Mesalands Community C (NM)
Miami Dade C (FL)
Middlesex County C (NJ)
Midland C (TX)
Modesto Junior C (CA)
Moreno Valley C (CA)
Morton C (IL)
Mountain View C (TX)
Mt. San Antonio C (CA)
Mt. San Jacinto C (CA)
Mt. St. Mary's U (CA)
Mt. St. Vincent, C of (NY)
Naugatuck Valley Community C (CT)
New Jersey City U

New Mexico Highlands U
New Mexico Institute of Mining &
  Technology
New Mexico Junior C
New Mexico State U
New Mexico State U, Alamogordo
New Mexico State U, Carlsbad
New Mexico State U, Dona Ana
  Community C
New Mexico State U, Grants
New Mexico, U of
New Mexico, U of, Valencia
New York, City C of
New York, City C of, C of Technology
New York, City C of, Eugenio Maria de
  Hostos Community C
New York, City C of, Lehman C
New York, City C of, Stella and Charles
  Guttman Community C
New York, City U of, Borough of
  Manhattan
New York, City U of, Bronx Community
  C
Norco C (CA)
North Orange County Community C
  (CA)
North Texas, U of, Dallas
Northeastern Illinois U
Northern Arizona U, Yuma Branch
Northern Essex Community C (MA)
Northern New Mexico C
Notre Dame de Namur U (CA)
Nova Southeastern U (FL)
Otero Junior C (CO)
Our Lady of the Lake U (TX)
Oxnard C (CA)
Pacific Oaks C (CA)
Palm Beach State C (FL)
Palo Alto C (TX)
Palomar C (CA)
Pasadena City C (CA)
Passaic County Community C (NJ)
Phoenix C (AZ)
Pima Community C (AZ)
Polytechnic U (Puerto Rico)
Porterville C (CA)
Pueblo Community C (CO)
Puerto Rico, American U of, Bayamon
Puerto Rico, EDP U of, Hato Rey
Puerto Rico, EDP U of, San Sebastian
Puerto Rico, Escuela de Artes Plásticas
  de
Puerto Rico, Inter American U of,
  Arecibo
Puerto Rico, Inter American U of,

Barranquitas
Puerto Rico, Inter American U of, Metro
  Campus
Puerto Rico, Inter American U of, San
  German
Puerto Rico, Inter American U of,
  System Central Office
Puerto Rico, Pontificia Universidad
  Católica de
Puerto Rico, U of, Cayey
Puerto Rico, U of, Mayaguez
Puerto Rico, U of, Rio Piedras
Reedley C (CA)
Richard J. Daley C (IL)
Riverside City C (CA)
Rutgers U, Newark (NJ)
Sagrado Corazón, Universidad del
  (Puerto Rico)
San Antonio C (TX)
San Bernardino Community C (CA)
San Bernardino Valley C (CA)
San Diego Community C (CA)
San Jacinto C (TX)
San Joaquin Delta C (CA)
San Jose City C (CA)
San Juan, C U of (Puerto Rico)
Santa Ana C (CA)
Santa Monica C (CA)
Santa Rosa Junior C (CA)
Schreiner U (TX)
South Mountain Community C (AZ)
South Texas C (TX)
Southern Nevada, C of
Southwest Texas Junior C
Southwest, U of (NM)
Southwestern Adventist U (TX)
Southwestern C (CA)
St. Augustine C (IL)
St. Edward's U (TX)
St. Mary's C (CA)
St. Mary's U (TX)
St. Peter's U (NJ)
St. Phillip's C (TX)
St. Thomas U (FL)
St. Xavier U (IL)
Sul Ross State U (TX)
Taft C (CA)
Tarrant County C (TX)
Texas A&M International U
Texas A&M U, Corpus Christi
Texas A&M U, Kingsville
Texas A&M U, San Antonio
Texas State Technical C, Harlingen
Texas State U
Texas, U of, Arlington

Texas, U of, El Paso
Texas, U of, Rio Grande Valley
Texas, U of, San Antonio
Trinidad State Junior C (CO)
Truckee Meadows Community C (NV)
Truman C (IL)
Turabo, Universidad del (Puerto Rico)
Union County C (NJ)
Universidad Adventista de las Antillas (Puerto Rico)
Universidad Carlos Albizu (Puerto Rico)
Universidad Central Del Caribe (Puerto Rico)
Universidad del Este, Carolina (Puerto Rico)
Universidad Metropolitana (Puerto Rico)
Universitario Ana G. Mendez (Puerto Rico)
Urban C (MA)
Valencia C (FL)

Vanguard U (CA)
Vaughn C of Aeronautics and Technology (NY)
Ventura C (CA)
Washington State U, Tri-Cities
Waubonsee Community C (IL)
Wenatchee Valley C (WA)
West Hills C, Coalinga (CA)
West Hills C, Lemoore (CA)
West Hills Community C (CA)
West Los Angeles C (CA)
West Texas A&M U (TX)
Western New Mexico U
Western Texas C
Whittier C (CA)
Wilbur Wright C (IL)
William Paterson U (NJ)
Woodbury U (CA)
Woodland Community C (CA)

States/Areas in the Country With High Hispanic College Degree Attainment

District of Columbia
Florida
Hawaii

Maryland
Virginia

Source: *The Hispanic Outlook in Higher Education* magazine (used with permission)

The Experts' Choice: Colleges That Are Welcoming to Latino Students

Experts were asked to name predominately Caucasian colleges that are particularly welcoming to Latino students.

Colorado C
Colorado, U of, Boulder
Loyola Marymount U (CA)
Miami, U of (FL)*
Occidental C (CA)

Oregon, U of
Santa Clara U (CA)
Texas, U of, Austin
Tulane U (LA)

* The Top Choice

States/Areas in the Country With the Lowest Hispanic College Degree Attainment

Arkansas
Idaho
Mississippi
Nebraska
Nevada

Source: *The Hispanic Outlook in Higher Education* magazine (used with permission)

Colleges Where the Highest Number of Hispanics Are Awarded Bachelor's Degrees in Ethnic, Cultural, or Gender Studies

1. California, U of, Los Angeles
2. California, U of, Santa Cruz
3. California, U of, Santa Barbara
4. California, U of, Berkeley
5. California, U of, Davis
6. California State U, Long Beach
7. North Carolina, U of, Chapel Hill
8. Washington, U of, Seattle
9. California State U, Fullerton
10. Florida International U

Source: *The Hispanic Outlook in Higher Education* magazine (used with permission)

Colleges Where the Highest Number of Hispanics Are Awarded Bachelor's Degrees in Engineering

1. Florida International U
2. California Polytechnic State U, Pomona
3. Texas, U of, El Paso
4. Texas A&M U, College Station
5. Florida, U of
6. Central Florida, U of
7. Texas, U of, Austin
8. Texas, U of, Pan America
9. California Polytechnic State U, San Luis Obispo
10. Texas, U of, San Antonio

Source: *The Hispanic Outlook in Higher Education* magazine

Four-Year Colleges Granting the Greatest Number of Health Care Profession Degrees to Hispanics

1. Miami Dade C (FL)
2. Keiser U (FL)
3. Texas, U of, Pan American
4. Florida International U
5. Nova Southeastern U (FL)
6. Texas, U of, Health Science Center, San Antonio
7. Texas, U of, El Paso
8. Texas Tech U, Health Sciences Center
9. Central Florida, U of
10. Grand Canyon U (AZ)
11. Florida National U
12. South Texas C
13. Texas, U of, Arlington
14. Texas, U of, Brownsville
15. Florida, U of
16. South Florida, U of
17. California State U, Fullerton
18. Dade Medical C, Miami (FL)
19. Monroe C (NY)
20. New Mexico, U of, Albuquerque
21. Chamberlain C of Nursing (IL)
22. Loma Linda U (CA)
23. California State U, Long Beach
24. Miami, U of (FL)
25. California State U, Fresno

Source: *The Hispanic Outlook in Higher Education* magazine

Colleges Where the Highest Number of Hispanics Are Awarded Bachelor's Degrees in the Liberal Arts & Sciences or General Studies and Humanities

1. Excelsior C (NY)
2. California State U, Northridge
3. California State U, San Bernardino
4. California State U, Long Beach

5. Northern Arizona U
6. Florida International U
7. California State U, Fresno

8. California State U, Dominguez Hills
9. Fairleigh Dickinson U (NJ)
10. Wayland Baptist U (TX)

Source: *The Hispanic Outlook in Higher Education* magazine (used with permission)

Colleges Where the Highest Number of Hispanics Are Awarded Bachelor's Degrees in the Social Sciences

1. Florida International U
2. California, U of, Riverside
3. California, U of, Los Angeles
4. California, U of, Santa Barbara
5. California State U, Northridge

6. California, U of, Irvine
7. California State U, Long Beach
8. California, U of, Berkeley
9. California, State U of, San Diego
10. California, U of, Davis

Source: *The Hispanic Outlook in Higher Education* magazine (used with permission)

Colleges Where the Highest Number of Hispanics Are Awarded Bachelor's Degrees in the Visual and Performing Arts

1. California State U, Long Beach
2. Columbia C (IL)
3. Arizona State U
4. Texas State U, San Marcos
5. California State U, Northridge
6. San Francisco State U (CA)

7. Texas, U of, Pan America
8. California State U, Fullerton
9. Florida International U (tie)
9. New York U (tie)
10. Texas, U of, El Paso

Source: *The Hispanic Outlook in Higher Education* magazine (used with permission)

Community Colleges with a Large Number of Hispanic Students

Austin Community C District (TX)
Bakersfield C (CA)
Central New Mexico Community C
Cerritos C (CA)
Chaffey C (CA)
Chicago, City C of, Richard J Daley C (IL)
Citrus C (CA)
East Los Angeles C (CA)
El Camino Community C District (CA)
El Paso Community C (TX)
Fresno City C (CA)
Fullerton C (CA)
Hillsborough Community C (FL)
Houston Community C (TX)
Imperial Valley C (CA)
Laredo Community C (TX)
Lone Star C System (TX)

Long Beach City C (CA)
Los Angeles Mission C (CA)
Los Angeles Pierce C (CA)
Los Angeles Trade Technical C (CA)
Los Angeles Valley C (CA)
Modesto Junior C (CA)
Mt. San Antonio C (CA)
New Mexico State U, Dona Ana
New York, City U of, Borough of
    Manhattan Community C
New York, City U of, Bronx Community
    C
New York, City U of, LaGuardia
    Community C
Northern Virginia Community C
Northwest Vista C (TX)
Palomar C (CA)
Pasadena City C (CA)

Pima Community C (AZ)
Reedley C (CA)
Rio Hondo C (CA)
Riverside City C (CA)
San Antonio C (TX)
San Bernardino Valley C (CA)
San Diego Mesa C (CA)
San Francisco, City C of (CA)

San Jacinto Community C (TX)
San Joaquin Delta C (CA)
Santa Ana C (CA)
Santa Barbara City C (CA)
Santa Monica C (CA)
Southwestern C (CA)
Tarrant County C District (TX)
Ventura C (CA)

Source: *The Hispanic Outlook in Higher Education* magazine (used with permission)

Four-Year Colleges That Award the Greatest Number of Associate Degrees to Hispanic Students

1. Miami Dade C (FL)
2. South Texas C
3. Valencia C (FL)
4. Broward C (FL)
5. Palm Beach State C (FL)
6. Keiser U (FL)
7. Texas, U of, Brownsville
8. Monroe C (NY)
9. Southern Nevada, C of
10. Seminole State C (FL)

Source: *The Hispanic Outlook in Higher Education* magazine (used with permission)

Community Colleges With the Greatest Number of Full-and Part-Time Hispanic Faculty

1. El Paso Community C (TX)
2. San Antonio C (TX)
3. Houston Community C (TX)
4. Laredo Community C (TX)
5. Central New Mexico Community C
6. St. Philip's C (TX)
7. Austin Community C District (TX)
8. Del Mar C (TX)
9. New York, City U of, LaGuardia Community C
10. New York, City U of, Hostos Community C
11. Northwest Vista C (TX)
12. New York, City U of, Bronx Community C
13. Southwest Texas Junior C
14. Texas State Technical C, Harlingen
15. Palo Alto C (TX)
16. Mt. San Antonio C (CA)
17. New York, City U of, Borough of Manhattan Community C
18. Tarrant County C District (TX)
19. Southwestern C (CA)
20. Santa Ana C (CA)
21. East Los Angeles C (CA)
22. New Mexico State U, Dona Ana
23. Hudson County Community C (NJ)
24. Hillsborough Community C (FL)
24. Rio Hondo C (CA)
25. Alamo Community C (TX)
26. Cerritos C (CA)
27. Pasadena City C (CA)
28. Fresno City C (CA)
29. San Francisco, City C of (CA)
30. Palomar C (CA)
32. Chaffey C (CA)
33. Santa Monica C (CA)
34. Passaic County Community C (NJ)
35. Long Beach City C (CA)
36. El Camino Community C District (CA)
37. Santa Fe Community C (NM)
38. New York, City U of, Queensborough Community C
39. Salt Lake Community C (UT)
40. Ivy Tech Community C (IN)
41. Reedley C (CA)
42. Glendale Community C (AZ)
43. El Centro C (TX)
44. Riverside City C (CA)
45. ASA C (NY)
46. Essex County C (NJ)
47. Phoenix C (AZ)
48. MiraCosta C (CA)
49. Northern Virginia Community C (VA)
50. Mesa Community C (AZ)

Source: *The Hispanic Outlook in Higher Education* magazine (used with permission)

Steven R. Antonoff

Two-Year Colleges Granting the Greatest Number of Health Care Profession Degrees to Hispanics

1. ASA C (NY)
2. Central New Mexico Community C
3. El Paso Community C (TX)
4. San Joaquin Valley C, Visalia (CA)
5. San Joaquin Valley C, Fresno (CA)
6. San Antonio C (TX)
7. Fresno City C (CA) (tie)
7. San Joaquin Valley C (CA) (tie)
8. Del Mar C (TX)
9. Mandl School, C of Allied Health (NY) (tie)
9. Saber C (FL) (tie)
10. Dade Medical C, Miami Lakes (FL)
11. Pima Community C (AZ)
12. Heald C, Hayward (CA)
13. San Jacinto Community C (TX)
14. San Joaquin Valley C, Hesperia (CA)
15. San Joaquin Valley C, Ontario (CA)
16. Lone Star C System (TX)
17. EDIC C (Puerto Rico)
18. Houston Community C (TX)
19. Ultimate Medical Academy, Tampa (FL)
20. Heald C, San Jose (CA) (tie)
20. St. Philip's C (TX) (tie)
21. Amarillo C (TX)
22. Mt. San Antonio C (CA)
23. Heald C, Salinas (CA)
24. New York, City U of, Bronx Community C (tie)
24. Heald C, Fresno (CA) (tie)
24. Texas State Technical C, Harlingen (tie)
25. Hillsborough Community C (FL)

Source: *The Hispanic Outlook in Higher Education* magazine (used with permission)

PACIFIC ISLANDER STUDENTS

Colleges With the Largest Enrollment of Pacific Islander Students

These numbers show the total enrollment of Pacific Islander students at each school.

Hawaii, U of, Manoa: 2,456
Pacific, U of (CA): 1,249
Hawaii, U of, Hilo: 1,124
California State U, San Marcos: 814
Hawaii, U of, West Oahu: 551
California State U, Sacramento: 398
American Public U System (WV): 390
Nevada, U of, Las Vegas: 386
Utah Valley U: 262
Florida, U of: 231
Chaminade U (HI): 196
Washington, U of, Seattle: 164
California State U, San Francisco: 159
Portland State U (OR): 150
Maryland, U of, University C: 147
Utah, U of: 144
Alaska, U of, Anchorage: 141
Thomas Edison State C (NJ): 139
California State U, East Bay: 136

Western Oregon U: 123
Dixie State U (UT): 123
Rutgers U, New Brunswick (NJ): 108
George Mason U (VA): 103
Oregon State U: 96
Washington State U: 95
Old Dominion U (VA): 95
Drexel U (PA): 94
Boise State U (ID): 91
Weber State U (UT): 89
Nevada, U of, Reno: 88
South Florida, U of: 88
California State U, Northridge: 85
California State U, Fullerton: 79
New York, City U of, C of Technology: 76
Northern Arizona U: 76
California, U of, Berkeley: 73
California, U of, Riverside: 72

Source: Wintergreen Orchard House

Colleges With the Highest Percentage of Pacific Islander Students

Hawaii, U of, Hilo: 32.51%
Pacific, U of the (CA): 32.22%
Hawaii, U of, West Oahu: 27.59%
Hawaii, U of, Manoa: 16.94%
Chaminade U (HI): 14.78%
California State U, San Marcos: 7.58%
Holy Names U (CA): 3.75%
Vaughn C of Aeronautics & Technology (NY): 3.48%
Northpoint Bible C (MA): 2.74%
Western Oregon U: 2.69%
DeVry U (WA): 2.66%
Notre Dame de Namur U (CA): 2.56%
Chamberlain C (IL): 2.44%
La Sierra U (CA): 2.38%
Menlo C (CA): 1.96%
Pacific Union C (CA): 1.88%
DeVry U (CA): 1.76%

Nevada, U of, Las Vegas: 1.67%
Concordia U (OR): 1.61%
Washington, U of, Tacoma: 1.60%
Warner Pacific C (OR): 1.59%
Alaska, U of, Southeast: 1.56%
Dixie State U (UT): 1.47%
Portland, U of (OR): 1.43%
California State U, Sacramento: 1.36%
Santa Fe U (NM): 1.33%
Oregon C of Art & Craft: 1.30%
Dominican U (CA): 1.29%
DeVry U (NJ): 1.24%
Southern Virginia U: 1.21%
Eastern Oregon U: 1.20%
Union C (NY): 1.16%
San Diego Christian C (CA): 1.13%
California State U, East Bay: 1.13%
Graceland U (IA): 1.03%

Source: Wintergreen Orchard House

FAITH/RELIGION

Anglican and Episcopal Colleges

Bard C (NY)
Bishop's U (Canada)
Clarkson C (NE)
Hobart C & William Smith C (NY)
Huron U C (Canada)
Kenyon C (OH)
King's C, U of (Canada)
Manitoba, U of (Canada)
Renison U C (Canada)

South, U of the (TN)
St. Augustine C (IL)
St. Augustine's U (NC)
St. Paul C (MN)
Thorneloe U (Canada)
Trinity C (Canada)
Voorhees C (SC)
Windsor, U of (Canada)

Source: Colleges and Universities of the Anglican Communion (cuac.anglicancommunion.org)

The Experts' Choice: Colleges Where Atheists Are Welcome

Experts identified these colleges as atheist-friendly.

Bard C (NY)
Beloit C (WI)
California, U of, Berkeley
Chicago, U of (IL)
Earlham C (IN)
Eckerd C (FL)
Evergreen State C (WA)

Goddard C (VT)
Grinnell C (IA)
Hampshire C (MA)
Kenyon C (OH)
New York U
Oberlin C (OH)
Reed C (OR)

Vassar C (NY)
Warren Wilson C (NC)

Wesleyan U (CT)

Baptist Colleges

Anderson U (SC)
Baptist C (FL)
Baptist C of Health Sciences (TN)
Baptist U of the Americas (TX)
Baylor U (TX)
Blue Mountain C (MS)
Bluefield C (VA)
California Baptist U
Campbell U (NC)
Campbellsville U (KY)
Carson-Newman U (TN)
Charleston Southern U (SC)
Chowan U (NC)
Clear Creek Baptist Bible C (KY)
Cumberlands, U of the (KY)
Dallas Baptist U (TX)
East Texas Baptist U
Fruitland Baptist Bible Institute (NC)
Georgetown C (KY)
Golden Gate Baptist Theological
   Seminary (CA)

Hannibal-LaGrange U (MO)
Hardin-Simmons U (TX)
Houston Baptist U (TX)
Howard Payne U (TX)
Judson C (AL)
Louisiana C
Mary Hardin-Baylor, U of (TX)
Mississippi C
Missouri Baptist U
North Greenville U (SC)
Oklahoma Baptist U
Ouachita Baptist U (AR)
Samford U (AL)
Seinan Gakuin U (Japan)
Shorter U (GA)
Southwest Baptist U (MO)
Union U (TN)
Wayland Baptist U (TX)
William Carey U (MS)
Williams Baptist C (AR)
Yellowstone Christian C (MT)

Source: International Association of Baptist Colleges and Universities (*baptistschools.org*)

Buddhist-Friendly Schools in the United States

These colleges are affiliated with or influenced by Buddhist teachings.

Dharma Realm Buddhist U (CA)
Maitripa C (OR)
Naropa U (CO)
Soka U (CA)
West, U of the (CA)

Catholic Colleges

These schools are members of the National Catholic College Admission Association.

Albertus Magnus C (CT)
Alvernia U (PA)
Anna Maria C (MA)
Aquinas C (MI)
Aquinas C (TN)
Assumption C (MA)
Ave Maria U (FL)

Avila U (MO)
Barry U (FL)
Bellarmine U (KY)
Belmont Abbey C (NC)
Benedictine C (KS)
Benedictine U (AZ)
Benedictine U (IL)

Boston C (MA)
Cabrini C (PA)
Caldwell U (NJ)
Calumet C (IN)
Canisius C (NY)
Carlow U (PA)
Carroll U (MT)
Catholic U (DC)
Chaminade U (HI)
Chestnut Hill C (PA)
Christian Brothers U (TN)
Creighton U (NE)
Dallas, U of (TX)
Dayton, U of (OH)
DePaul U (IL)
DeSales U (PA)
Detroit Mercy, U of (MI)
Dominican U (CA)
Dominican U (IL)
Duquesne U (PA)
Elms C (MA)
Emmanuel C (MA)
Fairfield U (CT)
Felician C (NJ)
Fontbonne U (MO)
Fordham U (NY)
Franciscan U (OH)
Gannon U (PA)
Gonzaga U (WA)
Great Falls, U of (MT)
Gwynedd Mercy U (PA)
Hilbert C (NY)
Holy Cross C (IN)
Holy Cross, C of the (MA)
Holy Family U (PA)
Incarnate Word, U of the (TX)
Iona C (NY)
John Carroll U (OH)
King's C (PA)
La Roche C (PA)
La Salle U (PA)
Le Moyne C (NY)
Lewis U (IL)
Loras C (IA)
Lourdes U (OH)
Loyola Marymount U (CA)
Loyola U (IL)
Loyola U (LA)
Loyola U (MD)
Manhattan C (NY)
Marian U (IN)
Marian U (WI)
Marquette U (WI)
Marymount U (CA)
Marymount U (VA)

Marywood U (PA)
Mercyhurst U (PA)
Merrimack C (MA)
Molloy C (NY)
Mt. Aloysius C (PA)
Mt. Mary U (WI)
Mt. St. Joseph U (OH)
Mt. St. Mary C (NY)
Mt. St. Mary's U (CA)
Mt. St. Mary's U (MD)
Mt. St. Vincent, C of (NY)
Newman U (KS)
Niagara U (NY)
Notre Dame C (OH)
Notre Dame de Namur U (CA)
Notre Dame U (MD)
Notre Dame, U of (IN)
Our Lady of the Lake C (LA)
Portland, U of (OR)
Providence C (RI)
Regis C (MA)
Regis U (CO)
Rosemont C (PA)
Sacred Heart U (CT)
Salve Regina U (RI)
San Diego, U of (CA)
San Francisco, U of (CA)
Santa Clara U (CA)
Scranton, U of (PA)
Seattle U (WA)
Siena C (NY)
Siena Heights U (MI)
Spring Hill C (AL)
St. Ambrose U (IA)
St. Anselm C (NH)
St. Benedict, C of/St. John's U (MN)
St. Bonaventure U (NY)
St. Catherine U (MN)
St. Edward's U (TX)
St. Elizabeth, C of (NJ)
St. Francis U (PA)
St. Francis, U of (IN)
St. John Fisher C (NY)
St. John's U (NY)
St. Joseph's C (IN)
St. Joseph's C (ME)
St. Joseph's U (PA)
St. Leo U (FL)
St. Louis U (MO)
St. Mary-of-the-Woods C (IN)
St. Mary, C of (NE)
St. Mary's C (CA)
St. Mary's C (IN)
St. Mary's U (MN)
St. Mary's U (TX)

St. Michael's C (VT)
St. Rose, C of (NY)
St. Thomas Aquinas C (NY)
St. Thomas U (FL)
St. Thomas, U of (MN)
St. Thomas, U of (TX)
St. Vincent C (PA)
Stonehill C (MA)

Thomas Aquinas C (CA)
Thomas More C (KY)
Villanova U (PA)
Viterbo U (WI)
Walsh U (OH)
Wheeling Jesuit U (WV)
Xavier U (LA)
Xavier U (OH)

The Newman Guide's Recommended Catholic Colleges

"*The Newman Guide to Choosing a Catholic College* recommends Catholic colleges, universities, and online programs both in the United States and abroad."

Aquinas C (MI)
Ave Maria U (FL)
Belmont Abbey C (NC)
Benedictine C (KS)
Catholic U (DC)
Christendom C (VA)
Dallas, U of (TX)
DeSales U (PA)
Franciscan U (OH)
Holy Apostles C & Seminary (CT)

John Paul the Great Catholic U (CA)
Mary, U of (ND)
Mt. St. Mary's U (MD)
Northeast Catholic C (NH)
St. Gregory's U (OK)
St. Thomas, U of (MN)
Thomas Aquinas C (CA)
Thomas More C (NH)
Walsh U (OH)
Wyoming Catholic C

Source: The Cardinal Newman Society (*cardinalnewmansociety.org*)

Christian Brothers Colleges

A Roman Catholic order, the Christian Brothers devote themselves exclusively to Christian education.

Christian Brothers U (TN)
La Salle U (PA)
Lewis U (IL)
Manhattan C (NY)
St. Mary's C (CA)
St. Mary's U (MN)

Franciscan Colleges and Universities

These colleges are members of the Association of Franciscan Colleges and Universities.

Alvernia U (PA)
Alverno C (WI)
Briar Cliff U (IA)
Cardinal Stritch U (WI)
Felician C (NJ)
Franciscan School of Theology (CA)
Franciscan U (OH)

Hilbert C (NY)
Lourdes U (OH)
Madonna U (MI)
Marian U (IN)
Neumann C (PA)
Our Lady of the Lake C (LA)
Quincy U (IL)

Siena C (NY)
Silver Lake C (WI)
St. Bonaventure U (NY)
St. Francis C (NY)
St. Francis U (PA)

St. Francis, U of (IL)
St. Francis, U of (IN)
St. John's C (MD)
Villa Maria C (NY)
Viterbo U (WI)

Source: Association of Franciscan Colleges and Universities (*franciscancollegesuniversities.org*)

Fastest-Growing Roman Catholic Doctoral Institutions

These are the percent increase in enrollment over a 10-year period, 2004-2014. Note: the average rate of growth in this category is 7.1%.

Benedictine U (IL): 95.1%
Spalding U (KY): 36.1%
Georgetown U (DC) 35.0%
San Francisco, U of (CA): 29.2%
Edgewood C (WI): 21.4%
St. Mary's U (MN): 19.8%
St. Louis U (MO): 17.2%
Loyola U (IL): 14.3%
St. John Fisher C (NY): 14.2%
Catholic U (DC): 11.9%

Source: *The Chronicle of Higher Education*

Fastest-Growing Roman Catholic Master's Institutions

These are the percent increase in enrollment over a 10-year period, 2004-2014. Note: the average rate of growth in this category is 3.7%.

Incarnate Word, U of the (TX): 86.1%
St. Mary, U of (KS): 74.3%
Newman U (KS): 69.2%
Walsh U (OH): 49.6%
Mt. St. Mary's U (CA): 45.9%
St. Francis U (PA): 44.4%
St. Joseph, U of (CT): 43.1%
St. Scholastica, C of (MN): 39.6%
Lewis U (IL): 38.0%
Sacred Heart U (CT): 37.6%

Source: *The Chronicle of Higher Education*

Fastest-Growing Roman Catholic Baccalaureate Institutions

These are the percent increase in enrollment over a 10-year period, 2004-2014. Note: the average rate of growth in this category is 7.4%.

Belmont Abbey C (NC): 95.0%
Elms C (MA): 78.3%
Notre Dame C (OH): 75.6%
Marian U (IN): 64.5%
Brescia U (KY): 56.7%

Benedictine C (KS): 48.4%
Great Falls, U of (MT): 46.2%
Merrimack C (MA): 41.9%
St. Catharine C (KY): 41.1%
Seton Hill U: 28.6%

Source: *The Chronicle of Higher Education*

The "Most Catholic" Catholic Schools

First Things is a conservative religious journal focused on creating a "religiously informed public philosophy for the ordering of society." These ratings were calculated from polls of students who were questioned about the academic, religious, and social lives of their schools. Ratings included variables such as academic reputation, graduation rates, friendliness to religious faith, the vibrancy of ministries, and student faith. In addition to polling, *First Things* conducted conversations with students, graduates, faculty, and chaplains.

According to *First Things* magazine, these Catholic schools are among those where Catholic roots are the most prominent.

1. Ave Maria U (FL)
2. Christendom C (VA)
3. Franciscan U (OH)
4. Thomas Aquinas C (CA)
5. Benedictine C (KS)
6. Belmont Abbey C (NC)
7. Thomas More C (NH)
8. Dallas, U of (TX)
9. Providence C (RI)
10. Mt. St. Mary's U (MD)
11. St. Thomas More, C of (TX)
12. St. Thomas, U of (TX)

Source: *First Things* (*firstthings.com*)

The "Least Catholic" Catholic Schools

First Things is a conservative religious journal focused on creating a "religiously informed public philosophy for the ordering of society." These ratings were calculated from polls of students who were questioned about the academic, religious, and social lives of their schools. Ratings included variables such as academic reputation, graduation rates, friendliness to religious faith, the vibrancy of ministries, and student faith. In addition to polling, *First Things* conducted conversations with students, graduates, faculty, and chaplains.

According to *First Things* magazine, these Catholic schools are among those where Catholic roots are the least prominent.

1. DePaul U (IL)
2. Detroit Mercy, U of (MI)
3. Seattle U (WA)

4. Niagara U (NY)
5. San Diego, U of (CA)
6. Lewis U (IL)
7. Georgetown U (DC)
8. D'Youville C (NY)
9. Molloy C (NY)
10. Lourdes C (OH)
11. Quincy U (IL)
12. San Francisco, U of (CA)

Members and Affiliates of the Council for Christian Colleges & Universities

These colleges are "intentionally Christ-centered" and qualified as members of the Council for Christian Colleges & Universities.

Abilene Christian U (TX)
Africa International U (Kenya)
Africa Nazarene U (Kenya)
Alphacrucis C (Australia)
Ambrose U (Canada)
Anderson U (IN)
Anderson U (SC)
Arizona Christian U
Asbury Theological Seminary (KY)
Asbury U (KY)
Avondale C of Higher Education
 (Australia)
Azusa Pacific U (CA)
Baylor U (TX)
Belhaven U (MS)
Bethel C (IN)
Bethel U (MN)
Biola U (CA)
Bluefield C (VA)
Booth U C (Canada)
Briercrest C and Seminary (Canada)
Bryan C (TN)
Cairn U (PA)
California Baptist U
Calvin C (MI)
Campbell U (NC)
Campbellsville U (KY)
Carson-Newman U (TN)
Central Christian C (KS)
Central University C (Ghana)
Charleston Southern U (SC)
Christ's C (Taiwan)
Christelijke Hogeschool Ede
 (Netherlands)
Christian Heritage C (Australia)
Colorado Christian U
Columbia International U (SC)
Concordia U (CA)

Corban U (OR)
Cornerstone U (MI)
Covenant C (GA)
Crandall U (Canada)
Crown C (MN)
CSI Bishop Appasamy College of Arts &
 Sciences (India)
Dallas Baptist U (TX)
Dallas Theological Seminary (TX)
Dordt C (IA)
East Texas Baptist U
Eastern Nazarene C (MA)
Eastern U (PA)
Emmanuel C (GA)
Erskine C (SC)
Evangel U (MO)
Excelsia C (Australia)
Faulkner U (AL)
Franciscan U (OH)
Fresno Pacific U (CA)
Friends U (KS)
Fuller Theological Seminary (CA)
Geneva C (PA)
George Fox U (OR)
Gordon C (MA)
Gordon-Conwell Theological Seminary
 (MA)
Grace C (IN)
Greenville C (IL)
Handong Global U (Korea)
Hannibal-LaGrange U (MO)
Hardin-Simmons U (TX)
Harding U (AR)
Hope International U (CA)
Houghton C (NY)
Houston Baptist U (TX)
Howard Payne U (TX)
Huntington U (IN)

Indiana Wesleyan U
Jerusalem U C (Israel)
John Brown U (AR)
John Wesley Theological C (Hungary)
Johnson U (TN)
Judson C (AL)
Judson U (IL)
Karoli Gaspar U (Hungary)
Kentucky Christian U (KY)
King U (TN)
King's C, The (NY)
King's U, The (Canada)
Kuyper C (MI)
Laidlaw C (New Zealand)
Lancaster Bible C (PA)
LCC International U (Lithuania)
Lee U (TN)
LeTourneau U (TX)
Life Pacific C (CA)
Lincoln Christian U (IL)
Lipscomb U (TN)
Louisiana C
Malone U (OH)
Mary Hardin-Baylor, U of (TX)
McMaster Divinity C (Canada)
Messiah C (PA)
MidAmerica Nazarene U (KS)
Milligan C (TN)
Mississippi C (MS)
Missouri Baptist U (MO)
Mobile, U of (AL)
Montreat C (NC)
Moody Bible Institute (IL)
Mt. Vernon Nazarene U (OH)
Multnomah U (OR)
Nazarene Theological C (United
  Kingdom)
New St. Andrews C (ID)
Newbold C (United Kingdom)
North Central U (MN)
North Greenville U (SC)
North Haiti Christian U
North Park U (IL)
Northwest Christian U (OR)
Northwest Nazarene U (ID)
Northwest U (WA)
Northwestern C (IA)
Northwestern, U of (MN)
Nyack C (NY)
Oklahoma Baptist U
Oklahoma Christian U
Olivet Nazarene U (IL)
Oral Roberts U (OK)
Ozarks, C of the (MO)
Palm Beach Atlantic U (FL)

Pepperdine U (CA)
Point Loma Nazarene U (CA)
Point U (GA)
Prairie C (Canada)
Providence Christian C (CA)
Providence U C (Canada)
Queensland U (Haiti)
Redeemer U C (Canada)
Regent U (VA)
Roberts Wesleyan C (NY)
Samford U (AL)
San Diego Christian C (CA)
Seattle Pacific U (WA)
Sheng-te Christian C (Taiwan)
Shorter U (GA)
Simpson U (CA)
Sioux Falls, U of (SD)
Southeastern Baptist Theological
  Seminary (NC)
Southeastern U (FL)
Southern Nazarene U (OK)
Southern Wesleyan U (SC)
Southwest Baptist U (MO)
Southwest, U of the (NM)
Southwestern Assemblies of God U
  (TX)
Southwestern Christian U (OK)
Spring Arbor U (MI)
Sterling C (KS)
Tabor C (KS)
Taylor U (IN)
Toccoa Falls C (GA)
Tokyo Christian U (Japan)
Trevecca Nazarene U (TN)
Trinity Christian C (IL)
Trinity International U (IL)
Trinity Western U (Canada)
Tyndale University C & Seminary
  (Canada)
Uganda Christian U (Uganda)
Universidad Evangélica Boliviana
  (Bolivia)
Universidad Nacional Evangélica
  (Dominican Republic)
Universitas Pelita Harapan (Indonesia)
Valley Forge, U of (PA)
Vanguard U (CA)
Walla Walla U (WA)
Warner Pacific C (OR)
Warner U (FL)
Waynesburg U (PA)
Westmont C (CA)
Wheaton C (IL)
Whitworth U (WA)
William Jessup U (CA)

Williams Baptist C (AR)
Wisconsin Lutheran C (WI)

Wycliffe Hall (United Kingdom)
York C (NE)

Source: Council for Christian Colleges and Universities, Washington, DC (*cccu.org*)

Christian College Consortium

The Christian College Consortium consists of colleges and universities united by a shared commitment to the liberal arts tradition and a common affirmation of faith.

Asbury C (KY)
Bethel U (MN)
George Fox U (OR)
Gordon C (MA)
Greenville C (IL)
Houghton C (NY)
Malone U (OH)

Messiah C (PA)
Seattle Pacific U (WA)
Taylor U (IN)
Trinity International U (IL)
Westmont C (CA)
Wheaton C (IL)

Source: Christian College Consortium (*ccconsortium.org*)

Faith on View Christian Colleges

Faith on View rates colleges on the following criteria: "Distinctively Christian and have this commitment at the core of their educational philosophy." The rankings are reputation, student success and satisfaction, faculty resources, and student selectivity. According to the website, Faith on View "is a great starting point for families looking into Christian education."

1. Thomas Aquinas C (CA)
2. St. Olaf C (MN)
3. Wheaton C (IL)
4. Hope C (MI)
5. Baylor U (TX)
6. Berea C (KY)
7. Providence C (RI)
8. Calvin C (MI)
9. Grove City C (PA)
10. Samford U (AL)
11. Cedarville U (OH)
12. Taylor U (IN)
13. Pepperdine U (CA)
14. Ozarks, C of the (MO)
15. Dallas, U of (TX)
16. Westmont C (CA)
17. Whitworth U (WA)
18. Goshen C (IN)
19. Mercer U (GA)
20. Union U (TN)
21. Belmont U (TN)
22. St. Thomas, U of (MN)
23. Gordon C (MA)
24. Messiah C (PA)

25. Gutenberg C (OR)
26. Azusa Pacific U (CA)
27. Dordt C (IA)
28. Ouachita Baptist U (AR)
29. Georgetown C (KY)
30. Asbury U (KY)
31. Abilene Christian U (TX)
32. Catholic U (DC)
33. Covenant C (GA)
34. Oklahoma Baptist U
35. Milligan C (TN)
36. Houghton C (NY)
37. Bethel U (MN)
38. John Brown U (AR)
39. Anderson U (IN)
40. Bethany Lutheran C (MN)
41. Christendom C (VA)
42. Northwestern, U of (MN)
43. Erskine C (SC)
44. Huntington U (IN)
45. Master's C, The (CA)
46. George Fox U (OR)
47. Northwest Nazarene U (ID)
48. Freed-Hardeman U (AR)

49. Harding U (AR)   50. Eastern Mennonite U (VA)

Source: Faith on View (*faithonview.com*)

25 Top Schools That Are Faith-Friendly

First Things is a conservative religious journal focused on creating a "religiously informed public philosophy for the ordering of society." These ratings were calculated from polls of students who were questioned about the academic, religious, and social lives of their schools. Ratings included variables such as academic reputation, graduation rates, friendliness to religious faith, the vibrancy of ministries, and student faith. In addition to polling, *First Things* conducted conversations with students, graduates, faculty, and chaplains.

These colleges and universities were selected by the Institute on Religion and Public Life ("an interreligious, nonpartisan research and educational 501(c)(3) organization") to be the ones that "cast a light on the place of religion or lack thereof on American college campuses today."

1.   Wheaton C (IL)
2.   Thomas Aquinas C (CA)
3.   Princeton U (NJ)
4.   U.S. Air Force Academy (CO)
5.   Brigham Young U (UT)
6.   Yeshiva U (NY)
7.   Virginia, U of
8.   Duke U (NC)
9.   Chicago, U of (IL)
10. Franciscan U (OH)
11. Hillsdale C (MI)
12. Dallas, U of (TX)
13. Calvin C (NI)
14. Columbia U (NY)
15. Stanford U (CA)
16. Notre Dame, U of (IN)
17. Baylor U (TX)
18. Benedictine C (KS)
19. Providence C (RI)
20. Grove City C (PA)
21. Taylor U (IN)
22. Wabash C (IN)
23. St. John's C (MD)
24. Davidson C (NC)
25. U.S. Naval Academy (MD)

Source: *First Things* (*firstthings.com*)

Colleges Where Chapel Attendance Is Required

Sometimes, that daunting engineering exam or biology paper requires the help of a higher power. At these schools, you'll be going to chapel every week and likely contemplating more important things than tests and papers.

Abilene Christian U (TX)
Azusa Pacific U (CA)
Baptist Bible C (PA)
Biola U (CA)
Bryn Athyn C (PA)
Cairn U (PA)
Colorado Christian U
Corban U (OR)
Cornerstone U (MI)
Crown C (MN)
Erskine C (SC)
Gardner-Webb U (NC)
George Fox U (OR)
Indiana Wesleyan U
La Sierra U (CA)
Lancaster Bible C (PA)
LeTourneau U (TX)
Mary Hardin-Baylor, U of (TX)
Master's C, The (CA)
Messiah C (PA)

Mobile, U of (AL)
Mt. Vernon Nazarene U (OH)
Northwest Christian U (OR)
Northwest U (WA)
Oklahoma Baptist U
Oklahoma Christian U
Oklahoma Wesleyan U
Patten U (CA)
Point Loma Nazarene U (CA)
Roberts Wesleyan C (NY)

San Diego Christian C (CA)
Simpson U (CA)
Southern Nazarene U (OK)
Southwestern Adventist U (TN)
Southwestern Assemblies of God U
   (TX)
Sterling C (KS)
Walla Walla U (WA)
Wayland Baptist U (TX)
Westmont C (CA)

Source: Wintergreen Orchard House

Colleges With Faith-Based Residence Halls

Florida Institute of Technology
Illinois, U of, Urbana
Nebraska, U of, Lincoln
Purdue U (IN) (men only)
Texas A&M U, Kingsville
Troy U (AL)

Source: *The College Finder* research, including: Campo-Flores, Arian. "Religious Dorms Sprout Up." *The Wall Street Journal,* 3 Sept. 2013: 1. Print.

Top Secular Colleges That Are the Least Unfriendly to Faith

First Things is a conservative religious journal focused on creating a "religiously informed public philosophy for the ordering of society." These ratings were calculated from polls of students who were questioned about the academic, religious, and social lives of their schools. Ratings included variables such as academic reputation, graduation rates, friendliness to religious faith, the vibrancy of ministries, and student faith. In addition to polling, *First Things* conducted conversations with students, graduates, faculty, and chaplains.

According to *First Things* magazine, these schools are the "least unfriendly to faith" among secular schools.

1. Princeton U (NJ)
2. Duke U (NC)
3. Virginia, U of
4. Chicago, U of (IL)
5. Stanford U (CA)
6. Columbia U (NY)
7. California Institute of Technology

Source: *First Things* (firstthings.com)

Steven R. Antonoff

First Things' Schools on the Rise, Filled With Excitement

First Things is a conservative religious journal focused on creating a "religiously informed public philosophy for the ordering of society." These ratings were calculated from polls of students who were questioned about the academic, religious, and social lives of their schools. Ratings included variables such as academic reputation, graduation rates, friendliness to religious faith, the vibrancy of ministries, and student faith. In addition to polling, *First Things* conducted conversations with students, graduates, faculty, and chaplains.

1. Belmont Abbey C (NC)
2. Wake Forest U (NC)
3. Houston Baptist U (TX)
4. King's C, The (NY)
5. Concordia U (WI)

Source: *First Things* (*firstthings.com*)

First Things' Schools in Decline, Filled With Gloom

First Things is a conservative religious journal focused on creating a "religiously informed public philosophy for the ordering of society." These ratings were calculated from polls of students who were questioned about the academic, religious, and social lives of their schools. Ratings included variables such as academic reputation, graduation rates, friendliness to religious faith, the vibrancy of ministries, and student faith. In addition to polling, *First Things* conducted conversations with students, graduates, faculty, and chaplains.

1. Valparaiso U (IN)
2. Gonzaga U (WA)
3. Dartmouth C (NH)
4. Azusa Pacific U (CA)
5. Notre Dame, C of (MD)

Source: *First Things* (*firstthings.com*)

Bible Colleges

These colleges, accredited by the Association for Biblical Higher Education, "assist men and women in the development of a biblical worldview, with a special emphasis upon preparation for church-related vocations."

Alaska Bible C	Baptist Bible C (MO)
Alaska Christian C	Baptist U of the Americas (TX)
Allegheny Wesleyan C (OH)	Barclay C (KS)
Ambrose U C (Canada)	Bethany C (Canada)
American Baptist C (TN)	Bethel C (VA)
American Evangelical U (CA)	Bethesda U (CA)
Appalachian Bible C (WV)	Bethlehem C (MN)
Arlington Baptist C (TX)	Beulah Heights U (GA)
B H Carroll Theological Institute (TX)	Biblical Studies, C of, Houston (TX)

Boise Bible C (ID)
Briercrest C & Seminary (SK)
Cairn U (PA)
Calvary Bible C & Theological Seminary (MO)
Canadian Southern Baptist Seminary
Carolina C of Biblical Studies (NC)
Carolina Christian C (NC)
Carver C (GA)
Central Christian C of the Bible (MO)
Cincinnati Christian U (OH)
Clear Creek Baptist Bible C (KY)
Columbia Bible C (Canada)
Columbia International U (SC)
Crossroads Bible C (IN)
Dallas Christian C (TX)
Davis C (NY)
Dominion C (WI)
Ecclesia C (AR)
Emmanuel Bible C (Canada)
Emmaus Bible C (IA)
Eston C (Canada)
Faith Baptist Bible C & Theological Seminary (IA)
Faith Bible C (VA)
Family of Faith C (OK)
God's Bible School & C (OH)
Grace Bible C (MI)
Grace C of Divinity (NC)
Grace Mission U (CA)
Grace U (NE)
Great Lakes Christian C (MI)
Heritage C & Seminary (ON)
Heritage Christian U (AL)
Hobe Sound Bible C (FL)
Hope International U (CA)
Horizon C & Seminary (SK)
Horizon U (CA)
Huntsville Bible C (AL)
International Reformed U & Seminary (CA)
Johnson U (TN)
Kentucky Mountain Bible C (KY)
King's U, The (TX)
Kingswood U (NB)
Kuyper C (MI)
Lancaster Bible C (PA)
Laurel U (NC)
Life Pacific C (CA)
Lincoln Christian U (IL)
Louisville Bible C (KY)
Luther Rice C & Seminary (GA)

Manhattan Christian C (KS)
Master's C & Seminary (Canada)
Mid-South Christian C (TN)
Midwest U (MO)
Montana Bible C (MT)
Moody Bible Institute (IL)
Multnomah U (OR)
Nazarene Bible C (CO)
Nebraska Christian C (NE)
New Hope Christian C (OR)
Northpoint Bible C (MA)
Oak Hills Christian C (MN)
Ohio Christian U
Olivet U (CA)
Ozark Christian C (MO)
Pacific Rim Christian U (HI)
Pillar C (NJ)
Prairie C (Canada)
Presbyterian Theological Seminary in America (CA)
Providence U C (Canada)
R. E. Webber Institute for Worship Studies (FL)
Rio Grande Bible Institute (TX)
Rocky Mountain C (Canada)
Rosedale Bible C (OH)
Selma U (AL)
Simmons C (KY)
South Florida Bible C & Theological Seminary
Southeastern Baptist C (MS)
Southeastern Bible C (AL)
St. Louis Christian C (MO)
Steinbach Bible C (Canada)
SUM Bible C & Theological Seminary (CA)
Summit Pacific C (Canada)
Summit U (PA)
Theological U of the Caribbean (Puerto Rico)
Trinity Bible C (ND)
Trinity C (FL)
Tri-State Bible C (OH)
Tyndale U C & Seminary (Canada)
Universidad Pentecostal Mizpa (Puerto Rico)
Vanguard C (Canada)
Washington U (VA)
Welch C (TN)
William Jessup U (CA)
Williamson C (TN)
World Mission U (CA)

Source: Association for Biblical Higher Education (*abhe.org*)

Bible Colleges and Seminaries

These schools are members of the International Association of Bible Colleges and Seminaries.

Bethesda Christian Bible Institute (MI)
Christian Leaders Institute (MI)
Christian Life School of Theology (GA)
Christian World C (MD)
Colegio Biblico (TX)
Faith School of Theology (ME)
Faith Theological Seminary & Christian C (FL)
Florida Beacon C & Seminary (FL)
Heart of America Bible C & Theological Seminary (MO)
Kingsway U & Theological Seminary (IA)
Logos Christian C & Graduate Schools (FL)
Mt. Olivet Theological Seminary (GA)
Temple Bible C & Seminary (OH)
The BBC School of Theology (GA)
True Standard Christian Bible C (NC)
United Theological Seminary (NY)
Vision Christian Bible C & Seminary (FL)
Vision International U (CA)

Source: International Association of Bible Colleges and Seminaries (*iabcs.org*)

Colleges With Many Jewish Students

At these colleges, either Jewish students are enrolled in high numbers or they represent a high percentage of the student population.

Boston U (MA)	Massachusetts, U of, Amherst
Brandeis U (MA)	Michigan, U of, Ann Arbor
Brown U (RI)	New York U
California, U of, Los Angeles	New York, City U of, Baruch
Chicago, U of (IL)	New York, City U of, Queens
Columbia U (NY)	Pennsylvania State U, University Park
Cornell U (NY)	Pennsylvania, U of
Dickinson C (PA)	Princeton U (NJ)
Drexel U (PA)	Rutgers U (NJ)
Harvard U (MA)	Toronto, U of (Canada)
Illinois, U of, Urbana	Wellesley C (MA)
Johns Hopkins U (MD)	Yale U (CT)
Kentucky, U of	Yeshiva U (NY)
Maryland, U of, College Park	York U (Canada)

Choices for Jewish Students

Dr. Mark Fisher, an independent educational consultant in Atlanta and researcher of colleges appropriate for Jewish students, lists the following as his favorites because they attract Jewish students and have an active Jewish community. In addition, many have kosher dining.

Public Universities

Arizona, U of
Central Florida U
Charleston, C of (SC)
Florida, U of
Illinois, U of, Urbana
Indiana U, Bloomington
Maryland, U of, College Park
Massachusetts, U of, Amherst
Michigan, U of, Ann Arbor
New York, State U of, Binghamton
Ohio State U, Columbus
Rutgers U (NJ)
Texas, U of, Austin
Vermont, U of
Wisconsin, U of, Madison

Private Colleges

American U (DC)
American Jewish U (CA)
Barnard C (NY)
Boston U (MA)
Bradley U (IL)
Brandeis U (MA)
Chicago, U of (IL)
Clark U (MA)
Columbia U (NY)
Cornell U (NY)
Dickinson C (PA)
Drexel U (PA)
Duke U (NC)
Elon C (NC)

Emory U (GA)
Franklin & Marshall C (PA)
George Washington U (DC)
Goucher C (MD)
Hartford, U of (CT)
Harvard U (MA)
Hofstra U (NY)
Ithaca C (NY)
Jewish Theological Seminary (NY)
Johns Hopkins U (MD)
Lynn U (FL)
Massachusetts Institute of Technology
Miami, U of (FL)
Muhlenberg C (PA)
New York U
Northeastern U (MA)
Northwestern U (IL)
Oberlin C (OH)
Pennsylvania, U of
Princeton U (NJ)
Rochester, U of (NY)
Southern California, U of
Stanford U (CA)
Syracuse U (NY)
Touro C/Lander C (NY)
Trinity (CT)
Tufts U (MA)
Tulane U (LA)
Vanderbilt U (TN)
Washington U (MO)
Wesleyan U (CT)
Yale U (CT)
Yeshiva U (NY)

The Experts' Choice: Jewish-Friendly Colleges

Experts were asked to name colleges with an active Jewish community or kosher meal options.

Brown U (RI)
California, U of, Los Angeles
Drexel U (PA)
Florida, U of
Kentucky, U of
New York, City U of, Baruch
New York, City U of, Queens
Pennsylvania State U, University Park

Rice U (TX)
Smith C (MA)
Southern California, U of
Toronto, U of (Canada)
Washington & Lee U (VA)
Wellesley C (MA)
Western U (Canada)
York U (Canada)

Colleges With Kosher Meals Available

Since the last edition of *The College Finder,* there has been an increase in colleges serving kosher meals. Dr. Mark Fisher, an independent educational consultant in Atlanta, identifies the following colleges as offering fresh, kosher dining (although a few have packaged meals), with most having kosher food available at lunch and/or dinner. Updated information is also available on a website operated by Hart Levine, director of Heart to Heart at the Orthodox Union (*theheart2heartproject.org/koshermap*) or by contacting the Hillel organization at individual colleges.

American Jewish U (CA)
Arizona, U of
Barnard C (NY)
Boston U (MA)
Bradley U (IL)
Brandeis U (MA)
Brown U (RI)
California, U of, San Diego
California, U of, Irvine
California, U of, Los Angeles
Carnegie Mellon U (PA)
Case Western Reserve U (OH)
Central Florida, U of
Charleston, C of (SC)
Chicago, U of (IL)
Clark U (MA)
Colorado, U of, Boulder
Columbia U (NY)
Connecticut, U of
Cornell U (NY)
Dartmouth C (NH)
Delaware, U of
Dickinson (PA)
Drexel U (PA)
Duke U (NC)
Emory U (GA)
Franklin & Marshall C (PA)
Goucher C (MD)
Hartford, U of (CT)
Harvard U (MA)
Hofstra U (NY)
Illinois, U of, Urbana
Indiana U, Bloomington
Ithaca C (NY)
Jewish Theological Seminary (NY)
Johns Hopkins U (MD)
Kansas, U of
Maryland, U of, Baltimore County
Maryland, U of, College Park
Massachusetts Institute of Technology
Massachusetts, U of, Amherst
McGill U (Canada)
Michigan State U

Michigan, U of, Ann Arbor
Mt. Holyoke C (MA)
Muhlenberg C (PA)
New Jersey, C of
New York U
New York, City U of, Baruch
New York, City U of, Brooklyn
New York, City U of, Queens
New York, State U of, Albany
New York, State U of, Binghamton
New York, State U of, Buffalo
New York, State U of, Geneseo
New York, State U of, Stony Brook
Northeastern U (MA)
Northwestern U (IL)
Oberlin C (OH)
Ohio State U, Columbus
Pennsylvania State U, University Park
Pennsylvania, U of
Pittsburgh, U of (PA)
Princeton U (NJ)
Rochester, U of (NY)
Rutgers U (NJ)
San Diego, U of (CA)
Stanford U (CA)
Syracuse U (NY)
Temple U (PA)
Touro C/Lander C (NY)
Towson U (MD)
Trinity C (CT)
Tufts U (MA)
Tulane U (LA)
Vanderbilt U (TN)
Vermont, U of
Washington U (MO)
Wayne State U (MI)
Wellesley C (MA)
Wesleyan U (CT)
Williams C (MA)
Wisconsin, U of, Madison
Yale U (CT)
Yeshiva U (NY)

These Colleges Have Many Kosher Meal Plan Options

American Jewish U (CA)
Arizona, U of
Barnard C (NY)
Boston U (MA)
Brandeis U (MA)
Brown U (RI)
California, U of, Irvine
California, U of, Los Angeles
Carnegie Mellon U (PA)
Case Western U (OH)
Chicago, U of (IL)
Clark U (MA)
Colorado, U of, Boulder
Columbia U (NY)
Connecticut, U of
Cornell U (NY)
Dartmouth C (NH)
Dickinson U (PA)
Drexel U (PA)
Duke U (NC)
Emory U (GA)
Florida, U of
Franklin & Marshall U (PA)
Goucher C (MD)
Hartford, U of (CT)
Harvard (MA)
Hofstra U (NY)
Illinois, U of, Urbana
Indiana U, Bloomington
Ithaca U (NY)
Johns Hopkins U (MD)
Kansas, U of
Maryland, U of, Baltimore County
Maryland, U of, College Park
Massachusetts Institute of Technology
Massachusetts, U of, Amherst
McGill U (Canada)
Michigan State U
Michigan, U of, Ann Arbor
Mt. Holyoke C (MA)
Muhlenberg U (PA)

New Jersey, C of
New York U
New York, City U of, Queens
New York, State U of, Albany
New York, State U of, Binghamton
New York, State U of, Buffalo
New York, State U of, Geneseo
New York, State U of, Stony Brook
Northeastern U (MA)
Northwestern U (IL)
Oberlin C (OH)
Ohio State U
Pennsylvania, U of
Pittsburgh, U of (PA)
Princeton (NJ)
Rice U (TX)
Rochester, U of (NY)
Rutgers U (NJ)
Smith C (MA)
Southern California, U of
Stanford U (CA)
Stern C (NY)
Syracuse U (NY)
Temple U (PA)
Touro C/Lander C (NY)
Towson U (MD)
Trinity C (CT)
Tufts U (MA)
Tulane U (LA)
Vanderbilt U (TN)
Vermont, U of
Washington & Lee U (VA)
Washington U (MO)
Wayne State U (MI)
Wellesley C (MA)
Western U (Canada)
Williams C (MA)
Wisconsin, U of, Madison
Yale U (CT)
Yeshiva U (NY)

Source: Heart 2 Heart (*theheart2heartproject.org*)

Lutheran Colleges and Universities

Augsburg C (MN)
Augustana C (IL)
Augustana C (SD)
Bethany C (KS)
California Lutheran U

Capital U (OH)
Carthage C (WI)
Concordia C (AL)
Concordia C (Canada)
Concordia C (MI)

Concordia C (MN)
Concordia C (NE)
Concordia C (NY)
Concordia C (OR)
Concordia U (CA)
Concordia U (IL)
Concordia U (TX)
Concordia U (WI)
Finlandia U (MI)
Gettysburg C (PA)
Grand View U (IA)
Gustavus Adolphus C (MN)
Lenoir-Rhyne U (NC)
Luther C (IA)
Midland U (NE)
Muhlenberg C (PA)

Newberry C (SC)
Pacific Lutheran U (WA)
Regina, U of, Luther C (Canada)
Roanoke C (VA)
St. Olaf C (MN)
Susquehanna U (PA)
Texas Lutheran U
Thiel C (PA)
Trinity Lutheran C (WA)
Valparaiso U (IN)
Wagner C (NY)
Waldorf C (IA)
Wartburg C (IA)
Wisconsin Lutheran C
Wittenberg U (OH)

Source: *lutherancolleges.org*

Methodist Colleges

Adrian C (MI)
Alaska Pacific U
Albion C (MI)
Albright C (PA)
Allegheny C (PA)
American U (DC)
Baker U (KS)
Baldwin-Wallace C (OH)
Bennett C (NC)
Bethune-Cookman U (FL)
Birmingham-Southern C (AL)
Boston U (MA)
Brevard C (NC)
Centenary C (LA)
Central Methodist U (MO)
Claflin U (SC)
Clark Atlanta U (GA)
Columbia C (SC)
Cornell C (IA)
Dakota Wesleyan U (SD)
Denver, U of (CO)
DePauw U (IN)
Dickinson C (PA)
Dillard U (LA)
Drew U (NJ)
Duke U (NC)
Emory & Henry C (VA)
Emory U (GA)
Evansville, U of (IN)
Ferrum C (VA)
Florida Southern C
Green Mountain C (VT)
Greensboro C (NC)

Hamline U (MN)
Hendrix C (AR)
High Point U (NC)
Huntingdon C (AL)
Huston-Tillotson U (TX)
Illinois Wesleyan U
Indianapolis, U of (IN)
Iowa Wesleyan C
Kansas Wesleyan U
Kendall C (IL)
Kentucky Wesleyan C
LaGrange C (GA)
Lambuth U (TN)
Lebanon Valley C (PA)
Lindsey Wilson C (KY)
Lycoming C (PA)
MacMurray C (IL)
Martin Methodist C (TN)
McKendree U (IL)
McMurry U (TX)
Methodist U (NC)
Millsaps C (MS)
Morningside C (IA)
Mt. Union C (OH)
Nebraska Methodist C
Nebraska Wesleyan U
North Carolina Wesleyan C
North Central C (IL)
Ohio Northern U
Ohio Wesleyan U
Oklahoma City U
Otterbein C (OH)
Pacific, U of the (CA)

Paine C (GA)
Pfeiffer U (NC)
Philander Smith C (AR)
Puget Sound, U of (WA)
Randolph-Macon C (VA)
Randolph C (VA)
Reinhardt C (GA)
Rocky Mountain C (MT)
Rust C (MS)
Shenandoah U (VA)
Simpson C (IA)
Southern Methodist U (TX)
Southwestern C (KS)

Southwestern U (TX)
Syracuse U (NY)
Tennessee Wesleyan C
Texas Wesleyan U
Union C (KY)
Virginia Wesleyan C
Wesley C (DE)
Wesleyan C (GA)
West Virginia Wesleyan C
Wiley C (TX)
Willamette U (OR)
Wofford C (SC)

Moravian Colleges

Moravian C (PA)
Salem C (NC)

Colleges for Mormon Students

Arizona State U
Boise State U (ID)
Brigham Young U (HI)*
Brigham Young U (ID)*
Brigham Young U (UT)*
California, U of, Davis
Colorado State U, Ft. Collins
Dixie State U (UT)
Eastern Arizona C
LDS Business C (UT)*

Nevada, U of, Reno
Northern Arizona U
Oregon State U
Snow C (UT)
Southern Utah U
Southern Virginia U
Utah State U
Utah Valley U
Washington, U of, Seattle
Weber State U (UT)

* Latter-Day Saints Church Colleges and Universities

Source: *The College Finder* research and The Church of Jesus Christ of Latter-Day Saints (*lds.org*)

Schools With Muslim Student Associations

The colleges and universities below are home to Muslim Student Associations recognized by the National Organization of Muslim Student Alliances.

Arizona State U
Arkansas, U of
Austin C (TX)
Bradley U (IL)
California State U, San Jose
California, U of, Berkeley
Central Florida, U of
Cincinnati, U of (OH)
Collin C (TX)

Delaware, U of
Des Moines U (IA)
Drexel U (PA)
Elmhurst C (IL)
Florida, U of
George Mason U (VA)
George Washington U (DC)
Georgia State U
Indiana U, Bloomington

Indiana U, Northwest
Indianapolis, U of (IN)
Langara C (Canada)
Marquette U (WI)
Massachusetts Institute of Technology
Michigan, U of, Ann Arbor
Michigan, U of, Dearborn
Michigan, U of, Flint
New York, State U of, Albany
New York, State U of, Binghamton
North Carolina State U
North Carolina, U of, Chapel Hill
North Carolina, U of, Greensboro
North Texas, U of
Ohio State U
Ohio Wesleyan U
Pittsburgh, U of (PA)

Rice U (TX)
Seton Hall U (NJ)
South Florida, U of
Tennessee, U of, Martin
Texas Christian U
Texas Tech U
Texas, U of, Arlington
Texas, U of, Austin
Texas, U of, Dallas
Toledo, U of (OH)
Wayne State U (MI)
West Virginia School of Osteopathic
  Medicine
William & Mary, C of (VA)
Winona State U (WI)
Xavier U (OH)

Source: MSA National (*msanational.org*)

Pentecostal Colleges

Apostolic Bible Institue (MN)
Centro Teologico Ministerial (TX)
Christian Life C (CA)
Emmanuel C (GA)
Indiana Bible C (IN)
Northeast Christian C (Canada)
Southwestern Christian U (OK)
Texas Bible C
Urshan C (MO)
W. L. Bonner C (SC)

Source: *The College Finder* research, including UPCI Division of Education

Presbyterian Colleges

These are members of the Association of Presbyterian Colleges and Universities.

Agnes Scott C (GA)
Alma C (MI)
Arcadia U (PA)
Austin C (TX)
Barber-Scotia C (NC)
Belhaven U (MS)
Blackburn C (IL)
Bloomfield C (NJ)
Buena Vista U (IA)
Carroll U (WI)
Centre C (KY)
Coe C (IA)
Davidson C (NC)

Davis & Elkins C (WV)
Dubuque, U of (IA)
Eckerd C (FL)
Hanover C (IN)
Hastings C (NE)
Idaho, C of
Illinois C
Jamestown C (ND)
Johnson C. Smith U (NC)
King C (TN)
Lake Forest C (IL)
Lees-McRae C (NC)
Lyon C (AR)

Macalester C (MN)
Mary Baldwin C (VA)
Maryville C (TN)
Missouri Valley C
Monmouth C (IL)
Montreat C (NC)
Muskingum U (OH)
Ozarks, U of the (AR)
Pikeville, U of (KY)
Presbyterian C (SC)
Queens U (NC)
Rhodes C (TN)
Rocky Mountain C (MT)
Schreiner U (TX)

St. Andrews U (NC)
Stillman C (AL)
Trinity U (TX)
Tulsa, U of (OK)
Tusculum C (TN)
Warren Wilson C (NC)
Waynesburg U (PA)
Westminster C (MO)
Westminster C (PA)
Westminster C (UT)
Whitworth C (WA)
William Peace U (NC)
Wilson C (PA)
Wooster, C of (OH)

Source: Association of Presbyterian Colleges and Universities (*presbyteriancolleges.org*)

Among the Best Seriously Protestant Schools

First Things is a conservative religious journal focused on creating a "religiously informed public philosophy for the ordering of society." These ratings were calculated from polls of students who were questioned about the academic, religious, and social lives of their schools. Ratings included variables such as academic reputation, graduation rates, friendliness to religious faith, the vibrancy of ministries, and student faith. In addition to polling, *First Things* conducted conversations with students, graduates, faculty, and chaplains.

1. Wheaton C (IL)
2. Calvin C (MI)
3. Taylor U (IN)
4. Gordon C (MA)
5. George Fox U (OR)
6. Westmont C (CA)
7. Seattle Pacific U (WA)
8. Houghton C (NY)
9. Grove City C (PA)
10. Whitworth C (WA)
11. Houston Baptist U (TX)
12. Union U (TN)

Source: *First Things* (*firstthings.com*)

Quaker Colleges

Barclay C (KS)
Bryn Mawr C (PA)
Earlham C (IN)
Earlham School of Religion (IN)
Friends Theological C (Kenya)
Friends U (KS)
George Fox U (OR)
Guilford C (NC)
Haverford C (PA)

Long Island U, (NY)
Malone U (OH)
Pendle Hill (PA)
Swarthmore C (PA)
Whittier C (CA)
William Penn U (IA)
Wilmington C (OH)
Woodbrooke Quaker Study Centre
    (United Kingdom)

Source: Friends Association for Higher Education (*quakerfahe.com*)

Seventh-Day Adventist Colleges

Adventist U of Health Sciences (FL)
Andrews U (MI)
Burman U (Canada)
Kettering C (OH)
La Sierra U (CA)
Loma Linda U (CA)
Oakwood U (AL)

Pacific Union C (CA)
Southern Adventist U (TN)
Southwestern Adventist U (TX)
Union C (NE)
Walla Walla U (WA)
Washington Adventist U (MD)

Source: Adventist Colleges and Universities (*adventistcolleges.org*)

FIRST-GENERATION/UNDOCUMENTED STUDENTS

I'm First: Schools Committed to Serving and Supporting First-Generation Students

Amherst C (MA)
Arcadia U (PA)
Arizona, U of
Avila U (MO)
Babson C (MA)
Baldwin Wallace U (OH)
Barnard C (NY)
Barry U (FL)
Bates C (ME)
Bay Path U (MA)
Belmont U (TN)
Bentley U (MA)
Boston U (MA)
Brandeis U (MA)
Bridgeport, U of (CT)
Brown U (RI)
Bucknell U (PA)
California Institute of Technology
California Lutheran U
California Polytechnic State U, San Luis
    Obispo
Catawba C (NC)
Catholic U (DC)
Central Connecticut State U
Centre C (KY)
Champlain C (VT)
Chapman U (CA)
Charleston, C of (SC)
Chicago, U of (IL)
Cincinnati, U of
Claremont McKenna C (CA)
Colby C (ME)
Colgate U (NY)
Colorado C
Colorado State U, Ft. Collins

Columbia C (IL)
Columbia U (NY)
Cooper Union (NY)
Cornell C (IA)
Cornell U (NY)
Dartmouth C (NH)
Davidson C (NC)
Denver, U of (CO)
Detroit Mercy, U of (MI)
Dickinson C (PA)
Duke U (NC)
Eastern Oregon U
Elmhurst C (IL)
Emory U (GA)
Ferris State U (MI)
Ferrum C (VA)
Fisk U (TN)
Florida, U of
Fordham U (NY)
Framingham State U (MA)
Franklin & Marshall C (PA)
Georgia State U (GA)
Georgia, U of
Gettysburg C (PA)
Grinnell C (IA)
Gwynedd Mercy U (PA)
Hamilton C (NY)
Hanover C (IN)
Harvard U (MA)
Harvey Mudd C (CA)
Haverford C (PA)
Holy Cross C (IN)
Houston, U of (TX)
Illinois C (IL)
Illinois, U of, Chicago

Illinois, U of, Springfield
Indiana State U
Indiana U, Bloomington
Indiana Wesleyan U
Iowa, U of
Jamestown, U of
Johns Hopkins U (MD)
Juniata C (PA)
Kalamazoo C (MI)
Keene State C (NH)
Kent State U (OH)
Kentucky, U of
King's C (PA)
Lehigh U (PA)
Lesley U (MA)
Lipscomb U (TN)
Loyola U (MD)
Lycoming C (PA)
MacMurray C (IL)
Manchester U (IN)
Manhattan C (NY)
Marymount U (CA)
Maryville C (TN)
Mercy C (NY)
Meredith C (NC)
Michigan, U of, Ann Arbor
Michigan, U of, Flint
Mills C (CA)
Missouri U of Science & Technology
Missouri Valley C
Mount Aloysius C (PA)
Nebraska, U of, Lincoln
New Mexico Highlands U
New York U
Newberry C (SC)
North Carolina A&T State U
North Carolina State U
North Carolina, U of, Greensboro
North Carolina, U of, Wilmington
North Park U (IL)
Northeastern U (MA)
Northern Arizona U
Northern Colorado, U of
Northwestern U (IL)
Notre Dame U (MD)
Notre Dame, U of (IN)
Occidental C (CA)
Ohio U, Athens
Oral Roberts U (OK)
Pennsylvania, U of
Pepperdine U (CA)
Pitzer C (CA)
Pomona C (CA)
Princeton U (NJ)
Quinnipiac U (CT)

Ramapo C (NJ)
Redlands, U of (CA)
Rensselaer Polytechnic Institute (NY)
Robert Morris U (PA)
Richmond, U of (VA)
Rochester Institute of Technology (NY)
Rochester, U of (NY)
Roosevelt U (IL)
Sacramento State U (CA)
San Diego, U of (CA)
San Francisco, U of (CA)
Sarah Lawrence C (NY)
Simpson U (CA)
Skidmore C (NY)
Soka U (CA)
South Florida, U of (FL)
Southern California, U of
Southern Illinois U, Carbondale
Southern Vermont C
Spring Hill C (AL)
St. Francis U (PA)
St. John Fisher C (NY)
St. Leo U (FL)
St. Mary's C (CA)
St. Mary's C (IN)
St. Michael's C (VT)
St. Norbert C (WI)
St. Vincent C (PA)
Stanford U (CA)
Stetson U (FL)
Susquehanna U (PA)
Swarthmore C (PA)
Temple U (PA)
Texas Christian U
Texas State U
Thomas C (ME)
Trinity C (CT)
Trinity U (DC)
Truman State U (MO)
Tufts U (MA)
Union C (KY)
Union U (TN)
U.S. Air Force Academy (CO)
U.S. Coast Guard Academy (CT)
Vanderbilt U (TN)
Virginia Commonwealth U
Virginia Polytechnic Institute & State U
Walsh U (OH)
Warner Pacific C (OR)
Washington U (MO)
Wellesley C (MA)
Wesleyan U (CT)
Western Illinois U
Westfield State U (MA)
Whitman C (WA)

Willamette U (OR)
Williams C (MA)
Winthrop U (SC)
Wisconsin, U of, Milwaukee

Wisconsin, U of, River Falls
Worcester Polytechnic Institute
Yale U (CT)

Source: *I'm First* is an online community supported by the Center for Student Opportunity to help first-generation students (*imfirst.org*).

Colleges for Undocumented Students to Consider

Colleges are listed here for a variety of reasons, including 1.) the college admits undocumented students without classification as international students; 2.) the college may have other ways of classifying and admitting undocumented students; 3.) the college may make no distinction between undocumented and documented students; 4.) grant offerings specifically targeted toward undocumented students may be available and/or private money may be offered to help finance undocumented student financial aid; and 5.) the college provides good administrative support for undocumented students.

Amherst C (MA)
Augsburg C (MN)
Bryn Mawr C (PA)
California Institute of Technology
California, U of, Berkeley
California, U of, Davis
California, U of, Los Angeles
California, U of, Merced
California, U of, Santa Cruz
Chicago, U of (IL)
Claremont McKenna C (CA)
Columbia U (NY)
Dartmouth C (NH)
Dominican U (CA)
Dominican U (IL)
Georgia Institute of Technology
Harvard U (MA)
Illinois, U of, Chicago

Illinois, U of, Springfield
Illinois, U of, Urbana
Indiana U-Purdue U, Indianapolis
Indiana, U of, Bloomington
Kenyon C (OH)
Loyola Marymount U (CA)
Mills C (CA)
Mt. St. Mary's U (CA)
National Hispanic U (CA)
Occidental C (CA)
Pitzer C (CA)
Pomona C (CA)
Ripon C (WI)
Santa Clara U (CA)
Stanford U (CA)
Tufts U (MA)
Whittier C (CA)
Yale U (CT)

Source: *The College Finder* research, including Get Me to College (*getmetocollege.org*), CNN Money (*money.cnn.com*), University of North Carolina Wilmington (*uncw.edu*), and Western Association for College Admission Counseling (*wacac.org*)

GENDER

Women's Colleges

Agnes Scott C (GA)
Alverno C (WI)
Assumption C for Sisters (NJ)
Barnard C (NY)
Bay Path C (MA)

Bennett C (NC)
Blue Mountain C (MS)
Brenau U (GA)
Brescia University C (Canada)
Bryn Mawr C (PA)

Carlow U (PA)
Cedar Crest C (PA)
Chatham U (PA)
Columbia C (SC)
Converse C (SC)
Cottey C (MO)
Denver, U of, Colorado Women's C
Douglass C of Rutgers U (NJ)
Georgian Court U (NJ)
Hollins U (VA)
Judson C (AL)
Lexington C (IL)
Mary Baldwin C (VA)
Meredith C (NC)
Midway C (NC)
Mills C (CA)
Moore C of Art & Design (PA)
Mt. Holyoke C (MA)
Mt. Mary C (WI)
Mt. St. Mary's C (CA)
New Rochelle, C of (NY)
Newcomb C of Tulane U (LA)
Notre Dame, C of (MD)
Peace C (NC)

Pine Manor C (MA)
Rosemont C (PA)
Russell Sage C (NY)
Salem C (NC)
Scripps C (CA)
Simmons C (MA)
Smith C (MA)
Spelman C (GA)
St. Benedict, C of (MN)
St. Catherine, C of (MN)
St. Elizabeth, C of (NJ)
St. Joseph C (CT)
St. Mary, C of (NE)
St. Mary-of-the-Woods C (IN)
St. Mary's C (IN)
Stephens C (MO)
Sweet Briar C (VA)
Texas Woman's U
Trinity U (DC)
Ursuline C (OH)
Wellesley C (MA)
Wesleyan C (GA)
Wilson C (PA)

Co-ed Colleges With the Highest Percentage of Women Students

Pacific Oaks C (CA): 95.95%
Trinity Washington U: 95.80%
Allen C (IA): 93.45%
LIM C (NY): 93.43%
Chatham U (PA): 90.99%
Nebraska Methodist C: 90.97%
Wheelock C (MA): 88.07%
New York School of Interior Design:
  87.78%
Resurrection U (IL): 87.54%
Our Lady of the Lake C (LA): 86.57%
Fashion Institute of Technology (NY):
  84.65%

Aquinas C (MI): 81.69%
Bastyr U (WA): 80.95%
Midway C (KY): 80.91%
Georgian Court U (NJ): 80.79%
Jefferson C of Health Sciences (VA):
  80.76%
Puerto Rico, U of, Medical Sciences
  Campus: 79.14%
Sage C (NY): 78.93%
Oregon C of Art & Craft: 77.27%
Keuka C (NY): 77.20%
Regis C (MA): 76.43%

Source: Wintergreen Orchard House

Years That Women's Colleges Became Co-ed

Albertus Magnus C (CT): 1985
Bennington C (VT): 1969
Brenau U (GA): 1997
Chestnut Hill C (PA): 2003
Colby-Sawyer C (NH): 1991
Connecticut C: 1969
Emmanuel C (MA): 2001

Endicott C (MA): 1997
Fisher C (MA): 1998
Goucher C (MD): 1986
Hood C (MD): 2002
Immaculata U (PA): 2005
Lasell C (MA): 1998
Lesley U (MA): 2005

Notre Dame C (OH): 2001
Our Lady of the Elms, C of (MA): 1998
Pitzer C (CA): 1971
Randolph-Macon Woman's C (became
    Randolph C) (VA): 2007
Regis C (MA): 2004
Salve Regina U (RI): 1972
Sarah Lawrence C (NY): 1968

Seton Hill U (PA): 2002
Skidmore C (NY): 1971
St. Mary, U of (KS): 1988
Vassar C (NY): 1967
Wells C (NY): 2005
Wheaton C (MA): 1990
William Woods U (MO): 2007

Men's Colleges

Beth Medrash Govoha (NJ)
Central State U (OH)
Conception Seminary C (MO)
Hampden Sydney C (VA)
Morehouse C (GA)
Ner Israel Rabbinical C (MD)
Pontifical C Josephinum (OH)
St. John Vianney C Seminary (CO)

St. John's Seminary (CA)
St. John's U (MN)
St. Joseph Seminary C (LA)
Talmudic U (FL)
Wabash C (IN)
Yeshiva Ohr Elchonon-Chabad/West
    Coast Talmudical Seminary (CA)

Source: Wintergreen Orchard House

Co-ed Colleges With the Highest Percentage of Male Students

Neumont U (UT): 89.89%
Virginia Military Institute: 89.49%
Massachusetts Maritime Academy: 88.23%
Embry-Riddle Aeronautical U, Worldwide (FL): 88.22%
Vaughn C of Aeronautics and Technology (NY): 87.65%
Embry-Riddle Aeronautical U, Daytona Beach (FL): 83.44%
U.S. Military Academy (NY): 83.40%
Kettering U (MI): 81.72%
Wentworth Institute of Technology (MA): 81.66%
Kennasaw State U (GA): 81.11%
Webb Institute (NY): 81.01%
Clear Creek Baptist Bible C (KY): 79.74%
Polytechnic U (Puerto Rico): 79.43%
U.S. Naval Academy (MD): 78.44%
Rose-Hulman Institute of Technology (IN): 78.32%
Embry-Riddle Aeronautical U, Prescott (AZ): 78.27%
Bowie State U (MD): 78.09%
U.S. Air Force Academy (CO): 77.61%
Capitol C (OH): 77.15%
South Dakota School of Mines & Technology: 76.94%
Missouri, U of, Science & Technology: 76.70%
Milwaukee School of Engineering (WI): 76.70%
New Jersey Institute of Technology: 76.37%
Arizona State U, Polytechnic: 75.69%
Lawrence Technological U (MI): 75.50%
National Intelligence U (DC): 75.00%
Michigan Technological U: 74.74%

Norwich U (VT): 73.98%
Colorado School of Mines: 73.10%
Florida Institute of Technology: 72.84%
Clarkson U (NY): 71.94%
American Baptist C (TN): 71.63%
DeVry U (NJ): 71.58%
DeVry U (AR): 70.49%
Rensselaer Polytechnic Institute (NY): 70.43%
Illinois Institute of Technology: 70.37%
Five Towns C (NY): 69.81%
New Mexico Institute of Technology: 69.64%

Source: Wintergreen Orchard House

Years That Men's Colleges Became Co-ed

Amherst C (MA): 1975
Bowdoin C (ME): 1971
Brown U (RI): 1971
Claremont McKenna C (CA): 1976
Colgate U (NY): 1970
Dartmouth C (NH): 1972
Davidson C (NC): 1972
Duke U (NC): 1972
Harvard U (MA): 1977
Haverford C (PA): 1980
Holy Cross, C of the (MA): 1972
Johns Hopkins U (MD): 1970
Kenyon C (OH): 1969

Lehigh U (PA): 1971
Princeton U (NJ): 1969
Rose-Hulman Institute (IN): 1991
Trinity C (CT): 1969
U.S. Military Academy (NY): 1976
Valley Forge Military Academy & C: 2006
Virginia Military Institute: 1997
Virginia, U of: 1970
Washington & Lee U (VA): 1985
Williams C (MA): 1970
Wofford C (SC): 1975
Yale U (CT): 1969

Great Places for LGBT Students

Listed here in alphabetical order are the top 20 LGBT schools as taken from the "best of the best" list published in *The Advocate College Guide for LGBT Students.* Geographic region, i.e., ensuring a balanced list across the United States, was only one of the variables used.

American U (DC)
California, U of, Berkeley
California, U of, Los Angeles
California, U of, Santa Cruz
Duke U (NC)
Indiana U
Massachusetts, U of, Amherst
Michigan, U of, Ann Arbor
Minnesota, U of, Twin Cities
New York U

Oberlin C (OH)
Ohio State U
Oregon, U of
Pennsylvania State U, University Park
Pennsylvania, U of
Princeton U (NJ)
Puget Sound, U of (WA)
Southern California, U of
Stanford U (CA)
Tufts U (MA)

Source: Shane L. Windmeyer, 2006. *The Advocate College Guide for LGBT Students.* Alyson Books, New York.

Schools That Are Gay-Friendly

This list is based on the LGBT (Lesbian, Gay, Bisexual, Transgender)-Friendly Campus Climate Index. These colleges received high scores (a 4 or 5 on a 5-point scale) on LGBT campus life based on their inclusive, welcoming, and respectful atmosphere toward LGBT students. The index was developed by Campus Pride, a nonprofit LGBT organization.

Amherst C (MA)
Augsburg C (MN)
California State U, Humboldt
California State U, San Diego
Carleton C (MN)
Case Western Reserve U (OH)
Central Connecticut State U
Central Florida, U of
Colorado, U of, Boulder
Connecticut C
Cornell U (NY)
Duke U (NC)
Gettysburg C (PA)
Grand Valley State U (MI)
Hofstra U (NY)
Iowa, U of
Ithaca C (NY)
Louisville, U of (KY)
Macalester C (MN)
Maine, U of, Machias
Maryland, U of, College Park
Massachusetts, U of, Amherst

Minnesota, U of, Morris
Montclair State U (NJ)
New Mexico, U of, Albuquerque
New York U
Ohio State U, Columbus
Ohio U, Athens
Oregon, U of
Pennsylvania, U of
Portland State U (OR)
Princeton U (NJ)
Purdue U (IN)
Rutgers U, New Brunswick (NJ)
Southern California, U of
Southern Oregon U
Tufts U (MA)
Vermont, U of
Warren Wilson C (NC)
Washington State U
Wisconsin, U of, Eau Claire
Wisconsin, U of, Madison
Wisconsin, U of, Milwaukee
Wright State U (OH)

Source: Campus Pride Index (*campusclimateindex.org*)

The Experts' Choice: Colleges Where LGBT Students Are Happy

Experts were asked to name colleges where the lesbian, gay, bisexual, or transgender student feels comfortable and welcomed.

Allegheny C (PA)
Bard C (NY)
California, U of, Berkeley
Chicago, U of (IL)
Hampshire C (MA)
Indiana U, Bloomington
Maine, U of
New Hampshire, U of
Pitzer C (CA)

Portland State U (OR)
Reed C (OR)
Sarah Lawrence C (NY)
Smith C (MA)
Stanford U (CA)
Vassar C (NY)
Vermont, U of
Wilmington C (DE)

The Experts' Choice: Colleges With Gender-Neutral/Gender-Inclusive Housing

Experts were asked to name colleges where students may choose to room with students regardless of gender.

Amherst C (MA)
Arizona State U
Augsburg C (MN)
Bard C (NY)
Bates C (ME)
Bennington C (VT)
Brown U (RI)
Bucknell U (PA)
California Institute of Technology
California State U, Humboldt
California State U, San Diego
California, U of, Berkeley
California, U of, Davis
California, U of, Irvine
California, U of, Riverside
California, U of, Santa Cruz
Chicago, U of (IL)
Claremont McKenna C (CA)
Colgate U (NY)
Colorado C
Cornell U (NY)
Dartmouth C (NH)
Dickinson C (PA)
Eastern Michigan U
Eckerd C (FL)
Evergreen State C (WA)
Ft. Lewis C (CO)
Gettysburg C (PA)
Grinnell C (IA)
Hamilton C (NY)
Hampshire C (MA)
Harvard U (MA)
Harvey Mudd C (CA)
Hawaii, U of, Manoa
Ithaca C (NY)
Juniata C (PA)
Kenyon C (OH)
Lawrence U (WI)
Macalester C (MN)
Maine C of Art
Marlboro C (VT)

Mary Washington, U of (VA)
Massachusetts C of Art
Massachusetts, U of, Amherst
Michigan State U
Michigan, U of, Ann Arbor
Montclair State U (NJ)
New York U
New York, State U of, Albany
New York, State U of, Binghamton
New York, State U of, Geneseo
New York, State U of, Stony Brook
Northwestern U (IL)
Oberlin C (OH)
Pacific Lutheran U (WA)
Pennsylvania State U
Pitzer C (CA)
Pomona C (CA)
Pratt Institute (NY)
Ramapo C (NJ)
Reed C (OR)
Rice U (TX)
Salem State U (MA)
Sarah Lawrence C (NY)
Scripps C (CA)
Southern California, U of
Southern Oregon U
St. Mary's C (MD)
Stetson U (FL)
Towson U (MD)
Vanderbilt U (TN)
Vassar C (NY)
Vermont, U of
Wellesley C (MA)
Western Washington U
Wisconsin, U of, Green Bay
Wisconsin, U of, La Crosse
Wisconsin, U of, Madison
Wisconsin, U of, Milwaukee
Wisconsin, U of, Platteville
Wisconsin, U of, Whitewater
Wooster, C of (OH)

Colleges and Universities With a Trans-Inclusive Intramural Athletic Policy

These are schools with supportive transgender athletic communities. Support might include such nondiscrimination policies as gender-neutral uniforms and private changing spaces.

Bates C (ME)	Maryland, U of, College Park
Carleton C (MN)	Massachusetts, U of, Amherst
Central Florida, U of	Miami U (OH)
Colorado, U of, Boulder	Oberlin C (OH)
Emory U (CA)	Springfield C (MA)
Houston, U of (TX)	Vermont, U of
Iowa State U	Washington State U
Louisiana State U	Williams U (MA)

Source: Campus Pride (*campuspride.org*)

LEARNING/PHYSICAL CHALLENGES

The Experts' Choice: Colleges Where Learning-Disabled Students Succeed

American U (DC)	Limestone C (SC)
Arizona, U of**	Loras C (IA)
Beacon C (FL)	Lynn U (FL)*
Clark U (MA)	Marist U (NY)
Cornell C (IA)	McDaniel C (MD)
Curry C (MA)	Mitchell C (CT)
Dean C (MA)	Muhlenberg C (PA)
Denver, U of (CO)	Ozarks, U of the (AR)
DePaul (IL)	Towson U (MD)
Eckerd C (FL)	Wisconsin, U of, Madison
Endicott C (MA)	Wooster, C of (OH)
Ft. Lewis C (CO)	Worcester Polytechnic Institute (MA)
Goucher C (MD)	
High Point U (NC)	* The Top Choice
Hofstra U (NY)	** The Second Choice
Landmark C (VT)	

For Students With Learning Disabilities

Dr. Rachel B. Sobel is an independent educational consultant in Philadelphia and an expert on colleges for students with learning disabilities. She has identified the following schools as strong colleges for students with learning disabilities.

Adelphi U (NY)*	Auburn U (AL)
Albright U (PA)	Beacon C (FL)
American U (DC)*	Bryant C (RI)
American International C (MA)*	Case Western Reserve U (OH)
Arizona, U of*	Charleston, C of (SC)

Cincinnati, U of (OH)
Curry C (MA)*
Denver, U of (CO)*
Drew U (NJ)
Drexel U (PA)
Earlham C (IN)
Eckerd C (FL)
Elizabethtown C (PA)
Endicott C (MA)
Gannon U (PA)*
George Mason U (VA)
Guilford C (NC)
Hartford, U of (CT)
High Point U (NC)
Hiram C (OH)
Hofstra U (NY)*
Hood C (MD)
Indiana U, Bloomington
Iona C (NY)*
Landmark C (VT)
Lesley U (MA)
Lewis & Clark C (OR)
Limestone C (SC)* (strong dyslexia support)
Long Island U, C.W. Post (NY)*

Lynn U (FL)*
Manhattanville C (NY)
Marist C (NY)
McDaniel C (MD)*
Muhlenberg C (PA)
Muskingum U (OH)*
New England C (NH)*
Nicholls State C (LA)* (strong dyslexia support)
Northeastern U (MA)*
Ohio Wesleyan U
Pace U (NY)
Rider U (NJ)
Rochester Institute of Technology (NY)
Roger Williams U (RI)
Savannah C of Art and Design (GA)
South Carolina, U of
Southern Illinois U
Southern New Hampshire U (strong dyslexia support)
Southern Vermont C
St. Joseph's U (PA)
Tampa, U of (FL)
Texas Tech U
West Virginia Wesleyan

* These colleges offer comprehensive support services for an additional cost.

The Experts' Choice: Colleges Where Teachers Work Well with Learning-Disabled Students

Experts named these colleges as ones where instructors are particularly good at working with students with learning disabilities.

Adelphi U (NY)
American U (DC)
Arizona, U of****
Curry C (MA)*
Dean C (MA)
Denver, U of (CO)
DePaul U (IL)
Guilford C (NC)
High Point U (NC)
Hofstra U (NY)
Iona C (NY)
Landmark C (VT)***
Lone Star C, Houston (TX)
Lynchburg C (VA)
Lynn U (FL)**

Marist C (NY)
McDaniel C (MD)
Miami U (OH)
Mitchell C (CT)
Muhlenberg C (PA)
Northeastern U (MA)
Ozarks, U of the (AR)
Roger Williams U (RI)
Wooster, C of (OH)

* The Top Choice
** The Second Choice
*** The Third Choice
**** The Fourth Choice

Steven R. Antonoff

The Experts' Choice: Colleges Sensitive to Students With Different Learning Styles

Top Choices

Arizona, U of
Curry C (MA)
Denver, U of (CO)
Landmark C (VT)
Lynn U (FL)*

* The Top Choice

Second Choices

Adelphi U (NY)
Alabama, U of, Tuscaloosa
Albright C (PA)
American U (DC)
Arizona State U
Augsburg C (MN)
California State U, Sonoma
Carroll U (WI)
Charleston, C of (SC)
Colorado State U, Ft. Collins
Colorado, U of, Colorado Springs
Dean C (MA)
Denver U (CO)
DePaul U (IL)
Eckerd C (FL)
Fairleigh Dickinson U (NJ)
Goucher C (MD)
Hampshire C (MA)

Hastings C (NE)
High Point U (NC)
Hofstra U (NY)
Iona C (NY)
Lake Forest C (IL)
Loras C (IA)
Marist C (NY)
Marymount C (CA)
McDaniel C (MD)
Mercyhurst U (PA)
Mitchell C (CT)
Muhlenberg C (PA)
Muskingum U (OH)
New Hampshire, U of
New York, State U of, Oswego
New York, State U of, Purchase
Ohio Wesleyan U
Ozarks, U of the (AR)
Puget Sound, U of (WA)
Quinnipiac U (CT)
Redlands, U of (CA)
Regis U (CO)
Rider U (NJ)
San Francisco, U of (CA)
Southern Methodist U (TX)
Susquehanna U (PA)
Syracuse U (NY)
Tampa, U of (FL)
Western Oregon U
Westminster C (MO)

Colleges for Students With Autism Spectrum Disorder: The Very Friendly Ones

Autism spectrum disorder (ASD) is a group of developmental disabilities that can cause significant social, communication, and behavioral challenges. Some of the behaviors associated with autism include delayed learning of language; difficulty making eye contact or holding a conversation; difficulty with executive functioning, which relates to reasoning and planning; narrow, intense interests; poor motor skills; and sensory sensitivities. A person on the spectrum might exhibit many of these behaviors or just a few or other behaviors as well. Dr. Rachel B. Sobel, an independent educational consultant in Philadelphia and an expert on colleges for students with learning disabilities and ASD, chose these colleges as supportive of students with ASD. These selections were based on such factors as acceptance of social and learning style differences, a good support system in residential life and academic affairs, easy access to disability support, and trained faculty and staff. Colleges with these characteristics might be appropriate for a wide range of students.

Adelphi U (NY): Bridges to Adelphi
Alabama, U of, Tuscaloosa: Autism Spectrum Disorders College Transition and Support
    Program (UA-ACTS)
Arkansas, U of: Autism Support Program

ABOUT ME

Austin Peay State U (TN): Launched a pilot program to improve college experience for students with autism
Bellevue C (WA): Autism Spectrum Navigators Program
Castleton U (VT): College Steps Program
Connecticut, U of: Strategic Education for Students with ASD (SEAD Program)
Defiance C (OH): ASD Affinity Program
Drexel U (PA): Autism Support Program
Eastern U (PA): The College Success Program for Students Living with Autism Spectrum Disorder (CSP Program)
Eastern Illinois U: Students with Autism Transitional Education Program (STEP)
Marshall U (WV): College Program for Students with ASD
Mercyhurst U (PA): AIM Program
Minnesota, U of, Morris: LINK Program
Nova Southeastern U (FL): Access Plus Program
Rochester Institute of Technology (NY): Spectrum Support Program
Rutgers U (NJ): College Support Program for Students on the Autism Spectrum (CSP)
Southern Vermont C: College Steps Program
St. Joseph's U (PA): Kinney Center for Autism ASPIRE Program
Virginia Polytechnic Institute & State U: Stepped Transition for Students with ASD (STEPS Program)
West Florida, U of: Autism Inclusion Program
Western Kentucky U: Kelly Autism Program
Wright State U (OH): Raiders on the Autism Spectrum Excelling (RASE Program)

Colleges for Students With Autism Spectrum Disorder: The Friendly Ones

Dr. Rachel B. Sobel, an independent educational consultant in Philadelphia, has identified the following colleges as sensitive to the needs of students with Autism Spectrum Disorder. A wide range of students might be attracted to the support and care provided by these colleges.

Allegheny C (PA)
Arcadia U (PA)
Auburn U (AL)
Augsburg C (MN)
Beacon C (FL)
Becker C (MA)
Boston U (MA)
Brevard C (NC)
California Polytechnic State U, San Luis Obispo
Case Western Reserve U (OH)
Clark U (MA)
Colorado, U of, Boulder
Davidson C (NC)
Denver, U of (CO)
DeSales U (PA)
Dickinson C (PA)
Earlham C (IN)
East Stroudsburg U (PA)
Eastern Michigan U
Elon U (NC)
Fairleigh Dickinson U (NJ)

Florida Atlantic U
Franklin Pierce C (NH)
Ft. Lewis C (CO)
George Mason U (VA)
Goucher C (MD)
Green Mountain C (VT)
Grinnell C (IA)
Guilford C (NC)
Hartwick C (NY)
Harvey Mudd C (CA)
Hiram C (OH)
Hofstra U (NY)
Holy Family U (PA)
Indiana Wesleyan U
Johnson & Wales U (RI) (CO)
Keene State C (NH)
Landmark C (VT)
Lebanon Valley C (PA)
Lasell C (MA)
Lesley U (MA)
Limestone C (SC)
Lynn U (FL)

Manhattanville C (NY)
Marymount Manhattan C (NY)
Massachusetts Institute of Technology
McDaniel C (MD)
Moravia C (PA)
Mt. Ida C (MA)
Muskingum U (OH)
Ozarks, U of (AR)
Pace U (NY)
Pennsylvania, U of
Pine Manor C (MA)
Puget Sound, U of (WA)
Redlands, U of (CA)
Rensselaer Polytechnic Institute (NY)
Rider U (NJ)
Rowan U (NJ)

Sacred Heart U (CT)
Southern Illinois U
Southern New Hampshire U
Stevens Institute of Technology (NJ)
St. John's C (MD) (NM)
Swarthmore C (PA)
Temple U (PA)
Tennessee, U of, Chattanooga
Ursinus C (PA)
Western New England U (MA)
Westminster C (UT)
Whitman C (WA)
Whittier C (CA)
Wilkes U (PA)
Worcester Polytechnic Institute (MA)

The Experts' Choice: Colleges Accommodating to the Student in a Wheelchair

Arizona, U of
California, U of, Los Angeles
Chapman U (CA)
Elon U (NC)
Evergreen State C (WA)
Florida, U of
Goucher C (MD)
High Point U (NC)

Hofstra U (NY)
Illinois, U of, Urbana
Indiana U, Bloomington
Loyola Marymount U (CA)
Lynn U (FL)
Minnesota, U of, Duluth
Southern California, U of
Stanford U (CA)

RECOVERY/SECOND CHANCE

Collegiate Recovery Communities

Universities and colleges are leading the way in supporting students in recovery from addiction. According to the Association of Recovery in Higher Education, the following schools incorporate recovery on their campus in a way that is unique to their population and culture.

Alabama, U of, Birmingham
Alabama, U of, Tuscaloosa
Augsburg C (MN)
Baylor U (TX)
California, U of, Riverside
California, U of, Santa Barbara
Carnegie Mellon U (PA)
Case Western Reserve U (OH)
Colorado, U of, Boulder
Delaware, U of
Emory U (GA)
Fairfield U (CT)
Florida, U of

George Washington U (DC)
Georgia Southern U
Georgia, U of
Gonzaga U (WA)
Houston, U of (TX)
Indiana U-Purdue U, Indianapolis
Kennesaw State U (GA)
Kentucky, U of
Longwood U (VA)
Lorain County Community C (OH)
Michigan State U
Michigan, U of, Ann Arbor
Minnesota, U of, Rochester

Mississippi State U
Mississippi, U of
Monmouth U (NJ)
Nebraska, U of, Omaha
Nevada, U of, Reno
New Jersey, C of
North Carolina A&T State U
North Carolina, U of, Ashville
North Carolina, U of, Chapel Hill
North Carolina, U of, Charlotte
North Carolina, U of, Wilmington
North Texas, U of
Northern State U (SD)
Ohio State U, Columbus
Ohio U, Athens

Oregon State U
Oregon, U of
Pennsylvania State U, University Park
Rutgers U, New Brunswick (NJ)
Southern Oregon U
St. Cloud State U (MN)
Texas Tech U
Texas, U of, Austin
Texas, U of, Dallas
Vanderbilt U (TN)
Vermont, U of
Virginia Commonwealth U
Washington & Lee U (VA)
West Virginia U

Source: Association of Recovery in Higher Education (*collegiaterecovery.org*)

For Students Who Need a Second Chance

Some students may not have made good choices in their lives but are now on track for success. These students may have had problems with substance abuse, oppositional behavior, or other issues. Dr. Rachel Sobel, an independent educational consultant in Philadelphia and an expert on learning issues and troubled teens, identifies the following colleges as ones where such students might succeed.

Augsburg C (MN) (sober living option)
Birmingham-Southern C (AL)
Case Western Reserve U (OH)
Champlain C (VT)
Colby-Sawyer C (NH)
Connecticut C
Curry C (MA)
Dean C (MA)
DePaul U (IL)
Earlham C (IN)
Eckerd C (FL)
Goucher C (MD)
Green Mountain C (VT)
Guilford C (NC)
Hartwick C (NY)
Hobart & William Smith C (NY)
Johnson State C (VT)
Lebanon Valley C (PA)

Lewis & Clark C (OR)
Lynchburg C (VA)
Lynn U (FL)
Memphis, U of (TN)
Messiah C (PA)
New England C (NH)
Northern Arizona U (AZ)
Oregon, U of
Prescott C (AZ)
Randolph-Macon C (VA)
Roanoke C (VA)
Rochester Institute of Technology (NY)
Southern New Hampshire U
Stetson U (FL)
St. Lawrence U (NY)
Texas Tech U (sober living option)
Widener U (PA)
Worcester Polytechnic Institute (MA)

Steven R. Antonoff

CHAPTER TWO
ACADEMICS

...AND SO, THE THE **FIRST STUDENT** TO SOLVE THE FORMULA **CORRECTLY** WILL SUB FOR ME WHILE I'M AT **COMIC-CON.**

FIELDS OF STUDY: A–Z

ACTING

The Experts' Choice: Colleges for the Aspiring Actor

American U (DC)
Arts, U of the (PA)
Bard C (NY)
Boston U (MA)
Brandeis U (MA)
California, U of, Los Angeles
Carnegie Mellon U (PA)
Catawba C (NC)
Chapman U (CA)
Columbia C Chicago (IL)
DePaul U (IL)
Elon U (NC)
Emerson C (MA)
Fordham U (NY)
Indiana U Bloomington
Ithaca C (NY)
Juilliard School (NY)
Kenyon C (OH)
Marymount Manhattan C (NY)

Michigan, U of, Ann Arbor
Muhlenberg C (PA)
New York, State U of, Purchase
New York U
Northern Colorado, U of
Northwestern U (IL)
Oberlin C (OH)
Pace U (NY)
Roosevelt U (IL)
Sarah Lawrence C (NY)
Skidmore C (NY)
Southern California, U of
Syracuse U (NY)
Temple U (PA)
Tulane U (LA)
Vassar C (NY)
Wesleyan U (CT)
Yale U (CT)

ADVERTISING AND PUBLIC RELATIONS

Colleges to Consider for Advertising and Public Relations

Jennifer Tabbush is an independent educational consultant and founder of Headed For College, a college advising firm in Los Angeles. She supplied this list exclusively for *The College Finder*.

Alabama, U of, Tuscaloosa
Auburn U (AL)
Boston U (MA)
Bradley U (IL)
Brigham Young U (UT)
California State U, Fresno
California State U, Fullerton
Central Florida, U of
Chapman U (CA)
Columbia C Chicago (IL)
Denver, U of (CO)
DePaul U (IL)
Drake U (IA)
Emerson C (MA)
Florida State U (FL)
Florida, U of

Georgetown U (DC)
Georgia, U of
Houston, U of (TX)
Illinois, U of, Urbana
Loyola U (IL)
Marist C (NY)
Marquette U (WI)
Miami U (OH)
Miami, U of (FL)
Michigan State U
Nebraska, U of, Lincoln
New York U
Oklahoma State U
Oklahoma, U of
Pennsylvania State U, University Park
Pepperdine U (CA)

Quinnipiac U (CT)
San Francisco, U of (CA)
San Jose State U (CA)
South Carolina, U of, Columbia
Southern California, U of
Southern Methodist U
Syracuse U (NY)

Temple U (PA)
Tennessee, U of
Texas Christian U
Texas Tech U
Texas, U of, Austin
Texas, U of, San Antonio
Xavier U (OH)

AIR TRAFFIC CONTROL

Keeping the Skies Safe: Air Traffic Control Programs

These colleges are approved to "broaden employment opportunities in the aviation industry. While graduates of these approved colleges are not guaranteed employment, the Federal Aviation Administration (FAA) considers graduation from one of these programs a valuable hiring source for Air Traffic Control Specialists."

Aims Community C (CO)
Alaska, U of, Anchorage
Arizona State U, Mesa (AZ)
Baltimore County, Community C of (MD)
Beaver County, Community C of (PA)
Broward C (FL)
Daniel Webster C (NH)
Dowling C (NY)
Eastern New Mexico U, Roswell
Embry-Riddle Aeronautical U, Daytona (FL)
Embry-Riddle Aeronautical U, Prescott (AZ)
Florida Institute of Technology
Florida State C, Jacksonville
Green River Community C (WA)
Hampton U (VA)
Hesston C (KS)
InterAmerican U of Puerto Rico
Jacksonville U (FL)

Kent State U (OH)
LeTourneau U (TX)
Lewis U (IL)
Metropolitan State U (CO)
Miami Dade C (FL)
Middle Georgia State C
Middle Tennessee State U
Minneapolis Community and Technical C (MN)
Mt. San Antonio C (CA)
North Dakota, U of
Oklahoma, U of
Purdue U (IN)
Sacramento City C (CA)
St. Cloud State U (MN)
Texas State Technical C, Waco
Tulsa Community C (OK)
Vaughn C of Aeronautics and Technology (NY)
Western Michigan U

Source: Federal Aviation Administration (faa.gov)

ANIMATION

Colleges for the Study of Animation

Academy of Art U (CA)
Academy of Interactive Entertainment (WA)
Academy of Performing Arts (Czech Republic)
Advancing Technology, U of (AZ)
Animation Portfolio Workshop (Canada)

Animation Workshop (Denmark)
Anomalia (Czech Republic)
ArtCenter C of Design (CA)
Brigham Young U (UT)
California Institute of the Arts
California State U, Long Beach
California State U, Northridge

California, U of, Los Angeles
Camera Obscura School of Art (Israel)
Carnegie Mellon U (PA)
Denison U (OH)
DePaul U (IL)
DigiPen Institute of Technology (WA)
Digital Animation & Visual Effects
    School (FL)
Digital Media Arts C (FL)
École Supérieure d'Informatique de
    Communication (France)
Emily Carr U of Art and Design
    (Canada)
Ex'pression C for Digital Arts (CA)
Florida International U (FL)
Gobelins School of the Image (France)
Hampshire C (MA)
LaSalle C (Canada)
Maryland Institute C of Art
Michigan State U
Museum of Fine Arts, School of the
    (MA)

Nanyang Technological U (Singapore)
National Institute of Design (India)
Northeastern U (MA)
Ohio Wesleyan U (OH)
Pratt Institute (NY)
Redhouse C of Animation (Canada)
Rensselaer Polytechnic Institute (NY)
Rhode Island School of Design
Ringling C of Art & Design (FL)
Rochester Institute of Technology (NY)
Savannah C of Art and Design (GA)
Sheridan C (Canada)
Southern California, U of
Southern Methodist U (TX)
Southern New Hampshire U (NH)
Southwest U of Visual Arts (AZ)
Texas, U of, Dallas
Utah, U of
Visual Arts, School of (NY)
West England, U of (United Kingdom)
Worcester Polytechnic Institute (MA)

Sources: *College Finder* research, including *Animation Career Review*

ARCHAEOLOGY

Colleges With Interesting Programs in Archaeology

Baylor U (TX)
Beloit C (WI)
Boston U (MA)
Bowdoin C (ME)
Brown U (RI)
Bryn Mawr C (PA)
California, U of, Berkeley
California, U of, Los Angeles
Columbia U (NY)
Dartmouth C (NH)
Evansville, U of (IN)
Haverford C (PA)
Michigan, U of, Ann Arbor
New York, City U of, Hunter C
New York U

North Carolina, U of, Chapel Hill
Oberlin C (OH)
Oregon, U of
Pennsylvania, U of
Princeton U (NJ)
St. Mary's C (CA)
Texas, U of, Austin
Tufts U (MA)
Washington C (MD)
Washington U (MO)
Wellesley C (MA)
Wooster, C of (OH)
Yale U (CT)

ARCHITECTURE

Schools Offering Bachelor's Degrees in Architecture

The schools listed below are bachelor's programs accredited by the National Architectural Accrediting Board (NAAB), the sole organization authorized to accredit American professional degrees in architecture.

American U (United Arab Emirates)
Arizona, U of
Arkansas, U of
Auburn U (AL)
Boston Architectural C (MA)
California C of the Arts
California Polytechnic State U, San Luis Obispo
California Polytechnic State U, Pomona
Carnegie Mellon U (PA)
Cooper Union (NY)
Cornell U (NY)
Drexel U (PA)
Florida A&M U
Florida Atlantic U
Houston, U of (TX)
Howard U (DC)
Illinois Institute of Technology
Iowa State U
Kennasaw State U (GA)
Louisiana State U, Baton Rouge
Miami, U of (FL)
Mississippi State U
New Jersey Institute of Technology
New School of Architecture & Design (CA)
New York, City U of, City C

New York Institute of Technology
North Carolina State U
North Carolina, U of, Charlotte
Notre Dame, U of (IN)
Oklahoma State U
Oklahoma, U of
Oregon, U of
Pennsylvania State U
Philadelphia U (PA)
Polytechnic U (Puerto Rico)
Pratt Institute (NY)
Tennessee, U of, Knoxville
Texas, U of, Austin
Tuskegee U (AL)
Southern California Institute of Architecture
Southern California, U of
Southern U (LA)
Syracuse U (NY)
Rensselaer Polytechnic Institute (NY)
Rhode Island School of Design
Rice U (TX)
Virginia Polytechnic Institute & State U
Woodbury U (CA)

Source: National Architectural Accrediting Board (naab.org)

Schools to Consider for a Career in Architecture

Arkansas, U of
Auburn U (AL)
Boston Architectural C (MA)
California Polytechnic State U, Pomona
California Polytechnic State U, San Luis Obispo
California, U of, Berkeley
Carnegie Mellon U (PA)
Cincinnati, U of (OH)
Clemson U (SC)
Columbia U (NY)
Cooper Union (NY)
Cornell U (NY)

Harvard U (MA)
Iowa State U
Kansas State U
Kansas, U of
Massachusetts Institute of Technology
Michigan, U of, Ann Arbor
Notre Dame, U of (IN)
Oregon, U of
Pennsylvania State U, University Park
Pennsylvania, U of
Pratt Institute (NY)
Princeton U (NJ)
Rensselaer Polytechnic Institute (NY)

Rhode Island School of Design
Rice U (TX)
Savannah C of Art & Design (GA)
Southern California Institute of
   Architecture
Southern California, U of

Syracuse U (NY)
Texas, U of, Austin
Virginia Polytechnic Institute & State U
Virginia, U of
Washington U (MO)
Yale U (CT)

Source: *College Finder* research, including *Design Intelligence*, *Architectural Record*, and archdaily.com

Colleges to Consider for Landscape Architecture

Ball State U (IN)
California Polytechnic State U, San Luis
   Obispo
California Polytechnic State U, Pomona
Cornell U (NY)
Georgia, U of
Iowa State U
Kansas State U

Louisiana State U
Michigan State U
Ohio State U
Pennsylvania State U
Purdue U (IN)
Texas A&M U, College Station
Texas Tech U
Virginia Polytechnic Institute & State U

Source: *College Finder* research

ART/FINE ART

Great Places to Study Fine Arts

These colleges are members of the Association of Independent Colleges of Art and Design, a nonprofit consortium of leading art schools in the United States and Canada. Most offer a specialized art degree such as the Bachelor of Fine Arts and are "free-standing" (not a department of a college or university).

Alberta C of Art & Design (Canada)
Art Academy of Cincinnati (OH)
Art Center C of Design (CA)
Art Institute of Chicago, School of the
   (IL)
Arts, U of the (PA)
Bezalel Academy of Arts & Design
   (Israel) (international affiliate)
Burren C of Art (Ireland) (international
   affiliate)
California C of the Arts
California Institute of the Arts
Cleveland Institute of Art
Columbus C of Art & Design (OH)
Cooper Union (NY)
Cornish C of the Arts (WA)
Cranbrook Academy of Art (MI)
Creative Studies, C for (MI)
Emily Carr U of Art & Design (Canada)
Kansas City Art Institute (MO)

Laguna C of Art & Design (CA)
Lesley U, C of Art & Design (MA)
Lyme Academy C of Fine Arts (CT)
Maine C of Art
Maryland Institute C of Art
Massachusetts C of Art & Design
Memphis C of Art (TN)
Milwaukee Institute of Art & Design (WI)
Minneapolis C of Art & Design (MN)
Montserrat C of Art (MA)
Moore C of Art & Design (PA)
Museum of Fine Arts, School of the
   (MA)
New Hampshire Institute of Art
NSCAD U (Canada)
OCAD U (Canada)
Oregon C of Art & Craft
Osaka U of Arts (Japan) (international
   affiliate)
Otis C of Art & Design (CA)

Pacific Northwest C of Art (OR)
Parsons School of Design (NY)
Pennsylvania Academy of the Fine Arts
Pennsylvania C of Art & Design
Pratt Institute (NY)

Rhode Island School of Design
Ringling C of Art & Design (FL)
San Francisco Art Institute CA)
Visual Arts, School of (NY)
Watkins C of Art, Design & Film (TN)

Source: Association of Independent Colleges of Art and Design (aicad.org)

The Experts' Choice: Colleges for the Aspiring Artist

Counselors selected colleges for a student interested in fine or studio arts but who does not necessarily want to go to a college specializing in art.

The Top Choices

Boston U (MA)
Brown U (RI)
California, U of, Los Angeles
Carnegie Mellon U (PA)
Cornell U (NY)
Kenyon C (OH)
Michigan, U of, Ann Arbor
New York U
Sarah Lawrence C (NY)

Next Choices

American U (DC)
Bard C (NY)
Boston C (MA)
Bryn Mawr C (PA)
California State U, Humboldt
California, U of, Santa Barbara

Chicago, U of (IL)
Colby-Sawyer C (NH)
Columbia U (NY)
Cooper Union (NY)
Goucher C (MD)
Macalester C (MN)
Middlebury C (VT)
Oregon, U of
Rochester, U of (NY)
Savannah C of Art & Design (GA)
Scripps C (CA)
Skidmore C (NY)
Southern Methodist U (TX)
Syracuse U (NY)
Tufts U (MA)
Vassar C (NY)
Washington U (MO)
Washington, U of
Wesleyan U (CT)
Yale U (CT)

ASTRONOMY

Great Colleges to Study Astronomy

These schools are members of the Association of Universities for Research in Astronomy, a consortium of universities and other institutions that operate astronomical observatories and telescopes.

Arizona, U of
Boston U (MA)
California Institute of Technology
California, U of, Berkeley
California, U of, Santa Cruz
Carnegie Institution for Science (MD)
Chicago, U of (IL)
Colorado, U of, Boulder

Fisk U (TN)
Florida, U of
Georgia State U
Harvard U (MA)
Hawaii, U of, Manoa
Illinois, U of, Urbana
Indiana U Bloomington
Iowa State U

Johns Hopkins U (MD)
Maryland, U of, College Park
Massachusetts Institute of Technology
Michigan State U
Michigan, U of, Ann Arbor
Minnesota, U of, Twin Cities
Montana State U, Bozeman
New Jersey Institute of Technology
New Mexico State U
New York, State U of, Stony Brook
North Carolina, U of, Chapel Hill
Ohio State U, Columbus
Pennsylvania State U, University Park
Pittsburgh, U of (PA)

Pontificia Universidad Católica (Chile)
Princeton U (NJ)
Rutgers U, New Brunswick (NJ)
Stanford U (CA)
Swinburne U (Australia)
Texas A&M U, College Station
Texas, U of, Austin
Tohoku U (Japan)
Universidad de Chile
Vanderbilt U (TN)
Virginia, U of
Washington, U of, Seattle
Wisconsin, U of, Madison
Yale U (CT)

Source: Association of Universities for Research in Astronomy (aura-astronomy.org)

ATHLETIC TRAINING

Accredited Athletic Training Colleges

These are the schools that are accredited by the Commission on Accreditation of Athletic Training Education. The institutions listed below are active and in good standing and offer programs leading into a bachelor's degree in athletic training and prepare students for the certification examination.

Akron, U of (OH)
Alabama, U of, Tuscaloosa
Albion C (MI)
Alma C (MI)
Alvernia U (PA)
Appalachian State U (NC)
Ashland U (OH)
Augustana C (IL)
Aurora U (IL)
Baldwin Wallace U (OH)
Ball State U (IN)
Baylor U (TX)
Bethany C (KS)
Bethel C (IN)
Bethel U (MN)
Boise State U (ID)
Bridgewater C (VA)
California State U, Fresno
California State U, Fullerton
California State U, Long Beach
California State U, Northridge
California State U, Sacramento
Campbell U (NC)
Canisius C (NY)
Capital U (OH)
Carroll U (MT)
Castleton State C (VT)

Catawba C (NC)
Cedarville U (OH)
Central Connecticut State U
Central Florida, U of
Central Michigan U
Central Missouri, U of
Charleston Southern U (SC)
Charleston, C of (SC)
Charleston, U of (WV)
Clarke C (IA)
Coe C (IA)
Colorado Mesa U
Colorado State U, Pueblo
Concord U (WV)
Concordia U (CA)
Connecticut, U of
Delaware, U of
Denison U (OH)
Duquesne U (PA)
East Carolina U (NC)
Eastern Kentucky U
Eastern U (PA)
Eastern Washington U
Endicott C (MA)
Evansville, U of (IN)
Florida Gulf Coast U
Florida State U

Florida, U of
Franklin C (IN)
Ft. Hays State U (KS)
Gardner-Webb U (NC)
George Fox U (NC)
George Mason U (VA)
Georgia C & State U
Georgia Southern U
Georgia, U of
Grand Valley State U (MI)
Gustavus Adolphus C (MN)
Hardin-Simmons U (TX)
Heidelberg U (OH)
High Point U (NC)
Hope C (MI)
Illinois State U
Immaculata U (PA)
Indiana State U
Indiana U Bloomington
Indiana Wesleyan U
Indianapolis, U of (IN)
Iowa State U
Iowa, U of
Ithaca C (NY)
James Madison U (VA)
Kansas, U of
Kean U (NJ)
Keene State C (NH)
Kent State U (OH)
King U (TN)
King's C (PA)
Lake Superior State U (MI)
Lasell C (MA)
Laverne, U of (CA)
Lee U (TN)
Lees-McRae C (NC)
Lindenwood U (MO)
Linfield C (OR)
Lock Haven U (PA)
Longwood U (VA)
Louisiana State U, Baton Rouge
Luther C (IA)
Lynchburg C (VA)
Maine, U of
Maine, U of, Presque Isle
Manchester U (IN)
Marietta C (OH)
Marist C (NY)
Marquette U (WI)
Mars Hill U (NC)
Marywood U (PA)
Massachusetts C of Liberal Arts
Mercyhurst U (PA)
Merrimack C (MA)
Messiah C (PA)

Methodist U (NC)
Metropolitan State U (CO)
Miami U (OH)
Miami, U of (FL)
Michigan State U
Michigan, U of, Ann Arbor
Middle Tennessee State U
Minnesota State U, Mankato
Minnesota State U, Moorhead
Missouri State U
Mt. St. Joseph U (OH)
Nebraska Wesleyan U
Nebraska, U of, Kearney
Nebraska, U of, Omaha
Nevada, U of, Las Vegas
New Hampshire, U of
New Mexico, U of, Albuquerque
New York, State U of, Brockport
New York, State U of, Cortland
New York, State U of, Stony Brook
Nicholls State U (KY)
North Carolina, U of, Chapel Hill
North Carolina, U of, Charlotte
North Carolina, U of, Wilmington
North Central C (IL)
North Dakota, U of
North Florida, U of
North Georgia, U of
North Park U (IL)
Northern Colorado, U of
Northern Illinois U
Northern Iowa, U of
Northern Kentucky U
Northern Michigan U
Northwestern C (IA)
Nova Southeastern U (FL)
Ohio Northern U
Ohio U, Athens
Oregon State U
Otterbein U (OH)
Pacific, U of the (CA)
Park U (MO)
Pennsylvania State U, University Park
Pittsburgh, U of, Bradford
Plymouth State U (NH)
Point Loma Nazarene U (CA)
Purdue U (IN)
Quinnipiac U (CT)
Roanoke C (VA)
Rowan U (NJ)
Sacred Heart U (CT)
Saginaw Valley State U (MI)
Salisbury U (MD)
San Diego State U (CA)
San Jose State U (CA)

Slippery Rock U (PA)
South Carolina, U of
South Dakota State U
Southeast Missouri State U
Southern Arkansas U
Southern Connecticut State U
Southern Maine, U of
Southern Mississippi, U of
Southwestern C (KS)
Springfield C (MA)
St. Cloud State U (MN)
Sterling C (VT)
Tampa, U of (FL)
Temple U (PA)
Texas Lutheran U
Texas State U
Texas, U of, Austin
Texas, U of, Permian Basin
Toledo, U of (OH)
Towson U (MD)
Troy U (AL)
Truman State U (MO)
Tusculum C (TN)
Union C (NY)

Union U (TN)
Upper Iowa U
Utah, U of
Valdosta State U (GA)
Washburn U (KS)
Waynesburg U (PA)
Weber State U (UT)
West Chester U (PA)
West Virginia U
Western Carolina U (NC)
Western Illinois U
Wheeling Jesuit U (WV)
Whitworth U (WA)
Wichita State U (KS)
Wilmington U (DE)
Winona U (MN)
Winthrop U (SC)
Wisconsin, U of, Eau Claire
Wisconsin, U of, Lacrosse
Wisconsin, U of, Madison
Wisconsin, U of, Oshkosh
Wisconsin, U of, Stevens Point
Wright State U (OH)
Xavier U (OH)

Source: Commission on Accreditation of Athletic Training Education (caate.net)

AUDIO TECHNOLOGY/ACOUSTIC ENGINEERING

Colleges to Consider for Audio Technology and/or Acoustic Engineering

Boston U (MA)
Carnegie Mellon U (PA)
Columbia C Chicago (IL)
Denver, U of (CO)
DePaul U (IL)
Drexel U (PA)
Emerson C (MA)
Fordham U (NY)
Full Sail U (FL)
Indianapolis, U of (IN)
Ithaca C (NY)

Massachusetts, U of, Lowell
New Haven, U of (CT)
New York U
Purdue U (IN)
Shenandoah U (VA)
Southern California, U of
Virginia Polytechnic Institute &
   State U
Webster U (MO)
Western Michigan U

Source: *College Finder* research

AUTO DESIGN

Colleges for Auto Design

Automotive designers work with the aesthetics of a vehicle's interior and exterior qualities.

Academy of Art U (CA)
Advanced Technology Institute (VA)
Appalachian State U (NC)
Arizona State U
Art Center C of Design (CA)
Auburn U (AL)
Broward C (FL)
California State U, Long Beach
Carleton U (Canada)
Central Florida, C of
Cincinnati, U of (OH)
Clemson U (SC)
Creative Studies, C of (MI)
Florida State C, Jacksonville
Georgia Institute of Technology
Houston, U of (TX)
Illinois, U of, Chicago
Illinois, U of, Urbana
Indian River State C (FL)

Ivy Tech Community C (IN)
Lincoln C of Technology (multiple states)
Louisiana, U of, Lafayette
Metropolitan State U (CO)
Michigan, U of, Ann Arbor
North Carolina State U, Raleigh
Ohio State U, Columbus
Royal C of Art (United Kingdom)
San Jose State U (CA)
Santa Fe C (NM)
Seminole State C (FL)
Virginia Polytechnic Institute & State U
Washington, U of, Seattle
Western Michigan U
Western Washington U
WyoTech (multiple states)

AVIATION

Colleges That Offer Aviation Studies

These programs are accredited based on educational quality and alignment with industry standards.

Alaska, U of, Anchorage
Arizona State U, Tempe
Auburn U (AL)
Baylor U (TX)
Bridgewater State U (CT)
California Baptist U
Central Missouri, U of
Central Washington U
Delaware State U
Delta State U (MS)
Dowling C (NY)
Dubuque, U of (IA)
Embry-Riddle Aeronautical U (AZ)
Embry-Riddle Aeronautical U (FL)
Florida Institute of Technology
Florida Memorial U
Hampton U (VA)
Interamerican U (Puerto Rico)

Jacksonville U (FL)
Kansas State U, Salina
Kent State U (OH)
Korea Aerospace U
Kwara State U (Nigeria)
Liberty U (VA)
Louisiana Tech U
Maine, U of, Augusta
Maryland, U of, Eastern Shore
Mercer County Community C (NJ)
Middle Georgia State C
Middle Tennessee State U
Minnesota State U, Mankato
Mt. Allison U (Canada)
Mt. Royal U (Canada)
Nebraska, U of, Omaha
Nigerian C of Aviation Technology
North Dakota, U of

Ohio State U
Oklahoma City Community C
Oklahoma State U
Oklahoma, U of
Purdue U (IN)
Rocky Mountain C (CO)
Seneca C of Applied Arts & Technology
 (Canada)
South Dakota State U
Southeastern Oklahoma State U
Southeastern Oklahoma State U, Rose
 State U

Southern Illinois U, Carbondale
Spartan C of Aeronautics & Technology
 (OK)
St. Gregory's U (OK)
St. Louis U (MO)
Utah Valley U
Vaughn C of Aeronautics & Technology
 (NY)
Vermont Technical C
Western Michigan U
Western U (Canada)
Westminster C (UT)

Source: Aviation Accreditation Board International (aabi.aero)

BIOLOGY

The Experts' Choice: Great Biology Programs

Experts were asked to name colleges for a student who wants to major in biology. As a basic and central college subject, biology is offered at most liberal arts and sciences colleges. Evaluation of undergraduate programs in biology, however, is difficult because of the varied approaches to assessing quality. Students should base their college selection decisions on numerous variables, both academic and social. The following colleges offer programs in biology that are worth a second look.

The Top Choices

Brown U (RI)
California Institute of Technology
California, U of, San Diego
Chicago, U of (IL)
Columbia U (NY)
Emory U (GA)
Grinnell C (IA)
Harvey Mudd C (CA)
Kalamazoo U (MI)
Massachusetts Institute of Technology*
Princeton U (NJ)
Reed C (OR)
Stanford U (CA)
Swarthmore C (PA)
Tufts U (MA)
Wake Forest U (NC)
Washington U (MO)
Washington, U of

*The Top Choice

Honorable Mention

Amherst C (MA)

Arizona State U
Austin C (TX)
Baker U (KS)
Barnard C (NY)
Baylor U (TX)
Boston U (MA)
Bowdoin C (ME)
Brandeis U (MA)
Bryn Mawr C (PA)
Bucknell U (PA)
California Polytechnic State U, San Luis
 Obispo
California Polytechnic State U, Pomona
California, U of, Berkeley
California, U of, Davis
California, U of, Irvine
California, U of, Los Angeles
California, U of, Riverside
California, U of, Santa Barbara
Carnegie Mellon U (PA)
Case Western Reserve U (OH)
Claremont McKenna C (CA)
Colorado, U of, Boulder
Connecticut, U of
Cornell U (NY)
Dartmouth C (NH)

Davidson C (NC)
Duke U (NC)
Earlham C (IN)
Fairfield U (CT)
Gonzaga U (WA)
Grove City C (PA)
Gustavus Adolphus C (MN)
Hamilton C (NY)
Harvard U (MA)
Hawaii, U of, Hilo
Illinois, U of, Urbana
Indiana U Bloomington
Iowa, U of
Johns Hopkins U (MD)
Kansas, U of
Kentucky, U of
Knox C (IL)
Lawrence U (WI)
Maryland, U of, College Park
Massachusetts, U of, Amherst
Miami, U of (FL)
Michigan State U
Michigan, U of, Ann Arbor
Middlebury C (VT)
Montana, U of
Morningside C (IA)
Nevada, U of, Las Vegas
New York U
New York, State U of, Albany
New York, State U of, Binghamton
New York, State U of, Buffalo
New York, State U of, Stony Brook

North Carolina, U of, Chapel Hill
Northwestern U (IL)
Notre Dame, U of (IN)
Oberlin C (OH)
Ohio State U, Columbus
Oklahoma, U of
Oregon, U of
Pennsylvania State U, University Park
Pennsylvania, U of
Philadelphia, U of the Sciences in (PA)
Pomona C (CA)
Purdue U (IN)
Rice U (TX)
Ripon C (WI)
Rutgers U, New Brunswick (NJ)
Shippensburg U (PA)
Skidmore C (NY)
Southern California, U of
St. Michael's C (VT)
Texas, U of, San Antonio
Tulsa, U of (OK)
Union C (NY)
Ursinus C (PA)
Vanderbilt U (TN)
Villanova U (PA)
Virginia, U of
Wellesley C (MA)
Wheaton C (MA)
Wisconsin, U of, Madison
Wooster, C of (OH)
Yale U (CT)

BLACKSMITHING

Blacksmithing Colleges

These are members of the Artist-Blacksmith's Association of North America. Blacksmiths create objects from wrought iron or steel.

Alma C (MI)
Appalachian Center for Craft (TN)
Austin Community C (TX)
Bibliotekstjanst AB (Sweden)
Fleming C (Canada)
Georgia, U of
Haywood Community C (NC)
Maine C of Art (Joanne Waxman
   Library)

Massachusetts C of Art
Northern Michigan U
Rochester Institute of Technology (NY)
Sheridan C (WY)
Southern Highland Craft Guild (NC)
Southern Illinois U, Carbondale
Touchstone Center for Crafts (PA)

Source: The Artist-Blacksmith's Association of North America (abana.org)

BOAT BUILDING

Boat Building Colleges

These trade schools offer traditional and contemporary boat building and craftsmanship.

Apprentice School (VA)
Arques School (CA)
Great Lakes Boat Building School (MI)
NorthWest School of Wooden Boat Building (WA)

BOOK ARTS

Schools for Book Arts

These colleges offer courses in image creation, typesetting, leather binding, book restoration, preservation, and related subjects.

Alabama, U of, Tuscaloosa
American Academy of Bookbinding
  (CO)
Arizona, U of
Art Institute of Chicago, School of the
  (IL)
Arts, U of the (PA)
Carroll U (WI)
Columbia C Chicago (IL)
Florence School of Fine Arts (Italy)
George Washington U, Corcoran School
  of the Arts & Design (DC)
Idaho, U of

Iowa, U of
Maine, U of, Machias
Mills C (CA)
Minnesota Center for Book Arts
Montserrat C of Art (MA)
North Bennet Street School (MA)
Oregon Center of Arts and Crafts
Penland School of Crafts (NC)
Rhode Island School of Design
Scripps C (CA)
Virginia Commonwealth U
Wells C (NY)

Source: *College Finder* research

BROADCASTING

Colleges to Consider for Broadcasting

Alabama, U of, Tuscaloosa
Arizona State U
Arizona, U of
Auburn U (AL)
Ball State U (IN)
Boston U (MA)
Brigham Young U (UT)
California State U, Northridge
Central Florida, U of
Drexel U (PA)
Florida, U of

Houston, U of (TX)
Maryland, U of, College Park
Massachusetts Institute of Technology
Michigan State U
Northwestern U (IL)
Pennsylvania State U, University Park
Southern California, U of
Syracuse U (NY)
Temple U (PA)
Texas, U of, Austin

Source: *College Finder* research

BUSINESS

The Experts' Choice: Great Places to Study Business

The Top Choices

Arizona, U of
Babson C (MA)
Baylor U (TX)
Clarkson U (NY)
Cornell U (NY)
Emory U (GA)
Houston, U of (TX)
Michigan, U of, Ann Arbor
New York, City U of, Baruch
North Carolina, U of, Chapel Hill
Northeastern U (MA)
Notre Dame, U of (IN)
Oklahoma, U of
Pennsylvania, U of
Southern California, U of
Syracuse U (NY)
Temple U (PA)
Texas Christian U
Texas, U of, Austin
Virginia, U of
Washington U (MO)
Washington, U of, Seattle

Second Choices

Alabama, U of, Tuscaloosa
Arizona State U
Belmont U (TN)
Bentley U (MA)
Boston C (MA)

Boston U (MA)
Bradley U (IL)
Bryant C (RI)
California, U of, Berkeley
California, U of, Irvine
California, U of, Los Angeles
Carnegie Mellon U (PA)
Florida, U of
Georgetown U (DC)
Georgia Institute of Technology
Georgia, U of
Illinois, U of, Urbana
Iowa, U of
Loyola Marymount U (CA)
Massachusetts Institute of Technology
Miami U (OH)
Miami, U of (FL)Michigan State U
Minnesota, U of, Twin Cities
Missouri, U of, Kansas City
New York, State U of, Buffalo
Ohio State U
Pennsylvania State U, University Park
Pittsburgh, U of (PA)
Purdue U (IN)
Rice U (TX)
Rochester, U of (NY)
Southern Methodist U (TX)
St. Louis U (MO)
Texas A&M U, College Station
Utah, U of
Vanderbilt U (TN)
Wisconsin, U of, Madison

Agricultural/Agriculture Business

The following are universities with agricultural business or agricultural economics programs.

Auburn U (AL)
Illinois State U
Illinois, U of, Urbana
Iowa State U
Minnesota, U of, Twin Cities
Mississippi State U
Pennsylvania State U, University Park
Purdue U (IN)

Sam Houston State U (TX)
South Dakota State U
New York, State U of, Cobleskill Y
Texas A&M U, College Station
Wisconsin, U of, Madison
Virginia Polytechnic Institute &
   State U
Wyoming, U of

Source: *College Finder* research, including AgWeb, an online agriculture news source

The Experts' Choice: Colleges for the Budding Entrepreneur

Arizona, U of
Babson C (MA)
Baylor U (TX)
Bentley U (MA)
Bradley U (IL)
Brigham Young U (UT)
Bryant U (RI)
Clarkson U (NY)
Dayton, U of (OH)
DePaul U (IL)
Drexel U (PA)
Eckerd C (FL)
Emerson C (MA)
Georgia Tech U
Houston, U of (TX)
Lehigh U (PA)

Maryland, U of, College Park
Miami U (OH)
Michigan, U of, Ann Arbor
New York, City U of, Baruch C
North Carolina, U of, Chapel Hill
Northeastern U (MA)
Oklahoma, U of
Rowan U (NJ)
South Carolina, U of, Columbia
Southern California, U of
St. Louis U (MO)
Stevenson U (MD)
Syracuse U (NY)
Temple U (PA)
Texas Christian U
Washington U (MO)

Colleges to Consider for E-commerce

E-commerce is the study of conducting business through electronic means via the Internet. E-commerce provides opportunities to reach populations globally that would have been difficult in the past.

Bloomfield C (NJ)
Boston U (MA)
California State U, Fullerton
Creighton U (NE)
Dalhousie U (Canada)
Denver, U of (CO)
DePaul U (IL)
Illinois Institute of Technology
La Verne, U of (CA)
Lancaster U (United Kingdom)
Maryland, U of, College Park

McMaster U (Canada)
New Brunswick, U of (Canada)
Purdue U (IN)
Rochester, U of (NY)
Scranton, U of (PA)
Stratford U (VA)
Temple U (PA)
Thiel C (PA)
Toledo, U of (OH)
Towson U (MD)

Source: *College Finder* research

Great Marketing Programs

Marketing is connecting customers with products. The following are among the small or medium-sized schools that have collegiate chapters affiliated with the American Marketing Association.

Abilene Christian U (TX)
Akron, U of (OH)
Alfred U (NY)
Assumption C (MA)
Belmont U (TN)
Bethune-Cookman U (FL)

Bloomsburg U (PA)
Bob Jones U (SC)
Bradley U (IL)
Bryant U (RI)
California Lutheran U
Cameron U (OK)

ACADEMICS

Canisius C (NY)
Carnegie Mellon U (PA)
Catawba C (NC)
Chapman U (CA)
Chatham U (PA)
Creighton U (NE)
DePaul U (IL)
Dillard U (MA)
Drake U (IA)
Drexel U (PA)
Duquesne U (PA)
Florida Atlantic U
Florida International U
Fordham U (NY)
Georgia Southern U
Grambling State U (LA)
Grove City C (PA)
Hartford, U of (CT)
Hofstra U (NY)
Illinois Institute of Art
Illinois Wesleyan U
Ithaca C (NY)
John Carroll U (OH)
John Hopkins U (MD)
Johnson & Wales U (NC)
Johnson & Wales U (RI)
Kutztown U (PA)
La Verne, U of (CA)
Lake Forest C (IL)
Lehigh U (PA)
Liberty U (VA)
Loyola Marymount U (CA)
Loyola U (LA)
Loyola U (MD)
Luther C (IA)
Manhattan C (NY)
Marshall U (WV)
Mercer U (GA)
Merrimack C (MA)
Monmouth U (NJ)
New Haven, U of (CT)
New Jersey, C of
New Orleans, U of (LA)
New York, State U of, Oneonta
Niagara U (NY)
Northeastern U (MA)
Northwood U (MI)
Oakland U (MI)
Oklahoma Christian U (OK)

Old Dominion U (VA)
Pace U (NY)
Pacific Lutheran U (WA)
Portland State U (OR)
Prairie View A&M U (TX)
Providence C (RI)
Quinnipiac U (CT)
Radford U (VA)
Rhode Island C
Richmond, U of (VA)
Rider U (NJ)
Robert Morris U (PA)
Rowan U (NJ)
Salisbury U (MD)
Salve Regina U (RI)
Samford U (AL)
San Diego, U of (CA)
San Francisco, U of (CA)
Schreiner U (TX)
Seattle U (WA)
Seton Hill U (PA)
Slippery Rock U (PA)
St. Benedict, C of /St. John's U (MN)
St. Bonaventure U (NY)
St. John Fisher C (NY)
St. Joseph's U (PA)
St. Leo U (FL)
St. Mary's C (CA)
St. Thomas, U of (MN)
Stetson U (FL)
Susquehanna U (PA)
Syracuse U (NY)
Tampa, U of (FL)
Texas Christian U
Texas Lutheran U
Tiffin U (OH)
Truman State U (MO)
Tulane U (LA)
Villanova U (PA)
Virginia Commonwealth U
Walsh U (OH)
Washington C (MD)
West Chester U (PA)
Western New England U (MA)
Winthrop U (SC)
Wisconsin, U of, Stout
Worcester Polytechnic Institute (MA)
Xavier U (LA)
Xavier U (OH)

Source: American Marketing Association (ama.org)

CABINETMAKING

Cabinetmaking Colleges

Many students who want to work as a cabinetmaker go to a traditional college and pursue this career after graduation. Some go to specialized schools such as those here that offer cabinetmaking and millwork studies.

Bakersfield C (CA)
Bates Technical C (WA)
Bucks Country Community C (PA)
Central Georgia Technical C (GA)
Cerritos C (CA)
GateWay Community C (AZ)
Harrisburg Area Community C (PA)
Hennepin Technical C (MN)
Humber C (Canada)
Ivy Tech Community C (IN)
Lee C (TX)
Milwaukee Area Technical C (WI)
Mineral Area C (MO)

Minneapolis Community & Technical C (MN)
Palomar C (CA)
Penn Foster Career School (PA)
Seattle Central C (WA)
Sierra C (CA)
Southern Idaho, C of
Thaddeus Stevens C of Technology (PA)
Upper Bucks County Technical School (PA)
Utah Valley U

CARTOONING

Schools for Those Preparing to be a Cartoonist

Academy of Art U (PA)
Center for Cartoon Studies (VT)
Kubert School (NJ)
London Art C (United Kingdom)
Ringling C of Art & Design (FL)
Visual Arts, School of (NY)

COMMUNICATIONS

The Experts' Choice: Great Communications Programs

Experts were asked to name colleges for a student who wants to major in communications.

Arizona State U
Boston U (MA)
Elon U (NC)
Emerson C (MA)
Georgia, U of
Ithaca C (NY)
John Carroll U (OH)

Missouri, U of, Columbia
New York U
Northwestern U (IL)
Quinnipiac U (CT)
Southern California, U of
Syracuse U (NY)
Texas, U of, Austin

COMPUTER ANIMATION

Colleges With Fine Programs in Computer Animation

Animators creatively set objects and characters in motion. The following schools offer artistic and technical programs in computer animation as well as areas such as new media, integrative media, design media, and digital design.

Academy of Art U (CA)
Advancing Technology, U of (AZ)
Akron, U of (OH)
ArtCenter C of Design (CA)
Art Institute of Chicago, School of the (IL)
Art Institute of Ft. Lauderdale (FL)
Art Institute of Southern California
Arts, U of the (PA)
Bowling Green State U (OH)
Bradley U (IL)
California Institute of the Arts
California State U, Fullerton
California, U of, Los Angeles
Central Florida, U of
Cerro Coso Community C (CA)
Champlain C (VT)
Chapman U (CA)
Cogswell C (CA)
Columbia C Chicago (IL)
Communication Arts at Digital Circus, School of (NC)
Connecticut C
DePaul U (IL)
DigiPen Institute of Technology (WA)
Drexel U (PA)
Emerson C (MA)
Full Sail U (FL)
Georgia Institute of Technology
Hartford, U of (CT)
Huntingdon C (AL)
Jacksonville U (FL)
Kent State U (OH)
Kingston U (United Kingdom)
Loyola Marymount U (CA)
Marist C (NY)
Massachusetts Institute of Technology
Memphis C of Art (TN)

New Jersey Institute of Technology
New York Institute of Technology
New York U
New York, State U of, Alfred
Northern Illinois U
Ohio State U, Columbus
Oregon, U of
Otis C of Art & Design (CA)
Parsons School of Design (NY)
Pennsylvania, U of
Philadelphia U (PA)
Pratt Institute (NY)
Rhode Island School of Design
Ringling C of Art & Design (FL)
Rochester Institute of Technology (NY)
SAE Expression C (CA)
San Francisco School of Digital Filmmaking (CA)
San Francisco State U (CA)
Savannah C of Art & Design (GA)
Sheridan C Institute of Technology & Advanced Learning (Canada)
Sierra Nevada C (NV)
Southern California, U of
Stetson U (FL)
Texas A&M U, College Station
Vancouver Film School (Canada)
Vancouver Institute of Media Arts (Canada)
Virginia Commonwealth U
Visual Arts, School of (NY)
Washington, U of
Webster U (MO)
Wilkes U (PA)
Woodbury U (CA)
Worcester Polytechnic Institute (MA)

COMPUTER SCIENCE

Colleges With Excellent Programs in Computer Science (Including Animation and Game Design)

Allegheny C (PA)
Arizona State U
Atlantic Union C (MA)
Boston C (MA)
Brandeis U (MA)
Brown U (RI)
Bucknell U (PA)
California Polytechnic State U, San Luis
 Obispo
California Polytechnic State U, Pomona
California, U of, Berkeley
California, U of, Los Angeles
California, U of, Santa Cruz
Carleton C (MN)
Carnegie Mellon U (PA)
Case Western Reserve U (OH)
Champlain C (VT)
Chapman U (CA)
Chicago, U of (IL)
Clarkson U (NY)
Colorado State U, Ft. Collins
Connecticut, U of
Dartmouth C (NH)
Denver, U of (CO)
DePaul U (IL)
George Washington U (DC)
Georgia Institute of Technology
Gonzaga U (WA)
Goucher C (MD)
Hawaii Pacific U
Illinois C
Illinois, U of, Urbana
Johns Hopkins U (MD)
Kansas State U
Lehigh U (PA)
Louisiana, U of, Lafayette

Marlboro C (VT)
Massachusetts Institute of Technology
Massachusetts, U of, Dartmouth
Miami U (OH)
Miami, U of (FL)
Michigan, U of, Ann Arbor
Minnesota State U, Mankato
Montana State U, Bozeman
New Hampshire, U of
New York, State U of, Binghamton
Northwestern U (IL)
Old Dominion U (VA)
Pennsylvania State U, University Park
Princeton U (NJ)
Purdue U (IN)
Rhode Island, U of
Rice U (TX)
Rochester Institute of Technology (NY)
Rochester, U of (NY)
Ryerson U (Canada)
Santa Clara U (CA)
Seattle U (WA)
Sheridan C Institute of Technology &
 Advanced Learning (Canada)
South Carolina, U of, Columbia
Stanford U (CA)
Suffolk U (MA)
Texas A&M U, College Station
Texas, U of, Austin
Tulsa, U of (OK)
Washington, U of
Wentworth Institute of Technology (MA)
William & Mary, C of (VA)
Wofford C (SC)
Worcester Polytechnic Institute (MA)

The Experts' Choice: Colleges for Computer Science/Computer Engineering

Experts were asked to identify colleges for a student who wants to major in computer science or computer engineering.

The Top Choices

Boston U (MA)
California Institute of Technology
California, U of, Berkeley
California, U of, Davis

California, U of, Los Angeles
California, U of, San Diego
California, U of, Santa Barbara
Carnegie Mellon U (PA)
Columbia U (NY)
Cornell U (NY)

Georgia Institute of Technology
Harvard U (MA)
Illinois, U of, Urbana
Johns Hopkins U (MD)
Maryland, U of, College Park
Massachusetts Institute of Technology
Michigan, U of, Ann Arbor
Minnesota, U of, Twin Cities
New York U
North Carolina State U, Raleigh
Northwestern U (IL)
Ohio State U
Pennsylvania State U, University Park
Pennsylvania, U of
Princeton U (NJ)
Purdue U (IN)
Rice U (TX)
Southern California, U of
Stanford U (CA)
Texas A&M U, College Station
Texas, U of, Austin
Virginia Polytechnic Institute & State
   U
Washington, U of
Wisconsin, U of, Madison
Yale U (CT)

Honorable Mention

Arizona State U

Arkansas, U of, Little Rock
Brigham Young U (UT)
Brown U (RI)
California Polytechnic State U, San Luis
   Obispo
California, U of, Irvine
Chicago, U of (IL)
Colorado State U
Colorado, U of, Boulder
Connecticut, U of
Dartmouth C (NH)
DigiPen Institute of Technology (WA)
Duke U (NC)
Florida, U of
Harvey Mudd C (CA)
Illinois, U of, Chicago
Indiana U Bloomington
Massachusetts, U of, Amherst
New York, State U of, Stony Brook
North Carolina, U of, Chapel Hill
Northeastern U (MA)
Pittsburgh, U of (PA)
Rensselaer Polytechnic Institute (NY)
Rochester Institute of Technology (NY)
Rutgers U (NJ)
Santa Clara U (CA)
Utah, U of
Vanderbilt U (TN)
Washington U (MO)
Worcester Polytechnic Institute (MA)

CRIMINOLOGY

Colleges to Consider for Criminology

American U (DC)
Arizona State U
California, U of, Irvine
Central Florida, U of
Cincinnati, U of (OH)
Delaware, U of
Florida State U
Florida, U of
George Mason U (VA)
Illinois, U of, Chicago
Indiana U Bloomington
Indiana U of Pennsylvania
Loyola U (LA)
Marquette U (WI)
Maryland, U of, College Park
Michigan State U
Missouri, U of, St. Louis

Nebraska, U of, Omaha
New York, City U of, John Jay C of
   Criminal Justice
New York, State U of, Albany
Northeastern U (MA)
Pennsylvania State U, University Park
Pennsylvania, U of
Regis U (CO)
Rutgers U, Newark (NJ)
St. Anselm C (NH)
Sam Houston State U (TX)
South Carolina, U of
South Florida, U of
Stonehill C (MA)
Temple U (PA)
Texas, U of, Dallas

Sources: *College Finder* research

CULINARY

Preparation for a Career in the Culinary World

FSR Magazine, which serves the full-service restaurant industry, identified these programs as top culinary schools, based on depth of internship offerings, culinary theory, and hands-on kitchen classes.

Art Institute of Atlanta (GA)
Art Institute of Austin (TX)
Art Institute of California, Hollywood
Art Institute of California, Inland Empire
Art Institute of California, Los Angeles
Art Institute of California, Orange County
Art Institute of California, Sacramento
Art Institute of California, San Diego
Art Institute of California, San Francisco
Art Institute of California, Silicon Valley
Art Institute of Charleston (SC)
Art Institute of Charlotte (NC)
Art Institute of Colorado
Art Institute of Dallas (TX)
Art Institute of Fort Lauderdale (FL)
Art Institute of Houston (TX)
Art Institute of Indianapolis (IN)
Art Institute of Jacksonville (FL)
Art Institute of Las Vegas (NV)
Art Institute of Ohio
Art Institute of Michigan
Art Institute of Philadelphia (PA)
Art Institute of Phoenix (AZ)
Art Institute of Pittsburgh (PA)
Art Institute of Portland (OR)
Art Institute of Raleigh-Durham (NC)
Art Institute of Salt Lake City (UT)
Art Institute of San Antonio (TX)
Art Institute of Seattle (WA)
Art Institute of St. Louis (MO)
Art Institute of Tampa (FL)
Art Institute of Tennessee
Art Institute of Tucson (AZ)
Art Institute of Vancouver (Canada)
Art Institute of Virginia Beach (VA)
Art Institute of Washington (VA)

Art Institute of Wisconsin
Art Institutes International Minnesota
Auguste Escoffier School of Culinary Arts (CO)
Auguste Escoffier School of Culinary Arts (TX)
Columbus State Community C (OH)
Culinary Institute of America, Hyde Park (NY)
Culinary Institute of America, San Antonio (TX)
Culinary Institute of America, St. Helena (CA)
El Centro C, Dallas (TX)
Faulkner State Community C, Gulf Shores (AL)
Florida State C, Jacksonville (FL)
Illinois Institute of Art
Indian Hills Community C (IA)
Institute of Culinary Education (NY)
International Culinary Center (CA)
International Culinary Center (NY)
Johnson & Wales U (CO)
Johnson & Wales U (FL)
Johnson & Wales U (NC)
Johnson & Wales U (RI)
Kapiolani Community C (HI)
Kendall C School Of Culinary Arts (IL)
L'Academie de Cuisine (MD)
Lincoln Culinary Institute (FL)
New England Culinary Institute (VT)
Secchia Institute for Culinary Education (MI)
St. Philips C (TX)
Sullivan U, National Center for Hospitality Studies (KY)

Source: *FRS Magazine* (foodnewsfeed.com)

CYBERSECURITY

Colleges to Consider for Cybersecurity

Bellevue U (NE)
Carnegie Mellon U (PA)
Colorado Technical U
DePaul U (IL)
George Mason U (VA)
Houston, U of (TX)
Iowa State U
Maryland, U of, University College
Massachusetts, U of, Amherst
Mississippi State U
New York, State U of, Buffalo
Northeastern U (MA)
Norwich U (VT)

Nova Southeastern U (FL)
Oklahoma State U
Pittsburgh, U of (PA)
Purdue U (IN)
Southern California, U of
Southern New Hampshire U
St. John's U (NY)
Syracuse U (NY)
Texas, U of, San Antonio
U.S. Military Academy (NY)
Washington, U of, Seattle
West Chester U (PA)

Source: *College Finder* research, including the Ponemon Institute, a "research center dedicated to privacy, data protection, and information security policy."

DANCE

Colleges to Consider for Dance

Arizona, U of
Arts, U of (PA)
Brigham Young U (UT)
California Institute of the Arts
California, U of, Berkeley
California, U of, Irvine
Dean C (MA)
Emerson C (MA)
Florida State U
Iowa, U of
Juilliard School (NY)
Mason Gross School of the Arts (NJ)
New York U

New York, State U of, Purchase
North Carolina, U of
Oberlin C & Conservatory (OH)
Ohio State U
Oklahoma City U
Point Park U (PA)
Rutgers U New Brunswick (NJ)
Skidmore C (NY)
Temple U (PA)
Texas State U
Utah, U of

Source: *College Finder* research, including backstage.com

Great Schools to Study Dance

These are accredited programs of the National Association of Schools of Dance (NASD). NASD develops standards and guidelines to ensure a high level of educational quality. This is but one of the many ways to determine the quality of dance programs.

Akron, U of (OH)
Alabama, U of, Tuscaloosa
Appalachian State U (NC)

Arizona, U of
Ball State U (IN)
Barnard C (NY)

Belhaven U (MS)
Brigham Young U (UT)
Butler U (IN)
California Institute of the Arts
California State U, Fullerton
California State U, Long Beach
California, U of, Santa Barbara
Casper C (WY)
Chapman U (CA)
Cincinnati, U of (OH)
Columbia C (NY)
Florida State U
Florida, U of
Georgia, U of
Hartt School, The (CT)
Hope C (MI)
Illinois, U of, Urbana
Iowa, U of
Jacksonville U (FL)
James Madison U (VA)
Kent State U (OH)
Loyola Marymount U (CA)
Maryland, U of, Baltimore County
Mercyhurst U (PA)
Michigan, U of, Ann Arbor
Minnesota, U of, Twin Cities
Missouri, U of, Kansas City
Montclair State U (NJ)
Nebraska, U of, Lincoln
New Mexico, U of
New World School of the Arts (FL)
New York, State U of, Brockport

North Carolina, U of, Greensboro
Nutmeg Conservatory (CT)
Oakland U (MI)
Ohio State U, Columbus
Ohio U, Athens
Point Park U (PA)
Rutgers U (NJ)
San Jose State U (CA)
Slippery Rock U (PA)
South Carolina, U of, Columbia
South Florida, U of
Southern Methodist U (TX)
Southern Mississippi, U of
Southern Utah U
St. Olaf C (MN)
Temple U (PA)
Texas Christian U
Texas Tech U
Texas Woman's U
Texas, U of, Austin
Towson U (MD)
Utah, U of
Virginia Commonwealth U
Wayne State U (MI)
Western Kentucky U
Western Michigan U
Wichita State U (KS)
Winthrop U (SC)
Wisconsin, U of, Madison
Wisconsin, U of, Milwaukee
Wisconsin, U of, Stevens Point

Source: National Association of Schools of Dance (nasd.arts-accredit.org)

DENTAL

Colleges With Dental Schools

Students who want to become dentists may go to any undergraduate institution, as long
as they make sure to take required pre-dental classes. These colleges have their own
dental schools and are part of the American Dental Education Association (ADEA).

Alabama, U of, Birmingham
Arizona School of Dentistry & Oral
  Health
Augusta U, Dental C of Georgia
Boston U (MA)
California, U of, Los Angeles
California, U of, San Francisco
Case Western Reserve U (OH)
Colorado, U of, Denver
Columbia U (NY)

Connecticut, U of
Creighton U (NE)
Dalhousie U (Canada)
Detroit, U of (MI)
East Carolina U (NC)
Florida, U of
Harvard U (MA)
Howard U (DC)
Illinois, U of, Chicago
Indiana U Bloomington

Iowa, U of
Kentucky, U of
Lake Erie C of Osteopathic Medicine
 (FL)
Loma Linda U (CA)
Louisiana State U, New Orleans
Louisville, U of (KY)
Marquette U (WI)
Maryland, U of, Baltimore County
Medical U (SC)
Meharry Medical C (TN)
Michigan, U of, Ann Arbor
Midwestern U (AZ)
Midwestern U (IL)
Minnesota, U of, Twin Cities
Mississippi, U of
Missouri School of Dentistry & Oral
 Health
Missouri, U of, Kansas City
Nebraska, U of, Lincoln
Nevada, U of, Reno
New England, U of (ME)
New York U
New York, State U of, Buffalo
New York, State U of, Stony Brook
North Carolina, U of, Chapel Hill
Nova Southeastern U (FL)

Ohio State U
Oklahoma, U of
Oregon Health & Science U
Pacific, U of the (CA)
Pennsylvania, U of
Pittsburgh, U of (PA)
Puerto Rico, U of
Roseman U of Health Sciences (UT)
Rutgers U, New Brunswick (NJ)
South Carolina, Medical U of
Southern California, U of
Southern Illinois U, Carbondale
Temple U (PA)
Tennessee, U of, Health Science Center
Texas, A&M U, Baylor C of Dentistry
Texas, U of, Health Science Center,
 Houston
Texas, U of, Health Science Center,
 San Antonio
Touro C (NY)
Tufts U (MA)
Utah, U of
Virginia Commonwealth U
Washington, U of, Seattle
West Virginia U
Western U of Health Sciences C (CA)

Source: American Dental Education Association (adea.org)

ECONOMICS

The Experts' Choice: Excellence in Economics

As a basic and central college subject, economics is offered at most liberal arts and sciences colleges. Evaluation of undergraduate programs in economics, however, is difficult because of the varied approaches to assessing quality. Students should base their college selection decisions on numerous variables, both academic and social. The following colleges offer programs in economics that are worth a second look.

American U (DC)
Amherst C (MA)
Babson C (MA)
Bentley C (MA)
Bowdoin C (ME)
Bryant U (RI)
Bucknell U (PA)
California, U of, Berkeley
California, U of, Los Angeles
Chicago, U of (IL)*
Claremont McKenna C (CA)
Colgate U (NY)
Columbia U (NY)

Cornell U (NY)
Davidson C (NC)
Duke U (NC)
George Washington U (DC)
Georgetown U (DC)
Georgia Institute of Technology
Gettysburg C (PA)
Johns Hopkins U (MD)
London School of Economics (United
 Kingdom)
Massachusetts Institute of Technology
Michigan, U of, Ann Arbor
New York U

Northwestern U (IL)
Pennsylvania, U of
Princeton U (NJ)
Rice U (TX)
Rochester, U of (NY)
Syracuse U (NY)

Villanova U (PA)
Washington & Lee (VA)
Wesleyan U (CT)
Williams C (MA)

*The Top Choice

EDUCATION

Colleges to Prepare for a Career in Education

Alverno C (WI)
Arcadia U (PA)
Arizona, U of
Baldwin-Wallace C (OH)
Ball State U (IN)
Baylor U (TX)
Berea C (KY)
Bethel C (IN)
Birmingham Southern U (AL)
Boston C (MA)
Boston U (MA)
Bradley U (IL)
Brigham Young U (UT)
Brown U (RI)
Butler U (IN)
California State U, Northridge
San Diego State U (CA)
California, U of, San Diego
Calvin C (MI)
Central Florida, U of
Cincinnati, U of (OH)
Clark Atlanta U (GA)
Clemson U (SC)
Coe C (IA)
Colby-Sawyer C (NH)
Colgate U (NY)
Columbia U (NY)
Connecticut, U of
Creighton U (NE)
Dayton, U of (OH)
DePaul U (IL)
Drake U (IA)
Elmira C (NY)
Elon U (NC)
Florida Southern C
Florida State U
Florida, U of
Fordham U (NY)
Ft. Hays State U (KS)
Furman U (SC)

George Mason U (VA)
Georgia, U of
Gonzaga U (WA)
Goucher C (MD)
Hamline U (MN)
Hobart and William Smith C (NY)
Illinois, U of, Urbana
James Madison U (VA)
John Carroll U (OH)
Johns Hopkins U (MD)
King's C (PA)
Lesley U (MA)
LeTourneau U (TX)
Lipscomb U (TN)
Louisville, U of (KY)
Loyola U (MD)
Loyola Marymount U (CA)
Manhattan C (NY)
Marquette U (WI)
Maryland, U of, College Park
McDaniel C (MD)
Memphis, U of (TN)
Mercyhurst C (PA)
Miami U (OH)
Miami, U of (FL)
Michigan, U of, Ann Arbor
Millikin U (IL)
Millsaps C (MS)
Minnesota, U of, Twin Cities
Missouri, U of, Columbia
Mt. St. Mary's U (CA)
Nebraska, U of, Kearney
Nebraska, U of, Lincoln
New Jersey, C of
New Mexico, U of, Albuquerque
New Orleans, U of (LA)
New York, City U of, Hunter C
New York, State U of, Geneseo
New York, State U of, New Paltz

New York, State U of, Oswego
New York, State U of, Stony Brook
North Carolina State U, Raleigh
North Carolina, U of, Asheville
North Carolina, U of, Chapel Hill
Northern Colorado, U of
Nova Southeastern U (FL)
Ohio State U
Ohio U, Athens
Oregon State U
Otterbein C (OH)
Ouachita Baptist U (AR)
Ozarks, C of the (MO)
Pacific Lutheran U (WA)
Pacific, U of the (CA)
Pennsylvania State U, University Park
Pittsburgh, U of (PA)
Point Loma Nazarene U (CA)
Purdue U (IN)
Rochester, U of (NY)
Rutgers U, New Brunswick (NJ)
Salisbury U (MD)
Silver Lake C of the Holy Family (WI)
Simmons C (MA)
Skidmore C (NY)
South Florida, U of
Southwestern U (TX)
Springfield C (MA)

St. Andrews Presbyterian C (NC)
St. Louis U (MO)
Susquehanna U (PA)
Swarthmore C (PA)
Texas C
Texas Christian U
Texas, U of, Austin
Towson U (MD)
Trinity U (DC)
Trinity U (TX)
Truman State U (MO)
Valparaiso U (IN)
Vanderbilt U (TN)
Vassar C (NY)
Vermont, U of
Washburn U (KS)
Washington, U of
Western Washington U
Wheelock C (MA)
Whitworth C (WA)
William & Mary, C of (VA)
William Jewell C (MO)
Wilmington U (DE)
Winona State U (MN)
Wisconsin, U of, Madison
Wittenberg U (OH)

ENGINEERING

Distinguished Engineering Programs

California Institute of Technology
California, U of, Berkeley
California, U of, Los Angeles
California, U of, San Diego
Carnegie Mellon U (PA)
Columbia U (NY)
Cornell U (NY)
Duke U (NC)
Franklin W. Olin C of Engineering (MA)
Georgia Institute of Technology
Illinois, U of, Urbana
Johns Hopkins U (MD)
Maryland, U of, College Park
Massachusetts Institute of Technology

Michigan, U of, Ann Arbor
Northwestern U (IL)
Pennsylvania State U, University Park
Princeton U (NJ)
Purdue U (IN)
Rice U (TX)
Stanford U (CA)
Texas A&M U, College Station
Texas, U of, Austin
Virginia Polytechnic Institute &
  State U
Washington, U of
Wisconsin, U of, Madison

Source: *College Finder* research

Strength in Aerospace Engineering

Alabama, U of, Huntsville
Alabama, U of, Tuscaloosa
Arizona State U
Arizona, U of
Auburn U (AL)
California Institute of Technology
California Polytechnic State U, San Luis
 Obispo
California Polytechnic State U, Pomona
California State U, Long Beach
California, U of, Davis (Aeronautical
 Engineering)
California, U of, Irvine
California, U of, Los Angeles
California, U of, San Diego
Capitol C (MD) (Astronautical
 Engineering)
Case Western Reserve U (OH)
Central Florida, U of
Cincinnati, U of (OH)
Clarkson U (NY) (Aeronautical
 Engineering)
Colorado, U of, Boulder
Embry-Riddle Aeronautical U (AZ)
Embry-Riddle Aeronautical U (FL)
Florida Institute of Technology
Florida, U of
Georgia Institute of Technology
Illinois Institute of Technology
Illinois, U of, Urbana
Iowa State U
Kansas, U of
Maryland, U of, College Park
Massachusetts Institute of Technology
Miami, U of (FL)
Michigan, U of, Ann Arbor
Minnesota, U of, Twin Cities
Mississippi State U

Missouri U of Science & Technology
New Mexico State U
New York U, Tandon School of
 Engineering
New York, State U of, Buffalo
North Carolina State U
Notre Dame, U of (IN)
Ohio State U, Columbia
Oklahoma State U
Oklahoma, U of
Pennsylvania State U
Princeton U (NJ)
Purdue U (IN)
Rensselaer Polytechnic Institute (NY)
 (Aeronautical Engineering)
Rutgers U, New Brunswick (NJ)
Southern California, U of (Astronautical
 Engineering; Aerospace Engineering)
St. Louis U (MO)
Stanford U (CA)
Syracuse U (NY)
Tennessee, U of, Knoxville
Texas A&M U, College Station
Texas, U of, Arlington
Texas, U of, Austin
Tuskegee U (AL)
U.S. Air Force Academy (CO)
U.S. Naval Academy (MD)
Virginia Polytechnic Institute &
 State U
Virginia, U of
Washington, U of
West Virginia U
Western Michigan U (Aeronautical
 Engineering)
Wichita State U (KS)
Worcester Polytechnic Institute (MA)

Source: *College Finder* research

Audio Engineering Programs

The Audio Engineering Society is devoted to uniting engineers, scientists, and students by prompting innovations in audio research. Professional areas of inquiry include recording and production, broadcast and streaming, game audio, live sound, networked audio, sound for picture, and post-production. These colleges are members of the Audio Engineering Society.

American River C (CA)
American U (DC)
Appalachian State U (NC)
Arkansas, U of, Pine Bluff
Art Institute of Las Vegas (NV)
Art Institute of Seattle (WA)
Art Institute of Tennessee, Nashville
Atlanta Student (GA)
Ball State U (IN)
Bay State C (MA)
Belmont U (TN)
Berklee C of Music (MA)
Boston U (MA)
Brigham Young U (UT)
California Polytechnic State U, Pomona
California Polytechnic State U, San Luis Obispo
California State U, Chico
Capital U (OH)
Carnegie Mellon U (PA)
Central Missouri, U of
Citrus C (CA)
Cogswell Polytechnical C (CA)
Colorado, U of, Denver
Columbia C Chicago (IL)
Conservatory of Recording Arts & Sciences (AZ)
Duquesne U (PA)
Emerson C (MA)
Expression C for Digital Arts (CA)
Finger Lakes Community C (NY)
Full Sail U (FL)
Hampton Roads Student (VA)
Hartford, U of (CT)
Illinois, U of, Urbana
Indiana U Bloomington
Institute of Audio Research (NY)
Institute of Production & Recording (MN)
Ithaca C (NY)
Kansas City Kansas Community C

Lethbridge, U of (Canada)
London Ontario Student (ON)
Long Beach City C (CA)
Loyola Marymount U (CA)
Massachusetts, U of, Lowell
McGill U (Canada)
McNally Smith C of Music (MN)
Memphis, U of (TN)
Miami, U of (FL)
Michigan Technological U
Michigan, U of, Ann Arbor
Middle Tennessee State U
New England Institute of Art (MA)
New England School of Communications (ME)
New Haven, U of (CT)
New York U (NY)
New York, State U of, Fredonia
North Carolina, U of, Asheville
Ohio U
Peabody Institute, Johns Hopkins U (MD)
Pennsylvania State U
Purdue U (IN)
Ridgewater C, Hutchinson Campus (MN)
SAE Nashville (TN)
Salt Lake Community C (UT)
San Francisco State U (CA)
Shenandoah U (VA)
Southern California, U of
Southern Illinois U
Southwestern C (CA)
Stanford U (CA)
Syracuse U (NY)
Tribeca Flashpoint C (IL)
Valencia C (FL)
Webster U (MO)
William Paterson U (NJ)

Source: Audio Engineering Society (aes.org)

Steven R. Antonoff

Soundness in Automotive Engineering

Edmunds.com is a website devoted to car buyers and people in the automotive industry. Edmunds.com states, "To come up with this list of the top 10 automotive colleges and universities, we interviewed representatives of several car companies, studied results from vehicle-building competitions, and considered our own experience."

California Polytechnic State U, San Luis Obispo
California Polytechnic State U, Pomona
California, U of, Davis
Clemson U (SC)
Cornell U (NY)
Georgia Institute of Technology
Indiana U-Purdue U Indianapolis

Kettering U (MI)
Michigan State U
Michigan Technological U
Michigan, U of, Ann Arbor
Texas A&M U
Texas, U of, Arlington
Texas, U of, Austin
Virginia Polytechnic Institute & State U

Source: Edmunds.com

The Experts' Choice: Excellence in Bioengineering

Experts were asked to identify colleges for the student who wants to major in bioengineering.

Boston U (MA)
Brown U (RI)
California Polytechnic State U, San Luis Obispo
California, U of, Los Angeles
California, U of, San Diego
Carnegie Mellon U (PA)
Cornell U (NY)
Drexel U (PA)
Duke U (NC)
Georgia Institute of Technology
Johns Hopkins U (MD)
Lafayette C (PA)

Lehigh U (PA)
Massachusetts Institute of Technology
Northeastern U (MA)
Oklahoma, U of
Pennsylvania State U, University Park
Purdue U (IN)
Rensselaer Polytechnic Institute (NY)
Rochester, U of (NY)
Stanford U (CA)
Union C (NY)
Washington U (MO)
Worcester Polytechnic Institute (MA)

Robust Programs in Biological/Agricultural Engineering

Biological engineers might design medical devices, find ways to clean our water, or develop methods to test body chemistry. Agricultural engineers tackle issues related to the production of agricultural products, environmental issues, and power supplies.

California, U of, Davis
Cornell U (NY)
Florida, U of
Illinois, U of, Urbana
Iowa State U
Nebraska, U of, Lincoln
North Carolina State U, Raleigh
Purdue U, West Lafayette (IN)

Texas A&M U, College Station
Virginia Polytechnic Institute & State U

Source: *College Finder* research

Colleges That Combine Engineering and Business Studies

A curriculum that combines business and engineering courses can lead to a variety of emerging careers. These colleges are members of the National Organization for Business and Engineering (NOBE).

Drexel U (PA)
Georgia Institute of Technology
Illinois, U of, Urbana
McGill U (Canada)
Minnesota, U of, Twin Cities
New York U
Pennsylvania State U, Behrend
Pennsylvania State U, University Park
Southern California, U of
Texas, U of, Austin
Wisconsin, U of, Madison

Source: National Organization for Business and Engineering (nobenational.org)

Strength in Chemical Engineering

Bucknell U (PA)
California Institute of Technology
California, U of, Berkeley
California, U of, Santa Barbara
Cooper Union (NY)
Delaware, U of
Georgia Institute of Technology
Massachusetts Institute of Technology

Minnesota, U of, Twin Cities
Princeton U (NJ)
Rose-Hulman Institute of Technology
  (IN)
Rowan U (NJ)
Stanford U (CA)
Texas, U of, Austin
Wisconsin, U of, Madison

Source: *College Finder* research

Notable Civil Engineering Programs

Bucknell U (PA)
California Institute of Technology
California Polytechnic State U, San Luis
  Obispo
California, U of, Berkeley
Carnegie Mellon U (PA)
Cooper Union (NY)
Cornell U (NY)
Georgia Institute of Technology
Harvey Mudd C (CA)
Illinois, U of, Urbana

Lafayette C (PA)
Massachusetts Institute of Technology
Michigan, U of, Ann Arbor
North Carolina State U, Raleigh
Northwestern U (IL)
Pennsylvania State U, University Park
Purdue U (IN)
Rose-Hulman Institute of Technology
  (IN)
Stanford U (CA)
Texas A&M U, College Station

Texas, U of, Austin
U.S. Military Academy (NY)
Villanova U (PA)

Virginia Polytechnic Institute &
  State U
Wisconsin, U of, Madison

Source: *College Finder* research

Notable Electrical and/or Communications Engineering

Electrical engineers have the skills necessary to design electronic components for commercial, industrial, or scientific purposes. Communication engineers design telecommunication systems.

Bucknell U (PA)
California Institute of Technology
California Polytechnic State U, San Luis
  Obispo
California, U of, Berkeley
California, U of, Los Angeles
Carnegie Mellon U (PA)
Cooper Union (NY)
Cornell U (NY)
Georgia Institute of Technology
Harvey Mudd C (CA)
Illinois, U of, Urbana
Massachusetts Institute of Technology

Michigan, U of, Ann Arbor
Princeton U (NJ)
Purdue U (IN)
Rensselaer Polytechnic Institute (NY)
Rose-Hulman Institute of Technology
  (IN)
Stanford U (CA)
Texas, U of, Austin
U.S. Air Force Academy (CO)
U.S. Military Academy (NY)
U.S. Naval Academy (MD)
Virginia Polytechnic Institute &
  State U

Source: *College Finder* research

Soundness in Environmental Engineering

Environmental engineers design, plan, and apply measures to prompt sustainability, pollution controls, and remedies for environmental hazards.

Arizona State U
California Institute of Technology
California, U of, Berkeley
California, U of, Los Angeles
Carnegie Mellon U (PA)
Colorado, U of, Boulder
Cornell U (NY)
Florida, U of
Georgia Institute of Technology
Illinois, U of, Urbana
Johns Hopkins U (MD)
Massachusetts Institute of Technology
Michigan, U of, Ann Arbor
Michigan Technological U

North Carolina State U, Raleigh
Northwestern U (IL)
Ohio State U, Columbus
Pennsylvania State U, University Park
Portland State U (OR)
Purdue U (IN)
Stanford U (CA)
Texas A&M U, College Station
Texas, U of, Austin
Virginia Polytechnic Institute &
  State U
Washington, U of
Yale U (CT)

Source: *College Finder* research

Distinguished Industrial/Manufacturing Engineering Colleges

Industrial engineers find effective ways to use people, machines, materials, and energy to create a product or provide a service.

California, U of, Berkeley
Clemson U (SC)
Columbia U (NY)
Cornell U (NY)
Florida, U of
Georgia Institute of Technology
Illinois, U of, Urbana
Iowa State U
Kettering U (MI)
Massachusetts Institute of Technology

Michigan, U of, Ann Arbor
North Carolina State U, Raleigh
North Dakota State U
Northwestern U (IL)
Pennsylvania State U, University Park
Purdue U (IN)
Stanford U (CA)
Texas A&M U, College Station
Virginia Polytechnic Institute & State U
Wisconsin, U of, Madison

Source: *College Finder* research

Notable Mechanical Engineering Programs

Boston U (MA)
Bucknell U (PA)
California Institute of Technology
California Polytechnic State U, San Luis
   Obispo
California, U of, Berkeley
California, U of, Los Angeles
Cambridge, U of (United Kingdom)
Carnegie Mellon U (PA)
Clarkson U (NY)
Columbia U (NY)
Cooper Union (NY)
Cornell U (NY)
Franklin W. Olin C of Engineering (MA)
Georgia Institute of Technology
Harvey Mudd C (CA)
Illinois, U of, Urbana
Johns Hopkins U (MD)
Lafayette C (PA)

Lehigh U (PA)
Kettering U (MI)
Massachusetts Institute of Technology
Michigan, U of, Ann Arbor
Princeton U (NJ)
Purdue U (IN)
Rensselaer Polytechnic Institute (NY)
Rice U (TX)
Rose-Hulman Institute of Technology
   (IN)
Rowan U (NJ)
Stanford U (CA)
St. Louis U (MO)
Texas A&M U
U.S. Military Academy (NY)
U.S. Naval Academy (MD)
Wisconsin, U of, Madison
Worchester Polytechnic U (MA)

Source: *College Finder* research

Schools to Consider for Robotics

See also: Notable Mechanical Engineering Programs

Robotics is the science and technology behind the design, manufacturing, and application of robots. Robots have wide applicability in fields such as industry, space, and health care.

Arizona State U
Arizona, U of
Brown U (RI)

California Institute of Technology
California Polytechnic State U, Pomona
California, U of, Berkeley

California, U of, San Diego
California, U of, Santa Cruz
Carnegie Mellon U (PA)
Cincinnati, U of (OH)
Colorado School of Mines
Columbia U (NY)
Cornell U (NY)
Dartmouth C (NH)
Detroit Mercy, U of (MI)
Drexel U (PA)
Florida A&M U
Florida International U
Florida State U
Florida, U of
Georgia Institute of Technology
Georgia, U of
Hawaii, U of, Manoa
Houston, U of (TX)
Idaho, U of
Indiana U Bloomington
Johns Hopkins U (MD)
Kansas State U
Lawrence Technological U (MI)
Leeds, U of (United Kingdom)
Long Beach City C (CA)
Maryland, U of, College Park
Massachusetts Institute of Technology
Massachusetts, U of, Amherst
Michigan, U of, Ann Arbor
Michigan, U of, Dearborn
Minnesota, U of, Twin Cities
Missouri, U of, Columbia
Nebraska, U of, Lincoln
New Hampshire, U of
New Mexico Institute of Technology

New Mexico, U of, Albuquerque
North Carolina State U
Northwestern Polytechnic U (CA)
Notre Dame, U of (IN)
Ohio State U
Oklahoma, U of
Oregon State U
Pennsylvania, U of
Portland State U
Purdue U (IN)
Rice U (TX)
Rochester, U of (NY)
South Florida, U of
Southern California, U of
Southern Illinois U, Carbondale
Stanford U (CA)
Temple U (PA)
Tennessee State U
Tennessee, U of, Knoxville
Texas A&M U, College Station
Texas, U of, Austin
Texas, U of, Dallas
Toronto, U of (Canada)
U.S. Air Force Academy (CO)
Utah State U
Utah, U of
Vanderbilt U (TN)
Villanova U (PA)
Virginia Polytechnic Institute & State U
Washington U (MO)
Washington, U of
Washington, U of, Bothell
Wellesley U (MA)
Wisconsin, U of, Madison
Worcester Polytechnic Institute (MA)

Source: *College Finder* research, including NASA and *Robot Magazine*

The Experts' Choice: Great Engineering and Liberal Arts

Experts were asked to identify colleges with a good balance of engineering and liberal arts.

Bucknell U (PA)
Lafayette C (PA)
Lehigh U (PA)
Princeton U (NJ)
Swarthmore C (PA)
Tufts U (MA)
Vanderbilt U (TN)

ENGLISH

The Experts' Choice: English/Creative Writing/Literature Programs

Experts were asked to name colleges for a student who wants to major in English. As a basic and central college subject, English is offered at most liberal arts and sciences colleges. Evaluation of undergraduate programs in English, however, is difficult because of the varied approaches to assessing quality. Students should base their college selection decisions on numerous variables, both academic and social. The following colleges offer programs in English that are worth a second look.

Top Choices

Amherst C (MA)
Arizona, U of
Bard C (NY)
Bennington C (VT)
Boston U (MA)
Brandeis U (MA)
Brown U (RI)
Bryn Mawr C (PA)
California, U of, Irvine
Carleton C (MN)
Chicago, U of (IL)
Colorado C
Columbia U (NY)
Emerson C (MA)
Emory U (GA)
George Washington U (DC)
Goucher C (MD)
Grinnell C (IA)
Hamilton C (NY)
Hollins U (VA)
Iowa, U of
Johns Hopkins U (MD)
Kenyon C (OH)
Lewis & Clark C (OR)
Michigan, U of, Ann Arbor
Mississippi, U of
New York U
North Carolina, U of, Chapel Hill
Northwestern U (IL)
Oberlin C (OH)
Pomona C (CA)
Princeton U (NJ)
Redlands, U of (CA)
Reed C (OR)
Sarah Lawrence C (NY)
St. John's C (MD) (NM)
Swarthmore C (PA)
Washington U (MO)
Williams C (MA)
Yale U (CT)

Earning Praise

Agnes Scott C (GA)
Allegheny C (PA)
Alverno C (WI)
Arcadia U (PA)
Baldwin-Wallace C (OH)
Bard C at Simon's Rock (MA)
Bates C (ME)
Beloit C (WI)
California, U of, Berkeley
California, U of, Riverside
California, U of, Santa Cruz
Carnegie Mellon U (PA)
Centre C (KY)
Chapman U (CA)
Clark C (WA)
Colby C (ME)
Colby-Sawyer C (NH)
Colgate U (NY)
Connecticut C
Creighton U (NE)
Dartmouth C (NH)
Denver, U of (CO)
DePaul U (IL)
DePauw U (IN)
Dickinson C (PA)
Drake U (IA)
Duke U (NC)
Earlham C (IN)
Eckerd C (FL)
Evansville, U of (IN)
Fairleigh Dickinson U (NJ)
Fordham U (NY)
Franklin & Marshall C (PA)
George Mason U (VA)
Gettysburg C (PA)
Goddard C (VT)
Gonzaga U (WA)
Green Mountain C (VT)
Guilford C (NC)
Hamline U (MN)
Hampshire C (MA)

Hartwick C (NY)
Haverford C (PA)
Hawaii, U of, Hilo
Holy Cross, C of the (MA)
Hope C (MI)
Howard U (DC)
Indiana U Bloomington
Ithaca C (NY)
Kean U (NJ)
Knox C (IL)
Lafayette C (PA)
Lawrence U (WI)
Loras C (IA)
Lycoming C (PA)
Macalester C (MN)
Maine, U of, Farmington
Marlboro C (VT)
Marquette U (WI)
Mary Baldwin C (VA)
Massachusetts C of Liberal Arts
McDaniel C (MD)
Middlebury C (VT)
Montana, U of
Mt. Holyoke C (MA)
Muhlenberg C (PA)
Naropa U (CO)
New Mexico, U of, Albuquerque
New School (NY)
New York, State U of, Binghamton
New York, State U of, New Paltz
New York, State U of, Purchase
North Carolina, U of, Asheville
North Carolina, U of, Wilmington
Oregon, U of
Otterbein C (OH)
Pittsburgh, U of (PA)
Pitzer C (CA)
Puget Sound, U of (WA)
Purdue U (IN)
Reed C (OR)
Rhodes C (TN)
Richmond, U of (VA)
Ripon C (WI)
Rochester, U of (NY)

Rollins C (FL)
San Francisco Conservatory of Music (CA)
Santa Fe, C of (NM)
Schreiner U (TX)
Shimer C (IL)
Skidmore C (NY)
Smith C (MA)
South Carolina, U of, Columbia
South, U of the (TN)
Southwestern U (TX)
Spelman C (GA)
St. Lawrence U (NY)
St. Mary's C (MD)
St. Mary's U (TX)
Stanford U (CA)
Stephens C (MO)
Susquehanna U (PA)
Syracuse U (NY)
Tampa, U of (FL)
Trinity C (CT)
Truman State U (MO)
Tufts U (MA)
Tulane U (LA)
Utah, U of
Vassar C (NY)
Virginia, U of
Wake Forest U (NC)
Warren Wilson C (NC)
Washington & Lee U (VA)
Washington C (MD)
Wellesley C (MA)
Wesleyan U (CT)
Western Michigan U
Wheaton C (MA)
Whitman C (WA)
Willamette U (OR)
William Jewell C (MO)
Wilson C (PA)
Wisconsin, U of, Madison
Wittenberg U (OH)
Wofford C (SC)
Wooster, C of (OH)
York U (Canada)

ENVIRONMENTAL SCIENCE

Places to Study Environmental Science

Mother Nature Network is a website devoted to environmental concerns. The following is their list of colleges offering a range of environmental programs in areas such as marine conservation, agriculture, sustainable building, and fisheries.

1. Northland C (WI)
2. New York, State U of, Syracuse
3. Middlebury C (VT)
4. Cornell U (NY)
5. Duke U (NC)
6. Atlantic, C of the (ME)
7. Arizona State U
8. Yale U (CT)
9. Green Mountain C (VT)
10. Montana State U

Source: Mother Nature Network (mnn.com)

Colleges That Offer Studies in the Environment and Sustainability

There are colleges with programs, majors, or minors in fields such as environmental sciences, sustainability, environmental politics, and environmental change. Most of these programs include study in fields such as biology, chemistry, philosophy, history, and environmental law and policy.

Albion C (MI)
Appalachian State U (NC)
Arizona State U
Arkansas, U of, Fayetteville
Art Institute of Portland (OR)
Auburn U (AL)
Baldwin Wallace U (OH)
Ball State U (IN)
Bay State C (MA)
Bentley U (MA)
California Polytechnic State U, Pomona
California, U of, Irvine
Central C (IA)
Central Carolina Community C (NC)
Central Piedmont Community C (NC)
Chatham U (PA)
Clarion U (PA)
Colorado Mountain C
Columbia U (NY)
Daemen C (NY)
Dalhousie U (Canada)
Denver, U of (CO)
Dominican U (CA)
Drexel U (PA)
Eastern New Mexico U, Roswell
Elon U (NC)
Emory U (GA)
Florida, U of
Frostburg State U (MD)
Furman U (SC)
George Mason U (VA)
Green Mountain C (VT)
Hawaii, U of, Maui

Hofstra U (NY)
Indiana U-Purdue U Indianapolis
James Cook U (Australia)
Kean U (NJ)
Lane Community C (OR)
Lipscomb U (TN)
Maharishi U of Management (IA)
Maine, U of, Machias
Maryland, U of, College Park
Massachusetts, U of, Dartmouth
McGill U (Canada)
Meredith C (NC)
Messiah C (PA)
Michigan State U
Minnesota, U of, Duluth
Missouri Southern State U
Murdoch U (Australia)
New Haven, U of (CT)
New Mexico, U of
New York, State U of, Oswego
New York, State U of, Stony Brook
North Carolina, U of, Chapel Hill
Northern Colorado, U of
Notre Dame, U of (IN)
Ohio State U, Columbus
Oregon, U of
Pacific, U of the (CA)
Philadelphia U (PA)
Portland Community C (OR)
Prescott C (AZ)
Rensselaer Polytechnic Institute (NY)
Rhode Island, U of
Rider U (NJ)

Roosevelt U (IL)
Ryerson U (Canada)
San Diego City C (CA)
San Diego State U (CA)
Savannah C of Art & Design (SC)
Simon Fraser U (Canada)
South Dakota, U of
St. Joseph's C (PA)
Temple U (PA)

Texas, U of, Arlington
Utah, U of
Virginia, U of
Washington U (MO)
Wellesley C (MA)
Western Kentucky U
Western New England U (MA)
Winona State U (MN)
Winthrop U (SC)

Source: *College Finder* research, including the Association for the Advancement of Sustainability in Higher Education (aashe.org)

EVENT PLANNING

Notable Places to Study Event Planning

Event planners work in hotels or restaurants or are self-employed to create, organize, orchestrate, and/or direct events.

Alabama, U of, Tuscaloosa
Auburn U (AL)
Boston U (MA)
Bowling Green State U (OH)
Central Florida, U of
Charleston, C of (SC)
Collins C (AZ)
California Polytechnic State U, Pomona
Cornell U (NY)
Denver, U of (CO)
Drexel U (PA)
Endicott C (MA)
Farleigh Dickenson U (NJ)
George Washington U (DC)
Wisconsin, U of, Madison
Houston, U of (TX)
Iowa State U
Ithaca C (NY)
Johnson & Wales U (RI)
Lynn U (FL)

Massachusetts, U of, Amherst
Memphis, U of (TN)
Michigan State U
Mississippi, U of
Mitchell C (CT)
Nevada, U of, Las Vegas
New Hampshire, U of
New York U
Ohio State U, Columbus
Oklahoma State U
Purdue U (IN)
Rochester Institute of Technology (NY)
South Carolina, U of, Columbia
Southern New Hampshire U
Tennessee, U of
Virginia Polytechnic Institute & State U
Warren Wilson U (NC)
Washington State U
Widener U (PA)

Source: *College Finder* research

FASHION MERCHANDISING/DESIGN

The Experts' Choice: Fashion Merchandising and/or Design

Fashion merchandising is where fashion meets business, connecting designers and consumers. Students majoring in fashion merchandising learn the creative and practical sides of the fashion industry from a business perspective. Fashion design merges fashion with art. Students majoring in fashion design learn about colors, fabric patterns, and styles in order to develop original designs for consumers.

Top Choices

Academy of Art U (CA)
Art Institute of Chicago, School of the
   (IL)
Auburn U (AL)
California C of the Arts
Cincinnati, U of (OH)
Columbia C Chicago (IL)
Columbus C of Art & Design (OH)
Delaware, U of
Drexel U (PA)
École de la Chambre Syndicale de la
Couture Parisienne (France)
Fashion Institute of Design &
Merchandising (CA)
Fashion Institute of Technology (NY)*
Iowa State U
Kent State U (OH)
London C of Fashion (United Kingdom)
Missouri, U of, Columbia
Nebraska, U of, Lincoln
Otis C of Art & Design (CA)
Parsons School of Design (NY)**
Pratt Institute (NY)
Rhode Island School of Design
Royal C of Art (United Kingdom)
Savannah C of Art & Design (GA)
Virginia Commonwealth U

*The Top Choice
**The Second Choice

Second Choices

Aalot U (Finland)
Antwerp Royal Academy of Fine Arts
   (Belgium)
Applied Arts, U of (Austria)
Baylor U (TX)
Boston U (MA)

Brighton, U of (United Kingdom)
Bunka Fashion C (Japan)
Central St. Martin's (England)
Copenhagen Academy of Fashion
   Design (Denmark)
ESMOD International (France)
Fordham U (NY)
George Brown C (Canada)
Indiana U Bloomington
Istituto Marangoni (Italy)
Kingston U (United Kingdom)
Koefia Fashion Academy (Italy)
La Cambre (Belgium)
LaSalle C (Canada)
LIM C (NY)
Massachusetts C of Art
Melbourne School of Fashion (Australia)
Michigan, U of, Ann Arbor
Mode Gakuen C (Japan)
New York U
Oregon State U
Pennsylvania State U, University Park
Polimoda International Institute (Italy)
Polytechnic U (Italy)
Raffles Design Institute
   (Singapore)
Royal Melbourne Institute of Technology
   (Australia)
Rutgers U (NJ)
Ryerson U (Canada)
Shenkar C of Engineering & Design
   (Israel)
Studio Bercot (France)
Syracuse U (NY)
TAFE (Australia)
Tshwane U of Technology (South
   Africa)
Westminster, U of (England)
Whitehouse Institute of Design
   (Australia)

FILM

Colleges to Study Film Making

American Film Institute (CA)
ArtCenter C of Design (CA)
Boston U (MA)

California Institute of the Arts
California, U of, Los Angeles
Chapman U (CA)
Colorado Film School

Columbia C Chicago (IL)
Columbia U (NY)
Emerson C (MA)
Florida State U
Ithaca C (NY)
Loyola Marymount U (CA)
New York U
North Carolina School of the Arts
Northwestern U (IL)
Rhode Island School of Design

Ringling C of Art & Design (FL)
San Francisco State U (CA)
Savannah C of Art & Design (GA)
Southern California, U of
Stanford U (CA)
Syracuse U (NY)
Texas, U of, Austin
Wesleyan U (CT)

Source: *College Finder* research including *The Hollywood Reporter*

FORENSIC SCIENCE/PSYCHOLOGY

Colleges for Forensic Science and Forensic Psychology

Forensic scientists use their knowledge of chemistry and technology to accurately analyze bodily fluids, DNA, and other evidence to solve crimes. Forensic psychologists apply psychological theories to issues relating to the legal system.

Anna Maria C (MA)
Barry U (FL)
Bay Path U (MA)
Boston U (MA)
Bryant U (RI)
California, U of, Davis
Carroll C (MT)
Cedar Crest C (PA)
Chestnut Hill C (PA)
Daemen C (NY)
Embry-Riddle Aeronautical U (AZ)
Emmanuel C (MA)
Farmingdale State C (NY)
Findlay, U of (OH)
Florida Institute of Technology
Gannon U (PA)
George Washington U (DC)
Gwynedd-Mercy U (PA)
Hamline U (MN)
Hofstra U (NY)
Keystone C (PA)
Marian U (WI)

McDaniel C (MD)
Mercy C (NY)
Miami Dade C (FL)
MidAmerica Nazarene U (KS)
New Haven, U of (CT)
Ohio State U
Pace U (NY)
Pennsylvania State U, University Park
Point Park U (PA)
Rhode Island, U of
Roger Williams U (RI)
Seton Hall U (NJ)
Simpson U (IA)
St. Francis U (PA)
St. Thomas Aquinas C (NY)
St. Vincent C (PA)
Stevenson U (MD)
Syracuse U (NY)
Thomas More C (KY)
Trine U (IN)
Truman State U (MO)

FORESTRY

Great Forestry Colleges

These colleges are accredited through the Society of American Foresters. Forestry majors engage in activities including timber harvesting, ecological restoration, and management of protected areas.

Alabama A&M U
Alaska, U of, Fairbanks
Arkansas, U of, Monticello
Auburn U (AL)
California Polytechnic State U, San Luis Obispo
California, U of, Berkeley
Clemson U (SC)
Colorado State U, Ft. Collins
Duke U (NC)
Florida, U of
Georgia, U of
California State U, Humboldt
Idaho, U of
Iowa State U
Kentucky, U of
Louisiana State U
Louisiana Tech U
Maine, U of
Maryland, U of, College Park
Massachusetts, U of, Amherst
Michigan State U
Michigan Technological U
Minnesota, U of, Twin Cities
Mississippi State U
Missouri, U of, Columbia

Montana, U of
New Hampshire, U of
New Mexico Highlands U
New York, State U of, Environmental Science & Forestry
North Carolina State U
Northern Arizona U
Ohio State U, Columbus
Oklahoma State U
Oregon State U
Paul Smith's C (NY)
Pennsylvania State U
Purdue U (IN)
Southern Illinois U, Carbondale
Stephen F. Austin State U (TX)
Tennessee, U of
Texas A&M U, College Station
Utah State U
Virginia Polytechnic Institute & State U
Washington, U of
West Virginia U
Wisconsin, U of, Madison
Wisconsin, U of, Stevens Point
Yale U (CT)

Source: Society of American Foresters (eforester.org)

GAME DESIGN

Colleges for Students Interested in Game Design or Video Game Design

These are colleges with programs in game-related areas such as video game studies, interactive media, digital media, game design, and digital arts. Game design combines computer science and mathematics with art and other related fields. Game studies can include storyboarding, game production, game artistry, and game programming. Although some schools offer programs that are very hands-on, the programs at other schools are more academic.

Academy of Art U (CA)
Academy of Interactive Entertainment (WA)
American Intercontinental U (Switzerland)

American U (DC)
ArtCenter C of Design (CA)
Art Institute of Atlanta (GA)
Art Institute of Los Angeles (CA)
Art Institute of San Francisco (CA)

Art Institute of Vancouver (Canada)
Art Institutes, The (multiple states)
Arts, U of the (PA)
Austin Community C (TX)
Baltimore, U of (MD)
Becker C (MA)
Bradley U (IL)
California Institute of Technology
California Institute of the Arts
California State U, Fullerton
California State U, Long Beach
California State U, Monterey Bay
California, U of, Irvine
California, U of, Los Angeles
California, U of, Santa Cruz
Carnegie Mellon U (PA)
Central Florida, U of
Champlain C (VT)
Chapman U (CA)
Clarkson U (NY)
Cleveland Institute of the Arts (OH)
Cogswell Polytechnical C (CA)
Columbia C Chicago (IL)
Daniel Webster C (NH)
Dartmouth C (NH)
Denver, U of (CO)
DePaul U, C of Computing & Digital
   Media (IL)
DeVry U (multiple states)
DigiPen Institute of Technology (WA)
Drexel U Westphal C of Media Arts &
   Design (PA)
Dubuque, U of (IA)
Elmhurst C (IL)
Emerson C (MA)
Endicott C (MA)
Full Sail U (FL) George Mason U (VA)
Georgia Institute of Technology
Gnomon School of Visual Effects (CA)
Hampshire C (MA) High Point U (NC)
Illinois Wesleyan U
International Centre for Digital Content
   (United Kingdom)
Ithaca C (NY)
ITT Technical Institute (multiple states)
Johnson & Wales U (RI)
Louisiana, U of, Lafayette
Loyola Marymount U (CA)
Loyola U (IL)
Loyola U (LA)
Lyndon State C (VT)
Madison Media Institute (WI)
Maryland, U of, Baltimore

Maryville U (MO)
Massachusetts C of Art & Design
Massachusetts Institute of Technology
Massachusetts, U of, Amherst
Metropolitan State U of Denver (CO)
Michigan State U
Michigan, U of, Dearborn
New Hampshire Technical Institute
New Orleans, U of (LA)
New York U
North Carolina State U
Northern Michigan U
Ohio U, Scripps C of Communication
Oregon Institute of Technology
Otis C of Art & Design (CA)
Parsons School of Design (NY)
Pennsylvania State U, University Park
Pratt Institute (NY)
Rensselaer Polytechnic Institute (NY)
Rhode Island School of Design
Ringling C of Art & Design (FL)
Rochester Institute of Technology (NY)
Royal C of Art (United Kingdom)
SAE Expression C (CA)
San Diego State U (CA)
San Francisco State U (CA)
San Francisco, U of (CA)
San Jose State U (CA)
Savannah C of Art & Design (GA)
Shawnee State U (OH)
Sheridan C Institute of Technology &
   Advanced Learning (Canada)
Southern California, U of
Southern Methodist U, the Guildhall
   (TX)
Southern New Hampshire U
Springfield C (MA)
Stanford U (CA)
Suffolk U (MA)
Syracuse U, C of Visual & Performing
Arts (NY)
Texas A&M U
Texas, U of, Dallas
Utah, U of
Vermont Technical C
Washington, U of
Webster U (MO)
Wentworth Institute of Technology (MA)
West Virginia U
Westchester, C of (NY)
Westwood C (multiple campuses)
Wisconsin, U of, Stout
Worcester Polytechnic Institute (MA)

GEOLOGY/EARTH SCIENCE

Colleges to Review in Geology/Earth Science

Arizona State U
Arizona, U of
Bristol, U of (United Kingdom)
Brown U (RI)
California Institute of Technology
California, U of, Berkeley
California, U of, Davis
California, U of, Irvine
California, U of, Los Angeles
California, U of, San Diego
California, U of, Santa Barbara
California, U of, Santa Cruz
Cambridge, U of (United Kingdom)
Carleton C (MN)
Chicago, U of (IL)
Colorado School of Mines
Colorado, U of, Boulder
Columbia U (NY)
Cornell U (NY)
Harvard U (MA)
Hong Kong, U of
Houston, U of (TX)
, Joseph Fourier U, Grenoble (France)
Leeds, U of (United Kingdom)

Maryland, U of, College Park
Massachusetts Institute of Technology
Michigan, U of, Ann Arbor
Mississippi State U
Mt. Holyoke C (MA)
Oxford, U of (United Kingdom)
Peking U (China)
Pennsylvania State U, University Park
Pierre & Marie Curie U (France)
Pomona C (CA)
Princeton U (NJ)
Stanford U (CA)
Swiss Federal Institute of Technology
  (Switzerland)
Texas A&M U
Texas, U of, Austin
Tokyo, U of (Japan)
Trinity U (TX)
Utrecht U (the Netherlands)
Washington, U of, Seattle
Wisconsin, U of, Madison
Wooster, C of (OH)
Yale U (CT)

Member Colleges of the Keck Geology Consortium

The Keck Consortium focuses on enriching undergraduate education through development of high-quality research experience.

Amherst C (MA)
Beloit C (WI)
Carleton C (MN)
Colgate U (NY)
Colorado C
Franklin & Marshall C (PA)
Macalester C (MN)
Mt. Holyoke C (MA)
Oberlin C (OH)

Pomona C (CA)
Smith C (MA)
Trinity U (TX)
Union C (NY)
Washington & Lee U (VA)
Wesleyan U (CT)
Whitman C (WA)
Williams C (MA)
Wooster, C of (OH)

Source: Keck Geology Consortium (keckgeology.org)

Steven R. Antonoff

GOLF-RELATED STUDIES

Colleges That Prepare for a Career in the Golf Industry

These colleges prepare students for careers as professionals in the golf industry. Careers include Head Golf Professional, Director of Golf, Teaching Professional, Association Management, College Golf Coach, Golf Course Maintenance, and Golf Equipment Specialist. Many of these programs are accredited by the Professional Golf Association of America.

Arizona State U, Polytechnic
Campbell U (NC)
Central Oklahoma, U of
Clemson U (SC)
Coastal Carolina U (SC)
Colorado, U of, Colorado Springs
Delaware Valley U (PA)
Eastern Kentucky U
Ferris State U (MI)
Florida Gulf Coast U
Florida State U
Georgia, U of
Golf Academy of the South (FL)
Idaho, U of
Keiser U (FL)
Maryland, U of, College Park
Maryland, U of, Eastern Shore
Massachusetts, U of, Amherst
Methodist U (NC)

Michigan State U
Mississippi State U
Nebraska, U of, Lincoln
Nevada, U of, Las Vegas
New Mexico State U
New York, State U of, Cobleskill
New York, State U of, Delhi
North Carolina State U
Ohio State U, Columbus
Pennsylvania State U, University Park
Professional Golfers Career C
Rhode Island, U of
Sam Houston State U (TX)
San Diego Golf Academy (a division of Virginia C)
South Carolina, U of, Aiken
Trine U (IN)
Virginia C (online)

Source: *College Finder* research

HISTORY

Colleges With Fine History Departments

As a basic and central college subject, history is offered at most liberal arts and sciences colleges. Evaluation of undergraduate programs in history, however, is difficult because of the varied approaches to assessing quality. Students should base their college selection decisions on numerous variables, both academic and social. The following colleges offer programs in history that are worth a second look.

Albion C (MI)
Allegheny C (PA)
Alma C (MI)
American U (DC)
Amherst C (MA)
Bates C (ME)
Beloit C (WI)
Birmingham-Southern C (AL)
Boston C (MA)

Brandeis U (MA)
Brown U (RI)
Bryn Mawr C (PA)
California, U of, Berkeley
California, U of, Davis
California, U of, Los Angeles
California, U of, Santa Cruz
Calvin C (MI)
Carleton C (MN)

Chicago, U of (IL)
Claremont McKenna C (CA)
Colgate U (NY)
Colorado C
Columbia U (NY)
Connecticut C
Cornell U (NY)
Dallas, U of (TX)
Dartmouth C (NH)
Davidson C (NC)
Dickinson C (PA)
Drake U (IA)
Drew U (NJ)
Duke U (NC)
Emory U (GA)
George Washington U (DC)
Georgetown U (DC)
Gettysburg C (PA)
Goucher C (MD)
Grace C (IN)
Grinnell C (IA)
Hamilton C (NY)
Hamline U (MN)
Hampden-Sydney C (VA)
Harvard U (MA)
Hiram C (OH)
Indiana U Bloomington
Johns Hopkins U (MD)
Kalamazoo C (MI)
Kansas, U of
Kenyon C (OH)
Lafayette C (PA)
Lake Forest C (IL)
Lawrence U (WI)
Lewis & Clark C (OR)
Macalester C (MN)
Mary Washington, U of (VA)
Michigan, U of, Ann Arbor
Middlebury C (VT)
Millersville U (PA)
Moravian C (PA)
Mt. Holyoke C (MA)
Muhlenberg C (PA)
New York, State U of, Binghamton

North Carolina, U of, Chapel Hill
Northeastern U (MA)
Oberlin C (OH)
Ohio Wesleyan U
Pennsylvania, U of
Pittsburgh, U of (PA)
Pomona C (CA)
Princeton U (NJ)
Reed C (OR)
Richmond, U of (VA)
Rochester, U of (NY)
Santa Clara U (CA)
Smith C (MA)
South Carolina, U of, Columbia
South, U of the (TN)
Southwestern U (TX)
St. Mary's C (CA)
St. Olaf C (MN)
Stanford U (CA)
Swarthmore C (PA)
Texas Christian U
Texas, U of, Austin
Trinity U (TX)
Tufts U (MA)
Union C (NY)
Vanderbilt U (TN)
Vassar C (NY)
Vermont, U of
Virginia, U of
Wabash C (IN)
Washington & Lee U (VA)
Washington U (MO)
Wellesley C (MA)
Wesleyan U (CT)
West Virginia, U of
Whitman C (WA)
William & Mary, C of (VA)
Williams C (MA)
Wisconsin, U of, Madison
Wittenberg U (OH)
Wooster, C of (OH)
Yale U (CT)

INDUSTRIAL DESIGN

Schools to Consider for Industrial Design

Industrial design integrates logic, science, and engineering with production considerations. Industrial designers work to produce or redesign products.

Arizona State U
ArtCenter C of Design (CA)
Auburn U (AL)
Creative Studies, C for (MI)
Carnegie Mellon U (PA)
Cincinnati, U of (OH)
Cranbrook Academy of Art (MI)
Georgia Institute of Technology
Illinois, U of, Urbana
Kansas, U of

Metropolitan State U (CO)
Ohio State U
Pratt Institute (NY)
Rhode Island School of Design
Savannah C of Art & Design (GA)
Stanford U (CA)
Syracuse U (NY)
Virginia Polytechnic Institute & State U

INTERIOR DESIGN

Interior Design Colleges

Many of these schools are accredited by the Council for Interior Design Accreditation.

Abilene Christian U (TX)
Academy of Art U (CA)
Akron, U of (OH)
Alabama, U of, Tuscaloosa
Appalachian State U (NC)
Arizona State U
Art Institute of Chicago, School of the (IL)
Auburn U (AL)
Ball State U (IN)
Baylor U (TX)
Boston Architectural Center (MA)
Brenau U (GA)
California C of the Arts
California Polytechnic State U, Pomona
California, State U of, Fresno
California, State U of, Northridge
California, State U of, Sacramento
Central Arkansas, U of
Central Michigan U
Central Missouri, U of
Central Oklahoma, U of
Chaminade U (HI)
Charleston, U of (WV)
Chatham U (PA)
Cincinnati, U of (OH)
Colorado State U, Ft. Collins

Columbia C Chicago (IL)
Converse C (SC)
Cornell U (NY)
Creative Studies, C for (MI)
Drexel U (PA)
East Carolina U (NC)
Eastern Michigan U
Endicott C (MA)
Fashion Institute of Technology (NY)
Florida State U
Florida, U of, Gainesville
George Washington U (DC)
Georgia Southern U
Georgia, U of, Athens
Harding U (AR)
High Point U (NC)
Idaho, U of
Illinois Institute of Art
Illinois State U
Incarnate Word, U of the (TX)
Indiana State U
Indiana U-Purdue U Indianapolis
Indiana U Bloomington
Iowa State U
James Madison U (VA)
Kansas State U
Kean U (NJ)

ACADEMICS

Kent State U (OH)
Kentucky, U of
Louisiana State U, Baton Rouge
Louisiana Tech U
Louisiana, U of, Lafayette
Louisville, U of (KY)
Marylhurst U (OR)
Marymount U (VA)
Memphis, U of (TN)
Meredith C (NC)
Miami U (OH)
Michigan State U
Middle Tennessee State U
Minnesota, U of, Twin Cities
Mississippi State U
Missouri, U of, Columbia
Moore C of Art & Design (PA)
Mt. Mary U (WI)
Mt. Royal U (Canada)
Nebraska, U of, Kearney
Nebraska, U of, Lincoln
Nevada, U of, Las Vegas
New England School of Art & Design
   (MA)
New Jersey Institute of Technology
New York Institute of Interior Design
New York Institute of Technology
New York, State U of, Buffalo
North Carolina, U of, Greensboro
North Dakota State U
North Texas, U of
O'More C of Design (TN)
Ohio State U, Columbus
Ohio U, Athens
Oklahoma Christian U
Oklahoma State U
Oklahoma, U of
Oregon, U of
Parsons School of Design (NY)
Philadelphia U (PA)
Pratt Institute (NY)
Purdue U (IN)

Radford U (VA)
Rhode Island School of Design
Ringling C of Art & Design (FL)
Rochester Institute of Technology (NY)
   Rocky Mountain C of Art & Design
   (CO)
Ryerson U (Canada)
Sam Houston State U (TX)
Samford U (AL)
Savannah C of Art & Design (GA)
South Dakota State U
Southern Illinois U, Carbondale
Southern Mississippi, U of
Stephen F. Austin State U (TX)
Suffolk U (MA)
Syracuse U (NY)
Tennessee, U of, Knoxville
Texas Christian U
Texas State U, San Marcos
Texas Tech U (TX)
Texas, U of, Arlington
Texas, U of, Austin
Texas, U of, San Antonio
Utah State U
Villa Maria C (NY)
Virginia C (multiple states)
Virginia Commonwealth U
   Virginia Polytechnic Institute &
   State U
Visual Arts, School of (NY)
Wade C (TX)
Washington State U
Weber State U (UT)
Wentworth Institute of Technology (MA)
Western Carolina U (NC)
Western Michigan U
Winthrop U (SC)
Wisconsin, U of, Madison
Wisconsin, U of, Stevens Point
Wisconsin, U of, Stout
Woodbury U (CA)

Source: *College Finder* research, including the Council for Interior Design Accreditation
(accredit-id.org)

INTERNATIONAL RELATIONS

The Experts' Choice: Fine Places to Study International Relations

Experts were asked to list colleges for the student who wants to study international
relations. As a basic and central college subject, international relations is offered at most
liberal arts and sciences colleges. Evaluation of undergraduate programs in international

relations, however, is difficult because of the varied approaches to assessing quality. Students should base their college selection decisions on numerous variables, both academic and social. The following colleges offer programs in international relations that are worth a second look.

American U (DC)
Boston U (MA)
Brandeis U (MA)
Claremont McKenna C (CA)
Clark U (MA)
Dickinson C (PA)
George Mason U (VA)
George Washington U (DC)

Georgetown U (DC)
Goucher C (MD)
Johns Hopkins U (MD)
Macalester C (MN)
Occidental C (CA)
South Carolina, U of, Columbia
Tufts U (MA)

JEWELRY MAKING

Notable Jewelry Making Colleges

Jewelry designers work with precious metals and gemstones. A student who pursues this major can opt for a broad-based liberal arts curriculum (with business courses) or can train at a career-oriented college. Some of the options are listed here.

Academy of Art U (CA)
American School of Jewelry (FL)
Arts, U of the (United Kingdom)
Birmingham City U (United Kingdom)
California C of the Arts
California Institute of Jewelry Training
China Academy of Art
Denver School of Metal Arts (CO)
Edinburgh C of Art (United Kingdom)
Estonian Academy of Arts (Estonia)

Gemological Institute of America (CA)
Illinois, U of, Urbana
Instituto Lorenzo De Medici (Italy)
Kansas, U of
New Approach School for Jewelers (TN)
Revere Academy of Jewelry Arts (CA)
Rochester Institute of Technology (NY)
San Diego State U (CA)
Texas Institute of Jewelry Technology
Wisconsin, U of, Madison

JOURNALISM

College Media Matters' Best Undergraduate Journalism Programs

College Media Matters is a "news site and innovation hub aiming to tell the story of college media 2.0 one day at a time and from as many perspectives as possible." It was created and maintained by journalism professor Dan Reimold, who passed away in 2015. These are the schools that Reimold chose as the "best undergraduate journalism programs at U.S. colleges and universities."

Alabama, U of, Tuscaloosa
Alaska, U of, Anchorage
American U (DC)
Arizona State U
Arizona, U of
Auburn U (AL)
Ball State U (IN)

Boston U (MA)
Bowling Green State U (OH)
Columbia C Chicago (IL)
Drake U (IA)
Duquesne U (PA)
Emerson C (MA)
Florida, U of

George Washington U (DC)
Georgia, U of
Gonzaga U (WA)
Idaho, U of
Illinois, U of, Urbana
Indiana U Bloomington
Iowa State U
Iowa, U of
Ithaca C (NY)
Kansas State U
Kansas, U of
Kent State U (OH)
Kentucky, U of
Loyola U (IL)
Maryland, U of, College Park
Miami, U of (FL)
Michigan State U
Middle Tennessee State U
Minnesota, U of, Twin Cities
Mississippi, U of
Missouri, U of, Columbia
Montana, U of

Nebraska, U of, Lincoln
Nevada, U of, Reno
New York U
New York, State U of, Stony Brook
North Carolina, U of, Chapel Hill
Northwestern U (IL)
Ohio U, Athens
Oklahoma State U
Oklahoma, U of
Oral Roberts U (OK)
Oregon, U of
Pennsylvania State U, University Park
San Jose State U (CA)
Southern California, U of
South Carolina, U of, Columbia
Syracuse U (NY)
Temple U (PA)
Texas, U of, Austin
Washington State U
Western Kentucky U
Wisconsin, U of, Madison

Source: *College Finder* research, collegemediamatters.com

LAW SCHOOL PREPARATION

Undergraduate Institutions Attended by Accepted Harvard Law School Students

Where did students accepted to Harvard Law School receive their undergraduate degrees? Here is the list from a recent year.

Alabama, U of, Birmingham
Alabama, U of, Tuscaloosa
Amherst C (MA)
Arizona State U
Auburn U (AL)
Barnard C (NY)
Beloit C (WI)
Beth Medrash Govoha (NJ)
Boise State U (ID)
Boston C (MA)
Boston U (MA)
Brandeis U (MA)
Brigham Young U (UT)
British Columbia, U of (Canada)
Brown U (RI)
California, U of, Berkeley
California, U of, Davis
California, U of, Irvine
California, U of, Los Angeles
California, U of, Riverside
California, U of, San Diego

California, U of, Santa Barbara
Carleton C (MN)
Case Western Reserve U (OH)
Chicago, U of (IL)
Claremont McKenna C (CA)
Clark U (MA)
Clemson U (SC)
Columbia U (NY)
Connecticut C
Cornell U (NY)
Dartmouth C (NH)
Delaware, U of
Denison U (OH)
DePauw U (IN)
Dickinson C (PA)
Drew U (NJ)
Duke U (NC)
Eastern Michigan U
Edinburgh, U of (United Kingdom)
Emory U (GA)
Excelsior C (online)

Fairfield U (CT)
Fairleigh Dickinson U (NJ)
Florida International U
Florida State U
Florida, U of
Fordham U (NY)
George Washington U (DC)
Georgetown U (DC)
Georgia Institute of Technology
Georgia State U
Gettysburg C (PA)
Harvard U (MA)
Hawaii, U of, Hilo
Hendrix C (AZ)
Hillsdale C (MI)
Holy Cross, C of the (MA)
Howard U (DC)
Indiana U Bloomington
International Business & Economics, U
    of (China)
Iowa, U of
James Madison U (VA)
Johns Hopkins U (MD)
Kentucky, U of, Lexington
London, U of (United Kingdom)
Maryland, U of, College Park
Marymount Manhattan C (NY)
Massachusetts Institute of Technology
McGill U (Canada)
Miami U (OH)
Miami, U of (FL)
Michigan, U of, Ann Arbor
Michigan, U of, Dearborn
Middlebury C (VT)
Minnesota, U of, Twin Cities
Missouri, U of, Kansas City
Morehouse C (GA)
Mt. Holyoke C (MA)
Nebraska, U of, Lincoln
New Jersey, C of
New Mexico, U of, Albuquerque
New York U
New York, City U of, Baruch C
New York, City U of, Brooklyn C
New York, City U of, Hunter C
New York, City U of, Queens C
New York, State U of, Binghamton
North Carolina, U of, Chapel Hill
North Carolina, U of, Pembroke
Northeastern U (MA)
Northwestern U (IL)
Notre Dame, U of (IN)
Oakwood U (AL)
Ohio State U, Columbus
Ohio U, Athens

Ohio Wesleyan U
Oklahoma City U
Oklahoma State U, Stillwater
Oklahoma, U of
Olivet Nazarene U (IL)
Oxford, U of (United Kingdom)
Patrick Henry C (VA)
Peking U (China)
Pennsylvania, U of
Pittsburgh, U of (PA)
Pomona C (CA)
Portland State U (OR)
Princeton U (NJ)
Purdue U (IN)
Queen's U (Canada)
Renmin U (China)
Rice U (TX)
Rochester, U of (NY)
Rutgers U, New Brunswick (NJ)
San Francisco State U (CA)
Sarah Lawrence C (NY)
Scripts C (CA)
South Carolina, U of, Columbia
Southern California, U of
Southern Methodist U (TX)
Spelman C (GA)
St. Anselm C (NH)
St. John's U (NY)
St. Louis U (MO)
St. Olaf C (MN)
Stanford U (CA)
Swarthmore C (PA)
Temple U (PA)
Tennessee, U of, Knoxville
Texas A&M U, College Station
Texas, U of, Austin
Texas, U of, Dallas
Toronto, U of (Canada)
Touro C (NY)
Transylvania U (KY)
Trinity C (CT)
Troy U (AL)
Tsinghua U (China)
Tufts U (MA)
Tulane U (LA)
U.S. Coast Guard Academy (CT)
U.S. Military Academy (NY)
U.S. Naval Academy (MD)
Utah, U of
Vanderbilt U (TN)
Vermont, U of
Villanova U (PA)
Virginia Polytechnic Institute &
    State U
Virginia, U of

Wake Forest U (NC)
Warren Wilson C (NC)
Washington State U
Washington U (MO)
Washington, U of, Seattle
Wayne State U (MI)
Weber State U (UT)
Wellesley C (MA)
Wesleyan C (GA)
Wesleyan U (CT)
Western Kentucky U

Western Ontario, U of (Canada)
Wheaton C (IL)
Wheaton C (MA)
William & Mary, C of (VA)
Williams C (MA)
Winnipeg, U of (Canada)
Wisconsin, U of, Madison
Yale U (CT)
Yeshiva U (NY)
York U (Canada)

Source: law.harvard.edu

MATHEMATICS

The Experts' Choice: Excellent Mathematics Programs

Experts were asked to name colleges for a student who wants to major in mathematics. As a basic and central college subject, mathematics is offered at most liberal arts and sciences colleges. Evaluation of undergraduate programs in mathematics, however, is difficult because of the varied approaches to assessing quality. Students should base their college selection decisions on numerous variables, both academic and social. The following colleges offer programs in mathematics that are worth a second look.

The Top Choices

Bryn Mawr C (PA)
California Institute of Technology
California, U of, Los Angeles
Carnegie Mellon U (PA)
Chicago, U of (IL)*
Harvey Mudd C (CA)**
Hendrix C (AR)
Illinois, U of, Urbana
Massachusetts Institute of Technology**
New York U
Pennsylvania, U of
Pomona C (CA)
Princeton U (NJ)
Reed C (OR)
Rice U (TX)
St. Olaf C (MN)
Washington U (MO)

*The Top Choice
**The Second Choice (tie)

The Next Choices

Bates C (ME)
Bowdoin C (ME)

Bucknell U (PA)
California Polytechnic State U, San Luis Obispo
California State U, Humboldt
California, U of, Berkeley
California, U of, San Diego
California, U of, Santa Cruz
Case Western Reserve U (OH)
Clarkson U (NY)
Colorado School of Mines
Columbia U (NY)
Cornell U (NY)
Dartmouth C (NH)
Georgia Institute of Technology
Grinnell C (IA)
Harvard U (MA)
Haverford C (PA)
Illinois Institute of Technology
Illinois Wesleyan U
Johns Hopkins U (MD)
Kansas State U
Lafayette C (PA)
Lebanon Valley C (PA)
Lehigh U (PA)
Louisiana State U, Baton Rouge
Louisiana Technological & State U
Michigan State U
Michigan, U of, Ann Arbor

Mt. Holyoke C (MA)
New York, City U of, Baruch C
New York, State U of, Buffalo
Northwestern U (IL)
Notre Dame, U of (IN)
Oberlin C (OH)
Occidental C (CA)
Oklahoma State U
Pittsburgh, U of (PA)
Rensselaer Polytechnic Institute (NY)
Seattle U (WA)

St. John's C (MD) (NM)
Stanford U (CA)
Swarthmore C (PA)
Texas A&M U, International
Texas, U of, Austin
Union C (NY)
Washington, U of
Wellesley C (MA)
Wisconsin, U of, Madison
Yale U (CT)

MEDICAL SCHOOL PREPARATION/HEALTH

The Experts' Choice: Superior Pre-med Programs

Amherst C (MA)
Brandeis U (MA)
Brown U (RI)
Carnegie Mellon U (PA)
Carroll C (MT)
Case Western Reserve U (OH)
Cornell U (NY)
Davidson C (NC)
Duke U (NC)
Emory U (GA)
Franklin & Marshall C (PA)
Georgetown U (DC)
Holy Cross, C of the (MA)

Johns Hopkins U (MD)
Kalamazoo C (MI)
North Carolina State U
Northwestern U (IL)
Rochester, U of (NY)
Stanford U (CA)
Tufts U (MA)
Tulane U (LA)
Ursinus C (PA)
Vanderbilt U (TN)
Washington U (MO)
Wooster, C of (OH)

The Experts' Choice: Great Pre-med Programs for B Students

Alabama, U of, Birmingham
Allegheny C (PA)
American U (DC)
Clark U (MA)
Creighton U (NE)
Dickinson C (PA)
Drexel U (PA)
Duke U (NC)
Franklin & Marshall C (PA)
Hobart C (NY)
Juniata C (PA)
Kalamazoo C (MI)
McDaniel C (MD)

Miami, U of (FL)
Minnesota, U of, Twin Cities
Montana State U, Bozeman
Muhlenberg C (PA)
Ohio Wesleyan U
Quinnipiac U (CT)
Ramapo C (NJ)
St. Louis U (MO)
Ursinus C (PA)
Vermont, U of
Washington, U of, Seattle
Wooster, C of (OH)

Colleges Providing a Fast Track to Becoming a Doctor

There are colleges that make it easier to become a medical doctor by cutting down the time it takes to get an undergraduate degree and also a medical degree. Some colleges admit students from high school into accelerated programs. Some colleges admit qualified freshmen or sophomore students into these programs. This is a listing of colleges that offer some form of "early assurance" to medical school for outstanding students. Some may be open only to traditionally underrepresented students or for those who intend to practice in rural America. Some are for in-state students only.

Akron, U of (OH)
Alabama, U of, Tuscaloosa
Bates C (ME)
Baylor U (TX)
Boston U (MA)
Bowdoin C (ME)
Brown U (RI)
Bucknell U (PA)
Caldwell C (NJ)
California, U of, San Diego
Case Western Reserve U (OH)
Central Florida, U of
Cincinnati, U of (OH)
Clarkson U (NY)
Colby C (ME)
Colorado, U of, Boulder
Connecticut, U of, Storrs
DeSales U (PA)
Drew U (NJ)
Drexel U (PA)
Duquesne U (PA)
East Carolina U (NC)
Elmira C (NY)
Fisk U (TN)
Florida Atlantic U
Florida Gulf Coast U
Florida Southern U
Florida State U
Florida, U of
George Washington U (DC)
Georgetown U (DC)
Grambling State U (LA)
Hampden-Sydney C (VA)
Hampton U (VA)
Hawaii, U of, Manoa
Hiram C (OH)
Hobart & William Smith C (NY)
Hofstra U (NY)
Houston, U of (TX)
Howard U (DC)
Illinois Institute of Technology
Juniata C (PA)
Kean U (NJ)
Kent State U (OH)

Kentucky, U of
Lehigh U (PA)
Louisville, U of (KY)
Loyola U (IL)
Maine, U of
Marshall U (WV)
Miami, U of (FL)
Missouri, U of, Kansas City
Monmouth U (NJ)
Montclair State U (NJ)
Moravian C (PA)
Muhlenberg C (PA)
New Jersey Institute of Technology
New York U Tandon School of
Engineering
New York, City U of, Brooklyn C
New York, City U of, Staten Island
New York, State U of, C of
Environmental Science & Forestry
New York, State U of, Cobleskill
New York, State U of, Geneseo
New York, State U of, Potsdam
New York, State U of, Stony Brook
North Carolina A&T State U
Northern Michigan U
Northwestern U (IL)
Oklahoma, U of
Pennsylvania State U, University Park
Pittsburgh, U of (PA)
Randolph-Macon C (VA)
Rensselaer Polytechnic Institute (NY)
Rice U (TX)
Robert Morris U (PA)
Rochester, U of (NY)
Rosemont C (PA)
Rutgers U (NJ)
Sciences, U of the (PA)
Shepherd U (WV)
Siena C (NY)
South Florida, U of
St. Bonaventure U (NY)
St. Lawrence U (NY)
St. Louis U (MO)
Stevens Institute of Technology (NJ)

Stockton U (NJ)
Temple U (PA)
Texas Tech U
Toledo, U of (OH)
Tufts U (MA)
Tulane U (LA)
Union C (NY)
Ursinus C (PA)
Villanova U (PA)
Virginia Commonwealth U

Wake Forest U (NC)
Washington & Jefferson C (PA)
Washington U (MO)
Wayne State U (MI)
West Chester U (PA)
West Virginia U
Widener U (PA)
Wilkes U (PA)
William & Mary, C of (VA)
Youngstown State U (OH)

Source: *College Finder* research

Colleges With Programs in Global Health, International Health, and/or International Public Health

Global or international health relates to health issues and concerns that extend beyond the borders of nations. The field includes study in such areas as demography, economics, epidemiology, political economy, and sociology. Career positions include health care practitioner, educator, researcher, and change agent.

Alabama, U of, Birmingham
Allegheny C (PA)
Arizona State U
Bethel C (IN)
California Baptist U
California, U of, San Diego
Catholic U of America (DC)
Central Michigan U
Clemson U (SC)
Cornell U (NY)
Duke U (NC)
Emory U (GA)
George Mason U (VA)
George Washington U (DC)
Georgetown U (DC)
Harvard U (MA)
Imperial C London (United Kingdom)
Indiana U-Purdue U Indianapolis
Iowa, U of
Johns Hopkins U (MD)
Kalamazoo C (MI)
Kent State U (OH)
Kentucky, U of

Loma Linda U (CA)
Macalester C (MN)
Mercer U (GA)
Muhlenberg C (PA)
Northwestern U (IL)
New York U
Ohio State U
Oregon State U
Pittsburgh, U of (PA)
Simon Fraser U (Canada)
Southern California, U of
St. Thomas, U of (MN)
Texas, U of, Austin
Toledo, U of (OH)
Tufts U (MA)
Tulane U (LA)
Union C (NE)
Utah, U of
Vanderbilt U (TN)
Washington U (MO)
Washington, U of, Seattle
Westminster C (UT)
Yale U (CT)

Source: *College Finder* research and the College Board's Big Future (bigfuture.collegeboard.org)

I Want to Be a Doctor...But Wait, I Forgot to Take Science!

Many individuals pursue medical careers after receiving a bachelor's degree. Sometimes these students have not taken the requisite number of science courses required to be successful in medical school. The following colleges offer post-baccalaureate pre-medical programs. Although some programs award a bachelor's degree (and a few award a master's degree), most are non-degree certificate programs.

Adelphi U (NY)
Agnes Scott C (GA)
Avila U (MO)
Bennington C (VT)
Boston U (MA)
Bryn Mawr C (PA)
Caldwell C (NJ)
California State U, Fullerton
California State U, San Marcos
California, U of, Berkeley (Extension)
California, U of, Davis (School of Medicine)
California, U of, Irvine (School of Medicine)
California, U of, Los Angeles (School of Medicine)
Carson-Newman C (TN)
Chapman U (CA)
Charles R. Drew U of Medicine & Science (CA)
Cleveland State U (OH)
Colorado State U
Colorado, U of, Boulder
Columbia U (NY)
Cornell U (NY)
Dominican U (IL)
Drew U (NJ)
Drexel U (PA)
Elms C (MA)
Florida, U of
Georgetown U (DC)
Goucher C (MD)
Guilford C (NC)
Harvard U (MA)
Hofstra U (NY)
Johns Hopkins U (MD)
Kansas, U of
LaSalle U (PA)
Lewis U (IL)
Louisville, U of (KY)
Loyola Marymount U (CA)
Manhattanville C (NY)

Maryland, U of
Massachusetts, U of, Dartmouth
Meredith C (NC)
MGH Institute of Health Professions (MA)
Miami, U of (FL)
Montana State U
Mt. Holyoke C (MA)
Nazareth C (NY)
New York U
New York, City U of, City C
New York, State U of, Purchase
New York, State U of, Stony Brook
North Carolina, U of, Greensboro
Northeastern State U (OK)
Northwestern Health Sciences U (MN)
Northwestern U (IL)
Ohio State U
Oregon State U
Oregon, U of
Pennsylvania State U, University Park
Pennsylvania, U of
Rider U (NJ)
Rochester, U of (NY)
Rockhurst U (MO)
Rosemont C (PA)
Rutgers U, New Brunswick (NJ)
San Francisco State U (CA)
Scripps C (CA)
Seattle U (WA)
Southern Illinois U, Carbondale
Southern Maine, U of
Stockton U (NJ)
Temple U (PA)
Thomas Jefferson U (PA)
Tufts U (MA)
Vermont, U of
Virginia, U of
Washington U (MO)
West Chester U (PA)
William Paterson U (NJ)
Worcester State U (MA)

Source: *College Finder* research, including the American Association of Medical Colleges

Steven R. Antonoff

MUSIC

The Experts' Choice: Fine Music Programs

Experts were asked to name colleges for the student who wants to major in music. The following colleges offer programs in music (instrumental, musical theater, voice, and/or music business) that are worth investigating.

The Very Top Choices

Berklee C of Music (MA)
Boston U (MA)
Carnegie Mellon U (PA)
Curtis Institute of Music (PA)
Hartford, U of (CT)
Ithaca C (NY)
James Madison U (VA)
Juilliard School (NY)
Loyola U (LA)
Manhattan School of Music (NY)
Miami, U of (FL)
Michigan, U of, Ann Arbor
New England Conservatory of Music
    (MA)
New York U
North Texas, U of
Rice U (TX)
Rochester, U of (NY)
Shenandoah U (VA)
Southern California, U of
Southern Methodist U (TX)

The Top Choices

Appalachian State U (NC)
Arts, U of the (PA)
Baldwin-Wallace C (OH)
Ball State U (IN)
Bard C (NY)
Belmont U (TN)
Boston Conservatory (MA)
California Institute of the Arts
California, U of, Los Angeles
Capital U (OH)
Catholic U of America (DC)
Cincinnati, U of (OH)
Cleveland Institute of Music (OH)
Colorado, U of, Boulder
Columbia C Chicago (IL)
Delaware, U of
DePaul U (IL)
DePauw U (IN)
Drexel U (PA)

Duquesne U (PA)
Elmhurst C (IL)
Emerson C (MA)
Emory U (GA)
Eugene Lang C (NY)
Evansville, U of (IL)
Five Towns C (NY)
Florida State U
Full Sail U (FL)
Gettysburg C (PA)
Gustavus Adolphus C (MN)
Illinois Wesleyan U
Indiana U Bloomington
Iowa, U of
Jacksonville U (FL)
Johns Hopkins U (MD)
Lawrence U (WI)
Lebanon Valley C (PA)
Lehigh U (PA)
Liverpool Institute for Performing Arts
    (United Kingdom)
Mannes School of Music (NY)
Maryland, U of, College Park
McNally Smith C of Music (MN)
Miami U (OH)
Michigan, U of, Ann Arbor
Middle Tennessee State U
Moravian C (PA)
Muhlenberg C (PA)
New York, State U of, Binghamton
New York, State U of, Buffalo
New York, State U of, Fredonia
New York, State U of, Potsdam
New York, State U of, Purchase
North Carolina School of the Arts
Northwestern U (IL)
Oberlin C (OH)
Ohio Northern U
Oregon, U of
Otterbein C (OH)
Pomona U (CA)
Redlands, U of (CA)
Reed C (OR)
Rider U (NJ)
San Francisco Conservatory (CA)
Smith C (MA)

Southern Illinois U, Carbondale
St. Olaf C (MN)
Stanford U (CA)
Susquehanna U (PA)
Syracuse U (NY)
Towson U (MD)
Yale U (CT)

Honorable Mention

Alabama, U of, Tuscaloosa
Alaska, U of, Anchorage
Allegheny C (PA)
American Conservatory of Music (IL)
American U (DC)
Amherst C (MA)
Arizona, U of
Arkansas, U of, Fayetteville
Babson C (MA)
Barnard C (NY)
Barry U (FL)
Baylor U (TX)
Berklee C of Music (MA)
Bethune-Cookman U (FL)
Bowling Green State U (OH)
Bradley U (IL)
Brandeis U (MA)
Brenau U (GA)
Brigham Young U (UT)
Bucknell U (PA)
California State U, Chico
California State U, Dominguez Hills
California State U, Long Beach
California State U, Northridge
California, U of, Berkeley
California, U of, Santa Barbara
Carleton C (MN)
Case Western Reserve U (OH)
Central Arkansas, U of
Chicago, U of (IL)
Clark U (MA)
Clemson U (SC)
Colburn School (CA)
Colorado, U of, Denver
Columbia C (SC)
Connecticut, U of
Conservatory of Recording Arts &
    Sciences (AZ)
Converse C (SC)
Cornell U (NY)
Cornish C of the Arts (WA)
Davidson C (NC)
Dayton, U of (OH)
Denison U (OH)
Denver, U of (CO)

Drake U (IA)
Duke U (NC)
Elon U (NC)
Florida Atlantic U
Furman U (SC)
George Mason U (VA)
Georgia State U
Goucher C (MD)
Guitar Institute (CA)
Hampshire C (MA)
Harvard U (MA)
Hofstra U (NY)
Illinois State U
Illinois, U of, Urbana
Johnson State C (VT)
Kent State U (OH)
LaGrange C (GA)
Leeds C of Music (United Kingdom)
Longwood U (VA)
Louisiana State U, Baton Rouge
Loyola Marymount U (CA)
Mary Washington, U of (VA)
Marymount Manhattan C (NY)
Massachusetts Institute of Technology
Massachusetts, U of, Lowell
Memphis, U of (TN)
Mercy C (NY)
Michigan State U
Millikin U (IL)
Mills C (CA)
Missouri State U
Missouri, U of, Kansas City
Montclair State U (NJ)
Musicians Institute (CA)
New Haven, U of (CT)
New Jersey, C of
New School (NY)
New World School of the Arts (FL)
New York, City U of, Brooklyn
New York, City U of, Queens C
New York, State U of, Albany
New York, State U of, Geneseo
New York, State U of, Stony Brook
North Carolina, U of, Asheville
North Carolina, U of, Chapel Hill
North Carolina, U of, Charlotte
North Carolina, U of, Greensboro
Northeastern U (MA)
Northern Colorado, U of
Northern Illinois U
Northern Virginia Community C
Notre Dame, U of (IN)
Occidental C (CA)
Ohio Wesleyan U
Oklahoma City U

Oklahoma, U of
Pace U (NY)
Pacific Lutheran U (WA)
Pacific Union C (CA)
Pennsylvania State U, University Park
Pepperdine U (CA)
Point Park U (PA)
Puget Sound, U of (WA)
Richmond, U of (VA)
Rockford C (IL)
Rollins C (FL)
Roosevelt U (IL)
SAE Expression C (CA)
Sarah Lawrence C (NY)
Scripps C (CA)
Seton Hall U (NJ)
Skidmore C (NY)
Southern Maine, U of
Southwestern U (TX)
St. Mary's C (MD)
St. Mary's U (MN)
St. Rose, C of (NY)
Stetson U (FL)
Stevens Institute of Technology (NJ)
Swarthmore C (PA)
Tampa, U of (FL)
Temple U (PA)
Texas, U of, Arlington
Texas, U of, Austin
Toronto, U of (Canada)

Trinity International U (IL)
Tufts U (MA)
Tulane U (LA)
Vanderbilt U (TN)
VanderCook C of Music (IL)
Vassar C (NY)
Virginia Commonwealth U
Virginia Polytechnic Institute & State U
Wagner C (NY)
Wake Forest U (NC)
Washington U (MO)
Washington, U of
Webster U (MO)
Wellesley C (MA)
Wesleyan U (CT)
West Georgia, U of
West Virginia U
Western Michigan U
Whitman C (WA)
Wilkes U (PA)
Willamette U (OR)
William & Mary, C of (VA)
William Paterson U (NJ)
Williams C (MA)
Winthrop U (SC)
Wisconsin, U of, Oshkosh
Wooster, C of (OH)
Wright State U (OH)
York U (Canada)

The Experts' Choice: Options for the Musician Who Doesn't Want to Attend a Conservatory

Belmont U (TN)
Boston C (MA)
Boston U (MA)
California, U of, Los Angeles
Case Western Reserve U (OH)
Columbia C Chicago (IL)
Denver, U of (CO)
Indiana U Bloomington
Lawrence U (WI)
Lebanon Valley C (PA)
New York U
North Texas, U of
Northwestern U (IL)

Oberlin C (OH)
Pacific, U of the (CA)
Puget Sound, U of (WA)
Rice U (TX)
Skidmore C (NY)
Southern California, U of
St. Olaf C (MN)
Susquehanna C (PA)
Vanderbilt U (TN)
Yale U (CT)

Colleges Where You Can Combine Music and Business

Music and business can be combined in lots of ways and can include study in music merchandising, copyright and publishing, and artist management.

Belmont U (TN)
Berklee C of Music (MA)
California State U, Chico
California State U, Northridge
Colorado, U of, Denver
Columbia C Chicago (IL)
Denver, U of (CO)
DePaul U (IL)
Drexel U (PA)

Loyola U (MD)
McNally Smith C (MN)
Memphis, U of (TN)
Miami, U of (FL)
Pacific, U of the (CA)
Skidmore C (NY)
Southern California, U of
Westminster C of the Arts, Rider U (NJ)
William Paterson U (NJ)

Colleges to Consider for Music Therapy

Jennifer Tabbush is an independent educational consultant and founder of Headed For College, a college advising firm in Los Angeles. She supplied this list exclusively for *The College Finder.*

Anna Maria C (MA)
Arizona State U
Baldwin-Wallace U (OH)
Berklee C of Music (MA)
California, U of, Berkeley
California, U of, Davis
California, U of, San Diego
California, U of, Santa Barbara
Chapman U (CA)
Dayton, U of (OH)
Duquesne U (PA)
Elizabethtown C (PA)
Florida State U
Georgia, U of

Indiana U-Purdue U Ft. Wayne
Kansas, U of
Louisville, U of (KY)
Loyola U (LA)
Miami, U of (FL)
Michigan State U
Minnesota, U of
New York, State U of, Fredonia
New York, State U of, New Paltz
Pacific, U of the (CA)
Sam Houston State U (TX)
Seton Hill U (PA)
Temple U (PA)
Wooster, C of (OH)

NANNYING

Trade Schools to Prepare to Be a Nanny

Many students who want to work as a nanny go to a traditional college and pursue this career after graduation. Some go to specialized schools such as these.

Ashton Warner Nanny Academy (New Zealand)
Chaffey Community C (CA)
English Nanny & Governess School (OH)
Merrill Palmer Institute (MI)
Nanny Academy (Nigeria)
Nanny Academy of America (MI)
Norland C (United Kingdom)

Source: *College Finder* research

NANOTECHNOLOGY

Colleges to Consider for Nanotechnology

Jennifer Tabbush is an independent educational consultant and founder of Headed For College, a college advising firm in Los Angeles. She supplied this list exclusively for *The College Finder*.

Arizona State U
Arkansas, U of, Fayetteville
California, U of, Riverside
California, U of, San Diego
Cornell U (NY)
Denver, U of (CO)
Drexel U (PA)
Duke U (NC)
Johns Hopkins U (MD)
Maryland, U of, College Park
Michigan, U of, Ann Arbor
Minnesota, U of, Twin Cities
New York, State of, Albany

North Carolina, U of, Chapel Hill
Northwestern U (IL)
Ohio State U, Columbus
Pennsylvania State U, University Park
Pennsylvania, U of
Purdue U (IN)
Rice U (TX)
Rutgers U (NJ)
Stevens Institute of Technology U (NJ)
Virginia Commonwealth U
Virginia, U of
Washington State U

NURSING

Colleges With Accredited Nursing Programs

These are the member institutions of the Accreditation Commission for Education in Nursing that grant baccalaureate degrees.

Adventist U of Health Sciences (FL)
Alaska, U of, Anchorage
Albany State U (GA)
Alcorn State U (MS)
Alderson Broaddus U (WV)
Andrews U (MI)
Angelo State U (TX)
Anna Maria C (MA)
Aquinas C (TN)
Arkansas State U
Arkansas Tech U
Arkansas, U of, Ft. Smith
Arkansas, U of, Little Rock
Arkansas, U of, Monticello
Augusta State U (GA)
Austin Peay State U (TN)
Baptist Health System, School of Health
    Professions (TX)
Becker C (MA)
Bethel C (IN)
Bethune-Cookman U (FL)
Boise State U (ID)

Bowie State U (MD)
Bradley U (IL)
Brookline C, Albuquerque (NM)
Brookline C, Phoenix (AZ)
Broward C (FL)
Bryan C of Health Sciences (NE)
Case Western Reserve U (OH)
Cedar Crest C (PA)
Central Oklahoma, U of
Charleston Southern U (SC)
Charleston, U of (WV)
Chicago State U (IL)
Chipola C (FL)
Clarion U (PA)
Clarkson C (NE)
Coastal Carolina U (SC)
Coastal Georgia, C of
Colorado State U, Pueblo
Cumberland U (TN)
Daemen C (NY)
Dalton State C (GA)
Darton State C (GA)

Davenport U (MI)
Daytona State C (FL)
Delaware State U
Denver School of Nursing (CO)
DeSales U (PA)
Dickinson State U (ND)
Dillard U (LA)
District of Columbia, U of the
Dixie State U (UT)
East Central U (OK)
East Stroudsburg U (PA)
Eastern New Mexico U
ECPI U, Virginia Beach (VA)
Elmira C (NY)
Emporia State U (KS)
Endicott C (MA)
Evansville, U of (IN)
Excelsior C (online)
Ferris State U (MI)
Florida A&M U
Florida Southwestern State C
Florida State C, Jacksonville
Florida, State C of, Manatee
Francis Marion U (SC)
Franciscan U (OH)
Franklin Pierce U (NH)
Grambling State U (LA)
Gardner-Webb U (NC)
Georgia C & State U
Georgia Highlands C
Georgia Southwestern State U
Good Samaritan C of Nursing & Health
  Science (OH)
Gordon State C (GA)
Governors State U (IL)
Great Basin C (NV)
Gwynedd-Mercy U (PA)
Harding U (AR)
Hawaii, U of, Hilo
Holy Cross, U of (LA)
Houston Baptist U (TX)
Indian River State C (FL)
Indiana U Northwest
Indiana State U
Indiana U-Purdue U Ft. Wayne
Indiana U-Purdue U Indianapolis
Indiana U East
Iowa Wesleyan C
Jamestown, U of (ND)
Kean U (NJ)
Kentucky State U
Kettering C (OH)
La Roche C (PA)
LaGrange C (GA)
Lake Superior State U (MI)

Lamar U (TX)
Langston U (OK)
Lincoln Memorial U (TN)
Lincoln U (MO)
Lipscomb U (TN)
Lock Haven U (PA)
Louisiana State U, Alexandria
Loyola U (LA)
Lubbock Christian U (TX)
Maine, U of, Augusta
Mansfield U (PA)
Maria C (NY)
Marshall U (WV)
Marywood U (PA)
Mercy C (OH)
Metropolitan State U (CO)
Miami Dade C (FL)
Middle Georgia State C
Midland U (NE)
Midway C (KY)
Millersville U (PA)
Minot State U (ND)
Missouri Southern State U
Montana State U, Northern
Mt. Aloysius C (PA)
Nebraska Wesleyan U
Neumann U (PA)
New England Institute of Technology
  (RI)
New England, U of (ME)
New Jersey City U
New York, City U of, City C of
  Technology
New York, City U of, Medgar Evers C
New York, City U of, Staten Island
New York, City U of, York
New York, State U of, Canton
New York, State U of, Delhi
Norfolk State U (VA)
North Carolina Agricultural & Technical
  State U
North Carolina Central U
North Carolina, U of, Greensboro
North Georgia, U of
Northeastern State U (OK)
Northern Kentucky U
Northwestern Oklahoma State U
Notre Dame of Maryland U
Oakwood U (AL)
Oklahoma City U
Oklahoma Panhandle State U
Oklahoma, U of, Health Science Center
Our Lady of the Lake C (LA)
Pacific Union C (CA)
Palm Beach State C (FL)

Park U (MO)
Pennsylvania C of Technology
Pennsylvania State U, University Park
Piedmont C (GA)
Pikeville, U of (KY)
Pittsburgh, U of, Bradford (PA)
Platt C (CO)
Polk State C (FL)
Prairie View A&M U (TX)
Presentation C (SD)
Purdue U, Calumet (IN)
Purdue U, North Central (IN)
Ramapo C (NJ)
Regis C (MA)
Rio Grande, U of (OH)
Rivier U (NH)
Rockford U (IL)
Rogers State U (OK)
Roseman U of Health Sciences (UT)
Salish Kootenai C (MT)
Sam Houston State U (TX)
Shawnee State U (OH)
Slippery Rock U (PA)
Sonoma State U (CA)
South C (TN)
South Georgia State C
Southern Adventist U (TN)
Southern Arkansas U
Southwest Baptist U (MO)
Southwestern Oklahoma State U
St. Catherine U (MN)
St. Elizabeth, C of (NJ)

St. Francis Medical Center C of Nursing
St. John's C (IL)
St. John's River State C (FL)
St. Joseph's C (NY)
St. Mary, C of (NE)
St. Vincent's C (CT)
Stephen F. Austin State U (TX)
Tampa, U of (FL)
Tennessee State U, Nashville
Tennessee, U of, Martin
Texas A&M U, International
Texas, U of, Brownsville
Thomas Edison State C (NJ)
Thomas More C (KY)
Thomas U (GA)
Trocaire C (NY)
Troy U (AL)
Tulsa, U of (OK)
Tuskegee U (AL)
Utah Valley U
Vermont Technical C (VT)
Vincennes U (IN)
Virginia Commonwealth U
Wagner C (NY)
Walla Walla U (WA)
Wayland Baptist U (TX)
Weber State U (UT)
Webster U (MO)
Wesley C (DE)
West Virginia Wesleyan C
Wingate U (NC)
Youngstown State U (OH)

Source: Accreditation Commission for Education in Nursing (acenursing.org)

The Experts' Choice: Colleges Offering Good Preparation for Nursing

Arizona State U
Arizona, U of
Boston C (MA)
California, U of, Los Angeles
Case Western Reserve U (OH)
Colorado, U of, Denver
Columbia U (NY)
Drexel U (PA)
Duke U (NC)
Emory U (GA)
Georgetown U (DC)
Illinois, U of, Chicago
Indiana U-Purdue Indianapolis
Iowa, U of
Johns Hopkins U (MD)
Maryland, U of, Baltimore

Michigan, U of, Ann Arbor
Minnesota, U of, Twin Cities
Molloy C (NY)
New York U
North Carolina, U of, Chapel Hill
Ohio State U, Columbus
Oregon Health & Science U
Pennsylvania, U of
Pittsburgh, U of (PA)
Quinnipiac U (CT)
Rochester, U of (NY)
Rush U (IL)
Simmons C (MA)
Texas, U of, Austin
Vanderbilt U (TN)
Virginia, U of

Washington U (MO)
Wisconsin, U of, Madison

Yale U (CT)

Ready to Start Your Nursing Training Right Now?

Sandy Aprahamian, Independent Educational Consultant, is owner of EdNavigators in Pennsylvania. What follows is her list of nursing schools providing "direct entry." Direct entry means that the college or university accepts students into the B.S.N. (Bachelor of Science in Nursing) program upon acceptance to the university—in other words, direct entry from high school. Students still need to meet individual college admission requirements, including grade point average, test scores, etc. In addition, college policies regarding direct entry and participation in the program change regularly, so interested students are encouraged to contact the college for current information. This list is not intended to be exhaustive.

Alabama, U of, Birmingham
California, U of, Irvine
California, U of, Los Angeles
Catholic U of America (DC)
Chamberlain C of Nursing (multiple
    states)
Clemson U (SC)
Connecticut, U of
D'Youville C (NY)
Delaware, U of
DeSales U (PA)
Drexel U (PA)
Duquesne U (PA)
East Stroudsburg U (PA)
Florida Southern C
Georgetown U (DC)
Grand Valley State U (MI)
Indiana U of Pennsylvania
Jacksonville U (FL)
Marquette U (WI)
Marymount U (VA)
Michigan, U of, Ann Arbor
Mississippi, U of
Moravian C (PA)
Mt. Mercy U (IA)
Neumann U (PA)

New Jersey, C of
New York U
New York, State U of, Plattsburgh
Pennsylvania State U, University Park
Pennsylvania, U of
Pittsburgh, U of (PA)
Quinnipiac U (CT)
Regis U (CO)
Rhode Island, U of
Robert Morris U (NJ)
Rutgers U (NJ)
Sacred Heart U (CT)
Scranton, U of (PA)
Seton Hall U (NJ)
Stevenson U (MD)
Temple U (PA)
Texas Christian U
Texas, U of, Austin
Villanova U (PA)
Virginia, U of
West Chester U (PA)
Widener U (PA)
Wilkes U (PA)
York C (PA)

The Experts' Choice: Nursing and Liberal Arts

Experts were asked to name general liberal arts colleges that are particularly good with nursing preparation.

Belmont U (TN)
Coe C (IA)
Gettysburg C (PA)
Morehead State U (KY)

Otterbein U (OH)
Wheaton C (IL)
Wisconsin, U of, Eau Claire
Wisconsin, U of, Oshkosh

Steven R. Antonoff

PHYSICAL THERAPY

Accredited Physical Therapy Programs

The following colleges and universities are those accredited by the American Physical Therapy Association's Commission on Accreditation in Physical Therapy Education.

Alabama State U
Alabama, U of, Birmingham
Alvernia U (PA)
American International C (MA)
Andrews U (MI)
Angelo State U (TX)
Arcadia U (PA)
Arizona School of Health Sciences
Arkansas State U
Armstrong State U (GA)
Azusa Pacific U (CA)
Baylor U (TX)
Bellarmine U (KY)
Belmont U (TN)
Boston U (MA)
Bradley U (IL)
Brenau U (GA)
Briar Cliff U (IA)
California State U, Fresno
California State U, Long Beach
California State U, Northridge
California State U, Sacramento
California, U of, San Francisco
Campbell U (NC)
Carroll U (WI)
Central Arkansas, U of
Central Florida, U of
Central Michigan U
Chapman U (CA)
Chatham U (PA)
Cincinnati, U of (OH)
Clarke U (IA)
Clarkson U (NY)
Cleveland State U (OH)
Colorado, U of, Boulder
Columbia U (NY)
Concordia U (MN)
Concordia U (WI)
Connecticut, U of
Creighton U (NE)
D'Youville C (NY)
Daemen C (NY)
Dayton, U of (OH)
Delaware, U of
DeSales U (PA)
Dominican C (NY)
Drexel U (PA)

Duke U (NC)
Duquesne U (PA)
East Carolina U (NC)
East Tennessee State U
Eastern Washington U
Elon U (NC)
Emory & Henry C (VA)
Emory U (GA)
Evansville, U of (IN)
Findlay, U of (OH)
Florida A&M U
Florida Gulf Coast U
Florida International U
Florida, U of
Franklin Pierce U (AZ)
Franklin Pierce U (NH)
Gannon U (PA)
George Fox U (OR)
George Washington U (DC)
Georgia Regents U
Georgia State U
Governors State U (IL)
Grand Valley State U (MI)
Hampton U (VA)
Hardin-Simmons U (TX)
Harding U (AR)
Hartford, U of (CT)
Howard U (DC)
Husson U (ME)
Idaho State U
Illinois, U of, Chicago
Incarnate Word, U of the (TX)
Indiana State U
Indiana U School of Health &
   Rehabilitation Sciences
Indianapolis, U of (IN)
Iowa, U of
Ithaca C (NY)
Jamestown, U of (ND)
Kansas, U of, Medical Center
Kentucky, U of
Langston U (OK)
Lebanon Valley C (PA)
Loma Linda U (CA)
Long Island U, Brooklyn (NY)
Louisiana State U Health Sciences
   Center, New Orleans

Louisiana State U Health Sciences
  Center, Shreveport
Lynchburg C (VA)
Marquette U (WI)
Marshall U (WV)
Mary, U of (ND)
Maryland, U of, Baltimore
Maryland, U of, Eastern Shore
Marymount U (VA)
Maryville U (MO)
Massachusetts, U of, Lowell
Mayo School of Health Sciences (MN)
Medical U of South Carolina
Mercer U (GA)
Mercy C (NY)
MGH Institute of Health Professions
  (MA)
Miami, U of (FL)
Michigan, U of, Flint
Midwestern U (AZ)
Midwestern U (IL)
Minnesota, U of, Twin Cities
Misericordia U (PA)
Mississippi, U of
Missouri State U
Missouri, U of, Columbia
Montana, U of, Missoula
Mt. St. Joseph U (OH)
Mt. St. Mary's U (MD)
Nazareth C (NY)
Nebraska, U of, Medical Center
Neumann U (PA)
Nevada, U of, Las Vegas
New England, U of (ME)
New Jersey, State U of, Rutgers
  (Newark/North Campus)
New Jersey, State U of, Rutgers
  (Stratford/South)
New Mexico, U of
New York Institute of Technology
New York Medical C
New York U
New York, City U of, Hunter C
New York, City U of, Staten Island
New York, State U of, Buffalo
New York, State U of, Downstate
  Medical Center
New York, State U of, Stony Brook
New York, State U of, Upstate
  Medical U
North Carolina, U of, Chapel Hill
North Dakota, U of
North Florida, U of
North Georgia, U of
North Texas, U of, Health Science

Center
Northeastern U (MA)
Northern Arizona U
Northern Illinois U
Northwestern U (IL)
Nova Southeastern U (FL)
Nova Southeastern U-Tampa
  (Hybrid Four-Year Program) (FL)
Oakland U (MI)
Ohio State U
Ohio U
Oklahoma, U of, Health Sciences
  Center
Old Dominion U (VA)
Pacific U (OR)
Pacific, U of the (CA)
Pittsburgh, U of (PA)
Puerto Rico, U of
Puget Sound, U of (WA)
Quinnipiac U (CT)
Radford U (VA)
Regis U (CO)
Rhode Island, U of
Rockhurst U (MO)
Rocky Mountain U of Health Professions
  (UT)
Rosalind Franklin U of Medicine &
  Science (IL)
Sacred Heart U (CT)
Sage C (NY)
Samford U (AL)
Samuel Merritt U (CA)
San Diego State U (CA)
San Francisco State U (CA)
Sciences, U of the (PA)
Scranton, U of (PA)
Seton Hall U (NJ)
Shenandoah U (VA)
Simmons C (MA)
Slippery Rock U (PA)
South Alabama, U of
South Carolina, U of
South Dakota, U of
South Florida, U of
South, U of the (TN)
Southern California, U of
Southwest Baptist U (MO)
Springfield C (MA)
St. Ambrose U (IA)
St. Catherine U (MN)
St. Francis U (PA)
St. Louis U (MO)
St. Mary, U of (KS)
St. Scholastica, C of (MN)
Stockton U (NJ)

Temple U (PA)
Tennessee State U
Tennessee, U of, Chattanooga
Tennessee, U of, Health Science Center
Texas State U, San Marcos
Texas Tech U, Health Sciences Center
Texas Woman's U
Texas, U of, Dallas, Southwestern
Medical Center
Texas, U of, El Paso
Texas, U of, Galveston, Medical Branch
Texas, U of, San Antonio, Health
Science Center
Thomas Jefferson U (PA)
Toledo, U of (OH)
Touro U (NV)
Touro U (NY)
Trine U (NY)
Utah, U of
Utica C (NY)

Vermont, U of
Virginia Commonwealth U
Walsh U (OH)
Washington U (MO)
Washington, U of, Seattle
Wayne State U (MI)
West Coast U (CA)
West Virginia U
Western Carolina U (NC)
Western Kentucky U
Western U of Health Sciences (CA)
Wheeling Jesuit U (WV)
Wichita State U (KS)
Widener U (PA)
Wingate U (NC)
Winston-Salem State U (NC)
Wisconsin, U of, La Crosse
Wisconsin, U of, Madison
Wisconsin, U of, Milwaukee
Youngstown State U (OH)

The Experts' Choice: Excellent Physical Therapy Programs

Arcadia U (PA)
Baylor U (TX)
Boston U (MA)
Daemen C (NY)
Delaware, U of
Duquesne U (PA)
Emory U (GA)
High Point U (NC)
Iowa, U of
Ithaca C (NY)
Marquette U (WI)
Miami, U of (FL)

Northeastern U (MA)
Northwestern U (IL)
Pittsburgh, U of (PA)
Puget Sound, U of (WA)
Quinnipiac U (CT)
Scranton, U of (PA)
South Carolina, U of, Columbia
Southern California, U of
Springfield C (MA)
St. Louis U (MO)
Washington U (MO)

Recognized Physical Therapy Programs

Colleges listed here have physical therapy programs worth checking out. Physical therapists treat disorders of the human body to improve physical function and relieve pain.

Alabama, U of, Birmingham
Arcadia U (PA)
Boston U (MA)
California, U of, San Francisco
Calvin C (MI)
Creighton U (NE)
Delaware, U of
Drexel U (PA)
Emory U (GA)
Florida, U of

Hawaii, U of, Manoa
Illinois, U of, Chicago
Iowa, U of
Kansas, U of, Medical Center
Lock Haven U (PA)
Marquette U (WI)
Maryland, U of, Baltimore
MGH Institute of Health Professions
   (MA)
Miami, U of (FL)

Minnesota, U of, Twin Cities
New Mexico, U of
New York, State U of, Brockport
New York, State U of, Upstate Medical U
North Alabama, U of
North Carolina, U of, Chapel Hill
Northeastern U (MA)
Northwestern U (IL)
Ohio State U
Pittsburgh, U of (PA)
Ramapo C (NJ)
Sacred Heart U (CT)
Sage C (NY)

Southern California, U of
Southern Florida, U of
St. Rose, C of (NY)
Temple U (PA)
Texas, U of, San Antonio
Thomas Jefferson U (PA)
Utah, U of
Virginia Commonwealth U
Washington U (MO)
William & Mary, C of (VA)
William Paterson U (NJ)
Wisconsin, U of, Madison
Wisconsin, U of, Milwaukee

PHYSICS

The Experts' Choice: Excellent Physics Departments

Experts were asked to name colleges for the student who wants to major in physics. As a basic and central college subject, physics is offered at most liberal arts and sciences colleges. Evaluation of undergraduate programs in physics, however, is difficult because of the varied approaches to assessing quality. Students should base their college selection decisions on numerous variables, both academic and social.

The Top Choices

California Institute of Technology
Harvey Mudd C (CA)
Massachusetts Institute of Technology
Princeton U (NJ)*

*The Top Choice

The Second Choices

Bryn Mawr C (PA)
California, U of, Berkeley
California, U of, Los Angeles
Carleton C (MN)
Cornell U (NY)
Harvard U (MA)
Reed C (OR)
Rensselaer Polytechnic Institute (NY)
Rice U (TX)

Honorable Mention

Amherst C (MA)
Arkansas, U of, Fayetteville
Bethel U (MN)
Boston U (MA)
Bradley U (IL)

Brandeis U (MA)
Brigham Young U (UT)
California Polytechnic State U, San Luis
  Obispo
California, U of, Santa Barbara
Carnegie Mellon U (PA)
Chicago, U of (IL)
Colorado School of Mines
Creighton U (NE)
Dartmouth C (NH)
George Washington U (DC)
Grinnell C (IA)
Grove City C (PA)
Houston, U of (TX)
Illinois, U of, Urbana
Johns Hopkins U (MD)
Kansas State U
Kettering U (MI)
Lafayette C (PA)
Lawrence U (WI)
Macalester C (MN)
Maryland, U of, College Park
McGill U (Canada)
New Hampshire, U of
New Mexico Institute of Technology
New York, City U of, City C
New York, State U of, Albany
New York, State U of, Geneseo

Oberlin C (OH)
Occidental C (CA)
Pomona C (CA)
Rochester, U of (NY)
Rutgers U, New Brunswick (NJ)
Sonoma State U (CA)
South Carolina, U of, Columbia
Swarthmore C (PA)
Texas, U of, Austin

Tulsa, U of (OK)
Tuskegee U (AL)
U.S. Naval Academy (MD)
Ursinus C (PA)
Vanderbilt U (TN)
Virginia, U of
Wake Forest U (NC)
Whitman C (WA)
Wisconsin, U of, Milwaukee

POLITICAL SCIENCE

Colleges With Excellent Political Science Programs

As a basic and central college subject, political science is offered at most liberal arts and sciences colleges. Evaluation of undergraduate programs in political science, however, is difficult because of the varied approaches to assessing quality. Students should base their college selection decisions on numerous variables, both academic and social. The following colleges offer programs in political science that are worth a second look.

American U (DC)
Beloit C (WI)
Brandeis U (MA)
California, U of, Berkeley
Catholic U of America (DC)
Chatham U (PA)
Claremont McKenna C (CA)
Clark U (MA)
Columbia U (NY)
Denver, U of (CO)
DePaul U (IL)
Dickinson C (PA)
Earlham C (IN)
Emory U (GA)
Eugene Lang C (NY)
Evergreen State C (WA)
George Mason U (VA)
George Washington U (DC)
Georgetown U (DC)
Georgia Institute of Technology
Goddard C (VT)
Grinnell C (IA)
Guilford C (NC)
Hampshire C (MA)
Harvard U (MA)
Hobart C (NY)
Hope C (MI)
Indiana U Bloomington
Ithaca C (NY)

James Madison U (VA)
Lewis & Clark C (OR)
London School of Economics (United Kingdom)
Macalester C (MN)
Michigan State U
Mills C (CA)
New York, State U of, Binghamton
Northern Arizona U
Ohio State U, Columbus
Oregon, U of
Pennsylvania State U, University Park
Pittsburgh, U of (PA)
Pitzer C (CA)
Princeton U (NJ)
Quinnipiac U (CT)
Sarah Lawrence C (NY)
St. Mary's C (MD)
Stanford U (CA)
Suffolk U (MA)
Syracuse U (NY)
Toronto, U of (Canada)
Tufts U (MA)
Virginia Polytechnic Institute & State U
Washington State U
Washington U (MO)
Wisconsin, U of, Madison

PSYCHOLOGY

The Experts' Choice: Colleges With Strong Programs in Psychology

Experts were asked to identify colleges for students interested in psychology. As a basic and central college subject, psychology is offered at most liberal arts and sciences colleges. Evaluation of undergraduate programs in psychology, however, is difficult because of the varied approaches to assessing quality. Students should base their college selection decisions on numerous variables, both academic and social. The following colleges offer programs in psychology that are worth a second look.

The Top Choices

Brandeis U (MA)
California, U of, Los Angeles
Chicago, U of (IL)
Clark U (MA)
Colgate U (NY)
Denver, U of (CO)
Duke U (NC)
George Washington U (DC)
Harvard U (MA)
Iowa, U of
Mt. Holyoke C (MA)
Northwestern U (IL)
New York U
Oregon, U of
Pitzer C (CA)
Princeton U (NJ)
Reed C (OR)
Stanford U (CA)
Tufts U (MA)
Vanderbilt U (TN)
Yale U (CT)

Honorable Mention

Albion C (MI)
Alverno C (WI)
Bard C (NY)
Barnard C (NY)
Bates C (ME)
Boston C (MA)
Bucknell U (PA)
California State U, Northridge
California, U of, Berkeley
California, U of, Davis
California, U of, Los Angeles
California, U of, Riverside
California, U of, San Diego
California, U of, Santa Barbara
California, U of, Santa Cruz
Carleton C (MN)
Carnegie Mellon U (PA)

Case Western Reserve U (OH)
Claremont McKenna C (CA)
Colorado C
Colorado State U, Ft. Collins
Columbia U (NY)
Cornell U (NY)
Dartmouth C (NH)
Denison U (OH)
Dickinson C (PA)
Drew U (NJ)
Earlham C (IN)
Elon U (NC)
Emory U (GA)
Franklin & Marshall C (PA)
George Mason U (VA)
Gettysburg C (PA)
Grinnell C (IA)
Hollins U (VA)
Indiana U Bloomington
James Madison U (VA)
Johns Hopkins U (MD)
Lewis & Clark C (OR)
Loyola U (MD)
Loyola U (IL)
Marquette U (WI)
Michigan, U of, Ann Arbor
Mills C (CA)
Montclair State U (NJ)
Muhlenberg C (PA)
New York, State U of, Binghamton
New York, State U of, Buffalo
Ohio State U, Columbus
Pennsylvania, U of
Pomona C (CA)
Richmond, U of (VA)
Rochester, U of (NY)
Rollins C (FL)
Rutgers U, New Brunswick (NJ)
San Diego State U (CA)
Santa Clara U (CA)
Smith C (MA)
Sonoma State U (CA)

Southern California, U of
Southern Illinois U, Carbondale
St. Anselm C (NH)
Syracuse U (NY)
Texas, U of, Austin
Towson U (MD)
Transylvania U (KY)
Tulane U (LA)
Union C (NY)
Utah, U of
Vassar C (NY)

Virginia, U of
Washington U (MO)
Washington, U of
Wesleyan U (CT)
Western Washington U
Westmont C (CA)
Wheaton C (MA)
William & Mary, C of (VA)
Williams C (MA)
Wisconsin, U of, Madison
Yeshiva U (NY)

PUBLIC POLICY/PUBLIC SERVICE

Colleges With Public Policy/Public Service Programs

Public policy refers to laws, regulations, and other programs developed by local, state, or national governments to solve community problems. Public policy is typically a multidisciplinary field of study. These schools are among those offering a major in public policy or public service.

Akron, U of (OH)
Albion C (MI)
American U (DC)
Anna Maria C (MA)
Arizona State U
Arizona, U of
Arkansas, U of, Little Rock
Atlantic, C of the (ME)
Bennington C (VT)
Bentley U (MA)
Bristol Community C (MA)
Brown U (RI)
Bryant U (RI)
California State U, East Bay
California, U of, Berkeley
California, U of, Los Angeles
California, U of, Riverside
California, U of, San Diego
Carnegie Mellon U (PA)
Central Washington U
Chatham U (PA)
Chicago, U of (IL)
Colorado, U of, Denver
Columbia U (NY)
Cornell U (NY)
Delaware, U of
Denver, U of (CO)
DePaul U (IL)
Dickinson C (PA)
Duke U (NC)
Elon U (NC)
Florida International U

George Mason U (VA)
Georgetown U (DC)
George Washington U (DC)
Georgia Institute of Technology
Georgia State U
Georgia, U of
Hamilton C (NY)
Hampshire C (MA)
Harvard U (MA)
Hobart & William Smith C (NY)
Houston Baptist U (TX)
Howard Payne U (TX)
Immaculata U (PA)
Indiana U Bloomington
Indiana U-Purdue U Indianapolis
Indiana Wesleyan U
Johns Hopkins U (MD)
Kentucky, U of
Lafayette C (PA)
Maryland, U of, College Park
Massachusetts C of Liberal Arts
Massachusetts, U of, Amherst
Massachusetts, U of, Boston
Michigan State U
Michigan, U of, Ann Arbor
Mills C (CA)
Minnesota, U of, Twin Cities
Mississippi, U of
New College of Florida
New York, City U of, Baruch
New York, City U of, School of
    Professional Studies

New York, State U of, Albany
New York U
North Carolina, U of, Chapel Hill
Northwestern U (IL)
Ohio U
Ohio State U
Olivet Nazarene U (IL)
Pennsylvania State U, Harrisburg
Pennsylvania, U of
Pittsburgh, U of (PA)
Pomona C (CA)
Princeton U (NJ)
Redlands, U of (CA)
Regent U (VA)
Rhode Island, U of
Rice U (TX)
Rochester Institute of Technology (NY)
Rutgers U, Camden (NJ)
Rutgers U, Newark (NJ)
Sage C (NY)
Scripps C (CA)
Simmons C (MA)
Southeastern U (FL)
Southern California, U of

Southern Methodist U (TX)
St. Joseph's U (CT)
St. Mary's C (MD)
St. Peter's U (NJ)
St. Vincent C (PA)
Stanford U (CA)
Susquehanna U (PA)
Texas A&M U, College Station
Texas, U of, Austin
Texas, U of, Dallas
Trevecca Nazarene U (TN)
Trinity C (CT)
Vanderbilt U (TN)
Virginia Polytechnic Institute & State U
Virginia Commonwealth U
Virginia, U of
Wagner C (NY)
Washington State U
Washington, U of, Seattle
William & Mary, C of (VA)
Wisconsin, U of, Madison
Wisconsin, U of, Superior
Wisconsin, U of, Whitewater

Source: *College Finder* research, including The College Board

SCIENCE

The Experts' Choice: Strong Science Programs

Experts were asked to list colleges for students looking for a great education in the sciences. As a basic and central college subject, sciences are offered at most liberal arts and sciences colleges. Evaluation of undergraduate programs in science, however, is difficult because of the varied approaches to assessing quality. Students should base their college selection decisions on numerous variables, both academic and social. The following colleges offer programs in science that are worth a second look, according to the experts.

California Institute of Technology
California, U of, Berkeley
California, U of, Davis
California, U of, Los Angeles
California, U of, San Diego
California, U of, San Francisco
Chicago, U of (IL)
Columbia U (NY)
Cornell U (NY)
Duke U (NC)
Harvard U (MA)
Illinois, U of, Urbana
Johns Hopkins U (MD)
Massachusetts Institute of Technology
Michigan, U of, Ann Arbor

North Carolina, U of, Chapel Hill
Northwestern U (IL)
Pennsylvania, U of
Princeton U (NJ)
Rockefeller U (NY)
Scripps Research Institute (CA)
Stanford U (CA)
Texas, U of, Austin
Texas, U of, Dallas, Southwestern
    Medical Center
Washington U (MO)
Washington, U of, Seattle
Wisconsin, U of, Madison
Yale U (CT)

The Experts' Choice: Unexpectedly Strong Science Programs

Colleges like Johns Hopkins U (MD), Massachusetts Institute of Technology, and California Institute of Technology are known for their great science programs. Experts were asked to go beyond these choices and identify colleges whose science programs may be overlooked.

As a basic and central college subject, sciences are offered at most liberal arts and sciences colleges. Evaluation of undergraduate programs in science, however, is difficult because of the varied approaches to assessing quality. Students should base their college selection decisions on numerous variables, both academic and social. The following colleges offer programs in science that are worth a second look.

Top Choices

Bowdoin C (ME)
Carleton C (MN)
Carnegie Mellon U (PA)
Case Western Reserve U (OH)
Chicago, U of (IL)
Colgate U (NY)
Davidson C (NC)
Duke U (NC)
Emory U (GA)
Harvey Mudd C (CA)
Lehigh U (PA)
Pomona C (CA)
Purdue U (IN)
Rochester Institute of Technology (NY)
Rochester, U of (NY)
Union C (NY)
Washington U (MO)
Wellesley C (MA)
Wooster, C of (OH)
Worcester Polytechnic Institute (MA)

Second Choices

Amherst C (MA)
Boston U (MA)
Brandeis U (MA)
Brown U (RI)
Bryn Mawr C (PA)
Bucknell U (PA)
California, U of, Berkeley
Colgate U (NY)
Colorado School of Mines
Connecticut, U of

Cornell U (NY)
Dartmouth C (NH)
Davidson C (NC)
Delaware, U of
Franklin & Marshall C (PA)
Georgia Institute of Technology
Harvard U (MA)
Haverford C (PA)
Juniata (PA)
Kenyon C (OH)
Lafayette C (PA)
Lawrence U (WI)
Miami, U of (FL)
Mt. Holyoke C (MA)
Muhlenberg C (PA)
Northwestern U (IL)
Oberlin C (OH)
Ohio State U, Columbus
Oregon, U of
Princeton U (NJ)
Reed C (OR)
Rensselaer Polytechnic Institute (NY)
Rhodes C (TN)
Rice U (TX)
Richmond, U of (VA)
Scranton, U of (PA)
Smith C (MA)
St. Olaf C (MN)
Stanford U (CA)
Swarthmore C (PA)
Tufts U (MA)
Vanderbilt U (TN)
Wake Forest U (NC)
Washington, U of
Williams C (MA)

SCREENWRITING

Colleges With High-Caliber Screenwriting Programs

American Film Institute (CA)
Boston U (MA)
California State U, Los Angeles
California, U of, Los Angeles
Chapman U (CA)
Chicago, U of (IL)
Columbia U (NY)
Emerson C (MA)

Florida State U
Ithaca C (NY)
Loyola Marymount U (CA)
New York Film Academy
New York U
Southern California, U of
Texas, U of, Austin

Source: *College Finder* research, screencraft.org, movieoutline.com

SOCIAL WORK

Quick Path to a Social Work Career

The colleges and universities listed below are among those offering some form of a combined Bachelor/Master of Social Work degree. These programs are typically five years.

Dominican U (CA)
Loyola U (IL)
Monmouth U (NJ)
New York, City U of, Hunter C
New York, State U of, Buffalo
Springfield C (MA)
St. Ambrose U (IA)

Source: *College Finder* research, including socialwork.dom.edu and individual college websites

SOCIOLOGY

The Experts' Choice: Excellent Sociology Programs

Experts were asked to name colleges for the student who wants to major in sociology. As a basic and central college subject, sociology is offered at most liberal arts and sciences colleges. Evaluation of undergraduate programs in sociology, however, is difficult because of the varied approaches to assessing quality. Students should base their college selection decisions on numerous variables, both academic and social. The following colleges offer programs in sociology that are worth a second look.

Amherst C (MA)
Arizona, U of
Auburn U (AL)
Beloit C (WI)
Brandeis U (MA)

Briar Cliff U (IA)
Brigham Young U (UT)
Brown U (RI)
Bryn Mawr C (PA)
California, U of, Berkeley

California, U of, Los Angeles
California, U of, Santa Cruz
Catholic U of America (DC)
Chicago, U of (IL)
Clark U (MA)
Clemson U (SC)
Coe C (IA)
Colorado State U, Ft. Collins
Colorado, U of, Boulder
Colorado, U of, Colorado Springs
Columbia U (NY)
Cornell C (IA)
Cornell U (NY)
Dartmouth C (NH)
Denison U (OH)
DePaul U (IL)
Duke U (NC)
Earlham C (IN)
Gettysburg C (PA)
Goucher C (MD)
Hartwick C (NY)
Harvard U (MA)
Hendrix C (AR)
Howard U (DC)
Illinois C
Illinois, U of, Urbana
Illinois, U of, Chicago
Indiana U Bloomington
Iowa, U of
Ithaca C (NY)
Kansas, U of
Knox C (IL)
Lake Forest C (IL)
Loyola Marymount U (CA)
McDaniel C (MD)
Michigan State U
Michigan, U of, Ann Arbor
Montana, U of
Moravian C (PA)

Morehouse C (GA)
New Mexico, U of
New York, City U of, Baruch
New York, State U of, Albany
New York, State U of, Stony Brook
North Carolina, U of, Chapel Hill
North Carolina, U of, Wilmington
Northwestern U (IL)
Oberlin C (OH)
Ohio U, Athens
Ohio Wesleyan U
Oklahoma City U
Oregon, U of
Pace U (NY)
Pennsylvania, U of
Pittsburgh, U of (PA)
Princeton U (NJ)
Quinnipiac U (CT)
San Francisco, U of (CA)
Simmons C (MA)
Smith C (MA)
Sonoma State U (CA)
South Florida, U of
St. Joseph's U (PA)
St. Lawrence U (NY)
Stanford U (CA)
Swarthmore C (PA)
Syracuse U (NY)
Tufts U (MA)
Washington State U
Washington, U of
Western Washington U
Wheaton C (MA)
Whitman C (WA)
Wisconsin, U of, Madison
Wisconsin, U of, Stevens Point
Wooster, C of (OH)
Yale U (CT)

THEATER

The Experts' Choice: Colleges With Excellent Theater Programs

Experts were asked to identify colleges for someone interested in theater arts.

The Top Choices

Bennington C (VT)
Boston U (MA)
Brandeis U (MA)
California Institute of the Arts

California, U of, Los Angeles
Carnegie Mellon U (PA)*
Case Western Reserve U (OH)
Chapman U (CA)
DePaul U (IL)
Drew U (NJ)

Emerson C (MA)
Fordham U (NY)
Ithaca C (NY)
Juilliard School (NY)
Kenyon C (OH)
Michigan, U of, Ann Arbor
Muhlenberg C (PA)
New York U
New York, State U of, Purchase**
North Carolina School of the Arts
Northwestern U (IL)
Sarah Lawrence C (NY)
Southern California, U of
Syracuse U (NY)
Vassar C (NY)
Wagner C (NY)
Wesleyan U (CT)
Yale U (CT)

*The Top Choice
**The Second Choice

Other Choices

American Musical & Dramatic Academy
    (NY)
Adelphi U (NY)
Agnes Scott C (GA)
American Academy of Dramatic Arts
    (NY)
American Conservatory Theater (CA)
American U (DC)
Arizona State U
Arts, U of the (PA)
Bard C (NY)
Barnard C (NY)
Beloit C (WI)
Bristol Old Vic Theatre School (United
    Kingdom)
California, U of, Irvine
California, U of, Santa Barbara
Catawba C (NC)
Catholic U of America (DC)
Cincinnati, U of (OH)
Colorado, U of, Boulder
Columbia C Chicago (IL)
Connecticut C
Cornish C of the Arts (WA)
DeSales U (PA)
Drama Centre London (United Kingdom)
Elon U (NC)
Evansville, U of (IN)
Georgetown U (DC)
Goucher C (MD)
Hampshire C (MA)

Hartford, U of (CT)
Hofstra U (NY)
Houston, U of (TX)
Idaho, U of
Illinois, U of, Urbana
Indiana U Bloomington
Iowa, U of
Jacksonville U (FL)
Kean U (NJ)
London Academy of Music & Dramatic
    Arts (United Kingdom)
Long Island U, Post (NY)
Loyola U (LA)
Manhattanville C (NY)
Marymount Manhattan C (NY)
Massachusetts C of Liberal Arts
Massachusetts, U of, Amherst
Memphis, U of (TN)
Miami, U of (FL)
Mills C (CA)
Minnesota, U of, Twin Cities
Missouri, U of, Kansas City
Moravian C (PA)
National Institute of Dramatic Art
    (Australia)
Nebraska Wesleyan U
New Hampshire, U of
New World School of the Arts (FL)
New York, State U of, New Paltz
Niagara U (NY)
North Carolina, U of, Chapel Hill
Northern Arizona U
Oberlin C (OH)
Occidental C (CA)
Otterbein C (OH)
Pace U (NY)
Roosevelt U (IL)
Royal Academy of Dramatic Art (United
    Kingdom)
Royal Central School of Speech &
    Drama (United Kingdom)
Rutgers U (NJ)
Savannah C of Art & Design (GA)
Shepherd U (WV)
Skidmore C (NY)
Southern California, U of
Southern Methodist U (TX)
Southern Oregon U
Stephens C (MO)
Temple U (PA)
Texas Christian U
Texas, U of, Austin
Trinity C (CT)
Tufts U (MA)
Viterbo U (WI)

Washington C (MD)
Wells C (NY)
Wheaton C (MA)
Whitman C (WA)

Wilkes U (PA)
Willamette U (OR)
Wittenberg U (OH)

UNDECIDED

Colleges to Consider as an Undecided Student

Jennifer Tabbush is an independent educational consultant and founder of Headed For College, a college advising firm in Los Angeles. She supplied this list exclusively for *The College Finder*.

American U (DC)
Amherst C (MA)
Boston U (MA)
Brown U (RI)
Claremont-McKenna C (CA)
Columbia U (NY)
Drexel U (PA)
Emory U (GA)
Grinnell C (IA)
George Washington U (DC)
Harvard U (MA)
Ithaca C (NY)
Macalester C (MN)

Massachusetts, U of, Amherst
New York U
Northeastern U (MA)
Oberlin C (OH)
Pittsburgh, U of (PA)
Pomona C (CA)
Princeton U (NJ)
Rochester, U of (NY)
Southern California, U of
Tufts U (MA)
Tulane U (LA)
Williams C (MA)

The Experts' Choice: Colleges Right for the Undecided Student

Experts were asked to identify colleges where it's perfectly fine for a student to be undecided about areas of study or career.

Beloit C (WI)
Bennington C (VT)
Brown U (RI)
Clark U (MA)
Colorado C
Evergreen State C (WA)
Grinnell C (IA)
Hampshire C (MA)

Ithaca C (NY)
Macalester C (MN)
New College of Florida
Oberlin C (OH)
Occidental C (CA)
Redlands, U of (CA)
Sarah Lawrence C (NY)

VETERINARY SCHOOL PREPARATION

Colleges With Veterinary Medicine Schools

Auburn U (AL)
Calgary, U of (Canada)
California, U of, Davis
Colorado State U, Ft. Collins
Cornell U (NY)
Edinburgh, U of (United Kingdom)

Florida, U of
Georgia, U of
Glasgow, U of (United Kingdom)
Guelph, U of (Canada)
Illinois, U of, Urbana
Iowa State U

ACADEMICS

Kansas State U
Lincoln Memorial U (TN)
Louisiana State U, Baton Rouge
Massey U (New Zealand)
Melbourne, U of (Australia)
Michigan State U
Midwestern U (AZ)
Minnesota, U of, Twin Cities
Mississippi State U
Missouri, U of, Columbia
Montréal, Université de (Canada)
Murdoch U (Australia)
North Carolina State U
Ohio State U, Columbus
Oklahoma State U
Oregon State U
Pennsylvania, U of
Prince Edward Island, U of, Atlantic
  Veterinary C (Canada)
Purdue U (IN)
Queensland, U of (Australia)

Ross U (West Indies)
Royal Veterinary C, U of London (United
  Kingdom)
Saskatchewan, U of, Western C of
  Veterinary Medicine (Canada)
St. George's U (West Indies)
Sydney, U of (Australia)
Tennessee, U of
Texas A&M U, College Station
Tufts U (MA)
Tuskegee U (AL)
Universidad Nacional Autónoma de
  México
University C Dublin (Ireland)
Utrecht U (the Netherlands)
VetAgro Sup (France)
Virginia-Maryland C of Veterinary
  Medicine
Washington State U
Western U of Health Sciences (OR)
Wisconsin, U of, Madison

Source: Association of American Veterinary Medical Colleges

ACADEMIC OPPORTUNITIES/CHARACTERISTICS

Colleges With the Highest Four-Year Graduation Rates

Numbers show the average percentage of students who graduate within four years.

Boston C (MA): 100.00%
St. Mary's C (CA): 96.07%
Neumont U (UT): 93.30%
Olin C (MA): 93.15%
Pomona C (CA): 92.80%
Davidson C (NC): 92.24%
Webb Institute (NY): 91.67%
Haverford C (PA): 91.11%
Williams C (MA): 90.81%
Columbia U (NY): 90.02%
Vassar C (NY): 89.66%
Amherst C (MA): 89.64%
Yale U (CT): 89.64%
Carleton C (MN): 89.59%
Juilliard School (NY): 89.58%
Notre Dame, U of (IN): 89.55%
Hamilton C (NY): 89.53%
Bates C (ME): 89.37%
Colby C (ME): 89.29%
Holy Cross, C of the (MA): 89.00%

Swarthmore C (PA): 88.77%
Washington U (MO): 88.23%
Princeton U (NJ): 88.17%
U.S. Coast Guard Academy (CT):
  88.10%
Georgetown U (DC): 87.95%
Pennsylvania, U of: 87.91%
Chicago, U of (IL): 87.89%
Johns Hopkins U (MD): 87.86%
Bowdoin C (ME): 87.58%
Middlebury C (VT): 87.54%
Duke U (NC): 87.29%
Bucknell U (PA): 87.26%
Tufts U (MA): 87.15%
U.S. Naval Academy (MD): 86.99%
Vanderbilt U (TN): 86.65%
Dartmouth C (NH): 86.62%
Cornell U (NY): 86.61%
Colgate U (NY): 86.56%

Source: Wintergreen Orchard House

Steven R. Antonoff

Colleges With the Highest Six-Year Graduation Rates

Numbers show the percentage of students who graduate within six years.

American Baptist C (TN): 100%
Norfolk State U (VA): 100%
Olin C (MA): 99%
North Florida, U of: 98%
Yale U (CT): 98%
Columbia U (NY): 97%
Harvard U (MA): 97%
Juilliard School (NY): 97%
Princeton U (NJ): 97%
Amherst C (MA): 96%
Pennsylvania, U of: 96%
Pomona C (CA): 96%
Webb Institute (NY): 96%
Williams C (MA): 96%
Dartmouth C (NH): 95%
Davidson C (NC): 95%
Notre Dame, U of (IN): 95%
Stanford U (CA): 95%
Brown U (RI): 94%
Duke U (NC): 94%

Middlebury C (VT): 94%
Vassar C (NY): 94%
Washington U (MO): 94%
Bates C (ME): 93%
Bowdoin C (ME): 93%
California Institute of Technology: 93%
Chicago, U of (IL): 93%
Claremont McKenna C (CA): 93%
Colby C (ME): 93%
Cornell U (NY): 93%
Hamilton C (NY): 93%
Haverford C (PA): 93%
Johns Hopkins U (MD): 93%
Massachusetts Institute of Technology: 93%
Neumont U (UT): 93%
Swarthmore C (PA): 93%
Vanderbilt U (TN): 93%
Virginia, U of: 93%
Georgetown U (DC): 92%

Source: Wintergreen Orchard House

Colleges With High Retention Rates

These are colleges where a high percentage of students stay on after freshman year rather than transfer to a different school.

Amherst C (MA)
Barnard C (NY)
Bowdoin C (ME)
Brown U (RI)
California Institute of Technology
California, U of, Berkeley
Chicago, U of (IL)
Claremont McKenna C (CA)
Colorado C
Columbia U (NY)
Cornell U (NY)
Dartmouth C (NH)
Duke U (NC)
Harvard U (MA)
Harvey Mudd C (CA)
Haverford C (PA)
Johns Hopkins U (MD)
Massachusetts Institute of Technology
Michigan, U of, Ann Arbor

Middlebury C (VT)
Notre Dame, U of (IN)
Pennsylvania, U of
Pomona C (CA)
Princeton U (NJ)
Rice U (TX)
Rochester, U of (NY)
Soka U of America (CA)
Stanford U (CA)
Swarthmore C (PA)
Tufts U (MA)
U.S. Naval Academy (MD)
Vanderbilt U (TN)
Virginia, U of
Washington & Lee U (VA)
Wellesley C (MA)
Williams C (MA)
Worcester Polytechnic Institute (MA)
Yale U (CT)

Source: Wintergreen Orchard House

Excellence in the First-Year College Experience

The John N. Gardner Institute for Excellence in Undergraduate Education recognized the followir colleges and universities as exemplifying best practices in the first year of college according to th following five criteria:

- Evidence of an intentional, comprehensive approach to the first year that is appropriate to the institution's type
- Evidence of assessment of the various initiatives that constitute this approach
- Evidence of broad impact on significant numbers of first-year students, including, but not limited to, special student sub-populations
- Strong administrative support for first-year initiatives, evidence of institutionalization, and durability over time
- Involvement of a wide range of faculty, student affairs professionals, academic administrators, and other constituent groups

Community Colleges:
Denver, Community C of (CO)
LaGuardia Community C (NY)
Four-Year Colleges and Universities (Enrollment Under 2,000):
Eckerd C (FL)
Kalamazoo C (MI)

Four-Year Colleges and Universities (Enrollment 2,000–5,000):
Drury U (MO)
Elon U (NC)
U.S. Military Academy (NY)

Four-Year Colleges and Universities (Enrollment 5,000–10,000):
New York, City U of, Lehman
Texas A&M U, Corpus Christi

Four-Year Universities (Enrollment 10,000–20,000):
Appalachian State U (NC)
Ball State U (IN)

Four-Year Universities (Enrollment Over 20,000):
Indiana U-Purdue U Indianapolis
South Carolina, U of, Columbia

Source: John N. Gardner Institute for Excellence in Undergraduate Education (jngi.org)

The Experts' Choice: Smaller Colleges Offering Students Plenty of Personal Attention

Experts were reminded that most smaller colleges have accessible teachers. Among all small colleges, these were identified as institutions where students receive close personal attention from professors.

Belmont Abbey C (NC)
Capital U (OH)
Central Piedmont Community C (NC)
Dickinson C (PA)
Fayetteville State U (NC)
Francis Marion U (SC)

Steven R. Antonoff

Marlboro C (VT)
Quinnipiac U (CT)
Swarthmore C (PA)
Western New England U (MA)
Winthrop U (SC)

The Experts' Choice: Colleges Where Students Are Decision-Makers

Experts were asked to pick schools that go the extra mile to allow students to govern and/or be involved in decision-making.

Antioch C (OH)
Bryn Mawr C (PA)
California Polytechnic State U, San Luis Obispo
Guilford C (NC)
Haverford C (PA)
Marlboro C (VT)
Pitzer C (CA)
Rice U (TX)
Swarthmore C (PA)
Whittier C (CA)

The Experts' Choice: Colleges Offering Stellar Undergraduate Research Opportunities

Experts singled out these colleges for providing outstanding undergraduate research opportunities.

Beloit C (WI)
Brandeis U (MA)
California Institute of Technology
California, U of, Los Angeles
Carnegie Mellon U (PA)
Case Western Reserve U (OH)
Chicago, U of (IL)
Clark U (MA)
Coe C (IA)
Cornell U (NY)
Duke U (NC)
Emory U (GA)
Georgia Institute of Technology
Harvard U (MA)
Hendrix C (AR)
Hope C (MI)
Johns Hopkins U (MD)**
Massachusetts Institute of Technology
Michigan, U of, Ann Arbor
Missouri, U of, Columbia
North Carolina State U
Northeastern U (MA)

Occidental C (CA)
Pitzer C (CA)
Pomona C (CA)
Princeton U (NJ)
Purdue U (IN)
Rensselaer Polytechnic Institute (NY)
Rhodes C (TN)
Rice U (TX)**
Richmond, U of (VA)
Rochester, U of (NY)
Stanford U (CA)
Swarthmore C (PA)
Tufts U (MA)
Tulane U (LA)
Washington U (MO)
Washington, U of
Wisconsin, U of, Madison
Wooster, C of (OH)*

*The Top Choice
**The Second Choice (tie)

Honors Colleges: Making a Large School Seem Smaller

Honors colleges come in a variety of shapes and sizes. Most provide enrichment for bright and determined students. Some offer special classes and resources. At certain schools, students apply to participate in these programs, whereas other colleges select students following a review of their application materials. The following represent colleges and universities with well-respected honors programs or honors colleges.

Alabama, U of, Tuscaloosa, Honors College
Arizona State U, Barrett Honors College
Arizona, U of, Honors College
Arkansas, U of, Fayetteville, Honors College
Arkansas, U of, Pine Bluff, Blakely Honors College
Auburn U (AL), Honors College
California, U of, Irvine, Campus-Wide Honors Program
California, U of, Los Angeles, Honors Program
Central Arkansas, U of, Schedler Honors College
Central Florida, U of, Burnett Honors College
Central Missouri State U, Honors College
Clemson U (SC), Calhoun Honors College
Colorado State U, Honors Program
Connecticut, U of, Honors Program
Delaware, U of, Honors Program
Florida Atlantic U, Honors College
Florida International U, Honors College
Florida State U, Honors Program
Florida, U of, Honors Program
Georgia, U of, Honors Program
Houston, U of (TX), Honors Program
Illinois, U of, Urbana, Campus Honors Program
Indiana U Bloomington, Hutton Honors College
Iowa State U, Honors Program
Iowa, U of, Honors Program
Kansas, U of, Honors Program
Kent State U (OH), Honors College
Kentucky, U of, Honors Program
Louisiana State U, Honors College
Maine, U of, Honors College
Maryland, U of, Baltimore County, Honors College
Massachusetts, U of, Amherst, Commonwealth Honors College
Miami U (OH), Honors Program
Michigan State U, Honors College
Michigan, U of, Ann Arbor, Literature, Science, and the Arts Honors Program
Minnesota, U of, Twin Cities, Honors Program
Mississippi, U of, Sally McDonnell Barksdale Honors College
Missouri, U of, Honors College
Montana, U of, Davidson Honors College
Nevada, U of, Las Vegas, Honors College
New Hampshire, U of, Honors Program
New Mexico, U of, Albuquerque, Honors College
New York, State U of, Albany, Honors College
New York, State U of, Binghamton, Scholars Program
New York, State U of, Buffalo, Honors College
North Carolina State U, Honors Program

North Carolina, U of, Chapel Hill, Honors Carolina
Ohio State U, Columbus, Honors & Scholars Program
Ohio U, Honors Tutorial College
Oklahoma State U, Honors College
Oklahoma, U of, Honors College
Old Dominion U (VA) Honors College
Oregon State U, Honors College
Oregon, U of, Clark Honors College
Pennsylvania State U, University Park, Schreyer Honors College
Purdue U (IN), Honors Program
Rhode Island, U of, Honors Program
Rutgers U (NJ), School of Arts & Sciences Honors Program
South Carolina, U of, Honors College
South Dakota State U, Fishback Honors College
South Florida, U of, Honors College
Southeast Missouri State U, Stephens Honors Program
Temple U (PA), Honors Program
Tennessee, U of, Knoxville, Chancellor's Honors Program, Haslam Scholars Program
Texas A&M U, Honors Program
Texas Tech U, Honors College
Texas, U of, Arlington, Honors College
Texas, U of, Austin, variety of honors programs within the various disciplines
Texas, U of, Dallas, Honors College
Texas, U of, San Antonio, Honors College
Tulane U (LA), Honors Program
Utah, U of, Honors College
Vermont, U of, Honors College
Virginia Polytechnic Institute & State U, University Honors is transitioning to an Honors College
Virginia, U of, Echols Scholars Program
Washington State U, Honors College
Washington, U of, Seattle, Honors Program
West Florida, U of, Kugelman Honors Program
West Georgia, U of, Honors College
Western Carolina U, Honors College
Western Michigan U, Lee Honors College
Wisconsin, U of, Madison, Letters & Science Honors Program

Source: *College Finder* research and John Willingham's *A Review of Fifty Public University Honors Programs* (2014), Public University Press, Charleston, SC

The Experts' Choice: Great Honors Colleges

Experts were asked to name public universities with exceptional honors colleges.

Alabama, U of, Tuscaloosa
Arizona State U
Arizona, U of
Colorado, U of, Boulder
Connecticut, U of
Delaware, U of
Florida, U of
Georgia, U of
Indiana U Bloomington

Iowa State U
James Madison U (VA)
Maryland, U of
Massachusetts, U of, Amherst
Michigan, U of, Ann Arbor**
Mississippi, U of
North Carolina, U of, Chapel Hill
Ohio State U
Oregon State U

Oregon, U of
Pennsylvania State U, University Park*
Pittsburgh, U of (PA)
South Carolina, U of
Texas, U of, Austin
Vermont, U of

Virginia, U of
Washington, U of, Seattle
Wisconsin, U of

*The Top Choice
**The Second Choice

The Experts' Choice: Colleges Where Double-Majoring Is Common

Experts were asked to identify colleges where having two majors is common and easy to do.

Allegheny C (PA)
Amherst C (MA)
Beloit C (WI)
Boston U (MA)
Bowdoin C (ME)
Brown U (RI)**
California, U of, Los Angeles
Case Western Reserve U (OH)
Chapman U (CA)
Davidson C (NC)
Duke U (NC)
Emory U (GA)
Goucher C (MD)
Hamilton C (NY)
Harvard U (MA)
Idaho, C of
Lawrence U (WI)
Michigan, U of, Ann Arbor

New York U
Northwestern U (IL)
Notre Dame, U of (IN)
Oberlin C (OH)
Rice U (TX)
Richmond, U of (VA)
Rochester, U of (NY)
Southern California, U of
St. Olaf C (MN)
Vanderbilt U (TN)
Vassar C (NY)
Washington U (MO)*
Williams C (MA)
Wooster, C of (OH)

*The Top Choice
**The Second Choice

The Experts' Choice: Are A's Really A's?

Experts were asked to list colleges with notable grade inflation, i.e., a trend of awarding higher grades than would have been awarded for similar work or exam results in the past. According to the online publication *Inside Higher Ed,* "The most common grade is A—at all kinds of colleges."

Bard C (NY)
Bates C (ME)
Boston U (MA)
Bowdoin C (ME)
California Institute of Technology
California, U of, Berkeley
California, U of, Davis
Carnegie Mellon U (PA)
Chicago, U of (IL)
Colorado C
Columbia U (NY)
Cornell U (NY)
Creighton U (NE)
Davidson C (NC)

Duke U (NC)
Furman U (SC)
Holy Cross, C of the (MA)
Johns Hopkins U (MD)
Kenyon C (OH)
Knox C (IL)
Macalester C (MN)
Massachusetts Institute of Technology
Michigan, U of, Ann Arbor
Oberlin C (OH)
Pennsylvania, U of
Pomona C (CA)
Princeton U (NJ)
Purdue U (IN)

Reed C (OR)
Rensselaer Polytechnic Institute (NY)
Roanoke C (VA)
Rochester, U of (NY)
St. Anselm C (NH)
St. John's U (MN)
Stanford U (CA)
Swarthmore C (PA)
U.S. Air Force Academy (CO)

U.S. Military Academy (NY)
U.S. Naval Academy (MD)
Vanderbilt U (TN)
Virginia, U of
Wake Forest U (NC)
Washington U (MO)
Wellesley C (MA)
Wesleyan U (CT)
William & Mary, C of (VA)

No Core Class Requirements

Some colleges have a series of required classes that all students must take in order to graduate. This is usually referred to as a "core curriculum." On the opposite end of the spectrum, these colleges are among those that have no specific requirements for graduation. As such, students have more choice in the classes they take.

Amherst C (MA)
Brown U (RI)
Grinnell C (IA)
Hamilton C (NY)
Hampshire C (MA)
Rochester, U of (NY)
Sarah Lawrence C (NY)
Vassar C (NY)

The Experts' Choice: Colleges With Few Course Requirements

Experts were asked for colleges that require students to take few, if any, core classes.

Amherst C (MA)
Bennington C (VT)
Brown U (RI)*
Columbia U (NY)
Hamilton C (NY)
Hampshire C (MA)
Rochester, U of (NY)
Smith C (MA)
Wesleyan U (CT)

*The Top Choice

Colleges With Comprehensive Course Requirements

These colleges have comprehensive general education requirements for graduation. In other words, at these colleges students may have more required classes as all students are asked to take courses in fields such as composition, mathematics, science, and foreign language.

Baylor U (TX)
Bluefield C (VA)
Boston C (MA)
California Polytechnic State U, San Luis

Obispo
Charleston, C of (SC)
Christopher Newport U (VA)
Citadel, The (SC)

Clark Atlanta U (GA)
Colorado Christian U
Columbia C (NY)
Dallas, U of (TX)
Davis & Elkins C (WV)
Gardner-Webb U (NC)
Georgia Southern U
Georgia, U of
Hillsdale C (MI)
Houston Baptist U (TX)
Kennesaw State U (GA)
McKendree U (IL)
Morehouse C (GA)
Pepperdine U (CA)

Point Loma Nazarene U (CA)
Regent U (VA)
Science & Arts, U of (OK)
Southwest Baptist U (MO)
St. Edward's U (TX)
St. John's C (MD) (NM)
Swarthmore C (PA)
Thomas Aquinas C (CA)
Thomas More C (KY)
U.S. Air Force Academy (CO)
U.S. Coast Guard Academy (CT)
U.S. Military Academy (NY)
Villanova U (PA)
Wellesley C (MA)

Source: *College Finder* research and whatwilltheylearn.com

The Experts' Choice: Colleges Committed to the Environment

Experts were asked to list colleges committed to the environment in one or more of these ways: academic offerings, environmental initiatives, campus policies, and student activities.

Most Notable

Atlantic, C of the (ME)
British Columbia, U of (Canada)
Cornell U (NY)
Dickinson C (PA)
Green Mountain C (VT)
Harvard U (MA)
Middlebury C (VT)

Notable

Allegheny C (PA)
American U (DC)
Amherst C (MA)
Aquinas C (MI)
Arizona State U
Bowdoin C (ME)
Brown U (RI)
Calgary, U of (Canada)
California Institute of Technology
California State U, Chico
California, U of, Davis
California, U of, San Diego
California, U of, Santa Barbara
Carleton C (MN)
Colorado C

Colorado State U, Ft. Collins
Dartmouth C (NH)
Denver, U of (CO)
Earlham C (IN)
EARTH U (Costa Rica)
Evergreen State C (WA)
Furman U (SC)
Georgia Institute of Technology
Georgia, U of
Glasgow, U of (United Kingdom)
Goucher C (MD)
Grand Valley State U (MI)
Leeds U (United Kingdom)
Lewis & Clark C (OR)
Loyola U (IL)
Luther C (IA)
Maryland, U of, College Park
New York, State U of, Stony Brook
Oberlin C (OH)
Pomona C (CA)
Portland State U (OR)
Tufts U (MA)
Vermont, U of
Washington, U of
Willamette U (OR)
Yale U (CT)

Colleges in the EcoLeague

Alaska Pacific U
Atlantic, C of the (ME)
Dickinson C (PA)

Green Mountain C (VT)
Northland C (WI)
Prescott C (AZ)

Source: EcoLeague (ecoleague.org)

Sun Grant Universities

The Sun Grant Initiative, established in 2008, is an association composed of land-grant universities and national laboratories that aim to develop better bio-based fuels and products through the use of farming stock from America's rural communities. There are five regional centers that lead the Sun Grant Initiative and one subcenter.

Hawaii, U of, Manoa (subcenter)
Oklahoma State U
Oregon State U
Pennsylvania State U, University Park
South Dakota State U
Tennessee, U of, Knoxville

Source: Sun Grant Initiative (sungrant.org)

Sea Grant Schools

The Sea Grant Directors lead the 33 Sea Grant programs based at top universities in every coastal and Great Lakes state, Puerto Rico, and Guam, working to put the robust intellectual capacity in place at these universities to bear on important societal problems. They coordinate program activities, setting local, regional, and national priorities and work as part of a national network to help citizens and businesses understand, conserve, and better utilize America's coastal, ocean, and Great Lakes resources.

Alaska, U of, Fairbanks
California, U of, San Diego
Connecticut, U of
Delaware, U of
Florida, U of
Georgia, U of
Guam, U of
Hawaii, U of, Manoa
Illinois, U of, Urbana
Louisiana State U, Baton Rouge
Maine, U of
Maryland, U of, College Park
Massachusetts Institute of Technology
Michigan, U of, Ann Arbor
Minnesota, U of, Twin Cities
Mississippi, U of

New Hampshire, U of
North Carolina State U
Ohio State U, Columbus
Oregon State U
Pennsylvania State U, University Park
Puerto Rico, U of
Rhode Island, U of
Southern California, U of
Texas A&M U, College Station
Vermont, U of
Virginia Institute of Marine Science
Washington, U of
Wisconsin, U of, Madison
Woods Hole Oceanographic Institute (MA)

Source: Sea Grant Colleges, National Oceanic and Atmospheric Administration (seagrant.noaa.gov)

Great Books Colleges

A "Great Book," in this context, is a work that has had significance for the first generation of readers and for readers in succeeding years. A Great Book can be in any field such as theology, philosophy, history, fiction, poetry, political science, or science. Although students at most colleges read many of the classics, the following colleges have optional or required programs emphasizing their use.

- Baylor U (TX): The Great Texts program focuses on foundational works from antiquity to the present.
- Benedictine C (KS): Great Books curriculum is an option for students to fulfill general education requirements.
- Biola U (CA): The Torrey Honors Institute focuses on teaching the Great Books and exploring ideas through Socratic discussion.
- Boston U (MA): An elective core curriculum is based on the Great Books.
- Brock U (Canada): The Liberal Studies Program is oriented toward the Great Books.
- Chicago, U of (IL): The curriculum consists of a four-year sequence of readings from the Great Books.
- Christendom C (VA): The core curriculum is based on the Great Books.
- Clemson U (SC): Great Works of Western Civilization is an undergraduate minor.
- Columbia U (NY): Masterpieces of Western Literature and Philosophy is a yearlong course.
- Concordia U (Canada): This liberal arts college focuses on the Great Books.
- Dallas, U of (TX): Constantin College of Liberal Arts core curriculum offers a comprehensive Great Books curriculum.
- East Carolina U (NC): Thomas Harriot College of Arts and Sciences sponsors an interdisciplinary program in the Great Books.
- Eastern U (PA): Templeton Honors College has a Great Books core.
- Faulkner U (AL): Great Books Honors provides an honors track that integrates with each undergraduate degree program.
- Franciscan U of Steubenville (OH): The Honors Program is centered on the close reading and discussion of the Great Books.
- Gutenberg C (OR): The College features a broad-based Great Books curriculum.
- Hillsdale C (MI): The core curriculum includes Great Books courses.
- Kansas State U: The University offers a primary texts certificate.
- Kentucky State U: The Great Books are a key component of the curriculum in the Whitney Young School of Honors and Liberal Studies.
- Lawrence U (WI): The freshman studies program focuses on the Great Books.
- Lynchburg C (VA): The Lynchburg College Symposium Readings Program revolves around the Great Books.
- Malaspina U (Canada): The liberal studies program focuses on the Great Books.
- Mercer U (GA): The Great Books program is one of two general education tracks in the College of Liberal Arts.
- Michigan, U of: With rare exceptions, first-year honor students are required to take a Great Books course in each semester.
- Middle Tennessee State U: A Great Books minor is available.
- New St. Andrews C (ID): The curriculum is related to the classics and Great Books.
- North Park U (IL): A two-semester chronological program is available to honors students.
- North Texas, U of: The Great Books program is an interdisciplinary major in the college of arts and sciences.
- Northeast Catholic C (NH): The Great Books form the foundation for all courses, in both core studies and individual majors.

- Northwestern State U (LA): The Louisiana Scholars College combines Great Books–based courses with other offerings.
- Notre Dame, U of (IN): The Program of Liberal Studies is a three-year, prescribed sequence of seminars and specialized courses or tutorials anchored in the Western and Catholic traditions.
- Ohio Wesleyan U: Offered through the classics major, Ohio Wesleyan's program focuses on classics of Greek and Roman thought and literature.
- Pepperdine U (CA): Seaver College offers the Great Books colloquium as a four-course sequence on masterpieces of Western civilization.
- Princeton U (NJ): The Great Books are part of the program of freshman seminars in the residential colleges.
- Quest U (Canada): The required first-year core includes many features of a classic Great Books approach.
- San Francisco, U of (CA): The Saint Ignatius Institute offers "rigorous academics rooted in the Great Books."
- Shimer C (IL): One of the more extensive Great Books colleges, Shimer uses original source readings rather than textbooks.
- Southern Virginia U: The College offers a comprehensive liberal arts education based on the Great Books.
- St. Anselm C (NH): A major is offered in liberal studies in the Great Books.
- St. John's C (MD) (NM): The model of the Great Books colleges, St. John's offers a four-year, non-elective curriculum in which students read, discuss, and write about the seminal works that have shaped the world.
- St. Mary's C (CA): The Integral Liberal Arts Program includes a Great Books emphasis.
- St. Olaf C (MN): The Great Conversation is an integrated sequence of five courses taken over two years.
- Temple U (PA): The Intellectual Heritage Program is a group of foundation courses required for students in the college of arts and sciences.
- Texas, U of, Austin: The Thomas Jefferson Center for Core Ideas and Texts offers serious study of original writings and in collaboration with the Liberal Arts Honors Humanities Program offers a major in the Great Books
- Thomas Aquinas C (CA): A full Great Books curriculum is in place, with no majors or minors, no electives, and no specializations.
- Thomas More C (NH): All students take a six-hour humanities course through the four years. Much of the learning is based on the Great Books, and students also are required to study Latin or Greek.
- Wesleyan U (CT): The College of Letters is an interdisciplinary major program for the study of Western literature, history, and philosophy. It has the Great Books as its core.
- Whitman C (WA): The General Studies Program is a two-semester exploration of the formation and transformation of some Western worldviews using the Great Books.
- Wisconsin, U of, Milwaukee: Through the College of Letters & Science, the University offers a certificate program grounded in the Great Books.
- Wyoming Catholic C: The curriculum is built around the Great Books, reflecting a philosophy that students should learn directly from the greatest thinkers.

Consortium for Innovative Environments in Learning

The colleges and universities listed below are members of the Consortium for Innovative Environments in Learning. According to the consortium, the 12 member schools are "deeply and richly student-centered in our practice. Our commitment is to discover the best means to produce engaged life-long learners and thoughtful citizens. Constantly seeking for authentic teaching, assessment, interdisciplinary, and experiential learning techniques, we've come together to learn from each other and maximize our impact on U.S. higher education."

Alverno C (WI)	New College of Florida
Berea C (KY)	New York U, Gallatin School of
Daemen C (NY)	Individualized Study
Evergreen State C (WA)	Pitzer C (CA)
George Mason U, New Century C (VA)	Prescott C (AZ)
Hampshire C (MA)	Stockton U (NJ)
Johnson C. Smith U (NC)	Western Washington U, Fairhaven C
Marlboro C (VT)	

Source: Consortium for Innovative Environments in Learning (cielearn.org)

Colleges With Innovative Academic Programs

Many schools have special features, but these colleges stand out for their atypical and/or nontraditional approaches to undergraduate education.

- Alverno C (WI): Alverno offers a competency-based curriculum and doesn't hand out traditional grades but instead uses a narrative transcript as a way of assessing students.
- Amherst C (MA): Amherst has no core curriculum or distribution requirements. First-year students are required to take an interdisciplinary seminar designed to stimulate "critical thinking and active learning at the college level."
- Atlantic, C of the (ME): In order to prepare its students to "make a difference in the world," the College offers interdisciplinary classes and independent study projects. Seniors must produce an original project considered the capstone of their college experience.
- Bard C (NY): The "pillars" of a Bard education are the yearlong first-year seminars that prepare students for rigorous intellectual exploration, sophomore year's moderation (i.e., a self-exploration as students transition to the Upper College), and an original, focused senior project.
- Bennington C (VT): Through the Plan Process, Bennington students specify what they want to study and how they intend to study it. In addition, students annually undertake a seven-week Field Work Term where, with help from the College, they pursue jobs and internships in their field of interest.
- Brown U (RI): With no curriculum requirements, Brown provides an open learning environment in which students define liberal education for themselves.
- California, U of, San Diego: Under UCSD's undergraduate college system, each college has its own programmatic theme, curricular requirements, and extracurricular activities. With this system, UCSD combines the intimacy of a small liberal arts college with the resources of a large research university.
- California, U of, Santa Barbara: A "graduate school for undergraduates," the College of Creative Studies offers select students innovative classes and one-on-one assistance that culminates in each participant producing a body of original work in the arts and sciences.
- California, U of, Santa Cruz: On enrollment, students are affiliated with one of 10 colleges that provide academic support and student activities. Performance evaluations are a part of the UC Santa Cruz grading system.
- Chicago, U of (IL): Chicago is noted for its emphasis on interdisciplinary education, critical thinking, and discussion of classic texts.
- Clarkson U (NY): The Clarkson School, an interdisciplinary program for high school seniors, enables students to obtain their high school diploma while finishing their first year of college.

- Dallas, U of (TX): UD has an intensive, integrated two-year core curriculum, and student participation in study abroad programs ranks among the highest in the nation.
- Deep Springs C (CA): An all-male two-year college that is tuition-free and very selective in admission, Deep Springs is perhaps the most unusual college in the U.S. The total enrollment numbers about 25 students, all working and living together on a cattle ranch in California's high desert.
- Eugene Lang C (NY): At this institution—whose formal name is Eugene Lang College The New School for Liberal Arts—all courses are seminars, integrated interdisciplinary learning is emphasized, and the curriculum is student-directed.
- Evergreen State C (WA): Evergreen's interdisciplinary learning contracts allow students to explore a subject at an advanced level, working closely with a faculty or staff sponsor.
- Goddard C (VT): In Goddard's low-residency model of education, students spend eight days on campus followed by 16 weeks of self-reflection and independent work with an advisor.
- Green Mountain C (VT): GMC's environmental focus is exemplified by its adventure programming and the Farm and Food Project, which both provide hands-on learning.
- Grinnell C (IA): Students design their own curriculum. The only required course is the first-year tutorial designed to expand students' writing, critical thinking, analysis, discussion, and oral presentation skills. For their tutorial, first-year students can choose from more than 35 topics.
- Hamilton C (NY): The College's open curriculum allows students to zero in on their passions. "Proseminars," small classes that provide interaction and collaboration with faculty and other students, are designed to promote student writing and critical thinking. A recently adopted requirement specifies that "all concentrations, or majors, feature relevant, mandatory course work on diversity."
- Hampshire C (MA): Hampshire's Divisional System offers students a framework for taking responsibility for their own learning and customizing their curriculum. Rather than declare a major, students build a concentration, choosing courses from among five interdisciplinary schools.
- Indiana U of Pennsylvania: Robert Cook Honors College features an integrated, cross-disciplinary curriculum of small core classes (with no tests) as well as opportunities for research, travel, and internships. To promote friendships and provide support for one another, all first-year Honors College students live together in a single residence hall.
- Kalamazoo C (MI): The *K-Plan* comprises four components: depth and breadth in the liberal arts, learning through doing, international and intercultural exposure, and independent scholarship.
- Long Island U (NY): At LIU's Global College, students live and learn in at least eight countries and then return to New York City for a final semester before receiving their bachelor's degree in global studies.
- Maharishi U of Management (IA): Oriented around a "consciousness-based curriculum" in which students are immersed in one full-time course a month, the University promotes active learning, transcendental meditation, and self-exploration and inner growth.
- Marlboro C (VT): Each student completes a self-designed Plan of Concentration that explores interdisciplinary subjects, incorporates tutorials and consistent faculty advising, and culminates in a major work of scholarship.
- Miami U (OH): An interdisciplinary option in the College of Arts and Sciences, the Western Program permits students to create their own major and is home to the Compass Living and Learning Community.
- Naropa U (CO): Based in the Buddhist tradition, this nonsectarian school encourages students to choose from a host of "curated majors" or create their own while expanding their learning through internships, service projects, global study, and creative projects.
- New College of Florida: New College of Florida, the state's honors college for the liberal arts, features academic learning contracts, tutorials, independent study, and a senior thesis.

ACADEMICS

- New York U: At the Gallatin School of Individualized Study, an independent interdisciplinary college within NYU, students create their own learning through seminars, tutorials, internships, and global opportunities.
- Oberlin C (OH): In addition to a curriculum exploration requirement encouraging students to broaden their interests, Oberlin requires that students demonstrate writing ability as well as quantitative and formal reasoning and take three courses with a cultural diversity designation. The Experimental College, both a student-run organization and a college department, sponsors courses taught by any member of the Oberlin community, whether faculty, staff, student, or resident.
- Pitzer C (CA): For Pitzer students, an interdisciplinary education means not just studying a variety of subjects but creating an individualized, self-directed program that incorporates learning outside the classroom.
- Prescott C (AZ): The focus at Prescott is on experiential education, collaborative learning, and student-designed study where grades are optional and narrative evaluations assess growth.
- Quest U (Canada): Quest operates on a block plan (i.e., students take one course at a time) so that an area of interest can be thoroughly explored. The flexibility of the block plan also facilitates experiential learning in environments outside the classroom.
- Redlands, U of (CA): The Johnston Center for Individualized Instruction allows students to shape their education, study abroad, connect with real-world issues, co-teach with a professor, and enjoy a community of like-minded scholars pursuing their individual interests as they support each other.
- Reed C (OR): Often characterized as one of the most intellectual colleges in the nation, Reed provides conference-style classes where student can pursue interdisciplinary studies, dual degrees, and special programs.
- Ripon C (WI): To develop the skills that employers look for, Ripon's five-seminar Catalyst Curriculum builds students' writing, collaboration, qualitative reasoning, communication, and intercultural competence. A Four-Year Career and Development Plan helps ensure that graduates are ready to make the most of life after college.
- Rochester, U of (NY): In lieu of complicated general education requirements, the Rochester Curriculum allows students to choose two clusters of three-course sequences within a division or department.
- Sarah Lawrence C (NY): Hallmarks of academics at Sarah Lawrence include small seminars, biweekly student-faculty conferences, and study abroad and exchange programs.
- Smith C (MA): There are no distribution requirements but a range of majors as well as numerous concentrations that allow students to combine and connect different areas of interest.
- Soka U of America (CA): Special features include a student-centered curriculum, seminar classes, and study abroad for all students, which is included in tuition fees.
- St. John's C (MD) (NM): St. John's program is based on reading and discussing the major works of Western civilization. Students can study in either Santa Fe or Annapolis or alternate between the two.
- St. Lawrence U (NY): A "domestic study abroad program," the Adirondack Semester is held at an off-the-grid yurt village where students study nature and human relationships through such courses as nature writing, ecology, environmental philosophy, and land-use change.
- St. Olaf C (MN): The Center for Integrative Studies offers a path for students to design their own majors to meet individual learning interests and goals.

- Sterling C (VT): Every student has a job and everyone gets their hands dirty at Sterling, which is dedicated to educating stewards of the environment and is one of seven federally recognized Work Colleges.
- Swarthmore C (PA): Swarthmore features small seminar-style classes and an interdisciplinary curriculum, plus an Honors Program that emphasizes independent learning and dialogue with peers, faculty, and outside scholars.
- Thomas Aquinas C (CA): Eschewing traditional majors, the College offers a four-year interdisciplinary curriculum focusing on original writings of philosophers, historians, scientists, poets, and theologians. The Discussion Method in the Socratic tradition compels students to grapple with big ideas and contribute their voice to every class meeting.
- Thomas More C (NH): The College focuses on the classics and emphasizes individualized education. Sophomores spend a semester in Rome exploring all that the Eternal City has to offer.
- Truman State U (MO): In addition to choosing a major, students at this public liberal arts university participate in the Liberal Studies Program. Here they focus on essential skills for success, modes of inquiry into problems and issues of different academic disciplines, and interconnecting perspectives to better understand how disciplines relate to and influence each other.
- Unity C (ME): Unity calls itself "America's environmental college" and backs it up by offering 16 environmentally focused majors and a liberal arts curriculum centered on sustainability science.
- Vassar C (NY): Vassar offers nine multidisciplinary programs and six interdepartmental programs. The Ford Scholars Program brings together students and faculty in collaborative work in the social sciences and humanities. Students may study off campus at Vassar-sponsored locations abroad or at U.S. institutions through the Twelve College Exchange and other programs. Each year some 500 students take on internships locally or in New York City.
- Warren Wilson C (NC): The Triad—academics, work, and service—is the foundation of a Warren Wilson education and ensures that learning takes place inside and outside the classroom. An integrative study option provides what is essentially a design-your-own-major experience.
- Wesleyan U (CT): Known for the diversity of both its student body and curriculum, Wesleyan offers service learning so that students can apply classroom knowledge to the real world. To incorporate service learning in their courses, faculty can draw support and resources from the Allbritton Center.
- Western Washington U: The Fairhaven College of Interdisciplinary Studies provides small seminar-style courses, narrative evaluations in lieu of grades, interdisciplinary majors, close faculty advising, and opportunities for independent study and study abroad.
- Wheaton C (MA): Beyond its 47 majors and 59 minors, the College encourages students to explore connections and delve into international and diverse cultural issues through the Center for Global Education and the Marshall Center for Intercultural Learning, respectively.

The Experts' Choice: Colleges Integrating Technology Into the Academic Experience

Experts were asked for colleges that integrate technology into the academic experience.

California Institute of Technology
Carnegie Mellon U (PA)
Georgetown U (DC)
Massachusetts Institute of Technology*

Rochester Institute of Technology (NY)
Worcester Polytechnic Institute (MA)

*The Top Choice

The Experts' Choice: Colleges With Unique Science Programs

- ArtCenter C of Design (CA): World-class automotive design program
- California, U of, Irvine: Gaming The System and Game Culture and Technology
- Carnegie Mellon U (PA): Machine Learning Department is multidisciplinary and includes science as well as psychology and philosophy. The Robotics Institute includes majors and minors and over 1,000 faculty, staff, students, and visitors.
- École Polytechnique Féderale de Lausanne (Switzerland): Provides unusual opportunities, through 250 laboratories, to conduct personalized research.
- Florida State U, Panama City: Unique Advanced Science Diving Program, including the ability to study underwater crime scene investigation
- Imperial C London (United Kingdom): The Centre for Bio-Inspired Technology focuses on inventing and developing devices in fields such as health care.
- Louisiana State U, Baton Rouge: Planning for the Worst and Disaster Science and Management
- Massachusetts Institute of Technology: Ready for Launch and Aeronautics and Astronautics
- Ohio State U: Spy School and Security and Intelligence
- Olin C (MA): Academic culture is collaborative, interdisciplinary, and focused on a broad approach to engineering.
- Tufts U (MA): Intelligent Design and Engineering Psychology

The Experts' Choice: Unusual Majors

Some colleges feature unusual majors such as glassblowing and anthrozoology. Experts were asked to identify colleges with a fairly specialized major.

- Alfred U (NY): Ceramics, Glassblowing
- Appalachian State U (NC): Fermentation Science
- Atlantic, C of the (ME): Human Ecology (only major offered)
- Barnard C (NY): Dramaturgy
- Brown U (RI): Applied Mathematics
- California Polytechnic State U, San Luis Obispo: Viticulture and Enology
- California State U, Chico: Glassblowing
- California, U of, Davis: Viticulture and Enology
- Carroll C (MT): Anthrozoology
- Centre C (KY): Glassblowing
- Chapman C (CA): Screenwriting
- Clark U (MA): International Development and Social Change
- Columbia C Chicago (IL): Poetry
- Delaware Valley U (PA): Animal Biotechnology and Conservation
- Georgia, U of: Scientific Illustration
- Hartwick C (NY): Glassblowing
- High Point U (NC): Interior Design
- Illinois Wesleyan U: Arts Management
- Naropa U (CO): Jack Kerouac School of Disembodied Poetics

Steven R. Antonoff

- New Hampshire, U of: EcoGastronomy
- North Carolina State U: Poultry Science
- North Texas, U of: Digital Retailing
- Otis C of Art & Design (CA): Toy Design
- Pennsylvania State U, University Park: Petroleum Engineering
- Prescott C (AZ): Equine-Assisted Learning (graduate degree)
- Ringling C of Art & Design (FL): Game Art
- Rochester Institute of Technology (NY): Packaging Science
- Rochester, U of (NY): Archaeology, Technology, and Historical Structures
- South Florida, U of: Cybersecurity (graduate degree)
- St. Joseph's U (PA): Food Marketing
- Sterling C (KS): Sustainable Food Systems
- Texas, U of, San Antonio: Cybersecurity
- Southern California, U of: Music Industry
- Washington U (MO): Fashion Design
- Washington, U of, Seattle: Interaction Design
- Wisconsin, U of, River Falls: Equine Animal Science

Work, Service, and Learning Colleges

Work Colleges offer students enhanced learning opportunities by integrating work, learning, and service throughout their college experience. Students earn a valuable degree plus important life and professional skills.

Alice Lloyd C (KY)
Berea C (KY)
Blackburn C (IL)
Ecclesia C (AR)
Ozarks, C of the (MO)
Sterling C (VT)
Warren Wilson C (NC)

Source: Work Colleges Consortium (workcolleges.org)

Colleges Where Physical Work Is Common

These schools encourage or require students to work on campus as part of the college experience.

Alice Lloyd C (KY)
Berea C (KY)
Berry C (GA)
Blackburn C (IL)
Deep Springs C (CA)
Ecclesia C (AR)
Goddard C (VT)
Ozarks, C of the (MO)
Sterling C (VT)
Warren Wilson C (NC)

College Members of the National Student Exchange

The National Student Exchange (NSE) is a "network for inter-university exchange within the United States, Canada, Guam, Puerto Rico, and the U.S. Virgin Islands. Member institutions provide exchange opportunities for undergraduate students for whom an overseas experience is not appropriate, comfortable, or affordable. NSE offers study opportunities at diverse university settings and provides access to a wide range of courses and programs; field experiences, co-op, and internship options; and resident assistant, honors, and study abroad opportunities of its member campuses. Work completed while on exchange at the host campus is brought back to the home institution and credited to the student's degree program."

Adams State U (CO)
Alabama A&M U
Alabama State U
Alabama, U of, Birmingham
Alabama, U of, Tuscaloosa
Alaska, U of, Anchorage
Alaska, U of, Fairbanks
Alaska, U of, Southeast, Juneau
Arizona, U of
Bishop's U (Canada)
Boise State U (ID)
Bowie State U (MD)
Brandon U (Canada)
Bridgewater State U (MA)
Calgary, U of (Canada)
California Polytechnic State U, San Luis Obispo
California State U, Bakersfield
California State U, Chico
California State U, East Bay
California State U, Monterey Bay
California State U, Northridge
California State U, San Bernardino
California U (PA)
Cape Breton U (Canada)
Central Washington U
Cleveland State U (OH)
Colorado Mesa U
Colorado State U, Pueblo
Colorado, U of, Colorado Springs
Dakota State U (SD)
East Central U (OK)
Eastern Connecticut State U
Eastern Illinois U
Eastern Oregon U
Emporia State U (KS)
Florida International U
Ft. Hays State U (KS)
Ft. Lewis C (CO)
Georgia, U of
Guam, U of
Hawaii, U of, Hilo

Hawaii, U of, Manoa
Indiana U of Pennsylvania
Indiana U-Purdue U Ft. Wayne
Indiana U-Purdue U Indianapolis
InterAmerican U of Puerto Rico, Barranquitas
InterAmerican U of Puerto Rico, San German
Iowa State U
Jackson State U (MS)
Johnson State C (VT)
Keene State C (NH)
Kent State U (OH)
Kentucky, U of
Kutztown U (PA)
Lewis-Clark State C (ID)
Longwood U (VA)
Louisiana State U, Baton Rouge
Louisville, U of (KY)
Maine, U of, Farmington
Maine, U of, Presque Isle
Marshall U (WV)
Massachusetts C of Liberal Arts
Massachusetts, U of, Amherst
Massachusetts, U of, Boston
Memorial U, Newfoundland (Canada)
Michigan, U of, Flint
Minnesota State U, Mankato
Minnesota State U, Moorhead
Minnesota, U of, Morris
Minnesota, U of, Rochester
Minnesota, U of, Twin Cities
Mississippi State U
Missouri, U of, Columbia
Montana State U, Bozeman
Montana, U of
Montevallo, U of (AL)
Murray State U (KY)
Nebraska, U of, Kearney
Nevada, U of, Las Vegas
New C of Florida
New Hampshire, U of

New Jersey City U
New Jersey, C of
New Mexico State U
New Mexico, U of, Albuquerque
New Orleans, U of (LA)
New York U
New York, City U of, Queens C
New York, State U of, Plattsburg
New York, State U of, Binghamton
New York, State U of, Buffalo
New York, State U of, Potsdam
New York, State U of, Stony Brook
North Carolina Central U
North Carolina State U
North Dakota State U
North Texas, U of
Northern Arizona U
Northern British Columbia, U of
  (Canada)
Northern Colorado, U of
Northern Iowa, U of
Northwestern State U (LA)
Oakland U (MI)
Oklahoma State U
Oregon, U of
Philadelphia U (PA)
Plymouth State U (NH)
Polytechnic U (Puerto Rico)
Portland State U (OR)
Prairie View A&M U (TX)
Puerto Rico, U of, Bayamon
Puerto Rico, U of, Cayey
Puerto Rico, U of, Humacao
Puerto Rico, U of, Mayaquez
Puerto Rico, U of, Rico Piedras
Ramapo C (NJ)
Regina, U of (Canada)
Rhode Island C
Rhode Island, U of
Rutgers U, New Brunswick (NJ)
Salem State U (MA)
Sonoma State U (CA)
South Carolina State U
South Carolina, U of, Columbia

South Dakota State U
South Dakota, U of
Southern Connecticut State U
Southern Oregon U
Southern U (LA)
Southern Utah U
St. Mary's C (MD)
Texas State U, San Marcos
Texas, U of, Pan America
Texas, U of, San Antonio
Toledo, U of (OH)
Towson U (MD)
Universidad del Sagrado Corazon
  (Puerto Rico)
Université de Montréal (Canada)
Université du Quebec a Montreal
  (Canada)
Université de Sherbrooke (Canada)
Utah Valley U
Utah, U of
Virgin Islands, U of the, St. Croix
Virgin Islands, U of the, St. Thomas
Virginia State U
Washington, U of, Seattle
West Chester U (PA)
West Virginia U
Western Kentucky U
Western Oregon U
Western State Colorado U
Westfield State U (MA)
William Paterson U (NJ)
Winthrop U (SC)
Wisconsin, U of, Eau Claire
Wisconsin, U of, Green Bay
Wisconsin, U of, La Crosse
Wisconsin, U of, Oshkosh
Wisconsin, U of, Platteville
Wisconsin, U of, River Falls
Wisconsin, U of, Stout
Wisconsin, U of, Superior
Wisconsin, U of, Whitewater
Wichita State U (KS)
Worcester State U (MA)
Wyoming, U of

Source: National Student Exchange (nse.org)

UN Semester

Diplomats start here. These are among the colleges that allow students to attend classes at UN headquarters in New York City and spend time observing UN operations.

Alfred U (NY)
Austin C (TX)
Bentley U (MA)
Carroll U (WI)
Drew U (NJ)
Duke U (NC)
Florida Southern C
Gettysburg C (PA)
Hobart & William Smith C (NY)
Hofstra U (NY)
Illinois Wesleyan U
Immaculata U (PA)
Iowa, U of
King's C (PA)
Lycoming C (PA)
McDaniel C (MD)
Meredith C (NC)
Millikin U (IL)
Millsaps C (MS)
Minnesota, U of, Morris
Morningside C (IA)
Mt. Union, U of (OH)
Muskingum U (OH)
Nebraska Wesleyan U
Nebraska, U of, Lincoln
Nevada, U of, Las Vegas

New College of Florida
New Hampshire, U of
New York, State U of, New Paltz
North Central C (IL)
North Dakota State U
Occidental C (CA)
Point Loma Nazarene U (CA)
Randolph-Macon C (VA)
Rockford U (IL)
Rutgers U, New Brunswick (NJ)
Sacred Heart U (CT)
Salem C (NC)
Seton Hill U (PA)
Southern New Hampshire U
St. Augustine's U (NC)
Susquehanna U (PA)
Texas, U of, Dallas
Thiel C (PA)
Utica C (NY)
Valparaiso U (IN)
Wabash C (IN)
Washington State U
Westminster C (UT)
Whittier C (CA)
William Woods U (MO)
Wooster, C of (OH)

Source: Wintergreen Orchard House

Colleges With Phi Beta Kappa Chapters

Less than 10 percent of the nation's liberal arts colleges are members of Phi Beta Kappa, the nation's oldest and most respected undergraduate honors organization. Note, however, that some colleges have rejected the offer of Phi Beta Kappa membership. For example, Bryn Mawr College rejected a Phi Beta Kappa membership on the principles that "special societies based on grades run counter to the principle of the college," according to the dean of the undergraduate college. The date the chapter was established is listed.

Agnes Scott C (GA): 1926
Alabama, U of, Tuscaloosa: 1851
Albion C (MI): 1940
Alfred U (NY): 2004
Allegheny C (PA): 1902
Alma C (MI): 1980
American U (DC): 1944
Amherst C (MA): 1853
Arizona State U: 1973
Arizona, U of: 1932

Arkansas, U of, Fayetteville: 1932
Auburn U (AL): 2001
Augustana C (IL): 1950
Austin C (TX): 2001
Barnard C (NY): 1901
Bates C (ME): 1917
Baylor U (TX): 1977
Beloit C (WI): 1911
Birmingham-Southern C (AL): 1937
Boston C (MA): 1971

Boston U (MA): 1899
Bowdoin C (ME): 1825
Bowling Green State U (OH): 1983
Brandeis U (MA): 1962
Brown U (RI): 1830
Bucknell U (PA): 1940
California State U, Long Beach: 1977
California, U of, Berkeley: 1898
California, U of, Davis: 1968
California, U of, Irvine: 1974
California, U of, Los Angeles: 1930
California, U of, Riverside: 1965
California, U of, San Diego: 1977
California, U of, Santa Barbara: 1968
California, U of, Santa Cruz: 1986
Carleton C (MN): 1914
Carnegie Mellon U (PA): 1995
Case Western Reserve U (OH): 1847
Catholic U of America (DC): 1941
Centre C (KY): 1971
Chatham U (PA): 1962
Chicago, U of (IL): 1899
Cincinnati, U of (OH): 1899
Claremont McKenna C (CA): 1983
Clark U (MA): 1953
Clemson U (SC): 2006
Coe C (IA): 1949
Colby C (ME): 1896
Colgate U (NY): 1878
Colorado C: 1904
Colorado State U, Ft. Collins: 1973
Colorado, U of, Boulder: 1904
Columbia U (NY): 1869
Connecticut C: 1935
Connecticut, U of: 1956
Cornell C (IA): 1923
Cornell U (NY): 1882
Dallas, U of (TX): 1989
Dartmouth C (NH): 1787
Davidson C (NC): 1923
Delaware, U of: 1956
Denison U (OH): 1911
Denver, U of (CO): 1940
DePauw U (IN): 1889
Dickinson C (PA): 1887
Drake U (IA): 1923
Drew U (NJ): 1980
Duke U (NC): 1920
Earlham C (IN): 1965
Eckerd C (FL): 2004
Elmira C (NY): 1940
Emory U (GA): 1929
Fairfield U (CT): 1995
Fisk U (TN): 1953
Florida International U: 2001

Florida State U: 1935
Florida, U of: 1938
Fordham U (NY): 1962
Franklin & Marshall C (PA): 1908
Furman U (SC): 1973
George Washington U (DC): 1938
Georgetown U (DC): 1965
Georgia, U of: 1914
Gettysburg C (PA): 1923
Goucher C (MD): 1905
Grinnell C (IA): 1908
Gustavus Adolphus C (MN): 1983
Hamilton C (NY): 1870
Hamline U (MN): 1974
Hampden-Sydney C (VA): 1949
Harvard U (MA): 1781
Haverford C (PA): 1899
Hendrix C (AR): 1998
Hiram C (OH): 1971
Hobart & William Smith C (NY): 1871
Hofstra U (NY): 1973
Hollins U (VA): 1962
Holy Cross, C of the (MA): 1974
Hope C (MI): 1971
Howard U (DC): 1953
Idaho, U of: 1926
Illinois C: 1932
Illinois Wesleyan U: 2001
Illinois, U of, Chicago: 1977
Illinois, U of, Urbana: 1907
Indiana U Bloomington: 1911
Iowa State U: 1973
Iowa, U of: 1895
Johns Hopkins U (MD): 1895
Kalamazoo C (MI): 1958
Kansas State U: 1974
Kansas, U of: 1890
Kent State U (OH): 1977
Kentucky, U of: 1926
Kenyon C (OH): 1858
Knox C (IL): 1917
Lafayette C (PA): 1890
Lake Forest C (IL): 1962
Lawrence U (WI): 1914
Lehigh U (PA): 1887
Lewis & Clark C (OR): 1998
Louisiana State U, Baton Rouge: 1977
Loyola U (MD): 1995
Loyola U (IL): 1995
Luther C (IA): 1983
Macalester C (MN): 1968
Maine, U of: 1923
Manhattan C (NY): 1971
Marietta C (OH): 1860
Marquette U (WI): 1971

ACADEMICS

Mary Baldwin C (VA): 1971
Mary Washington, U of (VA): 1971
Maryland, U of, Baltimore County: 1998
Maryland, U of, College Park: 1964
Massachusetts Institute of
    Technology: 1971
Massachusetts, U of, Amherst: 1965
McDaniel C (MD): 1988
Miami U (OH): 1911
Miami, U of (FL): 1983
Michigan State U: 1968
Michigan, U of, Ann Arbor: 1907
Middlebury C (VT): 1868
Mills C (CA): 1929
Millsaps C (MS): 1989
Minnesota, U of, Twin Cities: 1892
Mississippi, U of: 2001
Missouri, U of, Columbia: 1901
Morehouse C (GA): 1968
Mt. Holyoke C (MA): 1905
Muhlenberg C (PA): 1968
Nebraska, U of, Lincoln: 1895
New Hampshire, U of: 1952
New Jersey, C of: 2006
New Mexico, U of, Albuquerque: 1965
New York U: 1858
New York, City U of, Brooklyn: 1950
New York, City U of, City C: 1867
New York, City U of, Hunter C: 1920
New York, City U of, Lehman: 1971
New York, City U of, Queens C: 1950
New York, State U of, Albany: 1974
New York, State U of, Binghamton: 1971
New York, State U of, Buffalo: 1938
New York, State U of, Geneseo: 2004
New York, State U of, Stony Brook: 1974
North Carolina State U: 1995
North Carolina, U of, Chapel Hill: 1904
North Carolina, U of, Greensboro: 1934
North Dakota, U of: 1914
Northwestern U (IL): 1890
Notre Dame, U of (IN): 1968
Oberlin C (OH): 1907
Occidental C (CA): 1926
Ohio State U, Columbus: 1904
Ohio U, Athens: 1929
Ohio Wesleyan U: 1907
Oklahoma, U of: 1920
Oregon, U of: 1923
Pennsylvania State U, University
    Park: 1937
Pennsylvania, U of: 1892
Pittsburgh, U of (PA): 1953
Pomona C (CA): 1914
Princeton U (NJ): 1899

Puget Sound, U of (WA): 1986
Purdue U (IN): 1971
Randolph-Macon C (VA): 1923
Randolph C (VA): 1917
Redlands, U of (CA): 1977
Reed C (OR): 1938
Rhode Island, U of: 1977
Rhodes C (TN): 1949
Rice U (TX): 1929
Richmond, U of (VA): 1929
Ripon C (WI): 1952
Roanoke C (VA): 2004
Rochester, U of (NY): 1887
Rockford C (IL): 1953
Rutgers U, Douglass (NJ): 1921
Rutgers U, New Brunswick (NJ): 1869
Rutgers U, Newark (NJ): 1958
San Diego State U (CA): 1974
San Diego, U of (CA): 2003
San Francisco State U (CA): 1977
Santa Clara U (CA): 1977
Scripps C (CA): 1962
Skidmore C (NY): 1971
Smith C (MA): 1904
South Carolina, U of, Columbia: 1926
South Dakota, U of: 1926
South, U of the (TN): 1926
Southern California, U of: 1929
Southern Methodist U (TX): 1949
Southwestern U (TX): 1995
Spelman C (GA): 1997
St. Catherine U (MN): 1938
St. Joseph's U (PA): 2001
St. Lawrence U (NY): 1899
St. Louis U (MO): 1968
St. Mary's C (MD): 1998
St. Michael's C (VT): 2001
St. Olaf C (MN): 1949
Stanford U (CA): 1904
Stetson U (FL): 1982
Swarthmore C (PA): 1896
Sweet Briar C (VA): 1950
Syracuse U (NY): 1896
Temple U (PA): 1974
Tennessee, U of, Knoxville: 1965
Texas A&M U, College Station: 2004
Texas Christian U: 1971
Texas Tech U: 2006
Texas, U of, Austin: 1905
Trinity C (CT): 1845
Trinity U (TX): 1974
Trinity Washington U (DC): 1971
Truman State U (MO): 2001
Tufts U (MA): 1892
Tulane U (LA): 1909

Tulsa, U of (OK): 1989
Union C (NY): 1817
Ursinus C (PA): 1992
Utah, U of: 1935
Valparaiso U (IN): 2004
Vanderbilt U (TN): 1901
Vassar C (NY): 1899
Vermont, U of: 1848
Villanova U (PA): 1986
Virginia Polytechnic Institute & State U: 1977
Virginia, U of: 1908
Wabash C (IN): 1898
Wake Forest U (NC): 1941
Washington & Jefferson C (PA): 1937
Washington & Lee U (VA): 1911
Washington C (MD): 2006
Washington State U: 1929
Washington U (MO): 1914
Washington, U of, Seattle: 1914
Wayne State U (MI): 1953

Wellesley C (MA): 1904
Wells C (NY): 1932
Wesleyan U (CT): 1845
West Virginia U: 1910
Western Michigan U: 1998
Wheaton C (MA): 1932
Whitman C (WA): 1920
Willamette U (OR): 1997
William & Mary, C of (VA): 1776
Williams C (MA): 1864
Wilson C (PA): 1950
Wisconsin, U of, Madison: 1899
Wisconsin, U of, Milwaukee: 1974
Wittenberg U (OH): 1992
Wofford C (SC): 1941
Wooster, C of (OH): 1926
Wyoming, U of: 1940
Xavier U (OH): 2006
Yale U (CT): 1780

Source: Phi Beta Kappa Society

Colleges that Have Been Selected for Phi Beta Kappa Since 2000

The following colleges and universities have been selected to host Phi Beta Kappa chapters since 2000. Fewer than 10% of the nation's liberal arts colleges are members of Phi Beta Kappa, the nation's oldest and most respected undergraduate honors organization. Note, however, that some colleges have rejected the offer of Phi Beta Kappa membership. For example, Bryn Mawr College rejected a Phi Beta Kappa membership on the principle that "special societies based on grades run counter to the principle of the college," according to the dean of the undergraduate college. The date the chapter was established is listed.

Alfred U (NY): 2004
Auburn U (AL): 2001
Austin C (TX): 2001
Butler U (IN): 2010
Clemson U (SC): 2006
Creighton U (NE): 2012
Eckerd C (FL): 2004
Elon U (NC): 2010
Florida International U: 2001
George Mason U (VA): 2013
Houston, U of: TBA
Illinois Wesleyan U: 2001
James Madison U (VA): 2010
Mercer U (GA): TBA
Mississippi, U of: 2001
New Jersey, C of: 2006

New York, State U of, Geneseo: 2004
Oklahoma State U: 2013
Oregon State U: TBA
Pacific, U of the (CA): 2007
Roanoke C (VA): 2004
San Diego, U of (CA): 2003
St. Benedict, C of/St. John's U (MN):
2010
St. Joseph's U (PA): 2001
St. Michaels C (VT): 2001
Texas A&M U, College Station: 2004
Texas Tech U: 2006
Truman State U (MO): 2001
Valparaiso U (IN): 2004
Washington C (MD): 2006
Xavier U (OH): 2006

Colleges Graduating Rhodes Scholars in 2015

The highly prized Rhodes Scholarship enables the recipient to study at the University of Oxford in England for two years. Students from Australia, Bermuda, Canada, Germany, Hong Kong, India, Jamaica & the Commonwealth Caribbean, Kenya, New Zealand, Pakistan, Southern Africa, United States, Zambia, and Zimbabwe compete for the scholarship and are selected on the basis of their intellectual and academic excellence and their personal qualities, including leadership. These colleges enrolled one or more Rhodes Scholars in 2015.

Adelaide, U of (Australia)
Alabama, U of, Birmingham
Auckland, U of (New Zealand)
British Columbia, U of (Canada)
Brown U (RI)
Calgary, U of (Canada)
Cambridge, U of (United Kingdom)
Canterbury, U of (New Zealand)
Cape Town, U of (South Africa)
Copperbelt U (Zambia)
Cornell U (NY)
Dalhousie U (Canada)
Dartmouth C (NH)
Delhi, U of (India)
Edinburgh, U of (United Kingdom)
Exeter, U of (United Kingdom)
Harvard U (MA)
Hong Kong, U of
Johns Hopkins U (MD)
Jomo Kenyatta, U of, Agriculture & Technology (Kenya)
Lady Shri Ram C, Delhi U (India)
Malawi, U of
Manitoba, U of (Canada)
Maryland, U of, College Park
Massachusetts Institute of Technology
McGill U (Canada)
Melbourne, U of (Australia)
Memorial U of Newfoundland (Canada)
Michigan, U of, Ann Arbor
Mt. Allison U (Canada)
National Academy of Legal Studies & Research (India)

National Law School of India U, Bangalore (India)
National U of Science & Technology (Pakistan)
New South Wales, U of (Australia)
New York U, Abu Dhabi
North Carolina, U of, Chapel Hill
Notre Dame, U of (IN)
Pennsylvania, U of
Pretoria, U of (South Africa)
Princeton U (NJ)
Puget Sound, U of (WA)
Queensland U of Technology (Australia)
Rhodes U (South Africa)
Santa Clara U (CA)
St. John's National Academy of Health Sciences (India)
Stanford U (CA)
Tasmania, U of (Australia)
Tennessee, U of, Chattanooga
Texas, U of, Austin
Toronto, U of (Canada)
U.S. Air Force Academy (CO)
Wabash C (IN)
West Indies, U of the (Jamaica)
West Indies, U of the, St. Augustine (Trinidad & Tobago)
Western Australia, U of
Wisconsin, U of, Eau Claire
Yale U (CT)

Source: The Rhodes Scholarships (rhodeshouse.ox.ac.uk)

U.S. Institutions Graduating the Most Rhodes Scholars from 1904 to 2015

These institutions have graduated 25 or more Rhodes Scholars from 1904 to 2015.

Brown U (RI)
Chicago, U of (IL)
Columbia U (NY)

Cornell U (NY)
Dartmouth C (NH)
Duke U (NC)

Steven R. Antonoff

Harvard U (MA)
Kansas, U of
Massachusetts Institute of Technology
Mississippi, U of
Montana, U of
North Carolina, U of, Chapel Hill
Oklahoma, U of
Princeton U (NJ)
South, U of the (TN)
Stanford U (CA)
Swarthmore C (PA)

Texas, U of, Austin
U.S. Air Force Academy (CO)
U.S. Military Academy (NY)
U.S. Naval Academy (MD)
Vanderbilt U (TN)
Virginia, U of
Washington U (MO)
Washington, U of, Seattle
Williams C (MA)
Wisconsin, U of, Madison
Yale U (CT)

Source: The Rhodes Trust (rhodesscholar.org)

Colleges Producing the Most Fulbright Students

The Fulbright Program began in 1946 and is managed by the Institute of International Education. Almost 8,000 grants are awarded annually in an effort to promote cultural and international engagement through international academic exchange. Fulbright students undertake advanced research, graduate-level study, classroom teaching, etc. in more than 155 countries. Students are selected on the basis of their academic record, language abilities, and personal qualifications. Numbers show the total number of Fulbright awards by institution type for the 2015–2016.

Research Institutions

Harvard U (MA): 31
Michigan, U of, Ann Arbor: 29
Northwestern U (IL): 26
Yale U (CT): 26
Arizona State U: 22
Pennsylvania, U of: 21
Chicago, U of (IL): 20
Columbia U (NY): 20
Indiana U Bloomington: 19
Princeton U (NJ): 19
Southern California, U of: 19
Brown U (RI): 18
Georgetown U (DC): 17
Illinois, U of, Urbana: 15
Johns Hopkins U (MD): 15
North Carolina, U of, Chapel Hill: 15
Pittsburgh, U of (PA): 15
California, U of, Berkeley: 14
Minnesota, U of, Twin Cities: 14
Notre Dame, U of (IN): 14
Texas, U of, Austin: 14

Virginia, U of: 14
Cornell U (NY): 13
William & Mary, C of (VA): 13
Wisconsin, U of, Madison: 13
American U (DC): 12
California, U of, Los Angeles: 12
Duke U (NC): 12
Iowa, U of: 12
Massachusetts, U of, Amherst: 12
Ohio State U, Columbus: 12
Alabama, U of, Tuscaloosa: 11
Boston C (MA): 11
Florida State U: 11
Maryland, U of, College Park: 11
Rutgers U, New Brunswick (NJ): 11
Tufts U (MA): 11
George Washington U (DC): 10
Louisville, U of (KY): 10
Pennsylvania State U, University Park: 10
Stanford U (CA): 10
Washington, U of: 10

Master's Institutions

St. Edward's U (NY): 10
Villanova U (PA): 9

New York, City U of, Queens: 7
Portland, U of (OR): 6

Rollins C (FL): 5
Western Kentucky U: 5
Western Washington U: 5
Elon U (NC): 4
Marist C (NY): 4
Nazareth C (NY): 4
North Park U (IL): 4
Seattle U (WA): 4
Truman State U (MO): 4
Boise State U (ID): 3
Butler U (IN): 3

Chapman U (CA): 3
Drake U (IA): 3
Loyola U (LA): 3
Mills C (CA): 3
New Jersey, C of: 3
New York, City U of, Hunter C: 3
Redlands, U of (CA): 3
Rochester Institute of Technology (NY): 3
Santa Clara U (CA): 3
Wisconsin, U of, Eau Claire: 3

Bachelor's Institutions

Pitzer C (CA): 21
Smith C (MA): 19
Bates C (ME): 18
Bowdoin C (ME): 17
Williams C (MA): 15
Pomona C (CA): 14
Oberlin C (OH): 13
Amherst C (MA): 12
Occidental C (CA): 11
Wheaton C (MA): 10
Kenyon C (OH): 9
Scripps C (CA): 9
St. Olaf C (MN): 9
Carleton C (MN): 8
Claremont McKenna C (CA): 8
Davidson C (NC): 8
Hobart C & William Smith C (NY): 7
Lewis & Clark C (OR): 7
Macalester C (MN): 7
Middlebury C (VT): 7
Swarthmore C (PA): 7

Wellesley C (MA): 7
Whitman C (WA): 7
Barnard C (NY): 6
Hamilton C (NY): 6
Vassar C (NY): 6
Carthage C (WI): 5
Dickinson C (PA): 5
Franklin & Marshall C (PA): 5
Grinnell C (IA): 5
Haverford C (PA): 5
Mt. Holyoke C (MA): 5
Wesleyan U (CT): 5
Denison U (OH): 4
DePauw U (IN): 4
Doane C (NE): 4
Furman U (SC): 4
St. Benedict, C of (MN): 4
Transylvania U (KY): 4
Union C (NY): 4
Wooster, C of (OH): 4

Specialized Institutions

Princeton Theological Seminary (NJ): 3
Rhode Island School of Design: 3
Art Institute of Chicago, School of the
   (IL): 2

Maryland Institute C of Art: 2
California C of the Arts: 1
Cranbrook Academy of Art (MI): 1
Juilliard School (NY): 1

Sources: Institute of International Education (us.fulbrightonline.org) and *The Chronicle of Higher Education*

Steven R. Antonoff

Watson Fellowship Partner Colleges

The Thomas J. Watson Fellowship is a one-year grant for purposeful, independent exploration outside the United States, awarded to graduating seniors nominated by one of 40 partner colleges.

Amherst C (MA)
Atlantic, C of the (ME)
Bard C (NY)
Bates C (ME)
Berea C (KY)
Bowdoin C (ME)
Bryn Mawr C (PA)
California Institute of Technology
Carleton C (MN)
Colby C (ME)
Colgate U (NY)
Colorado C
Davidson C (NC)
Earlham C (IN)
Grinnell C (IA)
Hamilton C (NY)
Harvey Mudd C (CA)
Haverford C (PA)
Hendrix C (AR)
Lawrence U (WI)

Macalester C (MN)
Middlebury C (VT)
Oberlin C (OH)
Pitzer C (CA)
Pomona C (CA)
Puget Sound, U of (WA)
Reed C (OR)
Rhodes C (TN)
Rice U (TX)
Scripps C (CA)
South, U of the (TN)
Swarthmore C (PA)
Union C (NY)
Ursinus C (PA)
Vassar C (NY)
Wellesley C (MA)
Wesleyan U (CT)
Wheaton C (MA)
Whitman C (WA)
Williams C (MA)

Source: Thomas J. Watson Fellowship (watson.foundation)

Peace Corps

"As the preeminent international service organization of the United States, the Peace Corps sends Americans abroad to tackle the most pressing needs of people around the world. Peace Corps Volunteers work at the grassroots level toward sustainable change that lives on long after their service—at the same time becoming global citizens and serving their country. When they return home, Volunteers bring their knowledge and experiences—and a global outlook—that enriches the lives of those around them."

The following large colleges and universities (more than 15,000 students) had the most Peace Corps volunteers in 2015.

Washington, U of: 72
Wisconsin, U of, Madison: 68
Florida, U of: 59
Minnesota, U of, Twin Cities: 59
Colorado, U of, Boulder: 53
Michigan, U of, Ann Arbor: 48
Indiana U Bloomington: 47
California, U of, Santa Barbara: 43
Colorado State U, Ft. Collins: 43
Ohio State U, Columbus: 42
Maryland, U of, College Park: 41
North Carolina, U of, Chapel Hill: 39

California, U of, Berkeley: 37
California, U of, Davis: 36
California, U of, San Diego: 36
California, U of, Los Angeles: 35
Illinois, U of, Urbana: 35
James Madison U (VA): 35
Oregon, U of: 35
South Florida, U of: 35
California Polytechnic State U, San Luis Obispo: 34
Arizona State U: 33
Michigan State U: 33

San Diego State U (CA): 32   California, U of, Santa Cruz: 32

The following mid-sized colleges and universities (between 5,000 and 10,000 students) had the most Peace Corps volunteers in 2015.

George Washington U (DC): 43
American U (DC): 42
Western Washington U: 41
Cornell U (NY): 38
Virginia, U of: 36
Vermont, U of: 31
Georgetown U (DC): 29
Emory U (GA): 27
Humboldt State U (CA): 25
Montana, U of: 24
William & Mary, C of (VA): 24
Tulane U (LA): 19
New Hampshire, U of: 18
Montana State U: 16

San Diego, U of (CA): 16
Wisconsin, U of, Stevens Point: 16
Fordham U (NY): 15
New York, State U of, Geneseo: 15
Boston C (MA): 14
Hawaii, U of, Manoa: 14
Johns Hopkins U (MD): 14
Minnesota, U of, Duluth: 14
Wisconsin, U of, La Crosse: 14
Chicago, U of (IL): 13
Howard U (DC): 13
Miami, U of (FL): 13
North Carolina, U of, Wilmington: 13
Rhode Island, U of: 13

The following small colleges and universities (less than 5,000 students) had the most Peace Corps volunteers in 2015.

Gonzaga U (WA): 18
Puget Sound, U of (WA): 18
Macalester C (MN): 17
Carleton C (MN): 13
Evergreen State C (WA): 13
Middlebury C (VT): 12
New York, State U of, C of
Environmental Science & Forestry: 12
Willamette U (OR): 12
Dickinson C (PA): 11
Mary Washington, U of (VA): 11
Simmons C (MA): 11
Ft. Lewis C (CO): 10
Gettysburg C (PA): 10
North Carolina, U of, Asheville: 10
St. Michael's C (VT): 10
Allegheny C (PA): 9
Bowdoin C (ME): 9

Bucknell U (PA): 9
Denison U (OH): 9
Kalamazoo C (MI): 9
Knox C (IL): 9
Oberlin C (OH): 9
Richmond, U of (VA): 9
St. Lawrence U (NY): 9
Clark U (MA): 8
Drake U (IA): 8
Grinnell C (IA): 8
Lewis & Clark C (OR): 8
Seattle Pacific U (WA): 8
Smith C (MA): 8
Stonehill C (MA): 8
Wake Forest U (NC): 8
Wellesley C (MA): 8
Whitworth U (WA): 8
Wooster, C of (OH): 8

The following colleges and universities have had the most Peace Corps volunteers historically since 1961.

California, U of, Berkeley: 3,615
Wisconsin, U of, Madison: 3,184
Washington, U of: 2,937
Michigan, U of, Ann Arbor: 2,640
Colorado, U of, Boulder: 2,435

Source: Peace Corps (peacecorps.gov)

Colleges With Students Committed to Teaching

Teach for American is the national corps of college graduates who commit two years to teach in urban and rural public schools. Listed in order, these colleges had the highest number of alumni enter the 2014 corps.

Large Schools
Michigan, U of, Ann Arbor
California, U of, Berkeley
California, U of, Los Angeles
Texas, U of, Austin
Florida, U of
North Carolina, U of, Chapel Hill
Pennsylvania State U, University Park
Georgia, U of

Illinois, U of, Urbana
Wisconsin, U of, Madison
Arizona State U
Southern California, U of
Cornell U (NY)
Virginia, U of
Pennsylvania, U of

Medium Schools
Howard U (DC)
Vanderbilt U (TN)
George Washington U (DC)
Harvard U (MA)
Boston C (MA)
Florida A&M U
Georgetown U (DC)
Columbia U (NY)
Northwestern U (IL)

Duke U (NC)
Emory U (GA)
American U (DC)
Dartmouth C (NH)
Southern Methodist U (TX)
Rice U (TX)
Yale U (CT)
William & Mary, C of (VA)

Small Schools
DePauw U (IN)
Spelman C (GA)
Richmond, U of (VA)
Wesleyan U (CT)
Franklin & Marshall C (PA)
Williams C (MA)
Barnard C (NY)
Pomona C (CA)
Wheaton C (IL)
Washington & Lee U (VA)
Morehouse C (GA)

Clark Atlanta U (GA)
Holy Cross, C of the (MA)
Davidson C (NC)
Hamilton C (NY)
Whitman C (WA)
Agnes Scott C (GA)
Allegheny C (PA)
Colgate U (NY)
Denison U (OH)
Dickinson C (PA)

Source: Teach for America (teachforamerica.org)

Greatest Colleges to Work For

Students benefit when the people working for their college are happy. These colleges are the best to work for on the basis of such criteria as compensation, job satisfaction, and work/life balance.

Great Small, Four-Year Colleges to Work For
Gettysburg C (PA)
John Brown U (AR)
Lubbock Christian U (TX)
McPherson C (KS)

MGH Institute of Health Professions (MA)
Mississippi U for Women
New York Chiropractic C
Ozarks, C of the (MO)
Roberts Wesleyan C (NY)
West Virginia School of Osteopathic Medicine

Great Medium-Sized, Four-Year Colleges to Work For
Angelo State U (TX)
Eastern Connecticut State U
Elon U (NC)
Endicott C (MA)
Francis Marion U (SC)
Incarnate Word, U of the (TX)
McKendree U (IL)
Rollins C (FL)
West Texas A&M U
Western U of Health Sciences (CA)

Great Large, Four-Year Colleges to Work For
Baylor U (TX)
Central Oklahoma, U of
Florida International U
Hofstra U (NY)
Illinois State U
Maryland, U of, Baltimore County
Mississippi State U
Mississippi, U of
Southern New Hampshire U
Texas Christian U

Great Small, Two-Year Colleges to Work For
Morgan Community C (CO)
North Florida Community C
Panola C (TX)
Rappahannock Community C (VA)

Great Medium-Sized, Two-Year Colleges to Work For
Blue Ridge Community C (NC)
Crowder C (MO)
Lord Fairfax Community C (VA)
Mississippi Gulf Coast Community C

Great Large, Two-Year Colleges to Work For
Delaware County Community C (PA)
Miami Dade C (FL)
Santa Rosa Junior C (CA)
Santiago Canyon C (CA)

Source: *The Chronicle of Higher Education*

Steven R. Antonoff

Colleges to Consider for Online Learning

While many colleges offer classes online, these colleges are known for their online learning opportunities. Online education enables students to study from their homes. The quality of online programs varies widely, and students are encouraged to carefully check curriculum, accreditation, support services, and cost. Some colleges that offer online courses are nonprofit whereas others are for-profit. Many of the following colleges have multiple campuses, often in several states.

American Public U (WV)*
Argosy U (CA)
Arizona State U
Arizona, U of
Ashford U (CA)
Capella U (MN)
Central Florida, U of
Columbia C (MO)
DeVry U (IL)*
Ft. Hays State U (KS)
Grand Canyon U (AZ)
Granite State C (NH)
Kaplan U (IA)*
Liberty U (VA)
Maryland, U of, University C

New York, State U of (Open SUNY)
Northern Arizona U
Nova Southeastern U (FL)
Oregon State U
Pennsylvania State U, World Campus
Phoenix, U of (AZ)
Regis U (CO)
Southern New Hampshire U
Strayer U (DC)
Walden U (MN)
Washington State U Global Campus
Western Governors U (UT)

*Corporate headquarters location

Source: *College Finder* research

Military Colleges

Four Year

California Maritime Academy
Citadel, The (SC)
Great Lakes Maritime Academy (MI)
Maine Maritime Academy
Mary Baldwin C (Virginia Women's
    Institute for Leadership)
Massachusetts Maritime Academy
New York, State U of, Maritime C
North Georgia C & State U
Norwich U (VT)

Texas A&M U, College Station
    (Voluntary Corps of Cadets)
Texas Maritime Academy
U.S. Air Force Academy (CO)
U.S. Coast Guard Academy (CT)
U.S. Merchant Marine Academy (NY)
U.S. Military Academy (NY)
U.S. Naval Academy (MD)
Virginia Military Institute
Virginia Polytechnic Institute & State U

Two Year

Georgia Military C
Marion Military Institute (AL)
New Mexico Military Institute
Valley Forge Military Academy & C (PA)
Wentworth Military Academy & Junior C (MO)

CAREER PREPARATION

The Experts' Choice: Colleges With Excellent Career Counseling

The Top Choices

Butler U (IN)
Citadel, The (SC)
Colorado State U, Ft. Collins
Francis Marion U (SC)
Lebanon Valley C (PA)
Morehead State U (KY)
Rochester Institute of Technology (NY)
Union C (NY)

More Choices

American Jewish U (CA)
Barnard C (NY)
Bentley U (MA)
Blue Mountain C (MS)
Bridgewater State U (MA)
Brooks Institute (CA)
Caldwell C (ID)
Clark U (MA)
Clemson U (SC)
Cornell U (NY)
Davidson C (NC)

Dowling C (NY)
Florida, U of
Franklin & Marshall C (PA)
Kansas City Art Institute (MO)
Laguna C of Art & Design (CA)
Macalester C (MN)
Mississippi Valley State U
New York, City U of, Hunter C
North Carolina State U
Northeastern U (MA)
Notre Dame, U of (IN)
Oregon, U of
Pennsylvania State U, University Park
Richmond, U of (VA)
Rose-Hulman Institute of Technology (IN)
Southern Mississippi, U of
Southwestern U (TX)
Sweet Briar C (VA)
Texas, U of, Austin
Wake Forest U (NC)
Washington, U of
Waynesburg U (PA)
West Liberty U (WV)
Yale U (CT)

The Experts' Choice: Great Liberal Arts Education and Career Assistance

Experts were asked to name liberal arts and sciences colleges that do a particularly good job helping students find a career and land a job.

Amherst C (MA)
Barnard C (NY)
Claremont McKenna C (CA)
Clark U (MA)
Colorado School of Mines
Connecticut C
DePauw U (IN)
Dickinson C (PA)
Drexel U (PA)
Harvard U (MA)
Harvey Mudd C (CA)
Haverford C (PA)
Kenyon C (OH)
Lehigh U (PA)

Middlebury C (VT)
Northeastern U (MA)
Occidental C (CA)
Ohio Wesleyan U
Puget Sound, U of (WA)
Santa Clara U (CA)
Smith C (MA)
St. Olaf C (MN)
Swarthmore C (PA)
Union C (NY)
Wellesley C (MA)
Willamette U (OR)
Wooster, C of (OH)

The Experts' Choice: Colleges That Do a Great Job Helping Graduates Find Jobs

This list reflects the opinions of the experts as well as *College Finder* research.

Arizona State U
Babson C (MA)
Bentley U (MA)
Brigham Young U (UT)
California, U of, Berkeley
Carnegie Mellon U (PA)
Clarkson U (NY)
Cornell U (NY)
Dartmouth C (NH)
Denver, U of (CO)
Dickinson State U (ND)
Emory U (GA)
Florida, U of
Georgetown U (DC)
Georgia Institute of Technology
Illinois, U of, Urbana
Maryland, U of, College Park
Massachusetts Institute of Technology
Massachusetts, U of, Amherst
Michigan State U
Michigan, U of, Ann Arbor
New York U
Nichols C (MA)

North Carolina State U
North Carolina, U of, Chapel Hill
Northeastern U (MA)
Notre Dame, U of (IN)
Ohio State U, Columbus
Pennsylvania State U, University Park
Pennsylvania, U of
Princeton U (NJ)
Purdue U (IN)
Rutgers U, New Brunswick (NJ)
Southern California, U of
Southern Mississippi, U of
Southwestern U (TX)
Syracuse U (NY)
Texas A&M U
Texas Tech U
Virginia Polytechnic Institute & State U
Virginia, U of
Wake Forest U (NC)
Washington State U
Washington U (MO)
Wisconsin, U of, Madison

Sources: *College Finder* research, *Wall Street Journal*, and Online Schools Center

Top Cooperative Education Colleges

Cooperative education is a term that embraces different forms of experiential learning. At these colleges—all partners in the National Co-Op Scholarship Program—students apply what they learn in the classroom to an internship or job.

Cincinnati, U of (OH)
Clarkson U (NY)
Drexel U (PA)
Johnson & Wales U (multiple locations)
Massachusetts, U of, Lowell
Merrimack C (MA)
New York, State U of, Oswego
Rochester Institute of Technology (NY)
Toledo, U of (OH)
Wentworth Institute of Technology (MA)

Source: World Association for Cooperative and Work-Integrated Education (waceinc.org)

The Experts' Choice: Colleges Offering Hands-On Experience

Experts identified these colleges for the student who wants to obtain skills or knowledge by not simply reading or studying but by experiencing and doing.

Atlantic, C of the (ME)
Berea C (KY)
California Polytechnic State U, San Luis
 Obispo
Champlain C (VT)*
Cincinnati, U of (OH)
Colorado C
Deep Springs C (CA)
Drexel U (PA)*
Endicott C (MA)
Evergreen State C (WA)
Georgia Institute of Technology
Lamar U (TX)

Marlboro C (VT)
Northeastern U (MA)*
Prescott C (AZ)
Rochester Institute of Technology (NY)
Southern U (LA)
Sterling C (VT)
Stevens Institute of Technology (NJ)
Warren Wilson C (NC)
Wooster, C of (OH)
Worcester Polytechnic Institute (MA)

*Top Choice (tie)

Where Ph.D.s Received Their Undergraduate Degrees

Listed here are colleges ranked in order of the highest number of doctoral degrees per hundred B.A./B.S. degrees, signifying the success of the school in sending its graduates on to achieve doctorates. According to a Pomona study, "Ph.D. production rate is calculated as the number of doctorates (Ph.D., Sc.D., and Ed.D.) earned between 2003 and 2012 by the institution's baccalaureate alumni, divided by the number of B.A./B.S. degrees awarded by the institution between 1998 and 2007."

1. California Institute of Technology
2. Harvey Mudd C (CA)
3. Swarthmore C (PA)
4. Reed C (OR)
5. Carleton C (MN)
6. Massachusetts Institute of
 Technology
7. Grinnell C (IA)
8. Harvard U (MA)
9. Princeton U (NJ)
10. Chicago, U of (IL)
11. Haverford C (PA)
12. Oberlin C (OH)
13. Williams C (MA)
14. Pomona C (CA)
15. Amherst C (MA)
16. Bryn Mawr C (PA)
17. Yale U (CT)
18. Rice U (TX)
19. St. John's C (MD)
20. Macalester C (MN)
21. Brown U (RI)
22. Stanford U (CA)
23. Wesleyan U (CT)

24. Wellesley C (MA)
25. Lawrence U (WI)
26. Earlham C (IN)
27. Vassar C (NY)
28. Rochester, U of (NY)
29. Hendrix C (AR)
30. Duke U (NC)
31. Case Western Reserve U (OH)
32. Cornell U (NY)
33. Kalamazoo C (MI)
34. Dartmouth C (NH)
35. New Mexico Institute of Technology
36. Smith C (MA)
37. New England Conservatory of
 Music (MA)
38. Bowdoin C (ME)
39. Hampshire C (MA)
40. Mt. Holyoke C (MA)
41. Kenyon C (OH)
42. William & Mary, C of (VA)
43. Carnegie Mellon U (PA)
44. Brandeis U (MA)
45. Occidental C (CA)
46. Columbia U (NY)

47. Whitman C (WA)
48. Allegheny C (PA)
49. Wooster, C of (OH)

50. Davidson C (NC)
51. Spelman C (GA)

Sources: Baccalaureate Origins of Earned Doctoral Degrees (2003–2012) compiled by the Office of Institutional Research, Pomona College in July 2015 (https://www.pomona.edu/sites/default/files/bacorigins_2003-2012.pdf). Data available from National Science Foundation through WebCASPAR (https://ncsesdata.nsf.gov/webcaspar/). Two surveys were used to compile these statistics: the NSF Survey of Earned Doctorates (http://www.nsf.gov/statistics/srvydoctorates/) and the IPEDS Completions Survey coordinated by the National Center for Education Statistics (http://nces.ed.gov/ipeds/). The data were retrieved by the Higher Education Data Sharing Consortium.

Where Arts Ph.D.s Received Their Undergraduate Degrees

Listed here are colleges ranked in order of the highest number of doctoral degrees per hundred B.A./B.S. degrees, signifying the success of the school in sending its graduates on to achieve doctorates in the arts.

1. New England Conservatory of Music (MA)
2. Curtis Institute of Music (PA)
3. Juilliard School (NY)
4. Cleveland Institute of Music (OH)
5. Manhattan School of Music (NY)
6. San Francisco Conservatory of Music (CA)
7. Oberlin C (OH)
8. Boston Conservatory (MA)
9. Puerto Rico Conservatory of Music
10. Lawrence U (WI)
11. North Carolina, U of, School of the Arts
12. Bard C, Simon's Rock (MA)
13. Yale U (CT)
14. Swarthmore C (PA)
15. Rochester, U of (NY)
16. Grinnell C (IA)
17. Berklee C of Music (MA)
18. Williams C (MA)
19. Stetson U (FL)
20. Wellesley C (MA)
21. California Institute of the Arts
22. Barnard C (NY)
23. Carleton C (MN)
24. Reed C (OR)
25. Smith C (MA)

Sources: Baccalaureate Origins of Earned Doctoral Degrees (2003–2012) compiled by the Office of Institutional Research, Pomona College in July 2015 (https://www.pomona.edu/sites/default/files/bacorigins_2003-2012.pdf). Data available from National Science Foundation through WebCASPAR (https://ncsesdata.nsf.gov/webcaspar/). Two surveys were used to compile these statistics: the NSF Survey of Earned Doctorates (http://www.nsf.gov/statistics/srvydoctorates/) and the IPEDS Completions Survey coordinated by the National Center for Education Statistics (http://nces.ed.gov/ipeds/). The data were retrieved by the Higher Education Data Sharing Consortium.

Where Geoscience Ph.D.s Received Their Undergraduate Degrees

Listed here are colleges ranked in order of the highest number of doctoral degrees per hundred B.A./B.S. degrees, signifying the success of the school in sending its graduates on to achieve doctorates in geosciences.

1. California Institute of Technology
2. Carleton C (MN)
3. New Mexico Institute of Technology
4. Harvey Mudd C (CA)
5. Whitman C (WA)
6. Colorado School of Mines
7. Eckerd C (FL)
8. Williams C (MA)
9. Colorado C
10. Pomona C (CA)

11. Amherst C (MA)
12. Juniata C (PA)
13. Macalester C (MN)
14. Lyndon State C (VT)
15. Bates C (ME)
16. Texas A&M U, Galveston
17. Oberlin C (OH)
18. Brown U (RI)

19. Hampshire C (MA)
20. Rice U (TX)
21. Colgate U (NY)
22. Franklin & Marshall C (PA)
23. Lawrence U (WI)
24. Middlebury C (VT)
25. Massachusetts Institute of Technology

Source: Baccalaureate Origins of Earned Doctoral Degrees (2003–2012) compiled by the Office of Institutional Research, Pomona College in July 2015 (https://www.pomona.edu/sites/default/files/bacorigins_2003-2012.pdf). Data available from National Science Foundation through WebCASPAR (https://ncsesdata.nsf.gov/webcaspar/). Two surveys were used to compile these statistics: the NSF Survey of Earned Doctorates (http://www.nsf.gov/statistics/srvydoctorates/) and the IPEDS Completions Survey coordinated by the National Center for Education Statistics (http://nces.ed.gov/ipeds/). The data were retrieved by the Higher Education Data Sharing Consortium.

Where Humanities Ph.D.s Received Their Undergraduate Degrees

Listed here are colleges ranked in order of the highest number of doctoral degrees per hundred B.A./B.S. degrees, signifying the success of the school in sending its graduates on to achieve doctorates in humanities.

1. St. John's C (MD)
2. Reed C (OR)
3. Swarthmore C (PA)
4. Amherst C (MA)
5. Carleton C (MN)
6. Bryn Mawr C (PA)
7. St. John's C (NM)
8. Yale U (CT)
9. Thomas Aquinas C (CA)
10. Princeton U (NJ)
11. Bard C (NY)
12. Harvard U (MA)
13. Grinnell C (IA)

14. Chicago, U of (IL)
15. Wesleyan U (CT)
16. Pomona C (CA)
17. Haverford C (PA)
18. Vassar C (NY)
19. Kenyon C (OH)
20. Oberlin C (OH)
21. Williams C (MA)
22. Dallas, U of (TX)
23. Sarah Lawrence C (NY)
24. Smith C (MA)
25. Brown U (RI)

Sources: Baccalaureate Origins of Earned Doctoral Degrees (2003–2012) compiled by the Office of Institutional Research, Pomona College in July 2015 (https://www.pomona.edu/sites/default/files/bacorigins_2003-2012.pdf). Data available from National Science Foundation through WebCASPAR (https://ncsesdata.nsf.gov/webcaspar/). Two surveys were used to compile these statistics: the NSF Survey of Earned Doctorates (http://www.nsf.gov/statistics/srvydoctorates/) and the IPEDS Completions Survey coordinated by the National Center for Education Statistics (http://nces.ed.gov/ipeds/). The data were retrieved by the Higher Education Data Sharing Consortium.

Where Life Science Ph.D.s Received Their Undergraduate Degrees

Listed here are colleges ranked in order of the highest number of doctoral degrees per hundred B.A./B.S. degrees, signifying the success of the school in sending its graduates on to achieve doctorates in life sciences.

1. California Institute of Technology
2. Reed C (OR)
3. Carleton C (MN)
4. Swarthmore C (PA)
5. Grinnell C (IA)
6. Haverford C (PA)
7. Massachusetts Institute of Technology
8. Pomona C (CA)
9. Chicago, U of (IL)
10. Earlham C (IN)
11. Harvey Mudd C (CA)
12. Cornell U (NY)
13. Allegheny C (PA)
14. Harvard U (MA)
15. Duke U (NC)
16. Atlantic, C of the (ME)
17. New York, State U of, C of Environmental Science & Forestry
18. Brown U (RI)
19. Rochester, U of (NY)
20. Princeton U (NJ)
21. Stanford U (CA)
22. Oberlin C (OH)
23. Yale U (CT)
24. Rice U (TX)
25. Kalamazoo C (MI)

Sources: Baccalaureate Origins of Earned Doctoral Degrees (2003–2012) compiled by the Office of Institutional Research, Pomona College in July 2015 (https://www.pomona.edu/sites/default/files/bacorigins_2003-2012.pdf). Data available from National Science Foundation through WebCASPAR (https://ncsesdata.nsf.gov/webcaspar/). Two surveys were used to compile these statistics: the NSF Survey of Earned Doctorates (http://www.nsf.gov/statistics/srvydoctorates/) and the IPEDS Completions Survey coordinated by the National Center for Education Statistics (http://nces.ed.gov/ipeds/). The data were retrieved by the Higher Education Data Sharing Consortium.

Where Mathematics and Computer Science Ph.D.s Received Their Undergraduate Degrees

Listed here are colleges ranked in order of the highest number of doctoral degrees per hundred B.A./B.S. degrees, signifying the success of the school in sending its graduates on to achieve doctorates in mathematics and computer science.

1. Harvey Mudd C (CA)
2. California Institute of Technology
3. Massachusetts Institute of Technology
4. Carnegie Mellon U (PA)
5. Rice U (TX)
6. Harvard U (MA)
7. Chicago, U of (IL)
8. Princeton U (NJ)
9. Swarthmore C (PA)
10. New Mexico Institute of Technology
11. Reed C (OR)
12. Carleton C (MN)
13. Williams C (MA)
14. Rose-Hulman Institute of Technology (IN)
15. Haverford C (PA)
16. Rensselaer Polytechnic Institute (NY)
17. Stanford U (CA)
18. Pomona C (CA)
19. Grinnell C (IA)
20. Amherst C (MA)
21. Yale U (CT)
22. Brown U (RI)
23. Whitman C (WA)
24. Case Western Reserve U (OH)
25. Columbia U (NY)

Sources: Baccalaureate Origins of Earned Doctoral Degrees (2003–2012) compiled by the Office of Institutional Research, Pomona College in July 2015 (https://www.pomona.edu/sites/default/files/bacorigins_2003-2012.pdf). Data available from National Science Foundation through WebCASPAR (https://ncsesdata.nsf.gov/webcaspar/). Two surveys were used to compile these statistics: the NSF Survey of Earned Doctorates (http://www.nsf.gov/statistics/srvydoctorates/) and the IPEDS Completions Survey coordinated by the National Center for Education Statistics (http://nces.ed.gov/ipeds/). The data were retrieved by the Higher Education Data Sharing Consortium.

Where Physical Science Ph.D.s Received Their Undergraduate Degrees

Listed here are colleges ranked in order of the highest number of doctoral degrees per hundred B.A./B.S. degrees, signifying the success of the school in sending its graduates on to achieve doctorates in physical sciences (including subjects such as chemistry and physics).

1. California Institute of Technology
2. Harvey Mudd C (CA)
3. Reed C (OR)
4. New Mexico Institute of Technology
5. Massachusetts Institute of Technology
6. Carleton C (MN)
7. Wabash C (IN)
8. Swarthmore C (PA)
9. Lawrence U (WI)
10. Grinnell C (IA)
11. Wooster, C of (OH)
12. Haverford C (PA)
13. Rice U (TX)
14. Chicago, U of (IL)
15. Harvard U (MA)
16. Kalamazoo C (MI)
17. Allegheny C (PA)
18. Princeton U (NJ)
19. Franklin & Marshall C (PA)
20. Case Western Reserve U (OH)
21. Williams C (MA)
22. Bryn Mawr C (PA)
23. Hendrix C (AR)
24. Colorado School of Mines
25. Macalester C (MN)

Sources: Baccalaureate Origins of Earned Doctoral Degrees (2003–2012) compiled by the Office of Institutional Research, Pomona College in July 2015 (https://www.pomona.edu/sites/default/files/bacorigins_2003-2012.pdf). Data available from National Science Foundation through WebCASPAR (https://ncsesdata.nsf.gov/webcaspar/). Two surveys were used to compile these statistics: the NSF Survey of Earned Doctorates (http://www.nsf.gov/statistics/srvydoctorates/) and the IPEDS Completions Survey coordinated by the National Center for Education Statistics (http://nces.ed.gov/ipeds/). The data were retrieved by the Higher Education Data Sharing Consortium.

Where Psychology Ph.D.s Received Their Undergraduate Degrees

Listed here are colleges ranked in order of the highest number of doctoral degrees per hundred B.A./B.S. degrees, signifying the success of the school in sending its graduates on to achieve doctorates in psychology.

1. Puerto Rico, U of, Aguadilla
2. Wellesley C (MA)
3. Reed C (OR)
4. Barnard C (NY)
5. Vassar C (NY)
6. Pomona C (CA)
7. Swarthmore C (PA)
8. Hendrix C (AR)
9. Grinnell C (IA)
10. Haverford C (PA)
11. Williams C (MA)
12. Yale U (CT)
13. Southwestern U (TX)
14. Wesleyan U (CT)
15. Connecticut C
16. Claremont McKenna C (CA)
17. Duke U (NC)
18. Spelman C (GA)
19. Carleton C (MN)
20. Scripps C (CA)
21. Smith C (MA)
22. Brown U (RI)
23. Bryn Mawr C (PA)
24. Macalester C (MN)
25. Brandeis U (MA)

Source: Baccalaureate Origins of Earned Doctoral Degrees (2003–2012) compiled by the Office of Institutional Research, Pomona College in July 2015 (https://www.pomona.edu/sites/default/files/bacorigins_2003-2012.pdf). Data available from National Science Foundation through WebCASPAR (https://ncsesdata.nsf.gov/webcaspar/). Two surveys were used to compile these statistics: the NSF Survey of Earned Doctorates (http://www.nsf.gov/statistics/srvydoctorates/) and the IPEDS Completions Survey coordinated by the National Center for Education Statistics (http://nces.ed.gov/ipeds/). The data were retrieved by the Higher Education Data Sharing Consortium.

Where Social Science Ph.D.s Received Their Undergraduate Degrees

Listed here are colleges ranked in order of the highest number of doctoral degrees per hundred B.A./B.S. degrees, signifying the success of the school in sending its graduates on to achieve doctorates in social sciences (including subjects such as economics, political science, public policy, sociology, anthropology, linguistics, and area studies).

1. Swarthmore C (PA)
2. Reed C (OR)
3. Harvard U (MA)
4. Chicago, U of (IL)
5. Grinnell C (IA)
6. Bryn Mawr C (PA)
7. Amherst C (MA)
8. Macalester C (MN)
9. Oberlin C (OH)
10. Pomona C (CA)
11. Carleton C MN)
12. Wesleyan U (CT)
13. Williams C (MA)
14. Princeton U (NJ)
15. Yale U (CT)
16. St. John's C (MD)
17. Haverford C (PA)
18. Vassar C (NY)
19. Brown U (RI)
20. Stanford U (CA)
21. Wellesley C (MA)
22. Hampshire C (MA)
23. Dartmouth C (NH)
24. Beloit C (WI)
25. Bard C (NY)

Source: Baccalaureate Origins of Earned Doctoral Degrees (2003–2012) compiled by the Office of Institutional Research, Pomona College in July 2015 (https://www.pomona.edu/sites/default/files/bacorigins_2003-2012.pdf). Data available from National Science Foundation through WebCASPAR (https://ncsesdata.nsf.gov/webcaspar/). Two surveys were used to compile these statistics: the NSF Survey of Earned Doctorates (http://www.nsf.gov/statistics/srvydoctorates/) and the IPEDS Completions Survey coordinated by the National Center for Education Statistics (http://nces.ed.gov/ipeds/). The data were retrieved by the Higher Education Data Sharing Consortium.

CALENDARS

Colleges Where Students Take One Course at a Time

Taking one class at a time, typically for three or four weeks, is sometimes called a "block system."

Colorado C
Cornell C (IA)
Keiser U (FL)
Maharishi U of Management (IA)
Montana, U of, Western
Prescott C (AZ) (modified)
Quest U (Canada)
Spalding U (KY) (modified)
Tusculum C (TN)

Colleges Offering Unique Learning Opportunities in January

At these "four-one-four" colleges, a one-month "interim term" is incorporated between semesters, commonly in January. Although there are many variations, this January experience usually affords students opportunities for projects on and off campus, independent study or research, foreign study experiences, and internships.

Albright C (PA)
Augustana C (IL)
Austin C (TX)
Bethany C (KS)
Bethel C (KS)
Biola U (CA)
Cairn U (PA)
Chapman U (CA)
Colby C (ME)
Davis & Elkins C (WV)
Erskine C (SC)
Hartwick C (NY)
Idaho, C of
La Verne, U of (CA)
Linfield C (OR)
Luther C (IA)
Massachusetts Institute of Technology
Massachusetts Maritime Academy
McDaniel C (MD)
Mercyhurst U (PA)

Middlebury C (VT)
Midland U (NE)
Millersville U (PA)
Molloy C (NY)
Mt. Vernon Nazarene U (OH)
Oklahoma Baptist U
Pacific Lutheran U (WA)
Quinnipiac U (CT)
Rhode Island School of Design
San Diego, U of (CA)
Sioux Falls, U of (SD)
St. Norbert C (WI)
Sterling C (KS)
Trinity C (CT)
Washington & Jefferson C (PA)
Whitworth U (WA)
Williams C (MA)
Wilson C (PA)
Wofford C (SC)

Source: Wintergreen Orchard House

Colleges on a Quarter System

Under a quarter system, the academic year is divided into three terms (fall, winter, and spring) called quarters instead of the typical two semesters. Most schools also offer a fourth summer quarter. In other words, they divide the academic year (September to June) into three parts.

California Institute of Technology
California Polytechnic State U, San Luis Obispo
California Polytechnic State U, Pomona
California State U, Bakersfield
California State U, East Bay
California State U, Los Angeles
California State U, San Bernardino
California, U of, Davis
California, U of, Irvine
California, U of, Los Angeles
California, U of, Riverside
California, U of, San Diego
California, U of, Santa Barbara
California, U of, Santa Cruz
Capella U (MN)
Central Washington U (WA)
Chicago, U of (IL)
Dartmouth C (NH)
Denver, U of (CO)
DePaul U (IL)
Drexel U (PA)
Eastern Oregon U
Eastern Washington U
Evergreen State C (WA)
Johnson & Wales U (RI)
Kendall C (IL)
Loma Linda U (CA)
Louisiana Tech U

Marylhurst U (OR)
Milwaukee School of Engineering (WI)
North Central C (IL)
Northwestern U (IL)
Ohio State U, Lima
Ohio State U, Mansfield
Ohio State U, Marion
Ohio State U, Newark
Oregon Institute of Technology
Oregon State U
Oregon, U of
Pacific Union C (CA)
Portland State U (OR)
Rose-Hulman Institute of Technology (IN)
Rush U (IL)
Santa Clara U (CA)
Savannah C of Art & Design (GA)
Seattle Pacific U (WA)
Seattle U (WA)
Southern Oregon U
Stanford U (CA)
Texas Southern U
Walla Walla U (WA)
Washington, U of, Seattle
Western Oregon U
Western Washington U
Worcester Polytechnic Institute (MA)

Source: Wintergreen Orchard House

Colleges on a Trimester System

These are among the colleges that are on a trimester system. Three trimesters each academic year, 10 to 11 weeks per semester: it's different, but it works for these schools.

Augustana C (SD)
Carleton C (MN)
Carleton U (Canada)
Atlantic, C of the (ME)
Florida A&M U
Franklin U (OH)
Golden Gate U (CA)
Granite State C (NH)
Knox C (IL)
Lawrence U (WI)

Nova Southeastern U (FL)
Rocky Mountain C of Art & Design (CO)
Simon Fraser U (Canada)
Union C (NY)
U.S. Merchant Marine Academy (NY)
Louisiana, U of, Monroe
Michigan, U of, Ann Arbor
New South Wales, U of (Australia)
Science & Arts, U of (OK)
South Florida, U of

Toronto, U of (Canada)
Wilmington U (DE)

York U (Canada)

Source: Wintergreen Orchard House

The Experts' Choice: Colleges With Unique Calendars

Many colleges divide their academic year into two semesters of equal length while others segment the year into quarters and trimesters. Experts were asked to identify some schools that have instituted different ways of organizing time in the classroom.

- Alma C (MI): Alma uses a 4-4-1 academic calendar (fall and winter semesters of approximately 14 weeks each, followed by a one-month spring term in May). During their matriculation, students are required to take two spring term courses, one of which must cross geographical, cultural, or disciplinary boundaries.
- Bates C (ME): The Short Term is a five-week period of unusual courses (frequently conducted off campus) that cannot be accommodated during the regular semester.
- Colorado C: The academic calendar is organized around taking one class (or block) at a time, four blocks a semester, eight blocks per year. The College also offers a winter half-block and a summer session.
- Cornell C (IA): At this block-plan school, students take one class for 18 days, three to four hours a day, Monday through Friday, followed by a break of four and a half days.
- Dartmouth C (NH): The D-Plan, Dartmouth's flexible year-round system, allows students to choose which terms to enroll. First-year students and seniors may be required to be on campus during certain terms; sophomores have a required on-campus summer.
- Elmira C (NY): In April and May, Term III is a six-week study opportunity that allows for off-campus learning such as study abroad and internships as well as in-depth exploration of a topic or immersion in a project.
- Florida Southern C: Summer sessions (varying from five to 10 weeks each) enable students to take courses online, work toward early graduation, or retake a class to improve their GPA.
- Hanover C (IN): Fall and winter terms last 17 to 18 weeks each, whereas spring term is only the month of May.
- Kalamazoo C (MI): To accommodate experiential learning, the academic calendar provides blocks of time during which students can pursue career development, foreign study, internships, and research.
- Maharishi U of Management (IA): The University operates on a 12-blocks-per-year system, with students taking one course per month, followed by a three-and-a-half-day rest between each block.
- Quest U (Canada): As at other block-plan schools, studying a single subject every day over a three-week-plus period allows students to focus on and explore an area in depth. With two 16-week semesters of four blocks each and two additional summer blocks, students have the flexibility to tailor their schedule to their needs and interests.
- Tusculum C (TN): Under the Focused Calendar, another block plan, Tusculum students "live and breathe" every subject they study.
- Montana, U of, Western: With its Experience One program, Montana Western is the only public college in the nation where students take one course at a time.
- Worcester Polytechnic Institute (MA): The WPI academic calendar consists of six terms of approximately seven weeks each.

Steven R. Antonoff

INTERNATIONALISM/STUDY ABROAD

STUDY ABROAD

The Experts' Choice: Terrific Study Abroad Programs

Most colleges offer foreign study/study abroad programs. Experts were asked to identify colleges where many students study abroad and/or colleges with particularly strong programs.

Top Choices

Arcadia U (PA)
Boston U (MA)
Colgate U (NY)
Denver, U of (CO)
Dickinson C (PA)
Goucher C (MD)
Hamilton C (NY)
Holy Cross, C of the (MA)
Kalamazoo C (MI)
Lewis & Clark C (OR)
Middlebury C (VT)
New York U
St. Olaf C (MN)
Syracuse U (NY)

Honorable Mention

American Jewish U (CA)
American U (DC)
Beloit C (WI)
Bowdoin C (ME)
Calvin C (MI)
Carleton C (MN)
Colorado, U of, Boulder
Columbia U (NY)
Concordia C (MN)
Connecticut C
Covenant C (GA)
Dartmouth C (NH)
DePauw U (IN)
Earlham C (IN)

Eckerd C (FL)
Elon U (NC)
Evansville, U of (IN)
Franciscan U (OH)
Georgetown U (DC)
Goshen C (IN)
Grinnell C (IA)
Guilford C (NC)
Gustavus Adolphus C (MN)
Linfield C (OR)
Macalester C (MN)
Maryland, U of, College Park
New York U
Pacific Lutheran U (WA)
Pitzer C (CA)
Pomona C (CA)
Princeton U (NJ)
Queens U (NC)
Richmond, U of (VA)
Scripps C (CA)
Soka U of America (CA)
St. Benedict, C of (MN)
St. John's U (NY)
Stanford U (CA)
Trinity C (CT)
Tufts U (MA)
Union C (NY)
Westmont C (CA)
Whitman C (WA)
Worcester Polytechnic Institute (MA)
Yeshiva U (NY)

Highest Number of Students Studying Abroad From Colleges Offering Doctoral Degrees

1. New York U
2. Texas, U of, Austin
3. Southern California, U of
4. Minnesota, U of, Twin Cities
5. Michigan State U
6. Michigan, U of, Ann Arbor
7. Ohio State U, Columbus
8. Texas A&M U
9. Wisconsin, U of, Madison
10. Indiana U Bloomington

11. Boston U (MA)
12. Pennsylvania, U of
13. California, U of, Los Angeles
14. Washington, U of
15. Florida, U of

16. Illinois, U of, Urbana
17. Georgia, U of
18. Florida State U
19. Maryland, U of, College Park
20. George Washington U (DC)

Source: C. Farrugia and R. Bhandari, 2014. Open Doors 2014: *Report on International Educational Exchange*. New York: Institute of International Education. Data are for 2013–2014. Used with permission. This list includes only doctoral-granting institutions.

Where the Highest Percentage of Undergraduates Study Abroad From Colleges Offering Doctoral Degrees

1. Denver, U of (CO)
2. San Diego, U of (CA)
3. Wake Forest U (NC)
4. New York U
5. American U (DC)
6. Pepperdine U (CA)
7. Stanford U (CA)
8. St. Thomas, U of (MN)
9. Dartmouth C (NH)
10. Duke U (NC)

11. Yale U (CT)
12. Notre Dame, U of (IN)
13. Boston C (MA)
14. Georgetown U (DC)
15. Boston U (MA)
16. Washington U (MO)
17. Syracuse U (NY)
18. George Washington U (DC)
19. Tufts U (MA)
20. William & Mary, C of (VA)

Source: C. Farrugia and R. Bhandari, 2014. Open Doors 2014: *Report on International Educational Exchange*. New York: Institute of International Education. Data are for 2013–2014. Used with permission. This list includes only doctoral-granting institutions.

Highest Number of Students Studying Abroad From Colleges Offering Master's Degrees

1. Arcadia U (Canada)
2. Elon U (NC)
3. Dallas, U of (TX)
4. Lee U (TN)
5. Wingate U
6. Loyola U (MD)
7. Queens U (NC)
8. St. Mary's C (CA)
9. Bryant U (RI)
10. Whitworth U (WA)

11. Marist C (NY)
12. Rollins C (FL)
13. Stetson U (FL)
14. Pacific Lutheran U (WA)
15. Redlands, U of (CA)
16. Evansville, U of (IN)
17. Chapman U (CA)
18. Villanova U (PA)
19. Bentley U (MA)
20. Butler U (IN)

Source: C. Farrugia and R. Bhandari, 2014. Open Doors 2014: *Report on International Educational Exchange*. New York: Institute of International Education. Data are for 2013–2014. Used with permission.

Institutions by Total Number of Study Abroad Students: Top Associate Colleges 2012–2013

1. Orange Coast C (CA): 249
2. Du Page, C of (IL): 221
3. Miami Dade C (FL): 200
4. Pellissippi State Community C (TN): 182
5. Cabrillo C (CA): 139
6. Kirkwood Community C (IA): 137

Steven R. Antonoff

7. New York, State U of, Broome Community C: 130
8. San Francisco, City C of (CA): 116
9. Mesa Community C (AZ): 106
10. Valencia C (FL): 104
11. Citrus C (CA): 103
12. Santa Barbara City C (CA): 88
13. Riverside Community C (CA): 81
14. Cosumnes River C (CA): 78
15. Southwest Tennessee Community C: 70
16. Pasadena City C (CA): 69
17. Austin Community C (TX): 68
18. Diablo Valley C (TX): 66
18. Santa Rosa Junior (CA): 66
20. Tulsa Community C (OK): 61

Source: C. Farrugia and R. Bhandari, 2014. Open Doors 2014: *Report on International Educational Exchange.* New York: Institute of International Education. Data are for 2013–2014. Used with permission.

Colleges Where Freshman Year Study Abroad Is Common

Studying internationally is common. Most students study abroad during their junior (or even sophomore) year. At the colleges listed here, study abroad is available to freshmen as well.

Arcadia U (PA)
Colby C (ME)
Florida State U
Hamilton C (NY)
Michigan State U
Middlebury C (VT)
Mississippi, U of

New Haven, U of (CT)
New York U
Plymouth State U (NH)
Syracuse U (NY)
Wheaton C (IL)

Top 20 Leading Destinations of U.S. Study Abroad Students

1. United Kingdom
2. Italy
3. Spain
4. France
5. China
6. Germany
7. Costa Rica
8. Australia
9. Ireland
10. Japan

11. South Africa
12. Argentina
13. India
14. Brazil
15. Mexico
16. Czech Republic
17. Ecuador
18. Denmark
19. South Korea
20. Peru

Source: C. Farrugia and R. Bhandari, 2014. Open Doors 2014: *Report on International Educational Exchange.* New York: Institute of International Education. Data are for 2013–2014. Used with permission.

Colleges That Are Members of the Intercollegiate Center for Classical Studies in Rome

These are the members of the Intercollegiate Center for Classical Studies in Rome. This is a semester program in which the schools "provide undergraduate students with an opportunity in Rome to study ancient history, archaeology, Greek and Latin literature, Italian language, and ancient art."

Amherst C (MA)
Barnard C (NY)
Bates C (ME)
Beloit C (WI)
Boston C (MA)
Boston U (MA)
Bowdoin C (ME)
Brown U (RI)
Bryn Mawr C (PA)
California State U, Long Beach
California, U of, Berkeley
California, U of, Davis
California, U of, Los Angeles
California, U of, Riverside
California, U of, San Diego
California, U of, Santa Barbara
Carleton C (MN)
Centre C (KY)
Christopher Newport U (VA)
Cincinnati, U of (OH)
Claremont McKenna C (CA)
Colgate U (NY)
Colorado, U of, Boulder
Columbia U (NY)
Connecticut C
Cornell U (NY)
Creighton U (NE)
Davidson C (NC)
Denison U (OH)
DePauw U (IN)
Dickinson C (PA)
Duke U (NC)
Emory U (GA)
Fordham U (NY)
Franklin & Marshall C (PA)
Furman U (SC)
George Washington U (DC)
Georgetown U (DC)
Georgia, U of
Gettysburg C (PA)
Grand Valley State U (MI)
Grinnell C (IA)
Gustavus Adolphus C (MN)
Hamilton C (NY)
Harvard U (MA)
Haverford C (PA)
Hollins U (VA)

Holy Cross, C of the (MA)
Indiana U Bloomington
Iowa, U of
Johns Hopkins U (MD)
Kalamazoo C (MI)
Kansas, U of
Kenyon C (OH)
Knox C (IL)
Lawrence U (WI)
Lehigh U (PA)
Louisiana State U, Baton Rouge
Loyola U (MD)
Macalester C (MN)
Mary Washington, U of (VA)
Massachusetts, U of, Amherst
Michigan State U
Michigan, U of, Ann Arbor
Middlebury C (VT)
Millsaps C (MS)
Mississippi, U of
Missouri, U of, Columbia
Mt. Holyoke C (MA)
New Hampshire, U of
New York U
New York, State U of, Buffalo
North Carolina, U of, Chapel Hill
Northwestern State U (LA)
Northwestern U (IL)
Notre Dame, U of (IN)
Oberlin C (OH)
Ohio State U, Columbus
Ohio Wesleyan U
Pennsylvania, U of
Pittsburg, U of (PA)
Pitzer C (CA)
Pomona C (CA)
Princeton U (NJ)
Puget Sound, U of (WA)
Randolph C (VA)
Randolph-Macon C (VA)
Reed C (OR)
Rhodes C (TN)
Rice U (TX)
Richmond, U of (VA)
Rochester, U of (NY)
Rollins C (FL)
Rutgers U, New Brunswick (NJ)

San Diego State U (CA)
San Francisco State U (CA)
Scripps C (CA)
Skidmore C (NY)
Smith C (MA)
South, U of the (TN)
Southern California, U of
Southwestern U (TX)
St. Joseph's U (PA)
Stanford U (CA)
Swarthmore C (PA)
Sweet Briar C (VA)
Texas A&M U
Texas, U of, Austin
Trinity C (CT)
Trinity U (TX)
Tulane U (LA)
Union C (KY)

Vanderbilt U (TN)
Vassar C (NY)
Vermont, U of
Virginia Polytechnic Institute & State U
Virginia, U of
Wabash C (IN)
Wake Forest U (NC)
Washington & Lee U (VA)
Washington U (MO)
Wellesley C (MA)
Wesleyan U (CT)
Whitman C (WA)
Willamette U (OR)
William & Mary, C of (VA)
Williams C (MA)
Wisconsin, U of, Madison
Wooster, C of (OH)
Yale U (CT)

Source: Duke Global Education for Undergraduates (studyabroad.duke.edu)

Colleges in the Associated Kyoto Program

These schools are members of a consortium that sponsors students for study in Japan for one year.

Amherst C (MA)
Bates C (ME)
Bucknell U (PA)
Carleton C (MN)
Colby C (ME)
Connecticut C
Middlebury C (VT)
Mt. Holyoke C (MA)

Oberlin C (OH)
Pomona C (CA)
Smith C (MA)
Wellesley C (MA)
Wesleyan U (CT)
Whitman C (WA)
Williams C (MA)

INTERNATIONAL UNIVERSITIES FOR AMERICAN STUDENTS

Great Global Universities

Rankings are based on such variables as teaching, research, international outlook, and reputation.

1. California Institute of Technology
2. Oxford, U of (United Kingdom)
3. Stanford U (CA)
4. Cambridge, U of (United Kingdom)
5. Massachusetts Institute of Technology
6. Harvard U (MA)
7. Princeton U (NJ)
8. Imperial C London (United Kingdom)
9. ETH Zurich—Swiss Federal Institute of Technology Zurich (Switzerland)
10. Chicago, U of (IL)
11. Johns Hopkins U (MD)

12. Yale U (CT)
13. California, U of, Berkeley
14. U C London (United Kingdom)
15. Columbia U (NY)
16. California, U of, Los Angeles
17. Pennsylvania, U of
18. Cornell U (NY)
19. Toronto, U of (Canada)
20. Duke U (NC)
21. Michigan, U of, Ann Arbor
22. Carnegie Mellon U (PA)
23. London School of Economics & Political Science (United Kingdom)
24. Edinburgh, U of (United Kingdom)
25. Northwestern U (IL)
26. Singapore, National U of
27. King's C London (United Kingdom)
28. Karolinska Institute (Sweden)
29. LMU Munich (Germany)
30. New York U

Source: *Times Higher Education* World University Rankings (timeshighereducation.com)

American Universities Outside the United States

The Association of American International Colleges and Universities is "a leadership organization of American international universities, whose members provide responsible delivery and quality assurance of American higher education outside the United States."

Regular Members

American C of Greece
American C of Thessaloniki (Greece)
American U in Bulgaria
American U in Cairo (Egypt)
American U of Armenia
American U of Beirut (Lebanon)
American U of Central Asia (Kyrgyzstan)
American U of Paris (France)
American U of Rome (Italy)
American U of Sharjah (United Arab Emirates)

American Universities, Institute for (France)
Central European U (Hungary)
Franklin U (Switzerland)
Haigazian U (Lebanon)
Irish American U (Ireland)
John Cabot U (Italy)
Lebanese American U
Richmond, The American International U in London (United Kingdom)

Associate Members

Al Akhawayn U in Ifrane (AUI) (Morocco)
American College & University Programs in Italy, Association of (AACUPI)
American U of Afghanistan (AUAF)

American U of Iraq, Sulaimani
American U of Kosovo
American U of Nigeria (ABTI)
Forman Christian C (Pakistan)
St. Louis U (Spain)

Source: Association of American International Colleges and Universities (aaicu.org)

Steven R. Antonoff

Colleges With International Campuses

The location of the main campus is listed before the location of the international campus.

Carnegie Mellon U (PA) (Qatar)
Cornell Medical C (NY) (Qatar)
George Mason U (VA) (Seoul)
Georgetown U (DC) (Qatar)
Heriot-Watt U (United Kingdom) (Dubai)
INSEAD Business School of the World
  (France) (Abu Dhabi)
London Business School (United
  Kingdom) (Dubai)
Marist C (NY) (Florence)
Massachusetts, U of, Lowell (Kuwait)
Murdoch U (Australia) (Dubai)

New York U (Abu Dhabi, Shanghai)
Northwestern U (IL) (Qatar)
Paris-Sorbonne U (France) (Abu Dhabi)
Rochester Institute of Technology (NY)
  (Dubai)
Texas A&M U (Qatar)
Virginia Commonwealth U (Qatar)
Webster U (MO) (Accra, Athens,
  Bangkok, Beijing, Chengdu, Geneva,
  Jakarta, Leiden, London, Shanghai,
  Vienna)

Emerging International Universities

This is a ranking of the top 100 universities less than 50 years old. Rankings are based on such variables as teaching, research, international outlook, and reputation.

1. École Polytechnique Fédérale de Lausanne (Switzerland)
2. Nanyang Technological U (Singapore)
3. Hong Kong U of Science & Technology (Hong Kong)
4. Maastricht U (Netherlands)
5. Pohang U of Science & Technology (South Korea)
6. Korea Advanced Institute of Science & Technology (South Korea)
7. Konstanz, U of (Germany)
8. Karlsruhe Institute of Technology (Germany)
9. Pierre & Marie Curie U (France)
10. Scuola Superiore Sant'Anna (Italy)
11. Antwerp, U of (Belgium)
12. Barcelona, Autonomous U of (Spain)
13. Ulm U (Germany)
14. Luxembourg, U of
15. Pompeu Fabra U (Spain)
16. Dundee, U of (United Kingdom)
17. Duisburg-Essen, U of (Germany)
18. Calgary, U of (Canada)
18. Paris-Sud U (France)
20. Hong Kong, City U of (Hong Kong)
21. Sydney, U of Technology (Australia)
22. Rush U (IL)
23. Bielefeld U (Germany)
24. Texas, U of, Dallas
25. Paris Diderot U (France)
26. Swedish U of Agricultural Sciences
27. Hong Kong Polytechnic U (Hong Kong)
28. Aalto U (Finland)
28. Paris Descartes U (France)
28. Queensland U of Technology (Australia)

Source: *Times Higher Education* World University Rankings (timeshighereducation.com)

Notable Universities in Asia

Rankings are based on such variables as teaching, research, international outlook, and reputation.

1. Tokyo, U of (Japan)
2. Singapore, National U of
3. Hong Kong, U of (Hong Kong)
4. Peking U (China)
5. Tsinghua U (China)
6. Seoul National U (South Korea)
7. Hong Kong U of Science & Technology (Hong Kong)
8. Korea Advanced Institute of Science & Technology (South Korea)
9. Kyoto U (Japan)
10. Nanyang Technological U (Singapore)
11. Pohang U of Science & Technology (South Korea)
12. Middle East Technical U (Turkey)
13. Hong Kong, Chinese U of (Hong Kong)
14. Boğaziçi U (Turkey)
15. Tokyo Institute of Technology (Japan)
16. Sungkyunkwan U (South Korea)
17. National Taiwan U
18. Osaka U (Japan)
19. Istanbul Technical U (Turkey)
19. Tohoku U (Japan)
21. Sabancı U (Turkey)
22. Tel Aviv U (Israel)
23. Hong Kong, City U of (Hong Kong)
24. Fudan U (China)
25. Jerusalem, Hebrew U of (Israel)
26. Korea U (South Korea)
26. China, U of Science & Technology
28. Yonsei U (South Korea)
29. Hong Kong Polytechnic U (Hong Kong)
30. Bilkent U (Turkey)

Source: *Times Higher Education* World University Rankings (timeshighereducation.com)

The Experts' Choice: Great Canadian Colleges for American Students

Experts were asked to name colleges in Canada that are particularly welcoming to American students. Where not otherwise stated, the Canadian province is given in parentheses.

Acadia U (Nova Scotia)
Bishop's U (Quebec)
British Columbia, U of
Concordia U (Quebec)
Dalhousie U (Nova Scotia)
Guelph, U of (Ontario)
McGill U (Quebec)
Mt. Allison U (New Brunswick)

Queen's U (Ontario)
Quest U (British Columbia)
Ryerson U (Ontario)
Simon Fraser U (British Columbia)
Toronto, U of (Ontario)
Victoria, U of (British Columbia)
Waterloo, U of (Ontario)
Western Ontario, U

Canadian Residential Colleges

The Canadian colleges on this list have 15% or more of their students living on campus.

Acadia U (Canada)
Ambrose U (Canada)
Bishop's U (Canada)
Brescia University C (Canada)
Brock U (Canada)
Carleton U (Canada)
Dalhousie U (Canada)
Guelph, U of (Canada)
King's College, U of (Canada)
Laurentian U (Canada)
McMaster U (Canada)
Memorial U (Canada)
Mt. Allison U (Canada)

Mt. Saint Vincent U (Canada)
New Brunswick, U of, Fredericton (Canada)
New Brunswick, U of, St. John (Canada)
Nipissing U (Canada)
Queen's U (Canada)
St. Francis Xavier U (Canada)
St. Thomas U (Canada)
Trent U (Canada)
Université de Sherbrooke (Canada)
Waterloo, U of (Canada)
Western U (Canada)
Wilfrid Laurier U (Canada)

The Experts' Choice: Great Schools in China for American Students

Experts were asked to name colleges in China that are particularly welcoming to American students. Where not otherwise stated, the city name is given in parentheses.

Beijing Language & Cultural U
Chinese U of Hong Kong
Guizhou U (Guiyang)
Hong Kong Baptist U

New York U Shanghai
Peking U (Beijing)
Shanghai Jiao Tong U
Shanghai U

The Experts' Choice: Great Colleges in the British Isles for American Students

Experts were asked to name colleges in the British Isles that are particularly welcoming to American students.

Edinburgh, U of (United Kingdom)
Kings C London (United Kingdom)
Oxford, U of (United Kingdom)
Richmond, The American International U in London (United Kingdom)
St. Andrews, U of (United Kingdom)*
Trinity C, Dublin (United Kingdom)

*The Top Choice

The Experts' Choice: Colleges to Consider in England and Scotland

England

Bristol, U of (United Kingdom)
Camberwell C of Arts (United Kingdom)
Cambridge, U of (United Kingdom)
Central St. Martins (United Kingdom)
Chelsea C of Arts (United Kingdom)

Durham, U of (United Kingdom)
King's C London (United Kingdom)
London C of Communication (United Kingdom)
London C of Fashion (United Kingdom)
London School of Economics & Political Science (United Kingdom)
London, U of, Goldsmiths (United Kingdom)
London, U of, Royal Holloway (United Kingdom)
Nottingham, U of (United Kingdom)
Oxford, U of (United Kingdom)
Queen Mary U of London (United Kingdom)
Regent's U (United Kingdom)
Richmond, The American International U in London (United Kingdom)
Roehampton, U of (United Kingdom)
School of Oriental & Asian Studies (United Kingdom)
U C, London (United Kingdom)
Warwick, U of (United Kingdom)
Wimbledon C of Arts (United Kingdom)
York, U of (United Kingdom)

Scotland

Edinburgh C of Art (United Kingdom)
Edinburgh, U of (United Kingdom)
Glasgow C of Art (United Kingdom)
Glasgow, U of (United Kingdom)
St. Andrews, U of (United Kingdom)

Top Universities in the United Kingdom

Universities that are members of the Russell Group "provide an outstanding student experience for both undergraduates and postgraduates. Their combination of teaching and research excellence creates an ideal learning environment which attracts the most outstanding students from the U.K. and across the world."

Birmingham, U of (United Kingdom)
Bristol, U of (United Kingdom)
Cambridge, U of (United Kingdom)
Cardiff U (United Kingdom)
Durham U (United Kingdom)
Edinburgh, U of (United Kingdom)
Exeter, U of (United Kingdom)
Glasgow, U of (United Kingdom)
Imperial C London (United Kingdom)
King's C London (United Kingdom)
Leeds, U of (United Kingdom)
Liverpool, U of (United Kingdom)
London School of Economics & Political Science (United Kingdom)
Manchester, U of (United Kingdom)
Newcastle U (United Kingdom)
Nottingham, U of (United Kingdom)
Oxford, U of (United Kingdom)
Queen Mary U of London (United Kingdom)
Queen's U, Belfast (United Kingdom)

Sheffield, U of (United Kingdom)
Southampton, U of (United Kingdom)
University C London (United Kingdom)
Warwick, U of (United Kingdom)
York, U of (United Kingdom)

Source: Russell Group (russellgroup.ac.uk)

International Universities Distinguished in the Arts and Humanities

Rankings are based on such variables as teaching, research, international outlook, and reputation.

1. Stanford U (CA)
2. Harvard U (MA)
3. Massachusetts Institute of Technology
4. Oxford, U of (United Kingdom)
5. U C London (United Kingdom)
6. Cambridge, U of (United Kingdom)
7. California, U of, Berkeley
8. Chicago, U of (IL)
9. Columbia U (NY)
9. Princeton U (NJ)
11. Yale U (CT)
12. California, U of, Los Angeles
13. Pennsylvania, U of
14. Toronto, U of (Canada)
15. King's C London (United Kingdom)

16. Edinburgh, U of (United Kingdom)
17. Leiden U (Netherlands)
18. Berlin, Free U of (Germany)
19. Michigan, U of, Ann Arbor
20. New York U
21. Berlin, Humboldt U of (Germany)
22. Duke U (NC)
23. LMU Munich (Germany)
24. Heidelberg U (Germany)
25. Cornell U (NY)
25. York, U of (United Kingdom)
27. KU Leuven (Belgium)
28. Durham U (United Kingdom)
29. Sydney, U of (Australia)
30. Amsterdam, U of (Netherlands)
30. Warwick, U of (United Kingdom)

Source: *Times Higher Education* World University Rankings (timeshighereducation.com)

International Universities Distinguished in the Physical Sciences

Rankings are based on such variables as teaching, research, international outlook, and reputation.

1. California Institute of Technology
2. Stanford U (CA)
3. Massachusetts Institute of Technology
4. California, U of, Berkeley
5. Princeton U (NJ)
6. Cambridge, U of (United Kingdom) (tie)
6. Harvard U (MA) (tie)
8. Oxford, U of (United Kingdom)
9. Cornell U (NY)
10. Carnegie Mellon U (PA)
11. California, U of, Los Angeles
12. ETH Zurich—Swiss Federal Institute of Technology Zurich (Switzerland)
13. Yale U (CT)

14. École Polytechnique Fédérale de Lausanne (Switzerland)
15. Chicago, U of (IL)
16. Imperial C London (United Kingdom)
17. Illinois, U of, Urbana
18. Columbia U (NY)
19. Singapore, National U of
20. Toronto, U of (Canada)
21. Washington, U of
22. École Polytechnique (France)
23. Edinburgh, U of (United Kingdom)
24. Georgia Institute of Technology
25. École Normale Supérieure (France)
26. LMU Munich (Germany)
27. U C London (United Kingdom)
28. Peking U (China)

29. California, U of, Santa Barbara   30. Texas, U of, Austin

Source: *Times Higher Education* World University Rankings (timeshighereducation.com)

Reputation of International Universities

Only subjective judgment of reputation was considered in this ranking by *Times Higher Education*.

1. Harvard U (MA)
2. Massachusetts Institute of Technology
3. Stanford U (CA)
4. Cambridge, U of (United Kingdom)
5. Oxford, U of (United Kingdom)
6. California, U of, Berkeley
7. Princeton U (NJ)
8. Yale U (CT)
9. Columbia U (NY)
10. California Institute of Technology
11. Chicago, U of (IL)
12. Tokyo, U of (Japan)
13. California, U of, Los Angeles
14. Michigan, U of, Ann Arbor
15. Imperial C London (United Kingdom)
16. Pennsylvania, U of
17. Cornell U (NY)

18. Tsinghua U (China)
19. ETH Zurich—Swiss Federal Institute of Technology Zurich (Switzerland)
20. U C London (United Kingdom)
21. Peking U (China)
22. Johns Hopkins U (MD)
23. Toronto, U of (Canada)
24. London School of Economics & Political Science (United Kingdom)
25. New York U
26. Singapore, National U of
27. Kyoto U (Japan)
28. Duke U (NC)
29. Washington, U of
30. Illinois, U of, Urbana
30. Lomonosov Moscow State U (Russia)
30. Northwestern U (IL)

Source: *Times Higher Education* World University Rankings (timeshighereducation.com)

INTERNATIONAL ENROLLMENT

Colleges With the Largest Enrollment of International Students

We dug through our database to find the total enrollment of international students at each college.

Purdue U (IN): 4,981
Michigan State U: 4,798
Illinois, U of, Urbana: 4,504
York U (Canada): 4,299
Indiana U Bloomington: 3,706
Washington, U of, Seattle: 3,559
Ft. Hays State U (KS): 3,543
California, U of, Berkeley: 3,407
Ohio State U, Columbus: 3,343
New York, State U of, Buffalo: 3,285
New York U: 3,097
Minnesota, U of, Twin Cities: 3,073
Boston U (MA): 2,833
California State U, Northridge: 2,470

Southern California, U of: 2,335
Iowa, U of: 2,259
Iowa State U: 2,172
San Francisco State U (CA): 2,007
Michigan, U of, Ann Arbor: 1,954
Texas, U of, Austin: 1,888
Florida International U: 1,869
Arizona, U of: 1,807
Drexel U (PA): 1,735
New York, State U of, Stony Brook: 1,731
Utah, U of: 1,729
New York, City U of, Baruch C: 1,669
Oregon State U: 1,656

Kent State U (OH): 1,580
Georgia Institute of Technology: 1,544
California State U, Fullerton: 1,528
New York, State U of, Binghamton:
   1,482
Cornell U (NY): 1,418
Portland State U (OR): 1,399

Rutgers U, New Brunswick (NJ): 1,395
Kansas, U of: 1,285
Syracuse U (NY): 1,239
Carnegie Mellon U (PA): 1,215
Fashion Institute of Technology (NY):
   1,212
Central Oklahoma, U of: 1,205

Source: Wintergreen Orchard House

Colleges With the Highest Percentage of International Students

These colleges and universities aren't kidding around when it comes to diversity.

Knoxville C (TN): 92.73%
Soka U of America (CA): 38.59%
Southern California Institute of
Architecture: 34.36%
Northwood U (multiple campuses):
   32.90%
Ft. Hays State U (KS): 30.99%
Florida Institute of Technology: 30.94%
New England Conservatory of Music
   (MA): 29.47%
Babson C (MA): 26.35%
Tulsa, U of (OK): 25.99%
Art Institute of Chicago, School of the
   (IL): 25.97%
ArtCenter C of Design (CA): 25.30%
San Francisco Conservatory of Music
   (CA): 25.29%
Mt. Holyoke C (MA): 25.10%
Visual Arts, School of (NY): 24.37%
Illinois Institute of Technology: 23.92%
Santa Fe U (NM): 23.24%
Lynn U (FL): 23.14%
Pratt Institute (NY): 22.99%

Bryn Mawr C (PA): 22.89%
Juilliard School (NY): 19.28%
Carnegie Mellon U (PA): 19.27%
Suffolk U (MA): 19.25%
California C of the Arts: 18.62%
Earlham C (IN): 18.42%
San Francisco State U (CA): 18.34%
Cleveland Institute of Music (OH):
   18.22%
Principia C (IL): 17.92%
Purdue U (IN): 16.92%
Westminster C (UT): 16.86%
Andrews U (MI): 16.80%
Otis C of Art & Design (CA): 16.74%
New York, State U of, Buffalo: 16.56%
Boston U (MA): 15.60%
Atlantic, C of the (ME): 15.47%
Claremont McKenna C (CA): 14.67%
Oklahoma City U: 14.64%
Embry-Riddle Aeronautical U (FL):
   14.62%
Niagara U (NY): 14.41%
Chatham U (PA): 14.23%

Source: Wintergreen Orchard House

Colleges With the Most Foreign Countries Represented by their International Students

Is this the Student Union or the Olympic Village? Attending one of these colleges will give you chance to meet students from all over the world! Maybe learn how to say "hello" in a few languages? *Hej! Ciao! Merhaba!* Just a thought . . .

York U (Canada): 177
American Public U System (WV): 174
New York, City U of, Baruch C: 164
Tampa, U of (FL): 161
Georgia State U: 151
Toronto, U of (Canada): 150

Concordia U (OR): 150
British Columbia, U of (Canada): 148
Ryerson U (Canada): 147
McGill U (Canada): 136
Florida Atlantic U: 134
Texas, U of, Arlington: 123

Kennesaw State U (GA): 123
Georgia, U of: 122
Guelph, U of (Canada): 120
Anglia Ruskin U (United Kingdom): 120
Virginia, U of: 119
San Diego State U (CA): 118
Drexel U (PA): 118
Central Florida, U of: 116
Florida International U: 115
Dalhousie U (Canada): 115
American U (DC): 114
American U of Paris (France): 113
Miami, U of (FL): 113
Arkansas, U of, Fayetteville: 113
New York, City U of, York C: 112

New York, State U of, Stony Brook: 109
Ohio State U, Columbus: 109
Nuova Accademia di Belle Arti (Italy): 108
Oklahoma, U of: 107
Savannah C of Art & Design (GA): 107
Jacobs U (Germany): 107
Iowa State U: 106
Rochester Institute of Technology (NY): 105
Western Michigan U: 104
Pennsylvania, U of: 103
New York, City U of, C of Technology: 103
Texas, U of, San Antonio: 103

Source: Wintergreen Orchard House

Doctoral-Level Institutions with the Most International Students

1. New York U
2. Southern California, U of
3. Columbia U (NY)
4. Arizona State U
5. Illinois, U of, Urbana
6. Northeastern U (MA)
7. Purdue U, West Lafayette (IN)
8. California, U of, Los Angeles
9. Michigan State U
10. Washington, U of

Source: *Chronicle of Higher Education*

Master's-Level Institutions with the Most International Students

1. San Jose State U (CA)
2. California State U, Northridge
3. California State U, Fullerton
4. California State U, Long Beach
5. Rochester Institute of Technology (NY)
6. New York Institute of Technology, Old Westbury
7. San Francisco State U (CA)
8. Central Missouri, U of
9. New York, City U of, Baruch C
10. Johnson & Wales U (RI)

Source: *Chronicle of Higher Education*

Bachelor's Level Colleges With the Most International Students

Bard C (NY)
Brigham Young U (HI)
Brigham Young U (ID)

Steven R. Antonoff

Bryn Mawr C (PA)
Calvin C (MI)
Middlebury C (VT)
Mt. Holyoke C (MA)
Richmond, U of (VA)
Smith C (MA)
Utah Valley U

Source: Institute of International Education, *Chronicle of Higher Education*

Community Colleges With the Most International Students

1. Houston Community C (TX)
2. Santa Monica C (CA)
3. De Anza C (CA)
4. Seattle Central Community C (WA)
5. Lone Star College System (TX)
6. Diablo Valley C (CA)
7. Montgomery C (MD)
8. Johnson County Community C (KS)
9. Northern Virginia Community C
10. Green River Community C (WA)

Sources: Institute of International Education, *Chronicle of Higher Education*

Special-Focus Institutions with the Most International Students

1. Academy of Art U (CA)
2. Savannah C of Art & Design (GA)
3. Visual Arts, School of (NY)
4. New York Film Academy (CA)
5. Art Institute, School of the (IL)
6. Babson C (MA)
7. Berkeley C (NY)
8. Rhode Island School of Design
9. Massachusetts C of Pharmacy & Health Sciences
10. ArtCenter C of Design (CA)

States With the Most International College Students

1. California
2. New York
3. Texas
4. Massachusetts
5. Illinois
6. Pennsylvania
7. Florida
8. Ohio
9. Michigan
10. Indiana
11. Washington
12. Missouri
13. Georgia
14. Virginia
15. New Jersey

Source: C. Farrugia and R. Bhandari, *Open Doors*, Institute of International Education.

States with the Highest Percentage of International Students

1. Washington, DC: 11.1%
2. Massachusetts: 9.9%
3. New York: 7.6%
4. Delaware: 7.3%
5. Washington: 7.0%
6. Rhode Island: 6.6%
7. Indiana: 5.9%
8. Hawaii: 5.6%
9. Pennsylvania: 5.3%
10. Connecticut: 5.2%
10. Oregon: 5.2%
12. Kansas: 5.0%
12. North Dakota: 5.0%
14. Illinois: 4.9%
15. California: 4.6%
15. Ohio: 4.6%
17. Michigan: 4.5%
18. Maryland: 4.3%
19. Texas: 4.2%
20. Missouri: 4.1%

Source: C. Farrugia and R. Bhandari, *Open Doors*, Institute of International Education.

COMMUNITY COLLEGES

Community Colleges Awarding the Most Degrees: Two-Year Schools

This list includes degrees in all fields of study.

1. Ivy Tech Community C (IN)
2. Northern Virginia Community C
3. Tarrant County C District (TX)
4. Houston Community C (TX)
5. Lone Star C System (TX)
6. Salt Lake Community C (UT)
7. Suffolk County Community C (NY)
8. Portland Community C (OR)
9. El Paso Community C (TX)
10. Hillsborough Community C (FL)
11. New York, City U of, Borough of Manhattan Community C
12. Central New Mexico Community C
13. Nassau Community C (NY)
14. Cuyahoga Community C (OH)
15. Central Texas C
16. Tidewater Community C (VA)
17. San Jacinto Community C (TX)
18. New York, City U of, Kingsborough Community C
19. Macomb Community C (MI)
20. Pima Community C (AZ)

Source: *Community College Week*

Community Colleges Awarding the Most Degrees: Four-Year Schools

This list includes degrees in all fields of study. These are four-year schools that offer two-year degrees.

1. Phoenix, U of (AZ)
2. Miami Dade C (FL)
3. Valencia C (FL)
4. Broward C (FL)
5. Florida State C at Jacksonville
6. Palm Beach State C (FL)
7. St. Petersburg C (FL)
8. Keiser U (FL)
9. Kaplan U, Davenport (IA)
10. South Texas C
11. Everest U South Orlando (FL)
12. Seminole State C of Florida
13. Eastern Florida State C
14. Santa Fe C (FL)
15. Southern Nevada, C of
16. Indian River State C (FL)

17. Daytona State C (FL)
18. Utah Valley U

19. Florida SouthWestern State C
20. Bellevue C (WA)

Source: *Community College Week*

Community Colleges Awarding the Most Two-Year Certificates: Two-Year Schools

This list includes certificates in all fields of study. A certificate is a credential that is focused on a specific topic. It can mean you have the technical knowledge of a distinct field. Certificates usually require fewer credits as compared to degree programs.

1. Ivy Tech Community C (IN)
2. Guilford Technical Community C (NC)
3. Central New Mexico Community C
4. Porter & Chester Institute of Stratford (CT)
5. Vista C (TX)
6. Pima Community C (AZ)
7. United Education Institute, Huntington Park Campus (CA)
8. Mesa Community C (AZ)
9. Delgado Community C (LA)
10. Santa Monica C (CA)
11. Palomar C (CA)
12. Glendale Community C (AZ)
13. South Louisiana Community C
14. San Jacinto Community C (TX)
15. Saddleback C (CA)
16. Baton Rouge Community C (LA)
17. Mississippi Gulf Coast Community C
18. WyoTech Laramie (WY)
19. Santa Barbara City C (CA)
20. Pulaski Technical C (AR)

Source: *Community College Week*

Community Colleges Awarding the Most Two-Year Certificates: Four-Year Schools

These are the four-year schools that award the highest number of two-year certificates; the list encompasses all fields of study. A certificate is a credential focused on a specific topic, indicating technical knowledge of a distinct field. Certificates usually require fewer credits than degree programs.

1. Florida Career C, Miami
2. Florida Technical C
3. Charter C, Anchorage (AK)
4. Vincennes U (IN)
5. South Texas C
6. East Coast Polytechnic Institute U (VA)
7. Berkeley C, Woodland Park (NJ)
8. Florida Technical C
9. New York Film Academy (CA)

Source: *Community College Week*

Community Colleges That Are Growing Quickly

These are community colleges with enrollments of 10,000 or more students that have had the greatest increase in the last couple of years.

1. Des Moines Area Community C (IA)
2. Los Angeles Mission C (CA)

3. Wake Technical Community C (NC)
4. Western Idaho, C of
5. Pasco-Hernando State C (FL)
6. New York, City U of, Borough of Manhattan Community C
7. Ohlone C (CA)
8. Coastline Community C (CA)
9. Madison Area Technical C (WI)
10. Lone Star C System (TX)
11. Reedley C (CA)

12. Los Angeles Trade Technical C (CA)
13. San Joaquin Delta C (CA)
14. Pasadena City C (CA)
15. Bakersfield C (CA)
16. Southern Nevada, C of
17. San Bernardino Valley C (CA)
18. Santa Rosa Junior C (CA)
19. Los Angeles Pierce C (CA)
20. Fresno City C (CA)

Source: *Community College Week*

Community Colleges Awarding the Most Degrees to Minorities: Two-Year Schools

This list includes degrees in all fields of study. Minorities are defined as those who identify as Hispanic, African American, American Indian, or Asian American.

1. Houston Community C (TX)
2. El Paso Community C (TX)
3. Northern Virginia Community C
4. New York, City U of, Borough of Manhattan Community C
5. Tarrant County C District (TX)
6. Lone Star C System (TX)
7. Pasadena City C (CA)
8. New York, City U of, Kingsborough Community C
9. New York, City U of, LaGuardia Community C

10. San Joaquin Delta C (CA)
11. Central New Mexico Community C
12. San Jacinto Community C (TX)
13. East Los Angeles C (CA)
14. Mt. San Antonio C (CA)
15. San Joaquin Valley C (CA)
16. Central Texas C (TX)
17. Nassau Community C (NY)
18. El Camino Community C (CA)
19. Wayne County Community C (MI)
20. Santa Ana C (CA)

Source: *Community College Week*

Community Colleges Awarding the Most Degrees to Minorities: Four-Year Schools

This list includes degrees in all fields of study. These are four-year schools that offer two-year degrees. Minorities are defined as those who identify as Hispanic, African American, American Indian, or Asian American.

1. Miami Dade C (FL)
2. Phoenix, U of (AZ)
3. Broward C (FL)
4. Valencia C (FL)
5. South Texas C
6. Palm Beach State C (FL)
7. Keiser U (FL)
8. Florida State C
9. Monroe C (NY)
10. Everest U, South Orlando (FL)
11. Kaplan U, Davenport (IA)

12. Southern Nevada, C of
13. Seminole State C (FL)
14. St. Petersburg C (FL)
15. East Coast Polytechnic Institute (VA)
16. New York, City U of, New York City C of Technology
17. Indian River State C (FL)
18. Santa Fe C (FL)
19. Florida SouthWestern State C
20. Colorado Technical U

Source: *Community College Week*

Steven R. Antonoff

Community Colleges Working to Strengthen Academic and Career Opportunities

Pathways Project is a multiyear effort that strives to help community colleges design and implement structured academic and career pathways for all students. It is sponsored by the American Association of Community Colleges and funded by a grant from the Bill & Melinda Gates Foundation. These 30 colleges are taking part in the project.

Alamo C System (TX)
Bakersfield C (CA)
Broward C (FL)
Cleveland State Community C (TN)
Columbus State Community C (OH)
Community C of Philadelphia (PA)
Cuyahoga Community C (OH)
El Paso Community C (TX)
Front Range Community C (CO)
Indian River State C (FL)
Irvine Valley C (CA)
Jackson C (MI)
Lansing Community C (MI)
Linn-Benton Community C (OR)
Monroe Community C (NY)

Mt. San Antonio C (CA)
Northeast Wisconsin Technical C (WI)
Paris Junior C (TX)
Pierce C (WA)
Prince George's Community C (MD)
St. Petersburg C (FL)
San Jacinto C (TX)
Skagit Valley C (WA)
Stanly Community C (NC)
South Seattle C (WA)
Tallahassee Community C (FL)
Tulsa Community C (OK)
Wallace State Community C (AL)
Western Wyoming Community C
Zane State C (OH)

Source: *Community College Week*

CONNECTIONS TO OTHER UNIVERSITIES

Excellent Research Universities

The Association of American Universities (AAU) is an association of 62 leading public and private research universities in the United States and Canada. AAU members, and the year of each college's admission into the association, are listed here.

Arizona, U of (1985)
Boston U (MA) (2012)
Brandeis U (MA) (1985)
Brown U (RI) (1933)
California Institute of Technology (1934)
California, U of, Berkeley (1900)
California, U of, Davis (1996)
California, U of, Irvine (1996)
California, U of, Los Angeles (1974)
California, U of, San Diego (1982)
California, U of, Santa Barbara (1995)
Carnegie Mellon U (PA) (1982)
Case Western Reserve U (OH) (1969)
Chicago, U of (IL) (1900)
Colorado, U of, Boulder (1966)
Columbia U (NY) (1900)
Cornell U (NY) (1900)
Duke U (NC) (1938)

Emory U (GA) (1995)
Florida, U of (1985)
Georgia Institute of Technology (2010)
Harvard U (MA) (1900)
Illinois, U of, Urbana (1908)
Indiana U Bloomington (1909)
Iowa State U (1958)
Iowa, U of (1909)
Johns Hopkins U (MD) (1900)
Kansas, U of (1909)
Maryland, U of, College Park (1969)
Massachusetts Institute of Technology (1934)
McGill U (Canada) (1926)
Michigan State U (1964)
Michigan, U of, Ann Arbor (1900)
Minnesota, U of, Twin Cities (1908)
Missouri, U of, Columbia (1908)

New York U (1950)
New York, State U of, Buffalo (1989)
New York, State U of, Stony Brook (2001)
North Carolina, U of, Chapel Hill (1922)
Northwestern U (IL) (1917)
Ohio State U (1916)
Oregon, U of (1969)
Pennsylvania State U (1958)
Pennsylvania, U of (1900)
Pittsburgh, U of (PA) (1974)
Princeton U (NJ) (1900)
Purdue U (IN) (1958)
Rice U (TX) (1985)

Rochester, U of (NY) (1941)
Rutgers U, New Brunswick (NJ) (1989)
Southern California, U of (1969)
Stanford U (CA) (1900)
Texas A&M U, College Station (2001)
Texas, U of, Austin (1929)
Toronto, U of (Canada) (1926)
Tulane U (LA) (1958)
Vanderbilt U (TN) (1950)
Virginia, U of (1904)
Washington U (MO) (1923)
Washington, U of, Seattle (1950)
Wisconsin, U of, Madison (1900)
Yale U (CT) (1900)

Source: Association of American Universities (aau.edu)

Members of the Oak Ridge Consortium

Oak Ridge Associated Universities (ORAU) is a consortium of doctoral-granting academic institutions. Member universities strive to advance scientific research and education by creating collaborative partnerships involving academics, government, and industry.

Alabama A&M U
Alabama, U of, Birmingham
Alabama, U of, Huntsville
Alabama, U of, Tuscaloosa
Appalachian State U (NC)
Arkansas State U
Arkansas, U of, Fayetteville
Arkansas, U of, Medical Sciences
Auburn U (AL)
Berea C (KY)
Carnegie Mellon U (PA)
Catholic U of America (DC)
Central Florida, U of
Charleston, C of (SC)
Cincinnati, U of (OH)
Clark Atlanta U (GA)
Clemson U (SC)
Colorado State U, Ft. Collins
Colorado, U of, Boulder
Delaware, U of
District of Columbia, U of the
Duke U (NC)
East Carolina U (NC)
East Tennessee State U
Eastern Kentucky U
Embry-Riddle Aeronautical U (FL)
Emory U (GA)
Fayetteville State U (NC)
Florida Atlantic U
Florida Institute of Technology

Florida International U
Florida State U
Florida, U of
George Mason U (VA)
George Washington U (DC)
Georgetown U (DC)
Georgia Institute of Technology
Georgia Regents U
Georgia Southern U
Georgia State U
Georgia, U of
Houston, U of (TX)
Howard U (DC)
Idaho State U
Illinois Institute of Technology
Imperial C London (United Kingdom)
Indiana U Bloomington
Jackson State U (MS)
Johns Hopkins (MD)
Johnson C. Smith U (NC)
Kentucky State U
Kentucky, U of
Lehigh U (PA)
Lincoln Memorial U (TN)
Louisiana State U
Louisville, U of (KY)
Maryland, U of, College Park
Maryland, U of, Eastern Shore
Maryville C (TN)
Meharry Medical C (TN)

Memphis, U of (TN)
Miami, U of (FL)
Michigan State U
Michigan Technological U
Michigan, U of, Ann Arbor
Middle Tennessee State U
Mississippi State U
Mississippi, U of
Mississippi, U of, Medical Center
Missouri U of Science & Technology
Missouri, U of, Columbia
Morehouse C (GA)
Morgan State U (MD)
Nevada, U of, Las Vegas
Nevada, U of, Reno
New Mexico State U
New Mexico, U of, Albuquerque
New Orleans, U of (LA)
New York, City U of, City C
Norfolk State U (VA)
North Carolina A&T State U
North Carolina State U
North Carolina, U of, Chapel Hill
North Carolina, U of, Charlotte
North Dakota, U of
North Texas, U of
Notre Dame, U of (IN)
Ohio State U, Columbus
Oklahoma State U
Oklahoma, U of
Oklahoma, U of, Center for Health
    Sciences C of Osteopathic Medicine
Pennsylvania State U, University Park
Philadelphia U (PA)
Pittsburgh, U of (PA)
Polytechnic U of Puerto Rico
Polytechnic U of Puerto Rico (FL)
Purdue U (IN)
Rice U (TX)
Roanoke C (VA)
Rutgers U, New Brunswick (NJ)

South Alabama, U of
South Carolina State U
South Carolina, U of, Columbia
South Florida, U of
Southern Illinois U, Carbondale
Southern Methodist U (TX)
Southern Mississippi, U of
Syracuse U (NY)
Temple U (PA)
Tennessee State U
Tennessee Technological U
Tennessee, U of
Tennessee, U of, Chattanooga
Tennessee, U of, Health Science Center
Texas A&M U, College Station
Texas Christian U
Texas Tech U
Texas, U of, Arlington
Texas, U of, Austin
Texas, U of, Dallas
Texas, U of, Pan American
Texas, U of, San Antonio
Tulane U (LA)
Tulsa, U of (OK)
Tuskegee U (AL)
Utah State U
Utah, U of
Vanderbilt U (TN)
Virginia Commonwealth U
Virginia State U
Virginia Polytechnic Institute & State U
Virginia, U of
Wake Forest U (NC)
Washington U (MO)
Wayne State U (MI)
West Virginia U
Western Carolina U (NC)
Western Kentucky U
William & Mary, C of (VA)
Wisconsin, U of, Madison

Source: Oak Ridge Associated Universities (orau.org)

Colleges Cooperating

Colleges, particularly smaller ones, often find they can offer expanded academic and social programs by combining resources, programs, and personnel. Students at member schools may be able to cross-register, travel together, or make use of joint resources or facilities.

Associated Colleges of Illinois

Augustana C (IL)
Aurora U (IL)
Blackburn C (IL)
Concordia U Chicago (IL)
Dominican U (IL)
Elmhurst C (IL)
Eureka C (IL)
Greenville C (IL)
Illinois C
Knox C (IL)
Lake Forest C (IL)
Lewis U (IL)

McKendree U (IL)
Millikin U (IL)
Monmouth C (IL)
North Central C (IL)
North Park U (IL)
Olivet Nazarene U (IL)
Principia C (IL)
Quincy U (IL)
Rockford U (IL)
St. Francis, U of (IL)
Trinity Christian C (IL)

Associated Colleges of the Midwest

Beloit C (WI)
Carleton C (MN)
Coe C (IA)
Colorado C
Cornell C (IA)
Grinnell C (IA)
Knox C (IL)

Lake Forest C (IL)
Lawrence U (WI)
Luther C (IA)
Macalester C (MN)
Monmouth C (IL)
Ripon C (WI)
St. Olaf C (MN)

Associated Colleges of the South

Birmingham-Southern C (AL)
Centenary C (LA)
Centre C (KY)
Davidson C (NC)
Furman U (SC)
Hendrix C (AR)
Millsaps C (MS)
Morehouse C (GA)

Rhodes C (TN)
Richmond, U of (VA)
Rollins C (FL)
South, U of the (TN)
Southwestern U (TX)
Spelman C (GA)
Trinity U (TX)
Washington & Lee U (VA)

Associated Colleges of the St. Lawrence Valley

Clarkson U (NY)
New York, State U of, Canton
New York, State U of, Potsdam
St. Lawrence U (NY)

Associated Colleges of the Twin Cities

Augsburg C (MN)
Hamline U (MN)
Macalester C (MN)
St. Catherine U (MN)
St. Thomas, U of (MN)

Atlanta University Center Consortium

Clark Atlanta U (GA)
Morehouse C (GA)
Morehouse School of Medicine (GA)
Spelman C (GA)

Baltimore Collegetown Network

Baltimore County, Community C of (MD)
Baltimore, U of (MD)
Coppin State U (MD)
Goucher C (MD)
Johns Hopkins U (MD)
Loyola U (MD)
Maryland Institute C of Art
Maryland, U of, Baltimore
Maryland, U of, Baltimore County
McDaniel C (MD)
Morgan State U (MD)
Notre Dame of Maryland U
Stevenson U (MD)
Towson U (MD)

Birmingham Area Consortium for Higher Education

Alabama, U of, Birmingham
Birmingham-Southern C (AL)
Miles C (AL)
Montevallo, U of (AL)
Samford U (AL)

Central Pennsylvania Consortium

Dickinson C (PA)
Franklin & Marshall C (PA)
Gettysburg C (PA)

The Claremont Colleges

Claremont Graduate U (CA)
Claremont McKenna C (CA)
Harvey Mudd C (CA)
Keck Graduate Institute of Applied Sciences (CA)
Pitzer C (CA)
Pomona C (CA)
Scripps C (CA)

Colleges of the Fenway

Emmanuel C (MA)
Massachusetts C of Art & Design
Massachusetts C of Pharmacy & Health Sciences
Simmons C (MA)
Wentworth Institute of Technology (MA)
Wheelock C (MA)

Five College Consortium

Amherst C (MA)
Hampshire C (MA)
Massachusetts, U of, Amherst
Mt. Holyoke C (MA)
Smith C (MA)

Great Lakes Colleges Association

Albion C (MI)
Alleghany C (PA)
Antioch C (OH)
Denison U (OH)
DePauw U (IN)
Earlham C (IN)
Hope C (MI)

Kalamazoo C (MI)
Kenyon C (OH)
Oberlin C (OH)
Ohio Wesleyan U
Wabash C (IN)
Wooster, C of (OH)

Higher Education Consortium of Central Massachusetts

Anna Maria C (MA)
Assumption C (MA)
Becker C (MA)
Clark U (MA)
Holy Cross, C of the (MA)
Massachusetts C of Pharmacy & Health
 Science
Massachusetts, U of, Medical School

Nichols C (MA)
Quinsigamond Community C (MA)
Tufts U, Cummings School of Veterinary
 Medicine (MA)
Worcester Polytechnic Institute (MA)
Worcester State U (MA)

Lehigh Valley Association of Independent Colleges

Cedar Crest C (PA)
DeSales U (PA)
Lafayette C (PA)
Lehigh U (PA)
Moravian C (PA)
Muhlenberg C (PA)

The Ohio Five

Oberlin C (OH)
Denison U (OH)
Ohio Wesleyan U
Kenyon C (OH)
Wooster, C of (OH)

ACADEMICS

Pittsburgh Council on Higher Education

Carlow U (PA)
Carnegie Mellon U (PA)
Chatham U (PA)
Community C of Allegheny County (PA)
Duquesne U (PA)
La Roche C (PA)
Pittsburgh Theological Seminary (PA)
Pittsburgh, U of (PA)
Point Park U (PA)
Robert Morris U (PA)

Quaker Consortium

Bryn Mawr C (PA)
Haverford C (PA)
Swarthmore C (PA)
Pennsylvania, U of

Seven-College Exchange

Hampden-Sydney C (VA)
Hollins U (VA)
Mary Baldwin C (VA)
Randolph C (VA)

Randolph-Macon C (VA)
Sweet Briar C (VA)
Washington & Lee U (VA)

The Seven Sisters

The Seven Sisters are seven historically liberal arts women's colleges in the Northeastern United States. Both Radcliffe (now part of Harvard University) and Vassar are now co-ed.

Barnard C (NY)
Bryn Mawr C (PA)
Mt. Holyoke C (MA)
Radcliffe C (MA)
Smith C (MA)
Vassar C (NY)
Wellesley C (MA)

Twelve-College Exchange

Amherst C (MA)
Bowdoin C (ME)
Connecticut C
Dartmouth C (NH)
Mt. Holyoke C (MA)
National Theater Institute (CT)
Smith C (MA)

Trinity C (CT)
Vassar C (NY)
Wellesley C (MA)
Wesleyan U (CT)
Wheaton C (MA)
Williams C (MA)

Washington Consortium

American U (DC)
Catholic U of America (DC)
District of Columbia, U of the
Gallaudet U (DC)
George Mason U (VA)
George Washington U (DC)
Georgetown U (DC)
Howard U (DC)

Maryland, U of, College Park
Marymount U (VA)
National Defense U (DC)
National Intelligence U (DC)
Trinity U (DC)
Uniformed Services U of the Health
  Sciences (MD)

Liberal Arts Colleges Promoting Information Exchange

These colleges are members of the Consortium of Liberal Arts Colleges (CLAC) "chartered to explore and promote the use of information technology in the service of our liberal arts educational missions."

Albion C (MI)
Allegheny C (PA)
Alma C (MI)
Amherst C (MA)
Barnard C (NY)
Bates C (ME)
Beloit C (WI)
Bowdoin C (ME)
Bryn Mawr C (PA)
Bucknell U (PA)
Carleton C (MN)
Claremont McKenna C (CA)
Colby C (ME)
Colgate U (NY)
Colorado C
Connecticut C
Davidson C (NC)
Denison U (OH)
DePauw U (IN)
Dickinson C (PA)
Earlham C (IN)
Franklin & Marshall C (PA)
Gettysburg C (PA)
Grinnell C (IA)
Hamilton C (NY)
Hampshire C (MA)
Harvey Mudd C (CA)
Haverford C (PA)
Hobart & William Smith C (NY)
Holy Cross, C of the (MA)
Hope C (MI)
Kalamazoo C (MI)
Kenyon C (OH)
Lafayette C (PA)
Lake Forest C (IL)

Lawrence U (WI)
Luther C (IA)
Macalester C (MN)
Manhattan C (NY)
Middlebury C (VT)
Mills C (CA)
Mt. Holyoke C (MA)
Oberlin C (OH)
Occidental C (CA)
Ohio Wesleyan U
Pomona C (CA)
Reed C (OR)
Rhodes C (TN)
Skidmore C (NY)
Smith C (NY)
South, U of the (TN)
Southwestern U (TX)
St. Lawrence U (NY)
St. Olaf (MN)
Swarthmore C (PA)
Trinity C (CT)
Trinity U (TX)
Union C (NY)
Vassar C (NY)
Wabash C (IN)
Washington & Lee U (VA)
Washington C (MD)
Wellesley C (MA)
Wesleyan U (CT)
Wheaton C (IL)
Wheaton C (MA)
Whitman C (WA)
Whittier C (CA)
Williams C (MA)
Wooster, C of (OH)

Source: liberalarts.org

Steven R. Antonoff

Liberal Arts Colleges to Consider That Offer Great Sciences

The Oberlin Group is a consortium representing 80 selective liberal arts colleges. The idea for the Oberlin Group grew out of conferences held at Oberlin in the 1980s when the presidents of 50 liberal arts colleges met to discuss the role of private colleges in educating the nation's scientists.

Agnes Scott C (GA)
Albion C (MI)
Alma C (MI)
Amherst C (MA)
Augustana C (IL)
Austin C (TX)
Bard C (NY)
Barnard C (NY)
Bates C (ME)
Beloit C (WI)
Berea C (KY)
Bowdoin C (ME)
Bryn Mawr C (PA)
Bucknell U (PA)
Carleton C (MN)
Claremont Colleges Consortium (CA)
Clark U (MA)
Coe C (IA)
Colby C (ME)
Colgate U (NY)
Colorado C
Connecticut C
Davidson C (NC)
Denison U (OH)
DePauw U (IN)
Dickinson C (PA)
Drew U (NJ)
Earlham C (IN)
Eckerd C (FL)
Franklin & Marshall C (PA)
Furman U (SC)
Gettysburg C (PA)
Grinnell C (IA)
Gustavus Adolphus C (MN)
Hamilton C (NY)
Haverford C (PA)
Holy Cross, C of the (MA)
Hope C (MI)
Kalamazoo C (MI)
Kenyon C (OH)
Knox C (IL)

Lafayette C (PA)
Lake Forest C (IL)
Lawrence U (WI)
Macalester C (MN)
Manhattan C (NY)
Middlebury C (VT)
Mills C (CA)
Morehouse C (GA)
Mt. Holyoke C (MA)
Oberlin C (OH)
Occidental C (CA)
Ohio Wesleyan U
Randolph-Macon C (VA)
Reed C (OR)
Rhodes C (TN)
Rollins C (FL)
Sarah Lawrence C (NY)
Simmons C (MA)
Skidmore C (NY)
Smith C (MA)
South, U of the (TN)
Spelman C (GA)
St. Benedict, C of/St. John's U (MN)
St. Lawrence U (NY)
St. Olaf C (MN)
Swarthmore C (PA)
Trinity C (CT)
Trinity U (TX)
Union C (NY)
Vassar C (NY)
Wabash C (IN)
Washington & Lee U (VA)
Wellesley C (MA)
Wesleyan U (CT)
Wheaton C (MA)
Whitman C (WA)
Whittier C (CA)
Willamette U (OR)
Williams C (MA)
Wooster, C of (OH)

Source: oberlingroup.org

Great Public Liberal Arts Colleges

Recognizing the importance of liberal arts and sciences education for success in a complex global society, the Council of Public Liberal Arts Colleges (COPLAC) represents liberal arts education in the public sector. These are the member colleges and universities.

Alberta, U of, Augustana (Canada)
Charleston, C of (SC)
Eastern Connecticut State U
Evergreen State C (WA)
Ft. Lewis C (CO)
Georgia C & State U
Henderson State U (AR)
Illinois, U of, Springfield
Keene State C (NH)
Maine, U of, Farmington
Mansfield U (PA)
Mary Washington, U of (VA)
Massachusetts C of Liberal Arts
Midwestern State U (TX)
Minnesota, U of, Morris

Montevallo, U of (AL)
New College of Florida
New York, State U of, Geneseo
North Carolina, U of, Asheville
Ramapo C (NJ)
Science & Arts, U of (OK)
Shepherd U (WV)
Sonoma State U (CA)
South Carolina, U of, Aiken
Southern Oregon U
Southern Utah U
St. Mary's C (MD)
Truman State U (MO)
Virginia, U of, Wise
Wisconsin, U of, Superior

Source: coplac.org

Members of the Venture Consortium

Students who attend member colleges receive assistance in finding a job in nonprofit organizations after graduation or during a time off from college studies.

Brown U (RI)
Franklin & Marshall C (PA)
Holy Cross, C of the (MA)
Sarah Lawrence C (NY)
Vassar C (NY)
Wesleyan U (CT)

CHAPTER THREE
STUDENT LIFE

LOCATION/FACILITIES

The Experts' Choice: Most Beautiful Campuses

Top Choices

California, U of, San Diego
Colgate U (NY)
Colorado, U of, Boulder
Cornell U (NY)
Duke U (NC)
Elon U (NC)
Furman U (SC)
Indiana U Bloomington
Kenyon C (OH)
Lewis & Clark C (OR)
Miami U (OH)
Middlebury C (VT)
Pepperdine U (CA)
Princeton U (NJ)
Rice U (TX)

Richmond, U of (VA)
Rollins C (FL)
Scripps C (CA)
Southern Methodist U (TX)
Stanford U (CA)*
Swarthmore C (PA)
Vanderbilt U (TN)
Virginia, U of
Wake Forest U (NC)
Washington U (MO)
Washington, U of
Wellesley C (MA)
Yale U (CT)

*The Top Choice

Second Choices

Agnes Scott C (GA)
Alabama, U of, Tuscaloosa
Amherst C (MA)
Boston C (MA)
Bowdoin C (ME)
Bryn Mawr C (PA)
Bucknell U (PA)
California, U of, Berkeley
California, U of, Los Angeles
California, U of, Santa Cruz
Chicago, U of (IL)
Colby C (ME)
Columbia U (NY)
Dartmouth C (NH)
Denison U (OH)
Emory U (GA)
Florida Southern C
Haverford C (PA)
High Point U (NC)
Lehigh U (PA)

Maryland, U of
Mt. Holyoke C (MA)
Northwestern U (IL)
Notre Dame, U of (IN)
Pomona C (CA)
Rhodes C (TN)
South, U of the (TN)
Southern California, U of
St. John's C (MD)
St. John's U (MN)
St. Olaf C (MN)
Texas Christian U
Trinity C (CT)
Tufts U (MA)
Tulsa, U of (OK)
Vassar C (NY)
Vermont, U of
William & Mary, C of (VA)
Williams C (MA)

Travel + Leisure's Most Beautiful College Campuses

The following universities or colleges are most beautiful according to *Travel + Leisure* magazine.

Bard C (NY)

Berry C (GA)

Bryn Mawr C (PA)
California, U of, San Diego
Chicago, U of (IL)
Cincinnati, U of (OH)
Colorado, U of, Boulder
Cornell U (NY)
Duke U (NC)
Florida Southern C
Furman U (SC)
Indiana U Bloomington
Kenyon C (OH)
Lewis & Clark C (OR)
Notre Dame, U of (IN)
Princeton U (NJ)

Rice U (TX)
Scripps C (CA)
South, U of the (TN)
St. Olaf C (MN)
Stanford U (CA)
Swarthmore C (PA)
Vanderbilt U (TN)
Virginia, U of
Washington, U of
Wellesley C (MA)
William & Mary, C of (VA)
Wisconsin, U of, Madison
Yale U (CT)

Source: *Travel + Leisure* (travelandleisure.com)

UniversityParent's Beautiful College Campuses

According to UniversityParent, these institutions have the most beautiful campuses in the United States.

1. William & Mary, C of (VA)
2. California, U of, Berkeley
3. Hampshire C (MA)
4. Northwestern U (IL)
5. Lewis & Clark C (OR)
6. Colorado, U of, Boulder
7. Furman U (SC)
8. Atlantic, C of the (ME)
9. Cornell U (NY)
10. Texas, U of, Austin

Source: UniversityParent (universityparent.com)

25 Most Beautiful Christian Universities

1. Covenant C (GA)
2. Pepperdine U (CA)
3. Eastern U (PA)
4. Montreat C (NC)
5. Point Loma Nazarene U (CA)
6. Geneva C (PA)
7. Palm Beach Atlantic U (FL)
8. California Baptist U
9. Baylor U (TX)
10. Wheaton C (IL)
11. Franciscan U (OH)
12. Regent U (VA)
13. Westmont C (CA)
14. Seattle Pacific U (WA)
15. Samford U (AL)
16. Ozarks, C of the (MO)
17. Whitworth U (WA)
18. John Brown U (AR)
19. Waynesburg U (PA)
20. Colorado Christian U
21. Greenville C (IL)
22. Biola U (CA)
23. Nyack C (NY)
24. Campbell U (NC)
25. Houston Baptist U (TX)

Source: Christian Universities Online (christianuniversitiesonline.org)

Steven R. Antonoff

The Experts' Choice: Colleges Where Seeing is Believing

Experts were asked to list colleges where student visits to the campus are particularly essential to discovering the school's positive features.

California, U of, San Diego
California, U of, Santa Cruz
Case Western Reserve U (OH)
Chapman U (CA)
Colorado C
Colorado, U of, Boulder
Connecticut C
Denison U (OH)
DePauw U (IN)
Elon U (NC)
Furman U (SC)
Georgia Institute of Technology
Goucher C (MD)
Grinnell C (IA)*
Johns Hopkins U (MD)
Kalamazoo C (MI)
Kansas, U of
Kenyon C (OH)*

Knox C (IL)
Miami U (OH)
Millsaps C (MS)
Montana State U
Muhlenberg C (PA)
Pittsburgh, U of (PA)
Redlands, U of (CA)
Reed C (OR)
Santa Clara U (CA)
Tampa, U of (FL)
Wabash C (IN)
Warren Wilson C (NC)
Wellesley C (MA)
Wisconsin, U of, Madison
Wooster, C of (OH)*

*The Top Choice (tie)

S...p...r...e...a...d Out: Colleges with the Most Acreage

Here you may have to walk a mile to get to class. Don't worry, most of these schools provide buses. Check out the acreage on these colleges, where bigger really is better.

Berry C (GA): 27,000
U.S. Air Force Academy (CO): 18,000
U.S. Military Academy (NY): 16,080
South, U of the (TN): 13,000
Duke U (NC): 9,350
Stanford U (CA): 8,180
Pennsylvania State U, University Park: 7,264
Liberty U (VA): 6,819
California Polytechnic State U, San Luis Obispo: 6,000
California, U of, Davis: 5,300
Michigan State U: 5,200
Texas A&M U, College Station: 5,200
Tuskegee U (AL): 5,000
Mississippi State U: 4,200
Connecticut, U of: 4,093
New Mexico State U: 3,500
Oklahoma, U of: 3,481
Ohio State U, Columbus: 3,469
Mississippi, U of: 3,391

Maine, U of: 3,300
Sweet Briar C (VA): 3,250
Michigan, U of, Ann Arbor: 3,245
West Virginia U: 2,737
Rutgers U, New Brunswick (NJ): 2,695
Southern Illinois U, Edwardsville: 2,660
New Hampshire, U of: 2,600
Principia C (IL): 2,600
Virginia Polytechnic Institute & State U: 2,600
Purdue U (IN): 2,595
St. John's U (MD): 2,500
Alabama A&M U: 2,300
Regina, U of (Canada): 2,298
Alaska, U of, Fairbanks: 2,250
Delaware, U of: 2,011
California, U of, Santa Cruz: 2,000
Florida, U of: 2,000
Miami U (OH): 2,000
Minnesota, U of , Twin Cities: 2,000
Stockton U (NJ): 2,000

Source: Wintergreen Orchard House

The Experts' Choice: Great Residence Halls

Experts were asked to identify colleges offering students great living spaces in their residence halls or dormitories.

Arkansas, U of, Fayetteville
Boise State U (ID)
Brigham Young U (ID)
Colorado C
Colorado State U, Ft. Collins
Colorado, U of, Boulder
High Point U (NC)
Lamar U (TX)
Middlebury C (VT)

Northeastern U (MA)
Pomona C (CA)
Princeton U (NJ)
Salisbury U (MD)
Skidmore C (NY)
Trinity U (TX)
Virginia, U of
Washington U (MO)
Wofford C (SC)

Where Most Students Live On Campus

Do you mind shared bathrooms and showers? At these colleges, you'd better start learning to love walking down the hall in your bathrobe and slippers. The percentage of students who live on campus over four years is listed after the name of the college.

Alice Lloyd C (KY): 100%
Citadel, The (SC): 100%
DePauw U (IN): 100%
Frank Lloyd Wright School of Architecture (AZ): 100%
Jacobs U (Germany): 100%
Harvard U (MA): 100%
Olin C (MA): 100%
Pennsylvania State U, Abington: 100%
Pontifical C Josephinum (OH): 100%
St. Joseph Seminary C (LA): 100%
U.S. Air Force Academy (CO): 100%
U.S. Coast Guard Academy (CT): 100%
U.S. Merchant Marine Academy (NY): 100%
U.S. Military Academy (NY): 100%
U.S. Naval Academy (MD): 100%
Virginia Military Institute: 100%
Webb Institute (NY): 100%
Bethany C (KS): 99%
Connecticut C: 99%

Denison U (OH): 99%
Franklin & Marshall C (PA): 99%
Kenyon C (OH): 99%
Soka U of America (CA): 99%
Thomas Aquinas C (CA): 99%
Principia C (IL): 99%
Wesleyan U (CT): 99%
Wooster, C of (OH): 99%
Amherst C (MA): 98%
Centre C (KY): 98%
Harvey Mudd C (CA): 98%
Haverford C (PA): 98%
Lincoln U (MO): 98%
Pomona C (CA): 98%
South, U of the (TN): 98%
St. Lawrence U (NY): 98%
Hamilton C (NY): 97%
Middlebury C (VT): 97%
Princeton U (NJ): 97%
Wellesley C (MA): 97%

Source: Wintergreen Orchard House

The Experts' Choice: College or Resort? Schools With Unbelievable Amenities

Experts were asked name colleges that provide resort-style amenities.

Alabama, U of, Tuscaloosa: Lazy river
Bowdoin C (ME): Great food!

Steven R. Antonoff

Cincinnati, U of (OH): Three pools, more than 21,000 pounds of weights, a climbing wall, and a suspended track
Clemson U (SC): Miniature golf course for football players
Georgia Institute of Technology: Water park in the student center
Georgia Southern U: Lazy river and climbing wall
Gettysburg C (PA): Huge climbing wall
Grand Canyon U (AZ): Resort-style pool and cabanas in the middle of campus
High Point U (NC): Swimming pools, putting greens, and concierge services
Houston, U of (TX): Recreation center with pool and rock-climbing wall
Kenyon C (OH): Terrific swimming facilities
Miami, U of (FL): Great pool complex
Missouri, U of, Columbia: Boxing gym, Stalcup's Garage featuring TRX® Suspension Training systems, and other high-tech facilities
Montana State U, Bozeman: Climbing wall
Oregon, U of: Private hot tubs, tanning salon, yoga studio, and golf simulator
Purdue U (IN): State-of-the-art student recreation facility
San Diego State U (CA): Multiple outside pools
Southern Methodist U (TX): Tanning pool and rock-climbing wall
Texas, U of, Austin: Seven basketball courts, archery range, dance classes, and full-size Olympic swimming pools
Texas Tech U: Lazy river

Colleges With Respected Art Museums

Many colleges have outstanding art collections, some general and some specialized. Here are a few notable ones.

Arizona State U: Meteorite Museum
Bowdoin C (ME): Peary MacMillan Arctic Museum & Arctic Studies Center
Brandeis U (MA): Rose Art Museum
California, U of, Berkeley: Berkeley Art Museum & Pacific Film Archive
California, U of, Los Angeles: Franklin D. Murphy Sculpture Garden & Hammer Museum
Colby C (ME)
Cornell U (NY)
Florida Southern C: Frank Lloyd Wright Building
Florida, U of: Museum of Natural History
Harvard U (MA)
Indiana U Bloomington
Iowa, U of
Kansas, U of: Natural History Museum
Michigan, U of, Ann Arbor
Nebraska, U of, Lincoln
North Carolina, U of, Chapel Hill: Morehead Planetarium & Science Center
Notre Dame, U of (IN)
Oberlin C (OH)
Pennsylvania, U of: Museum of Archaeology & Anthropology
Pepperdine U (CA)
Princeton U (NJ)
Smith C (MA)
Stanford U (CA)
Virginia, U of
Western Washington U: Outdoor Sculpture Collection
William & Mary, C of (VA)

STUDENT LIFE

Williams C (MA)
Wisconsin, U of, Madison: Chazen Museum
Yale U (CT)

Beach Colleges

Not all beach colleges are situated near the coast in places such as California and Florida. While many are, there are also numerous colleges located close to large bodies of water. The following institutions are a sampling of schools within an hour or so of a beach or a lake.

Atlantic, C of the (ME)
Bethune-Cookman U (FL)
Bowdoin C (ME)
Brigham Young U (HI)
California Polytechnic State U, San Luis Obispo
California State U, Long Beach
California State U, Monterey Bay
California State U, San Marcos
California, U of, San Diego
California, U of, Santa Barbara
California, U of, Santa Cruz
Caribbean Medical U (Curaçao)
Charleston, C of (SC)
Citadel, The (SC)
Clemson U (SC)
Coastal Carolina U (SC)
Deakin U, Geelong (Australia)
Eckerd C (FL)
Endicott C (MA)
Flagler C (FL)
Florida Atlantic U
Florida Gulf Coast U
Florida Institute of Technology
Goa U (India)
Hawaii Pacific U
Hawaii, U of, Hilo
Hawaii, U of, Manoa
Higher Polytechnic School of Gandia (Spain)
Humboldt State U (CA)
Kingsborough Community C (NY)
Lake Forest C (IL)
Laurentian U (Canada)
Loyola Marymount U (CA)
Madras, U of (India)
Malaysia U Sabah
Malaysia U Terengganu
Medical U of the Americas (Federation of Saint Kitts and Nevis)

Miami, U of (FL)
Mitchell C (CT)
Monmouth U (NJ)
Nelson Mandela Metropolitan U (South Africa)
New C of Florida
New England, U of (ME)
New York U
North Carolina, U of, Wilmington
Northwestern U (IL)
Notre Dame Australia, U of
Old Dominion U (VA)
Oregon Coast Community C
Palm Beach Atlantic U (FL)
Pepperdine U (CA)
Point Loma Nazarene U (CA)
Pondicherry U (India)
Rhode Island, U of
Ruhuna, U of (Sri Lanka)
Salve Regina U (RI)
San Diego State U (CA)
San Francisco, U of (CA)
Seattle Pacific U (WA)
Seattle U (WA)
Seychelles, U of
St. Mary's C (MD)
St. Benedict, C of/St. John's U (MN)
St. George's U (Grenada)
St. Matthew's U (Cayman Islands)
Tampa, U of (FL)
Texas A&M U, Corpus Christi
Texas A&M U, Galveston
Virgin Islands, U of the, St. Thomas
Washington, U of
Wells C (NY)
West Florida, U of
Western Washington U
Wisconsin, U of, Madison
Wollongong, U of (Australia)

Colleges With the Most Computers Available to Students

Sure, you probably have 17 different devices right now that can reach the Internet. But sometimes, you just can't beat hunkering down in the computer lab with the rest of your class to finish up that project or final paper.

Minnesota, U of, Twin Cities: 20,000
St. John's U (MD): 13,222
Troy U (AL): 12,792
Texas, U of, El Paso: 10,100
U.S. Naval Academy (MD): 9,000
Drexel U (PA): 8,000
Dayton, U of (OH): 7,675
Clemson U (SC): 7,500
Wisconsin, U of, Madison: 7,100
Rensselaer Polytechnic Institute (NY): 7,000
Northwest Missouri State U: 6,650
Pennsylvania State U, University Park: 6,150
Monterrey Institute of Technology & Higher Education (Mexico): 6,077
Washington, U of, Seattle: 6,000
Seton Hall U (NJ): 5,000
Toledo, U of (OH): 5,000
Temple U (PA): 4,908
U.S. Military Academy (NY): 4,591
Oklahoma, U of: 4,500

Bentley U (MA): 4,493
Central Florida, U of: 4,005
Florida A&M U: 4,000
James Madison U (VA): 4,000
California, U of, Los Angeles: 3,930
Maryland, U of, College Park: 3,890
Brigham Young U (UT): 3,800
Montclair State U (NJ): 3,797
McGill U (Canada): 3,730
Georgia Southern U: 3,722
Arkansas, U of, Fayetteville: 3,626
Rochester Institute of Technology (NY): 3,530
Syracuse U (NY): 3,500
Arkansas, U of, Little Rock: 3,500
New York, State U of, Buffalo: 3,400
Iowa State U: 3,400
North Carolina State U: 3,217
National U (CA): 3,200
Lawrence Technological U (MI): 3,170
Bowie State U (MD): 3,144

Source: Wintergreen Orchard House

Schools With Farms

These are some universities and colleges that provide students with the opportunity to use a farm.

Dickinson C (PA)
Green Mountain C (VT)
Hampshire C (MA)
Ozarks, C of the (MO)
Pomona C (CA)
St. Lawrence U (NY)
Sterling C (VT)
Willamette U (OR)

Source: *College Finder* research

The 25 Largest College Football Stadiums

1. Michigan, U of, Ann Arbor: Michigan Stadium, 109,901 seats
2. Pennsylvania State U, University Park: Beaver Stadium, 106,572 seats
3. Ohio State U, Columbus: Ohio Stadium, 104,944 seats
4. Texas A&M U: Kyle Field, 102,733 seats
5. Tennessee, U of: Neyland Stadium, 102,455 seats
6. Louisiana State U, Baton Rouge: Tiger Stadium, 102,321 seats
7. Alabama, U of, Tuscaloosa: Bryant-Denny Stadium, 101,821 seats
8. Texas, U of, Austin: Darrell K Royal Stadium, 100,119 seats
9. Southern California, U of: LA Memorial Coliseum, 93,607 seats
10. Georgia, U of, Athens: Sanford Stadium, 92,746 seats
11. California, U of, Los Angeles: The Rose Bowl, 92,542 seats
12. Florida, U of: Ben Hill Griffin Stadium at Florida Field, 88,548 seats
13. Auburn U (AL): Jordan-Hare Stadium, 87,451 seats
14. Florida State U: Doak Campbell Stadium, 79,560 seats
15. Oklahoma, U of: Gaylord Family Oklahoma Memorial Stadium, 82,112 seats
16. Clemson U (SC): Memorial Stadium, 81,500 seats
17. Notre Dame, U of (IN): Notre Dame Stadium, 80,795 seats
18. Wisconsin, U of, Madison: Camp Randall Stadium, 80,321 seats
19. South Carolina, U of, Columbia: Williams-Brice Stadium, 80,250 seats
20. Arkansas, U of: Donald W. Reynolds Razorback Stadium, 80,000 seats
21. Michigan State U: Spartan Stadium, 75,005 seats
22. Alabama, U of, Birmingham: Legion Field, 71,594 seats
23. Missouri, U of: Faurot Field, 71,168 seats
24. Iowa, U of: Kinnick Stadium, 70,585 seats
25. San Diego State U (CA): Qualcomm Stadium, 70, 561 seats

Source: *College Finder* research, including *Sporting News*

Colleges With Golf Courses

Clemson U (SC)
Colgate U (NY)
Cornell U (NY)
Duke U (NC)
Florida, U of
Georgia, U of
Grand Valley State U (MI)
Kansas State U
Louisiana State U, Baton Rouge
Michigan, U of, Ann Arbor
Mt. Holyoke C (MA)
New Mexico, U of, Albuquerque
New York, State U of, Delhi
North Carolina, U of, Chapel Hill
Notre Dame, U of (IN)

Ohio State U, Columbus
Oklahoma State U
Oklahoma, U of
Pennsylvania State U, University Park
Purdue U (IN)
Stanford U (CA)
Texas Tech U
U.S. Air Force Academy (CO)
Virginia Polytechnic Institute & State U
Virginia, U of
Washington State U
Williams C (MA)
Wisconsin, U of, Madison
Yale U (CT)

Source: *College Finder* research, including *Links Golf Magazine* (linksmagazine.com)

Top 50 Largest College Libraries

Colleges are listed in order of the number of volumes in the university library.

Harvard U (MA): 16,832,952
Illinois, U of, Urbana: 13,158,748
Yale U (CT): 12,787,962
California, U of, Berkeley: 11,545,418
Columbia U (NY): 11,189,036
Michigan, U of, Ann Arbor: 10,778,736
Texas, U of, Austin: 9,990,941
Chicago, U of (IL): 9,837,021
California, U of, Los Angeles: 9,151,964
Indiana U Bloomington: 8,677,974
Stanford U (CA): 8,500,000
Wisconsin, U of, Madison: 8,421,198
Cornell U (NY): 8,173,778
Princeton U (NJ): 7,226,744
Washington, U of, Seattle: 7,203,156
Minnesota, U of, Twin Cities: 7,111,311
North Carolina, U of, Chapel Hill:
    7,012,787
Pennsylvania, U of: 6,438,305
Duke U (NC): 6,174,814
Ohio State U, Columbus: 6,161,657
Pittsburgh, U of (PA): 6,148,036
Arizona, U of: 5,998,148
Oklahoma, U of: 5,662,666
Michigan State U: 5,609,761
Virginia, U of: 5,607,915
Iowa, U of: 5,490,825
Pennsylvania State U, University
    Park: 5,441,121

New York U: 5,382,424
Northwestern U (IL): 5,047,970
Georgia, U of: 4,810,192
Rutgers U (NJ): 4,722,407
Colorado, U of, Boulder: 4,681,261
Texas A&M U, College Station:
    4,577,498
Arizona State U: 4,497,114
Florida, U of: 4,414,450
Cincinnati, U of: 4,379,445
North Carolina State U: 4,332,899
Washington U (MO): 4,323,958
Kansas, U of: 4,318,644
Brigham Young U (UT): 4,292,056
Brown U (RI): 4,187,257
Southern California, U of: 4,180,515
California, U of, Davis: 4,175,047
Tulane U (LA): 4,155,793
Louisiana State U, Baton Rouge:
    4,128,626
Connecticut, U of: 4,096,396
New York, State U of, Buffalo:
    4,029,865
Temple U (PA): 3,990,379
South Carolina, U of, Columbia:
    3,963,958
Maryland, U of, College Park: 3,930,013

Source: American Library Association (ala.org)

The Experts' Choice: Best College Cities

Experts were asked to list cities where it's great to be a college student.

Ann Arbor, MI
Athens, GA
Atlanta, GA
Austin, TX
Bloomington, IN
Boston, MA*
Boulder, CO
Burlington, VT
Chapel Hill, NC
Charleston, SC
Charlottesville, VA
Chicago, IL
College Station, TX

Columbus, OH
Denver, CO
Eugene, OR
Ft. Collins, CO
Greenville, SC
Houston, TX
Iowa City, IA
Ithaca, NY
Los Angeles, CA
Madison, WI
Nashville, TN
New York City, NY
Norman, OK

Oxford, OH
Philadelphia, PA
San Luis Obispo, CA
Saratoga Springs, NY
Seattle, WA
St. Paul, MN

State College, PA
Stillwater, OK
Washington, DC

*The Top Choice

The Experts' Choice: Friendly College Cities

Experts were asked to go beyond famous college cities like Ann Arbor, Michigan, and Boulder, Colorado, to identify other cities that are particularly friendly to college students.

Amherst, MA
Athens, GA
Austin, TX
Baltimore MD
Bloomington, IN
Boston, MA
Burlington, VT
Chapel Hill, NC
Charleston, SC
Charlottesville, VA
Chicago, IL
Columbia, MO
Eugene, OR
Evanston, IL

Hanover, NH
Ithaca, NY
Madison, WI
Nashville, TN
New York City, NY
Philadelphia, PA
Pittsburgh, PA
Portland, OR
Seattle, WA
St. Louis, MO
St. Paul, MN
Tampa, FL
Washington, DC

Great College Destinations: Major Metropolitan Cities (More Than 2.5 Million Residents)

According to the American Institute for Economic Research, these are the best major metropolitan cities for college students. Ratings are based on social or cultural factors including cost of rent, city accessibility, arts and entertainment, culture, bars and restaurants, diversity, and cost of living minus rent, and four work opportunities: youth unemployment, percent of residents who are college educated, economic activity, and workers in technology.

1. San Francisco, CA
2. Boston, MA
3. Seattle, WA
4. Denver, CO
5. Houston, TX
6. Minneapolis, MN
7. Washington, DC
8. Dallas, TX
9. San Diego, CA
10. New York City, NY
11. Baltimore, MD
12. Los Angeles, CA
13. Atlanta, GA
14. St. Louis, MO
15. Tampa, FL

Source: American Institute for Economic Research, *The AIER 2016 College Destinations Index* (aier.org)

Great College Destinations: Midsized Metropolitan Cities (1 to 2.5 Million Residents)

According to the American Institute for Economic Research, these are the best midsized metropolitan cities for college students. Ratings are based on social or cultural factors including cost of rent, city accessibility, arts and entertainment, culture, bars and restaurants, diversity, and cost of living minus rent, and four work opportunities: youth unemployment, percent of residents who are college-educated, economic activity, and workers in technology.

1. San Jose, CA
2. Austin, TX
3. Pittsburgh, PA
4. Raleigh, NC
5. Salt Lake City, UT
6. Portland, OR
7. Nashville, TN
8. Columbus, OH
9. Grand Rapids, MI
10. Milwaukee, WI
11. Cincinnati, OH
12. Buffalo, NY
13. New Orleans, LA
14. Cleveland, OH
15. Kansas City, MO
16. San Antonio, TX
17. Indianapolis, IN
18. Rochester, NY
19. Hartford, CT
20. Orlando, FL

Source: American Institute for Economic Research, *The AIER 2016 College Destinations Index* (aier.org)

Great College Destinations: Small Metropolitan Cities (250,000 to 1 Million Residents)

According to the American Institute for Economic Research, these are the best small metropolitan cities for college students. Ratings are based on social or cultural factors including cost of rent, city accessibility, arts and entertainment, culture, bars and restaurants, diversity, and cost of living minus rent, and four work opportunities: youth unemployment, percent of residents who are college-educated, economic activity, and workers in technology.

1. Boulder, CO
2. Durham, NC
3. Ann Arbor, MI
4. Madison, WI
5. Fort Collins, CO
6. Santa Barbara, CA
7. Provo, UT
8. Naples, FL
9. Trenton, NJ
10. Huntsville, AL
11. Lincoln, NE
12. Asheville, NC
13. Des Moines, IA
14. Omaha, NE
15. Portland, ME
16. Gainesville, FL
17. San Luis Obispo, CA
18. Honolulu, HI
19. Myrtle Beach, SC
20. Lexington, KY

Source: American Institute for Economic Research, *The AIER 2016 College Destinations Index* (aier.org)

Great College Destinations: College Towns (Fewer Than 250,000 Residents)

According to the American Institute for Economic Research, these are the best towns for college students. Ratings are based on social or cultural factors including cost of rent, city accessibility, arts and entertainment, culture, bars and restaurants, diversity, and cost of living minus rent, and four work opportunities: youth unemployment, percent of residents who are college-educated, economic activity, and workers in technology.

1.	Ames, IA	11. Manhattan, KS
2.	Ithaca, NY	12. Bloomington, IN
3.	Iowa City, IA	13. College Station, TX
4.	Charlottesville, VA	14. Rochester, MN
5.	Columbia, MO	15. Lawrence, KS
6.	Santa Fe, NM	16. Champaign-Urbana, IL
7.	Corvallis, OR	17. State College, PA
8.	Missoula, MT	18. Morgantown, WV
9.	Fargo, ND	19. Blacksburg, VA
10.	Lafayette, ID	20. Mankato, MN

Source: American Institute for Economic Research, *The AIER 2016 College Destinations Index* (aier.org)

Populations of Some College Towns

New York, NY: 8,400,000; home to dozens of colleges
Los Angeles, CA: 3,900,000; home to dozens of colleges
Austin, TX: 885,000; Texas, U of, Austin
Tucson, AZ: 526,116; Arizona, U of
Durham, NC: 245,000; Duke U
Ann Arbor, MI: 117,000; Michigan, U of
Peoria, IL: 116,000; Bradley U
Boulder, CO: 103,100; Colorado, U of
South Bend, IN: 100,000; Notre Dame, U of
Bozeman, MT: 40,000; Montana State U
Richmond, IN: 40,000; Earlham C
Ithaca, NY: 30,000; Cornell U and Ithaca C
Walla Walla, WA: 30,000; Whitman C
Northfield, MN: 20,000; Carleton C and St. Olaf C
Norton, MA: 19,000; Wheaton C
Arcata, CA: 18,000; Humboldt State U
Durango, CO: 17,557; Ft. Lewis C
Hanover, NH: 11,200; Dartmouth C
Williamstown, MA: 7,754; Williams C
Henniker, NH: 4,800; New England C
Hamilton, NY: 4,100; Colgate U
Gambier, OH: 2,400; Kenyon C
Sewanee, TN: 2,400; South, U of the
Big Pine, CA: 1,700; Deep Springs C

College Cities With Many Bike Riders

This list shows college cities with a population greater than 5,000, followed by the percentage of people who bike to work.

Stanford, CA: 41.7%; home of Stanford U
Isla Vista, CA: 19.6%; home of California, U of, Santa Barbara
Davis, CA: 14.4%; home of California, U of, Davis
Key West, FL: 12.7%; home of Florida Keys Community C

Steven R. Antonoff

Corvallis, OR: 7.1%; home of Oregon State U
Boulder, CO: 6.9%; home of Colorado, U of, Boulder
Gunnison, CO: 6.7%; home of Western State Colorado U
Oberlin, OH: 6.5%; home of Oberlin C
Twin Lakes, CA: 6.2%; home of California, U of, Santa Cruz
Missoula, MT: 5.6%; home of Montana, U of
Berkeley, CA: 5.6%; home of California, U of, Berkeley

Source: The website City-Data.com collects data from many sources and on issues from weather to crime.

College Cities With Vibrant Music Scenes

Looking for top-notch record stores, late-night venues with quality musicians, and a healthy culture of concerts and performances? These college cities feature a lively music scene, with some cities specializing in particular genres such as jazz or punk and some featuring a blend of different genres. This list was compiled from several websites and music magazines online.

Asheville, NC; home of North Carolina, U of
Athens, GA; home of Georgia, U of
Austin, TX; home of Texas, U of, Austin
Berkeley, CA; home of California, U of, Berkeley
Boston, MA; home of many colleges
Boulder, CO; home of Colorado, U of, Boulder
Cambridge, MA; home of Harvard U and Massachusetts Institute of Technology
Chapel Hill, NC; home of North Carolina, U of, Chapel Hill
Chicago, IL; home of many colleges
Columbus, OH; home of Ohio State U
Denton, TX; home of North Texas, U of
Los Angeles, CA; home of California, U of, Los Angeles
Madison, WI; home of Wisconsin, U of, Madison
Minneapolis, MN; home of Minnesota, U of
Nashville, TN; home of many colleges
New Haven, CT; home of Yale U
New York City, NY; home of many colleges
Olympia, WA; home of Evergreen State C
Omaha, NE; home of Creighton U
Pittsburgh, PA; home of many colleges
Portland, OR; home of many colleges
San Francisco, CA; home of many colleges
Seattle, WA; home of many colleges
Washington, DC; home of many colleges

Source: *College Finder* research

States Where College Students Make Up the Highest Proportion of the Population

The U.S. average for college students as a percentage of state population is 4.1%. The following states have the highest percentage of college students in their populations.

1. District of Columbia; about 9.9%
2. Iowa; about 7.4%
3. Arizona; about 7.1%
4. Utah; about 6.3%

5. Rhode Island; about 5.9%
6. Massachusetts; about 5.5%
7. North Dakota; about 5.3%
8. Vermont; about 5.2%
9. Nebraska; about 4.8%
10. New York; about 4.7%

11. New Hampshire; about 4.5%
12. Minnesota; about 4.4%
13. Missouri; about 4.4%
14. Kansas: about 4.3%
15. Mississippi; about 4.3%

Source: *The Huffington Post,* Huffpost College

WEATHER

Ten Snowiest Colleges

These are the snowiest colleges in the United States, based on snowfall in inches in a recent winter.

1. Michigan Technological U: 200 inches
2. Syracuse U (NY): 124 inches
3. Rochester, U of (NY): 99 inches
4. New York, State U of, Buffalo: 94 inches
5. Minnesota, U of, Duluth: 86 inches
6. Vermont, U of: 81 inches
7. Southern New Hampshire U: 69 inches
8. Western Michigan U: 67 inches
9. Cornell U (NY): 65 inches
10. Alaska, U of, Fairbanks: 62 inches

Source: AccuWeather (accuweather.com)

Top 25 Snowiest Cities in America

Niche compiled a list of the snowiest cities in the contiguous United States—those boasting the most snowfall during the winter months. This ranking uses the 30-year average monthly snowfall totals for December through March, as reported by NOAA and only includes U.S. cities with a population above 50,000.

1. Syracuse, NY: 110.0 inches
2. Erie, PA: 89.0 inches
3. Rochester, NY: 87.8 inches
4. Buffalo, NY: 82.9 inches
5. Flagstaff, AZ: 81.7 inches
6. Utica, NY: 77.5 inches
7. Grand Rapids, MI: 65.8 inches
8. Duluth, MN: 62.7 inches
9. Cleveland, OH: 60.3 inches
10. South Bend, IN: 60.0 inches
11. Worcester, MA: 58.5 inches
12. Portland, ME: 57.2 inches
13. Boulder, CO: 55.0 inches

14. Albany, NY: 53.9 inches
15. Manchester, NH: 52.0 inches
16. Ann Arbor, MI: 51.3 inches
17. Battle Creek, MI: 50.5 inches
18. Pocatello, ID: 50.3 inches
19. Kalamazoo, MI: 45.6 inches
20. Provo, UT: 45.0 inches
21. Milwaukee, WI: 44.0 inches
22. Green Bay, WI: 44.1 inches
23. Madison, WI: 44.0 inches
24. Fargo, ND: 42.8 inches
25. Flint, MI: 42.2 inches

Source: niche.com. "Niche is a website that helps you discover the schools and neighborhoods that are right for you. We rigorously analyze dozens of public data sets and millions of reviews to produce comprehensive rankings, report cards, and profiles for every K-12 school, college, and neighborhood in the U.S."

America's 20 Coldest Major Cities

According to The Weather Channel (Jon Erdman, January 27, 2014): "Using 30-year average temperatures from NOAA's National Climatic Data Center during the months of December, January, and February, we compiled the 20 coldest major U.S. cities. We didn't rank cities based on their record coldest temperatures but rather which cities are persistently the coldest in those three core winter months." The number after the city name is the average December, January, and February temperature in degrees Fahrenhelt.

1. Minneapolis/St. Paul, MN: 18.7
2. Anchorage, AK: 18.8
3. Madison, WI: 21.6
4. Milwaukee, WI: 24.9
5. Omaha, NE: 25.9
6. Chicago, IL: 26.4
7. Lincoln, NE: 26.8
8. Rochester, NY: 27.0
9. Buffalo, NY: 27.1
10. Ft. Wayne, IN: 27.4

11. Toledo, OH: 27.8
12. Detroit, MI: 27.9
13. Akron, OH: 28.5
14. Cleveland, OH: 30.3
15. Indianapolis, IN: 30.6
16. Colorado Springs, CO: 30.8
17. Pittsburgh, PA: 31.1
18. Denver, CO: 31.2
19. Kansas City, MO: 31.3
20. Boston, MA: 31.8

Source: The Weather Channel (weather.com)

Clear Days in Major Cities

After the name of the city is the average number of days per year that the sky is clear.

Phoenix, AZ: 211
Las Vegas, NV: 210
Sacramento, CA: 188
San Francisco, CA: 160
Los Angeles, CA: 147
San Diego, CA: 146
Oklahoma City, OK: 139
Dallas, TX: 135
Salt Lake City, UT: 125
Kansas City, MO: 120
Memphis, TN: 118
Austin, TX: 115
Denver, CO: 115
Raleigh, NC: 111
Atlanta, GA: 110
Charlotte, NC: 109
New York, NY: 107
Virginia Beach, VA: 106
Baltimore, MD: 105
San Antonio, TX: 105

Nashville, TN: 102
New Orleans, LA: 101
St. Louis, MO: 101
Tampa, FL: 101
Richmond, VA: 100
Birmingham, AL: 99
Boston, MA: 98
Providence, RI: 98
Washington, DC: 96
Minneapolis, MN: 95
Jacksonville, FL: 94
Louisville, KY: 93
Philadelphia, PA: 93
Houston, TX: 90
Milwaukee, WI: 90
Indianapolis, IN: 88
Chicago, IL: 84
Hartford, CT: 82
Cincinnati, OH: 81
Detroit, MI: 75

Miami, FL: 74
Columbus, OH: 72
Portland, OR: 68
Cleveland, OH: 66

Rochester, NY: 61
Pittsburgh, PA: 59
Seattle, MO: 58
Buffalo, NY: 54

Source: Current Results (currentresults.com)

COLLEGES BY CITY

Excellent Colleges In or Near Albany

These are among the fine schools located in or near Albany, New York.

Hartwick C (NY)
New York, State U of, Albany
New York, State U of, Oneonta
Rensselaer Polytechnic Institute (NY)
Skidmore C (NY)
Union C (NY)
Williams C (MA)

Excellent Colleges In or Near Albuquerque

These are among the fine schools located in or near Albuquerque, New Mexico.

New Mexico Highlands U
New Mexico Institute of Mining and Technology
New Mexico, U of
Santa Fe U of Art and Design (NM)
St. John's C (NM)

Excellent Colleges In or Near Atlanta

These are among the fine schools located in or near Atlanta, Georgia.

Agnes Scott C (GA)
Berry C (GA)
Clark Atlanta U (GA)
Emory U (GA)
Emory U/Oxford C (GA)
Georgia Institute of Technology
Georgia Southern U
Georgia State U
Georgia, U of
Mercer U (GA)
Morehouse C (GA)
Oglethorpe U (GA)
Spelman C (GA)

Excellent Colleges In or Near Austin

These are among the fine schools located in or near Austin, Texas. (Also see colleges in or near Houston, Texas, and San Antonio, Texas.)

Concordia U (TX)
Schreiner U (TX)
Southwestern U (TX)
St. Edward's U (TX)
Texas, U of, Austin

Excellent Colleges In or Near Baltimore

These are among the fine schools located in or near Baltimore, Maryland. Also see colleges in or near Washington, D.C.

Coppin State U (MD)
Goucher C (MD)
Hood C (MD)
Johns Hopkins U (MD)
Loyola C (MD)
Maryland Institute C of Art
Maryland, U of, Baltimore
Maryland, U of, College Park
Maryland, U of, Eastern Shore

McDaniel C (MD)
Morgan State U (MD)
St. John's C (MD)
Salisbury U (MD)
Stevenson U (MD)
Towson U (MD)
United States Naval Academy (MD)
Washington C (MD)

Excellent Colleges In or Near Birmingham

These are among the fine schools located in or near Birmingham, Alabama.

Alabama A&M U
Alabama, U of, Birmingham
Alabama, U of, Huntsville
Alabama, U of, Tuscaloosa
Auburn U (AL)
Birmingham-Southern C (AL)
Samford U (AL)
Stillman C (AL)
Tuskegee U (AL)

Excellent Colleges In or Near Boston

These are among the fine schools located in or near Boston, Massachusetts. Also see colleges in or near Providence, Rhode Island.

Amherst C (MA)
Assumption C (MA)
Babson C (MA)
Bentley C (MA)

Berklee C of Music (MA)
Boston C (MA)
Boston U (MA)
Brandeis U (MA)

Bridgewater State C (MA)
Brown U (RI)
Bryant U (RI)
Clark U (MA)
Curry C (MA)
Emerson C (MA)
Emmanuel C (MA)
Endicott C (MA)
Fisher C (MA)
Framingham State C (MA)
Gordon C (MA)
Hampshire C (MA)
Harvard U (MA)
Holy Cross, C of the (MA)
Johnson & Wales U (RI)
Lasell C (MA)
Lesley U (MA)
Massachusetts Institute of Technology
Massachusetts, U of, Amherst
Massachusetts, U of, Boston
Merrimack C (MA)

Mt. Holyoke C (MA)
Mt. Ida C (MA)
Northeastern U (MA)
Olin C of Engineering (MA)
Providence C (RI)
Regis C (MA)
Rhode Island School of Design
Rhode Island, U of
Roger Williams U (RI)
Salve Regina U (RI)
Simmons C (MA)
Smith C (MA)
Stonehill C (MA)
Suffolk U (MA)
Tufts U (MA)
Wellesley C (MA)
Wentworth Institute of Technology (MA)
Wheaton C (MA)
Wheelock C (MA)
Worcester Polytechnic Institute (MA)

Excellent Colleges In or Near Buffalo

These are among the fine schools located in or near Buffalo, New York. Also see colleges in or near Rochester, New York; Syracuse, New York; and Toronto, Ontario, Canada.

Canisius C (NY)
Daemen C (NY)
New York, State U of, Buffalo
Niagara U (NY)
Toronto, U of (Canada)

Excellent Colleges In or Near Cedar Rapids

These are among the fine schools located in or near Cedar Rapids, Iowa.

Coe C (IA)
Cornell C (IA)
Drake U (IA)
Grinnell C (IA)

Iowa State U
Iowa, U of
Loras C (IA)

Excellent Colleges In or Near Charleston

These are among the fine schools located in or near Charleston, South Carolina.

Charleston, C of (SC)
Charleston Southern U (SC)
Citadel, The (SC)
Coastal Carolina U (SC)
South Carolina, U of, Columbia

Steven R. Antonoff

Excellent Colleges In or Near Charlotte

These are among the fine schools located in or near Charlotte, North Carolina. Also see colleges in or near Greenville, North Carolina.

Anderson U (SC)
Brevard C (NC)
Catawba C (NC)
Clemson U (SC)
Davidson C (NC)
Duke U (NC)
East Carolina U (NC)
Elon U (NC)
Furman U (SC)
Greensboro C (NC)
Guilford C (NC)
High Point U (NC)

Johnson C. Smith U (NC)
North Carolina School of the Arts
North Carolina State U
North Carolina, U of, Asheville
North Carolina, U of, Chapel Hill
North Carolina, U of, Charlotte
North Carolina, U of, Greensboro
Presbyterian C (SC)
Queens U of Charlotte (NC)
Wake Forest U (NC)
Western Carolina U (NC)
Wofford C (SC)

Excellent Colleges In or Near Chicago

These are among the fine schools located in or near Chicago, Illinois.

Art Institute of Chicago, School of the
(IL)
Bradley U (IL)
Chicago, U of (IL)
Columbia C Chicago (IL)
DePaul U (IL)
Illinois Institute of Technology
Illinois, U of, Chicago

Lake Forest C (IL)
Loyola U (IL)
North Park U (IL)
Northwestern U (IL)
Robert Morris C (IL)
Roosevelt U (IL)
Wheaton C (IL)

Excellent Colleges In or Near Cincinnati

These are among the fine schools located in or near Cincinnati, Ohio. Also see colleges in or near Cleveland, Ohio; Columbus, Ohio; and Louisville, Kentucky.

Antioch C (OH)
Cincinnati, U of (OH)
Dayton, U of (OH)
Miami U (OH)
Mt. St. Joseph U (OH)
Wilberforce U (OH)
Wilmington C (OH)
Xavier U (OH)

Excellent Colleges In or Near Cleveland

These are among the fine schools located in or near Cleveland, Ohio. Also see colleges in or near Cincinnati, Ohio, and Columbus, Ohio.

Akron, U of
Baldwin Wallace U (OH)
Case Western Reserve U (OH)
John Carroll U (OH)
Kent State U (OH)
Oberlin C (OH)

Excellent Colleges In or Near Columbus

These are among the fine schools located in or near the greater Columbus, Ohio, area. Also see colleges in or near Cincinnati, Ohio, and Cleveland, Ohio.

Capitol U (OH)
Denison U (OH)
Kenyon C (OH)
Miami U (OH)
Ohio State U, Columbus
Ohio U, Athens
Ohio Wesleyan U
Otterbein C (OH)
Wilberforce U (OH)
Wittenberg U (OH)
Wooster, C of (OH)

Excellent Colleges In or Near Dallas/Fort Worth

These are among the fine schools located in or near the Dallas/Fort Worth, Texas, area.

Austin C (TX)
Baylor U (TX)
Dallas, U of (TX)
LeTourneau U (TX)
North Texas, U of
Southern Methodist U (TX)
Stephen F. Austin State U (TX)
Texas Christian U
Texas, U of, Dallas
Texas Women's U

Excellent Colleges In or Near Denver

These are among the fine schools located in or near the greater Denver, Colorado, area.

Colorado C
Colorado Christian U
Colorado School of Mines
Colorado State U, Ft. Collins
Colorado, U of, Boulder

Colorado, U of, Colorado Springs
Colorado, U of, Denver
Denver, U of (CO)
Johnson & Wales U (CO)
Metropolitan State C (CO)

Steven R. Antonoff

Naropa U (CO)
Northern Colorado, U of

Regis U (CO)
U.S. Air Force Academy (CO)

Excellent Colleges In or Near Detroit

These are among the fine schools located in or near Detroit, Michigan.

Adrian C (MI)
Albion C (MI)
Creative Studies, C of (MI)
Detroit, U of, Mercy (MI)
Eastern Michigan U
Hillsdale C (MI)
Kettering U (MI)
Madonna U (MI)

Marygrove C (MI)
Michigan State U
Michigan, U of, Ann Arbor
Michigan, U of, Dearborn
Oakland U (MI)
Rochester C (MI)
Wayne State U (MI)
William Tyndale C (MI)

Excellent Colleges In or Near Greenville

These are among the fine schools located in or near Greenville, South Carolina. Also see colleges in or near Charlotte, North Carolina.

Anderson U (SC)
Clemson U (SC)
Converse C (SC)
Furman C (SC)
North Carolina, U of, Asheville
Presbyterian C (SC)
South Carolina, U of, Columbia
Warren Wilson C (NC)
Western Carolina U (NC)
Winthrop U (SC)
Wofford C (SC)

Excellent Colleges In or Near Harrisburg

These are among the fine schools located in or near Harrisburg, Pennsylvania.

Albright C (PA)
Bucknell U (PA)
Dickinson C (PA)
Elizabethtown C (PA)
Franklin & Marshall C (PA)
Gettysburg C (PA)
Lafayette C (PA)
Lehigh U (PA)
Muhlenberg C (PA)
Susquehanna U (PA)

Excellent Colleges In or Near Hartford

These are among the fine schools located in or near Hartford, Connecticut.

Amherst C (MA)
Connecticut C
Connecticut, U of
Fairfield U (CT)
Hartford, U of (CT)
Hampshire C (MA)
Massachusetts, U of, Amherst
Mitchell C (CT)
Mt. Holyoke C (MA)
New Haven, U of (CT)

Quinnipiac U (CT)
Sacred Heart U (CT)
Smith C (MA)
Springfield C (MA)
St. Joseph C (CT)
Trinity C (CT)
U.S. Coast Guard Academy (CT)
Wesleyan U (CT)
Western New England C (MA)
Yale U (CT)

Excellent Colleges In or Near Honolulu

These are among the fine schools located in or near Honolulu, Hawaii.

Brigham Young U (HI)
Chaminade, U of, Honolulu (HI)
Hawaii Pacific U
Hawaii, U of, Hilo
Hawaii, U of, Manoa

Excellent Colleges In or Near Houston

These are among the fine schools located in or near Houston, Texas. Also see colleges in or near Austin, Texas, and San Antonio, Texas.

Houston, U of (TX)
Rice U (TX)
St. Thomas, U of (TX)
Texas, U of, Austin

Excellent Colleges In or Near Indianapolis

These are among the fine schools located in or near Indianapolis, Indiana.

Anderson U (IN)
Ball State U (IN)
Butler U (IN)
DePauw U (IN)
Earlham C (IN)
Franklin C (IN)
Indiana, U of

Indiana U-Purdue U Indianapolis
Indianapolis, U of
Purdue U (IN)
Rose-Hulman Institute of Technology
   (IN)
Wabash C (IN)

Excellent Colleges In or Near Jacksonville

These are among the fine schools located in or near Jacksonville, Florida. Also see colleges in or near Orlando, Florida, and Tampa, Florida.

Bethune-Cookman C (FL)
Embry-Riddle Aeronautical U (FL)
Flagler C (FL)
Florida State U
Florida, U of
Jacksonville U (FL)
North Florida, U of
Stetson U (FL)

Excellent Colleges In or Near Kansas City

These are among the fine schools located in or near Kansas City, Kansas, or Kansas City, Missouri.

Baker U (KS)
Kansas State U
Kansas, U of
Missouri, U of, Kansas City
Washburn U (KS)
William Jewell C (MO)

Excellent Colleges In or Near Los Angeles

These are among the fine schools located in or near Los Angeles, California. Also see colleges in or near San Diego, California.

American Jewish U (CA)
ArtCenter C of Design (CA)
Azusa Pacific U (CA)
Biola U (CA)
California Institute of the Arts
California Institute of Technology
California Lutheran U
California State U, Northridge
California, U of, Los Angeles
California, U of, Santa Barbara
Chapman U (CA)
Claremont McKenna C (CA)
Harvey Mudd C (CA)
La Verne, U of (CA)

Loyola Marymount U (CA)
Master's C, The (CA)
Mt. St. Mary's U (CA)
Occidental C (CA)
Pepperdine U (CA)
Pitzer C (CA)
Pomona C (CA)
Redlands, U of (CA)
Scripps C (CA)
Southern California, U of
Westmont C (CA)
Whittier C (CA)
Woodbury U (CA)

Excellent Colleges In or Near Louisville

These are among the fine schools located in or near Louisville, Kentucky. Also see colleges in or near Cincinnati, Ohio.

Bellarmine U (KY)
Berea C (KY)
Centre C (KY)
Kentucky, U of
Louisville, U of (KY)
Transylvania U (KY)

Excellent Colleges In or Near Manchester

These are among the fine schools located in or near Manchester, New Hampshire.

Bennington C (VT)
Colby-Sawyer C (NH)
Dartmouth C (NH)
Franklin Pierce U (NH)
Marlboro C (VT)
New England C (NH)
New Hampshire, U of
Southern New Hampshire U
St. Anselm C (NH)
Thomas More C of Liberal Arts (NH)

Excellent Colleges In or Near Memphis

These are among the fine schools located in or near Memphis, Tennessee.

Christian Brothers U (TN)
Memphis, U of (TN)
Mississippi, U of
Rhodes C (TN)

Excellent Colleges In or Near Miami

These are among the fine schools located in or near Miami, Florida.

Barry U (FL)
Florida Atlantic U
Florida International U
Lynn U (FL)
Miami, U of (FL)
Nova Southeastern U (FL)

Excellent Colleges In or Near Milwaukee

These are among the fine schools located in or near Milwaukee, Wisconsin.

Alverno C (WI)
Carroll U (WI)
Lawrence U (WI)
Marquette U (WI)
Ripon C (WI)
Wisconsin, U of, Madison
Wisconsin, U of, Milwaukee

Excellent Colleges In or Near Minneapolis

These are among the fine schools located in or near Minneapolis, Minnesota.

Augsburg C (MN)
Bethel U (MN)
Carleton C (MN)
Gustavus Adolphus C (MN)
Hamline U (MN)
Macalester C (MN)
Minnesota, U of, Twin Cities
St. Catherine U (MN)
St. Olaf C (MN)
St. Thomas, U of (MN)

Excellent Colleges In or Near Montreal

These are among the fine schools located in or near Montreal, Quebec, Canada.

Bishop's U (Canada)
Concordia U (Canada)
McGill U (Canada)

Excellent Colleges In or Near Nashville

These are among the fine schools located in or near Nashville, Tennessee.

Aquinas C (TN)
Belmont U (TN)
Fisk U (TN)
Lipscomb U (TN)
South, U of the (TN)
Tennessee State U
Trevecca Nazarene U (TN)
Vanderbilt U (TN)
Watkins C of Art, Design & Film (TN)
Welch C (TN)

Excellent Colleges In or Near New Orleans

These are among the fine schools located in or near New Orleans, Louisiana.

Dillard U (LA)
Louisiana State U, Baton Rouge
Loyola U (LA)
New Orleans, U of (LA)
Southeastern Louisiana U
Tulane U (LA)
Xavier U (LA)

Excellent Colleges In or Near New York City

These are among the fine schools located in or near New York City, New York. Also see colleges in or near Newark, New Jersey.

Adelphi U (NY)
Barnard C (NY)
Centenary C (NJ)
Columbia U (NY)
Connecticut C
Cooper Union (NY)
Dominican C (NY)
Drew U (NJ)
Eugene Lang C (NY)
Fairfield U (CT)
Fairleigh Dickinson U (NJ)
Fashion Institute of Technology (NY)
Fordham U (NY)
Hofstra U (NY)
Iona C (NY)
Juilliard School (NY)
Kean U (NJ)
Long Island U (NY)
Manhattan C (NY)
Manhattanville C (NY)
Marist C (NY)
Marymount Manhattan C (NY)
Monmouth U (NJ)
Montclair State U (NJ)

New Haven, U of (CT)
New Jersey Institute of Technology
New Jersey, C of
New Rochelle, C of (NY)
New York, State U of, Purchase
New York, State U of, Stony Brook
New York U
Pace U (NY)
Pratt Institute (NY)
Princeton U (NJ)
Quinnipiac U (CT)
Ramapo C (NJ)
Rider U (NJ)
Rutgers U, New Brunswick (NJ)
Sacred Heart U (CT)
Sarah Lawrence C (NY)
Seton Hall U (NJ)
St. John's U (NY)
St. Thomas Aquinas C (NY)
Stevens Institute of Technology (NJ)
Vassar C (NY)
Visual Arts, School of (NY)
Wagner C (NY)
Yeshiva U (NY)

Excellent Colleges In or Near Newark

These are among the fine schools located in or near Newark, New Jersey. Also see colleges in or near New York City, New York.

Drew U (NJ)
Fairleigh Dickinson U (NJ)
Kean U (NJ)
Monmouth U (NJ)
Montclair State U (NJ)
New Jersey, C of

New Jersey Institute of Technology
Princeton U (NJ)
Rider U (NJ)
Rutgers U, New Brunswick (NJ)
Seton Hall U (NJ)
Stevens Institute of Technology (NJ)

Excellent Colleges In or Near Norfolk

These are among the fine schools located in or near Norfolk, Virginia. Also see colleges in or near Richmond, Virginia.

Christopher Newport U (VA)
Hampton U (VA)
Mary Washington, U of (VA)
Old Dominion U (VA)
Richmond, U of (VA)
William & Mary, C of (VA)

Excellent Colleges In or Near Oklahoma City

These are among the fine schools located in or near Oklahoma City, Oklahoma.

Oklahoma City U
Oklahoma State U
Oklahoma, U of
Oral Roberts U
Tulsa, U of (OK)

Excellent Colleges In or Near Omaha

These are among the fine schools located in or near Omaha, Nebraska.

Creighton U (NE)
Nebraska, U of, Lincoln
Nebraska, U of, Omaha

Excellent Colleges In or Near Orlando

These are among the fine schools located in or near Orlando, Florida. Also see colleges in or near Jacksonville, Florida, and Tampa, Florida.

Bethune-Cookman U (FL)
Central Florida, U of
Embry-Riddle Aeronautical U (FL)
Florida Institute of Technology
Florida Southern C
Rollins C (FL)
Stetson U (FL)

Excellent Colleges In or Near Peoria

These are among the fine schools located in or near Peoria, Illinois.

Bradley U (IL)
Eureka C (IL)
Illinois, U of, Urbana

Illinois Wesleyan U
Knox C (IL)
Monmouth C (IL)

Excellent Colleges In or Near Philadelphia

These are among the fine schools located in or near Philadelphia, Pennsylvania.

Arcadia U (PA)
Arts, U of the (PA)
Bryn Mawr C (PA)
Cabrini C (PA)
Chestnut Hill C (PA)
Cheyney U (PA)
Curtis Institute of Music (PA)
Delaware, U of
DeSales U (PA)
Drexel U (PA)
Haverford C (PA)
Immaculata U (PA)
La Salle U (PA)

Lehigh U (PA)
Moravian C (PA)
Muhlenberg C (PA)
Pennsylvania, U of (PA)
Philadelphia U (PA)
Philadelphia, U of the Sciences in (PA)
St. Joseph's U (PA)
Swarthmore C (PA)
Temple U (PA)
Ursinus C (PA)
Villanova U (PA)
West Chester U (PA)
Widener U (PA)

Excellent Colleges In or Near Phoenix

These are among the fine schools located in or near Phoenix, Arizona.

Arizona State U
Arizona, U of
Grand Canyon U (AZ)
Northern Arizona U
Prescott C (AZ)

Excellent Colleges In or Near Pittsburgh

These are among the fine schools located in or near the greater Pittsburgh, Pennsylvania, area.

Allegheny C (PA)
Carlow U (PA)
Carnegie Mellon U (PA)
Chatham U (PA)
Duquesne U (PA)
Grove City C (PA)
Indiana U of Pennsylvania
Pittsburgh, U of (PA)
Robert Morris U (PA)
Slippery Rock U (PA)
Washington & Jefferson C (PA)

Steven R. Antonoff

Excellent Colleges In or Near Portland, Maine

These are among the fine schools located in or near Portland, Maine.

Atlantic, C of the (ME)
Bates C (ME)
Bowdoin C (ME)
Colby C (ME)
Maine, U of
Southern Maine, U of

Excellent Colleges In or Near Portland, Oregon

These are among the fine schools located in or near the greater Portland, Oregon, area.

Concordia C (OR)
George Fox U (OR)
Lewis & Clark C (OR)
Linfield C (OR)
Oregon State U

Oregon, U of
Portland State U (OR)
Portland, U of (OR)
Reed C (OR)
Willamette U (OR)

Excellent Colleges In or Near Providence

These are among the fine schools located in or near Providence, Rhode Island. Also see colleges in or near Boston, Massachusetts.

Brown U (RI)
Bryant U (RI)
Johnson & Wales U (RI)
Providence C (RI)
Rhode Island C
Rhode Island School of Design
Rhode Island, U of
Roger Williams U (RI)
Salve Regina U (RI)

Excellent Colleges In or Near Raleigh-Durham

These are among the fine schools located in or near Raleigh-Durham, North Carolina.

Duke U (NC)
East Carolina U (NC)
Elon U (NC)
Greensboro C (NC)
Guilford C (NC)
North Carolina A&T State U
North Carolina State U
North Carolina, U of, Chapel Hill

Excellent Colleges In or Near Richmond

These are among the fine schools located in or near Richmond, Virginia. Also see colleges in or near Norfolk, Virginia.

Christopher Newport U (VA)
Liberty U (VA)
Lynchburg C (VA)
Randolph-Macon C (VA)
Richmond, U of (VA)

Virginia Commonwealth U
Virginia, U of
Virginia Union U
William & Mary, C of (VA)

Excellent Colleges In or Near Rochester

These are among the fine schools located in or near Rochester, New York. Also see colleges in or near Buffalo, New York; Syracuse, New York; and Toronto, Ontario, Canada.

Hobart & William Smith C (NY)
New York, State U of, Geneseo
Rochester Institute of Technology (NY)
Rochester, U of (NY)
Syracuse U (NY)

Excellent Colleges In or Near Sacramento

These are among the fine schools located in or near Sacramento, California. Also see colleges in or near San Francisco, California.

California State U, Sacramento
California, U of, Davis
Pacific, U of the (CA)
Sonoma State U (CA)

Excellent Colleges In or Near Salt Lake City

These are among the fine schools located in or near Salt Lake City, Utah.

Brigham Young U (UT)
Utah, U of
Weber State U (UT)
Westminster C (UT)

Excellent Colleges In or Near San Antonio

These are among the fine schools located in or near San Antonio, Texas. Also see colleges in or near Austin, Texas, and Houston, Texas.

Our Lady of the Lake U (TX)
St. Mark's U (TX)
Texas Lutheran U

Texas, U of, San Antonio
Texas, U of, San Marcos
Trinity U (TX)

Excellent Colleges In or Near San Diego

These are among the fine schools located in or near San Diego, California. Also see colleges in or near Los Angeles, California.

California, U of, Irvine
California, U of, San Diego
Chapman U (CA)
Point Loma Nazarene U (CA)

San Diego State U (CA)
San Diego, U of (CA)
Whittier C (CA)

Excellent Colleges In or Near San Francisco

These are among the fine schools located in or near San Francisco, California. Also see colleges in or near Sacramento, California.

Art Institute of San Francisco (CA)
California, U of, Berkeley
California, U of, Davis
California, U of, Santa Cruz
Holy Names U (CA)
Menlo C (CA)
Mills C (CA)
Notre Dame de Namur U (CA)

Pacific, U of the (CA)
San Francisco, U of (CA)
San Jose State U (CA)
Santa Clara U (CA)
Sonoma State U (CA)
St. Mary's C (CA)
Stanford U (CA)

Excellent Colleges In or Near Seattle

These are among the fine schools located in or near Seattle, Washington. Also see colleges in or near Vancouver, British Columbia, Canada.
Evergreen State C (WA)
Pacific Lutheran U (WA)
Puget Sound, U of (WA)
Seattle Pacific U (WA)
Seattle U (WA)
Washington, U of, Seattle
Western Washington U

Excellent Colleges In or Near Spokane

These are among the fine schools located in or near Spokane, Washington.

Eastern Washington U
Gonzaga U (WA)
Washington State U
Whitworth U (WA)

Excellent Colleges In or Near St. Louis

These are among the fine schools located in or near St. Louis, Missouri.

Missouri, U of, St. Louis
St. Louis U (MO)
Washington U (MO)
Westminster C (MO)
William Woods U (MO)

Excellent Colleges In or Near Syracuse

These are among the fine schools located in or near Syracuse, New York. Also see colleges in or near Buffalo, New York; Rochester, New York, and Toronto, Ontario, Canada.

Cazenovia C (NY)
Colgate U (NY)
Cornell U (NY)
Hamilton C (NY)
Hobart & William Smith C (NY)
Ithaca C (NY)
Keuka C (NY)

New York, State U of, Geneseo
New York, State U of, Oswego
Rochester Institute of Technology (NY)
Rochester, U of (NY)
Syracuse U (NY)
Wells C (NY)

Excellent Colleges In or Near Tampa

These are among the fine schools located in or near Tampa, Florida. Also see colleges in or near Jacksonville, Florida, and Orlando, Florida.

Eckerd C (FL)
Florida Southern C
New C of Florida
Ringling C of Art & Design (FL)
South Florida, U of
St. Leo U (FL)
Tampa, U of (FL)

Excellent Colleges In or Near Toronto

These are among the fine schools located in or near Toronto, Ontario, Canada. Also see colleges in or near Buffalo, New York; Rochester, New York; and Syracuse, New York.

Brock U (Canada)
Guelph, U of (Canada)
New York, State U of, Buffalo
Ryerson Polytechnic U (Canada)
Toronto, U of (Canada)
York U (Canada)

Excellent Colleges In or Near Vancouver

These are among the fine schools located in or near Vancouver, British Columbia, Canada. Also see colleges in or near Seattle, Washington.

British Columbia, U of (Canada)
Quest U (Canada)
Selkirk C (Canada)
Simon Fraser U (Canada)
Trinity Western U (Canada)

Excellent Colleges In or Near Washington, D.C.

These are among the fine schools located in or near the greater Washington D.C. area. Also see colleges in or near Baltimore, Maryland.

American U (DC)
Catholic U of America (DC)
Gallaudet U (DC)
George Mason U (VA)
George Washington U (DC)
Georgetown U (DC)
Howard U (DC)

James Madison U (VA)
Mary Washington, U of (VA)
Maryland, U of, College Park
Richmond, U of (VA)
St. Mary's C (MD)
Trinity Washington U (DC)
Virginia, U of

ACTIVITIES

Colleges With the Largest Number of Registered Student Organizations

At these colleges, you won't be just hanging out in your dorm playing solitaire. These are the colleges with the most school-recognized organizations, from Greek life to hacky sack clubs. You'll never be bored. Seriously.

Ohio State U, Columbus: 1,493
Michigan, U of, Ann Arbor: 1,435
Toronto, U of (Canada): 1,134
Cornell U (NY): 1,017
Texas, U of, Austin: 1,000
Illinois, U of, Urbana: 1,000
California, U of, Los Angeles: 1,000
Purdue U (IN): 948
Wisconsin, U of, Madison: 888
Iowa State U: 827
Maryland, U of, College Park: 818
Pennsylvania State U, University Park: 816
Florida, U of: 800
Virginia Polytechnic Institute & State U: 792
Southern California, U of: 764

Monterrey Institute of Technology & Higher Education (Mexico): 761
Vanderbilt U (TN): 724
Texas A&M U, College Station: 700
Indiana U Bloomington: 700
Missouri, U of, Columbia: 700
Minnesota, U of, Twin Cities: 680
Arizona State U, Tempe: 673
Georgia, U of: 639
Nebraska, U of, Lincoln: 629
Stanford U (CA): 625
Kansas, U of: 615
Colorado State U: 611
North Carolina State U: 608
Michigan State U: 600
New York U: 595

North Carolina, U of, Chapel Hill: 592
South Florida, U of: 591
Virginia Commonwealth U: 583
Connecticut, U of: 582
California, U of, Irvine: 554

Florida State U: 550
Central Florida, U of: 550
Georgia Institute of Technology: 529
Iowa, U of: 512

Source: Wintergreen Orchard House

Colleges With Highly Ranked Debate Teams

These are winning teams in recent years, according to the International Debate Education Association. Schools participate in policy, parliamentary, and world schools debate (British Parliamentary) events.

Ateneo de Manila U (Philippines)
Babes-Bolyai U (Romania)
Cambridge, U of (United Kingdom)
Cork, U C (Ireland)
Cornell U (NY)
Dublin, U C (Ireland)
Durham U (United Kingdom)
Harvard U (MA)
Leiden U (Netherlands)
London School of Economics (United Kingdom)
McGill U (Canada)

Monash U (Australia)
Nanyang Technological U (Singapore)
New South Wales, U of (Australia)
Oxford, U of (United Kingdom)
Queen's U (Canada)
Queensland, U of (Australia)
Toronto, U of (Canada)
Trinity C, Dublin (Ireland)
Vermont, U of
Warwick, U of (United Kingdom)
Witwatersrand, U of the (South Africa)
Yale U (CT)

Source: *College Finder* research including the International Debate Education Association (idebate.org)

Colleges With Dress Codes

These schools take away the guesswork when figuring out what to wear on the first day of school.

Abilene Christian U (TX)
Advancing Technology, U of (AZ)
Benedict C (SC)
Biola U (CA)
Brigham Young U (HI)
Brigham Young U (ID)
Cairn U (PA)
California Maritime Academy
Calvary Bible C (MO)
Crown C (MN)
East Texas Baptist U
Embry-Riddle Aeronautical U (AZ)
Embry-Riddle Aeronautical U (FL)
Great Falls, U of (MT)
Gwynedd Mercy U (PA)
Hannibal-LaGrange U (MO)
Johnson C. Smith U (NC)
La Sierra U (CA)
Lancaster Bible C (PA)

Maine Maritime Academy
Malone U (OH)
Mary Baldwin C (VA)
Mary Hardin-Baylor, U of (TX)
Maryland, U of, Eastern Shore
Massachusetts Maritime Academy
Master's C (Canada)
Mobile, U of (AL)
Mt. Vernon Nazarene U (OH)
Oklahoma Christian U
Oklahoma Wesleyan U
Patten U (CA)
San Diego Christian C (CA)
Southwestern Adventist U (TX)
Southwestern Assemblies of God U (TX)
Stillman C (AL)
Thomas Aquinas C (CA)
U.S. Air Force Academy (CO)

U.S. Coast Guard Academy (CT)   U.S. Military Academy (NY)
U.S. Merchant Marine Academy (NY)   Union C (NY)

Source: Wintergreen Orchard House

Colleges With Excellent Ethics Bowl Teams

These colleges and universities are ranked highly in the International Intercollegiate Ethics Bowl. In an ethics bowl, teams discuss their moral assessment of interpersonal and societal problems.

Alabama, U of, Birmingham   Oklahoma Christian U
Alaska, U of, Anchorage   Oklahoma, U of
Azusa Pacific U (CA)   Providence C (RI)
California Polytechnic State U, Pomona Richmond, U of (VA)
Ft. Lewis C (CO)   Santa Clara U (CA)
Gonzaga U (WA)   Taylor U (IN)
Harper C (IL)   U.S. Naval Academy (MD)
Indiana U Bloomington   Villanova U (PA)
Michigan, U of, Ann Arbor   Westminster C (UT)
North Carolina, U of, Charlotte   Whitworth U (WA)

Source: Association for Practical and Professional Ethics (appe.indiana.edu)

Colleges Gamers Might Consider

These colleges have active gaming clubs.

Arizona State U   Nebraska, U of, Lincoln
California, U of, Irvine   Pennsylvania State U, University Park
California, U of, Los Angeles   Princeton U (NJ)
Carnegie Mellon U (PA)   Rensselaer Polytechnic Institute (NY)
DigiPen Institute of Technology (WA)   Rochester Institute of Technology (NY)
Full Sail U (FL)   Southern California, U of
Georgia Institute of Technology   Texas, U of, Austin
Massachusetts Institute of Technology Virginia Polytechnic Institute & State U
Michigan, U of, Dearborn   Virginia, U of
Minnesota, U of, Twin Cities

Source: *College Finder* research, including Global Gaming League

More Colleges for Gamers

These colleges are members of Tespa, "a network of college clubs founded to promote gaming and host the best college e-sports events and competitions."

Abilene Christian U (TX)   Arizona, U of
Academy of Art U (CA)   Arkansas, U of
Alabama, U of, Huntsville   Ball State U (IN)
Appalachian State U (NC)   Berklee C of Music (MA)

Boston U (MA)
Bowling Green State U (OH)
California Polytechnic State U, Pomona
California State U, Chico
California State U, Fullerton
California State U, Long Beach
California State U, Los Angeles
California, U of, Berkeley
California, U of, Irvine
California, U of, Los Angeles
California, U of, Riverside
California, U of, San Diego
California, U of, Santa Cruz
Carnegie Mellon U (PA)
Central Connecticut State U
Central Missouri, U of
Central Oklahoma, U of
Chapman U (CA)
Clemson U (SC)
Collin College (TX)
Colorado, U of, Boulder
Colorado, U of, Colorado Springs
Columbia U (NY)
Connecticut, U of
Cornell U (NY)
Dawson C (Canada)
Drexel U (PA)
École de Technologie Supérieure
  (Canada)
Florida Gulf Coast U
George Mason U (VA)
Georgia State U
Harvard U (MA)
Hofstra U (NY)
Huntington U (Canada)
Husson U (ME)
Idaho, U of
Illinois, U of, Urbana
Indiana U-Purdue U Ft. Wayne
Indiana U-Purdue U Indianapolis
Indiana U Bloomington
Johns Hopkins U (MD)
Johnson & Wales U (FL)
Kansas State U
Kansas Wesleyan U
Kansas, U of
LaVerne, U of (CA)
Lehigh U (PA)
Liberty U (VA)
Los Medanos C (CA)
Louisiana, U of, Monroe
Mary Hardin-Baylor, U of (TX)
Mendocino C (CA)
Miami U (OH)
Michigan, U of, Ann Arbor

Minnesota, U of, Duluth
Montana State U
Montana, U of
Murray State U (KY)
Neumont U (UT)
Nevada, U of, Las Vegas
Nevada, U of, Reno
New Haven, U of (CT)
New York, State U of, Oneonta
New York, State U of, Polytechnic
  Institute
New York, State U of, Stony Brook
North Carolina State U
North Carolina, U of, Chapel Hill
North Carolina, U of, Charlotte
North Carolina, U of, Greensboro
North Texas, U of
Northern Arizona U
Northern Illinois U
Northern Virginia Community C
Ohio State U
Ohlone Community C (CA)
Oklahoma State U
Ontario, U of, Institute of Technology
  (Canada)
Orange Coast C (CA)
Pennsylvania State U, University Park
Point Loma Nazarene U (CA)
Portland State U (OR)
Rensselaer Polytechnic Institute (NY)
Rochester Institute of Technology (NY)
Rowan U (NJ)
Rutgers U (NJ)
Ryerson U (Canada)
Sam Houston State U (TX)
San Diego, U of (CA)
San Jose State U (CA)
South Alabama, U of
South Carolina, U of
Southern California, U of
Southern Illinois U, Edwardsville
Southwestern C (CA)
St. Louis C of Pharmacy (MO)
St. Scholastica, C of (MN)
Stevens Institute of Technology (NJ)
Tarleton State U (TX)
Temple U (PA)
Tennessee Technological U
Texas A&M U
Texas Tech U
Texas, U of, Austin
Texas, U of, Dallas
Texas, U of, Rio Grande Valley
Texas, U of, San Antonio
Utah State U

Utah Valley U
Utah, U of
Virginia, U of
Washington, U of

Waterloo, U of (Canada)
Wilfrid Laurier U (Canada)
Wisconsin, U of, Milwaukee
Word of Life Bible Institute (NY)

Source: Tespa (tespa.org)

Colleges Where a High Percentage of Students Join Fraternities

If John Belushi screaming "TOGA!" and doing the gator on the dance floor is your idea of
the perfect college, check out these schools.

Welch C (TN): 84%
Washington & Lee U (VA): 82%
DePauw U (IN): 78%
South, U of the (TN): 67%
Dartmouth C (NH): 66%
Millsaps C (MS): 60%
Wabash C (IN): 60%
Transylvania U (KY): 55%
Harding U (AR): 50%
Massachusetts Institute of Technology:
  49%
Franklin C (IN): 49%
Whitman C (WA): 46%
York C (NE): 46%
Westminster C (MO): 45%
Bucknell U (PA): 44%
Hanover C (IN): 44%
Ohio Wesleyan U: 44%
Washington & Jefferson C (PA): 43%
Wofford C (SC): 43%

Texas Christian U: 42%
Centre C (KY): 42%
Presbyterian C (SC): 41%
Lehigh U (PA): 40%
Sam Houston State U (TX): 40%
Case Western Reserve U (OH): 40%
Rhodes C (TN): 40%
Union C (NY): 39%
Lyon C (AR): 39%
Wake Forest U (NC): 39%
Oklahoma Christian U: 38%
Gettysburg C (PA): 38%
Culver-Stockton C (MO): 38%
Florida Southern C: 37%
Kettering U (MI): 37%
Beacon C (FL): 37%
Rose-Hulman Institute (IN): 36%
Westminster C (UT): 35%
Birmingham-Southern C (AL): 35%

Source: Wintergreen Orchard House

Colleges With the Most Fraternities

Whether it's an academic fraternity or an *Animal House*–like brotherhood, you might find
your perfect frat-fit at one of these schools.

Illinois, U of, Urbana: 60
Pennsylvania State U, University Park:56
Purdue U (IN): 50
Ohio State U, Columbus: 47
Cornell U (NY): 42
Indiana U Bloomington: 40
Michigan, U of, Ann Arbor: 40
Texas, U of, Austin: 40
Georgia Institute of Technology: 39
Southern California, U of: 37
Georgia, U of: 36

Maryland, U of, College Park: 36
Arizona State U, Tempe: 34
Georgia Southern U: 34
Methodist U (NC): 34
New York, State U of, Binghamton: 34
Texas Tech U: 33
Alabama, U of, Tuscaloosa: 32
Iowa State U: 32
Missouri, U of, Columbia: 32
North Carolina, U of, Chapel Hill: 32
Pennsylvania, U of: 32

Michigan State U: 31
North Carolina State U: 31
Syracuse U (NY): 31
Virginia, U of: 31
Auburn U (AL): 30
Florida State U: 30
Nebraska, U of, Lincoln: 30
Oklahoma State U: 30
Oklahoma, U of: 30

Arizona, U of: 29
Kansas, U of: 29
Miami U (OH): 29
Minnesota, U of, Twin Cities: 29
Rensselaer Polytechnic Institute (NY): 29
Washington State U: 29
California, U of, Los Angeles: 28
Washington, U of, Seattle: 28

Colleges Where a High Percentage of Students Join Sororities

At these schools, the sorority scene can't be beat. Think *Legally Blonde*.

Texas, U of, Pan American: 100%
Washington & Lee U (VA): 82%
Welch C (TN): 81%
South, U of the (TN): 72%
Millsaps C (MS): 64%
Dartmouth C (NH): 64%
DePauw U (IN): 63%
Rhodes C (TN): 60%
Wake Forest U (NC): 58%
Wofford C (SC): 55%
Transylvania U (KY): 55%
Vanderbilt U (TN): 55%
Furman U (SC): 54%
Franklin C (IN): 54%
York C (PA): 54%
Texas Christian U: 53%
Birmingham-Southern C (AL): 53%
Harding U (AR): 51%
Southern Methodist U (TX): 48%
Clemson U (SC): 48%

Presbyterian C (SC): 47%
Washington & Jefferson C (PA): 46%
Mt. Union, U of (OH): 46%
Denison U (OH): 45%
Missouri State U: 45%
Centenary C (LA): 44%
Creighton U (NE): 43%
Lehigh U (PA): 43%
Tulane U (LA): 43%
Duke U (NC): 42%
Bethany C (WV): 42%
Baker U (KS): 42%
Bucknell U (PA): 41%
Worcester Polytechnic Institute (MA): 41%
Oklahoma Christian U: 41%
Whitman C (WA): 40%
Centre C (KY): 40%
Huntingdon C (AL): 40%
Hillsdale C (MI): 40%

Source for both Franternities and Sororities data: Wintergreen Orchard House

Colleges With the Most Sororities

Check out these schools to find those gals who will most likely be your lifelong friends.

Methodist U (NC): 39
Illinois, U of, Urbana: 36
Texas A&M U, College Station: 36
Texas, U of, Austin: 32
Indiana U Bloomington: 31
Pennsylvania State U, University Park: 31
Purdue U (IN): 31
California, U of, Los Angeles: 30
Florida State U: 27

Georgia, U of: 27
Maryland, U of, College Park: 27
Arizona State U: 25
California, U of, Irvine: 25
Michigan, U of, Ann Arbor: 25
Southern California, U of: 25
Tennessee State U: 25
Syracuse U (NY): 24
Alabama, U of, Tuscaloosa: 23
North Carolina, U of, Chapel Hill: 23

South Florida, U of: 23
California, U of, Santa Barbara: 22
Central Florida, U of: 22
Iowa, U of: 22
Ohio State U, Columbus: 22
Arizona, U of: 21
Miami U (OH): 21
North Carolina State U: 21
California, U of, Riverside: 20
Iowa State U: 20
Nebraska, U of, Lincoln: 20

New York, State U of, Albany: 20
New York, State U of, Environmental
Science & Forestry: 20
Oregon State U: 20
San Diego State U (CA): 20
Texas Christian U: 20
California State U, Sacramento: 19
Cornell U (NY): 19
Houston, U of (TX): 19
Washington State U: 19

Source: Wintergreen Orchard House

The Experts' Choice: Colleges Where Fraternities and Sororities Are Important

The experts named these colleges as places where fraternities and sororities play a central role in campus life.

Arizona, U of
Arkansas State U
Bucknell U (PA)
Central Arkansas, U of
Colorado State U, Ft. Collins
Colorado, U of, Boulder
Gettysburg C (PA)

Indiana U Bloomington
Iowa State U
Northern Colorado, U of
Texas A&M U
Texas, U of, Austin
Washington & Lee U (VA)

The Experts' Choice: Gap Between Students Who Join Fraternities and Sororities and Students Who Do Not

Experts were asked to identify colleges that have a clear division between those who participate in fraternities and sororities and those who do not.

Alabama, U of, Tuscaloosa
Auburn U (AL)
Bucknell U (PA)
California, U of
Clemson U (SC)
DePauw U (IN)
Duke U (NC)
Emory U (GA)
Georgia, U of
Gettysburg C (PA)
Lehigh U (PA)
Michigan, U of, Ann Arbor
Mississippi, U of
Northwestern U (IL)

Oklahoma, U of
Richmond, U of (VA)
South Carolina, U of, Columbia
Southern California, U of
Southern Methodist U (TX)
Syracuse U (NY)
Texas Christian U
Texas, U of
Union C (NY)
Vanderbilt U (TN)
Virginia, U of
Wake Forest U (NC)
Washington & Lee U (VA)

Colleges With Great Marching Bands

Alabama, U of, Tuscaloosa
Arizona, U of
Auburn U (AL)
Baylor U (TX)
Florida A&M U
Florida, U of
Georgia, U of, Athens
Grambling State U (LA)
Jackson State U (MS)
Jacksonville State U (AL)
James Madison U (VA)
Louisiana State U, Baton Rouge
Michigan State U
Michigan, U of, Ann Arbor
Minnesota, U of, Twin Cities
North Texas, U of
Northwestern State U (LA)

Notre Dame, U of (IN)
Ohio State U, Columbus
Ohio U
Oklahoma, U of
Pennsylvania State U, University Park
Purdue U (IN)
Southern California, U of
Southern U (LA)
Stanford U (CA)
Tennessee, U of, Knoxville
Texas A&M U
Texas Tech U
Texas, U of, Austin
Western Carolina U (NC)
Wisconsin, U of, Eau Claire
Wisconsin, U of, Madison

Source: *College Finder* research and *USA Today*'s College Football Fan Index

Colleges With Outstanding Model United Nations Programs

The colleges listed below have particular strength in Model United Nations as judged by recent national successes.

California, U of, Berkeley
Chicago, U of (IL)
Claremont McKenna C (CA)
Clark U (MA)
Columbia U (NY)
Cornell U (NY)
Emory U (GA)
Florida International U
Florida State U
George Washington U (DC)
Georgetown U (DC)
Harvard U (MA)
McGill U (Canada)

Miami, U of (FL)
Michigan State U
Mt. Holyoke C (MA)
New York U
Pennsylvania, U of
Princeton U (NJ)
Rutgers U (NJ)
Stanford U (CA)
U.S. Military Academy (NY)
Vanderbilt U (TN)
William & Mary, C of (VA)
Yale U (CT)

Source: Best Delegate (bestdelegate.com)

Colleges With Notable Radio Stations

These radio stations boast such features as online streaming capabilities, community involvement, and studio facilities. Some have won Collegiate Broadcasters awards.

Alabama, U of, Tuscaloosa
American U (Egypt)
Appalachian State U (NC)

Azusa Pacific U (CA)
Bates C (ME)
Boston U (MA)

Bowling Green State U (OH)
California Polytechnic State U, San Luis Obispo
California State U, Long Beach
California, U of, Berkeley
California, U of, Riverside
California, U of, Santa Barbara
Carnegie Mellon U (PA)
Central Michigan U
Central Washington U
Cincinnati, U of (OH)
Colorado State U, Ft. Collins
Columbia C Chicago (IL)
Dakota State U (SD)
DePaul U (IL)
Five Towns C (NY)
Florida International U
Florida State U
Foothill-De Anza Community C (CA)
Georgetown U (DC)
Georgia Institute of Technology
Gettysburg C (PA)
Goshen C (IN)
Hawaii, U of, Manoa
Hofstra U (NY)
Husson U (ME)
Illinois State U
Illinois, U of, Urbana
Indiana State U
Iowa, U of
Ithaca C (NY)
Kansas State U
Kansas, U of
Keene State C (NH)
Kent State U (OH)
Lasell C (MA)
Lyndon State C (VA)
Marshall U (WV)
Mercer County Community C (NJ)
Michigan State U
Michigan Technological U (MI)
Millikin U (IL)
Milwaukee School of Engineering (WI)
Muskingum U (OH)
Nevada, U of, Reno
New Hampshire, U of
New York U
New York, City U of, Staten Island

New York, State U of, Brockport
New York, State U of, Plattsburgh
New York, State U of, Stony Brook
North Carolina Central U
North Carolina, U of, Chapel Hill
North Central C (IL)
Northeastern Illinois U
Northern Arizona U
Northern Michigan U
Northwest Missouri State U
Northwestern U (IL)
Occidental C (CA)
Oklahoma, U of
Oregon State U
Oregon, U of
Otterbein U (OH)
Puget Sound, U of (WA)
Randolph C (VA)
Richmond, U of (VA)
Rochester Institute of Technology (NY)
Roosevelt U (IL)
Rowan U (NJ)
Rutgers U, New Brunswick (NJ)
Santa Clara U (CA)
Savannah C of Art & Design (GA)
Southeastern Louisiana U
Southern Indiana, U of
St. Cloud State U (MN)
St. John's U (MN)
Stanford U (CA)
Stevens Institute of Technology (NJ)
Tarleton State U (TX)
Texas State U, San Marcos
Texas, U of, Arlington
Trinity C (CT)
Valparaiso U (IN)
Washington, U of, Seattle
Wayne State C (NE)
Waynesburg U (PA)
Wellesley C (MA)
West Chester U (PA)
Western Kentucky U
Western Washington U
Wilkes U (PA)
Wisconsin, U of, Madison
Wright State U (OH)

Source: *College Finder* research including Collegiate Broadcasters, Inc. Awards (collegebroadcasters.org)

Colleges That Have Radio Stations on iHeartRadio

These schools have radio stations available to stream from iHeartRadio.com.

Academy of Art U (CA)
Appalachian State U (NC)
Chicago State U (IL)
Connecticut C
Dartmouth C (NH)
DePaul U (IL)
Denison U (OH)
Embry-Riddle Aeronautical U (FL)
Emerson C (MA)
Fairleigh Dickinson U (NJ)
Flagler C (FL)
Freed-Hardeman U (TN)
Green River C (WA)
Hampton U (VA)
Indianapolis, U of (IN)

Ithaca C (NY)
Lehigh Community C (PA)
Lewis U (IL)
Lincoln C (IL)
North Central C (IL)
Pittsburgh, U of (PA)
Rice U (TX)
Seton Hall U (NJ)
Siena C (NY)
Stanford U (CA)
Syracuse U (NY)
Temple U (PA)
Texas, U of, Arlington
Vanderbilt U (TN)
Wooster, C of (OH)

Source: iHeartRadio (iheart.com)

Colleges With Sexual Health Education and Preparedness

Below are the top 20 U.S. colleges and universities from the 2015 Trojan™ Sexual Health Report Card. Colleges were chosen on the basis of such factors as quality of sexual health information, strength of sexual assault programs, and outreach programs in sexual health education and preparedness.

Arizona, U of
Brown U (RI)
Columbia U (NY)
Colorado State U
Connecticut, U of
Cornell U (NY)
Florida, U of
Georgia, U of
Indiana U Bloomington
Iowa, U of

Maryland, U of, College Park
Michigan State U
Michigan, U of, Ann Arbor
Minnesota, U of, Twin Cities
Northwestern U (IL)
Oregon State U
Oregon, U of
Princeton U (NJ)
Stanford U (CA)
Texas, U of, Austin

Source: Trojan™ Brand Condoms (trojanbrands.com)

Colleges With Great Sustainability Programs

Sierra Club listed these colleges and universities as the ones with the best sustainability programs. The Sierra Club is a grassroots environmental organization.

1. California, U of, Irvine
2. American U (DC)
3. Dickinson C (PA)
4. Loyola U (IL)
5. Lewis & Clark C (OR)
6. Stanford U (CA)
7. South Florida, U of
8. Green Mountain C (VT)
9. Connecticut, U of
10. Georgia Institute of Technology
11. Colorado State U, Ft. Collins
12. George Washington U (DC)

Steven R. Antonoff

13. Maryland, U of, College Park
14. San Diego, U of (CA)
15. North Carolina, U of, Chapel Hill
16. Cornell U (NY)

17. California, U of, San Diego
18. Middlebury C (VT)
19. Harvard U (MA)
20. Chatham U (PA)

Source: Sierra Club (sierraclub.org)

Colleges Competing in the Solar Decathlon

According to its website, "The U.S Department of Energy Solar Decathlon challenges collegiate teams to design, build, and operate solar-powered houses that are cost-effective, energy-efficient, and attractive." These colleges have competed in recent years.

California Polytechnic State U, San Luis Obispo
California State U, Sacramento
California, U of, Davis
California, U of, Irvine
Chapman U (CA)
Clemson U (SC)
Crowder C (MO)
Drury U (MO)
Florida, U of
Middle Tennessee State U
Missouri U of Science & Technology

New York, City U of, C of Technology
New York, State U of, Alfred
New York, State U of, Buffalo
Roma Tor Vergata, U of (Italy)
Santa Fe C (FL)
Singapore, National U of (Singapore)
Stevens Institute of Technology (NJ)
Texas, U of, Austin
Vanderbilt U (TN)
West Virginia U
Western New England U (MA)
Yale U (CT)

Colleges With Great Television Stations

These stations won awards in recent years from either the Collegiate Broadcasters or the Academy of Television Arts & Sciences.

American Film Institute (CA)
ArtCenter C of Design (CA)
Berry C (GA)
Boston U (MA)
Brigham Young U (UT)
Brown U (RI)
Chapman U (CA)
Connecticut, U of
Emerson C (MA)
Florida State U
George Mason U (VA)
Hastings C (NE)
Hobart & William Smith C (NY)
Ithaca C (NY)
Kansas, U of
Kent State U (OH)
Midwestern State U (TX)
Montana State U, Bozeman
Muskingum U (OH)
Neumann U (PA)

New York, State U of, Binghamton
North Carolina State U
North Texas, U of
Northwestern U (IL)
Oklahoma, U of
Oregon State U
Oregon, U of
Pennsylvania State U, University Park
Pittsburgh State U (PA)
Rowan U (NJ)
Saddleback C (CA)
Savannah C of Art & Design (GA)
Southeastern Louisiana U
Southern California, U of
St. Cloud State U (MN)
Virginia State U
Visual Arts, School of (NY)
Washington State U
West Virginia U
Wisconsin, U of, Oshkosh

Source: College Finder research including Collegiate Broadcasters, Inc. Awards (collegebroadcasters.org) and Academy of Television Arts & Sciences, Annual College Television Award Winners (emmys.tv)

ENROLLMENT

Colleges That Focus on the Undergraduate

Students preparing for undergraduate study should weigh the advantages and the disadvantages of the proportion of undergraduate students (those working on their first college degree) to graduate students at colleges they are considering. Colleges with a high percentage of graduate students tend to be larger and may not provide the support and personal attention that colleges more oriented toward undergraduate students provide. Furthermore, at colleges with a high percentage of graduate students, a greater proportion of the instructors may be students working on an advanced degree. On the other hand, colleges with a higher percentage of graduate students may feature more depth in course offerings and greater availability of instructors. Depending on the needs and interests of the individual undergraduate student, an emphasis on graduate studies will constitute either a boost or a disadvantage. The following lists, grouped by athletic conference, illustrate the variation in these proportions.

Ivy League Conference Colleges Ranked by Percentage of Undergraduates to Total Enrollment

- Brown U (RI): 6,100 undergrads, 8,500 total, 72%
- Dartmouth C (NH): 4,100 undergrads, 6,100 total, 67%
- Princeton U (NJ): 5,300 undergrads, 7,900 total, 66%
- Cornell U (NY): 14,200 undergrads, 21,800 total, 65%
- Yale U (CT): 5,400 undergrads, 11,800 total, 46%
- Pennsylvania, U of: 9,800 undergrads, 21,800 total, 45%
- Harvard U (MA): 6,600 undergrads, 20,500 total, 32%
- Columbia U (NY): 6,100 undergrads, 24,600 total, 25%

Big Ten Conference Colleges Ranked by Percentage of Undergraduate Students to Total Enrollment

- Pennsylvania State U, University Park: 38,500 undergrads, 44,900 total, 86%
- Nebraska, U of, Lincoln: 19,100 undergrads, 23,500 total, 81%
- Indiana U Bloomington: 32,000 undergrads, 41,400 total, 78%
- Michigan State U: 37,000 undergrads, 47,300 total, 78%
- Purdue U (IN): 30,000 undergrads, 38,900 total, 77%
- Ohio State U, Columbus: 41,900 undergrads, 54,800 total, 76%
- Rutgers U (NJ): 42,327 undergrads, 56,868 total, 74%
- Illinois, U of, Urbana: 31,300 undergrads, 43,200 total, 72%
- Iowa, U of: 21,300 undergrads, 29,400 total, 72%
- Maryland, U of, College Park: 25,800 undergrads, 35,900 total, 72%
- Wisconsin, U of, Madison: 29,000 undergrads, 41,000 total, 71%
- Michigan, U of, Ann Arbor: 27,800 undergrads, 43,000 total, 64%
- Minnesota, U of, Twin Cities: 30,400 undergrads, 47,400 total, 64%
- Northwestern U (IL): 8,300 undergrads, 19,600 total, 42%

Atlantic Coast Conference Colleges Ranked by Percentage of Undergraduate Students to Total Enrollment

- Clemson U (SC): 16,500 undergrads, 20,500 total, 82%
- Florida State U: 31,700 undergrads, 39,800 total, 80%

- Virginia Polytechnic Institute & State U: 23,900 undergrads, 31,100 total, 77%
- North Carolina State U: 23,300 undergrads, 31,800 total, 73%
- Notre Dame, U of (IN): 8,500 undergrads, 11,900 total, 71%
- Syracuse U (NY): 14,500 undergrads, 20,500 total, 71%
- Virginia, U of: 14,500 undergrads, 21,000 total, 69%
- Louisville, U of (KY): 14,800 undergrads, 21,700 total, 68%
- Georgia Institute of Technology: 14,000 undergrads, 21,000 total, 67%
- Miami, U of (FL): 10,300 undergrads, 15,800 total, 67%
- Boston C (MA): 9,100 undergrads, 13,700 total, 66%
- North Carolina, U of, Chapel Hill: 18,000 undergrads, 27,900 total, 65%
- Wake Forest U (NC): 4,800 undergrads, 7,400 total, 65%
- Pittsburgh, U of (PA): 18,100 undergrads, 28,100 total, 64%
- Duke U (NC): 6,500 undergrads, 15,000 total, 43%

Big 12 Conference Colleges Ranked by Percentage of Undergraduate Students to Total Enrollment

- Texas Christian U: 8,400 undergrads, 9,700 total, 87%
- Baylor U (TX): 12,800 undergrads, 15,300 total, 84%
- Iowa State U: 25,000 undergrads, 29,800 total, 84%
- Kansas State U: 19,400 undergrads, 23,400 total, 83%
- Texas Tech U: 26,300 undergrads, 31,900 total, 82%
- Oklahoma State U: 19,900 undergrads, 25,000 total, 80%
- Texas, U of, Austin: 39,200 undergrads, 51,500 total, 76%
- West Virginia U: 22,300 undergrads, 29,200 total, 76%
- Kansas, U of: 19,200 undergrads, 26,900 total, 71%
- Oklahoma, U of: 21,600 undergrads, 30,700 total, 70%

Source: *College Finder* research, including College Board *College Handbook*

The Largest Colleges

We're not going to insult your intelligence by describing this list.

Toronto, U of (Canada): 66,370
Central Florida, U of: 51,269
York U (Canada): 48,069
Ohio State U, Columbus: 44,201
Texas A&M U, College Station: 44,072
American Public U System (WV): 43,964
Pennsylvania State U, University Park: 40,085
Texas, U of, Austin: 39,979
Florida International U: 39,045
Arizona State U: 38,735
Michigan State U: 37,988
Indiana U Bloomington: 36,862
Athabasca U (Canada): 36,622
Minnesota, U of, Twin Cities: 34,449
British Columbia, U of (Canada): 34,098
Rutgers U, New Brunswick (NJ): 33,900
California State U, Northridge: 33,398

Grand Canyon U (AZ): 33,194
Florida, U of: 33,168
California State U, Fullerton: 33,116
Florida State U: 32,528
Illinois, U of, Urbana: 32,281
Western State U (CO): 31,903
Arizona, U of: 31,670
Alberta, U of (Canada): 31,648
Houston, U of (TX): 31,587
St. Petersburg C (FL): 31,547
Wisconsin, U of, Madison: 31,319
South Florida, U of: 31,100
Texas State U: 31,005
California State U, Long Beach: 30,474
Utah Valley U: 30,370
North Texas, U of: 29,481
Alabama, U of, Tuscaloosa: 29,440
Purdue U (IN): 29,440
Washington, U of, Seattle: 28,933

California, U of, Los Angeles: 28,674 Temple U (PA): 28,068
Michigan, U of, Ann Arbor: 28,283

Source: Wintergreen Orchard House

The Experts' Choice: Large Universities That Feel Small

Some students worry that if they attend a large university they will be merely a number. Experts were asked to identify larger colleges that feel smaller than they are.

Alabama, U of
Arizona, U of
Clemson U (SC)
Colorado, U of, Boulder
Delaware, U of
Georgia, U of
Indiana U Bloomington
Kansas, U of
Maryland, U of, College Park
Massachusetts, U of, Amherst
Miami U (OH)
Michigan, U of, Ann Arbor

Montana State U
New Hampshire, U of
North Carolina, U of, Chapel Hill
Northwestern U (IL)
Ohio State U
Oregon, U of
South Carolina, U of
Vermont, U of
Virginia Polytechnic Institute & State U
Wisconsin, U of, Madison
Yale U (CT)

Colleges With the Smallest Student-Faculty Ratios

If you attend one of these schools, you won't need to jockey for attention in class or pray that there isn't a wait during office hours.

Bard C at Simon's Rock (MA)
Boston Conservatory (MA)
Burlington C (VT)
California Institute of Technology
Chicago, U of (IL)
Columbia U (NY)
Conservatory of Music (Puerto Rico)
Harvard U (MA)
Juilliard School (NY)
Knoxville C (TN)
Manhattan School of Music (NY)
Marlboro C (VT)
Marylhurst U (OR)
Morris Brown C (GA)
National Intelligence U (DC)
New England Conservatory of Music (MA)
New York, State U of, Korea
North Carolina School of the Arts
Otis C of Art & Design (CA)

Paier C of Art (CT)
Pennsylvania, U of Princeton U (NJ)
Principia C (IL)
Puerto Rico, U of, Medical Sciences Campus
Rice U (TX)
San Francisco Conservatory of Music (CA)
Shasta C (CA)
Sojourner-Douglass C (MD)
St. John's C (MD)
St. Mary, C of (NE)
Stanford U (CA)
U.S. Coast Guard Academy (CT)
U.S. Military Academy (NY)
Webb Institute (NY) Wellesley C (MA)
Williams C (MA)
VanderCook C of Music (IL)
Yale U (CT)
Yeshiva U (NY)

Source: Wintergreen Orchard House

Steven R. Antonoff

Public Schools With the Greatest Percentage of Out-of-State First-Year Students

What is it that draws so many out-of-state students to these universities? For some—the service academies, for example—the admission process is designed to produce a class that represents the nation. For other schools, it's an area of expertise (e.g., the arts, fashion, or technology) that attracts out-of-state students. Location may play a part as well, with public universities in remote areas without many other college choices drawing students from nearby states. Whatever the reason, these are the schools that students are willing to go the distance to attend.

U.S. Military Academy (NY): 93%
U.S. Naval Academy (MD): 93%
U.S. Coast Guard Academy (CT): 92%
U.S. Air Force Academy (CO): 90%
Vermont, U of: 76%
North Dakota, U of: 65%
North Dakota State U: 63%
Delaware State U: 60%
Kentucky State U: 60%
Lincoln U (MO): 57%
South Dakota School of Mines & Technology: 57%
Alabama, U of, Tuscaloosa: 56%
New Hampshire, U of: 56%
Rhode Island, U of: 56%
North Carolina School of the Arts: 55%
West Virginia U: 54%
Coastal Carolina U (SC): 53%
New York, State U of, Empire State C: 53%
Central State U (OH): 52%

Plymouth State U (NH): 52%
Wisconsin, U of, River Falls: 51%
Arkansas, U of, Fayetteville: 49%
Mayville State U (ND): 49%
Mississippi, U of: 49%
Colorado State U, Ft. Collins: 48%
South Carolina, U of, Columbia: 48%
Wyoming, U of: 48%
Citadel, The (SC): 46%
Colorado, U of, Boulder: 45%
Montana State U, Bozeman: 45%
Virginia Military Institute: 45%
Wisconsin, U of, Superior: 45%
Charleston, C of (SC): 43%
Evergreen State C (WA): 43%
Oregon, U of: 43%
Fashion Institute of Technology (NY): 42%
Colorado School of Mines: 41%
Iowa, U of: 41%
New Mexico Highlands U: 40%

Source: Wintergreen Orchard House

Percentage of Out-of-State Students at Public Universities

No brilliant description needed: This list is just the facts.

U.S. Coast Guard Academy (CT): 97%
U.S. Military Academy (NY): 94%
U.S. Naval Academy (MD): 93%
U.S. Air Force Academy (CO): 92%
Elizabeth City State U (NC): 89%
Vermont, U of: 66%
Plymouth State U (NH): 58%
North Dakota, U of: 58%
North Dakota State U: 56%
Kentucky State U: 52%
Lincoln U (MO): 52%
North Carolina School of the Arts: 51%
Wisconsin, U of, River Falls: 51%
South Dakota School of Mines & Technology: 50%
West Virginia U: 49%
Coastal Carolina U (SC): 47%
Wisconsin, U of, Superior: 47%
New Hampshire, U of: 46%
Alabama, U of, Tuscaloosa: 46%
Delaware State U: 46%

Colorado State U, Ft. Collins: 43%
Valley City State U (ND): 43%
Maryland, U of, University C: 43%
Citadel, The (SC): 42%
Rhode Island, U of: 41%
Virginia Military Institute: 41%
Mayville State U (ND): 40%
Troy U (AL): 40%
Institute of American Indian Arts (NM): 40%
Montana State U, Bozeman: 39%
Johnson State C (VT): 39%
Arkansas, U of, Pine Bluff: 39%
Shepherd U (WV): 38%
Central State U (OH): 38%
South Dakota, U of: 37%
Arkansas, U of, Fayetteville: 37%
Auburn U (AL): 37%
Charleston, C of (SC): 37%
Mississippi, U of: 37%

Source: Wintergreen Orchard House

Fastest-Growing Private Nonprofit Doctoral Institutions

The number given is the percent increase in enrollment over a 10-year period, 2004–2014. Note: the average rate of growth in this category is 11.2%.

Alliant International U (CA): 134.0%
Wilmington U (DE): 103.0%
Benedictine U (KS): 95.1%
Maryville U (MO): 88.9%
Regent U (VA): 71.7%
Worcester Polytechnic Institute (MA): 67.2%
Drexel U (PA): 49.3%
Florida Institute of Technology: 36.5%
Rice U (TX): 36.4%
Spalding U (KY): 36.1%
Georgetown U (DC): 35.0%

Rochester, U of (NY): 32.8%
Stevens Institute of Technology (NJ): 32.1%
Southern California, U of: 32.0%
San Francisco, U of (CA): 29.2%
Carnegie Mellon U (PA): 28.4%
California Institute of Integral Studies: 27.7%
Columbia U (NY): 27.4%
Emory U (GA): 25.4%
New York U: 25.0%

Source: *Chronicle of Higher Education*

Steven R. Antonoff

Fastest-Growing Public Doctoral Institutions

The number given is the percent increase in enrollment over a 10-year period, 2004–2014. Note: the average rate of growth in this category is 14.0%.

Texas A&M U, Kingsville: 85.9%
Alabama, U of, Tuscaloosa: 72.2%
Utah State U: 71.5%
New York, City U of, Graduate Center: 65.6%
Texas, U of, Dallas: 63.9%
Missouri U of Science & Technology: 59.9%
Texas, U of, Arlington: 57.1%
Mississippi, U of: 55.2%
Massachusetts, U of, Lowell: 54.9%

Arkansas, U of, Fayetteville: 51.9%
Oregon State U: 50.8%
Colorado School of Mines: 45.4%
Ohio U: 45.1%
Northern Arizona U: 44.8%
Massachusetts, U of, Boston: 43.4%
Central Florida, U of: 43.1%
Florida International U: 42.3%
Texas A&M U, Commerce: 40.5%
Texas Woman's U: 40.2%
Rutgers U, New Brunswick (NJ): 39.4%

Source: *Chronicle of Higher Education*

Fastest-Growing Public Master's Institutions

The number given is the percent increase in enrollment over a 10-year period, 2004–2014. Note: the average rate of growth in this category is 12.4%.

Washington, U of, Bothell: 208.6%
California State U, Channel Islands: 190.9%
Florida Gulf Coast U: 143.0%
Washington, U of, Tacoma: 113.2%
Thomas Edison State U (NJ): 95.4%
Arkansas Tech: 85.1%
Houston-Victoria, U of (TX): 82.3%
Kennasaw State U (GA): 78.5%
Texas A&M International U: 77.0%

Texas, U of, Permian Basin: 69.0%
Maryland, U of, University C: 68.8%
California State U, Monterey Bay: 68.1%
California State U, San Marcos: 65.0%
Ft. Hays State U (KS): 62.7%
Rowan U (NJ): 52.5%
Texas, U of, Tyler: 51.5%
West Alabama, U of: 49.4%
Eastern New Mexico U: 49.3%
Peru State C (NE): 48.5%
Wisconsin, U of, Platteville: 44.1%

Source: *Chronicle of Higher Education*

STUDENT LIFE

SAFETY

Campus Safety: The Non-List

There are no lists of colleges included here. Studies show that the safest colleges are those with 10,000–20,000 students in a city with a population under 100,000. The colleges most prone to violent crime are those with fewer than 10,000 students in a city with populations of more than 500,000. The size of the town or city is often the best predictor of violent crime on campus.

Campus crime statistics can be misleading given that colleges report data in different ways and crime patterns vary at different times of the year. Furthermore, because offenses are not always reported on a per-student basis, larger schools often show higher incidences of crime. Because the Student Right-to-Know and Campus Security Act of 1990 requires that colleges report crime information, the latest facts on campus safety are available from each college. Prospective students are encouraged to speak with college officials and current students to determine both the reality of crime as well as the perception of safety at chosen campuses.

The Office of Postsecondary Education of the U.S. Department of Education reports crime data on campuses through its Campus Safety and Security Data Analysis Cutting Tool (ope.ed.gov/campussafety). Additional resources include StopHazing (stophazing.org), Clery Center for Security on Campus (clerycenter.org), and College Drinking: Changing the Culture (collegedrinkingprevention.gov).

Steven R. Antonoff

CHAPTER FOUR
ATHLETICS

ATHLETICS

Major Athletic Conferences

The Atlantic Coast Conference

Boston C (MA)
Clemson U (SC)
Duke U (NC)
Florida State U
Georgia Institute of Technology
Louisville, U of (KY)
Miami, U of (FL)
North Carolina State U

North Carolina, U of, Chapel Hill
Notre Dame, U of (IN)
Pittsburgh, U of (PA)
Syracuse U (NY)
Virginia Polytechnic Institute & State U
Virginia, U of
Wake Forest U (NC)

Atlantic 10

Davidson C (NC)
Dayton, U of (OH)
Duquesne U (PA)
Fordham U (NY)
George Mason U (VA)
George Washington U (DC)
La Salle U (PA)
Lock Haven U (PA) (field hockey only)

Massachusetts, U of, Amherst
Rhode Island, U of
Richmond, U of (VA)
St. Bonaventure U (NY)
St. Francis (PA) (field hockey only)
St. Joseph's U (PA)
St. Louis U (MO)
Virginia Commonwealth U

The Big East

Butler U (IN)
Cincinnati, U of (OH) (women's lacrosse only)
Connecticut, U of (field hockey & women's lacrosse only)
Creighton U (NE)
Denver, U of (CO) (men's lacrosse only)
DePaul U (IL)
Florida, U of (women's lacrosse only)
Georgetown U (DC)
Marquette U (WI)

Old Dominion U (VA) (field hockey only)
Providence C (RI)
Seton Hall U (NJ)
St. John's U (NY)
Temple U (PA) (field hockey & women's lacrosse only)
Vanderbilt U (TN) (women's lacrosse only)
Villanova U (PA)
Xavier U (OH)

Big Sky

California Polytechnic State U, San Luis Obispo (football only)
California State U, Sacramento
California, U of, Davis (football only)
Eastern Washington U
Hartford, U of (CT) (men's golf only)
Idaho State U
Idaho, U of
Montana State U

Montana, U of
New York, State U of, Binghamton (men's golf only)
North Dakota, U of
Northern Arizona U
Northern Colorado, U of
Portland State U (OR)
Southern Utah U
Weber State U (UT)

The Big Ten

Illinois, U of, Urbana
Indiana U, Bloomington
Iowa, U of
Johns Hopkins U (MD) (men's lacrosse only)
Michigan State U
Michigan, U of, Ann Arbor
Minnesota, U of, Twin Cities

Nebraska, U of, Lincoln
Northwestern U (IL)
Ohio State U, Columbus
Pennsylvania State U, University Park
Purdue U (IN)
Rutgers U, New Brunswick (NJ)
Wisconsin, U of, Madison

Big 12

Alabama, U of, Tuscaloosa (women's rowing only)
Baylor U (TX)
Denver, U of (CO) (women's gymnastics only)
Iowa State U
Kansas State U
Kansas, U of
North Dakota State U (wrestling only)
Northern Colorado, U of (wrestling only)
Oklahoma State U
Oklahoma, U of

Old Dominion U (VA) (women's rowing only)
South Dakota State U (wrestling only)
Tennessee, U of, Knoxville (women's rowing only)
Texas Christian U
Texas Tech U
Texas, U of, Austin
U.S. Air Force Academy (CO) (wrestling only)
Utah Valley U (wrestling only)
West Virginia U
Wyoming, U of (wrestling only)

Conference USA

Alabama, U of, Birmingham
Florida Atlantic U
Florida International U
Kentucky, U of (men's soccer only)
Louisiana Tech U
Marshall U (WV)
Middle Tennessee State U
New Mexico, U of, Albuquerque (men's soccer only)
North Carolina, U of, Charlotte

North Texas, U of
Old Dominion U (VA)
Rice U (TX)
South Carolina, U of, Columbia (men's soccer only)
Southern Mississippi, U of (TX)
Texas, U of, El Paso
Texas, U of, San Antonio
Western Kentucky U

The Ivy League

Brown U (RI)
Columbia U (NY)
Cornell U (NY)
Dartmouth C (NH)

Harvard U (MA)
Pennsylvania, U of
Princeton U (NJ)
Yale U (CT)

Mid-American Conference

Akron, U of (OH)
Ball State U (IN)
Binghamton U (NY) (men's tennis only)
Bowling Green State U (OH)
Central Michigan U
Eastern Michigan U
Evansville, U of (IN) (men's swimming

only)
Kent State U (OH)
Longwood U (VA) (field hockey only)
Miami U (OH)
Massachusetts, U of (football only)
Missouri State U (field hockey & men's swimming only)

Missouri, U of, Columbia (wrestling only)
New York, State U of, Buffalo
Northern Illinois U
Northern Iowa, U of (wrestling only)
Ohio U, Athens
Old Dominion U (VA) (wrestling only)
Southern Illinois U, Carbondale (men's

swimming only)
Toledo, U of (OH)
West Virginia U (men's soccer only)
Western Michigan U

Mountain West Conference

Boise State U (ID)
California State U, Fresno
Colorado C (women's soccer)
Colorado State U, Ft. Collins
Hawaii, U of, Manoa
Nevada, U of, Las Vegas
Nevada, U of, Reno

New Mexico, U of, Albuquerque
San Diego State U (CA)
San Jose State U (CA)
U.S. Air Force Academy (CO)
Utah State U
Wyoming, U of

Pac-12

Arizona State U
Arizona, U of
Boise State U (ID) (wrestling only)
California Polytechnic State U (wrestling
  only)
California State U, Bakersfield (wrestling
  only)
California, U of, Berkeley
California, U of, Los Angeles
Colorado, U of, Boulder

Oregon State U
Oregon, U of
San Diego State U (CA) (men's soccer
  only)
Southern California, U of
Stanford U (CA)
Utah, U of
Washington State U
Washington, U of, Seattle

Patriot League

American U (DC)
Boston U (MA)
Bucknell U (PA)
Colgate U (NY)
Fordham U (NY) (football only)
Georgetown U (DC) (football & women's
  rowing only)
Holy Cross, C of the (MA)
Lafayette C (PA)

Lehigh U (PA)
Loyola U (MD)
Massachusetts Institute of Technology
  (women's rowing only)
Richmond, U of (VA) (women's golf
  only)
U.S. Military Academy (NY)
U.S. Naval Academy (MD)

The Southeastern Conference

Alabama, U of, Tuscaloosa
Arkansas, U of, Fayetteville
Auburn U (AL)
Florida, U of
Georgia, U of
Kentucky, U of
Louisiana State U, Baton Rouge

Mississippi State U
Mississippi, U of
Missouri, U of
South Carolina, U of, Columbia
Tennessee, U of, Knoxville
Texas A&M U, College Station
Vanderbilt U (TN)

ATHLETICS

Southwestern Athletic Conference

Alabama A&M U
Alabama State U
Alcorn State U (MS)
Arkansas, U of, Pine Bluff
Grambling State U (LA)

Jackson State U (MS)
Mississippi Valley State U
Prairie View A&M U (TX)
Southern U (LA)
Texas Southern U

Western Athletic Conference

California State U, Bakersfield
California State U, Sacramento
  (baseball only)
Chicago State U (IL)
Grand Canyon U (AZ)
Houston Baptist U (TX) (men's soccer
  only)
Idaho, U of (women's swimming only)
Incarnate Word, U of the (TX) (men's
  soccer only)
Nevada, U of, Las Vegas (men's
  swimming & men's soccer only)
Missouri, U of, Kanas City
New Mexico State U
North Dakota, U of (baseball, men's

swimming & women's swimming
  only)
Northern Arizona U (women's swimming
  only)
Northern Colorado, U of (baseball &
  women's swimming only)
San Jose State U (CA) (men's soccer
  only)
Seattle U (WA)
Texas, U of, Rio Grande Valley
U.S. Air Force Academy (CO) (men's
  swimming & men's soccer only)
Utah Valley U
Wyoming, U of (men's swimming only)

Colleges Where a High Percentage of Students Participate in Intercollegiate Sports

Your sport is your life—and likely one of the big considerations in your selection of a college. If you like being surrounded by other athletes, you just might fit in perfectly at one of these schools.

U.S. Merchant Marine Academy (NY):
  90%
New York, State U of, Maritime C: 80%
U.S. Coast Guard Academy (CT): 80%
Webber International U (FL): 80%
Central Christian C of Kansas: 79%
Mid-America Christian U (OK): 75%
Mt. Marty C (SD): 75%
Waldorf C (IA): 72%
Siena Heights U (MI): 70%
Virginia Military Institute: 70%
Webb Institute (NY): 70%
William Penn U (IA): 70%
Limestone C (SC): 69%
Thiel C (PA): 68%
Cumberlands, U of the (KY): 61%
Bethany C (KS): 60%
Cornell U (NY): 60%
Dubuque, U of (IA): 60%
Indiana Institute of Technology: 60%

Missouri Valley C: 60%
Sterling C (KS): 60%
Notre Dame C (OH): 58%
Tabor C (KS): 57%
Bluefield C (VA): 56%
Graceland U (IA): 56%
Iowa Wesleyan C: 56%
Brevard C (NC): 55%
Jamestown, U of (ND): 55%
Lake Erie C (OH): 55%
Missouri Baptist U: 55%
Oklahoma Wesleyan U: 55%
Pfeiffer U (NC): 55%
Post U (CT): 55%
Union C (NY): 55%
Ottawa U (KS): 54%
Defiance C (OH): 52%
Southwest, U of the (NM): 52%
Adrian C (MI): 51%
Eureka C (IL): 51%

Source: Wintergreen Orchard House

Colleges That Give Lots of Aid to Female Athletes in Division I

Baker U (KS)
Benedictine C (KS)
Biola U (CA)
Brenau U (GA)
Campbellsville U (KY)
Central Methodist U (MO)
Concordia U (CA)
Corban U (OR)
Cumberland U (TN)
Cumberlands, U of the (KY)
Embry-Riddle Aeronautical U (FL)
Faulkner U (AL)
Great Falls, U of (MT)
Hope International U (CA)
Lindsey Wilson C (KY)
Lyon C (AR)

Martin Methodist C (TN)
MidAmerica Nazarene U (KS)
Missouri Baptist U
Missouri Valley C
Mobile, U of (AL)
Oklahoma Baptist U
Oklahoma City U
Robert Morris U (IL)
Rocky Mountain C (MT)
San Diego Christian C (CA)
St. Francis, U of (IN)
St. Gregory's U (OK)
Texas Wesleyan U (TX)
Vanguard U (CA)
Wayland Baptist U (TX)
William Woods U (MO)

Source: The College Finder research

Colleges That Give Lots of Aid to Female Athletes in Division II

Ave Maria U (FL)
Bethel U (TN)
Concordia U (NE)
Concordia U (OR)
Culver-Stockton C (MO)
Davenport U (MI)
Doane C (NE)
Hastings C (NE)
Indiana Institute of Technology
Lawrence Technological U (MI)
Marian U (IN)
Midland U (NE)
Milligan C (TN)

Oklahoma Wesleyan U
Olivet Nazarene U (IL)
Ottawa U (KS)
Point Park U (PA)
Savannah C of Art & Design (GA)
Simpson U (CA)
St. Andrews U (NC)
St. Francis, U of (IL)
Tennessee Wesleyan C
Union C (KY)
Webber International U (FL)
William Penn U (IA)

Source: The College Finder research

Colleges That Give Lots of Aid to Male Athletes in Division I

Bacone C (OK)
Baker U (KS)
Belhaven U (MS)
Benedictine C (KS)
Campbellsville U (KY)
Carroll C (MT)
Central Methodist U (MO)
Concordia U (CA)
Corban U (OR)
Cumberland U (TN)
Cumberlands, U of the (KY)

Embry-Riddle Aeronautical U (FL)
Evangel U (MO)
Faulkner U (AL)
Georgetown C (KY)
Great Falls, U of (MT)
Hope International U (CA)
Lindsey Wilson C (KY)
Martin Methodist C (TN)
Master's C and Seminary (CA)
MidAmerica Nazarene U (KS)
Missouri Baptist U

Missouri Valley C
Mobile, U of (AL)
Oklahoma Baptist U
Oklahoma City U
Pikeville, U of (KY)
Robert Morris U (IL)
Rocky Mountain C (MT)
San Diego Christian C (CA)

St. Francis-Fort Wayne, U of (IN)
St. Gregory's U (OK)
St. Xavier U (IL)
Texas Wesleyan U
Trinity International U (IL)
Wayland Baptist U (TX)
William Woods U (MO)

Source: The College Finder research

Colleges That Give Lots of Aid to Male Athletes in Division II

Ave Maria U (FL)
Bethany C (KS)
Bethel C (IN)
Bethel C (KS)
Bethel U (TN)
Bluefield C (VA)
Briar Cliff U (IA)
Concordia U (MI)
Concordia U (NE)
Concordia U (OR)
Culver-Stockton C (MO)
Dakota Wesleyan U (SD)
Doane C (NE)
Dordt C (IA)
Graceland U (IA)
Grand View U (IA)
Hastings C (NE)
Indiana Institute of Technology
Jamestown, U of (ND)
Judson U (IL)
Marian U (IN)
McPherson C (KS)
Menlo C (CA)
Midland U (NE)

Milligan C (TN)
Morningside C (IA)
Northwestern C (IA)
Oklahoma Wesleyan U
Olivet Nazarene U (IL)
Ottawa U (KS)
Point Park U (PA)
Point U (GA)
Reinhardt U (GA)
Savannah C of Art & Design (GA)
Siena Heights U (MI)
Spring Arbor U (MI)
St. Ambrose U (IA)
St. Andrews U (NC)
St. Francis, U of (IL)
Sterling C (KS)
Tabor C (KS)
Taylor U (IN)
Tennessee Wesleyan C
Union C (KY)
Waldorf C (IA)
Warner U (FL)
Webber International U (FL)
William Penn U (IA)

Source: The College Finder research

Colleges With the Highest Total Athletic Budgets

Alabama, U of, Tuscaloosa
Arizona State U
Arizona, U of
Arkansas, U of, Fayetteville
Auburn U (AL)
Baylor U (TX)
California, U of, Berkeley
California, U of, Los Angeles
Clemson U (SC)
Connecticut, U of

Duke U (NC)
Florida State U
Florida, U of
Georgia, U of
Indiana U, Bloomington
Iowa, U of
Kansas, U of
Kentucky, U of
Louisiana State U, Baton Rouge
Louisville, U of (KY)

Miami, U of (FL)
Michigan State U
Michigan, U of, Ann Arbor
Minnesota, U of, Twin Cities
Mississippi, U of
Missouri, U of, Columbia
Nebraska, U of, Lincoln
North Carolina, U of, Chapel Hill
Northwestern U (IL)
Notre Dame, U of (IN)
Ohio State U, Columbus
Oklahoma State U
Oklahoma, U of
Oregon, U of
Pennsylvania State U, University Park

Purdue U (ID)
Rutgers U, New Brunswick (NJ)
South Carolina, U of, Columbia
Southern California, U of
Stanford U (CA)
Syracuse U (NY)
Tennessee, U of, Knoxville
Texas A&M U, College Station
Texas Christian U
Texas, U of, Austin
Virginia Polytechnic Institute & State U
Virginia, U of,
Washington, U of, Seattle
West Virginia U
Wisconsin, U of, Madison

Colleges Where a High Percentage of Students Participate in Intramural Sports

You love sports enough to play them year-round, right? Stick with IM teams to meet your fellow hardcore rugby/bowling/floor hockey hooligans.

InterAmerican U of Puerto Rico,
   Aguadilla: 100%
U.S. Coast Guard Academy (CT): 100%
U.S. Military Academy (NY):
   100%
Virginia, U of: 94%
Notre Dame, U of (IN): 93%
Gettysburg C (PA): 92%
Texas Christian U: 92%
Carleton C (MN): 90%
Coe C (LA): 90%
Emmaus Bible C (IA): 90%
Gonzaga U (WA): 90%
Graceland U (IA): 90%
St. John's U (MD): 90%
Capital U (OH): 88%
Creighton U (NE): 86%
Bethany C (KS): 85%
Colorado School of Mines: 85%
Davis C (NY): 85%
Georgia Southern U: 85%

Michigan, U of, Ann Arbor: 85%
Monmouth C (IL): 85%
Rochester, U of (NY): 82%
California Institute of Technology: 80%
California, U of, Los Angeles: 80%
Principia C (IL): 80%
Puget Sound, U of (WA): 80%
Ramapo C (NJ): 80%
Springfield C (MA): 80%
Taylor U (IN): 80%
Tennessee, U of, Knoxville: 80%
Tulsa, U of (OK): 80%
Wesleyan U (CT): 80%
Western State Colorado U: 80%
Whitman C (WA): 80%
William & Mary, C of (VA): 80%
Wabash C (IN): 77%
Ball State U (IN): 76%
West Virginia U: 76%
New Jersey, C of: 75%

Source: Wintergreen Orchard House

ARCHERY

Colleges With Great Archery Clubs

Arizona State U
Arizona, U of
Atlantic Cape Community C (NJ)
Brandeis U (MA)
California State U, Fullerton
California State U, Humboldt
California State U, Sonoma
California, U of, Berkeley
California, U of, Davis
California, U of, Merced
California, U of, San Diego
Columbia U (NY)
Connecticut, U of
Florida Atlantic U
Emmanuel C (GA)
Fashion Institute of Technology (NY)
Florida, U of
Georgia Institute of Technology
Georgia Southern U
Harvard U (MA)
James Madison U (VA)

Massachusetts Institute of Technology
Michigan State U
Missouri State U
North Carolina, U of, Charlotte
Ohio U, Athens
Oklahoma State U
Pennsylvania State U, University Park
Pennsylvania, C of, Technology
Prince William Sound Science Center
  (AK)
Princeton U (NJ)
Purdue U (IN)
South Carolina, U of, Columbia
Southern California, U of
Southern Utah U
Stanford U (CA)
Texas A&M U, College Station
Texas, U of, Austin
Texas, U of, Dallas
Wellesley C (MA)
Wisconsin, U of, La Crosse

Source: Team USA (teamusa.org)

ARM WRESTLING

Colleges With Winning Co-ed Arm Wrestling Teams

Connecticut, U of
Pennsylvania State U, University Park
Rutgers U, New Brunswick (NJ)
Syracuse U (NY)

Source: CAWL to Arms (cawltoarms.com)

BADMINTON

Colleges With Badminton Clubs

These universities and colleges have strong badminton clubs.

Amherst C (MA)
California State U, San Francisco
California State U, San Jose
California, U of, Berkeley

California, U of, Davis
California, U of, Irvine
California, U of, Los Angeles
California, U of, San Diego

Columbia U (NY)
Drexel U (PA)
Duke U (NC)
George Mason (VA)
Johns Hopkins (MD)
Loyola U (MD)
Maryland, U of, College Park
Massachusetts, U of, Amherst
Miami, U of (FL)
Mississippi, U of

New York U
New York, State U of, Stony Brook
Pennsylvania, U of
Princeton U (NJ)
Rensselaer Polytechnic Institute (NY)
Stanford U (CA)
Worcester Polytechnic Institute (MA)
Yale U (CT)
New York U

Source: The College Finder research, including Team USA (teamusa.org)

BASEBALL

Colleges With Winning Division I Baseball Teams

These colleges and universities have had the most championships in recent years.

Southern California, U of: 12
Louisiana State U, Baton Rouge: 6
Texas, U of, Austin: 6
Arizona State U: 5
Arizona, U of: 4
California State U, Fullerton: 4
Miami, U of (FL): 4
Minnesota, U of, Twin Cities: 3
California, U of, Berkeley: 2
Michigan, U of, Ann Arbor: 2
Oklahoma, U of: 2
Oregon State U: 2
South Carolina, U of, Columbia: 2
Stanford U (CA): 2

California State U, Fresno: 1
California, U of, Los Angeles: 1
Georgia, U of: 1
Holy Cross, C of the (MA): 1
Missouri, U of, Columbia: 1
Ohio State U, Columbus: 1
Oklahoma State U: 1
Pepperdine U (CA): 1
Rice U (TX): 1
Vanderbilt U (TN): 1
Virginia, U of: 1
Wake Forest U (NC): 1
Wichita State U (KS): 1

Source: National Collegiate Athletic Association (ncaa.org)

Colleges With Winning Division II Baseball Teams

These colleges have had the most baseball championships in NCAA Division II in the past 50 years.

Florida Southern C: 7
Tampa, U of (FL): 7
California State Polytechnic U, Pomona: 3
California State U, Chico: 2
California State U, Northridge: 2
California, U of, Irvine: 2
California, U of, Riverside: 2
Central Missouri, U of: 2
Jacksonville U (FL): 2
Troy U (AL): 2

California Polytechnic State U, San Luis
    Obispo: 1
Chapman U (CA): 1
Columbus State U (GA): 1
Delta State U (MS): 1
Illinois State U: 1
Kennesaw State U (GA): 1
Lynn U (FL): 1
Mt. Olive, U of (NC): 1
Southeastern Oklahoma State U: 1

ATHLETICS

Southern Indiana, U of: 1
St. Mary's U (TX): 1
Valdosta State U (GA): 1

West Chester U (PA): 1
West Florida, U of: 1

Source: Sports Illustrated Almanac

Colleges With Winning Division III Baseball Teams

These colleges have had the most baseball championships in the past 40 years in NCAA Division III.

Marietta C (OH): 6
Eastern Connecticut State U: 4
Montclair State U (NJ): 3
California State U, Stanislaus: 2
Glassboro U (NJ): 2
Ithaca C (NY): 2
Marietta C (OH): 2
North Carolina Wesleyan C: 2
Southern Maine, U of: 2
St. Thomas, U of (MN): 2
William Paterson U (NJ): 2

Wisconsin, U of, Oshkosh: 2
Wisconsin, U of, Whitewater: 2
Chapman U (CA): 1
Illinois Wesleyan U: 1
Kean U (NJ): 1
La Verne, U of (CA): 1
Linfield C (OR): 1
New York, State U of, Cortland: 1
Ramapo C (NJ): 1
Trinity C (CT): 1
Wisconsin, U of, Stevens Point: 1

Source: Sports Illustrated 2014 Almanac

BASKETBALL

Men's Division I Basketball Champions and Runners-Up

These colleges were champions or runners-up in the past 30 years.

Arizona, U of
Arkansas, U of, Fayetteville
Butler U (IN)
California, U of, Los Angeles
Connecticut, U of
Duke U (NC)
Florida, U of
Georgetown U (DC)
Georgia Institute of Technology
Illinois, U of, Urbana
Indiana U, Bloomington
Kansas, U of
Kentucky, U of
Louisville, U of (KY)

Maryland, U of, College Park
Memphis, U of (TN)
Michigan, U of, Ann Arbor
Michigan State U
Nevada, U of, Las Vegas
North Carolina, U of, Chapel Hill
Ohio State U
Oklahoma, U of
Seton Hall U (NJ)
Syracuse U (NY)
Utah, U of
Villanova U (PA)
Wisconsin, U of, Madison

Source: National Collegiate Athletic Association (ncaa.org)

Men's Division II Basketball Champions and Runners-Up

These colleges were champions or runners-up in the past 30 years.

Augustana C (SD)
Augusta State U (GA)
Barton C (NC)
Bellarmine U (KY)
Bridgeport, U of (CT)
Brigham Young U (HI)
Bryant U (RI)
California, U of, Davis
California, U of, Riverside
California State Polytechnic U, Pomona
California State U, Bakersfield
Central Missouri, U of
Drury U (MO)
Findlay, U of (OH)
Florida Southern C
Ft. Hays State U (KS)
Gannon U (PA)
Indiana U (PA)
Jacksonville State U (AL)

Kennesaw State U (GA)
Kentucky Wesleyan C
Lincoln Memorial U (TN)
Metropolitan State U (CO)
Montevallo, U of (AL)
North Alabama U
North Carolina Central U
Northeastern State U (OK)
Northern Kentucky U
Sacred Heart U (CT)
South Dakota State U
Southeast Missouri State U
Southern Indiana, U of
Troy U (AL)
Virginia Union U
Washburn U (KS)
Western Washington U
West Liberty U (WV)
Winona State U (MN)

Source: National Collegiate Athletic Association (ncaa.org)

Men's Division III Basketball Champions and Runners-Up

These colleges were champions or runners-up in the past 30 years.

Amherst C (MA)
Augustana C (IL)
Benedictine U (IL)
Cabrini C (PA)
Calvin C (MI)
Catholic U (DC)
Clark U (MA)
DePauw U (IN)
Elizabethtown C (PA)
Franklin & Marshall C (PA)
Gustavus Adolphus C (MN)
Hampden Sydney C (VA)
Hope C (MI)
Illinois Wesleyan U
Lebanon Valley C (PA)
Lemoyne-Owen C (TN)
Manchester U (IN)
Mary Hardin-Baylor, U of (TX)
Nebraska Wesleyan U
New Jersey, C of
New York, State U of, Potsdam

New York U
North Park U (IL)
Ohio Northern U
Ohio Wesleyan U (OH)
Otterbein U (OH)
Richard Stockton C (NJ)
Rochester U (NY)
Rowan U (NJ)
Scranton, U of (PA)
St. Thomas, U of (MN)
Virginia Wesleyan C
Washington U (MO)
William Peterson U (NJ)
Williams C (MA)
Wisconsin, U of, Eau Claire
Wisconsin, U of, Platteville
Wisconsin, U of, Stevens Point
Wisconsin, U of, Whitewater
Wittenberg U (OH)
Wooster, C of (OH)

Source: National Collegiate Athletic Association (ncaa.org)

Women's Division I Basketball Champions and Runners-Up

These colleges were champions or runners-up in the past 30 years.

Auburn U (AL)
Baylor U (TX)
Connecticut, U of
Duke U (NC)
Georgia, U of
Louisiana Tech U
Louisville, U of (KY)
Maryland, U of, College Park
Michigan State U
North Carolina, U of, Chapel Hill
Notre Dame, U of (IN)
Ohio State U
Oklahoma, U of

Old Dominion U (VA)
Purdue U (IN)
Rutgers U (NJ)
Southern California, U of
Stanford U (CA)
Syracuse U (NY)
Tennessee, U of, Knoxville
Texas, U of, Austin
Texas A&M U, College Station
Texas Tech U
Virginia, U of
Western Kentucky U

Source: National Collegiate Athletic Association (ncaa.org)

Women's Division II Basketball Champions and Runners-Up

These colleges were champions or runners-up in the past 30 years.

American International C (MA)
Arkansas Tech U
Ashland U (OH)
Bentley C (MA)
California State Polytechnic U, Pomona
California U (PA)
Central Missouri, U of
Clayton State U (GA)
Delta State U (MS)
Dowling C (NY)
Drury U (MO)
Emporia State U (KS)
Florida Gulf Coast U
Franklin Pierce U (NH)
Ft. Lewis C (CO)
Grand Valley State U (MI)
Hampton U (VA)
Michigan Technological U

Minnesota State U, Mankato
New Haven, U of (CT)
North Dakota State U
North Dakota, U of
Northern Kentucky U
Portland State U (OR)
Seattle Pacific U (WA)
Shaw U (NC)
Shippensburg U (PA)
South Dakota State U
South Dakota, U of
Southeast Missouri State U
Southeastern Oklahoma State U
Southern Connecticut State U
Southern Indiana, U of
Washburn U (KS)
West Texas A&M U

Source: National Collegiate Athletic Association (ncaa.org)

Women's Division III Basketball Champions and Runners-Up

These colleges were champions or runners-up in the past 30 years.

Alma C (MI)
Amherst C (MA)

Bishop's U (Canada)
Bowdoin C (ME)

ATHLETICS

California State U, Stanislaus
Capital U (OH)
Central U (IA)
Concordia U (MN)
DePauw U (IN)
Eastern Connecticut State U
Elizabethtown C (PA)
Fairleigh Dickinson U, Florham (NJ)
George Fox U (OR)
Hope C (MI)
Howard Payne U (TX)
Illinois Wesleyan U
Messiah C (PA)
Millikin U (IL)
Moravian C (PA)
Mt. Union C (OH)
Muskingum U (OH)
New Rochelle, C of (NY)
New York U

Randolph-Macon C (VA)
Salem State C (MA)
Scranton, U of (PA)
Southern Maine, U of
St. Benedict, C of (MN)
St. John Fisher C (NY)
St. Lawrence U (NY)
St. Thomas, U of (MN)
Thomas More C (KY)
Trinity U (TX)
Tufts U (MA)
Washington U (MO)
Whitman C (WA)
Wilmington C (OH)
Wisconsin, U of, Eau Claire
Wisconsin, U of, Oshkosh
Wisconsin, U of, Stevens Point
Wisconsin, U of, Whitewater

Source: National Collegiate Athletic Association (ncaa.org)

BOWLING

Colleges With a Winning Tradition in Bowling

Alabama, U of, Birmingham
Arkansas State U
Central Missouri U
Delaware State U
Fairleigh Dickinson U (NJ)
Kutztown U (PA)
Maryland, U of, Eastern Shore
McKendee U (IL)
Nebraska, U of, Lincoln

Norfolk State U (VA)
North Carolina A&T State U
Sam Houston State U (TX)
St. Francis U (PA)
Stephen F. Austin U (TX)
Valparaiso U (IN)
Vanderbilt U (TN)
Wisconsin, U of, Whitewater

Source: National Collegiate Athletic Association (ncaa.org)

CLIMBING

Colleges With Strength in Climbing

These are colleges that participated in a recent USA Climbing Collegiate series. USA Climbing offers competitions in bouldering, sport, and speed climbing.

Adams State C (CO)
Akron, U of (OH)
Alabama, U of, Tuscaloosa
Appalachian State U (NC)
Arizona State U

Arizona, U of
Baylor U (TX)
Belmont U (TN)
Bowdoin C (ME)
Brevard C (NC)

California Baptist U
California Polytechnic State U, San Luis
 Obispo
California State U, Chico
California State U, Humboldt
California State U, Northridge
California State U, San Diego
California, U of, Irvine
California, U of, Riverside
California, U of, San Diego
California, U of, Santa Barbara
Carleton C (MN)
Central Florida, U of
Clemson U (SC)
Colgate U (NY)
Colorado State U, Ft. Collins
Colorado State U, Pueblo
Colorado, U of, Boulder
Colorado, U of, Colorado Springs
Columbia U (NY)
Dallas, U of (TX)
Denver, U of (CO)
Florida Atlantic U
Florida Institute of Technology
Florida State U
Florida, U of
Ft. Lewis C (CO)
George Mason U (VA)
Georgia Institute of Technology
Georgia Southern U
Georgia State U
Harvard U (MA)
Houston, U of (TX)
Indiana U, Bloomington
Kansas State U
Kennesaw State U (GA)
Massachusetts Institute of Technology
Metropolitan State U (CO)
Minnesota, U of, Twin Cities
Mississippi State U
New York, State U of, Buffalo
New York, State U of, Plattsburgh
North Carolina State U
North Carolina, U of, Chapel Hill
North Florida, U of

Northeastern U (MA)
Northern Arizona U
Northern Colorado, U of
Notre Dame, U of (MD)
Pennsylvania, U of
Portland Community C (OR)
Princeton U (NJ)
Ramapo C (NJ)
Riverside Community C (CA)
Rochester Institute of Technology (NY)
Rochester, U of (NY)
Rutgers U, New Brunswick (NJ)
San Diego, U of (CA)
Sierra Nevada C (NV)
Smith C (MA)
South Dakota State U
South Dakota, U of
South Florida, U of
Southern California, U of
Southern Indiana, U of
Stanford U (CA)
Stevens Institute of Technology (NJ)
Temple U (PA)
Tennessee, U of, Chattanooga
Tennessee, U of, Knoxville
Texas A&M U, College Station
Texas A&M U, Commerce
Texas Tech U
Texas, U of, Austin
Texas, U of, Dallas
Texas, U of, San Antonio
Tufts U (MA)
Tyler Junior C (TX)
U.S. Air Force Academy (CO)
U.S. Military Academy (NY)
U.S. Naval Academy (MD)
Utah, U of
Virginia Polytechnic Institute & State U
Virginia, U of
Warren Wilson C (NC)
Washington U (MO)
West Georgia, U of
Western Carolina U (NC)
Worcester Polytechnic Institute (MA)
Yale U (CT)

Source: USA Climbing (usaclimbing.net)

CRICKET

Colleges With Strong Cricket Teams

The following colleges competed in a recent College Cricket National Championship.

Arkansas State U
Auburn U (AL)
Boston U (MA)
Carnegie Mellon U (PA)
Drexel U (PA)
Embry-Riddle Aeronautical U (FL)
Florida Institute of Technology
Florida, U of
Fraser Valley, U of (Canada)
Georgia Institute of Technology
Harvard U (MA)
Houston, U of, Downtown (TX)
Iowa State U
Maryland, U of, College Park
McGill U (Canada)
New York, State U of, Buffalo

Northeastern U (MA)
Northern Illinois U
Pennsylvania State U, University Park
Pennsylvania, U of
Rutgers U (NJ)
Ryerson U (Canada)
South Alabama, U of
South Florida, U of
Texas A&M U, College Station
Texas Tech U
Texas, U of, Arlington
Texas, U of, Austin
Texas, U of, Dallas
Virginia Polytechnic Institute & State U
Wayne State U (MI)
West Virginia U

Source: American College Cricket (americancollegecricket.com)

CROSS-COUNTRY

Colleges With High Rankings in Men's Cross-Country

These Division I colleges had the highest rankings in a recent year, according to the U.S. Track & Field and Cross Country Coaches Association.

1. Colorado, U of, Boulder
2. Syracuse U (NY)
3. Oregon, U of
4. Oklahoma State U
5. Villanova U (PA)
6. Wisconsin, U of, Madison
7. Portland, U of (OR)
8. Iona C (NY)
9. Stanford U (CA)
10. Northern Arizona U
11. Providence C (RI)
12. California, U of, Los Angeles
13. Virginia, U of
14. Georgetown U (DC)
15. Brigham Young U (UT)
16. Washington, U of
17. Michigan State U
18. Michigan, U of, Ann Arbor
19. Furman U (SC)
20. Tulsa, U of (OK)
21. Arkansas, U of, Fayetteville
22. Southern Utah U
23. North Carolina, U of, Chapel Hill
24. Mississippi, U of
25. Indiana U, Bloomington

Source: National Collegiate Athletic Association (ncaa.org)

Colleges With High Rankings in Women's Cross-Country

These Division I colleges had the highest rankings in a recent year, according to the U.S. Track & Field and Cross Country Coaches Association.

1.	Michigan State U	14.	William & Mary, C of (VA)
2.	Georgetown U (DC)	15.	North Carolina, U of, Chapel
3.	Oregon, U of		Hill
4.	Arkansas, U of	16.	Iona C (NY)
5.	Iowa State U	17.	Virginia, U of
6.	Wisconsin, U of, Madison	18.	Michigan, U of, Ann Arbor
7.	West Virginia U	19.	Washington, U of
8.	Colorado, U of, Boulder	20.	Minnesota, U of, Twin Cities
9.	New Mexico, U of	21.	Toledo, U of (OH)
10.	Stanford U (CA)	22.	Ohio State U, Columbus
11.	Boise State U (ID)	23.	Providence C (RI)
12.	Vanderbilt U (TN)	24.	North Carolina State U
13.	Florida State U	25.	Syracuse U (NY)

Source: National Collegiate Athletic Association (ncaa.org)

CURLING

Colleges With Strength in Curling

Boston U (MA)
Carroll C (MT)
Colgate U (NY)
Hamilton C (NY)
Harvard U (MA)
Massachusetts Institute of Technology
Minnesota, U of, Duluth
Nebraska, U of, Lincoln

Pennsylvania State U, University Park
Rensselaer Polytechnic Institute (NY)
Rochester Institute of Technology (NY)
Tennessee, U of, Knoxville
Villanova U (PA)
Wisconsin, U of, Green Bay
Wisconsin, U of, Stevens Point
Yale U (CT)

Source: USA Curling College Central (collegecurlingusa.org)

CYCLING

Colleges That Have USA Collegiate Cycling Teams

Collegiate cycling is governed by USA Cycling.

Abilene Christian U (TX)
Adams State U (CO)
Alabama, U of, Huntsville
Alabama, U of, Tuscaloosa
American U (DC)
Appalachian State U (NC)
Arizona State U
Arizona, U of

Arkansas State U
Arkansas, U of
Auburn U (AL)
Bard C (NY)
Baylor U (TX)
Boise State U (ID)
Boston C (MA)
Boston U (MA)

Bowdoin C (ME)
Brevard C (NC)
Brown U (RI)
Bucknell U (PA)
Butler U (IN)
California Polytechnic State U, San Luis Obispo
California State U, Channel Islands
California State U, Fresno
California State U, Fullerton
California State U, Humboldt
California State U, Long Beach
California State U, Sacramento
California State U, San Francisco
California State U, San Jose
California State U, San Marcos
California, U of, Berkeley
California, U of, Davis
California, U of, Irvine
California, U of, Los Angeles
California, U of, Merced
California, U of, San Diego
California, U of, Santa Barbara
California, U of, Santa Cruz
Carleton C (MN)
Carnegie Mellon U (PA)
Case Western Reserve U (OH)
Central Florida, U of
Central Washington U
Charleston, C of (SC)
Chicago, U of (IL)
Cincinnati, U of
Claremont Colleges Consortium (CA)
Clarkson U (NY)
Clemson U (SC)
Colorado C
Mesa State U (CO)
Colorado School of Mines
Colorado State U, Ft. Collins
Colorado, U of, Boulder
Colorado, U of, Colorado Springs
Colorado, U of, Denver
Columbia U (NY)
Connecticut, U of
Cornell U (NY)
Dartmouth C (NH)
Davidson C (NC)
Delaware, U of
Denver, U of (CO)
DePaul U (IL)
DePauw U (IN)
Drexel U (PA)
Duke U (NC)
East Tennessee State U
Eastern Washington U

Florida International U
Florida State U
Florida, U of
Franklin & Marshall C (PA)
Ft. Lewis C (CO)
Furman U (SC)
George Mason U (VA)
George Washington U (DC)
Georgia Institute of Technology
Georgia State U
Georgia, U of
Gonzaga U (WA)
Grand Valley State U (MI)
Hamilton C (NY)
Harvard U (MA)
Houston, U of (TX)
Idaho, U of
Illinois Institute of Technology
Illinois, U of, Chicago
Illinois, U of, Urbana
Indiana U (PA)
Indiana U, Bloomington
Iowa State U
Iowa, U of
James Madison U (VA)
Johns Hopkins U (MD)
Johnson & Wales U (RI)
Johnson State C (VT)
Juniata C (PA)
Kansas State U
Kansas, U of
Kennesaw State U (GA)
Kentucky, U of
King U (TN)
Lawrence Technological U (MI)
Lees-McRae C (NC)
Lehigh U (PA)
Liberty U (VA)
Lindenwood U (MO)
Lindsey Wilson C (KY)
Louisiana State U
Louisiana Tech U
Louisiana, U of, Lafayette
Louisville, U of (KY)
Marian U (IN)
Marquette U (WI)
Mars Hill U (NC)
Marshall U (WV)
Maryland, U of, Baltimore
Maryland, U of, Baltimore County
Maryland, U of, College Park
Massachusetts Institute of Technology
Massachusetts, U of, Amherst
Massachusetts, U of, Dartmouth
McKendree U (IL)

ATHLETICS

Metropolitan State U (CO)
Miami U (OH)
Michigan Institute of Aviation &
  Technology
Michigan State U
Michigan Technological U
Michigan, U of, Ann Arbor
Michigan, U of, Flint
Middlebury C (VT)
Midwestern State U (AZ)
Millersville U (PA)
Milligan C (TN)
Minnesota State U, Mankato
Minnesota, U of, Duluth
Minnesota, U of, Twin Cities
Mississippi, U of
Missouri, U of, Science & Technology
Missouri, U of, Columbia
Montana State U
Montana, U of
Mt. Vernon Nazarene U (OH)
Murray State U (KY)
Naval Postgraduate School (CA)
Nebraska, U of, Lincoln
Nevada, U of, Reno
New Hampshire, U of
New Mexico, U of
New Orleans, U of (LA)
New River Community C (VA)
New York U
New York, City U of, Hunter
Nicholls State U (LA)
North Carolina State U
North Carolina, U of, Chapel Hill
North Carolina, U of, Greensboro
North Carolina, U of, Wilmington
North Central C (IL)
North Dakota State U
North Georgia, U of
North Texas, U of
Northeastern U (MA)
Northern Arizona U
Northern Colorado, U of
Northern Michigan U
Northwestern U (IL)
Notre Dame, U of (IN)
Oberlin C (OH)
Ohio State U
Oklahoma State U
Oklahoma, U of
Oregon State U
Oregon, U of
Pennsylvania State U, C of Medicine
Pennsylvania State U, Lehigh Valley
Pennsylvania State U, University Park

Pennsylvania, U of
Pittsburgh, U of (PA)
Portland State U (OR)
Portland, U of (OR)
Prescott C (AZ)
Princeton U (NJ)
Providence C (RI)
Providence Christian C (CA)
Puget Sound, U of (WA)
Purdue U (IN)
Rensselaer Polytechnic Institute (NY)
Rhode Island School of Design
Rice U (TX)
Ripon C (WI)
Rochester Institute of Technology (NY)
Rochester, U of (NY)
Rutgers U, New Brunswick (NJ)
San Diego State U (CA)
San Francisco, U of (CA)
Santa Clara U (CA)
Seattle U (WA)
Shippensburg U (PA)
South Carolina, U of, Columbia
South Dakota School of Mines &
  Technology
South Florida, U of
Southern California, U of
Southern Illinois U, Carbondale
Southern Methodist U (TX)
St. Benedict, C of/St. John's U (MN)
St. Louis U (MO)
St. Mary's C (CA)
St. Olaf C (MN)
Stanford U (CA)
Stephen F. Austin State U (TX)
Syracuse U (NY)
Temple U (PA)
Tennessee, U of, Chattanooga
Tennessee, U of, Knoxville
Texas A&M U, College Station
Texas State U, San Marcos
Texas Tech U
Texas, U of, Austin
Texas, U of, Dallas
Texas, U of, San Antonio
Tufts U (MA)
Tulane U (LA)
U.S. Air Force Academy (CO)
U.S. Military Academy (NY)
U.S. Naval Academy (MD)
Union C (KY)
Utah State U
Utah Valley U
Utah, U of
Vermont, U of

Villanova U (PA)
Virginia Commonwealth U
Virginia Polytechnic Institute & State U
Virginia, U of
Wake Forest U (NC)
Walla Walla U (WA)
Warren Wilson C (NC)
Washington State U
Washington U (MO)
Washington, U of, Seattle
Wentworth Institute of Technology (MA)
West Virginia U
Western Carolina U (NC)

Western State U (CO)
Western Washington U
Whitman C (WA)
Willamette U (OR)
William & Mary, C of (VA)
Williams C (MA)
Wisconsin, U of, Eau Claire
Wisconsin, U of, Madison
Wisconsin, U of, Platteville
Wisconsin, U of, Whitewater
Worcester Polytechnic Institute (MA)
Wyoming, U of
Yale U (CT)

Source: USA Cycling (usacycling.org)

Colleges With Strength in Division I Cycling

These colleges performed well at a recent Mountain National tournament. The competition included downhill biking, cross-country, dual slalom, team relay, and short-track cross-country.

Appalachian State U (NC)
Arizona, U of
California State U, San Diego
California State U, San Jose
California Polytechnic State U, San Luis Obispo
California, U of, Berkeley
California, U of, Santa Barbara
California, U of, Santa Cruz
Central Florida, U of
Clemson U (SC)
Colorado State U, Ft. Collins
Colorado, U of, Boulder
Connecticut, U of
Drexel U (PA)
Florida, U of
Georgia State U
Lees-McRae C (NC)
Lindenwood U (MO)
Lindsey Wilson C (KY)

Marian U (IN)
Metropolitan State U (CO)
Midwestern State U (TX)
Nevada, U of, Reno
New Hampshire, U of
North Carolina State U
North Carolina, U of, Chapel Hill
Northeastern U (MA)
Northern Arizona U
South Carolina, U of, Columbia
Stanford U (CA)
Texas A&M U, College Station
Texas Tech U
Texas, U of, San Antonio
Vermont, U of
Virginia Polytechnic Institute & State U
Virginia, U of
Wisconsin, U of, Madison
Wyoming, U of

Source: USA Cycling (usacycling.org)

Colleges With Strength in Division II Cycling

These colleges performed well at a recent Mountain National tournament. The competition included downhill biking, cross-country, dual slalom, team relay, & short-track cross-country.

Adams State U (CO)
Baylor U (TX)
Brevard C (NC)
California State U, Chico
Colorado School of Mines
Duke U (NC)
East Tennessee State U
Humboldt State U (CA)
King U (TN)
Lehigh U (PA)
Mars Hill U (NC)
Massachusetts Institute of Technology
Mesa State U (CO)

Michigan Technological U
Milligan C (TN)
Oregon State U
Prescott C (AZ)
Ripon C (WI)
Rochester Institute of Technology (NY)
U.S. Air Force Academy (CO)
Union C (KY)
Wake Forest U (NC)
Warren Wilson C (NC)
Wentworth Institute of Technology (MA)
Western State U (CO)
William & Mary, C of (VA)

Source: USA Cycling (usacycling.org)

Great Colleges for Cyclists

According to Bicycling magazine, these colleges have an enthusiastic cycling culture.

Arizona, U of
Bowdoin C (ME)
California, U of, Davis
Colorado, U of, Boulder
Louisville, U of (KY)

Michigan State U
Minnesota, U of, Twin Cities
Portland State U (OR)
Stanford U (CA)

Source: Bicycling (bicycling.com)

EQUESTRIAN

Equestrian - Hunter Seat and Western

Intercollegiate Horse Shows Association

IHSA provides collegiate riders of all skills the opportunity to compete individually and as teams in equestrian competition. It was founded on the principle that any college student should be able to participate in horse shows regardless of his or her riding ability or financial status.

Adelphi U (NY)
Adrian C (MI)
Akron, U of (OH)
Alabama, U of, Tuscaloosa
Albion C (MI)
Alfred State C (NY)

Alfred U (NY)
Allegheny C (PA)
Alma C (MI)
American U (DC)
Amherst C (MA)
Appalachian State U (NC)

Arcadia U (PA)
Arizona State U
Arizona, U of
Arkansas, U of, Fayetteville
Assumption C (MA)
Auburn U (AL)
Augustana C (IL)
Ave Maria U (FL)
Averett U (VA)
Ball State U (IN)
Becker C (MA)
Belmont U (TN)
Bennington C (VT)
Bentley U (MA)
Berry C (GA)
Bethany C (WV)
Black Hawk C (IL)
Bloomsburg U (PA)
Boston C (MA)
Boston U (MA)
Bowdoin C (ME)
Bowling Green State U (OH)
Brandeis U (MA)
Bridgewater C (VA)
Bridgewater State U (MA)
British Columbia, U of (Canada)
Brockport C (NY)
Brown U (RI)
Bucknell U (PA)
Bucks County Community C (PA)
Butler U (IN)
California Polytechnic State U, San Luis
　Obispo
California State Polytechnic U, Pomona
California State U, Sonoma
California U (PA)
California, U of, Berkeley
California, U of, Davis
California, U of, Los Angeles
California, U of, San Diego
Calvin C (MI)
Campbell U (NC)
Canisius C (NY)
Case Western Reserve U (OH)
Castleton U (VT)
Cazenovia C (NY)
Centenary U (NJ)
Central Connecticut State U
Central Florida, U of
Central Washington U
Chapman U (CA)
Charleston, C of (SC)
Chestnut Hill C (PA)
Christopher Newport U (VA)
Cincinnati, U of (OH)

Claremont Colleges Consortium (CA)
Clarion U, Venango (PA)
Clark U (MA)
Clemson U (SC)
Cloud Community C (KS)
Coastal Carolina U (SC)
Colby Community C (KS)
Colby Sawyer C (NH)
Colgate U (NY)
Colorado Academy of Veterinary
　Technology
Colorado C
Colorado School of Mines
Colorado State U, Ft. Collins
Colorado, U of, Boulder
Colorado, U of, Colorado Springs
Columbia U (NY)
Connecticut C (CT)
Connecticut, U of
Converse C (SC)
Cornell U (NY)
Curry C (MA)
Dartmouth C (NH)
Dayton, U of (OH)
Delaware Valley U (PA)
Delaware, U of
Denison U (OH)
DeSales U (PA)
Dickinson C (PA)
Drew U (NJ)
Drexel U (PA)
Duke U (NC)
Duquesne U (PA)
Earlham C (IN)
East Carolina U (NC)
East Stroudsburg U (PA)
Eastern Illinois U
Edinboro U (PA)
Elmira C (NY)
Elon U (NC)
Emory & Henry C (VA)
Emory U (GA)
Endicott C (MA)
Fairfield U (CT)
Ferris State U (MI)
Ferrum C (VA)
Findlay, U of (OH)
Florida Atlantic U
Florida Gulf Coast U
Florida International U
Florida Southern C
Florida State U
Florida, U of
Franciscan U (OH)
Franklin & Marshall C (PA)

ATHLETICS

Furman U (SC)
George Mason U (VA)
George Washington U (MD)
Georgetown C (KY)
Georgetown U (DC)
Georgia C & State U
Georgia Institute of Technology
Georgia Southern U
Georgia State U
Georgia, U of
Gettysburg C (PA)
Goucher C (MD)
Grand Valley State U (MI)
Grove City C (PA)
Guelph, U of (Canada)
Gustavus Adolphus C (MN)
Hampshire C (MA)
Hartwick C (NY)
High Point U (NC)
Hillsdale C (MI)
Hiram C (OH)
Hobart C & William Smith C (NY)
Hofstra U (NY)
Hollins U (VA)
Holy Cross, C of the (MA)
Hood C (MD)
Illinois State U
Illinois, U of, Urbana
Indiana U (IN)
Indiana U of Pennsylvania
Indiana U, South Bend
Indiana U-Purdue U, Indianapolis
Iowa State U
Ithaca C (NY)
James Madison U (VA)
Johns Hopkins U (MD)
Johnson & Wales U (RI)
Judson C (AL)
Kalamazoo C (MI)
Kansas State U
Kansas, U of
Kennesaw State U (GA)
Kent State U (OH)
Kentucky, U of
Kenyon C (OH)
Keuka C (NY)
Kutztown U (PA)
Lafayette C (PA)
Lake Erie C (OH)
Lake Forest C (IL)
Lakehead U (Canada)
Lander U (SC)
Laramie County Community C (WY)
Le Moyne C (NY)
Lebanon Valley C (PA)

Lehigh U (PA)
Liberty U (VA)
Linn-Benton Community C (OR)
Long Island U, C.W. Post (NY)
Longwood U (VA)
Louisiana State U, Baton Rouge
Louisville, U of (KY)
Lycoming C (PA)
Lynchburg C (VA)
Maine, U of
Marist C (NY)
Martin Community C (NC)
Mary Baldwin U (VA)
Mary Washington, U of (VA)
Maryland, U of, Baltimore County
Maryland, U of, College Park
Maryville C (TN)
Massachusetts, U of, Amherst
Massachusetts, U of, Dartmouth
Mercyhurst U (PA)
Miami U (OH)
Miami, U of (FL)
Michigan State U
Michigan, U of, Ann Arbor
Middle Tennessee State U
Middlebury C (VT)
Midway U (KY)
Millersville U (PA)
Minnesota, U of, Crookston
Minnesota, U of, Twin Cities
Mississippi C
Mississippi State U
Mississippi, U of
Missouri State U
Molloy C (NY)
Montana State U, Bozeman
Montana, U of
Montana, U of, Western
Moravian C (PA)
Morehead State U (KY)
Morrisville State C (NY)
Mt. Holyoke C (MA)
Mt. Ida C (MA)
Mt. San Antonio C (CA)
Mt. St. Mary's U (MD)
Murray State U (KY)
Nazareth C (NY)
Nebraska, U of, Lincoln
New England, U of (ME)
New Hampshire, U of
New York U
New York, State U of, Albany
New York, State U of, Binghamton
New York, State U of, Buffalo
New York, State U of, Cobleskill

Steven R. Antonoff

New York, State U of, Geneseo
New York, State U of, New Paltz
New York, State U of, Oneonta
New York, State U of, Stony Brook
North Alabama, U of
North Carolina State U
North Carolina, U of, Asheville
North Caroline, U of, Chapel Hill
North Carolina, U of, Charlotte
North Carolina, U of, Greensboro
North Carolina, U of, Wilmington
North Central Texas C
North Dakota State U
North Florida, U of
North Georgia, U of
North Texas, U of
Northeastern Oklahoma C
Northeastern U (MA)
Northern Arizona U
Northern Illinois U
Northern Kentucky U
Northwestern U (IL)
Norwich U (VT)
Nova Southeastern U (FL)
Oberlin C (OH)
Ohio State U, Columbus
Ohio U
Ohio Wesleyan U
Oklahoma Panhandle State U
Oklahoma, U of
Old Dominion U (VA)
Oregon State U
Oregon, U of
Ottawa, U of (Canada)
Otterbein U (OH)
Parkland C (IL)
Pennsylvania State U, Berks
Pennsylvania State U, Erie
Pennsylvania State U, Harrisburg
Pennsylvania State U, University Park
Pennsylvania, U of
Pittsburgh, U of (PA)
Post U (CT)
Princeton U (NJ)
Purdue U (IN)
Purdue U, North Central (IN)
Purdue U, Northwest (IN)
Radford U (VA)
Randolph C (VA)
Randolph-Macon C (VA)
Reedley C (CA)
Rensselaer Polytechnic Institute (NY)
Rhode Island C
Rhode Island, U of
Rhodes C (TN)

Richmond, U of (VA)
Rider U (NJ)
Ripon C (WI)
Roanoke C (VA)
Rochester Institute of Technology (NY)
Rocky Mountain C (MT)
Roger Williams U (RI)
Rowan U (NJ)
Rutgers U (NJ)
Sacred Heart U (CT)
Saginaw Valley State U (MI)
Salisbury U (MD)
Salve Regina U (RI)
Santa Clara U (CA)
Sarah Lawrence C (NY)
Savannah C of Art & Design (GA)
Scranton, U of (PA)
Sequoias, C of the (CA)
Seton Hill U (PA)
Shippensburg U (PA)
Siena C (NY)
Skidmore C (NY)
Slippery Rock U (PA)
Smith C (MA)
South Carolina, U of, Aiken
South Carolina, U of, Columbia
South Florida, U of
South, U of (TN)
Southeast Missouri State U
Southern California, U of
Southern Illinois U, Carbondale
Southern Nazarene U (OK)
Springfield C (MA)
St. Cloud State U (MN)
St. Andrews U (NC)
St. Joseph's C (NY)
St. Mary's C (IN)
St. Mary's C (MD)
St. Mary-of-the-Woods C (IN)
St. Vincent C (PA)
Stanford U (CA)
Stetson U (FL)
Stevens Institute of Technology (NJ)
Stonehill C (MA)
Suffolk County Community C (NY)
Susquehanna U (PA)
Sweet Briar C (VA)
Syracuse U (NY)
Tampa, U of (FL)
Tarleton State U (TX)
Taylor U (IN)
Temple U (PA)
Tennessee Technological U
Tennessee, U of, Knoxville
Texas A&M U, Commerce

Texas State U, San Marcos
Texas Technology U
Thiel C (PA)
Tiffin U (OH)
Towson U (MD)
Trinity C (CT)
Trinity U (TX)
Truman State U (MO)
Tufts U (MA)
U.S. Air Force Academy (CO)
U.S. Military Academy (NY)
Union C (NY)
Utah State U
Valley Forge Military C (PA)
Vanderbilt (TN)
Vassar C (NY)
Vermont, U of
Villanova U (PA)
Virginia Commonwealth U
Virginia Polytechnic Institute & State U
Virginia, U of
Wake Forest U (NC)
Washington & Jefferson C (PA)
Washington & Lee U (VA)
Washington C (MD)
Washington State U
Washington U (MO)
Washington, U of
Wellesley C (MA)
Wesleyan C (GA)

West Chester U (PA)
West Florida, U of
West Georgia, U of
West Texas U
West Virginia U
Western Carolina U (NC)
Western Illinois U
Western Kentucky U
Western Michigan U
Western Ontario, U of (Canada)
Western Washington U
Westfield State U (MA)
Wheaton C (MA)
William & Mary, C of (VA)
William Paterson U (NJ)
Williams C (MA)
Wilmington C (OH)
Wilson C (PA)
Wisconsin, U of, Eau Claire
Wisconsin, U of, La Crosse
Wisconsin, U of, Madison
Wisconsin, U of, Milwaukee
Wisconsin, U of, Platteville
Wisconsin, U of, River Falls
Wofford C (SC)
Wooster, C of (OH)
Worcester State U (MA)
Wyoming, U of
Youngstown State U (OH)

Source: Intercollegiate Horse Shows Association (ihsainc.com)

Colleges With Equestrian Intercollegiate Dressage Teams

These colleges are members of the Intercollegiate Dressage Association.

Albion C (MI)
Appalachian State U (NC)
Averett U (VA)
Bethany C (WV)
Bridgewater C (VA)
California Polytechnic State U, San Luis
  Obispo
California, U of, Davis
California, U of, Santa Cruz
Cazenovia C (NY)
Centenary C (NJ)
Central Florida, C of (FL)
Connecticut, U of
Cornell U (NY)
Dartmouth C (NH)
Delaware Valley U (PA)

Elon U (NC)
Emory & Henry C (VA)
Ferrum C (VA)
Findlay, U of (OH)
Florida State U
Florida, U of
Guelph, U of (Canada)
Johnson & Wales U (RI)
Kentucky, U of
Lake Erie C (OH)
Longwood U (VA)
Maine, U of
Marquette U (WI)
Massachusetts, U of, Amherst
Meredith Manor International Equestrian
  Centre (WV)

Miami U (OH)
Michigan State U
Mt. Holyoke C (MA)
New Hampshire, U of
North Carolina State U
Otterbein U (OH)
Pennsylvania State U, University Park
Post U (CT)
Radford U (VA)
Rhode Island, U of
Rutgers U, New Brunswick (NJ)

Santa Clara U (CA)
St. Andrews U (NC)
Stanford U (CA)
Vermont Technical C
Vermont, U of
Virginia Polytechnic Institute & State U
Virginia, U of
Wake Forest U (NC)
Western U (Canada)
Wilson C (PA)
Wooster, C of (OH)

Source: Intercollegiate Dressage Association (teamdressage.com)

FLAG FOOTBALL

Colleges With Strength in Flag Football

These colleges have had winning seasons in recent years in men's, women's, or co-ed divisions.

Angelo State U (TX)
Central Florida, U of
Florida A&M U
Kennesaw State U

Nebraska, U of, Lincoln
Nuevo León, U of (Mexico)
Valdosta State U (GA)

Source: NIRSA: Leaders in Collegiate Recreation (nirsa.net)

FOOTBALL

Colleges With Championships and/or Strong Records in Division I Football

Alabama, U of, Tuscaloosa
Arizona, U of
Arizona State U
Auburn U (AL)
Baylor U (TX)
Boise State U (ID)
California, U of, Los Angeles
Clemson U (SC)
Colorado, U of, Boulder
Florida, U of
Florida State U
Georgia, U of
Georgia Institute of Technology
Kansas State U
Louisiana State U
Louisville, U of (KY)
Miami, U of (FL)
Michigan, U of, Ann Arbor

Michigan State U
Minnesota, U of, Twin Cities
Mississippi, U of
Mississippi State U
Missouri, U of, Columbia
Nebraska, U of, Lincoln
Notre Dame, U of (IN)
Ohio State U, Columbus
Oklahoma, U of
Oregon, U of
Pennsylvania State U, University Park
Southern California, U of
Tennessee, U of, Knoxville
Texas, U of, Austin
Texas Christian U
Utah, U of
Washington, U of
Wisconsin, U of, Madison

Source: National Collegiate Athletic Association (ncaa.org)

ATHLETICS

Colleges With Championships and/or Strong Records in the Football Division I Subdivision

Appalachian State U (NC)
Arkansas State U
Boise State U (ID)
Coastal Carolina U (SC)
Colgate U (NY)
Delaware, U of
Eastern Illinois U
Eastern Kentucky U
Eastern Washington U
Fordham U (NY)
Furman U (SC)
Georgia Southern U
Harvard U (MA)
Idaho State U
Illinois State U
Indiana State U
Jacksonville State U (AL)
James Madison U (VA)
Liberty U (VA)
Louisiana, U of, Monroe

Marshall U (WV)
Massachusetts, U of, Amherst
McNeese State U (LA)
Montana, U of
Montana State U
Nevada, U of, Las Vegas
New Hampshire, U of
North Dakota State U
Northern Iowa, U of
Richmond, U of (VA)
Sam Houston State U (TX)
South Dakota State U
Southeastern Louisiana U
Stephen F. Austin State U (TX)
Tennessee, U of, Chattanooga
Towson U (MD)
Villanova U (PA)
Western Kentucky U
Youngstown State U (OH)

Source: National Collegiate Athletic Association (ncaa.org)

Colleges With Championships and/or Strong Records in Division II Football

Angelo State U (TX)
Azusa Pacific U (CA)
Bloomsburg U (PA)
Carson-Newman U (TN)
Colorado School of Mines
Colorado State U, Pueblo
Concord U (MV)
Delta State U (MS)
Ferris State U (MI)
Grand Valley State U (MI)
Harding U (AR)
Henderson State U (AK)
Indiana U (PA)
Jacksonville State U (AL)
Lenoir-Rhyne U (NC)
Michigan Technological U
Minnesota, U of, Duluth
Minnesota State U, Mankato
Mississippi C
New Haven, U of (CT)

North Alabama, U of
North Dakota, U of
North Dakota State U
Northern Colorado, U of
Northwest Missouri State U
Ohio Dominican U
Ouachita Baptist U (AR)
Pittsburg State U (KS)
Portland State U (OR)
Shepherd U (WV)
Sioux Falls, U of (SD)
South Dakota, U of
Texas A&M U, Kingsville
Troy U (AL)
Valdosta State U (GA)
Virginia State U
Wayne State U (MI)
West Chester U (PA)
West Georgia, U of
Winston-Salem State U (NC)

Source: National Collegiate Athletic Association (ncaa.org)

Steven R. Antonoff

Colleges With Championships and/or Strong Records in Division III Football

Albion C (MI)
Allegheny C (PA)
Augustana C (IL)
Bridgewater (VA)
Central C (IA)
Centre C (KY)
Chapman U (CA)
Concordia C (MN)
Dayton, U of (OH)
Delaware Valley U (PA)
Hobart C (NY)
Ithaca C (NY)
John Carroll U (OH)
Johns Hopkins U (MD)
Linfield C (OR)
Lycoming C (PA)
Mary Hardin-Baylor, U of (TX)
Massachusetts Institute of Technology
Mt. Union, U of (OH)
Muhlenberg C (PA)

North Central C (IL)
Pacific Lutheran U (WA)
Rowan U (NJ)
Salisbury U (MD)
St. John's U (MN)
St. John Fisher C (NY)
St. Thomas, U of (MN)
Texas Lutheran U
Trinity U (TX)
Union C (NY)
Wabash C (IN)
Wagner C (NY)
Wartburg C (IA)
Washington & Jefferson C (PA)
Wesley C (DE)
Wheaton C (IL)
Widener U (PA)
Wisconsin, U of, La Crosse
Wisconsin, U of, Whitewater
Wittenberg U (OH)

Source: National Collegiate Athletic Association (ncaa.org)

Colleges With Football Game Day Madness

Schools on the list were ranked by the "Best College Game Day Ambience" as "chosen by a panel of experts and then voted on by the public."

1. Clemson U (SC)
2. South Carolina, U of, Columbia
3. Tennessee, U of, Knoxville
4. Texas A&M U, College Station
5. Michigan, U of, Ann Arbor
6. Nebraska, U of, Lincoln
7. Pennsylvania State U, University Park
8. Ohio State U, Columbus
9. Louisiana State U, Baton Rouge
10. Alabama, U of, Tuscaloosa

Source: USA Today

Colleges That Produce the Greatest Numbers of Professional Football Players

These are the schools with the most NFL draft picks in recent years.

Southern California, U of: 493
Notre Dame, U of (IN): 486
Ohio State U: 418
Oklahoma, U of: 373
Nebraska, U of, Lincoln: 353
Michigan, U of, Ann Arbor: 348
Pennsylvania State U, University Park: 338

Tennessee, U of, Knoxville: 337
Texas, U of, Austin: 337
Alabama, U of, Tuscaloosa: 326
Miami, U of (FL): 325
Florida, U of: 324
Louisiana State U: 315
Georgia, U of: 311
Michigan State U: 303

California, U of, Los Angeles: 303
Washington, U of: 285
Purdue U (IN): 277
Pittsburgh, U of (PA): 272
Texas A&M U, College Station: 271
Wisconsin, U of, Madison: 268
Colorado, U of, Boulder: 266
Auburn U (AL): 262
Minnesota, U of, Twin Cities: 262
Arkansas, U of, Fayetteville: 258
Florida State U: 256
Stanford U (CA): 249
Iowa, U of: 245

Illinois, U of, Urbana: 241
Arizona State U: 239
Baylor U (TX): 229
Clemson U (SC): 229
California, U of, Berkeley: 228
Mississippi, U of: 227
North Carolina, U of, Chapel Hill: 226
Oregon, U of: 212
Georgia Institute of Technology: 211
Maryland, U of, College Park: 209
Missouri, U of, Columbia: 209
Boston C (MA): 198

Source: The College Finder research, including drafthistory.com

FRISBEE GOLF

Colleges With Frisbee Golf Teams

These are recent rankings for colleges with club competition disc golf teams.

1. Ferris State U (MI)
2. Colorado State U, Ft. Collins
3. Nevada, U of, Reno
4. Georgia Regents U
5. Arkansas, U of, Fayetteville
6. Oregon, U of
7. Liberty U (VA)
8. South Alabama, U of
9. Wisconsin, U of, Stout
10. Eastern Michigan, U of
11. Alabama, U of, Tuscaloosa
12. Mississippi State U
13. Kennesaw State U (GA)
14. South Carolina, U of, Columbia
15. North Carolina State U
16. Massachusetts, U of, Amherst
17. Kansas, U of
18. Northern Iowa, U of
19. Texas, U of, Austin
20. East Tennessee State U
21. Western Michigan, U of
22. Grand Valley State U (MI)
23. California State U, Monterey Bay
24. Iowa State U
25. Oregon State U

Source: College Disc Golf (college.discgolf.io)

HANDBALL

Colleges With Strength in Co-ed Handball

Angelo State U (TX)
Blinn C (TX)
California State U, San Jose
California, U of, Berkeley
California, U of, Irvine
Colorado School of Mines
De Anza C (CA)
Dublin City U (Ireland)
Dublin Institute of Technology (Ireland)
Florida, U of

Illinois, U of, Urbana
Institute of Technology (Ireland)
Lake Forest C (IL)
Limerick, U of (Ireland)
Michigan State U
Michigan, U of, Ann Arbor
Minnesota State U, Mankato
Minnesota, U of, Twin Cities
Missouri State U
New York, State U of, New Paltz

New York, State U of, Stony Brook
Pacific U (OR)
Rochester, U of (NY)
San Mateo, C of (CA)
Southwestern U (TX)
St. Louis U (MO)
St. Mary's C (CA)
Syracuse U (NY)

Texas A&M U, College Station
Texas, U of, Austin
Texas, U of, El Paso
Trinity C, Dublin (Ireland)
University C, Dublin (Ireland)
Utah State U
Western Washington U
Whatcom Community C (WA)

Source: United States Handball Association (ushandball.org)

HOCKEY

Colleges With Great Men's Hockey Division I

These colleges have been champions over the past 70 years.

Michigan, U of, Ann Arbor: 9
North Dakota, U of: 7
Denver, U of (CO): 6
Wisconsin, U of, Madison: 6
Boston C (MA): 5
Boston U (MA): 5
Minnesota, U of, Twin Cities: 4
Lake Superior State U (MI): 3
Michigan State U: 3
Michigan Technological U: 3
Colorado C: 2

Cornell U (NY): 2
Maine, U of: 2
Rensselaer Polytechnic Institute (NY): 2
Bowling Green State U (OH): 1
Harvard U (MA): 1
Minnesota, U of, Duluth: 1
Northern Michigan U: 1
Providence C (RI): 1
Union C (NY): 1
Yale (CT): 1

Source: Sports Illustrated Almanac

Colleges With Great Men's Ice Hockey Division III

These colleges have been champions over the past 30 years.

Middlebury C (VT): 8
St. Norbert C (WI): 4
Wisconsin, U of, Stevens Point: 4
Norwich U (VT): 3
New York, State U of, Plattsburgh: 2
Wisconsin, U of, River Falls: 2
Babson C (MA): 1

Bemidji State U (MN): 1
Neumann U (PA): 1
New York, State U of, Oswego: 1
Rochester Institute of Technology (NY): 1
Trinity C (CT): 1
Wisconsin, U of, Eau Claire: 1
Wisconsin, U of, Superior: 1

Source: Sports Illustrated 2014 Almanac

Colleges With Great Women's Ice Hockey Teams

These colleges had winning records in Division I women's ice hockey in a recent year.

Bemidji State U (MN)
Boston C (MA)

Boston U (MA)
Clarkson U (NY)

ATHLETICS

Connecticut, U of
Cornell U (NY)
Dartmouth C (NH)
Harvard U (MA)
Mercyhurst U (PA)
Minnesota, U of, Duluth
Minnesota, U of, Twin Cities
New Hampshire, U of
North Dakota, U of
Northeastern U (MA)
Ohio State U, Columbus

Pennsylvania State U, University Park
Princeton U (NJ)
Quinnipiac U (CT)
Robert Morris U (PA)
Rochester Institute of Technology (NY)
St. Lawrence U (NY)
Syracuse U (NY)
Vermont, U of
Wisconsin, U of, Madison
Yale U (CT)

Source: National Collegiate Athletic Association (ncaa.org)

JUDO

Colleges With Judo Clubs

Ball State U (IN)
California State U, Fresno
California State U, Stanislaus
California, U of, Berkeley
California, U of, Davis
California, U of, San Diego
Colorado School of Mines
Colorado, U of, Colorado Springs
Drexel U (PA)
Florida State U
Georgia, U of
Hawaii Tokai U
Indiana U, Bloomington
Iowa State U
Johnson & Wales U (RI)
Massachusetts, U of, Amherst
New York U
New York, City U of, Queens
Pennsylvania State U, University Park

Rutgers U, New Brunswick
San Francisco, U of
San Jose State U (CA)
Sarah Lawrence C (NY)
Schenectady Community C (NY)
South Florida, U of
South Kentucky U
Southeast Missouri U
St John's U (NY)
Tennessee, U of, Knoxville
Texas A&M U, College Station
Texas State U
Texas Tech U
Texas, U of, Austin
U.S. Air Force Academy (CO)
U.S. Military Academy (NY)
U.S. Naval Academy (MD)
Washington, U of
York C (NE)

Source: National Collegiate Judo Association (ncjajudo.org)

LACROSSE

Colleges With Winning Men's Lacrosse Teams

These are colleges that had winning records in men's Division I lacrosse in a recent year.

Brown U (RI)
Bucknell U (PA)
Colgate U (NY)
Cornell U (NY)
Denver, U of (CO)
Duke U (NC)
Georgetown U (DC)

Harvard U (MA)
Johns Hopkins U (MD)
Loyola U (MD)
Marist C (NY)
Marquette U (WI)
Maryland, U of, College Park
New York, State U of, Albany

New York, State U of, Stony Brook
North Carolina, U of, Chapel Hill
Notre Dame, U of (IN)
Ohio State U, Columbus
Princeton U (NJ)
Syracuse U (NY)

Towson U (MD)
U.S. Military Academy (NY)
U.S. Naval Academy (MD)
Virginia, U of
Yale U (CT)

Source: National Collegiate Athletic Association (ncaa.org)

Colleges With Winning Women's Lacrosse Teams

These are colleges that had recent winning records in women's Division I lacrosse.

Cornell U (NY)
Duke U (NC)
Florida, U of
Johns Hopkins U (MD)
Louisville, U of (KY)
Maryland, U of, College Park
Massachusetts, U of, Amherst
New York, State U of, Stony Brook
North Carolina, U of, Chapel Hill
Northwestern U (IL)

Notre Dame, U of (IN)
Ohio State U, Columbus
Pennsylvania State U, University Park
Pennsylvania, U of
Princeton U (NJ)
Southern California, U of
Stanford U (CA)
Syracuse U (NY)
Towson U (MD)
Virginia, U of

Source: National Collegiate Athletic Association (ncaa.org)

PAINTBALL

Colleges With Club Paintball Teams

Connecticut, U of
Cornell U (NY)
East Carolina U (NC)
Illinois State U
Indiana U, Bloomington
Iowa State U
Kennesaw State U (GA)
Liberty U (VA)
Massachusetts, U of, Amherst
New York, State U of, Oswego
Northeastern U (MA)
North Texas, U of
Pennsylvania State U, University Park

Saginaw Valley State U (MI)
Temple U (PA)
Texas, U of, Austin
Texas, U of, San Antonio
Texas A&M U, College Station
Texas Tech U
U.S. Military Academy (NY)
U.S. Naval Academy (MD)
Virginia Polytechnic Institute & State U
Wisconsin, U of, Madison
Wisconsin, U of, Milwaukee
Wisconsin, U of, Whitewater

Source: National Collegiate Paintball Association

QUIDDITCH

Colleges With Quidditch Teams

The following colleges have recently qualified for the Quidditch World Cup.

Appalachian State U (NC)
Arizona State U
Arkansas, U of, Fayetteville
Ball State U (IN)
Baylor U (TX)
Boston U (MA)
Bowling Green State U (OH)
Brigham Young U (UT)
British Columbia, U of (Canada)
California, U of, Santa Barbara
California, U of, Los Angeles
Central Michigan U
Charleston, C of (SC)
Emerson C (MA)
Florida, U of
George Mason U (DC)
Harvard U (MA)
Hofstra U (NY)
Illinois State U
Indiana U, Bloomington
Kansas, U of
Lock Haven U (PA)
Loyola U (LA)
Macaulay Honors C (NY)
Maryland, U of
Miami U (FL)
Michigan, U of, Ann Arbor
Michigan State U
Minnesota, U of
Missouri, U of

New York U
North Carolina, U of, Chapel Hill
Northern Arizona U
Ohio State U, Columbus
Ohio U, Athens
Oklahoma Baptist U
Oklahoma State U
Pennsylvania State U, University Park
Purdue U (IN)
Rensselaer Polytechnic Institute (NY)
Richmond, U of (VA)
Rochester, U of (NY)
Rochester Institute of Technology (NY)
Rollins C (FL)
Salt Lake Community C (UT)
Sam Houston State U (TX)
South Carolina, U of
South Florida, U of
Tennessee Technological U
Texas, U of, Austin
Texas, U of, San Antonio
Texas A&M U, College Station
Texas State U
Texas Tech U
Tufts U (MA)
Utah, U of
Utah State U
Villanova U (PA)
Virginia Commonwealth U
Western Washington U

RACQUETBALL

Colleges With Racquetball Teams

Akron, U of (OH)
Alabama, U of, Tuscaloosa
Appalachian State U
Arizona State U
Arizona, U of
Auburn U (AL)
Baldwin Wallace U (OH)
Binghamton U (NY)
Blue Ridge Community C (VA)
Brigham Young U (UT)

Bryant U (RI)
California Polytechnic State U, San Luis
  Obispo
California State U, Monterey Bay
California, U of, Berkeley
California, U of, Davis
California, U of, Santa Cruz
Central Florida, U of
Cincinnati, U of (OH)
Clarkson U (NY)

Clemson U (SC)
Cleveland State U (OH)
Colorado School of Mines
Colorado State U, Pueblo
Colorado, U of, Boulder
Colorado, U of, Colorado Springs
Colorado, U of, Denver
Connecticut, U of
Dayton, U of (OH)
Delaware, U of
Denver, U of (CO)
Duke U (NC)
Eastern Illinois U
Florida State U
Florida, U of
Fort Lewis C (CO)
George Washington U (DC)
Georgia Institute of Technology
Georgia Southwestern U
Georgia, U of
Grove City C (PA)
Howard U (DC)
Kennasaw State U (GA)
Lafayette C (PA)
Liberty U (VA)
Lindenwood U (MO)
Maryland, U of, Baltimore
Massachusetts, U of, Amherst
Massachusetts, U of, Lowell
Memphis, U of (TN)
Miami U (OH)
Miami, U of (FL)
Michigan Technical U
Missouri, U of, Columbia
New Mexico, U of
Nichols C (MA)
North Carolina State U
North Carolina, U of, Chapel Hill
North Carolina, U of, Wilmington
Northern Arizona U
Northern Colorado, U of
Northern Illinois U
Ohio State U, Columbus
Ohio U, Athens
Oregon State U
Pennsylvania State U, University Park

Providence C (RI)
Purdue U (IN)
Queensborough Community C (NY)
Rensselaer Polytechnic Institute (NY)
Rhode Island, Community C of
Rochester Institute of Technology (NY)
Rowan U (NJ)
Rutgers U, New Brunswick (NJ)
Sacramento State U (CA)
Scranton U (PA)
Slippery Rock U (PA)
South Carolina, U of
South Florida, U of
St. Louis U (MO)
Stanford U (CA)
Syracuse U (NY)
Temple U (PA)
Tennessee, U of, Chattanooga
Tennessee, U of, Knoxville
Texas A&M U, College Station
Texas Christian U
Texas State U
Texas Tech U
Texas, U of, Austin
Texas, U of, Dallas
U.S. Military Academy (NY)
Utah State U
Utah Valley U
Utah, U of
Vanderbilt U (TN)
Virginia Military Institute
Virginia Western Community C
Virginia, U of
Wake Forest U (NC)
Washington & Lee U (VA)
Weber State U (UT)
Western Michigan U
Western New England U (MA)
William & Mary, C of (VA)
Wisconsin, U of, Madison
Wisconsin, U of, Oshkosh
Wyoming, U of
Youngstown State U (OH)

Source: Team USA (teamusa.org)

ATHLETICS

RIFLE

Colleges With Strong Rifle Programs

These colleges were ranked highly by the Collegiate Rifle Coaches Association in a recent year.

1.	West Virginia U	11.	U.S. Naval Academy (MD)
2.	Alaska, U of, Fairbanks	12.	U.S. Military Academy (NY)
3.	Texas Christian U	13.	Tennessee, U of, Martin
4.	Nebraska, U of, Lincoln	14.	Akron, U of (OH)
5.	Jacksonville State U (AL)	15.	Nevada, U of, Reno
6.	Kentucky, U of	16.	North Carolina State U
7.	U.S. Air Force Academy (CO)	17.	Morehead State U (KY)
8.	Murray State U (KY)	18.	Mississippi, U of
9.	Memphis, U of (TN)	19.	North Georgia, U of
10.	Ohio State U, Columbus	20.	Columbus State U (GA)

Source: National Collegiate Athletic Association (ncaa.org)

RODEO

Colleges With Rodeo Programs

These colleges are separated into the following regions according to the National Intercollegiate Rodeo Association.

Big Sky

Blackfeet Community C (MT)
Dawson Community C (MT)
Great Falls, U of (MT)
Miles Community C (MT)
Montana State U

Montana State U, Northern
Montana, U of
Montana, U of, Western
Northwest C (WI)
Salish Kootenai C (MT)

Central Plains

Bacone C (OK)
Coffeyville Community C (KS)
Colby Community C (KS)
Connors State C (OK)
Dodge City Community C (KS)
Fort Hays State U (KS)
Fort Scott Community C (KS)
Garden City Community C (KS)
Kansas State U

Northeastern Oklahoma A&M C
Northwest Kansas Technical C
Northwestern Oklahoma State U
Oklahoma State U
Panhandle State U (OK)
Pratt Community C (KS)
Southeastern Oklahoma State U
Southwestern Oklahoma State U
Western Oklahoma State C

Central Rocky Mountain

Casper C (WY)
Central Wyoming C
Chadron State C (NE)
Colorado State U, Ft. Collins
Eastern Wyoming C
Gillette C (WY)
Lamar Community C (CO)

Laramie County Community C (WY)
Northeastern Junior C (CO)
Otero Junior C (CO)
Sheridan C (WY)
U.S. Air Force Academy (CO)
Wyoming, U of

Grand Canyon

Adams State C (CO)
Arizona, U of
Central Arizona C
Cochise C (AZ)

Dine C (AZ)
Mesalands Community C (NM)
Navajo Technical C (NM)
New Mexico State U

Great Plains

Black Hills State U (SD)
Dickinson State U (ND)
Hastings C (NE)
Iowa Central Community C
Iowa State U
Mid-Plains Community C (NE)
Mitchell Technical Institute (SD)

Nebraska College of Technical
  Agriculture
Nebraska, U of, Lincoln
North Dakota State U
South Dakota State U
Wisconsin, U of, River Falls

Northwest

Blue Mountain Community C (OR)
Boise State U (ID)
Central Oregon Community C
Central Washington U

Eastern Oregon U
Eastern Washington U
Treasure Valley Community C (OR)
Walla Walla Community C (WA)

Ozark

Arkansas, U of, Cossatot
Arkansas, U of, Monticello
East Mississippi Community C
Michigan State U
Missouri Valley C
Murray State U (KY)

Northwest Mississippi Community C
Southern Arkansas U
Tennessee, U of, Martin
Three Rivers C (MO)
West Alabama, U of

Rocky Mountain

Colorado Northwestern Community C
Idaho State U
Mesa State U (CO)
Snow C (UT)
Southern Idaho, C of

Southern Utah U
Utah State U
Utah Valley U
Weber State U (UT)

ATHLETICS

Southern

Hill C (TX)
Louisiana State U, Alexandria
McNeese State U (LA)
Northeast Texas Community C
Panola Junior C (TX)
Sam Houston State U (TX)
Southwest Texas Junior C

Stephen F. Austin State U (TX)
Texas A&M U, College Station
Texas A&M U, Commerce
Texas A&M U, Kingsville
Trinity Valley Community C (TX)
Wharton County Junior C (TX)

Southwest

Clarendon C (TX)
Eastern New Mexico U
Frank Phillips C (TX)
Howard County Junior C (TX)
New Mexico Junior C
Odessa C (TX)
Ranger C (TX)
South Plains C (TX)

Sul Ross State U (TX)
Tarleton State U (TX)
Texas Tech U
Vernon C (TX)
Weatherford C (TX)
West Texas A&M U
Western Texas C

West Coast

California Polytechnic State U, Pomona
California Polytechnic State U, San Luis
Obispo
California State U, Fresno
Cuesta C (CA)

Feather River C (CA)
Lassen C (CA)
Nevada, U of, Las Vegas
West Hills C (CA)

Source: National Intercollegiate Rodeo Association (collegerodeo.com)

RUGBY

Great Rugby Schools

These colleges are members of the USA Rugby Division 1A.

Arizona State U
Arizona, U of
Arkansas State U
Arkansas, U of, Fayetteville
Baylor U (TX)
California Polytechnic U, San Luis Obispo
California, U of, Berkeley
California, U of, Los Angeles
California, U of, San Diego
California, U of, Santa Barbara
Clemson U (SC)
Colorado State U, Ft. Collins
Colorado, U of, Boulder
Davenport U (MI)
Delaware, U of
Houston, U of (TX)
Illinois, U of, Urbana

Indiana U, Bloomington
Iona C (NY)
Iowa, U of
Kutztown U (PA)
Life U (GA)
Lindenwood U (MO)
Louisiana State U, Baton Rouge
Michigan State U
Michigan, U of, Ann Arbor
Minnesota, U of, Twin Cities
New Mexico, U of
New York, State U of, Buffalo
Ohio State U
Oklahoma, U of
Pennsylvania State U, University Park
Purdue U (IN)
Santa Clara U (CA)

Southern California, U of
St. Bonaventure U (NY)
St. Mary's C (CA)
Stanford U (CA)
Texas A&M U, College Station
Texas Christian U
Texas Tech U
Texas, U of, Austin

U.S. Air Force Academy (CO)
U.S. Military Academy (NY)
Utah State U
Utah, U of
West Virginia U
Wheeling Jesuit U (WV)
Wisconsin, U of, Madison
Wyoming, U of

Source: D1A College Rugby (d1arugby.com)

SAILING

Colleges With Club Sailing Teams

Boston C (MA)
Boston U (MA)
Bowdoin C (ME)
Brown U (RI)
Charleston, C of (SC)
Cornell U (NY)
Dartmouth C (NH)
Fordham U (NY)
Georgetown U (DC)
Harvard U (MA)
New York, State U of, Maritime

Old Dominion U (VA)
Pennsylvania, U of
Roger Williams U (RI)
Stanford U (CA)
St. Mary's U (TX)
Tufts U (MA)
U.S. Coast Guard Academy (CT)
U.S. Naval Academy (MD)
Vermont C
Yale U (CT)

SKEET

Schools With Skeet Shooting

Arizona, U of
Cameron U (OK)
Colorado State U, Ft. Collins
Delaware, U of
Delta State U (MS)
Eastern Kentucky U
Emmanuel C (GA)
Ferrum C (VA)
Florida, U of
Ft. Hays State U (KS)
George Mason U (VA)
Hillsdale C (MI)
Illinois, U of, Urbana
Iowa State U
Kentucky, U of
Lindenwood U (MO)
Louisiana, U of, Baton Rouge
Maine, U of, Machias
Missouri, U of, Columbia
Middle Tennessee State U

Missouri State U
Missouri, U of, Science & Technology
Nebraska, U of, Omaha
Northwest C (WY)
Pine Tech C (MN)
Purdue U (IN)
Schreiner U (TX)
South Carolina, U of, Aiken
Southeastern Illinois C
Texas A&M U, College Station
Trinity U (TX)
U.S. Air Force Academy (CO)
U.S. Merchant Marine Academy (NY)
U.S. Military Academy (NY)
U.S. Naval Academy (MD)
Vermont, U of
Virginia Polytechnic Institute & State U
Washington C (MD)
Wyoming, U of
Yale U (CT)

Source: NRA Competitive Shooting Programs (competitions.nra.org)

SKIING

Colleges With Club Competition Snow Sports

The United States Collegiate Ski & Snowboard Association is the sports federation for collegiate team ski racing and snowboarding. The USCSA has alpine, cross-country, freestyle, jumping, and snowboard collegiate competitions.

Akron, U of (OH): Alpine
Alexandria Technical C (MN): Alpine
Alfred U (NY): Alpine
Alma C (MI): Alpine
American Military U (WV): Alpine
Amherst C (MA): Alpine
Appalachian State U (NC): Alpine, Snowboarding
Babson C (MA): Alpine
Binghamton U (NY): Alpine
Boston U (MA): Alpine
Brandeis U (MA): Alpine
Bridgewater State U (MA): Alpine
Brigham Young U (UT): Alpine
British Columbia, U of (Canada): Alpine
Brown U (RI): Alpine
Bucknell U (PA): Alpine
California Polytechnic U, Pomona: Alpine, Snowboarding, Freestyle
California State U, Fullerton: Alpine, Snowboarding, Freestyle
California State U, Long Beach: Alpine, Snowboarding, Freestyle
California State U, San Diego: Alpine, Snowboarding, Freestyle
California, U of, Berkeley: Alpine, Snowboarding
California, U of, Davis: Alpine, Snowboarding, Freestyle
California, U of, Irvine: Alpine, Snowboarding, Freestyle
California, U of, Los Angeles: Alpine, Snowboarding, Freestyle
California, U of, San Diego: Alpine, Snowboarding, Freestyle
California, U of, Santa Barbara: Alpine, Snowboarding, Freestyle
Carnegie Mellon U (PA): Alpine
Castleton U (VT): Alpine
Central Michigan U: Alpine, Snowboarding
Central Oregon Community C: Freestyle
Cincinnati, U of (OH): Alpine, Snowboarding
Clarkson U (NY): Alpine, Cross-Country
Colby C (ME): Snowboarding
Colgate U (NY): Alpine
Colorado C: Alpine
Colorado School of Mines: Alpine
Colorado State U, Ft. Collins: Alpine, Snowboarding
Colorado, U of, Boulder: Snowboarding, Freestyle
Columbia U (NY): Alpine, Snowboarding
Connecticut C: Alpine
Connecticut, U of: Alpine
Cornell U (NY): Alpine, Cross-Country
Davis & Ekins C (WV): Alpine
DeSales U (PA): Alpine Snowboarding
Duke U (NC): Alpine, Snowboarding
East Carolina U (NC): Alpine, Snowboarding

ATHLETICS

Eastern Nazarene C (MA): Alpine
Fairfield U (CT): Alpine, Snowboarding
Fordham U (NY): Alpine
Ft. Lewis C (CO): Alpine
Gordon C (MA): Alpine
Grand Valley State U (MI): Alpine, Snowboarding
Green Mountain C (VT): Alpine
Hamilton C (NY): Alpine, Cross-Country
Hobart & William Smith C (NY): Alpine
Holy Cross, C of (MA): Alpine
Idaho, C of: Alpine, Cross-Country, Snowboarding, Freestyle
Idaho, U of: Alpine, Cross-Country, Snowboarding, Freestyle
Iowa State U: Alpine, Snowboarding
Ithaca C (NY): Alpine, Cross-Country
James Madison U (VA): Alpine, Snowboarding
John Carroll U (OH): Alpine, Snowboarding
Kent State U (OH): Alpine, Snowboarding
Keuka C (NY): Alpine
Lafayette C (PA): Alpine, Snowboarding
Lakehead U (Canada): Alpine
Lehigh U (PA): Alpine
Loyola Marymount U (CA): Alpine, Cross-Country, Snowboarding, Freestyle
Madison Area Technical C (WI): Alpine
Maine, U of, Farmington: Alpine, Cross-Country, Snowboarding
Maine, U of, Fort Kent: Alpine, Cross-Country
Maine, U of: Alpine, Cross-Country
Maine, U of, Presque Isle: Cross-Country
Marist C (NY): Alpine
Marquette U (WI): Alpine, Snowboarding
Massachusetts Institute of Technology: Alpine
Massachusetts, U of, Amherst: Alpine
Massachusetts, U of, Lowell: Alpine
Mesa State U (CO): Alpine, Nordic
Michigan State U: Alpine, Snowboarding
Michigan Technological U: Alpine, Cross-Country, Snowboarding, Freestyle
Michigan, U of, Ann Arbor: Alpine, Snowboarding
Minnesota State U, Mankato: Alpine
Minnesota, U of, Duluth: Alpine
Minnesota, U of, Twin Cities: Alpine
Montana, U of: Alpine
New York, State U of, Albany: Alpine
New York, State U of, Binghamton: Alpine
New York, State U of, Brockport: Alpine
New York, State U of, Buffalo: Alpine
New York, State U of, Geneseo: Alpine
North Carolina State U: Alpine, Snowboarding
North Carolina, U of, Chapel Hill: Alpine, Snowboarding
Northeastern U (MA): Alpine
Northern Michigan U: Alpine
Northwestern U (IL): Alpine, Snowboarding
Notre Dame, U of (IN): Alpine, Snowboarding
Ohio State U, Columbus: Alpine, Snowboarding, Freestyle
Oregon State U: Alpine
Oregon, U of: Alpine
Paul Smith's C (NY): Cross-Country

ATHLETICS

Pennsylvania State U, Wilkes Barre: Alpine
Pennsylvania State U, York: Alpine
Pennsylvania State U: Alpine
Pennsylvania, U of: Alpine
Princeton U (NJ): Alpine, Snowboarding
Puget Sound, U of (WA): Alpine
Rensselaer Polytechnic Institute (NY): Alpine, Cross-Country
Rhode Island, U of: Alpine
Rochester Institute of Technology (NY): Alpine
Rochester, U of (NY): Alpine
Rocky Mountain C (MT): Alpine
Rutgers U, New Brunswick (NJ): Alpine, Snowboarding
Scranton, U of (PA): Alpine
Sierra C (CA): Alpine
Sierra Nevada C (NV): Alpine, Snowboarding
Skidmore C (NY): Alpine, Cross-Country
Smith C (MA): Alpine
Southern California, U of: Alpine, Snowboarding, Freestyle
Springfield C (MA): Alpine
St. Anselm C (NH): Alpine
St. Cloud State U (MN): Alpine, Snowboarding
St. Olaf C (MN): Alpine, Cross-Country
St. Thomas, U of (MN): Alpine
Stanford U (CA): Alpine
Stevens Institute of Technology (NJ): Alpine, Snowboarding
Syracuse U (NY): Alpine
Trinity C (CT): Alpine
Tufts U (MA): Alpine
U.S. Air Force Academy (CO): Alpine, Cross-Country, Snowboarding, Freestyle
U.S. Merchant Marine Academy (NY): Alpine, Snowboarding
U.S. Military Academy (NY): Alpine, Cross-Country
U.S. Naval Academy (MD): Alpine
Vassar C (NY): Alpine, Cross-Country, Nordic
Villanova U (PA): Alpine
Virginia Military Institute: Alpine, Snowboarding
Virginia Polytechnic Institute & State U: Alpine, Snowboarding
Virginia, U of: Alpine, Snowboarding
Washington State U: Alpine
Washington, U of: Alpine
Weber State U (UT): Alpine
Wellesley C (MA): Alpine, Cross-Country
Wesleyan U (CT): Alpine
West Chester U (PA): Alpine
West Virginia U: Alpine, Snowboarding
West Virginia Wesleyan C: Alpine
Western Michigan U: Alpine, Snowboarding
Western State U (CO): Alpine, Cross-Country
Westminster C (UT): Alpine, Snowboarding
Whitman C (WA): Alpine, Cross-Country, Snowboarding, Freestyle
Wisconsin, U of, La Crosse: Alpine, Snowboarding
Wisconsin, U of, Madison: Alpine, Snowboarding
Wisconsin, U of, River Falls: Alpine
Worcester Polytechnic Institute (MA): Alpine, Cross-Country, Snowboarding
Wyoming, U of: Cross-Country
Yale U (CT): Alpine, Cross-Country

Steven R. Antonoff ·

Colleges With Strength in Skiing

These are rankings from a poll of coaches in a recent year.

Alaska, U of, Anchorage
Colorado, U of, Boulder
Dartmouth C (NH)
Denver, U of (CO)
Montana State U

New Hampshire, U of
New Mexico, U of
Northern Michigan U
Utah, U of
Vermont, U of

Source: National Collegiate Athletic Association (ncaa.org)

Top 10 Universities for Skiing & Snowboarding

1.   Colorado, U of, Boulder
2.   Utah, U of
3.   Vermont, U of
4.   Dartmouth C (NH)
5.   Montana State U
6.   Washington, U of
7.   Oregon State U
8.   Boise State U (ID)
9.   Southern California, U of
10. California, U of, Berkeley

Source: The Ski Channel (theskichannel.com)

SOCCER

Colleges With the Most Men's Division I Soccer Championships

The name of the school is followed by the number of men's soccer Division I championships in the past 55 years.

St. Louis U (MO): 10
Indiana U, Bloomington: 8
Virginia, U of: 6
California, U of, Los Angeles: 4
San Francisco, U of (CA): 4
Maryland, U of, College Park: 3
Clemson U (SC): 2
Connecticut, U of: 2
Michigan State U: 2
North Carolina, U of, Chapel Hill: 2
Akron, U of (OH): 1

California, U of, Santa Barbara: 1
Duke U (NC): 1
Hartwick C (NY): 1
Howard U (DC): 1
Pennsylvania, U of, West Chester: 1
Santa Clara U (CA): 1
Southern Illinois U, Edwardsville: 1
St. John's U (NY): 1
U.S. Naval Academy (MD): 1
Wake Forest U (NC): 1
Wisconsin, U of, Madison: 1

Source: Sports Illustrated Almanac

Colleges With the Most Division II Men's Soccer Championships

The name of the school is followed by the number of men's soccer Division II championships in the past 40 years.

Southern Connecticut State U: 6
Seattle Pacific U (WA): 5
Ft. Lewis C (CO): 3
Lynn U (FL): 3
Tampa, U of (FL): 3
Alabama A&M U: 2
California State U, Dominguez Hills: 2
Florida Institute of Technology: 2
Florida International U: 2
Adelphi U (NY): 1
Baltimore, U of (MD): 1
California State U, Bakersfield: 1

California State U, Sonoma: 1
Dowling C (NY): 1
Franklin Pierce U (NH): 1
Grand Canyon U (AZ): 1
Loyola U (MD): 1
Missouri, U of, St. Louis: 1
Northern Kentucky U: 1
Pennsylvania, U of, Lock Haven: 1
Seattle U (WA): 1
Southern Illinois U, Edwardsville: 1
Southern New Hampshire U: 1

Source: Sports Illustrated Almanac

Colleges With the Most Men's Division III Soccer Championships

The name of the school is followed by the number of men's soccer Division III championships over the past 40 years.

Messiah C (PA): 10
North Carolina, U of, Greensboro: 5
Babson C (MA): 3
California, U of, San Diego: 3
Ohio Wesleyan U: 2
Pennsylvania, U of, Lock Haven: 2
Rowan U (NJ): 2
Wheaton C (IL): 2
Bethany C (WV): 1
Brandeis U (MA): 1

Elizabethtown C (PA): 1
Kean U (NJ): 1
Middlebury C (VT): 1
New Jersey, C of: 1
New York, State U of, Brockport: 1
Richard Stockton C (NJ): 1
St. Lawrence U (NY): 1
Trinity U (TX): 1
Williams C (MA): 1

Source: Sports Illustrated Almanac

Colleges With the Most Women's Division I Soccer Championships

The name of the school is followed by the number of women's soccer Division I championships in the past 30 years.

North Carolina, U of, Chapel Hill: 21
Notre Dame, U of (IN): 3
Portland, U of (OR): 2
California, U of, Los Angeles: 1
Florida State U: 1

Florida, U of: 1
George Mason U (VA): 1
Santa Clara U (CA): 1
Southern California, U of: 1
Stanford U (CA): 1

Source: Sports Illustrated Almanac

Steven R. Antonoff

Colleges With the Most Women's Division II Soccer Championships

The name of the school is followed by the number of women's soccer Division II championships in the past 25 years.

Franklin Pierce U (NH): 5
Grand Valley State U (MI): 4
Barry U (FL): 3
California, U of, San Diego: 2
Metro State U (CO): 2
California State U, Dominguez Hills: 1
California State U, Hayward: 1
California State U, Sonoma: 1

Christian Brothers U (TN): 1
Kennesaw State U (GA): 1
Lynn U (FL): 1
Nebraska, U of, Omaha: 1
Seattle Pacific U (WA): 1
St. Rose, C of (NY): 1
Tampa, U of (FL): 1
West Florida, U of: 1

Source: Sports Illustrated Almanac

Colleges With the Most Women's Division III Soccer Championships

The name of the school is followed by the number of women's soccer Division III championships over the past 30 years.

California, U of, San Diego: 5
Messiah C (PA): 5
New Jersey, C of: 3
Wheaton C (IL): 3
Ithaca C (NY): 2
Ohio Wesleyan U: 2
Rochester, U of (NY): 2

William Smith C (NY): 2
Hardin-Simmons U (TX): 1
Lynchburg C (VA): 1
Macalester C (MN): 1
New York, State U of, Cortland State: 1
New York, State U of, Oneonta: 1

Source: Sports Illustrated

Colleges With Great Club Soccer Teams

Arkansas, U of, Fayetteville
Arizona, U of
Bloomsburg U (PA)
Boston U (MA)
Brigham Young U (UT)
California, U of, Berkeley
Cincinnati, U of (OH)
Colorado, U of, Boulder
Cornell U (NY)
Dickinson C (PA)
Houston, U of (TX)
Indiana U (PA)
James Madison U (VA)
Kansas State U
Messiah C (PA)
Michigan State U

Michigan, U of, Ann Arbor
North Dakota State U
Northeastern U (MA)
Pennsylvania, U of
Rice U (TX)
Southwestern Oklahoma State U
Syracuse U (NY)
Texas A&M U, College Station
Texas, U of, Austin
Truman State U (MO)
Virginia, U of
Oregon, U of
Washington U (MO)
West Virginia U
Yale U (CT)

Source: NIRSA: Leaders in Collegiate Recreation (nirsa.net)

ATHLETICS

SOFTBALL

Colleges With Successful Women's Division I Softball

These colleges were either champions and/or runners-up within the past 30 years.

Alabama, U of, Tuscaloosa
Arizona, U of
Arizona State U
California, U of, Berkeley
California, U of, Los Angeles
California State U, Fresno
California State U, Fullerton
California State U, Northridge

Florida, U of
Michigan, U of, Ann Arbor
Nebraska, U of, Lincoln
Northwestern U (IL)
Oklahoma, U of
Tennessee, U of, Knoxville
Texas A&M U, College Station
Washington, U of

Source: National Collegiate Athletic Association (ncaa.org)

Colleges With Successful Women's Division II Softball

The following colleges were champions and/or runners-up in the past 30 years.

California State U, Sacramento
California U of Pennsylvania
Central Oklahoma, U of
Dixie State U (UT)
Emporia State U (KS)
Florida Southern C
Georgia C
Grand Valley State U (MI)
Hawaii Pacific U
Humboldt State U (CA)
Kennesaw State U (GA)
Kutztown U (PA)
Lewis U (IL)
Lock Haven U (PA)

Lynn U (FL)
Merrimack C (MA)
Missouri Southern State U
Nebraska, U of, Omaha
Nebraska, U of, Kearney
Nebraska, U of, Omaha
North Dakota State U
North Georgia C & State U
Southern Illinois U, Edwardsville
St. Mary's U (TX)
Stephen F. Austin State U (TX)
Valdosta State U (GA)
West Texas A&M U
Wisconsin, U of, Parkside

Source: National Collegiate Athletic Association (ncaa.org)

SQUASH

Colleges With Strength in Squash

Amherst C (MA)
Bard C (NY)
Bates C (ME)
Boston C (MA)
Boston U (MA)
Bowdoin C (ME)
Brandeis U (MA)
Brown U (RI)

Bryant U (RI)
Bucknell U (PA)
California, U of, Berkeley
Charleston, C of (SC)
Chicago, U of (IL)
Colby C (ME)
Colgate U (NY)
Columbia U (NY)

Connecticut C
Cornell U (NY)
Dartmouth C (NH)
Davidson C (NC)
Denison U (OH)
Dickinson C (PA)
Drexel U (PA)
Duke U (NC)
Fordham U (NY)
Franklin & Marshall C (PA)
George Washington U (DC)
Georgetown U (DC)
Hamilton C (NY)
Harvard U (MA)
Haverford C (PA)
Illinois, U of, Urbana
Illinois, U of, Springfield
Ithaca C (NY)
Johns Hopkins U (MD)
Kenyon C (OH)
Lafayette C (PA)
Lehigh U (PA)
Maryland, U of, College Park
Miami, U of (FL)
Middlebury C (VT)
Minnesota, U of, Twin Cities
Massachusetts Institute of Technology
Mt. Holyoke C (MA)
U.S. Naval Academy (MD)
New York U
North Carolina, U of, Chapel Hill
Northeastern U (MA)

Northwestern U (IL)
Notre Dame, U of (IN)
Ohio State U, Columbus
Oregon, U of
Pennsylvania State U, University Park
Pennsylvania, U of
Princeton U (NJ)
Purdue U (IN)
Rhodes C (TN)
Richmond, U of (VA)
Rochester, U of (NY)
South, U of the (TN)
Siena C (NY)
Smith C (MA)
Southern California, U of
St. Lawrence U (NY)
Stanford U (CA)
Swarthmore C (PA)
Trinity C (CT)
Tufts U (MA)
Vanderbilt U (TN)
Vassar C (NY)
Vermont, U of
Virginia, U of
Washington U (MO)
Washington, U of
Wellesley C (MA)
Wesleyan U (CT)
Western Ontario, U of (Canada)
William Smith C (NY)
Williams C (MA)
Yale U (CT)

Source: College Squash Association (collegesquashassociation.com)

SURFING

Colleges With Strong Surfing Teams

These colleges are a part of the National Scholastic Surfing Association.

California State U, Channel Islands
California State U, San Diego
California State U, San Marcos
California, U of, San Diego
California, U of, Santa Barbara
Central Florida, U of
Daytona State C (FL)

Flagler C (FL)
Florida Atlantic U
Florida Institute of Technology
Mira Costa C (CA)
North Florida, U of
Point Loma Nazarene U (CA)
Saddleback C (CA)

SWIMMING

Colleges With Highly Ranked Men's Division I Swimming & Diving

These Division I colleges had the highest rankings in a recent year, according to the College Swimming Coaches Association of America.

Alabama, U of, Tuscaloosa
Arizona, U of
Auburn U (AL)
California, U of, Berkeley
Florida, U of
Georgia, U of
Harvard U (MA)
Indiana U, Bloomington
Iowa, U of
Louisville, U of (KY)
Michigan, U of, Ann Arbor
Minnesota, U of, Twin Cities
Missouri, U of, Columbia

North Carolina State U
North Carolina, U of, Chapel Hill
Ohio State U, Columbus
Pennsylvania State U, University Park
Southern California, U of
Stanford U (CA)
Tennessee, U of, Knoxville
Texas, U of, Austin
Utah, U of
Virginia Polytechnic Institute & State U
Virginia, U of
Wisconsin, U of, Madison

Source: National Collegiate Athletic Association (ncaa.org)

Colleges With Highly Ranked Women's Division I Swimming & Diving

These Division I colleges had the highest rankings in a recent year, according to the College Swimming Coaches Association of America.

Arizona, U of
Auburn U (AL)
California State U, San Diego
California, U of, Berkeley
California, U of, Los Angeles
Florida, U of
Georgia, U of
Indiana U, Bloomington
Louisiana State U, Baton Rouge
Louisville, U of (KY)
Michigan, U of, Ann Arbor
Minnesota, U of, Twin Cities
Missouri, U of, Columbia

North Carolina State U
North Carolina, U of, Chapel Hill
Ohio State U, Columbus
Purdue U (IN)
Southern California, U of
Southern Methodist U (TX)
Stanford U (CA)
Tennessee, U of, Knoxville
Texas A&M U, College Station
Texas, U of, Austin
Virginia, U of
Wisconsin, U of, Madison

Source: National Collegiate Athletic Association (ncaa.org)

Colleges With Notable Synchronized Swimming Teams

Arizona State U
Arizona, U of
Boston U (MA)
Canisius C (NY)
Carleton C (MN)
Central Florida, U of

Colorado State U, Ft. Collins
Florida, U of
Incarnate Word, U of the (TX)
Lindenwood U (MO)
Miami U (OH)
Michigan, U of, Ann Arbor

Minnesota, U of, Twin Cities
Ohio State U, Columbus
Ohio U, Athens
Pennsylvania State U, University Park
Pennsylvania, U of

Richmond, U of (VA)
Smith C (MA)
Stanford U (CA)
Wheaton C (MA)
William & Mary, C of (VA)

Source: Team USA (teamusa.org)

TABLE TENNIS

Schools With Strength in Table Tennis

Alabama, U of, Birmingham
Central Michigan U
Colorado State U, Ft. Collins
Colorado, U of, Boulder
Florida Atlantic U
Greenville C (IL)
Johns Hopkins U (MD)

New Jersey, C of
New York, State U of, Geneseo
Santa Fe C (FL)
Shippensburg U (PA)
Texas A&M U, College Station
Valparaiso U (IN)
Vanderbilt U (TN)

Source: National Collegiate Table Tennis Association (nctta.org)

TENNIS

Highly Ranked Men's Division I Tennis Teams

These Division I colleges had the highest rankings in a recent year, according to the Intercollegiate Tennis Association.

Baylor U (TX)
California, U of, Los Angeles
Columbia U (NY)
Duke U (NC)
Florida, U of
Georgia, U of
Illinois, U of, Urbana
Minnesota, U of, Twin Cities
Mississippi State U
Mississippi, U of
North Carolina, U of, Chapel Hill
Ohio State U, Columbus
Oklahoma, U of

San Diego, U of (CA)
South Florida, U of
Southern California, U of
Stanford U (CA)
Texas A&M U, College Station
Texas Christian U
Texas Tech U
Texas, U of, Austin
Vanderbilt U (TN)
Virginia Polytechnic Institute & State U
Virginia, U of
Wake Forest U (NC)

Source: National Collegiate Athletic Association (ncaa.org)

Highly Ranked Women's Division I Tennis Teams

These Division I colleges had the highest rankings in a recent year, according to the Intercollegiate Tennis Association.

Alabama, U of, Tuscaloosa
Baylor U (TX)
California, U of, Berkeley
California, U of, Los Angeles
Clemson U (SC)
Duke U (NC)
Florida, U of
Georgia Institute of Technology
Georgia, U of
Kentucky, U of
Louisiana State U
Miami, U of (FL)
Michigan, U of, Ann Arbor

Mississippi, U of
North Carolina, U of, Chapel Hill
Ohio State U
Oklahoma State U
Pepperdine U (CA)
Southern California, U of
Stanford U (CA)
Texas A&M U, College Station
Texas Christian U
Texas Tech U
Vanderbilt U (TN)
Virginia, U of

Source: National Collegiate Athletic Association (ncaa.org)

TRACK & FIELD

Prominent Men's Track & Field Teams

Akron, U of (OH)
Alabama, U of, Tuscaloosa
Arizona State U
Arkansas, U of, Fayetteville
Baylor U (TX)
Brigham Young U (UT)
Clemson U (SC)
Colorado, U of, Boulder
Florida, U of
Florida State U
Georgetown U (DC)
Georgia, U of
Illinois, U of, Urbana
Iowa State U
Kansas State U
Louisiana State U
Nebraska, U of

Ohio State U, Columbus
Oklahoma State U
Oregon, U of
Pennsylvania State U, University Park
South Carolina, U of
Southern California, U of
Stanford U (CA)
Syracuse U (NY)
Tennessee, U of, Knoxville
Texas, U of, Arlington
Texas, U of, Austin
Texas A&M U, College Station
Texas Christian U
Texas Tech U
Virginia, U of
Virginia Polytechnic Institute & State U
Washington, U of

Source: National Collegiate Athletic Association (ncaa.org)

ATHLETICS

Winning Women's Track & Field Teams

These Division I colleges had the highest rankings in a recent year, according to the U.S.
Track & Field and Cross Country Coaches Association.

Akron, U of (OH)
Alabama, U of, Tuscaloosa
Arizona State U
Arkansas, U of, Fayetteville
Baylor U (TX)
Clemson U (SC)
Florida State U
Florida, U of
Georgetown U (DC)
Georgia, U of
Kansas State U
Kansas, U of
Kentucky, U of
Louisiana State U, Baton Rouge
Miami, U of (FL)
Michigan, U of, Ann Arbor

Michigan State U
Mississippi State U
Missouri, U of, Columbia
Nebraska, U of, Lincoln
Notre Dame, U of (IN)
Oklahoma, U of
Oregon, U of
Providence C (RI)
Southern California, U of
Southern Illinois U, Carbondale
Stanford U (CA)
Texas A&M U, College Station
Texas Tech U
Texas, U of, Austin
Virginia Polytechnic Institute & State U
Wisconsin, U of, Madison

Source: National Collegiate Athletic Association (ncaa.org)

TRAP SHOOTING

Schools With Trap Shooting

Alaska, U of, Southeast
Arizona, U of
Cameron U (OK)
Colby Community C (KS)
Colorado State U, Ft. Collins
Delaware, U of
Delta State U (MS)
Eastern Kentucky U
Ecclesia C (AR)
Emmanuel C (GA)
Ferrum C (VA)
Florida, U of
Ft. Hays State U (KS)
Garden City Community C (KS)
George Mason U (VA)
Hillsdale C (MI)
Idaho, U of
Illinois, U of, Urbana
Iowa State U
Kansas State U
Kentucky, U of
Lindenwood U (MO)
Louisiana Tech U
Louisiana, U of, Baton Rouge

Maine, U of, Machias
Missouri, U of, Columbia
Middle Tennessee State U
Missouri State U
Missouri, U of, Science & Technology
Montana, U of
Nebraska, U of, Omaha
New York, State U of, Cortland
North Dakota State U
Northwest C (WY)
Pine Technical C (MN)
Purdue U (IN)
Schreiner U (TX)
Seattle U (WA)
South Carolina, U of, Aiken
Southeastern Illinois C
Texas A&M U, College Station
Trinity U (TX)
U.S. Air Force Academy (CO)
U.S. Merchant Marine Academy (NY)
U.S. Military Academy (NY)
U.S. Naval Academy (MD)
Vermont, U of
Virginia Polytechnic Institute & State U

Washington C (MD)
Wisconsin, U of, Platteville

Wyoming, U of
Yale U (CT)

Source: NRA Competitive Shooting Programs (competitions.nra.org)

ULTIMATE FRISBEE

Colleges With Strength in Ultimate Frisbee

Brown U (RI)
California, U of, Berkeley
California, U of, San Diego
California, U of, Santa Barbara
California, U of, Santa Cruz
Carleton C (MN)
Carnegie Mellon U (PA)
Central Florida, U of
Chabot C (CA)
Colorado, U of, Boulder
Cornell U (NY)
Delaware, U of
East Carolina U (NC)
Florida, U of
Georgia Institute of Technology
Georgia, U of
Harvard U (MA)
Illinois, U of, Urbana
Indiana, U of, Bloomington
Iowa, U of

Kansas, U of
Massachusetts, U of, Amherst
Michigan State U
Michigan, U of, Ann Arbor
Missouri State U
New York, State U of, Purchase
North Carolina State U
North Carolina, U of, Chapel Hill
North Carolina, U of, Wilmington
Oregon, U of
Pennsylvania State U, University Park
Pittsburgh, U of (PA)
Princeton U (NJ)
Stanford C (CA)
Texas, U of, Austin
Tufts U (MA)
Wesleyan U (CT)
William & Mary, C of (VA)
Williams C (MA)
Wisconsin, U of, Madison

Source: Ultimate Frisbee (ultimatefrisbee.com)

VOLLEYBALL

Winning Men's Division I Volleyball Teams

Ball State U (IN)
Brigham Young U (UT)
California State U, Long Beach
California State U, Northridge
California, U of, Irvine
California, U of, Los Angeles
California, U of, Santa Barbara
Erskine C (SC)
George Mason U (VA)
Grand Canyon U (AZ)
Harvard U (MA)
Hawaii, U of, Manoa
Indiana U-Purdue U, Ft. Wayne

Lewis U (IL)
Limestone C (SC)
Lindenwood U (MO)
Loyola U (IL)
Mt. Olive, U of (NC)
Ohio State U, Columbus
Pennsylvania State U, University Park
Pepperdine U (CA)
Pfeiffer U (NC)
Quincy U (IL)
Southern California, U of
Stanford U (CA)

Source: National Collegiate Athletic Association (ncaa.org)

Winning Women's Division I Volleyball Teams

These colleges were either champions and/or runners-up in the past 30 years.

Brigham Young U (UT)
California State U, Long Beach
California, U of, Berkeley
California, U of, Los Angeles
Florida, U of
Hawaii, U of, Manoa
Illinois, U of, Urbana
Minnesota, U of, Twin Cities
Nebraska, U of, Lincoln

Oregon, U of
Pacific, U of the (CA)
Pennsylvania State U, University Park
Southern California, U of
Stanford U (CA)
Texas, U of, Austin
Washington, U of
Wisconsin, U of, Madison

Source: National Collegiate Athletic Association (ncaa.org)

Winning Women's Division II Volleyball Teams

These colleges were either champions and/or runners-up in the past 30 years.

Augustana C (SD)
Barry U (FL)
Brigham Young U (HI)
California State U, Bakersfield
California State U, Northridge
California State U, Sacramento
California State U, San Bernardino
California, U of, Riverside
Central Missouri, U of
Concordia C (MN)
Grand Valley State U (MI)
Hawaii Pacific U

Nebraska, U of, Kearney
Nebraska, U of, Omaha
North Alabama, U of
North Dakota State U
Northern Michigan U
Portland State U (OR)
South Dakota State U
Southwest Minnesota State U
Tampa, U of (FL)
Truman State U (MO)
West Texas A&M U
Western Washington U

Source: National Collegiate Athletic Association (ncaa.org)

Winning Women's Division III Volleyball Teams

These colleges were either champions and/or runners-up in the past 30 years.

Benedictine U (IL)
California Lutheran U
California, U of, San Diego
Calvin C (MI)
Central C (IA)
Christopher Newport U (VA)
Elmhurst C (IL)
Emory U (GA)
Hope C (MI)
Juniata C (PA)

La Verne, U of (CA)
New York U
Ohio Northern U
St. Thomas U (MN)
Trinity U (TX)
Washington U (MO)
Wisconsin, U of, Oshkosh
Wisconsin, U of, Whitewater
Wittenberg U (OH)

Source: National Collegiate Athletic Association (ncaa.org)

ATHLETICS

WATER POLO

Highly Ranked Men's Water Polo Teams

These colleges had the highest rankings in a recent year.

Brown U (RI)
Bucknell U (PA)
California Baptist U
California State U, Long Beach
California, U of, Berkeley
California, U of, Davis
California, U of, Irvine
California, U of, Los Angeles
California, U of, San Diego
California, U of, Santa Barbara
Loyola Marymount U (CA)

Pacific, U of the (CA)
Pepperdine U (CA)
Princeton U (NJ)
Santa Clara U (CA)
Southern California, U of
St. Francis U (PA)
Stanford U (CA)
U.S. Air Force Academy (CO)
U.S. Naval Academy (MD)
Whittier C (CA)

Source: National Collegiate Athletic Association (ncaa.org)

Highly Ranked Women's Water Polo Teams

These colleges had the highest rankings in a recent year.

Arizona State U
California State U, Northridge
California State U, San Diego
California State U, San Jose
California, U of, Berkeley
California, U of, Davis
California, U of, Irvine
California, U of, Los Angeles
California, U of, San Diego
California, U of, Santa Barbara

Hartwick C (NY)
Hawaii, U of, Manoa
Indiana U, Bloomington
Long Beach State U (CA)
Loyola Marymount U (CA)
Pacific, U of the (CA)
Princeton U (NJ)
Stanford U (CA)
Wagner C (NY)

Source: National Collegiate Athletic Association (ncaa.org)

WATER SKIING

Schools With Division I Water Skiing Teams

Arizona State U
Cincinnati, U of (OH)
Florida Southern C
Grand Valley State U (MI)
Iowa State U
Kansas, U of

Louisiana, U of, Lafayette
Louisiana, U of, Monroe
Michigan State U
Ohio State U
Rollins C (FL)

Schools With Division II Water Skiing Teams

Auburn U (AL)
California State U, Chico
California State U, San Diego
California, U of, Davis
California, U of, Los Angeles
Michigan, U of, Ann Arbor

Texas A&M U, College Station
Texas State U
Texas, U of, Austin
Wisconsin, U of, La Crosse
Wisconsin, U of, Madison

WEIGHTLIFTING

Colleges With Weightlifting Programs

California State U, Sacramento
East Tennessee State U
Lindenwood U (MO)
Louisiana State U, Shreveport
Northern Michigan U

Oklahoma City U
Texas A&M U, College Station
West Virginia U
Wisconsin, U of, Whitewater

Source: Team USA (teamusa.org)

Colleges With Powerlifting Programs

Angelo State U (TX)
Ashland U (OH)
Ball State (IN)
Baton Rouge Community C (LA)
Benedictine C (KS)
California, U of, Los Angeles
Central Michigan U
Clemson U (SC)
Connecticut, U of
Florida, U of
Florida Gulf Coast U
Florida State U
Georgia, U of
Georgia State U
Houston, U of, Downtown (TX)
Illinois, U of, Urbana
Indiana U-Purdue U, Ft. Wayne
Kansas State U
Kansas, U of
Louisiana, U of, Lafayette
Louisiana State U, Baton Rouge
Missouri, U of, Columbia
Nebraska, U of, Lincoln

New York, State U of, Stony Brook
Nicholls State U (LA)
Northeastern U (MA)
Northwestern U (IL)
Ohio State U, Columbus
Our Lady of the Lake C (LA)
Pennsylvania, U of
Pennsylvania State U, University Park
Rutgers U, New Brunswick (NJ)
Sam Houston State U (TX)
Southeastern Louisiana U
Temple U (PA)
Texas, U of, Austin
Texas, U of, San Antonio
Texas A&M U, College Station
Texas Tech U
U.S. Air Force Academy (CO)
U.S. Military Academy (NY)
U.S. Naval Academy (MD)
Virginia Military Institute
West Virginia U
Wisconsin, U of, La Crosse
Yale U (CT)

Source: Powerlifting Watch (powerliftingwatch.com)

WRESTLING

Colleges With High Rankings in NCAA Division I Wrestling

Bucknell U (PA)
Cornell U (NY)
Edinboro U (PA)
Illinois, U of, Urbana
Iowa State U
Iowa, U of
Lehigh U (PA)
Michigan, U of, Ann Arbor
Minnesota, U of, Twin Cities
Missouri, U of, Columbia
North Carolina State U
North Dakota State U

Ohio State U, Columbus
Oklahoma State U
Old Dominion U (VA)
Oregon State U
Pennsylvania State U, University Park
Pittsburgh, U of (PA)
Purdue U (IN)
Rutgers U (NJ)
Virginia Polytechnic Institute & State U
Virginia, U of
Wisconsin, U of, Madison
Wyoming, U of

CHAPTER FIVE
COSTS

AFFORDABILITY/VALUE

The Experts' Choice: Great Value Colleges: The Top Choices

Experts were asked to list colleges that represented top choices based on a comparison of the college's comprehensive cost versus the overall quality of the institution's academic strength and student experience.

Agnes Scott C (GA)
Appalachian State U (NC)
Arizona State U
Arizona, U of
Atlantic, C of the (ME)
Baldwin Wallace U (OH)
Beloit C (WI)
Berea C (KY)
Bethune-Cookman U (FL)
Brigham Young U (UT)
California Polytechnic State U, Pomona
California State U, Bakersfield
California State U, Chico
California State U, Fresno
California State U, Fullerton
California State U, Long Beach
California State U, Sacramento
California State U, Sonoma
California State U, Stanislaus
California, U of, Irvine
California, U of, Riverside
Central Florida, U of
Central Washington U
Citadel, The (SC)
Clemson U (SC)
Colorado State U, Ft. Collins
Cooper Union (NY)
Davidson C (NC)
Delaware, U of
Doane C (NE)
Dominican U (IL)
Eastern Washington U
Evergreen State C (WA)
Fisk U (TN)
Florida State U
Florida, U of
Fresno Pacific U (CA)
George Mason U (VA)
Georgia Institute of Technology
Georgia, U of
Goshen C (IN)
Grand Valley State U (MI)
Grove City C (PA)
Harding U (AR)
Hawaii, U of, Hilo

Hillsdale C (MI)
Holy Family U (PA)
Howard U (DC)
Idaho, C of
Idaho, U of
Illinois C
Illinois State U
Illinois Wesleyan U
Illinois, U of, Chicago
Illinois, U of, Springfield
Jackson State U (MS)
James Madison U (VA)
Keystone C (PA)
La Verne, U of (CA)
Livingstone C (NC)
Longwood U (VA)
Loras College (IA)
Maine, U of, Farmington
Mary Washington, U of (VA)
Marygrove C (MI)
Maryland, U of, College Park
Maryland, U of, Eastern Shore
Michigan Jewish Institute
Michigan State U
Middle Tennessee State U
Midland U (NE)
Minnesota, U of, Twin Cities
Mississippi C
Mississippi State U
Mississippi, U of
Monmouth C (IL)
Montana State U, Bozeman
Montana State U, Northern
Montana, U of
Montclair State U (NJ)
Mt. Vernon Nazarene U (OH)
Murray State U (KY)
New C (FL)
New Hampshire, U of
New Jersey City U
New York, City U of, Brooklyn
New York, City U of, City C
New York, City U of, Hunter
New York, City U of, Lehman
New York, State U of, Binghamton

New York, State U of, Buffalo
Nicholls State U (LA)
North Carolina Central U
North Carolina State U, Raleigh
North Carolina, U of, Asheville
North Carolina, U of, Chapel Hill
North Carolina, U of, Wilmington
Northland C (WI)
Northwestern C (IA)
Northwestern Oklahoma State U
Ohio State U
Oklahoma State U
Oklahoma, U of
Oregon State U
Oregon, U of
Ozarks, C of the (MO)
Pennsylvania State U, Abington
Pennsylvania State U, Wilkes-Barre
Pennsylvania State U, Schuylkill
Pittsburg State U (KS)
Pittsburgh, U of (PA)
Pittsburgh, U of, Greensburgh (PA)
Plymouth State U (NH)
Prairie View A&M U (TX)
Presbyterian C (SC)
Richmond, U of (VA)
Ripon C (WI)
Robert Morris U (IL)
Rutgers U, Newark (NJ)
Salem C (NC)
Sam Houston State U (TX)
Seton Hill U (NJ)
Shippensburg U (PA)
Simpson C (IA)
Slippery Rock U (PA)
Soka U (CA)
South Carolina, U of, Columbia
South Dakota State U
South, U of the (TN)
Southern U (LA)
St. Edward's U (TX)
St. Joseph's C (NY)
St. Mary-of-the-Woods C (IN)

Tennessee State U
Tennessee, U of, Fayetteville
Texas A&M International U
Texas A&M U, College Station
Texas A&M U, Kingsville
Texas State U, San Marcos
Texas Tech U
Texas Woman's U
Texas, U of, Austin
Texas, U of, Pan-American
Towson U (MD)
Transylvania U (KY)
Trinity Lutheran C (WA)
Truman State U (MO)
U.S. Air Force Academy (CO)
U.S. Coast Guard Academy (CT)
U.S. Merchant Marine Academy (NY)
U.S. Military Academy (NY)
U.S. Naval Academy (MD)
Ursuline C (OH)
Utah, U of
Vanderbilt U (TN)
Vermont, U of
Virginia, U of
Virginia Military Institute
Virginia Polytechnic Institute & State U
Virginia State U
Washington, U of, Bothell
Washington, U of, Seattle
Wayland Baptist U (TX)
Wayne State C (NE)
Western Michigan U
Western Washington U
Westminster C (MO)
Wheaton C (IL)
Willamette C (OR)
William & Mary, C of (VA)
Wisconsin, U of, Eau Claire
Wisconsin, U of, Green Bay
Wisconsin, U of, Madison
Wisconsin, U of, Stevens Point
Wyoming, U of

Steven R. Antonoff

The Experts' Choice: Great Value Colleges: The Second Choices

Experts were asked to list colleges that represented good choices based on a comparison of the college's comprehensive cost versus the overall quality of the institution's academic strength and student experience.

Alice Lloyd C (KY)
Asbury U (KY)
Augustana C (SD)
Belhaven U (MS)
California State U, Channel Islands
California State U, East Bay
California State U, Northridge
California State U, San Bernardino
California State U, San Diego
California State U, San Marcos
Christian Brothers U (TN)
Claflin U (SC)
Coker C (SC)
Colorado State U, Pueblo
Concordia U (NE)
Crown C (MN)
East Carolina U (NC)
East Stroudsburg U (PA)
Elizabeth City State U (NC)
Elmhurst C (IL)
Fayetteville State U (NC)
Florida Memorial U
Geneva C (PA)
Georgian Court U (NJ)
Hannibal-LaGrange U (MO)
Hanover C (IN)
Humphreys C (CA)
Huntington U (IN)
Lane C (TN)
Le Moyne-Owen C (TN)
Lincoln Memorial U (TN)
Lincoln U (CA)
Maharishi U of Management (IA)
Maine Maritime Academy
Marian U (IN)
Martin Luther C (MN)
Martin Methodist C (TN)
Michigan, U of, Dearborn
MidAmerica Nazarene U (KS)
Monroe C (NY)
Morningside C (IA)
Morris College (SC)
Mt. Olive C (NC)
New York, City U of, Baruch
New York, City U of, Queens
New York, State U of, C at Brockport

North Carolina A&T State U
North Carolina, U of, Charlotte
North Carolina, U of, Greensboro
Northeastern State U (OK)
Northern Iowa, U of
Northland International U (WI)
Northwest Christian U (OR)
Ouachita Baptist U (AR)
Pennsylvania State U, Fayette-Eberly
Pennsylvania State U, New Kensington
Pennsylvania State U, Shenango
Pittsburgh, U of, Johnstown (PA)
Principia C (IL)
Radford U (VA)
Ramapo C (NJ)
Rhode Island C
Rust C (MS)
Rutgers U, Camden (NJ)
Savannah State U (GA)
South Carolina, U of, Upstate
Southeastern Oklahoma State U
Southern Wesleyan U (SC)
St. Francis, U of (IN)
St. Peter's U (NJ)
St. Thomas U (FL)
St. Vincent C (PA)
Tennessee Technological U
Texas, U of, Dallas
Texas, U of, El Paso
Tougaloo C (MS)
Utah State U
Virginia, U of, Wise
Voorhees C (SC)
Warner U (FL)
Washington, U of, Tacoma
Waynesburg U (PA)
Webb Institute (NY)
Wells C (NY)
Wesleyan C (GA)
Western Illinois U
Westfield State U (MA)
William Carey U (MS)
Williams Baptist C (AR)
Winston-Salem State U (NC)
Wisconsin, U of, La Crosse

Educate To Career Ranking of Good Value Colleges

The ETC College Rankings Index places major emphasis on the workforce preparedness and the improvement in earnings and employability that graduates derive from attending a particular college. The index empirically determines the economic value added by each of the 1,182 colleges ranked within its system.

1. North Carolina, U of, Chapel Hill
2. California, U of, Irvine
3. Virginia, U of
4. William & Mary, C of (VA)
5. Citadel, The (SC)
6. Michigan, U of, Ann Arbor
7. Florida, U of
8. New Hampshire, U of
9. Vermont, U of
10. California, U of, Los Angeles
11. James Madison U (VA)
12. Bob Jones U (SC)
13. California State U, San Marcos
14. Berea C (KY)
15. New Jersey, C of
16. California, U of, Merced
17. California State U, Los Angeles
18. St. John's U (NY)
19. California, U of, Berkeley
20. Connecticut, U of
21. Brigham Young U (UT)
22. New York, State U of, Geneseo
23. Truman State U (MO)
24. St. Benedict, C of (MN)
25. St. Vincent C (PA)
26. California, U of, Riverside
27. Iowa, U of
28. California State U, Stanislaus
29. Mary Washington, U of (VA)
30. Westminster C (PA)
31. St. Michael's C (VT)
32. California, U of, Santa Barbara
33. St. Mary's C (IN)
34. Wofford C (SC)
35. Moravian C (PA)
36. California, U of, San Diego
37. Maryland, U of, College Park
38. Massachusetts Maritime Academy
39. Maine, U of, Farmington
40. Gustavus Adolphus C (MN)
41. Brigham Young U (ID)
42. Northern Iowa, U of
43. California, U of, Santa Cruz
44. Delaware, U of
45. Stonehill C (MA)
46. New York, State U of, Brockport
47. Wisconsin, U of, Madison
48. Messiah C (PA)
49. California, U of, Davis
50. Virginia Polytechnic Institute & State U
51. Harvard U (MA)
52. DeSales U (PA)
53. New York, State U of, Cortland
54. Clemson U (SC)
55. Susquehanna U (PA)
56. California State U, Fresno
57. East Carolina U (NC)
58. Baldwin Wallace U (OH)
59. Georgia, U of
60. Illinois, U of, Springfield
61. North Carolina State U, Raleigh
62. La Salle U (PA)
63. Bentley U (MA)
64. New York, State U of, Binghamton
65. DePauw U (IN)
66. Bryant U (RI)
67. John Brown U (AR)
68. Vanderbilt U (TN)
69. Vassar C (NY)
70. Shippensburg U (PA)
71. St. Olaf C (MN)
72. Portland, U of (OR)
73. Creighton U (NE)
74. Clarkson U (NY)
75. Wellesley C (MA)
76. Texas A&M U, College Station
77. Wheaton C (IL)
78. Notre Dame, U of (IN)
79. Washington, U of, Seattle
80. Nebraska, U of, Kearney
81. John Carroll U (OH)
82. North Carolina, U of, Greensboro
83. Concordia C (MN)
84. Keene State C (NH)
85. California State U, Dominguez Hills
86. Yale U (CT)
87. Appalachian State U (NC)
88. Plymouth State U (NH)
89. Bloomsburg U (PA)
90. California State U, San Bernardino
91. Bethel U (MN)
92. North Carolina, U of, Charlotte
93. Massachusetts C of Pharmacy & Health Sciences
94. California State U, San Diego

Steven R. Antonoff

95. New York, State U of, Buffalo
96. Babson C (MA)
97. St. Norbert C (WI)

98. Slippery Rock U (PA)
99. Providence C (RI)
100. South Carolina, U of, Columbia

Sources:
ETC College Rankings Index
Copyright 2015
By Educate To Career *www.educatetocareer.org*
Link to rankings *https://www.jobsearchintelligence.com/etc/college-rankings.php*

Colleges That Meet the Financial Needs of Students

The percentage listed represents the amount of need that was met for students who were awarded need-based aid. We like the sound of "one hundred percent." It just has a nice ring to it, you know?

Amherst C (MA): 100%
Arlington Baptist C (TX): 100%
Barnard C (NY): 100%
Bates C (ME): 100%
Blessing-Rieman C of Nursing (IL): 100%
Boston C (MA): 100%
Bowdoin C (ME): 100%
Brown U (RI): 100%
Bryn Mawr C (PA): 100%
California Institute of Technology: 100%
Carleton C (MN): 100%
Chicago, U of (IL): 100%
Claremont McKenna C (CA): 100%
Colby C (ME): 100%
Colgate U (NY): 100%
Columbia U (NY): 100%
Cornell U (NY): 100%
Dartmouth C (NH): 100%
Davidson C (NC): 100%
Georgetown U (DC): 100%
Grinnell C (IA): 100%
Hamilton C (NY): 100%
Harvard U (MA): 100%
Harvey Mudd C (CA): 100%
Haverford C (PA): 100%
Holy Cross, C of the (MA): 100%
Johns Hopkins U (MD): 100%
Macalester C (MN): 100%
Massachusetts Institute of Technology: 100%
Middlebury C (VT): 100%

Mt. Holyoke C (MA): 100%
North Carolina, U of, Chapel Hill: 100%
Northwestern U (IL): 100%
Notre Dame, U of (IN): 100%
Oberlin C (OH): 100%
Occidental C (CA): 100%
Pennsylvania, U of: 100%
Pitzer C (CA): 100%
Pomona C (CA): 100%
Princeton U (NJ): 100%
Reed C (OR): 100%
Rice U (TX): 100%
Richmond, U of (VA): 100%
Scripps C (CA): 100%
Smith C (MA): 100%
Southern California, U of: 100%
Stanford U (CA): 100%
Swarthmore C (PA): 100%
Thomas Aquinas C (CA): 100%
Trinity C (CT): 100%
Tufts U (MA): 100%
Vanderbilt U (TN): 100%
Vassar C (NY): 100%
Virginia, U of: 100%
Wake Forest U (NC): 100%
Washington & Lee U (VA): 100%
Washington U (MO): 100%
Wellesley C (MA): 100%
Wesleyan U (CT): 100%
Williams C (MA): 100%
Yale U (CT): 100%

Source: Wintergreen Orchard House

COSTS

The Experts' Choice: Affordable State Universities

Experts named quality state universities that are affordable to an out-of-state student.

Alabama, U of, Tuscaloosa
Appalachian State U (NC)
Auburn U (AL)
Clemson U (SC)
Delaware, U of
Florida State U
Georgia, U of
Kansas, U of
Kentucky, U of
Louisiana, U of, Monroe
Massachusetts, U of, Amherst
Miami U (OH)
Minnesota, U of, Twin Cities

Mississippi, U of
Montana State U
Montana, U of
North Carolina State U
North Carolina, U of, Chapel Hill
Pennsylvania State U
Rutgers U (NJ)
South Carolina, U of
Truman State U (MO)
Utah, U of
Vermont, U of
West Virginia U
Wyoming, U of

Colleges Doing the Most for Low-Income Students

Pell Grants are federal grants awarded to undergraduate students on the basis of a student's financial need. Pell Grants are usually awarded to families earning less than $70,000. The following colleges had the highest product of the "average share of the freshman class that received a Pell Grant in 2011–2015" and "graduation rate for recent Pell recipients."

1. California, U of, Irvine: 40%
2. California, U of, Davis: 31%
3. California, U of, Santa Barbara: 31%
4. California, U of, Los Angeles: 28%
5. California, U of, San Diego: 28%
6. Westminster C: 27%
7. Florida U: 24%
8. Knox C (IL): 24%
9. California, U of, Berkeley: 23%
10. Vassar C (NY): 22%
11. Amherst C (MA): 20%
12. North Carolina, U of, Chapel Hill: 18%
13. Pomona C (CA): 18%
14. Washington, U of, Seattle: 17%
15. Wellesley C (MA): 17%
16. Massachusetts Institute of Technology: 15%
17. Harvard U (MA): 15%
18. Davidson C (NC): 14%
19. Princeton U (NJ): 13%
20. Stanford U (CA): 13%

Sources: *The New York Times*, "California's Universities, Still a Source of Opportunity," September 17, 2015; individual colleges; U.S. Department of Education

QuestBridge College Partners

QuestBridge is a nonprofit organization that works to increase the percentage of talented low-income students attending selective colleges and universities. Students fill out an online application, and finalists are chosen on factors including academic performance, financial need, and personal experiences such as having to work while attending school to help support their families. The following "college partners" offer four-year scholarships and admission to selected students.

Amherst C (MA)

Bowdoin C (ME)

Steven R. Antonoff

Brown U (RI)
California Institute of Technology
Carleton C (MN)
Chicago, U of (IL)
Claremont McKenna C (CA)
Colby C (ME)
Colorado C
Columbia U (NY)
Dartmouth C (NH)
Davidson C (NC)
Duke U (NC)
Emory U (GA)
Grinnell C (IA)
Haverford C (PA)
Macalester C (MN)
Massachusetts Institute of Technology
Northwestern U (IL)
Notre Dame, U of (IN)

Oberlin C (OH)
Pennsylvania, U of
Pomona C (CA)
Princeton U (NJ)
Rice U (TX)
Scripps C (CA)
Southern California, U of
Stanford U (CA)
Swarthmore C (PA)
Tufts U (MA)
Vanderbilt U (TN)
Vassar C (NY)
Virginia, U of
Washington & Lee U (VA)
Wellesley C (MA)
Wesleyan U (CT)
Williams C (MA)
Yale U (CT)

Source: QuestBridge (*questbridge.org*)

The Experts' Choice: Meeting the Need of Underrepresented Students

The most selective colleges typically meet the financial requirements of needy students. For this list, experts were asked to name colleges that "try hard to meet the financial need of traditionally underrepresented students."

Albright C (PA)
Arizona State U
Arizona, U of
Bates C (ME)
Beloit C (WI)
Berea C (KY)
Bowdoin C (ME)
Bucknell U (PA)
Case Western Reserve U (OH)
Centre C (KY)
Dartmouth C (NH)
Davidson C (NC)
Denison U (OH)
Earlham C (IN)
Emory U (GA)
Franklin & Marshall C (PA)
Grinnell C (IA)

Haverford C (PA)
Howard U (DC)
Illinois State U
Juniata C (PA)
Lafayette C (PA)
Lake Forrest C (IL)
Minnesota, U of, Twin Cities
Muhlenberg C (PA)
Richmond, U of (VA)
St. Olaf C (MN)
Syracuse U (NY)
Vassar C (NY)
Wabash C (IN)
Westminster C (UT)
Wheaton C (MA)
Wooster, C of (OH)

States Offering Tuition Discounts to Students in Neighboring States

Residents of a state that belongs to one of the clusters listed here may be able to attend a public college in another state at a reduced tuition charge. Programs vary considerably in tuition discounts provided, colleges participating, academic programs available, and admission criteria.

Academic Common Market

Alabama
Arkansas
Delaware
Florida (graduate only)
Georgia
Kentucky
Louisiana
Maryland

Mississippi
North Carolina
Oklahoma
South Carolina
Tennessee
Texas (graduate only)
Virginia
West Virginia

Source: Southern Regional Education Board (*sreb.org*)

Midwest Student Exchange Program

Illinois
Indiana
Kansas
Michigan
Minnesota
Missouri
Nebraska
North Dakota
Wisconsin

Source: Midwest Student Exchange (*mhec.org*)

New England Regional Student Program

Connecticut
Maine
Massachusetts
New Hampshire
Rhode Island
Vermont

Source: New England Board of Higher Education (*nebhe.org*)

Western Undergraduate Exchange

Alaska
Arizona
California
Colorado
Commonwealth of the Northern Mariana
  Islands
Hawaii
Idaho
Montana

Nevada
New Mexico
North Dakota
Oregon
South Dakota
Utah
Washington
Wyoming

Source: Western Undergraduate Exchange (*wiche.edu*)

Colleges and Universities Offering Generous Merit Aid

These colleges have historically provided merit aid to 20% or more of undergraduates. Merit awards are not influenced by financial need of a family but rather are given on the basis of academic performance; qualities such as leadership and community service; or skills and talents in such areas as music, athletics, and art.

Agnes Scott C (GA)
Alabama, U of, Tuscaloosa
Allegheny C (PA)
Auburn U (AL)
Baylor U (TX)
Beloit C (WI)
Bennington C (VT)
Bentley U (MA)
Biola U (CA)
Brigham Young U (UT)
Bryant U (RI)
Butler U (IN)
California Lutheran U
Case Western Reserve U (OH)
Catholic U (DC)
Centre C (KY)
Chapman U (CA)
Clark U (MA)
Clemson U (SC)
Colorado School of Mines
Colorado, U of, Boulder
Cornell C (IA)
Creighton U (NE)
Dayton, U of (OH)
Delaware, U of
Denison U (OH)
Denver, U of (CO)
DePauw U (IN)
Drew U (NJ)
Elon U (NC)
Fairfield U (CT)
Furman U (SC)
George Washington U (DC)
Georgia Institute of Technology
Gonzaga U (WA)
Goucher C (MD)
Gustavus Adolphus C (MN)
Hampshire C (MA)
Harvey Mudd C (CA)
Hendrix C (AR)
Hillsdale C (MI)
Hobart C and William Smith C (NY)
Hofstra U (NY)
Indiana U, Bloomington
Iowa State U
Ithaca C (NY)
Juniata C (PA)
Kalamazoo C (MI)

Kentucky, U of
Lawrence U (WI)
Lewis & Clark C (OR)
Linfield C (OR)
Loyola Marymount U (CA)
Loyola U (IL)
Loyola U (LA)
Manhattan C (NY)
Marquette U (WI)
Menlo C (CA)
Miami, U of (FL)
Millsaps C (MS)
Muhlenberg C (PA)
Nevada, U of, Reno
New C (FL)
Northeastern U (MA)
Oberlin C (OH)
Oklahoma State U
Olin C (MA)
Pepperdine U (CA)
Portland, U of (OR)
Puget Sound, U of (WA)
Quinnipiac U (CT)
Rensselaer Polytechnic Institute (NY)
Rhodes C (TN)
Rider U (NJ)
Rochester, U of (NY)
Rose-Hulman Institute (IN)
Santa Clara U (CA)
Sarah Lawrence C (NY)
South Carolina, U of, Columbia
South, U of the (TN)
Southern Methodist U (TX)
Southwestern U (TX)
St. Anselm C (NH)
St. Benedict, C of/St. John's U (MN)
St. Lawrence U (NY)
St. Louis U (MO)
St. Mary's C (MD)
St. Michael's C (VT)
St. Olaf C (MN)
Stonehill C (MA)
Texas Christian U
Transylvania U (KY)
Trinity U (TX)
Tulane U (LA)
Union C (NY)
Utah, U of

Vermont, U of	Whitworth U (WA)
Wabash C (IN)	Willamette U (OR)
Webb Institute (NY)	Wofford C (SC)
Westmont C (CA)	Wooster, C of, (OH)
Wheaton C (IL)	Worcester Polytechnic Institute (MA)
Wheaton C (MA)	Xavier U (LA)
Whitman C (WA)	

Source: College Kickstart LLC (*college-kickstart.com*)

The Experts' Choice: Money for Excellent Students

Experts identified these colleges as schools that give grants (and not loans) to excellent students.

Case Western Reserve U (OH)	Southern California, U of
Davidson C (NC)	Texas Christian U
Harvard U (MA)	Tulane U (LA)
Miami, U of (FL)	Villanova U (PA)
Northeastern U (MA)	Washington U (MO)
Princeton U (NJ)	Yale U (CT)
Rochester, U of (NY)	

Where Money Is Given to Students Without Financial Need

Smart, talented, driven students deserve a tuition break, whether they have financial need or not. You know the kids we're talking about—the ones who are impossibly brainy, play soccer and the flute, volunteer with blind orphans, and have a perfect smile.

North Greenville U (SC): 98.60%	Oberlin C (OH): 39.04%
Chaminade U (HI): 94.22%	Birmingham-Southern C (AL): 38.74%
Cooper Union (NY): 71.80%	Rhodes C (TN): 38.53%
Newman U (KS): 58.31%	Marquette U (WI): 38.43%
San Francisco Art Institute (CA): 53.32%	Denver, U of (CO): 37.89%
Patrick Henry C (VA): 49.03%	Dayton, U of (OH): 37.74%
Hillsdale C (MI): 48.89%	St. Mary's C (CA): 37.67%
Furman U (SC): 48.37%	Mississippi C: 37.66%
Olin C (MA): 48.10%	Gonzaga U (WA): 37.36%
Denison U (OH): 44.92%	Hendrix C (AR): 37.14%
Samford U (AL): 43.18%	Lindenwood U (MO): 36.95%
Trinity U (TX): 42.40%	Centre C (KY): 36.66%
New England Conservatory of Music (MA): 42.21%	Ouachita Baptist U (AR): 36.33%
Tulsa, U of (OK): 42.15%	Augustana C (IL): 35.92%
Art Institute of Chicago, School of the (IL): 42.09%	Truman State U (MO): 35.86%
Millsaps C (MS): 40.14%	Sierra Nevada C: 35.80%
Henderson State U (AR): 40.09%	Eckerd C (FL): 35.77%
Westminster C (UT): 39.51%	Tulane U (LA): 35.76%
Wooster, C of (OH): 39.17%	Southwestern Oklahoma State U: 35.55%
	Andrews U (MI): 34.95%

Source: Wintergreen Orchard House

Steven R. Antonoff

The Experts' Choice: Merit Money for B Students

Experts identified these colleges as ones that have proven particularly reliable in providing merit scholarships for B students.

Alabama, U of, Tuscaloosa
Allegheny C (PA)
Beloit C (WI)
Birmingham-Southern C (AL)
Carroll C (MT)
Chapman U (CA)
Clark U (MA)
Denver, U of (CO)
Earlham C (IN)
Gonzaga U (WA)
Goucher C (MD)
Hartford, U of (CT)
Hendrlx C (AR)
High Point U (NC)
Hofstra U (NY)
Ithaca C (NY)
Knox C (IL)
Lake Forest C (IL)
Le Moyne C (NY)
Loyola U (IL)
Loyola U (LA)
Marquette U (WI)

Maryville U (MO)
Miami, U of (FL)
Mississippi, U of
Ohio Wesleyan U
Portland, U of (OR)
Puget Sound, U of (WA)
Quinnipiac U (CT)
Redlands, U of (CA)
Rhodes C (TN)
Roanoke C (VA)
Seattle U (WA)
St. Louis U (MO)
Stetson U (FL)
Susquehanna U (PA)
Syracuse U (NY)
Tampa, U of (FL)
Tulane U (LA)
Ursinus C (PA)
Whittier C (CA)
Whitworth C (WA)
Willamette U (OR)
Wooster, C of (OH)

The Experts' Choice: Money for Special Talent to Non-majors

Experts were asked to name colleges known to award talent scholarships (in music, art, theater, etc.) to non-majors.

Carnegie Mellon U (PA)
Ithaca C (NY)
Rochester, U of (NY)
Skidmore C (NY)
St. Olaf C (MN)
Stetson U (FL)

Colleges Offering Community Service Scholarships

Entering first-year students who are active in high school community service projects are eligible to be Bonner Scholars. The following list of colleges include both those that are part of the Bonner Scholar Program and those that are part of the Bonner Leader program. Bonner Scholars receive full-need scholarships from the Bonner Foundation and are expected to engage in 10 hours of community service per week. Financial support in the Bonner Leader Program comes from the institution directly in the form of work-study or scholarships.

Allegheny C (PA)

Augsburg C (MN)

Bates C (ME)
Berea C (KY)
Berry C (GA)
Birmingham-Southern C (AL)
California State U, Sonoma
California, U of, Berkeley
Carson-Newman U (TN)
Centre C (KY)
Charleston, C of (SC)
Christopher Newport U (VA)
Concord U (WV)
Converse C (SC)
Davidson C (NC)
DePauw U (IN)
Earlham C (IN)
Edgewood C (WI)
Emory & Henry C (VA)
Guilford C (NC)
High Point U (NC)
Houston, U of (TX)
Lindsey Wilson C (KY)
Lynchburg C (VA)
Macalester C (MN)
Mars Hill U (NC)
Maryville C (TN)
Middlesex County C (NJ)
Montclair State U (NJ)
Morehouse C (GA)
New Jersey, C of

New Mexico, U of
North Carolina, U of, Chapel Hill
Notre Dame, U of (MD)
Oberlin C (OH)
Our Lady of the Lake C (LA)
Pfeiffer U (NC)
Rhodes C (TN)
Richmond, U of (VA)
Rider U (NJ)
Rollins C (FL)
Rutgers U, Camden (NJ)
Rutgers U, New Brunswick (NJ)
Rutgers U, Newark (NJ)
Siena C (NY)
South, U of the (TN)
Spelman C (GA)
St. Benedict, C of (MN)
Stetson U (FL)
Tampa, U of (FL)
Tusculum C (TN)
Union C (KY)
Ursinus C (PA)
Wagner C (NY)
Warren Wilson C (NC)
Washburn U (KS)
Washington & Lee U (VA)
Waynesburg U (PA)
Widener U (PA)
Wofford C (SC)

Source: Bonner Scholars Program (*bonner.org*)

STICKER PRICE

Colleges With No Tuition

No tuition means just what you think it means: 100% free tuition. (At some of these colleges, it may not include room and board.) Keep in mind that the students who attend these schools are the cream of the crop and have earned their free ride.

Curtis Institute of Music (PA)
Haskell Indian Nations U (KS)
National Intelligence U (DC)
Ozarks, C of the (MO)
U.S. Air Force Academy (CO)
U.S. Coast Guard Academy (CT)
U.S. Merchant Marine Academy (NY)
U.S. Military Academy (NY)
U.S. Naval Academy (MD)

Source: Wintergreen Orchard House

Colleges With No Application Fee

And no fee waivers needed. When it comes to submitting your application, these schools are 100% free! Tuition, however, is another story...

Allegheny C (PA)	Northwest Christian U (OR)
American C of Greece	Prescott C (AZ)
Augustana C (IL)	Rosemont C (PA)
Austin C (TX)	Scranton, U of (PA)
Bethany C (KS)	St. Bonaventure U (NY)
Bryn Athyn C (PA)	St. Peter's U (NJ)
Colby C (ME)	Texas A&M International U
Concordia U (OR)	Texas, U of, Permian Basin
Concordia U, Nebraska	Thiel C (PA)
Eastern New Mexico U	U.S. Air Force Academy (CO)
Eastern Oregon U	U.S. Coast Guard Academy (CT)
Grand Canyon U (AZ)	U.S. Merchant Marine Academy (NY)
Green Mountain C (VT)	U.S. Military Academy (NY)
Holy Names U (CA)	Union C (NE)
Houston Baptist U (TX)	Union C (NY)
Idaho, C of	Wellesley C (MA)
Jamestown, U of (ND)	Whitworth U (WA)
Johnson & Wales U (CO)	Wilson C (PA)
Mercyhurst U (PA)	York C (PA)
Midland U (NE)	

Source: Wintergreen Orchard House

The Experts' Choice: Top-Notch, Reasonable Price

In-state public universities are often more affordable than private universities. Experts were asked to look beyond these in-state options and name colleges that are top-notch yet offer a reasonable price tag for the out-of-state student.

Alabama, U of, Tuscaloosa	Idaho, U of
Arizona State U	Mary Washington, U of (VA)
Austin C (TX)	Miami U (OH)
British Columbia, U of (Canada)	Minnesota, U of, Twin Cities
California Polytechnic State U, San Luis Obispo	Montana State U
California State U, Long Beach	Montana, U of
Case Western Reserve U (OH)	New York, U of, Binghamton
Christopher Newport U (VA)	Olin C (MA)
Clark U (MA)	Rice U (TX)
Cooper Union (NY)	Texas, U of, Austin
Earlham C (IN)	Utah, U of
Elon U (NC)	Virginia, U of
Georgia, U of	Westminster C (MO)
Grove City C (PA)	Wisconsin, U of, Madison
High Point U (NC)	Wooster, C of (OH)

The Experts' Choice: Colleges Worth Every Penny

Amherst C (MA)
Brown U (RI)
California Polytechnic State U, San Luis
   Obispo
California, U of, Los Angeles
Carleton C (MN)
Dartmouth C (NH)
Harvard U (MA)
Kenyon C (OH)
Macalester C (MN)

Massachusetts Institute of Technology
Middlebury C (VT)
North Carolina State U
Northwestern U (IL)
Pennsylvania State U, University Park
Pomona C (CA)
Princeton U (NJ)
Stanford U (CA)
Swarthmore C (PA)

The Experts' Choice: Colleges Worth Taking Out a Second Mortgage

Experts were asked to name colleges for which securing a second mortgage to pay tuition and fees "is particularly justified."

Amherst C (MA)
Boston C (MA)
Boston U (MA)
Brown U (RI)
Bryn Mawr C (PA)
California Polytechnic State U, San Luis
Obispo
Carleton C (MN)
Carnegie Mellon U (PA)
Chicago, U of (IL)
Columbia U (NY)
Cornell U (NY)
Duke U (NC)
Emory U (GA)
Harvard U (MA)

Harvey Mudd C (CA)
Kenyon C (OH)
Massachusetts Institute of Technology
New York U
Northwestern U (IL)
Pomona C (CA)
Princeton U (NJ)
Rice U (TX)
Stanford U (CA)
Washington U (MO)
Wellesley C (MA)
Wesleyan U (CT)
Williams C (MA)
Yale U (CT)

The Experts' Choice: Overpriced Colleges

Experts were asked to list colleges that they considered not worth the expense.

Boston U (MA)
Duke U (NC)
George Washington U (DC)
New York U
Sarah Lawrence C (NY)
Stanford U (CA)
Vanderbilt U (TN)

Colleges That Charge the Most for Room and Board

A high price tag for room and board does not necessarily mean luxurious dorms or gourmet meals. These costs for room and board may reflect the higher cost of living in the area where the school is located.

Hebrew C (MA): $20,000
LIM C (NY): $19,850
Berklee C of Music (MA): $17,372
New York U: $16,782
Hellenic C (MA): $16,192
Jacksonville U (FL): $16,020
Harvey Mudd C (CA): $15,833
Fordham U (NY): $15,810
Bastyr U (WA): $15,550
California, U of, Berkeley: $15,180
Emerson C (MA): $15,096
New York, City U of, Baruch C: $15,048
Cooper Union (NY): $15,000
Marymount Manhattan C (NY): $15,000
Dean C (MA): $14,760

California State U, San Diego: $14,745
California, U of, Merced: $14,718
Fisher C (MA): $14,714
Pomona C (CA): $14,700
Harvard U (MA): $14,669
Southern Methodist U (TX): $14,645
California, U of, Los Angeles: $14,571
Scripps C (CA): $14,562
Manhattanville C (NY): $14,520
Catholic U (DC): $14,518
St. Joseph's U (PA): $14,513
Babson C (MA): $14,494
Quinnipiac U (CT): $14,490
Syracuse U (NY): $14,460

Source: Wintergreen Orchard House

Colleges Known for High Room and Board Charges

American Jewish University (CA)
Art Institute, School of the (IL)
Berklee C of Music (MA)
Boston Conservatory (MA)
California State U, San Diego
California, U of, Berkeley
California, U of, Los Angeles
California, U of, Merced
California, U of, Riverside
California, U of, Santa Cruz
Catholic U (DC)
Claremont McKenna C (CA)
Cooper Union (NY)
Dean C (MA)
Drexel U (PA)
Emerson C (MA)
Eugene Lang C (NY)
Fisher C (MA)
Fordham U, Lincoln Center (NY)
Harvey Mudd C (CA)
Hellenic C (MA)

Lesley U (MA)
Marymount Manhattan C (NY)
New School (NY)
New York School of Interior Design
New York U
New York, State U of, C of
 Environmental Science and Forestry
Olin C (MA)
Pace U (NY)
Pepperdine U (CA)
Pitzer C (CA)
Pomona C (CA)
Quinnipiac U (CT)
Roger Williams U (RI)
San Francisco Art Institute (CA)
Sarah Lawrence C (NY)
Smith C (MA)
St. John's U (NY)
Stevens Institute of Technology (NJ)
Vanderbilt U (TN)

Source: *The College Finder* research

Expensive Public Colleges for an Out-of-State Student

California, U of, Berkeley
California, U of, Davis
California, U of, Irvine
California, U of, Los Angeles
California, U of, Merced
California, U of, Riverside
California, U of, San Diego
California, U of, Santa Barbara
California, U of, Santa Cruz
Colorado School of Mines
Illinois, U of, Urbana
Miami U (OH)
Montclair State U (NJ)
New Hampshire, U of
New Jersey, C of

New Jersey Institute of Technology
Pennsylvania C of Technology
Pennsylvania State U, Altoona
Pennsylvania State U, Berks County
Pennsylvania State U, Erie
Pennsylvania State U, Harrisburg
Pennsylvania State U, University Park
Pittsburgh, U of (PA)
Rutgers U, Camden (NJ)
Rutgers U, New Brunswick (NJ)
Rutgers U, Newark (NJ)
St. Mary's C (MD)
Temple U (PA)
Vermont, U of
William & Mary, C of (VA)

Source: *The College Finder* research, including the College Board

Steven R. Antonoff

CHAPTER SIX
ADMISSION

Factors That Colleges Consider Most Important in Admission

1. Grades in College Preparatory Courses
2. Grades in All Courses
3. Strength of Curriculum
4. Admission Test Scores (SAT, ACT)
5. Essay or Writing Sample
6. Counselor Recommendation
7. Student's Demonstrated Interest
8. Teacher Recommendation
9. Class Rank
10. Subject Test Scores (AP, IB)

Source: National Association for College Admission Counselors (NACAC)

How Selective Is College Admission?

It's not as difficult as you might think. Only a handful of colleges are ultra-selective. Some facts about admission selectivity are provided here.

Less than One   Percent of colleges that accept less than 10% of those who apply

20   Percent of colleges that accept less than 45% of those who apply

65+   Average percent acceptance rate for first-time freshmen

80+   Percent of colleges that admit the majority of students who apply

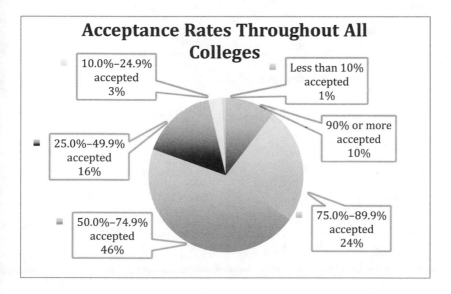

Acceptance Rates Throughout All Colleges

- 10.0%–24.9% accepted 3%
- Less than 10% accepted 1%
- 90% or more accepted 10%
- 25.0%–49.9% accepted 16%
- 75.0%–89.9% accepted 24%
- 50.0%–74.9% accepted 46%

The Experts' Choice: Hottest U.S. Colleges

A college's popularity goes up and down over time. Experts were asked to name one or two schools that are considered "hot" right now.

Alabama, U of, Tuscaloosa
California Polytechnic State U, San Luis
  Obispo
Charleston, C of (SC)
Claremont McKenna C (CA)
Colorado C
Delaware, U of
Duke U (NC)
Elon U (NC)*
George Washington U (DC)
High Point U (NC)
Indiana U Bloomington
Maryland, U of, Baltimore
Massachusetts Institute of Technology
Michigan, U of, Ann Arbor
Muhlenberg C (PA)
New York U
Northeastern U (MA)**
Northwestern U (IL)

Oregon, U of
Rice U (TX)
Richmond, U of (VA)
Santa Clara U (CA)
Southern California, U of
Southern Methodist U (TX)
Stanford U (CA)
Texas State U
Tulane U (LA)
Vanderbilt U (TN)***
Virginia, U of
Wake Forest U (NC)
Washington U (MO)
Wisconsin, U of, Madison

*The Top Choice
**The Second Choice
***The Third Choice

The Drool Schools™: The Most Selective Colleges and/or Most Unpredictable in Terms of Admission

Amherst C (MA)
Brown U (RI)
California Institute of Technology
Chicago, U of (IL)
Columbia U (NY)
Harvard U (MA)
Massachusetts Institute of Technology

Pomona C (CA)
Princeton U (NJ)
Stanford U (CA)
Swarthmore C (PA)
Williams C (MA)
Yale U (CT)

The Drool Schools™: The Second-Most Selective and/or Unpredictable Colleges

Barnard C (NY)
Bates C (ME)
Boston C (MA)
Bowdoin C (ME)
Bryn Mawr C (PA)
Bucknell U (PA)
California, U of, Berkeley
California, U of, Los Angeles
California, U of, San Diego
Carleton C (MN)
Carnegie Mellon U (PA)
Claremont McKenna C (CA)
Colby C (ME)
Colgate U (NY)

Cornell U (NY)
Curtis Institute of Music (PA)
Dartmouth C (NH)
Duke U (NC)
Emory U (GA)
Franklin W. Olin C of Engineering
Georgetown U (DC)
Harvey Mudd C (CA)
Haverford C (PA)
Johns Hopkins U (MD)
Juilliard School (NY)
Michigan, U of, Ann Arbor
Middlebury C (VT)

Steven R. Antonoff

New York U
North Carolina, U of, Chapel Hill
Northwestern U (IL)
Notre Dame, U of (IN)
Oberlin C (OH)
Pennsylvania, U of
Rice U (TX)
Southern California, U of

Tufts U (MA)
Vanderbilt U (TN)
Vassar C (NY)
Virginia, U of
Washington U (MO)
Wellesley C (MA)
Wesleyan U (CT)
William & Mary, C of (VA)

The Drool Schools™: The Third-Most-Selective and/or Unpredictable Colleges

Babson C (MA)
Boston U (MA)
Brandeis U (MA)
California Polytechnic State U, San Luis
    Obispo
California, U of, Davis
California, U of, Irvine
Case Western Reserve U (OH)
Colorado C
Cooper Union (NY)
Connecticut C
Davidson C (NC)
Dickinson C (PA)
Earlham C (IN)
Franklin & Marshall C (PA)
George Washington U (DC)
Georgia Institute of Technology
Grinnell C (IA)
Hamilton C (NY)
Holy Cross, C of the (MA)
Howard U (DC)
Illinois, U of, Urbana
Indiana U Bloomington
Kalamazoo C (MI)
Kenyon C (OH)
Lafayette C (PA)
Lawrence U (WI)
Lehigh U (PA)
Lewis & Clark C (OR)
Macalester C (MN)

Miami U (OH)
Mt. Holyoke C (MA)
New York, State U of, Binghamton
Occidental C (CA)
Oregon, U of
Ozarks, C of the (MO)
Pennsylvania State U, University Park
Pepperdine U (CA)
Pitzer C (CA)
Reed C (OR)
Rensselaer Polytechnic Institute (NY)
Rhode Island School of Design
Richmond, U of (VA)
Rochester, U of (NY)
Scripps C (CA)
Skidmore C (NY)
Smith C (MA)
Texas, U of, Austin
Trinity C (CT)
Tulane U (LA)
U.S. Air Force Academy (CO)
U.S. Military Academy (NY)
U.S. Naval Academy (MD)
Union C (NY)
Villanova U (PA)
Wake Forest U (NC)
Washington, U of, Seattle
Whitman C (WA)
Wisconsin, U of, Madison

The Experts' Choice: Colleges That Have Become More Selective

Experts were asked to identify colleges that have become more selective (in terms of admission) in the last few years.

Boston C (MA)
Case Western Reserve U (OH)
Chicago, U of (IL)

Colorado C
Elon U (NC)
Georgia Institute of Technology

ADMISSION

Northeastern U (MA)*
Richmond, U of (VA)
Santa Clara U (CA)
Southern California, U of
Southern Methodist U (TX)
Texas Christian U

Tulane U (LA)
Vanderbilt U (TN)
Villanova U (PA)
Washington U (MO)

*The Top Choice

Colleges Where the Highest Percentages of Accepted Students Enroll

For a variety of reasons, students admitted to these colleges usually accept their offer of enrollment.

Cambridge C (MA): 100%
City U (WA): 100%
New York, State U of, Oswego: 100%
St. Joseph Seminary C (LA): 100%
Southwest U of Visual Arts (AZ): 98.39%
Middle Georgia State C: 98.27%
InterAmerican U of Puerto Rico, San German: 96.74%
Ozarks, C of the (MO): 96.23%
Rocky Mountain C of Art & Design (CO): 95.52%
Touro C (NY): 93.69%
Guam, U of: 93.67%
InterAmerican U of Puerto Rico, Fajardo: 93.63%
Puerto Rico, U of, Ponce: 93.58%
Puerto Rico, U of, Humacao: 92.99%
Puerto Rico, U of, Mayaguez: 92.99%
Southeastern Baptist Theological Seminary (NC): 92.68%
InterAmerican U of Puerto Rico, Aguadilla: 92.61%
Puerto Rico, U of, Arecibo: 92.10%
Caribbean U (Puerto Rico): 91.53%
New Mexico Institute of Mining and Technology: 90.86%
Puerto Rico, U of, Bayamon: 89.57%
Dalton State C (GA): 88.01%
Laurel U (NC): 87.72%
St. Louis Christian C (MO): 87.50%
Hodges U (FL): 87.18%
Florida C: 87.17%
InterAmerican U of Puerto Rico, Ponce: 86.18%
U.S. Naval Academy (MD): 85.23%
U.S. Military Academy (NY): 85.22%
Universidad Adventista de las Antillas (Puerto Rico): 84.12%
Robert Morris U (PA): 83.90%
Shasta C (CA): 83.33%
Nebraska Methodist C: 83.02%
Trinity Baptist C (FL): 82.98%
American C of Greece: 82.79%
Marshall U (WV): 82.47%
Mayville State U (ND): 82.21%
Harvard U (MA): 81.05%

Source: Wintergreen Orchard House

Colleges That Accept Many Students Through Early Decision

If you always meet your deadlines or even hand in assignments early, you might want to look at these schools. Procrastinators should move on to another list. Listed are the percentages of students applying early decision who were accepted.

Hollins U (VA): 100%
Marlboro C (VT): 100%
Puerto Rico, U of, Arecibo: 100%
Universidad Adventista de las Antillas
  (Puerto Rico): 100%
Kalamazoo C (MI): 96.30%
Virginia Polytechnic Institute & State U:
  95.86%
Merrimack C (MA): 95.65%
Warren Wilson C (NC): 93.18%
Earlham C (IN): 92.86%
Alfred U (NY): 91.84%
DePauw U (IN): 91.80%
Marist C (NY): 90.42%
Ithaca C (NY): 89.89%
St. Lawrence U (NY): 89.53%
High Point U (NC): 89.01%
Furman U (SC): 88.69%
Wabash C (IN): 88.33%
Albany C of Pharmacy & Health
  Sciences (NY): 88.07%

Providence C (RI): 87.65%
Lawrence U (WI): 87.10%
Stonehill C (MA): 87.10%
St. Mary's C (MD): 86.92%
Wagner C (NY): 86.76%
Sacred Heart U (CT): 86.40%
Rhodes C (TN): 85.71%
Puget Sound, U of (WA): 85.00%
Elon U (NC): 84.92%
Hobart & William Smith C (NY): 84.55%
Wittenberg U (OH): 83.98%
Wheaton C (IL): 83.19%
St. Mary's C (CA): 82.76%
Muhlenberg C (PA): 82.15%
Champlain C (VT): 81.96%
Nazareth C (NY): 81.94%
Hampshire C (MA): 81.88%
Grove City C (PA): 81.82%
St. Louis C of Pharmacy (MO): 80.30%
Denison U (OH): 79.82%
Atlantic, C of the (ME): 78.72%

Source: Wintergreen Orchard House

The Experts' Choice: Great Colleges for the A-/B+ Student Who Wants a Balanced Life

Experts were asked to identify colleges for the fine (A-/B+) student who also wants to have fun in college.

Top Choices

Boston U (MA)
Delaware, U of
Elon U (NC)
Indiana U Bloomington
Miami U (OH)
Miami, U of (FL)
Michigan State U
Pennsylvania State U, University Park
Southern Methodist U (TX)

Syracuse U (NY)
Texas Christian U
Texas, U of, Austin
Tulane U (LA)*
Vanderbilt U (TN)
Wisconsin, U of, Madison*

*The Top Choice (tie)

More Choices

Alabama, U of, Tuscaloosa
American U (DC)
Bates C (ME)

California, U of, San Diego
Chapman U (CA)
Clemson U (SC)

Colgate U (NY)
Colorado State U
Colorado, U of, Boulder
Connecticut, U of
Denison U (OH)
Denver, U of (CO)
DePaul U (IL)
Dickinson C (PA)
Drew U (NJ)
Emory U (GA)
Florida State U
Furman U (SC)
George Washington U (DC)

Georgia, U of
New York U
Ohio State U
Oregon State U
Richmond, U of (VA)
Rollins C (FL)
San Diego State U (CA)
Southern California, U of
Trinity U (TX)
Vermont, U of
Villanova U (PA)
Virginia Polytechnic Institute & State U
Wake Forest U (NC)

The Experts' Choice: Great Reputation but Not Too Selective

Experts were asked to name colleges that are less selective (in terms of admission) than might be expected, given their reputations.

American U (DC)
Baylor U (TX)
Boston U (MA)
Bryn Mawr C (PA)
California, U of, Los Angeles
Case Western Reserve U (OH)
Chapman U (CA)
Charleston, C of (SC)
Colorado, U of, Boulder
Delaware, U of
Denver, U of (CO)
DePaul U (IL)
Drexel U (PA)
Furman U (SC)
Gettysburg C (PA)
Goucher C (MD)
Indiana U Bloomington
Iowa, U of
Kansas, U of

Loyola Marymount U (CA)
Miami U (OH)
Miami, U of (FL)
Michigan, U of, Ann Arbor
Missouri, U of, Columbia
Mt. Holyoke C (MA)
Muhlenberg C (PA)
Oregon, U of
Puget Sound, U of (WA)
Purdue U (IN)
Rutgers U (NJ)
Smith C (MA)
South Carolina, U of
Southern Methodist U (TX)
Syracuse U (NY)
Trinity C (CT)
Tulane U (LA)
Vermont, U of

The Experts' Choice: Amazing Colleges That Above Average and Average Students Can Get Into

Experts listed the following colleges as "amazing" ones to which average and above average students can be admitted.

American U (DC)
Appalachian State U (NC)
Boston U (MA)
Case Western Reserve U (OH)
Charleston, C of (SC)
Colorado, U of, Boulder
Creighton U (NE)

Dayton, U of (OH)
Denison U (OH)
Drexel U (PA)
Elon U (NC)
Furman U (SC)
George Mason U (VA)
Hampshire C (MA)

High Point U (NC)
Indiana U Bloomington
Kansas, U of
Lawrence U (WI)
Lewis & Clark C (OR)
Loyola Marymount U (CA)
Miami U (OH)
Montana, U of
Oregon, U of
Pittsburgh, U of (PA)
Puget Sound, U of (WA)
Purdue U (IN)
Rhodes C (TN)

Rochester, U of (NY)**
San Francisco, U of (CA)
Southern Methodist U (TX)
St. Olaf C (MN)
Syracuse U (NY)
Ursinus C (PA)
Vermont, U of
Washington, U of
Willamette U (OR)
Wooster, C of (OH)*

*The Top Choice
**The Second Choice

The Experts' Choice: Terrific Private Universities for a B Student

Experts identified great private universities for a B student with a strong desire for college success.

American U (DC)
Baylor U (TX)
Beloit C (WI)
Brandeis U (MA)
Carroll C (MT)
Case Western Reserve U (OH)
Clark U (MA)
Coe C (IA)
Denison U (OH)
Denver, U of (CO)
DePaul U (IL)
Drake U (IA)
Drew U (NJ)
Drexel U (PA)
Elon U (NC)
Florida Southern C
Fordham U (NY)
Gonzaga U (WA)
Hartford, U of (CT)
Hendrix C (AR)
High Point U (NC)
Hobart C (NY)
Hofstra U (NY)
Indiana U Bloomington
Juniata C (PA)
Lawrence C (WI)
Lewis & Clark C (OR)
Linfield C (OR)

Loyola Marymount U (CA)
Loyola U (MD)
Marquette U (WI)
McDaniel C (MD)
Mercer U (GA)
Muhlenberg C (PA)
Ohio Wesleyan U
Pace U (NY)
Portland, U of (OR)
Providence C (RI)
Puget Sound, U of (WA)
Quinnipiac U (CT)
Redlands, U of (CA)
Rider U (NJ)
Salve Regina U (RI)
San Francisco, U of (CA)
Scranton, U of (PA)
St. Anselm C (NH)
St. Benedict, C of/St. John's U (MN)
St. Joseph's U (PA)
St. Mary's C (CA)
Suffolk U (MA)
Syracuse U (NY)
Texas Christian U
Tulane U (LA)
Ursinus C (PA)
Willamette U (OR)
Wooster, C of (OH)

ADMISSION

The Experts' Choice: Great Private Colleges for the Average Student

Top Choices

Beloit C (WI)
Clark C (WA)
Eckerd C (FL)
Goucher C (MD)
Guilford C (NC)
High Point U (NC)
Hobart C (NY)
Ithaca C (NY)
Lake Forest C (IL)
Linfield C (OR)
Marist C (NY)

Ohio Wesleyan U
Puget Sound, U of (WA)
Redlands, U of (CA)
Ripon C (WI)
Seattle U (WA)
Syracuse U (NY)
Ursinus C (PA)
Wheaton C (IL)
Whittier C (CA)
Willamette U (OR)
Wooster, C of (OH)

Earning Praise

Bentley U (MA)
Bethune-Cookman U (FL)
Bryant U (RI)
California Lutheran U
Champlain C (VT)
Charleston, C of (SC)
Denison U (OH)
Denver, U of (CO)
Dickinson C (PA)
Drew U (NJ)
Earlham C (IN)
Endicott C (MA)
Gettysburg C (PA)
Grand Canyon U (AZ)
Hardwick C (NY)
Juniata C (PA)
Kalamazoo C (MI)
Lawrence U (WI)
Loyola C (MD)
Loyola U (IL)
Lynn U (FL)
McDaniel C (MD)
Muhlenberg C (PA)
Occidental C (CA)

Pacific Lutheran U (WA)
Pacific U (OR)
Point Loma Nazarene (CA)
Portland, U of (OR)
Providence C (RI)
Quinnipiac U (CT)
Regis U (CO)
Roanoke C (VA)
Roger Williams U (RI)
Rollins C (FL)
San Diego, U of (CA)
San Francisco, U of (CA)
Scranton, U of (PA)
Siena C (NY)
St. Anselm C (NH)
St. Joseph's U (PA)
Stevenson U (MD)
Stonehill C (MA)
Susquehanna U (PA)
Tulsa, U of (OK)
Union C (NY)
Washington C (MD)
Wittenberg U (OH)

The Experts' Choice: Amazing Colleges for the Improving Student

Experts were asked to list colleges for students on the rise, i.e., those whose grades have really improved in the last year or so.

Allegheny C (PA)
Beloit C (WI)
Chapman U (CA)
Clark U (MA)
Colorado C

Dickinson C (PA)
Drake U (IA)
Elon U (NC)**
Endicott C (MA)
Guilford C (NC)

High Point U (NC)
Indiana U Bloomington
Lawrence U (WI)
Lewis & Clark C (OR)
Loyola U (IL)
Ohio Wesleyan U
Puget Sound, U of (WA)
Redlands, U of (CA)*

St. Michael's C (VT)
Syracuse U (NY)
Washington C (MD)
Whittier C (CA)
Wooster, C of (OH)

*The Top Choice
**The Second Choice

Colleges That Accept the Highest Percentage of Students in the Bottom Half of Their Secondary School Class

You didn't crack the top 50%. That's okay. College is a clean slate, and you'll get a chance to prove yourself at one of these schools.

Dean C (MA): 78%
Chaminade U of Honolulu (HI): 77%
Maine, U of, Ft. Kent: 77%
Shaw U (NC): 77%
Pennsylvania C of Technology: 74%
Albertus Magnus C (CT): 73%
St. Mary, U of (KS): 68%
Webber International U (FL): 68%
Elizabeth City State U (NC): 67%
Morris C (SC): 67%
Texas A&M U, Galveston: 67%
Kentucky Mountain Bible C: 66%
Stephens C (MO): 66%
Bob Jones U (SC): 64%
New England C (NH): 64%
Morgan State U (MD): 62%
Robert Morris U (PA): 62%
Catawba C (NC): 61%
Chowan U (NC): 61%
Clarion U (PA): 61%

East Stroudsburg U (PA): 61%
Lane C (TN): 61%
Roosevelt U (IL): 61%
Cairn U (PA): 60%
Northeastern Illinois U: 60%
Lynn U (FL): 59%
Alabama State U: 58%
Georgia Gwinnett C: 58%
Paine C (GA): 58%
Faith Baptist Bible C (IA): 57%
South Carolina State U: 57%
Cameron U (OK): 56%
Lewis-Clark State C (ID): 56%
Lincoln U (MO): 56%
Utah Valley U: 56%
Lincoln U (MO): 55%
Missouri Valley C: 55%
Wesley C (DE): 55%
Burlington C (VT): 54%

Source: Wintergreen Orchard House

Colleges That Do Not Consider Standardized Test Scores

Standardized tests aren't for every student, and increasingly, they aren't for every college either. These schools do not require the SAT or ACT, or other standardized test scores to be considered for admission. However, they may require graded writing samples or other examples of student work instead.

Academy of Art U (CA)
Bellevue U (NE)
Boston Architectural C (MA)
California Institute of the Arts
City Vision C (MO)
Cogswell Polytechnical C (CA)
Concordia U (OR)

Fashion Institute of Technology (NY)
Guam, U of
Hampton U (VA)
Hartwick C (NY)
Houston, U of, Clear Lake (TX)
Juilliard School (NY)
Lincoln U (MO)

Mannes C (NY)
Marylhurst U (OR)
Mercy C (NY)
Merrimack C (MA)
Missouri Western State U
Morris C (SC)
National American U (CO)
National U (CA)
New Mexico Highlands U
Ohio State U, Lima
Ohio State U, Mansfield
Ohio State U, Marion
Ohio State U, Newark
Phoenix, U of (AZ)

Pikeville, U of (KY)
Ringling C of Art & Design (FL)
Sage C (NY)
San Francisco Conservatory of Music
 (CA)
Santa Fe U (NM)
Sarah Lawrence C (NY)
School of the Museum of Fine Arts,
 Boston (MA)
St. Joseph Seminary C (LA)
Trinity Washington U (DC)
Wayne State C (NE)
Wheaton C (IL)

Source: Wintergreen Orchard House

The Experts' Choice: Super Colleges for the Poor Test-Taker

Beyond those colleges that are test-optional, experts identified selective colleges that are good choices for students whose test scores often don't reflect their knowledge.

Top Choices

Colorado, U of, Boulder
Elon U (NC)
High Point U (NC)
Houston Community C (TX)
Kenyon C (OH)
Knox C (IL)

Lone Star C (TX)
Montana State U, Bozeman
Vermont, U of
Whitman C (WA)
Wooster, C of (OH)

Other Choices

Albion C (MI)
American U (DC)
Arkansas, U of
Austin Community C (TX)
Bard C (NY)
Barnard C (NY)
Bennett C (NC)
Biola U (CA)
Birmingham-Southern C (AL)
Bowdoin C (ME)
California Polytechnic State U, San Luis
Obispo
Charleston, C of (SC)
Colorado C
Colorado Mountain C
Colorado State U
Connecticut C
Cornell U (NY)
Delaware, U of
Denver, U of (CO)

DePauw U (IN)
Emmanuel C (MA)
Emory U (GA)
George Washington U (DC)
Goucher C (MD)
Hampshire C (MA)
Hobart C (NY)
Hofstra U (NY)
Holy Cross, C of the (MA)
Indiana U Bloomington
James Madison U (VA)
Kansas, U of
Liberty U (VA)
Loyola C (MD)
Lycoming C (PA)
Macalester C (MN)
Marquette U (WI)
Maryland, U of, Eastern Shore
McDaniel C (MD)
Nebraska Wesleyan U

New Hampshire, U of
New Mexico, U of
New York U
Oberlin C (OH)
Occidental C (CA)
Ohio Wesleyan U
Oregon State U
Oregon, U of
Ozarks, U of the (MO)
Pacific, U of the (CA)
Pennsylvania State U, Schreyer
Pomona C (CA)
Purdue U (IN)
Salve Regina U (RI)
Scripps C (CA)
Siena C (NY)
Skidmore C (NY)

Southern Oregon U
St. Mary's C (CA)
St. Olaf C (MN)
Suffolk U (MA)
Tampa, U of (FL)
Tarleton State U (TX)
Texas Christian U
Texas Southern U
Texas State U
Toledo, U of (OH)
Tulsa, U of (OK)
Western New England U (MA)
Whitworth U (WA)
Willamette U (OR)
Wisconsin, U of, River Falls
Wisconsin, U of, Stout

Colleges Participating in the Coalition for Access, Affordability, and Success

This is a list of the members of the Coalition for Access, Affordability, and Success. The Coalition was created to improve the fairness of the application process for students seeking to apply to multiple institutions. According to the Coalition, "The platform provides a single, centralized toolkit for students to organize, build, and refine their applications to numerous institutions."

American U (DC)
Amherst C (MA)
Bates C (ME)
Bowdoin C (ME)
Brown U (RI)
Bryn Mawr C (PA)
California Institute of Technology
Carleton C (MN)
Chicago, U of (IL)
Claremont McKenna C (CA)
Clemson U (SC)
Colby C (ME)
Colgate U (NY)
Colorado C
Columbia U (NY)
Connecticut C
Connecticut, U of
Cornell U (NY)
Dartmouth C (NH)
Davidson C (NC)
Denison U (OH)
Duke U (NC)
Emory U (GA)
Florida State U
Florida, U of
Franklin & Marshall C (PA)
Georgia Institute of Technology

Georgia, U of
Grinnell C (IA)
Hamilton C (NY)
Harvard U (MA)
Haverford C (PA)
Holy Cross, C of the (MA)
Illinois State U
Illinois, U of, Urbana
Indiana U Bloomington
Iowa, U of
James Madison U (VA)
Johns Hopkins U (MD)
Mary Washington, U of (VA)
Maryland, U of, College Park
Miami U (OH)
Michigan State U
Michigan, U of
Middlebury C (VT)
Minnesota, U of, Twin Cities
Missouri, U of, Columbia
Mt. Holyoke C (MA)
New Hampshire, U of
New Jersey, C of
New York, State U of, Binghamton
New York, State U of, Buffalo
New York, State U of, Geneseo
North Carolina State U

North Carolina, U of, Chapel Hill
Northeastern U (MA)
Northwestern U (IL)
Notre Dame, U of (IN)
Oberlin C (OH)
Ohio State U
Olin C (MA)
Pennsylvania State U, University Park
Pennsylvania, U of
Pittsburgh, U of (PA)
Pomona C (CA)
Princeton U (NJ)
Purdue U (IN)
Ramapo C (NJ)
Reed C (OR)
Rice U (TX)
Rochester, U of (NY)
Rutgers U, New Brunswick (NJ)
Skidmore C (NY)
Smith C (MA)

South Carolina, U of
St. Olaf C (MN)
Stanford U (CA)
Swarthmore C (PA)
Texas A&M U
Tufts U (MA)
Union C (NY)
Vanderbilt U (TN)
Vassar C (NY)
Vermont, U of
Virginia Polytechnic Institute & State U
Virginia, U of
Wake Forest U (NC)
Washington U (MO)
Washington, U of
Wellesley C (MA)
Wesleyan U (CT)
William & Mary, C of (VA)
Williams C (MA)
Yale U (CT)

Source: Coalition for Access, Affordability, and Success (coalitionforcollegeaccess.org)

CHAPTER SEVEN
EXPERT OPINIONS

GREAT GAP YEAR PROGRAMS

Sandy Furth, M.S., an independent educational consultant at World Student Support in Colorado, researches gap year programs. She suggests the following programs for students taking time out between high school and college (a gap year) or those wanting a unique experience during college. Furth also identifies the following as important gap year organizations.

American Gap Association: AGA is a standards-setting organization for gap years and is recognized as such by the U.S. Department of Justice and the Federal Trade Commission. Website includes links for parents, professionals, and students as well as a list of specific professionals who can assist in organizing a gap year (americangap.org). USA Gap Year Fairs: Every year, usually starting in January, this organization hosts events across the U.S. to showcase 30 or more gap year programs (usagapyearfairs.org).

Gap Year Programs Based in the United States

* American U (DC) Gap Program: Offers academics and internship experience in Washington, DC; great for students completing high school early or wanting a unique experience before transitioning to college (american.edu/spexs/augap).
* AmeriCorps: Citizens Schools National (citizenschools.org/careers/teaching-fellowship); included under the AmeriCorps umbrella are National Civilian Community Corp and City Year (nationalservice.gov/programs/americorps).
* Dynamy: Students participate in internships and live in apartments in Worcester, MA; program has relationships with various universities in the area, e.g., Becker C and Clark U (dynamy.org).
* Expedition Education Institute: Gap year and other programs where students participate in learning communities with an ecological focus (getonthebus.org).
* Kroka Expeditions: Semester programs within and outside the U.S. (kroka.org/page/index.shtml).
* National Outdoor Leadership School: NOLS is a wilderness education school offering gap year expedition-length courses in the U.S. and worldwide; college credit is available (nols.edu).
* Outward Bound: Courses in mountaineering, dog sledding, canoeing, rock climbing, and backpacking lasting from 35 days to a semester; student outcomes include developing decision-making, group management, and leadership skills (outwardbound.org).
* Ridge Mountain Academy: Co-ed athletic program in Whitefish, MT, helps students strengthen skills and learn new skills centered on mountain sports (ridgeacademy.com).

International Gap Year Programs Based in the United States

* Aarvark Israel: Semester and yearlong options in Israel for Jewish students ages 17–21 interested in urban experiences in Tel Aviv and Jerusalem (aardvarkisrael.com).
* AFS: Semester and yearlong programs for recent high school graduates to experience full immersion through living with a host family and attending a local high school abroad; volunteer abroad and college credit programs available (afsusa.org/study-abroad/gap-year).
* AMIGOS International: AMIGO's high school, gap year, and college programs feature cultural immersion through volunteer activities in Latin America (amigosinternational.org/volunteeropportunities).

- Carpe Diem: Offers culturally authentic gap year options to remote areas—East Africa, Central and South America, South Pacific—to provide volunteer service in a responsible manner; college credit available (carpediemeducation.org).
- CIEE: Offers recent U.S. high school graduates international experiences through classes with students from around the word, life with host families, and volunteer opportunities (ciee.org/gap-year-abroad/students).
- First Abroad: This sister company to the United Kingdom–based Gap 360 offers programs from study abroad (high school or college) to internships and volunteer opportunities (goabroad.com/providers/first-abroad).
- Global Citizen Year: Calling itself a bridge year rather than a gap year, Abby Falik's unique program encourages students to take a year off to do good for others. Financial aid and scholarships are available, but students must interview in order to gain acceptance (globalcitizenyear.org).
- Habitat for Humanity: Students can assist with building sites internationally or close to home, for long- or short-term volunteer work (habitat.org/ivp).
- InterExchange: InterExchange Working Abroad gives young North Americans the opportunity to discover another culture while gaining valuable international and working experience (interexchange.org).
- LeapNow Transforming Education: For participation in this academic year of experiential learning, students can opt in for credit through Naropa U in Boulder, CO (leapnow.org).
- Magic Carpet Rides: A nonprofit gap year for international service and travel (magiccarpetrides.org).
- Map the Gap International: Works with graduating high school students interested in a structured and purposeful time out before college (mapthegapinternational.com/index.html).
- MASA Israel Journey: Gap year, study abroad, internships, and other options for Jewish students to connect to their Jewish culture via a plethora of programs in jazz and contemporary music, art and design, history, sustainable living, and more (masaisrael.org).
- Rustic Pathways: Ability to take a gap year, semester, or one-month block devoted to service, exploration, and language immersion (gap.rusticpathways.com/programs).
- Thinking Beyond Borders: Offering high school, gap year, and study abroad options, this program places participants within communities to work alongside local leaders to develop a deeper understanding of the world (thinkingbeyondborders.org).
- Where There Be Dragons: Authentic student travel programs exposing the beautiful and complex realities of developing countries (wheretherebedragons.com).
- Youth International: An experiential learning program that combines rugged international travel, intercultural exchange, homestays with local families, volunteer community service work, and outdoor adventure (youthinternational.org).

The University and the Gap Year

Several universities will defer students who opt to take a gap year. Some of these institutions will accept credits earned during a gap year or semester, but always verify individual university policy. The universities designated here as "One Plus Three" may award a full year's credit for a gap year; "One Plus Four" schools may give credit, but in order to graduate, students must attend for four years. Again, always read the fine print. This list should be considered a work in progress; it is not a comprehensive listing. With every year, more schools may be added, while other schools may delete the gap year option. See the AGA website for a state-by-state listing of school deferral policies (americangap.org/fav-colleges.php) but most importantly, visit the individual school website or contact the university directly.

EXPERT OPINIONS

One Plus Three
Elon U (NC)
Naropa U (CO)
New School (NY)
Portland State U (OR)
Savannah C of Art & Design (GA)
St. Norbert's C (WI)

One Plus Four
American U (DC)
North Carolina, U of, Chapel Hill
Princeton U (NJ)
Tufts U (MA)

Gap Year Programs Based Outside the United States

- African Impact: Projects range from lion rehabilitation to child and orphan care. Based in the United Kingdom, this charitable organization also has a U.S. office africanimpact.com).
- Altitude Futures: This instructor training in Verbier, Switzerland, is aimed at competent skiers and snowboarders who want to acquire instructor certification (altitude-futures.com).
- Art History Abroad: Founded in 1983, Art History Abroad (AHA) focuses on Italian art and the connections among art, philosophy, music, literature, and history (arthistoryabroad.com/The-AHA-Gap-Year-Course.html).
- Flying Fish: Gap year programs for those who love water sports and want to gain certification or experience in such areas as sailing, scuba, and windsurfing (flyingfishonline.com/gap-year-adventures).
- Frontier: Variety of gap opportunities for the do-it-yourselfer, with options ranging from teaching English in Cambodia to working as a skiing instructor to volunteering in an elephant sanctuary (frontier.ac.uk/Volunteer/Gap-Year.aspx).
- Gap 360: Based in the United Kingdom, this sister company to First Abroad features a variety of options in more than 40 countries worldwide (gap360.com).
- Gap Force: Programs range from two weeks to three months in duration and have included orangutan protection in Borneo, South Africa wildlife volunteering, and European touring (gapforce.org/us).
- Gap Guru: Gap year travel specialists offering volunteering and internships abroad for independent travelers in such regions as India, Southeast Asia, South America, and Tanzania (gapguru.com).
- Pacific Discovery: Located in New Zealand but has an office in the U.S.; offers summer, semester, and gap year experiences to help participants gain the skills, confidence, and insights needed in a global society (pacificdiscovery.org).
- Projects Abroad: United Kingdom–based organization with a New York City office; provides teaching, volunteer, and other opportunities in Africa, Asia, Eastern Europe, Latin America, and the South Pacific (projects-abroad.co.uk).
- Quest Overseas: Options include adventure travel and working with animals and children. Participants are interviewed before acceptance into the program, and groups are no larger than 10 to 14 (questoverseas.com).

Culinary Gap Year Programs

- Le Cordon Bleu: Each school worldwide may offer short courses or longer ones; students can also attend one-day "taster" courses. (cordonbleu.edu).

- Leiths School of Food and Wine: Students can sign up for short or long courses to earn a certificate or just take special interest courses (leiths.com).
- Tante Marie Gap Year: Gap year students can do anything from short cooking courses to a Cordon Bleu certificate to hospitality certification; week-long food camps also available (tantemarie.co.uk).

The Experts' Choice: Great Summer and Gap Year Programs

- Brown U (RI) Pre-College Programs: Summer on-campus academic program offerings focus on online courses, global programs, environmental leadership, and entrepreneurship (brown.edu/academics/pre-college).
- California Institute of Technology Summer Undergraduate Research Fellowships (SURF): Students develop a research project with a grant and 10-week research period (sfp.caltech.edu/programs/surf).
- California State Summer School for the Arts: Sessions in animation, creative writing, dance, film and video, visual arts, theater, and music (csssa.org).
- California State Summer School for Mathematics and Science: High school students interested in STEM subjects can pursue summer studies at one of four University of California campuses (cosmos-ucop.ucdavis.edu).
- Carpe Diem: Emphasizes personal growth through international travel (carpediemeducation.org).
- City Year: AmeriCorps-affiliated program dedicated to providing support to high-poverty communities (cityyear.org).
- Concordia Language Schools: Summer program offering intensive preparation in 15 world languages (concordialanguagevillages.org).
- Dynamy: A gap year providing internships and hands-on learning (dynamy.org).
- Economics for Leaders: This residential program offered by the Foundation for Economics focuses on leadership and an understanding of the "economics way of thinking" (fte.org/student-programs).
- Envoys—Preparing Youth for the World: A summer program designed to help students become global citizens (envoys.com).
- Georgetown U (DC) School of Continuing Studies: Summer at Georgetown offers both precollege and college credit courses (scs.georgetown.edu).
- Global Citizen Year: A volunteer-based gap year in Brazil, Ecuador, India, and Senegal (globalcitizenyear.org).
- Great Books Summer Program: High school students discuss and debate the classics of literature in this program offered at Amherst C (MA); Stanford U (CA); Oxford, U of (United Kingdom); and Trinity C, Dublin (Ireland) (greatbookssummer.com).
- Illinois, U of, Urbana Media U: Weeklong summer camps for high school students focused on careers in the media industry (media.illinois.edu).
- Illinois, U of, Urbana Worldwide Youth in Science and Engineering (WYSE): Weeklong sessions allow high school students to explore mechanical engineering, bioengineering, and other topics (wyse.engineering.illinois.edu).
- Interlochen Arts Camp: Focuses on creative writing, dance, general arts, motion picture arts, music, theater, and visual arts (camp.interlochen.org).
- International Studies Abroad (ISA): Offers a wide array of study abroad opportunities (studiesabroad.com).
- Kenyon C (OH) Young Writers Workshop: Sponsored by *The Kenyon Review,* this intensive summer program for aspiring writers helps students improve their writing and become more insightful thinkers (kenyonreview.org/workshops/young-writers).
- Kivunim: An Israel-based gap year program offering Jewish and Middle East studies as well as travel programs in Europe, Northern Africa, and Asia (kivunim.org).

- Leap Now: Offers group travel and individual internships around the world (leapnow.org).
- Michigan, U of, Ann Arbor Math and Science Scholars: Two-week sessions introduce high school students to current research and developments in mathematics and science (math.lsa.umich.edu/mmss).
- Middlebury C (VT) Summer Language Academy: Four weeks of language and cultural immersion (middleburyinteractive.com/summer-language-academy).
- Midreshet Lindenbaum: Based in Israel, this program for young women offers courses in Hebrew, Jewish studies, and Middle Eastern studies (midreshet-lindenbaum.org.il).
- National Outdoor Leadership School: Wilderness education, outdoor ethics, and leadership (nols.edu).
- Northwestern U (IL) Summer at NU: High school students can enroll in undergraduate courses for college credit and also participate in a range of programs in such areas as journalism, film production, and English competency (sps.northwestern.edu/program-areas/summer).
- Oberlin C (OH) Summer Music Programs: Sessions in bass, flute, organ, percussion, piano, sonic arts, trombone, trumpet, and vocal arts (new.oberlin.edu/conservatory/summer).
- Outward Bound: Programs take place in city and suburban classrooms as well as wilderness areas around the globe (outwardbound.org).
- Oxford, U of (United Kingdom) Summer Courses: A summer program on a historic campus offers numerous courses in a wide range of subject areas (oxfordsummercourses.com).
- Rustic Pathways: Summer and gap year service programs (rusticpathways.com).
- School for International Training: Students travel, learn, and analyze critical issues facing communities across the world (sit.edu).
- Stevens Institute of Technology (NJ) Precollege Programs: Summer learning experiences in business; engineering and science; and technology, society, and the arts (stevens.edu/admissions/pre-college-programs).
- Students Shoulder to Shoulder: This "international school of global citizenship" immerses students in work in the field with nonprofit organizations in countries across the globe (shouldertoshoulder.com).
- Summer Discovery: Precollege enrichment and business institutes offered at universities in the United States and England (summerdiscovery.com).
- Thinking Beyond Borders: Summer and gap year programs focused on the challenges of living in a global society (thinkingbeyondborders.org).
- Where There Be Dragons: Experiential summer and gap year programs to foster global citizenship and leadership, with programs worldwide but mostly centered in Asia (wherethcrcbedragons.com).

The Experts' Choice: Best Undergraduate Education

Experts were asked to select those colleges with the highest academic standards and also those offering students an energized student experience and vocational success.

Bates C (ME)	Grinnell C (IA)
Bowdoin C (ME)	Haverford C (PA)
Carleton C (MN)	Harvey Mudd C (CA)
Chicago, U of (IL)	Holy Cross, C of the (MA)
Claremont McKenna C (CA)	Macalester C (MN)
Dartmouth C (NH)	Massachusetts Institute of Technology
Davidson C (NC)	Middlebury C (VT)
Duke U (NC)	Northwestern U (IL)

Pennsylvania State U, University Park
Pomona C (CA)
Princeton U (NJ)
Rochester, U of (NY)
St. John's C (NM) (MD)
Smith C (MA)
Stanford U (CA)

Swarthmore C (PA)
Wake Forest U (NC)
Wesleyan U (CT)
William & Mary, C of (VA)
Williams C (MA)
Wooster, C of (OH)

The Experts' Choice: Colleges That Should Be Ivies

The eight colleges in the Ivy League Athletic Association are Brown, Columbia, Cornell, Dartmouth, Harvard, Pennsylvania, Princeton, and Yale. Experts were asked, "As a result of their quality of undergraduate education, what colleges should be Ivies even though they are not."

Definitely Should Be Ivy

Amherst C (MA)
Chicago, U of (IL)**
Duke U (NC)*
Northwestern U (IL)
Pomona C (CA)
Rice U (TX)

Stanford U (CA)*
Swarthmore C (PA)
Vanderbilt U (TN)
Washington U (MO)*
Williams C (MA)

*The Top Choice (tie)
**The Second Choice

Should Be Ivy

Boston C (MA)
Bowdoin C (ME
Brandeis U (MA)
Bryn Mawr C (PA)
California Institute of Technology
California, U of, Berkeley
California, U of, Los Angeles
Carleton C (MN)*
Carnegie Mellon U (PA)
Colorado C
Davidson C (NC)
Emory U (GA)
Franklin & Marshall C (PA)
Georgetown U (DC)*
Grinnell C (IA)
Harvey Mudd C (CA)
Haverford C (PA)
Johns Hopkins U (MD)

Lawrence U (WI)
Macalester C (MN)
Massachusetts Institute of Technology
Michigan, U of, Ann Arbor
Middlebury C (VT)
Notre Dame, U of (IN)
Oberlin C (OH)
Reed C (OR)
Rochester, U of (NY)
Smith C (MA)
Southern California, U of
Tufts U (MA)
Tulane U (LA)
Virginia, U of
Wellesley C (MA)
Wesleyan U (CT)*
Whitman C (WA)
William & Mary, C of (VA)

*The Top Choice (tie)

Steven R. Antonoff

Honorable Mention

Barnard C (NY)
Bucknell U (PA)
Case Western Reserve U (OH)
Claremont McKenna C (CA)
Colgate U (NY)
Denison U (OH)
Furman U (SC)
Hamilton C (NY)
Kalamazoo C (MI)
Kenyon C (OH)

Lafayette C (PA)
Lehigh U (PA)
Muhlenberg C (PA)
New Jersey, C of
North Carolina, U of, Chapel Hill
St. Louis U (MO)
Vassar C (NY)
Wisconsin, U of, Madison
Wooster, C of (OH)
Worcester Polytechnic Institute (MA)

The Experts' Choice: The Public Ivies

The Ivy League colleges are private. Experts were asked to identify public colleges and universities they considered to be outstanding, the so-called "Public Ivies."

California, U of, Berkeley
California, U of, Los Angeles
California, U of, San Diego
Georgia, U of
Louisiana State U
Miami U (OH)
Michigan, U of, Ann Arbor
Minnesota, U of, Twin Cities

North Carolina, U of, Chapel Hill
Texas A & M U, College Station
Texas, U of, Austin
Vermont, U of
Virginia, U of
Washington, U of
William & Mary, C of (VA)
Wisconsin, U of, Madison

The Hidden Ivies

These are exceptional colleges that are on a par with the better-known Ivy schools according to Howard Greene and Matthew W. Greene, authors of The Hidden Ivies: Fifty Top Colleges from Amherst to Williams That Rival the Ivy League.

Amherst C (MA)
Barnard C (NY)
Bates C (ME)
Boston C (MA)
Bowdoin C (ME)
Bryn Mawr C (PA)
Bucknell U (PA)
Carleton C (MN)
Chicago, U of (IL)
Claremont McKenna C (CA)
Colby C (ME)
Colgate U (NY)
Colorado C
Davidson C (NC)
Duke U (NC)
Emory U (GA)
Georgetown U (DC)
Grinnell C (IA)

Hamilton C (NY)
Haverford C (PA)
Johns Hopkins U (MD)
Kenyon C (OH)
Lafayette C (PA)
Lehigh U (PA)
Macalester C (MN)
Middlebury C (VT)
Mt. Holyoke C (MA)
Northwestern U (IL)
Notre Dame, U of (IN)
Oberlin C (OH)
Pomona C (CA)
Reed C (OR)
Rice U (TX)
Richmond, U of (VA)
Rochester, U of (NY)
Smith C (MA)

Southern California, U of	Vassar C (NY)
Stanford U (CA)	Wake Forest U (NC)
Swarthmore C (PA)	Washington & Lee U (VA)
Trinity C (CT)	Washington U (MO)
Tufts U (MA)	Wellesley C (MA)
Tulane U (LA)	Wesleyan U (CT)
Vanderbilt U (TN)	Williams C (MA)

Source: The Hidden Ivies: Fifty Top Colleges from Amherst to Williams That Rival the Ivy League, 2009 (2nd ed.), Collins Reference, New York.

The Experts' Choice: Colleges Students Rave About

Experts were asked to name colleges that consistently win students' enthusiasm and praise.

Top Choices

Boston U (MA)**	Northwestern U (IL)
Brown U (RI)	Pennsylvania State U, University Park
California Polytechnic State U, San Luis Obispo	Pittsburgh, U of (PA)
	Puget Sound, U of (WA)
Chapman U (CA)	Rhodes C (TN)
Chicago, U of (IL)	South Carolina, U of
Claremont McKenna C (CA)	Southern California, U of
Colorado C***	Southern Methodist U (TX)
Cornell U (NY)	St. Lawrence U (NY)
Duke U (NC)	Texas Christian U***
Elon U (NC)	Tufts U (MA)
Georgia, U of	Tulane U (LA)
James Madison U (VA)	Vanderbilt U (TN)***
Miami U (OH)	Virginia, U of
Miami, U of (FL)	Wake Forest U (NC)
Michigan, U of, Ann Arbor	Washington U (MO)*
Middlebury C (VT)	Wheaton C (MA)
Northeastern U (MA)	Yale U (CT)

*The Top Choice
**The Second Choice
***The Third Choice (tie)

Second Choices

Alabama, U of, Tuscaloosa	Harvey Mudd C (CA)
American U (DC)	High Point U (NC)
Bates C (ME)	Marist C (NY)
Bowdoin C (ME)	Maryland, U of, College Park
California, U of, Los Angeles	New York U
Case Western Reserve U (OH)	Oberlin C (OH)
Charleston, C of (SC)	Occidental C (CA)
Dartmouth C (NH)	Pomona C (CA)
Delaware, U of	Quest U (Canada)
Denver, U of (CO)	Rice U (TX)
Georgetown U (DC)	Richmond, U of (VA)

Steven R. Antonoff

Santa Clara U (CA)
Scripps C (CA)
Stanford U (CA)
Susquehanna U (PA)
Tampa, U of (FL)

Virginia Polytechnic Institute & State U
Whitman C (WA)
Williams C (MA)
Wisconsin, U of, Madison

The Experts' Choice: Colleges Where Students Have a Positive Experience

Students tell counselors about their college experience. Experts then listed the colleges most often mentioned as ones at which their students reported having had the most positive experiences.

Barnard C (NY)
Beloit C (WI)
Boston C (MA)
Brown U (RI)
Bryn Mawr C (PA)
California Polytechnic State U, San Luis Obispo
California, U of, Berkeley
California, U of, Davis
California, U of, Santa Barbara
Chapman U (CA)
Cornell C (IA)
Davidson C (NC)
Denver, U of (CO)
Duke U (NC)
Elon U (NC)
Florida, U of
Furman U (SC)
Georgia, U of
Gonzaga U (WA)
Indiana U, Bloomington
Kalamazoo C (MI)
Kenyon C (OH)
Lehigh U (PA)
Miami U (OH)
Michigan, U of, Ann Arbor*

Middlebury C (VT)
North Carolina, U of, Chapel Hill
Northeastern U (MA)
Oregon, U of
Pittsburgh, U of (PA)
Puget Sound, U of (WA)
Richmond, U of (VA)
Rochester, U of (NY)
Santa Clara U (CA)
Southern California, U of
St. Louis U (MO)
St. Olaf C (MN)
Syracuse U (NY)
Texas A & M U, College Station
Texas Christian U
Trinity U (TX)
Tufts U (MA)
Tulane U (LA)
Vanderbilt U (TN)
Vermont, U of
Villanova U (PA)
Washington U (MO)
Wellesley C (MA)
Whitman C (WA)
Wisconsin, U of, Madison

*The Top Choice

EXPERT OPINIONS

The Experts' Choice: Overrated Colleges

Experts were asked to list colleges they considered consistently overrated.

Boston C (MA)
Boston U (MA)
Brown U (RI)
California, U of, Berkeley
California, U of, Los Angeles
Columbia U (NY)
Cornell U (NY)
Duke U (NC)
Emory U (GA)
Florida, U of
Georgetown U (DC)
Harvard U (MA)
High Point U (NC)
Massachusetts Institute of Technology

Michigan, U of, Ann Arbor
New York U
North Carolina, U of, Chapel Hill
Northeastern U (MA)
Pennsylvania State U, University Park
Pennsylvania, U of
Princeton U (NJ)
Southern California, U of
Stanford U (CA)
Vanderbilt U (TN)
Virginia, U of
Washington U (MO)
Yale U (CT)

The Experts' Choice: Great Underrated Colleges

Experts were asked to name great colleges that are of high quality, yet lack the name recognition they deserve.

American U (DC)
Baylor U (TX)
Belmont U (TN)
Bryn Mawr C (PA)
Carleton C (MN)
Carroll U (WI)
Case Western Reserve U (OH)*
Champlain C (VT)
Chapman U (CA)
Charleston, U of (SC)
Chicago, U of (IL)
Clark U (MA)
Colorado C
Davidson C (NC)
Delaware, U of
Denison U (OH)
Denver, U of (CO)
Dickinson C (PA)
Drew U (NJ)
Earlham C (IN)
Elon U (NC)
Florida Southern C
Furman U (SC)
Grand Valley State U (MI)
Hendrix C (AR)
IESEG School of Management (France)
Juniata C (PA)
Kenyon C (OH)
Lawrence U (WI)
Lehigh U (PA)

Lewis & Clark C (OR)
Loyola C (MD)
Macalester C (MN)
Mary Washington, U of (VA)
Mercer U (GA)
Minnesota, U of, Twin Cities
Montana State U
Muhlenberg C (PA)
Ohio Wesleyan U
Pacific U (OR)
Redlands, U of (CA)
Rensselaer Polytechnic Institute (NY)
Rhodes C (TN)
Richmond, U of (VA)
Rochester, U of (NY)
San Francisco, U of (CA)
Santa Clara U (CA)
Seattle U (WA)
South, U of the, Sewanee (TN)
St. Lawrence U (NY)
St. Olaf C (MN)
Syracuse U (NY)
Tennessee Technological U
Tulane U (LA)
Tulsa, U of (OK)
Washington U (MO)
West Chester U (PA)
Wheaton C (MA)
Whitman C (WA)
Whittier C (CA)

Wofford C (SC)
Wooster, C of (OH)

*The Top Choice

The Experts' Choice: The Hidden Gems

Experts defined a hidden gem as a college having strength in terms of the academic and social experience, yet one that is not well known.

Top Choices

Austin C (TX)
Beloit C (WI)
Colorado C
Dominican U (CA)
Elon U (NC)
Endicott C (MA)
Furman U (SC)
Hampshire C (MA)
High Point U (NC)
Knox C (IL)
Lawrence U (WI)*
Miami U (OH)
Muhlenberg C (PA)*

Puget Sound, U of (WA)
Redlands, U of (CA)
South, U of the (TN)
St. Anselm C (NH)
St. John's C (NM) (MD)
St. Lawrence U (NY)
Ursinus C (PA)
Washington C (MD)
Whitman C (WA)
Wofford C (SC)
Wooster, C of (OH)*

*The Top Choice (tie)

Second Choices

Albright C (PA)
Allegheny C (PA)
Baldwin-Wallace U (OH)
Bentley U (MA)
Birmingham-Southern C (AL)
Bradley U (IL)
Carroll C (MT)
Centre C (KY)
Chapman U (CA)
Clark U (MA)
Cornell C (IA)
Davidson C (NC)
Dayton, U of (OH)
Delaware, U of
DePauw U (IN)
Dickinson C (PA)
Drew U (NJ)
Earlham C (IN)
Florida Southern U
Franklin & Marshall C (PA)
George Mason U (VA)
Gettysburg C (PA)
Grove City C (PA)
Hendrix C (AR)
Hope C (MI)
Kalamazoo C (MI)
Kenyon C (OH)

Lewis & Clark C (OR)
Linfield C (OR)
Luther C (IA)
Marist C (NY)
McDaniel C (MD)
Montana State U
New C (FL)
Olin C (MA)
Pomona C (CA)
Portland, U of (OR)
Presbyterian C (SC)
Quest C (Canada)
Richmond, U of (VA)
Ripon C (WI)
Roger Williams U (RI)
Rollins C (FL)
Santa Clara U (CA)
Scranton U (PA)
Seattle U (WA)
Siena C (NY)
Southwestern U (TX)
St Thomas, U of (MN)
St. Benedict, C of/ St. John's U (MN)
St. Edwards U (TX)
St. Mary's C (CA)
St. Mary's C (MD)
St. Michael's C (VT)

St. Olaf C (MN)	Western Washington U
Stetson U (FL)	Wheaton C (MA)
Stevenson U (MA)	Whittier C (CA)
Tampa, U of (FL)	William Jewell C (MO)
Trinity U (TX)	Wittenberg U (OH)
Tulsa, U of (OK)	Worcester Polytechnic Institute (MA)
Union C (NY)	

Colleges That Change Lives

In *Colleges That Change Lives: 40 Schools That Will Change the Way You Think About College* (Penguin Books), educational consultant and former *New York Times* education editor Loren Pope profiles 40 colleges that "excel at developing potential, values, initiative, and risk-taking in a wide range of students." The book is currently edited by Hilary Oswald.

Agnes Scott C (GA)	Kalamazoo C (MI)
Allegheny C (PA)	Knox C (IL)
Antioch C (OH)	Lawrence U (WI)
Austin C (TX)	Lynchburg C (VA)
Beloit C (WI)	Marlboro C (VT)
Birmingham-Southern C (AL)	McDaniel C (MD)
Centre C (KY)	Millsaps C (MS)
Clark U (MA)	New C (FL)
Cornell C (IA)	Ohio Wesleyan U
Denison U (OH)	Puget Sound, U of (WA)
Earlham C (IN)	Reed C (OR)
Eckerd C (FL)	Rhodes C (TN)
Emory & Henry C (VA)	Southwestern U (TX)
Evergreen State C (WA)	St. John's C (MD)
Goucher C (MD)	St. Mary's C (CA)
Guilford C (NC)	St. Olaf C (MN)
Hampshire C (MA)	Ursinus C (PA)
Hendrix C (AR)	Wabash C (IN)
Hillsdale C (MI)	Wheaton C (IL)
Hiram C (OH)	Whitman C (WA)
Hope C (MI)	Willamette U (OR)
Juniata C (PA)	Wooster, C of (OH)

The Experts' Choice: Colleges That Inspire Success ®

There are "Colleges That Change Lives," but experts were asked, "If you developed a new list of similar colleges, and called them 'Colleges That Inspire Success®,' what schools would you include?"

American U (DC)	Colorado C
Amherst C (MA)	Connecticut C
Babson C (MA)	Davidson C (NC)
Bates C (ME)	Denison U (OH)
Bentley U (MA)	DePauw U (IN)
Bucknell U (PA)	Dickinson C (PA)
Carleton C (MN)	Elon U (NC)*
Chapman U (CA)	Franklin & Marshall C (PA)
Claremont McKenna C (CA)	Gettysburg C (PA)
Clark U (MA)	Gonzaga U (WA)

Steven R. Antonoff

Grinnell C (IA)
High Point U (NC)
Idaho, C of
Johns Hopkins U (MD)
Kenyon C (OH)
Lafayette C (PA)
Lawrence U (WI)
Macalester C (MN)
Marist C (NY)
Mt. Holyoke C (MA)
Muhlenberg C (PA)
Northeastern U (MA)*
Occidental C (CA)
Olin C (MA)
Pitzer C (CA)
Pomona C (CA)
Puget Sound, U of (WA)
Redlands, U of (CA)
Rensselaer Polytechnic Institute (NY)

Rochester, U of (NY)
Santa Clara U (CA)
Scripps C (CA)
Smith C (MA)
South, U of the (TN)
St. Olaf C (MN)
Susquehanna U (PA)
Trinity U (TX)
Union C (NY)
Villanova U (PA)
Washington & Lee U (VA)
Wesleyan U (CT)
Whitman C (WA)
Wofford C (SC)
Wooster, C of (OH)
Worcester Polytechnic Institute (MA)

* The Top Choice (tie)

Colleges That Foster Student Success

Researchers have identified the following 20 schools as colleges that "create a campus culture shown to foster student success."

Alverno C (WI)
California State U, Monterey Bay
Evergreen State C (WA)
Fayetteville State U (NC)
George Mason U (VA)
Gonzaga U (WA)
Kansas, U of
Longwood U (VA)
Macalester C (MN)
Maine, U of, Farmington

Miami U (OH)
Michigan, U of, Ann Arbor
South, U of the (TN)
Sweet Briar C (VA)
Texas, U of, El Paso
Ursinus C (PA)
Wabash C (IN)
Wheaton C (MA)
Winston-Salem State U (NC)
Wofford C (SC)

Source: George D. Kuh, et al., 2005. *Student Success in College: Creating Conditions That Matter.* Jossey-Bass, San Francisco.

Colleges of Distinction

For this designation, colleges are selected "...from a national team of educators and admissions professionals who identify schools that excel in the four areas of distinction: engaged students, great teaching, vibrant communities, and successful outcomes." A poll of high school guidance counselors is also part of selection process.

Abilene Christian U (TX)
Adelphi U (NY)
Adrian C (MI)
Agnes Scott C (GA)
Alabama, U of, Huntsville
Allegheny C (PA)

Alma C (MI)
Anna Maria C (MA)
Appalachian State U (NC)
Assumption C (MA)
Aurora U (IL)
Averett U (VA)

Azusa Pacific U (CA)
Baker U (KS)
Ball State U (IN)
Barry U (FL)
Bay Path U (MA)
Baylor U (TX)
Belhaven U (MS)
Belmont U (TN)
Bennington C (VT)
Berry C (GA)
Bethany C (WV)
Bethel C (IN)
Bethel C (KS)
Birmingham-Southern C (AL)
Brescia U (KY)
Butler U (IN)
Caldwell U (NJ)
California Baptist U
California C of the Arts
California Polytechnic State U, San Luis
  Obispo
California, U of, Santa Barbara
California, U of, Santa Cruz
Calvin C (MI)
Canisius C (NY)
Capital U (OH)
Carroll C (MT)
Carson-Newman U (TN)
Carthage C (WI)
Cazenovia C (NY)
Cedar Crest C (PA)
Cedarville U (OH)
Centre C (KY)
Champlain C (VT)
Chapman U (CA)
Charleston Southern U (SC)
Charleston, C of (SC)
Chatham U (PA)
Christian Brothers U (TN)
Coastal Carolina U (SC)
Coker C (SC)
Colorado Christian U
Colorado Mesa U
Concordia C (NY)
Concordia U (NE)
Concordia U, Chicago (IL)
Concordia U, Wisconsin
Cornell C (IA)
Cornerstone U (MI)
Creighton U (NE)
Culver-Stockton C (MO)
Curry C (MA)
D'Youville C (NY)
Daemen C (NY)
Dakota Wesleyan U (SD)

Dallas, U of (TX)
Davis & Elkins C (WV)
Dayton, U of (OH)
Defiance C (OH)
Denison U (OH)
Denver, U of (CO)
DePauw U (IN)
Dickinson C (PA)
Doane U (NE)
Dominican C (NY)
Dominican U of California
Dordt C (IA)
Drake U (IA)
Drew U (NJ)
Drexel U (PA)
Eastern Connecticut State U
Eastern Oregon U
Eastern U (PA)
Elmhurst C (IL)
Elon U (NC)
Emerson C (MA)
Emmanuel C (MA)
Emory & Henry C (VA)
Erskine C (SC)
Fairfield U (CT)
Fisher C (MA)
Flagler C (FL)
Florida Southern C
Fontbonne U (MO)
Fordham U (NY)
Friends U (KS)
Frostburg State U (MD)
Furman U (SC)
Gannon U (PA)
Geneva C (PA)
George Fox U (OR)
Georgetown C (KY)
Georgia C
Georgia Gwinnett C
Georgian Court U (NJ)
Gettysburg C (PA)
Gonzaga U (WA)
Gordon C (MA)
Goshen C (IN)
Grinnell C (IA)
Grove City C (PA)
Gwynedd Mercy U (PA)
Hardin-Simmons U (TN)
Hendrix C (AR)
High Point U (NC)
Hillsdale C (MI)
Hiram C (OH)
Hobart & William Smith C (NY)
Hofstra U (NY)
Hollins U (VA)

Steven R. Antonoff

Holy Cross C (IN)
Holy Cross, C of the (MA)
Holy Names U (CA)
Huntington U (IN)
Idaho, the C of
Illinois C
Illinois Wesleyan U
Immaculata U (PA)
Iona C (NY)
James Madison U (VA)
John Brown U (AR)
Judson U (IL)
Kalamazoo C (MI)
Kansas Wesleyan U
Keene State C (NH)
Kenyon C (OH)
Keuka C (NY)
King U (TN)
La Roche C (PA)
La Sierra U (CA)
Lafayette C (PA)
Lasell C (MA)
LaVerne, U of (CA)
Lawrence U (WI)
Le Moyne C (NY)
Lebanon Valley C (PA)
Lee U (TN)
Lewis & Clark C (OR)
Lewis U (IL)
Lipscomb U (TN)
Long Island U, Post (NY)
Louisville, U of (KY)
Loyola Marymount U (CA)
Loyola U (IL)
Loyola U (LA)
Loyola U (MD)
Lubbock Christian U (TX)
Luther C (IA)
Lynn U (FL)
Macalester C (MN)
MacMurray C (IL)
Maine, U of, Fort Kent
Maine, U of, Orono
Malone U (OH)
Manchester U (IN)
Manhattan C (NY)
Manhattanville C (NY)
Mansfield U (PA)
Marquette U (WI)
Mary Baldwin C (VA)
Mary Hardin-Baylor, U of (TX)
Mary, U of (ND)
Maryland, U of, Baltimore County
Maryville C (TN)
Master's C, the (CA)

McKendree U (IL)
Mercer U (GA)
Mercyhurst U (PA)
Meredith C (NC)
Messiah C (PA)
Miami U (OH)
Miami, U of (FL)
Michigan Technological U
Millersville U (PA)
Millsaps C (MS)
Minnesota, U of, Morris
Missouri U of Science and Technology
Molloy C (NY)
Monmouth C (IL)
Montevallo, U of (AL)
Mt. Aloysius C (PA)
Mt. Marty C (SD)
Mt. Olive, U of (NC)
Mt. St. Mary's U (MD)
Muhlenberg C (PA)
Naropa U (CO)
Nebraska Wesleyan U
Neumann U (PA)
New C (FL)
New Hampshire, U of
New Haven, U of (CT)
New Jersey, C of
New Rochelle, the C of (NY)
New York, State U of Oneonta
New York, State U of, Binghamton
New York, State U of, Buffalo
New York, State U of, Geneseo
New York, State U of, Oswego
Newbury C (MA)
Niagara U (NY)
Nichols C (MA)
North Carolina, U of, Wilmington
North Central C (IL)
Northeastern U (MA)
Northern Illinois U
Northern Iowa, U of
Northern Michigan U
Northwest Nazarene U (ID)
Occidental C (CA)
Oglethorpe U (GA)
Ohio Wesleyan U
Oklahoma Baptist U
Oklahoma U of Science and Arts
Olivet Nazarene U (IL)
Ottawa U (KS)
Pacific Lutheran U (WA)
Pacific Union C (CA)
Park U (MO)
Pepperdine U (CA)
Pfeiffer U (NC)

Piedmont C (GA)
Pittsburgh, U of, Bradford (PA)
Pittsburgh, U of, Greensburg (PA)
Portland, U of (OR)
Presbyterian C (SC)
Providence C (RI)
Puget Sound, U of (WA)
Quincy U (IL)
Quinnipiac U (CT)
Radford U (VA)
Ramapo C (NJ)
Randolph C (VA)
Regis C (MA)
Reinhardt U (GA)
Rhode Island C
Rhodes C (TN)
Richmond, U of (VA)
Rivier U (NH)
Rockhurst U (MO)
Rollins C (FL)
Rosemont C (PA)
Sacred Heart U (CT)
Sage C (NY)
Salem C (NC)
Salisbury U (MD)
Sam Houston State U (TX)
Samford U (AL)
San Diego, U of (CA)
Santa Clara U (CA)
Seattle U (WA)
Seton Hall U (NJ)
Shepherd U (WV)
Siena Heights U (MI)
Sierra Nevada C
Slippery Rock U (PA)
South, U of the (TN)
Southern Methodist U (TX)
Southwestern U (TX)
Spring Arbor U (MI)
Spring Hill C (AL)
Springfield C (MA)
St. Edward's U (TX)
St. Elizabeth, C of (NJ)
St. Francis U (PA)
St. Francis, U of (IL)
St. Joseph's C (NY)
St. Joseph's U (PA)
St. Leo U (FL)
St. Louis U (MO)
St. Norbert C (WI)
St. Olaf C (MN)
St. Thomas Aquinas C (NY)
St. Thomas, U of (MN)

St. Xavier U (IL)
Stephen F. Austin State U (TX)
Stonehill C (MA)
Suffolk U (MA)
Susquehanna U (PA)
Taylor U (IN)
Tennessee, U of, Chattanooga
Texas Christian U
Texas, U of, Dallas
Thiel C (PA)
Toccoa Falls C (GA)
Transylvania U (KY)
Trinity U (TX)
Truman State U (MO)
Tulane U (LA)
Tulsa, U of (OK)
Union U (TN)
Unity C (ME)
Vermont, U of
Villanova U (PA)
Virginia Wesleyan C
Virginia, U of, Wise
Viterbo U (WI)
Wake Forest U (NC)
Walsh U (OH)
Warner Pacific C (OR)
Washington C (MD)
Wayne State C (NE)
Waynesburg U (PA)
Wentworth Institute of Technology
West Chester U (PA)
Western Connecticut State U
Western New England U (MA)
Western State Colorado U
Western Washington U
Westminster C (UT)
Westmont C (CA)
Wheaton C (IL)
Whitman C (WA)
Whittier C (CA)
Whitworth U (WA)
Willamette U (OR)
William & Mary, C of (VA)
William Jewell C (MO)
Wisconsin Lutheran C
Wisconsin, U of, La Crosse
Wittenberg U (OH)
Wofford C (SC)
Woodbury U (CA)
Xavier U (LA)
Xavier U (OH)
Young Harris C (GA)

Princeton Review's Colleges That Create Futures

According to the authors, these colleges launch careers by going beyond the classroom. They may have excellent career centers, internship opportunities, cooperative education, service learning, and experiential learning programs. They involve undergrads in collaborative research with faculty.

Arizona State U
Babson C (MA)
Bryn Mawr C (PA)
California, U of, San Diego
Charleston, C of (SC)
Claremont McKenna C (CA)
Columbia U (NY)
Dayton, U of (OH)
DePauw U (IN)
Drew U (NJ)
Duke U (NC)
Florida, U of
Franklin & Marshall C (PA)
George Washington U (DC)
Gettysburg C (PA)
Harvey Mudd C (CA)
Haverford C (PA)
Hobart & William Smith C (NY)
Houston, U of (TX)
Lehigh U (PA)
Marist C (NY)
Massachusetts Institute of Technology
Michigan, U of, Ann Arbor
Middlebury C (VT)
New York, City U of, Hunter

New York, State U of, Binghamton
Northeastern U (MA)
Notre Dame, U of (IN)
Oberlin C (OH)
Pennsylvania, U of
Pittsburgh, U of (PA)
Pitzer C (CA)
Pomona C (CA)
Princeton U (NJ)
Rhodes C (TN)
Rice U (TX)
Smith C (MA)
Southern California, U of
St. Lawrence U (NY)
Stanford U (CA)
Stevens Institute of Technology (NJ)
Swarthmore C (PA)
Texas, U of, Austin
Vassar C (NY)
Villanova U (PA)
Wagner C (NY)
Wake Forest U (NC)
Washington U (MO)
William & Mary, C of (VA)
Worcester Polytechnic Institute (MA)

Source: Robert Franek and the staff of The Princeton Review, *Colleges That Create Futures: 50 Schools That Launch Careers By Going Beyond the Classroom* (Penguin Random House/Princeton Review).

STATE-BY-STATE HIDDEN GEMS

Sixty counselors nationwide—both independent educational consultants and school-based counselors—were selected and invited to participate in a special survey. The survey asked counselors to list and describe schools in their state that offered great quality but might be overlooked by students looking for colleges. These counselors responded with reviews, raves, and reports on their favorite "hidden gems."

The entry for each school is drawn from these responses, either as direct quotes from the counselors or as compilations of counselors' comments about the same school. Some entries include additional *College Finder* research. Readers should keep in mind that the information provided here reflects the subjective opinions of experts and that not all comments have been checked for accuracy.

The names of the counselors who participated in this section are listed in the acknowledgments on page ix.

Alabama

Birmingham-Southern C: In addition to high acceptance rates to med school, Birmingham-Southern boasts caring and engaged faculty and students who maintain a healthy balance of social life and academics.

Montevallo, U of: Montevallo has excellent support services for learning challenges, superb fine arts programs, and an array of merit scholarships.

Samford U: Samford is home to a strong faith-based community, beautiful facilities, and a superb music department.

Alaska

Alaska Pacific U: A small university with around 200 full-time undergraduates, APU is situated on the edge of wilderness in Anchorage, which provides for an intimate educational setting, minutes from the expansive outdoors of Alaska's mountains, seas, and wilderness.

Alaska, U of, Southeast: UAS delivers a small-college, residential experience akin to a liberal arts college for the price of a public university. Located right on the ocean, this compact campus in the northernmost temperate rain forest abounds in educational and recreational opportunities despite its size.

California

California Lutheran U: Previously focused primarily on its low-key suburban surroundings, CLU has recently turned its attention to the greater Los Angeles area. This has resulted in a new wave of adjunct faculty and curricula as well as a revitalized energy on campus, sparked by the wealth of opportunities available in this major metropolis.

California Polytechnic State U, San Luis Obispo: Located in the great college town of San Luis Obispo, Cal Poly SLO combines small class sizes with a focus on hands-on learning.

Steven R. Antonoff

California State University, Sonoma: CSU Sonoma is situated just north of San Francisco in beautiful Sonoma, a small-size city with a hometown feel. With its dedicated faculty, excellent resources for students with learning disabilities, and attractive dorms, the university is a pleasant exception to the commuter college reputation of the California State University system. In addition to a vibrant residential community and incredible natural surroundings, CSU Sonoma offers a generous admission policy.

Redlands, U of: Located in a lovely town in a beautiful part of Southern California, Redlands provides a range of resources for students with learning disabilities. The University's Johnston Center for Integrative Studies enables students to design their own majors.

California, U of, Riverside: Because of UC Riverside's relatively low number of graduate students, faculty here are more dedicated to undergraduate learning than is typical at other University of California campuses. Additionally, UC Riverside has an incredible engineering program that is accessible to a B/B- student.

St Mary's College: With a beautiful campus in a small suburban location, St. Mary's offers a community of friendly students and a welcoming vibe, as well as easy access to nearby San Francisco should the campus ever feel too confining.

Whittier College: Its comfortable, medium-sized campus in a beautiful setting near Los Angeles is only part of Whittier's appeal. The college also offers generous merit aid, and its admissions are friendly to the B student.

Colorado

Colorado, U of, Colorado Springs: UCCS boasts a beautiful, newly built campus and offers a great, nonselective engineering program.

Colorado School of Mines: Colorado School of Mines is known for its responsiveness to students and their families, as well as outstanding engineering academics and career placement opportunities.

Fort Lewis C: With its small enrollment, great facilities, and magnificent views, Fort Lewis offers the best of a private liberal arts college in a public state university. The school's academics are consistently growing stronger, with professors who are often described as "over-qualified" in their fields.

Connecticut

Connecticut C: Connecticut College not only provides its students with a wonderful liberal arts education but also sets itself apart from other colleges with its Career Enhancing Life Skills (CELS) Program to help students attain and fund internships in the US and abroad. Additionally, the on-campus arboretum and nearby Long Island Sound make for tons of opportunities for students in the environmental sciences.

Connecticut, U of: UConn's newly invigorated STEM program is a result of the Next Generation Connecticut Program, which aims to expand educational opportunities in STEM fields. For students with excellent grades and test scores, the Honors program and STEM scholars program offer scholarships and many other perks. Additionally,

EXPERT OPINIONS

construction has begun on Storrs Center, a new "downtown" area with restaurants and student-centered shopping, making Storrs a wonderful college town.

New Haven, U of: With an emphasis on experiential learning, the University of New Haven has top-notch programs in criminal justice, fire science, and forensic science. Dr. Henry Lee (of OJ Simpson trial fame) is a member of the faculty and heads the Lee Institute on campus.

Quinnipiac U: A spirited student body and numerous attractive new programs and buildings on campus have only increased Quinnipiac's popularity, which has been growing steadily in recent years.

Delaware

Wesley C: This private four-year college awards both bachelor's and associate's degrees and serves a racially and geographically diverse campus of about 1,200 students.

Wilmington U: A commuter school that attracts 23% of its students from out of state, Wilmington offers directed career-oriented academics and good athletics. Though there are no plans for Wilmington to begin to offer on-campus housing, the university is expanding by building a new campus in North Wilmington.

Florida

Florida Polytechnic, Lakeland: This newest addition to Florida's public university system boasts state-of-the-art, nearly futuristic buildings—the perfect setting for preparing students for the world of technology through hands-on experience in small classes.

Georgia

Berry C: This small liberal arts college founded on Christian values is set in rural northeast Georgia, about 75 miles from Atlanta on the world's largest college campus (27,000 acres). Berry encourages on-campus student employment as well as community service and offers extensive academic support for students with learning disabilities and good scholarships for high-achieving students.

Georgia C & State U: This public liberal arts college in the beautiful college town of Milledgeville features a full liberal arts curriculum.
Georgia Southern U: Located in rural Georgia (approximately three hours south of Atlanta), Georgia Southern has been named one of the top fashion merchandising schools in the United States, holding the ninth spot in the "Top 15 Fashion Schools in the South."

Georgia State University: This rapidly growing, up-and-coming diverse university in downtown Atlanta is transitioning from a commuter campus to a traditional one. Georgia State is building new dorms and recently received a large grant to start a film, music, and game design program.

Mercer U: Mercer provides great scholarships and fosters amazing relationships among faculty and students. Among the university's most impressive aspects are its excellent medical school and law school feeder programs.

Oglethorpe U: With a campus dominated by gothic architecture and nestled just outside the Atlanta city limits, Oglethorpe offers the kind of setting that many students may not want to leave, but this university guarantees that its students will graduate in four years or the fifth year is free. Students at Oglethorpe can intern locally in leading top-tier companies and be known by each professor by name.

Toccoa Falls C: Nestled in the foothills of the Northeast Georgia mountains, this small, Christian liberal arts college is ideally situated for outdoor activity while offering a taste of big cities (Atlanta and Greenville) just over an hour away. Particularly strong are the college's programs in sports management and outdoor leadership and education.

Hawaii

Hawaii Pacific U: HPU, a private university in Honolulu, has undergone tremendous growth in the last 20 years. In addition to strong programs in business, nursing, and the liberal arts, HPU is the only college in Hawaii that offers undergraduate degrees in marine biology and marine science. The university is famous for its low cost—$35,000 a year for tuition, room, and board. HPU dorms are located in oceanfront properties in downtown Honolulu and Waikiki beach. The college has unusually high number of foreign students due to its aggressive recruitment in European countries. Courses and classes are very flexible, with courses available on campus, at satellite campuses, and online. One unique aspect of HPU class scheduling is flexibility to work around a student's schedule by offering classes during the day, at night, and on weekends; three summer semesters and one winter break semester allow students to speed up credit completion. The main campus location in downtown Honolulu makes attending classes while working that much easier.

Hawaii, U of, Hilo: Located in the small town of Hilo on the big island of Hawaii, UHH offers a solid liberal arts program. The campus is also home to a new Pharmacy School where students can obtain a pharmacy degree in three years. Low cost and a beautiful natural environment make UHH a wonderful alternative for students who want to get away from the big city and enjoy incredible recreational outdoor activities.

Hawaii, U of, Manoa: Reasonable tuition costs, high admission rate, and location make UH very attractive. The major state university of Hawaii, UH is a member of the Western Undergraduate Exchange, which allows students in eligible western states to request reduced tuition costs. Additionally, UH's eight community college campuses offer one of the lowest tuitions in the nation for both in-state and out-of-state students. UH boasts a Law School, Business School, and Medical School as well as programs in architecture and public health and is famous for its astronomy, marine science, and Asian language programs as well as its high population of minority students. With a study abroad program that is particularly strong in Asian countries, UH is a top choice for anyone who would like to study in an Asian country but wants to obtain a US bachelor's degree.

Idaho

Boise State: Boise State has the large campus feel of many other western universities, but with a lower admission index. The university has a great connection to downtown Boise and is in the process of transforming itself into a research campus with additional PhD programs.

Idaho, U of, Moscow: An Idaho state flagship, U of I features outstanding departments in environmental studies, music, and geology. Situated in the lovely town of Moscow, the university is only seven miles from Washington State University in Pullman; the large mass of students in the region creates a youthful vibe and draws numerous businesses catering to the college crowd.

North Idaho C: A wonderful two-year college with on-campus housing and a beautiful location in Coeur d'Alene, North Idaho College feels more like a small private liberal arts college than a community college. Adding to its appeal is the college's joint program with the University of Idaho leading to a bachelor's degree.

Indiana

Earlham C: Earlham students and faculty alike say that the college's most impressive aspect is the close-knit relationship between students and professors, raving about the lifetime bonds that form over the course of their studies.

Evansville, U of: This medium-sized private liberal arts university boasts a wonderful musical theater program and a beautiful campus as well as a satellite campus in Grantham, England.

Valparaiso U: Just an hour east of Chicago, Valparaiso is home to professors and deans who are passionate about their work and devoted to sharing that passion with students.

Illinois

Illinois Wesleyan U: Great science programs, a warm and friendly student body, and terrific theater arts make Illinois Wesleyan one of the Midwest's most popular up-and-coming universities.

Lake Forest C: With Chicago accessible via a 45-minute train ride and a location in one of northern Illinois' great upscale towns, Lake Forest is a hidden midwestern gem offering a strong liberal arts education.

Kentucky

Bellarmine U: A small, comprehensive, Catholic university in Louisville, Bellarmine offers excellent career preparation, involved faculty, and an attractive campus with the burgeoning city of Louisville at its doorstep.

Transylvania U: Transylvania is a rigorous yet supportive small liberal arts college in the heart of Lexington.

Berea C: Berea provides a rigorous liberal arts education with a creative emphasis as well as training in crafts, and all this at an unbeatable price. A "work college," Berea is alone among top US colleges to award every student enrolled a no-tuition promise.

Steven R. Antonoff

Louisiana

Loyola U: A small university in the heart of New Orleans, Loyola boasts both small classes with caring professors and a geographically diverse student body that makes the school a "not-just-southern" experience. It is "application friendly" in that students need not be in the top 50% of their class. Loyola Students enjoy easy access to all that The Big Easy has to offer, including eateries, coffee shops, and street life.

Maryland

Hood C: Set in a beautiful, compact campus, Hood College has particularly strong programs in music, education, and business.

Goucher C: Located in the Baltimore suburb of Towson, Goucher is an excellent choice, particularly for those interested in the arts or international relations.

Salisbury U: Salisbury is an excellent value and a good choice for the student intending to study business, communications, or education.

Stevenson U: Focused on preparing young people for professional careers, Stevenson is an excellent option for the less-competitive student and offers good support for first-generation college students.

Washington C: The beautiful historic town of Chestertown on the eastern shore of the Chesapeake Bay is home to Washington College, a school offering particularly strong programs in international relations, political science, and environmental studies.

Massachusetts

Assumption C: Assumption's strong science programs offering research opportunities both on campus and at nearby medical and technology institutions make it an excellent choice for budding scientists. Located on the outskirts of Worcester, the college's suburban campus stretches well beyond its unassuming front entrance. Tucked out of sight are many new buildings including living/learning dorms, state-of-the-art biological science facilities, and apartment-style options for upper classmen. A new campus in Rome, Italy, was introduced in 2013 as part of the college's effort to expand its global focus. From either campus, Assumption offers students a tightly knit community with a commitment to service and plenty of school spirit.

Emmanuel C: Because of its collaboration with Merck Research Labs, Emmanuel is the "only college in the country with a private pharmaceutical research lab on campus." A location in the heart of Boston allows students to explore the opportunities of a big city from a small liberal arts college setting.

Endicott C: This small liberal arts college has a distinctive pre-professional focus, with standout nursing and hospitality programs. Additionally, the college is pioneering an integrated internship component of its curriculum that is required of every student. Located on the North Shore of Massachusetts Bay, Endicott is just a 30-minute train ride from Boston and boasts incredible oceanfront views.

EXPERT OPINIONS

Wentworth Institute of Technology: Wentworth has strong technology programs in a variety of fields, appealing to a wide range of student interests and abilities.

Minnesota

Augsburg C: Located in the heart of the Twin Cities of Minneapolis and St. Paul and next door to the University of Minnesota campus, Augsburg is a small liberal arts college that offers outstanding support for students with learning disabilities, amazing opportunities for first-generation students, and one of the most noted sober living programs in the nation.

Gustavus Adolphus C: The college's Lutheran and Swedish heritage make up a huge part of the student experience, giving Gustavus Adolphus a distinctive and welcoming environment. The college hosts the annual Nobel Conference, which focuses on bringing cutting-edge science issues to both students and interested members of the surrounding community.

Hamline U: Another notable Twin Cities institution, Hamline focuses on hands-on education, with 100% of its students completing an internship, collaborative research, service learning project, or field-based research.

McNally Smith C of Music: A nonresidential college situated in St. Paul, McNally Smith offers certificates and four-year programs in many facets of music and the music business.

Minnesota, U of, Morris: Two hours west of the Twin Cities, the UMN Morris is a branch of the University of Minnesota, only much smaller and friendlier than the Twin Cities campus. By offering greater access to professors, UMN Morris is able to provide a small, liberal arts college experience. The university is home to the funky, granola-y, artsy students often associated with such private schools as Beloit, Macalester, and Knox, but without the hefty price tag. Additionally, UMN Morris students enjoy the professors, library system, and research opportunities of UMN Morris's flagship sibling in the Twin Cities. Admission-friendly, UMN Morris has also been designated an A+ school for B students.

St. Benedict, C/St. John's U: By sharing each other's resources and creating an open and collaborative community, these two separate universities give students double the college experience for the price of a single admission. St. Benedict/St. John's U are among the top 10 schools sending students abroad.

St. Mary's U: From a pretty setting in southern Minnesota, St. Mary's offers both liberal arts and pre-professional programs for B/B- students. Its excellent Division III sports do well in the very competitive Minnesota Intercollegiate Athletic Conference.

Missouri

Drury U: This medium-sized university is home to an innovative undergraduate architecture department.

Webster U: A midsized university in suburban St. Louis, Webster boasts excellent theater and music departments.

Westminster C: Westminster is particularly strong in its extensive programs for students with learning disabilities.

Missouri U of Science & Technology: Missouri Tech provides exceptional job placement and strong summer programs in engineering and technology at an affordable price.

William Jewell C: William Jewell offers incredible special opportunities such as the Journey Grant and Oxbridge Honors program. Secluded in the town of Liberty, the college is only 20 minutes from the attractions of Kansas City.

Nevada

Nevada State C: This four-year, public commuter college is located in Henderson, only 12 miles from downtown Las Vegas. The school is strong in the health professions (especially nursing), business, education, and the liberal arts and also provides extensive career counseling.

Sierra Nevada C: This very small, private, four-year, residential liberal arts college is located on the beautiful north shore of Lake Tahoe. Boasting an 11:1 ratio of students to faculty, Sierra Nevada is a great school for outdoorsy students (especially skiers) and features robust programs in business, interdisciplinary studies, and the visual and performing arts.

New Jersey

Centenary C. Known for its equestrian programs (particularly its equine business major) Centenary also offers a comprehensive learning program, Project ABLE—Academic Bridges to Learning Effectiveness.

Drew U: Drew is an excellent liberal arts university that has dedicated many of its resources in recent years to enhancing that image.

Rider U: Located in Lawrenceville, just down the road from Princeton, Rider offers solid accounting and business majors along with new majors in global supply chain management and fine and performing arts. One of Rider's gems is its musical theater program, which is connected with the Westminster Choir College of Rider University in Princeton.

New Jersey, C of: The College of New Jersey boasts outstanding academic programs that are less costly than those at other comparable schools. TCNJ's location near both Lawrenceville and Princeton ensures that there are plenty of college students and ongoing activities close by. The newly opened $120-million College Town across from the main campus entrance is a public–private partnership that includes one-, two-, and four-bedroom apartments, shops, and restaurants for students. TCNJ has spent significant time and money to position itself as a powerful academic competitor and has been pulling top students in the state away from Rutgers. The college's academics, size (6,000), and professor/student interactions provide for a positive learning atmosphere, and it is particularly strong in sciences, education, business, and music.

Monmouth U: A private university near the Jersey shore, Monmouth offers a pleasant campus setting and a strong academic program.

EXPERT OPINIONS

New Mexico

St. John's C: Nestled in the mountains surrounding Santa Fe, St. John's College is a perfect fit for the student who is passionate about knowledge. Taught by "tutors" rather than professors, St. John's discussion-based classes in the liberal arts are grounded in the Great Books curriculum. This institution, along with its sister campus in Annapolis, Maryland, is ideal for those who desire not just a degree but also an education.

New York

Adelphi U, Garden City: A midsized university in an upscale New York suburb, Adelphi boasts robust programs in liberal arts, the performing arts, speech pathology and communication disorders, as well as several well-regarded signature pre-professional programs including nursing (with a cutting-edge facility under construction). A 75-acre protected arboretum offers students a quiet haven, while the campus location—just 20 miles from Manhattan—provides easy access to internships and weekend entertainment/nightlife. Given that the new and first female president of the university comes from a STEM background, it is expected that health and science will remain strong draws for students at Adelphi.

Marist C: Marist has established premier programs in fashion, communications, computer science, the health sciences, and study abroad. Students can take advantage of most of these offerings on the beautiful Hudson River campus with its state-of-the-art facilities. The Freshmen Florence Experience is truly unique, allowing first-year students to begin their studies with a year abroad or even opt to earn their degree from the fully accredited overseas branch.

Stevens Institute of Technology: Stevens is an exceptional academic and technology school with specialized programs such as naval engineering. Its lovely campus in fashionable Hoboken overlooks Manhattan and is home to a wonderfully warm and welcoming culture.

North Carolina

North Carolina, U of, Asheville: A public liberal arts college with strong academics, UNC Asheville is located in a lively midsized city renowned for its vibrant arts community, burgeoning culinary scene, and historic architecture.

Ohio

Bowling Green State U: Bowling Green State enjoys a great reputation for education, business, athletic training, and performing arts. It has also developed a new entrepreneurial program with seed business opportunities and one of the nation's best programs in college student personnel, which facilitates many extracurricular activities and encourages high participation/engagement rates among students.

Cincinnati, U of: Currently experiencing a renaissance of sorts, U Cincinnati has undertaken new brick and mortar projects, including a fitness center, residence halls, a Greek village, a renovated football stadium, and a newly developed program to help at-risk students succeed. The area within walking distance of the university has been

Steven R. Antonoff

upgraded substantially, and U Cincinnati's graduation rate has increased significantly in recent years, as has its reputation for programs in the DAAP (Design, Art, Architectural, and Planning) School and the College Conservatory of Music.

Dayton, U of: University of Dayton alumni consistently rate their undergraduate experience as positive and are very financially supportive, crediting their alma mater for their success. Current students are just as enthusiastic about the university. Students live in residence halls in the first two years and then branch out into university-owned houses in an adjacent residential neighborhood. Social life on campus tends to stay within this neighborhood, rather than migrating to bars and nightclubs. Additionally, there are many off-campus food choices that are supported on the student dining plan.

Oklahoma

Tulsa, U of: University of Tulsa is known for its dedicated and involved professors and its top programs in computer science, engineering, business, and in recent years, film.

Oregon

Linfield C: A college with tons of school spirit, Linfield is a perennial Division III national competitor. In addition to strong athletics, Linfield has caring faculty and solid academic programs that include an excellent nursing program.
Portland, U of: Situated on a lovely campus overlooking the Willamette River, this Catholic university is administered by the same Catholic order as Notre Dame. Students rave about the campus life and solid academics, especially in business, engineering, and nursing.

Willamette U: Willamette's noteworthy characteristics are its vibrant community, solid academics, and an impressively successful program that monitors students for possible graduate opportunities (such as a Fulbright) and helps those selected students apply.

Pennsylvania

Allegheny C: A liberal arts college in picturesque western Pennsylvania, Allegheny aims to better prepare its students for an interdisciplinary world by offering an innovative curriculum in which students must major and minor in two somewhat unrelated fields (i.e., not chemistry and biology but chemistry and philosophy).

Chestnut Hill C: A small, nurturing, Catholic liberal arts college located in a historic neighborhood of Philadelphia, Chestnut Hill offers many interesting combined programs as well as a particularly solid elementary education program. This is an environment where formerly reticent students "come out of their shells" and thrive socially.

Immaculata U: Immaculata features a faculty invested in student learning and success, a curriculum embedded with programs to provide academic support, and a beautiful campus near Philadelphia.

EXPERT OPINIONS

Juniata C: Central Pennsylvania's Juniata College has created a unique system of advisement to help students make the most of their college experience. In January of freshmen year, every student chooses two faculty advisors: a program advisor to assist with issues related to the student's program of emphasis matters and a general advisor to deal with broader academic issues.

Lebanon Valley C: With its friendly environment and approachable professors, Lebanon Valley is a very viable option for students who need a second chance.

Millersville U: One of 14 Pennsylvania State System of Higher Education (PASSHE) colleges, Millersville is located in historic Lancaster and provides great value for both in-state and out-of-state students.

Muhlenberg C: A small college only an hour's drive from Philadelphia, Muhlenberg offers robust academic options and lively social life.
Susquehanna U: With particularly strong programs in music and creative writing, Susquehanna is an appealing environment for the student with a passion for the arts.

York C: York is a private liberal arts college experience with a public school price and a direct admit nursing program.

Rhode Island

Bryant U: Bryant's suburban Providence location makes for excellent internship opportunities and academic experiences for its students.

Rhode Island C: Rhode Island College is home to an especially fine nursing program, small class sizes, and approachable professors.

South Carolina

Coker C: At Coker College, all classes are small and discussion-based. In addition, the campus is home to a wide variety of active organizations, helping to ensure that all students find meaningful social connection with peers.

Erskine C: Erskine's enrollment of about 600 means that all classes are small and that faculty can actively engage students throughout their four years. Perhaps as a result, Erskine graduates have a very high placement rate into graduate and professional school.

Presbyterian C: Faculty members at Presbyterian interact with students both in small classes as well as outside the classroom, giving students a solid liberal arts experience. The college also offers a generous merit aid program.

Tennessee

Belmont U: With Nashville enjoying a meteoric rise in popularity and growth, money is pouring into Belmont, making it a rising star in Tennessee. As might be expected given Belmont's location, its music and music business programs are particularly excellent. The university is Christian-based but less noticeably so than other Christian colleges in the state.

Steven R. Antonoff

Union U: This Christian university in western Tennessee has good programs in theology, nursing, and pharmacy. It is a great private college option for kids who live in the west of the state and don't want to be too far from home.

Lipscomb U: This Christian-centered university in Nashville boasts stellar programs in nursing and theology, and a new College of Entertainment and the Arts.

Texas

Trinity U: A midsized San Antonio university with a $1-billion endowment, Trinity offers housekeeping in its dorm rooms, all new buildings, and a test-optional admissions policy. In addition to a new STEM focus, the university has excellent neuroscience and early childhood research programs.

Southwestern U: Southwestern may be the best-kept secret in Texas. One of the university's standout features is the Paideia Learning Experience where students work with professors to determine subject material to study or research, connect different classes in new ways, and collaborate with other students, faculty, and staff. It is not uncommon for the university president to invite students to dine at his home to discuss topics or meet special guests. A small campus with good merit awards and solid liberal arts curriculum, Southwestern has been named one of Loren Pope's "Colleges that Change Lives."

St. Edward's U: A former commuter school, St. Edward's U has transformed itself with a solid liberal arts curriculum, good merit aid, and strong study abroad. Its location in the heart of Austin provides for good internship and shadowing opportunities and a diverse student culture. Professors at St. Edward's are engaged, and the university's business program is really taking off.

Vermont

Bennington C: Known for creating a small, intimate community of scholars, Bennington is home to an innovative curriculum where professors give narrative evaluations.

Castleton U: Until recently known as Castleton State, the rechristened Castleton University has increased its investment in infrastructure and academics and is led by a dynamic new president who is breathing new life into the school.

Champlain C: With an innovative curriculum, Champlain is always seeking ways to stay ahead of the curve in terms of programs and technology. The college also fosters excellent relationships with the business community and has a faculty that cares about the development of the whole student (including personal finance and life skills).

Lyndon State C: Lyndon State's strong points include happy, satisfied students and unique programs in graphic design and outdoor recreation and ski resort management. Its meteorology program has trained many of the meteorologists appearing on The Weather Channel.

Sterling C: This rural Vermont liberal arts college is an excellent choice for the student who wants a very hands-on education and is passionate about the environment and sustainability.

EXPERT OPINIONS

Virginia

Hollins U: Standout features of this central Virginia liberal arts college include a top-notch riding program and exceptional science research opportunities.

Lynchburg College: Lynchburg is known for its exceptionally close-knit community and beautiful campus.

Mary Washington, U of: This public midsized university has the feel of a classic liberal arts college. Located in the historic town of Fredericksburg halfway between Washington, D.C., and Richmond, Virginia, the university enjoys easy access via Amtrak to DC for day trips or internships. Costs are reasonable, even for out-of-state students. The liberal arts curriculum includes business and education majors as well as a first-rate theater program and an excellent historic preservation major. Small classes, faculty who are dedicated teachers, and plentiful research opportunities help students stay engaged in learning. Mary Washington's beautiful campus is an eye-pleasing combination of classical brick buildings and new construction and is home to friendly non-pretentious students.

Roanoke C: Actually located in Salem just a short drive from the larger city of Roanoke, this campus provides a wonderful location for students interested in taking advantage of the attractions of a small city and its surrounding mountains. Roanoke is a small college where professors act as mentors and take an interest in students, often bringing them into research projects. The college offers majors in liberal arts, business, and education as well as an honors program for those who want to push themselves. Sizeable merit aid is available for top applicants. Roanoke's community is close-knit and its students friendly.

Washington

Central Washington U: Central Washington University is home to an excellent program in construction management.

Puget Sound, U of: Puget Sound has a successful history of writing curriculum across disciplines as well as a well-regarded honors business program and School of Physical Therapy. The university's campus is beautiful, with themed dorms and easy access to Seattle.

Washington State U: Washington State is home to a fantastic honors program plus a seven-year program in veterinary medicine. A setting just seven miles west of the University of Idaho in Moscow makes for a lively community and plenty of student-oriented businesses, restaurants, and venues.

Washington, U of, Bothel: Students at UW Bothel reap the benefits of UW Seattle's excellent curriculum without the flagship's large class sizes. UW Bothel's excellent business program offers both BA and MBA degrees.

Whitman C: Whitman is a rigorous liberal arts college with exceptional geology and English programs. Its unique curriculum includes a first-year sequence that every Whitman student completes.

Wisconsin

Beloit C: Not exactly a hidden gem, Beloit deserves much more credit than it gets! It touts its liberal arts as "amplified" and allows students to choose from more then 50 majors or create their own.

Carroll U: Friendly and caring Carroll is a Catholic university, but students of all faiths are truly welcomed here and will find a home on this lovely, leafy suburban campus just outside of Milwaukee. This small Midwestern university has developed excellent physical therapy and physician's assistant programs as well as a superior program in athletic training.

Ripon C: Ripon describes its education style as "intensely personal," with a focus on personal academic development. The curriculum emphasizes the practical application of liberal arts skills, leading to good job and career counseling. Close mentoring by faculty members helps students hone their ability to articulate and advocate for themselves. Ripon has a specific mission to educate first-generation college students, and a first-rate disabilities office and program provides support for those who need it. The student body is a mix of rural farm kids, urban minority students, students with LDs, and suburban kids from both Milwaukee and Chicago. The college awards financial aid to almost every student and has strong Bridge, Trio, and McNair Scholars programs. Ripon even provides a bike for every student, making it easy to get around campus. The college has a deep-rooted sense of tradition and provides opportunities for all its students to shine through research, plays, athletics, and more. This is a perfect place for students who are not quite sure if college is for them.

Wisconsin, U of, Whitewater: A lovely rural campus of the University of Wisconsin, UW-Whitewater is situated not far from Milwaukee, Chicago, and Madison. It is small in size, so students get the feel of a liberal arts college for the price of a public institution. The university even lets Illinois students pay the same cost of attendance as in-state students. UW-Whitewater is particularly well respected for how well it helps first-year students transition into college.

EXPERT OPINIONS

CHAPTER EIGHT
TIDBITS AND TRIVIA

Educational Attainment of Adults

Eighth Grade or Less: 4.3%
Some High School, No Diploma: 8%
High School Diploma: 29.6%
Some College, No Degree: 19.4%
Associate Degree: 5.3%
Bachelor's Degree: 18.9%
Master's Degree: 7.5%
Professional Degree: 1.3%
Doctoral Degree: 1.6%

Source: U.S. Census Bureau

The Oldest Colleges (and When They Were Founded)

These are the oldest U.S. universities and colleges.

Harvard U (MA): 1636
William & Mary, C of (VA): 1693
St. John's C, Annapolis (MD): 1693
Yale U (CT): 1701
Delaware, U of: 1743
Princeton U (NJ): 1746
Washington & Lee U: 1749
Columbia U (NY): 1754
Pennsylvania, U of: 1757
Brown U (RI): 1764
Rutgers U, New Brunswick (NJ): 1766
Dartmouth C (NH): 1769

Fairly New Colleges (and When They Were Founded)

Northern California, U of: 1993
New St. Andrews C (ID): 1994
Catholic Pacific (Canada): 2000
Our Lady Seat of Wisdom Academy: 2000
Patrick Henry C (VA): 2000
Soka U (CA): 2001
California, U of, Merced: 2005
Wyoming Catholic C: 2005
John Paul the Great (CA): 2006
Ave Maria U (FL): 2007
Quest U (Canada): 2007
Living Water C (Canada): 2009
Singapore U of Technology & Design: 2009
New York U, Abu Dhabi: 2010
Chicago, U of, Institute of Politics: 2013
Florida Polytechnic U: 2013
Texas, U of, Rio Grande Valley: 2013
Webster U, Ghana Campus: 2013

TIDBITS AND TRIVIA

Xavier U Bhubanesawr: 2013
Ambrose Treacy C (Australia): 2015
Central Florida, U of, C of Undergraduate Studies: 2015

Nicknames for Colleges or Students at Particular Schools

Babson C (MA): Babsonites
Bard C (NY): Bardie
Bates C (ME): Batesies
Bennington C (VT): Bennies
Bryn Mawr C (PA): Mawrters
California Polytechnic State U,
   San Luis Obispo: Cal Poly/SLO
California, U of, Berkeley: Cal
Carleton C (MN): Carls
Clark U (MA): Clarkies
Colgate U (NY): 'Gate
Connecticut C: Conn
Drew U (NJ): Drewids
Duke U (NC): Dukies
Earlham C (IN): Earlhamites
Emory U (GA): Emeroids
Evergreen State C (WA): Greeners
Florida A & M U: Fam-You
Franklin & Marshall C (PA): Fummers
Gustavus Adolphus C (MN): Gusties
Hampden-Sydney C (VA): Hampsders
Hartwick C (NY): The Wick
Harvey Mudd C (CA): Mudders
Haverford C (PA): The Ford
Heidelberg C (OH): The Berg
Kalamazoo C (MI): known simply as "K"
Lake Forest C (IL): Foresters
Lewis & Clark C (OR): LC
Massachusetts Institute of Technology: The Tute
Mississippi U for Women: The W
Missouri, U of, Columbia: Mizzou
Morehouse C (GA): The House
Muhlenberg C (PA): The Berg
North Carolina, U of, Chapel Hill: Carolina
Oberlin C (OH): Obie/Oberliners
Occidental C (CA): Oxy
Pittsburgh, U of (PA): Pitt
Pitzer C (CA): Pitzies
Reed C (OR): Reedies
Rhode Island School of Design: Rizdee
St. John's C (MD) (NM): Johnnies
St. John's U (MN): Johnnies
St. Lawrence U (NY): Larries
St. Mary-of-the-Woods C (IN): Woodsies
St. Michael's C (VT): St. Mike's
St. Olaf C (MN): Ole
Scripps C (CA): Scrippsies
Skidmore C (NY): Skiddies
Smith C (MA): Smithies

South Carolina, U of, Columbia: Carolina
South, U of the (TN): Sewanee
Swarthmore C (PA): Swatties
Transylvania U (KY): Transy
U.S. Coast Guard Academy (CT): Coasties
U.S. Military Academy (NY): West Point
U.S. Naval Academy (MD): Annapolis
Valparaiso U (IN): Valpo
Vanderbilt U (TN): Vandy
Villanova U (PA): Nova
Wabash C (IN): Wallies
Washington State U: Wah-sue
Washington, U of: U-Dub
Wheaton C (IL): Wheaties
Wheaton C (MA): Wheaties
Whitman C (WA): Whitties
Williams C (MA): Ephs (shortened first name of the college founder)
Wittenberg U (OH): Witt
Worcester Polytechnic Institute (MA): Whoopies
Yale U (CT): Yalies/Elis (shortened first name of the college founder)

Interesting Team Mascots

Akron, U of (OH): Zips
Alabama, U of, Birmingham: Blazers
Alaska, U of, Southeast: Humpback Whales
Alaska, U of, Fairbanks: Nanooks
Amherst C (MA): Lord Jeffs
Arkansas State U: Red Wolves
Arkansas Tech: Wonder Boys
Arkansas, U of, Monticello: Boll Weevils
Atlantic, C of the (ME): Black Flies
Brooklyn College (NY): Bridges
Brandeis U (MA): Judges
California, U of, Santa Cruz: Banana Slugs
California, U of, Irvine: Anteaters
California State U Long Beach: Dirtbags
Campbell U (NC): Fighting Camels
Canisius C (NY): Griffins
Columbia C (CA): Claim Jumpers
Connecticut C: Camels
Delaware, U of: Blue Hens
Delta State U (MS): Fighting Okra
Drexel U (PA): Dragons
Elon U (NC): The Phoenix
Evansville, U of (IN): Purple Aces
Evergreen State C (WA): Geoducks
Fairfield U (CT): Stags
Grand Valley State U (MI): Lakers
Heidelberg C (OH): Student Princes
Indiana State U: Sycamores
Kent State U (OH): Golden Flashes
LaSalle U (PA): Explorers
Lincoln Memorial U (TN): Railsplitters

Lubbock Christian U (TX): Chaparrals
Marshall U (WV): Thundering Herd
Mary Baldwin C (VA): Squirrels
Mary, U of (ND): Marauders
Minnesota State U: Dragons
Missouri, U of, Kansas City: Kangaroos
Central Missouri State U: Mules
New York U: Violets
New York, State U of, C of Environmental Science and Forestry: Stumpies
North Carolina School of the Arts: Fighting Pickles
North Florida, U of: Ospreys
Northern Kentucky U: Norse
Oglethorpe U (GA): Stormy Petrel
Ohio Wesleyan U: Battling Bishops
Oklahoma, U of: Sooners
Pace U (NY): Setters
Pittsburg State U (KS): Gorillas
Presbyterian C (SC): Blue Hose
Rhode Island School of Design: basketball team (The Balls),
    ice hockey team (The Nads), Women's Soccer (The Jugs), Fencing (The Pricks)
Rose-Hulman Institute (IN): Fightin' Engineers
Rowan U (NJ): Professors
San Diego, U of (CA): Toreros
San Francisco, U of (CA): Dons
Scottsdale Community C (AZ): Artichokes
Slippery Rock U (PA): Pride
South Carolina, U of, Columbia: Gamecocks
South Carolina, U of, Spartanburg: Running Rifles
South Carolina, U of, Sumter: Fire Ants
Southern Arkansas U: Muleriders
Southern Illinois U, Carbondale: Salukis
Southwestern C (KS): The Moundbuilders
Southwestern Louisiana, U of: Ragin' Cajuns
Stetson U (FL): Hatters
St. Louis U (MO): Billikens
St. Louis C of Pharmacy (MO): Eutectic
Sweet Briar C (VA): Vixens
Texas Christian U: Horned Frogs
Thomas Jefferson U (PA): Medics
Trinity Christian C (IL): Trolls
Virginia Polytechnic Institute & State U: Hokies
Wake Forest U (NC): Demon Deacons
Washburn U (KS): Ichabods
Webster U (MO): Gorlocks
Western Carolina U (NC): Catamounts
Western Illinois U: Leathernecks
Whitman C (WA): The Fighting Missionaries
Whittier C (CA): Poets
Wichita State U (KS): Shockers
Williams College (MA): Ephs
Youngstown State U (OH): Emperor Penguins

Steven R. Antonoff

Top College Fight Songs

William E. Studwell and Bruce R. Schueneman, authors of *College Fight Songs II, A Supplementary Anthology,* rated college fight songs and summed up what made each special.

1. Notre Dame, U of (IN): "Notre Dame Victory March" ("the best-known and perhaps the most-borrowed")
2. Michigan, U of, Ann Arbor: "The Victors" ("most rousing and stunning; a very proud song")
3. Wisconsin, U of, Madison: "On Wisconsin" ("smooth and much-borrowed old classic")
4. Yale U (CT): "Down The Field" ("another smooth and much-borrowed old classic")
5. U.S. Naval Academy (MD): "Anchors Aweigh" ("very dynamic and uplifting")
6. Maine, U of, Orono: "The Maine Stein Song" ("great melody, but it's a drinking song")
7. Southern California, U of: "Fight on, USC" ("brilliant, sparkling, and innovative")
8. Georgia Institute of Technology: "Ramblin' Wreck from Georgia Tech" ("fine tune, great sense of humor")
9. Texas, U of, Austin: "The Eyes of Texas" ("tune borrowed from 'I've been working on the railroad,' but has a lot of sweep and energy")
10. Ohio State U, Columbus: "Across the Field" ("smooth and active; takes one pleasantly across the field")
11. Minnesota, U of, Twin Cities: "Minnesota Rouser" ("dynamic and rousing, as the title suggests")
12. Indiana U, Bloomington: "Indiana, Our Indiana" ("tugs at the heart while causing foot-tapping")
13. Illinois, U of, Urbana: "Illinois Loyalty" ("smooth, sensitive, and flowing")
14. Washington & Lee U (VA): "Washington & Lee Swing" ("very catchy and likable; well-named")
15. Pennsylvania, U of: "Fight on, Pennsylvania" ("creative and different from the rest of the pack")
16. Oklahoma, U of: "Boomer Sooner" ("borrowed from 'Yale Boola,' but rocks the stadium")
17. Georgia, U of: "Glory, Glory to Old Georgia" ("uses the rouser 'Battle Hymn of the Republic' as a tune; a passing mention to the University of Colorado, which also uses the tune for its 'Glory, Glory, Colorado' ")
18. U.S. Air Force Academy (CO): "U.S. Air Force Song" ("excellent uplifting march; also used as the Air Force's song")
19. U.S. Coast Guard Academy (CT): "Semper Paratus" ("lesser-known but quite stirring march; also used as the Coast Guard's song")
20. Clemson U (SC): "Clemson Fight Song" ("uses the delightful 'Tiger Rag' as its tune")
21. Tennessee, U of, Knoxville: "Down the Field" ("uses the exact same title and tune as Yale's 'Down the Field': F for originality, but A+ for taste")
22. U.S. Military Academy (NY): "On, Brave Old Army Team" ("We don't want to forget the Army; a good song with one terrific passage")
23. Northern Illinois U: "Huskie Fight Song" ("lively and distinctive")
24. Cornell U (NY): "Far Above the Cayuga's Waters" ("This is really an alma mater rather than a fight song, but is such a collegiate classic, how can one overlook it? If played with a lively enough tempo, it becomes a pretty good fight song")
25. Harvard U (MA), Rice U (TX) and Furman U (SC): "Our Director March" ("These three universities all use this excellent tune, but not always as a fight song; if the melody had a clearer institutional identity, it would be in the top fifteen. Many other schools also use the tune, including the University of Southern California, for its 'Victory Song'")
26. Oregon, U of: "Mighty Oregon" ("a very smooth song")

Honorable Mentions

Alabama, U of, Tuscaloosa: "Yea, Alabama"
Auburn U (AL): "War Eagle"
Boston C (MA): "For Boston"
California, U of, Los Angeles: "Sing UCLA"
Columbia U (NY): "Roar, Lion, Roar"
Dartmouth C (NH): "As the Backs Go Tearing By"
Duke U (NC): " Duke Blue and White"
Harvard U (MA): "The Gridiron King"
Illinois, U of, Urbana: "Pride of the Illini"
Kentucky, U of, Knoxville: "On, On, U of K"
Lamar U (TX): "Big Red"
Michigan State U: "Michigan State Fight Song"
Missouri, U of, Columbia: "Fight Tiger"
Nebraska, U of, Lincoln: "Dear Old Nebraska U"
Northwestern U (IL): "Go U Northwestern"
Ohio State U, Columbus: "Le Regiment"
Pennsylvania State U, University Park: "The Nittany Lion"
Pennsylvania, U of: "Fight on Pennsylvania"
Pittsburgh, U of (PA): "Hail to Pitt"
Princeton U (NJ): "The Princeton Cannon Song"
Stanford U (CA) "Come Join The Band"
South Carolina, U of, Columbia: "Carolina Fight Song"
Syracuse U (NY): "Down, Down The Field"
Texas A & M U, College Station: "The Aggie War Hymn"
Tulane U (LA): "Roll on, Tulane"
Washington, U of, Seattle: "Bow Down to Washington"
Yale U (CT): "Bingo, Eli Yale"

Notable or Exceptional Songs in Order of Superiority

1. Yale U (CT): "Down the Field"; "Yale Boola"; "Bingo Eli Yale"
2. Harvard U (MA): "Our Director"; "The Gridiron King"
3. Ohio State U, Columbus: "Across the Field"; "Le Regiment"
4. Illinois, U of, Urbana: "Illinois Loyalty"; "Pride of Illini"

Source: William E. Studwell and Bruce R. Schueneman, *College Fight Songs II, A Supplementary Anthology,* Binghamton, New York 13904, The Haworth Press, Inc., and personal conversation with Mr. Studwell.

Campuses Where Movies Were Filmed

These colleges served as at least one of the locations for the film or television series listed; some movies may have been filmed at more than one college. The year given is the year of the film's release or first season of the series. For each institution, films/series are listed by release date, starting with the most recent.

Acadia U (Canada): *Dolores Claiborne* (1995)
Agnes Scott C (GA): *Scream II* (1998); *Fried Green Tomatoes* (1991); *Driving Miss Daisy* (1989): *The Bear* (1983); *The Four Seasons* (1981)
Arizona State U: *Jerry Maguire* (1996)
Arizona, U of: *Glory Road* (2006); *Revenge of the Nerds* (1984)

Bentley C (MA): *Game Plan* (2007)
Boston C (MA): *The Program* (1993)
Berry C (GA): *Sweet Home Alabama* (2002); *Remember the Titans* (2000)
Boston U (MA): *21* (2008)
British Columbia, U of (Canada): *Fifty Shades of Grey* (2015); *X-Men Origins: Wolverine* (2009); *88 Minutes* (2007); *Good Luck Chuck* (2007); *She's the Man* (2006); *X-Men: The Last Stand* (2006); *The Exorcism of Emily Rose* (2005); *The Butterfly Effect* (2004); *Miracle* (2004); *Perfect Score* (2004); *Josie and the Pussycats* (2001); *Battlestar Galactica* television series (2004); *Antitrust* (2001); *Smallville* television series (2001)
Bryn Mawr C (PA): *How to Get Away With Murder* television series (2014)
Bunker Hill Community C (MA): *Good Will Hunting* (1997)
California Institute of Technology: *Orange County* (2002); *Legally Blonde* (2001); *Kiss the Girls* (1997); *Beverly Hills Cop* (1984)
California Polytechnic State U, San Luis Obispo: *Personal Best* (1982)
California State U, Fullerton: *The Comebacks* (2007)
California State U, Long Beach: *American Pie* (1999); *Ferris Bueller's Day Off* (1986)
California State U, Northridge: *Legally Blonde 2* (2003)
California State U, San Diego: *Bring It On* (2000)
California, U of, Berkeley: *Boys and Girls* (2000); *Patch Adams* (1998)
California, U of, Los Angeles: *Water for Elephants* (2011); *Live Free or Die Hard* (2007); *Art School Confidential* (2006); *Click* (2006); *First Daughter* (2004); *Old School* (2003); *Orange County* (2002); *How High* (2001); *Legally Blonde* (2001); *Erin Brockovich* (2000); *The Nutty Professor* (1996); *Higher Learning* (1995); *Final Analysis* (1992); *Happy Together* (1989)
Carleton C (MN): *D3, The Mighty Ducks* (1996)
Carnegie Mellon U (PA): *The Dark Knight Rises* (2012); *Smart People* (2008); *Wonder Boys* (1999); *Lorenzo's Oil* (1992)
Carthage C (WI): *Fever Lake* (1996)
Case Western Reserve U (OH): *Air Force One* (1997)
Centenary C (LA): *Welcome Home Roscoe Jenkins* (2008)
Centennial C (Canada): *Degrassi Junior High* television series (1987)
Central Florida, U of: *The Ten Avatars* (2008); *Sydney White* (2007); *Out of Time* (1998)
Chapman U (CA): *The Newest Pledge* (2012); *Accepted* (2006); *Crimson Tide* (1995)
Charleston, C of (SC): *The Notebook* (2004); *American Wedding* (2003): *Cold Mountain* (2003); *The Patriot* (2000)
Chicago, U of (IL): *The Express* (2008); *Proof* (2005); *When Harry Met Sally* (1989)
Claremont McKenna C (CA): *Lions for Lambs* (2007)
Clark Atlanta U (GA): *Stomp the Yard* (2007); *Drumline* (2002)
Columbia U (NY): *Still Alice* (2014); *August Rush* (2008); *Spider-Man 3* (2007); *Hitch* (2005); *Eternal Sunshine of the Spotless Mind* (2004); *Spider-Man 2* (2004); *Anger Management* (2003); *Mona Lisa Smile* (2003); *Spider-Man 1* (2002); *The Mirror Has Two Faces* (1996); *Malcolm X* (1992); *Hannah and Her Sister* (1986); *Altered States* (1980); *Marathon Man* (1976)
Drew U (NJ): *Spinning Into Butter* (2007); *The Family Stone* (2005)
Duke U (NC): *I Know What You Did Last Summer* (1997); *Kiss the Girls* (1997); *The Program* (1993); *The Handmaid's Tale* (1990); *Brainstorm* (1983)
Eckerd C (FL): *Misconceptions* (2008)
El Camino C (CA): *The Longest Yard* (2005)
Elon U (NC): *He Got Game* (1998)
Emory U (GA): *Into the Wild* (2007); *Road Trip* (2000)
Fairfield U (CT): *Hear My Song* (2014)
Fairleigh Dickinson U (NJ): *The Family Stone* (2005); *A Beautiful Mind* (2001)

Fordham U (NY): *Wall Street: Money Never Sleeps* (2010); *Solitary Man* (2009); *Kinsey* (2004); *A Beautiful Mind* (2001); *Center Stage* (2000); *Quiz Show* (1994); *The Verdict* (1982); *Love Story* (1970)

George Fox U (OR): *Into the Wild* (2007)

Georgia Institute of Technology: *One Missed Call* (2007); *Stomp the Yard* (2007); *Drumline* (2002); *Road Trip* (2000)

Georgia, U of: *Road Trip* (2000)

Harvard U (MA): *The Great Debaters* (2007); *The Firm* (1993); *Love Story* (1970)

Holy Cross, C of the (MA): *Game Plan* (2007)

Illinois, U of, Chicago: *Stranger Than Fiction* (2006)

Illinois, U of, Urbana: *With Honors* (1994)

Indiana U, Bloomington: *Breaking Away* (1979)

Iowa, U of: *The Program* (1993)

Johns Hopkins U (MD): *The Social Network* (2010); *Head of State* (2003); *The Curve* (1998)

Johnson & Wales U (RI): *27 Dresses* (2008)

Juilliard School (NY): *Center Stage* (2000)

Kenyon C (OH): *Liberal Arts* (2012)

Lake Forest C (IL): *Ordinary People* (1980)

Louisiana State U: *Pitch Perfect* (2012)

Manhattan C (NY): *A Beautiful Mind* (2001); *Six Degrees of Separation* (1993)

Massachusetts Institute of Technology: *Good Will Hunting* (1997)

McGill U (Canada): *The Human Stain* (2003)

McMaster U (Canada): *American Pie Presents Beta House* (2007); *American Pie Presents the Naked Mile* (2006); *Nemesis Game* (2003)

Michigan, U of: *The Program* (1993)

Minnesota, U of, Twin Cities: *With Honors* (1994); *Ice Castles* (1978)

Morehouse C (GA): *Stomp the Yard* (2007)

Morris Brown C (GA): *Stomp the Yard* (2007); *Drumline* (2002)

Mt. St. Mary's C (CA): *Alex & Emma* (2003)

New York U: *In Good Company* (2004); *The Freshman* (1990)

New York, City U of, Baruch: *Devil's Own* (1997)

New York, City U of, Bronx: *Mona Lisa Smile* (2003)

New York, City U of, Brooklyn: *Spinning Into Butter* (2007)

New York, City U of, City C: *Reversal of Fortune* (1990)

New York, City U of, Hunter C: *Devil's Own* (1997)

New York, City U of, Lehman: *Private Parts* (1997)

North Carolina, U of, Chapel Hill: *The Roommate* (2011); *Greek* television series (2007); *Patch Adams* (1998)

North Carolina, U of, Wilmington: *Dawson's Creek* television series (1998)

North Texas, U of: *Necessary Roughness* (1991)

Northwestern U (IL): *Road to Perdition* (2002)

Notre Dame, U of (IN): *Rudy* (1993)

Occidental C (CA): *Glee* television series (2013); *Arrested Development* television series (2012); *CSI* television series (2012); *NCIS* television series (2011); *The Kids Are All Right* (2010); *Private Practice* television series (2007); *Orange County* (2002); *Jurassic Park III* (2001); *Boys and Girls* (2000); *West Wing* television series (1999); *Don't Be a Menace to South Central While Drinking Your Juice in the Hood* (1996); *Clueless* (1995); *Beverly Hills 90210* television series (1990); *Real Genius* (1985); *Star Trek III* (1984); *Tall Story* (1960); *Pat and Mike* (1952); *Goodbye, Mr. Fancy* (1951)

Oregon, U of: *Without Limits* (1998); *Prefontaine* (1997); *Personal Best* (1982); *National Lampoon's Animal House* (1978)

Steven R. Antonoff

Pacific, U of the (CA): *Switched at Birth* television series (2011); *Parenthood* television series (2010); *Indiana Jones and the Kingdom of the Crystal Skull* (2008); *Raiders of the Lost Ark* (1981)

Pennsylvania, U of: *Transformers: Revenge of the Fallen* (2009); *Invincible* (2006); *Unbreakable* (2000); *Philadelphia* (1993)

Pierce C (CA): *The Comebacks* (2007)

Pomona C (CA): *Gilmore Girls* television series (2000); *Beaches* (1988); *Over the Top* (1987); *Eleanor and Franklin* television movie (1976); *The Absent Minded Professor* (1961)

Princeton U (NJ): *Admission* (2013); *Ye Maaya Chesave* (2010); *Transformers: Revenge of the Fallen* (2009); *Across The Universe* (2007); *Annapolis* (2006); *A Beautiful Mind* (2001); *I.Q.* (1994)

Reed C (OR): *Into the Wild* (2007)

Rollins C (FL): *Sydney White* (2007)

Ryerson U (Canada): *My Big Fat Greek Wedding* (2002); *True Blue* (2001)

Sarah Lawrence C (NY): *Baby It's You* (1983)

Simon Fraser U (Canada): *Underworld Awakening* (2012); *Personal Effects* (2009); *Fringe* television series (2008); *Battlestar Galactica* television series (2004); *Agent Cody Banks* (2003); *My Life Without Me* (2003); *Spy Game* (2001)

Smith C (MA): *Malice* (1993); *Who's Afraid of Virginia Woolf* (1966)

South Carolina, U of: *The Program* (1993)

Southern California, U of: *The Social Network* (2010); *The Number 23* (2007); *Harold and Kumar Go to White Castle* (2004); *Perfect Opposites* (2004); *Legally Blonde 2* (2003); *Old School* (2003); *Legally Blonde* (2001); *Road Trip* (2000); *Kiss the Girls* (1997); *Blue Chips* (1994); *Forrest Gump* (1994); *The Graduate* (1967)

Spelman C (GA): *School Daze* (1988)

St. Catherine, C of (MN): *D3, The Mighty Ducks* (1996)

St. Mary's U (Canada): *The Elizabeth Smart Story* television movie (2003)

St. Peter's C (NJ): *The Interpreter* (2005)

Stetson U (FL): *Water Boy* (1998)

Tennessee, U of: *Road Trip* (2000)

Texas A & M U, College Station: *Revenge of the Nerds* (1984)

Texas, U of, Austin: *Cheer Up* (2003); *Miss Congeniality* (2000); *DOA* (1988)

Toronto, U of (Canada): *Crimson Peak* (2015); *Total Recall* (2012); *Shadowland* (2008); *The Time Traveler's Wife* (2008); *Take the Lead* (2006); *Mean Girls* (2004); *The Prince and Me* (2004); *Degrassi: The Next Generation* television series (2001); *Dracula* (2000); *Skulls* (2000); *The Bride of Chucky* (1998); *The Mighty* (1998); *Good Will Hunting* (1997); *Tommy Boy* (1995); *PCU* (1994); *Searching for Bobby Fischer* (1993); *Paper Chase* (1973)

Trent U (Canada): *Urban Legends: Final Cut* (2000)

Tulane U (LA): *Our Brand is Crisis* (2015); *Pelican Brief* (1993)

U.S. Naval Academy (MD): *Patriot Games* (1992)

Union C (NY): *The Way We Were* (1973)

Ursinus C (PA): *How to Get Away With Murder* television series (2014)

Virginia, U of: *For Sale by Owner* (2009); *True Colors* (1991)

Wagner C (NY): *The Rewrite* (2014); *School of Rock* (2003)

Wake Forest U (NC): *The Longest Ride* (2015)

Washington State U: *At Middleton* (2013)

Washington, U of, Seattle: *21 and Over* (2011)

Waterloo, U of (Canada): *Degrassi: The Next Generation* television series (2001)

Wellesley C (MA): *Mona Lisa Smile* (2003)

Wesleyan U (CT): *PCU* (1994)

Wheaton C (MA): *Prozac Nation* (2001); *Soul Man* (1986)

Wiley C (TX): *The Great Debaters* (2007)

Wisconsin, U of, Madison: *Back to School* (1986)

Yale U (CT): *College Musical* (2014); *Hear My Song* (2014); *The Sisterhood of the Traveling Pants 2* (2008); *Indiana Jones and the Kingdom of the Crystal Skull* (2008); *Mona Lisa Smile* (2003)

Sources: *College Finder* research including imdb.com.

More Than Beer, Football, or Music: Unique Traditions

Jay McCann, a college counselor at Valor Christian High School in Highlands Ranch, Colo., and a researcher of college traditions, identifies these schools as ones that have creative and unique campus rituals.

Bates C (ME): During the week-long Winter Carnival, students go sledding, skating, compete in a snow sculpture contest, and even participate in an annual midwinter Polar Bear Swim in a nearby lake to celebrate the end of the semester.

California Institute of Technology: On Ditch Day (which arrives unannounced each year), seniors create complicated puzzles, called "stacks," which the underclassmen spend the whole day trying to solve. The problem solving leads to activities that range from diving for clues in the school pool, building Ikea furniture, playing human Hungry Hungry Hippos, and of course food and other fun.

Chicago, U of (IL): According to the Guinness Book of World Records, the Scav Hunt (or colloquially, Scav) has been considered the largest scavenger hunt in the world. Every May, teams of students vie to complete tasks that could take them as far as 1,000 miles away from campus! According to the website, "there are many other items that must be built, performed, written, programmed, drawn, eaten, designed, painted, solved, won, and (sometimes) endured." The 2016 list boasted 284 challenges to be met between Wednesday at midnight and Sunday.

Cornell U (NY): A tradition spanning more than a century, Dragon Day is celebrated to welcome the spring season and over the years has evolved into a friendly rivalry between the College of Architecture and the College of Engineering. Freshmen architecture students design a full-sized dragon that is paraded around the campus accompanied by a troupe of students in ridiculous costumes. At the conclusion of its journey, the dragon does battle with the gigantic phoenix created by the engineering students.

Dartmouth C (NH): Although there are countless college streaking traditions (including Hamilton College's varsity streaking team), the Ledyard Challenge boasts its own storied history and unique perspective. Those undertaking this feat must shed their clothes, swim across the Connecticut River to Vermont, run back across the bridge to New Hampshire (which has a state public indecency law). The goal is to not only swim and run as fast as possible but also avoid getting nabbed by local law enforcement.

Flagler C (FL): This campus, situated some two hours by car from Universal Studio's Harry Potter World, has instituted an annual Harry Potter Month. Students take their love of Hogwarts to a higher level by donning costumes, competing in trivia and quidditch, and binge-watching all eight Harry Potter films.

George Fox U (OR): A stuffed leather bear known as Bruin Jr. is the focus of the Bruin Brawl, a student government-organized competition that has become "the university's oldest and oddest tradition." As soon as Bruin Jr. is seen on campus, the bear is an instant object of obsession as students vie, wrestling and clawing, to claim the coveted mascot for their respective class.

Steven R. Antonoff

Haverford C (PA): Staying true to their Quaker ethos, Haverford students make decisions by community consensus. On Fall and Spring Plenary days, the entire campus stops in order to allow all members to discuss the college honor code and make any ratifications to school policies as one body.

Indiana U, Bloomington: In the Little 500, the largest collegiate bike race in the U.S., teams of four bikers circle a quarter-mile track seemingly endlessly as they compete in this all-day event. The men's race is 200 laps (50 miles), and the women's race totals 100 laps. The event inspired the 1979 movie "Breaking Away" as well as an '80s era TV show of the same name.

Juniata C (PA): The annual Storming of the Arch, organized by the men's and women's rugby teams, is a rite of passage for Juniata freshmen. As the first years try mightily to pass through the historic campus arch, hundreds of upperclassmen struggle just as hard to defend the arch from the freshmen. Both sides toil until all freshmen have conceded defeat or a lucky first-year student breaks through to the other side—a feat that thus far has never officially been accomplished.

North Carolina State U: For the Krispy Kreme Challenge, students compete by running 2.5 miles from campus to a local Krispy Kreme, gobbling a dozen donuts, and racing back to the start in under an hour. In addition to being a feat of gastrointestinal fortitude, the challenge functions as a fundraiser for a nearby children's hospital.

Pennsylvania State U, University Park: At THON—billed as the largest student-run philanthropic event in the world—thousands of students assemble for a 46-hour, nonstop, no-sleeping-or-sitting dance marathon. The indefatigable dancers raise money for cancer organizations and increase awareness of childhood cancer.

Reed C (OR): When Reed seniors finish their senior theses, they parade from the library to the registrar's office to turn in their work, an event that marks the conclusion of their academic requirements and the beginning of Renn Fayre. Once an authentic Renaissance festival, today this weekend of activities is characterized by costumes, slip-n-slides, music, bicycle jousting, fireworks, and plenty of food and fun. A more recent Renn Fayre tradition features the Picts, students who race across campus clad only in bright blue paint (and maybe running shoes).

Taylor U (IN): For the Boxer Run, which celebrates the first snowfall of the year, male students from one dorm run a loop around campus wearing nothing but boxers, gloves, and shoes. Meanwhile, men from a rival dorm confront the runners in their celebratory romp, tackling as many as they can. The result is a playful brawl that inevitably leads to quotes from war movies and vast entertainment for the assembled female spectators.

Transylvania U (KY): Following his firing from Transylvania in the 1800s, botany professor Constantine Rafinesque was said to put a curse on the college. Now four "lucky" student winners of an annual raffle drawing "enjoy" the privilege of Tombstay and the opportunity to sleep in the Rafinesque's tomb. In this hauntingly unique tradition, the students are treated to fun and food, and those who survive the evening become members of the very select Rafinesque Society.

Wooster, C of (OH): The tradition of Snow Arch requires that during snowy winters, students attempt to completely pack the arched entrance of Kauke Hall with snow. Legend has it that if they succeed, classes will be cancelled. For those who participate in the challenge, Snow Arch is no doubt a memorable part of their college experience but not a guarantee of a holiday. Following a recent successfully filled Snow Arch, the college president sent a campus-wide e-mail: "The arch is filled. A spirited Wooster tradition lives

TIDBITS AND TRIVIA

on. As a reward for your industry, we want to confirm that you will have further opportunities for learning this morning in classes."

Honorable Mention

Agnes Scott C (GA): Black Cat
California, U of, Berkeley: InVenture prize/Global Social Venture Competition
California, U of, Davis: Picnic Day
Carnegie Mellon U (PA): Buggy Race
Georgia Tech U: InVenture prize/Global Social Venture Competition
Hope C (MI): The Pull
Lawrence U (WI): The Great Midwest Trivia Contest
Rice U (TX): Beer Bike
Swarthmore C (PA): Crum Regatta

The Experts' Choice: Interesting Traditions and Fun Facts

Alvernia U (PA): The university has give-back days where the freshman do volunteer work for the surrounding community.

Auburn U (AL): Auburn has two mascots: War Eagle and Tigers.

Augustana U (SD): A "Viking Score" gives points to students for attending career fairs, resume workshops, meeting with advisors etc. A certain score by graduation has been tracked and led to job-finding success. Built in accountability.

Bates C (ME): Each year for the Puddle Jump, a hole is cut in the ice on Lake Andrews so students can jump into the cold water.

Beloit C (WI): Each year the college releases the Beloit College Mindset List, which explores the "cultural touchstones" that shape the lives of each new class of students.

Boise State U (ID): The football stadium for Boise State University has blue turf.

Bowdoin C (ME): Commodore Perry's Portrait is in the Library. In addition, the "College House" system links first year students to upperclassmen students and social opportunities.

Brandeis U (MA): There are three chapels on campus that never cast a shadow on each other.

Carleton C (MN): Broomball is played on the quad. In addition, there is a house where students can bake cookies.

Carnegie Mellon U (PA): This school paves the way for many Broadway stars.

Centre C (KY): All students enter without a declared major, which is determined by the end of the sophomore year. If the student follows advising recommendations and is unable to graduate in four years, tuition is waived to complete the undergraduate degree. Every student is also promised study abroad and a research or internship experience.

Chicago, U of (IL): The Scavenger Hunt includes items that must be found, built, programmed, eaten, solved, written, endured, etc.

Columbia C (IL): It is required that everyone take and pass a swimming test.

Dartmouth C (NH): One must see a moose before graduating.

Davidson C (NC): Freshmen are encouraged to "get into school spirit" by participating in the annual freshman cake race—a run around campus with the winners receiving an entire cake for themselves.

Duke U (NC): Students "tent" in Krzyzewski-ville for the six weeks leading up to the Duke-Carolina basketball game. They have elaborate guidelines and tent checks to establish priority seating for the game.

Erwin Technical C (FL): The main building was originally a Sears department store.

Georgia Institute of Technology: in 1927 Georgia Tech accidently sent two enrollment forms to William Edgar Smith, an incoming student. Smith decided to enroll a fictitious person named George P. Burdell in the school, using the extra enrollment form. Smith enrolled Burdell in the same classes as himself and turned in extra copies of homework assignments with the help of some friends. Burdell received a Bachelor of Science degree in Mechanical Engineering and later got a Master's Degree in Mechanical Engineering. Burdell has been carried on through the years by being enrolled at Georgia Tech on several more occasions and serving in almost every war since WWII. Burdell lives on at Georgia Tech through a Facebook page and is often found on sign-up sheets around campus. On campus there is a birthday celebration for George P. Burdell on April 1st every year.

Georgia, U of: Students are warned not to walk under the arch between campus and downtown Athens or they won't graduate. For four years or more, students walk around it until they graduate. Then they take their picture in cap and gown under the arch.

Gonzaga U (WA): Gonzaga surprises new prospective students by filling the gym with current students who cheer for them as they enter the venue. They also match prospective students with current students who have similar interests for tours and communication.

Jackson State U (FL): Their marching band is called the Sonic Boom of the South.

Juniata C (PA): All freshman try to storm through the arch which is guarded by the upperclassmen. None have successfully made it, but it's a memorable tradition.

Loyola Marymount U (LA): There is a large round sundial-like place on the ground, at the bluff end of the residence hall path. In the middle of a sundial a person can speak and be heard clearly from many yards away. The place overlooks a valley with many houses in it. People suspect the voice bounces off the buildings and the valley below. It's pretty weird to be talking as if using a megaphone.

Maryland, U of, College Park: Students rub the terrapin's nose on campus for good luck.

Michigan, U of, Ann Arbor: This school provides a high road to the Broadway stage.

Middlebury C (VT): Midyear graduates get their diplomas at the end of the on-campus ski slope.

New Hampshire, U of: The university has the oldest undergraduate research program in the country.

New York U, Gallatin School of Individualized Study: This is the smallest college at NYU and has the most academically diverse faculty, most personalized attention and no grad students or TA's teaching underclassmen.

Northern Arizona U: Alumni are welcomed back for a week of activities during homecoming.

Oberlin C (OH): There is a sculpture on campus that commemorates Oberlin as a stop on the Underground Railroad.

Ohio U, Athens: Every year there is a huge Halloween street party in and around Ohio University.

Pacific, U of the: There is one rock that is repainted nearly every night (sometimes multiple times in one night) by different campus groups: members of fraternities and sororities, clubs, athletic teams, etc.

Pennsylvania State U, University Park: Penn State has a student-run philanthropy dedicated to enhancing the lives of children and their families that are impacted by cancer. Also, Penn State's colors were originally Pink and Black. (They faded to blue and white).

Pennsylvania, U of: At home football games, toast is thrown onto the sidelines after the third quarter as the line, "Here's a toast to dear old Penn" is sung.

Princeton U (NJ): Princeton has a tremendous underground library.

Salem C (NC): The college began conferring degrees in the 1890's and is the oldest women's college in the nation by founding date. In 1766, sixteen girls and women walked more than 500 miles from Bethlehem, Pennsylvania to join the new community of the village of Salem in North Carolina.

Smith C (MA): There are Japanese lanterns and Scottish bagpipers at Smith's graduation.

South, U of the (TN): Honors students wear robes to class. In addition, when you leave the domain, you invoke the "angel."

Southern Methodist U (TX): There is a door that students walk through only twice—one as freshmen on the opening day, then back through at graduation.

St. Lawrence (NY): There is a Freshmen Run.

Taylor U (IN): At an annual basketball game, students crowd the gym in outrageous outfits while remaining in complete silence. After the tenth TU basket, the entire crowd erupts to start the weekend of Christmas festivities.

Texas Tech U: All the university gathers at winter holiday to celebrate the lighting of the campus by the "Carol of Lights."

Tulane U (LA): Administrators teach classes on campus.

Whittier C (CA): The college has Faculty Midnight Dinner during finals.

Wisconsin, U of, Madison: Jump Around. When "Jump Around" is played in-between the third and fourth quarters of home football games, fans go crazy doing as the song instructs. After every football game, the Badger Band presents a post-game performance

Steven R. Antonoff

called the Fifth Quarter. Thousands of fans stay after games to witness and sometimes participate in the post-game antics.

Wooster, C of (OH): Students can get a "snow day" if they pack a certain archway of a building with so much snow no one can proceed. They work so hard on it; they sleep most of that snow day. Too funny!

Wooster, C of (OH): There is parade through town for senior thesis celebration. In addition, Wooster has the highest enrollment of college professor's children in attendance.

College Traditions and Tidbits

Alvernia U (PA): Reflecting its Franciscan heritage, Alvernia tries to foster a sense of social justice and strong principles in its students. Service-learning courses help students grow professionally and as members of society, while receiving credit for their work with community-based partners such as food banks, mentoring programs, environmental projects, and other causes.

Arizona State U: For the ASU BB (Bras and Boxers) Run, more than 15,000 students celebrate the end of classes by running across the Tempe campus in nothing more than their underwear. The festivities are accompanied by plenty of music and entertainment. After shedding their clothing, students can donate it to Goodwill Arizona.

Auburn U (AL): Some mistakenly believe that Auburn has two mascots—the War Eagle and the Tigers. In fact, the university mascot is Aubie the Tiger and its men's and women's athletic teams are the Tigers. War Eagle is Auburn's motto and battle cry, as well as the name of university's golden eagle and a greeting among the Auburn "family."

Augustana U (SD): Augustana students add to their Viking Score by attending career fairs, resume workshops, meeting with advisors, etc. The higher the score, the better prepared you are to embark on your career. Attaining a certain score by graduation has been tracked and been found to lead to greater success at finding a job.

Barnard C (NY): During finals week, the college president, deans, and other members of the administration serve a Midnight Breakfast to students. Every breakfast has its own theme, and the whole community gets involved. Even more impressive, however, may be the traditional construction and consumption of The Big Sub. Each year, students make a gigantic sandwich that literally snakes across the campus, with everyone chowing down once the gargantuan dish has been assembled. With every passing year, another foot is added to the length of the sub, which has already surpassed one mile in length.

Bates C (ME): St. Patrick's Day marks the annual Puddle Jump, when a hole is cut in the ice on Lake Andrews so students can celebrate by plunging into the bone-chilling cold water.

Boise State U (ID): The football stadium for Boise State University features blue turf (aka Smurf Turf) of a distinctive blue.

Boston U (MA): For runners worldwide, the third Monday in April, the day of the Boston Marathon, represents the apex in a career of grueling physical strain and unwavering mental determination. For BU students, Marathon Monday marks the high point of the social season. Thanks to the Patriot's Day holiday that commemorates the anniversary of the battles of Lexington and Concord, Bostonians have a day off to throw parties, cheer for the runners, and roam the warming streets. The day's festivities kick off with 5:30 a.m. wake-up calls, pre-marathon beer-pong marathons, and waffle breakfasts at sunrise. The fun doesn't stop until the last runner crosses the finish line, which BU students assume happens sometime early the following morning, thus ensuring that the celebrations continue throughout the night.

Bowdoin C (ME): In the College House system, every Bowdoin student is assigned to one of eight houses that provide a ready-made group of friends, connections with upperclassmen, and unique house traditions. According to the college's director of residential life, "The College Houses serve, in a sense, as Bowdoin's living rooms."

Brandeis U (MA): The three chapels on campus (each celebrating a different faith) were designed and constructed so that one never casts a shadow on the other two. About a quarter of Brandeis students are annual participants in Liquid Latex, a body art fashion show in which models sport paint designs and nothing else.

Brown U (RI): Each spring the admissions office hosts A Day on College Hill to provide regular decision admittances a look at the opportunities at Brown in the classroom, on campus, and in the community.

Bryn Mawr C (PA): At Parade Night, the completion of the first week of classes, freshmen and sophomores celebrate with their sister classes, the juniors and seniors, respectively. As juniors and seniors, these same students will, in turn, receive their younger sister classes. For fall semester's Lantern Night, first-year students assemble in the cloisters where the sophomores present them with their lanterns in their class color or the McBride color of purple. Lantern Night is a visual representation of the light of knowledge is being passed from one class to the other. Welcome the First Years (formerly known as Hell Week and now irreverently referred to as WTF) encompasses seven days of fun and bonding between the first years and the upper classes. It not only breaks up the monotonous stretch between winter and spring breaks, but more importantly, serves as the true welcoming of the first-year class. The entire Bryn Mawr community comes together for May Day for medieval festivities and a general good time. The day concludes with the traditional showing of the classic film "The Philadelphia Story," starring fellow Mawrter Katharine Hepburn.

Bucknell U (PA): Candlelighting is held the week before classes start and repeated the night before commencement. Students stand side by side in the Academic Quad while the university president lights a candle. That light, representing the light of knowledge, is that passed from student to student. Singing is also a part of the tradition of first-year students serenading the university president in the first week of their second semester.

California Institute of Technology: What distinguishes CalTech's legendary Ditch Day from the typical high school Senior Skip Day can be summed up in one word: puzzles. Every year the seniors vanish from campus, leaving behind elaborate mind games that, according to campus myth, so occupy the underclasses that they are too engrossed to intrude into seniors' rooms when they make the mass migration off campus. In true Cal Tech form, the puzzles are complicated posers that only genius engineering nerds could conjure or solve. Pranks, science jokes, and general rowdiness round out the day.

California State U, Chico: Over Labor Day weekend, thousands of students at Chico State "float" up the Sacramento River to Beer Can Beach, the aptly named setting for the resulting freak show and party.

California, U of, Davis: In the late night Undie Run, the UC Davis track team and friends get nearly naked to make an annual streak across the campus.

California, U of, Los Angeles: Midnight Yell is exactly what it sounds like: to relieve stress during finals week, students pour outside at midnight and yell as loudly as they can. The Janss Steps, an 87-step expanse of stairs, served as the original entrance to the university. The land on which the university was built had been owned by the Janss brothers, and it was proposed that a structure be built in their honor. Edwin, the practical younger brother, lobbied for a parking garage, but older brother Hans insisted on something more aesthetic: sloping lawns with majestic steps leading up to the main quad. Suspecting that after he died, his little brother would simply replace the steps with parking, Hans had himself buried under the sixth step. Janss Steps traditions hold that students must never set foot on the sixth step from the bottom or they will spend an extra quarter (or longer) on campus. Fraternities sometimes hold séances on the step, easily identified by the drippings from their candles. In other traditions, students hoping for better luck with their exams rub the Bruin Paw, the right hind paw on a large statue of the UCLA mascot, the Bruin. And finally, UCLA tour guides like to point out Jim Morrison's locker, purported to be that of a student who briefly attended the university before achieving rock 'n roll glory as lead singer of The Doors.

California, U of, Santa Barbara: USCB students hold a Halloween extravaganza that draws attendees from across the United States.

Carleton C (MN): During the snowy winter months, Carls go "traying," using cafeteria trays as sleds on the hill behind Evans Hall. They also flood the Bald Spot, an open grassy spot in a central campus location, let it ice over and voila!—Bald Spot rink, where students play broomball, a game like hockey but played with shoes instead of skates, a ball instead of a puck, and brooms instead of hockey sticks. Silent Dance Party, another Carleton tradition, takes place at 11 p.m. on one of the two reading days before final exams. Partygoers receive an hour-long playlist composed by the party organizer before meeting on the first floor of the library. They then put on their headphones and press play at the same time and proceed to dance through the library and other campus locations. Additionally, at 10 p.m. on the night before finals begin, students stick their heads out the window and give a heartfelt (or desperate) Primal Scream. Carleton is also home to Rotblatt, an annual softball game that lasts as many innings as years that Carleton College has been in existence. Given that the college was founded in 1866, the game goes on seemingly forever and requires a certain stamina, especially since rules stipulate players must have a beverage in their hands at all times.

Carnegie Mellon U (PA): In Carnegie Mellon's Sweepstakes (more commonly known as Buggy) teams from campus organizations build torpedo-shaped vehicles and compete to finish first in a relay race. The race has taken place every year since 1920.

Central Florida, U of: At the end of October, Central Florida students stampede into the campus's Reflecting Pond for Spirit Splash, a celebration of homecoming weekend. The tradition was launched in 1995 when someone pushed the student body president into the pond. Spirit Splash has won the Best Campus Tradition award from the National Association for Campus Activities.

Chicago, U of (IL): The Scavenger Hunt specifies items that must be found, built, programmed, eaten, solved, written, endured, etc., and has included blood drives and road trips that may take participants as far as 1,000 miles from Chicago. This event currently holds the Guinness World Record for the world's largest scavenger hunt.

Clark U (MA): On Spree Day, classes are spontaneously cancelled, and the entire student body heads to the Green for a celebration that includes entertainment and activities.

Colgate U (NY): In the Torchlight Ceremony, incoming freshmen are led up Colgate's hill accompanied by torch-toting members of the school's honor society. Four years later (with any luck), they walk down the hill as outgoing seniors, carrying their own torches and tossing them into a bonfire to celebrate their last night together as a class. For athletic competitions against pitting Colgate against rival Cornell, students from the two schools throw Colgate toothpaste and Big Red gum, respectively.

Columbia U (NY): Orgo Night is a twice-yearly event that has become a popular campus tradition (although not with all students). Each semester on the night before the organic chemistry final, the university's marching band bursts into Butler Library and plays the alma mater at full volume. Orgo Night purportedly is meant to be a distraction to relieve stress the night before a critical test, but for some students, the ritual only increases their stress levels by driving them crazy.

Connecticut, U of: UConn students are passionate about their athletics, especially the men's and women's basketball teams. Like any school with a deep love of competitive sports, UConn has a plethora of fight songs and chants that students can break into during a game. As great their support of NCAA-sanctioned sports, Huskies are just as devoted to their unusual athletic traditions. For more than three decades, UConn students have celebrated spring by playing OOzeball. Teams of six—in recent years, always three males and three females—compete in mud volleyball that takes place in eight inches of ooze created especially for the game. Hundreds of spectators (presumably anyone who'd rather stay clean) watch their classmates compete. After the day's competition, the winning team walks away with a cash prize and enough mud caked on their bodies that they'll be washing it off for days. OOzeball has become so popular among college students that the tradition has been adopted by other schools.

Cornell U (NY): Dragon Day originated as a rivalry between the architecture and engineering departments. Every St. Patrick's Day, first-year architectural students design and build a several-story-high dragon (originally a snake with St. Patrick chasing after it) and parade it through campus, guided by costumed students. In the past, the dragon was set afire in the Arts Quad (a tradition now abandoned), which resulted in the north end of the quad being littered with the eerie framework remains of past dragon heads. Slope Day has changed a lot since its inception in 1901, but it's still an opportunity for Cornell students to celebrate spring's arrival. In recent years, students have welcomed the return of warm weather with a picnic and a rock concert featuring such performers as Kanye West, Snoop Dogg, and Ben Folds. Legends surrounding the Fall Creek suspension bridge claim that any couple that kisses in the middle of the suspension bridge will get married and if a kiss is refused on the bridge, the bridge will collapse into the gorge.

Dartmouth C (NH): The annual Winter Carnival, a tradition for more than a century, celebrates the season with events such as ski races, an ice sculpture contest, and a human dog sled race. In recent years, the carnival has included the popular Polar Bear Swim, where students leap into a hole cut out of ice on the Occom Pond. Fittingly, participants can take the chill off at the Alpha Chi Alpha Beach Party, a tradition since 1976.

Davidson C (NC): First years are encouraged to get into school spirit by participating in the annual freshman Cake Race, a tradition for more than 75 years. Winners of the 1.7-mile race around campus receive an entire cake for themselves.

Drake U (IA): The renowned Drake Relays have taken place for more than a century and annually attract more than 40,000 spectators every year to watch both Olympic-level athletes and college teams compete. The event includes an ever-growing number of community and university traditions. One of the most popular among Drake students is Street Painting, in which student organizations paint a square along the road in front of Cowles Library (and inevitably decorate each other as much as the concrete).

Duke U (NC): To obtain free student tickets to the most-fiercely fought basketball games (i.e., Duke versus University of North Carolina), students "tent" in Krzyzewskiville (or K-ville), an area outside Cameron Stadium that is named for Mike Krzyzewski, Duke's beloved Coach K. Tenting is governed by elaborate guidelines that include day and night tent checks to establish that the required number of students are present in the tent. Given that tenting may go on for weeks at a time, on-line access is provided so participants can keep up with their studies (although the Internet connection is reputed to be unreliable). There are also said to be five unofficial graduate requirements: explore the utilities tunnels running under the East and West Campuses, drive backwards around the traffic circle, climb atop Baldwin Auditorium, and take part in sexual escapades in both Perkins Library and the Sara P. Duke Gardens.

Emory U (GA): The spirit of Emory and unofficial mascot of the university is Dooley, the Lord of Misrule and a tradition dating back to 1899. In the spring during Dooley's Week, that spirit "comes alive" as an Emory student dressed as a skeleton wanders the campus, dismissing classes. The entire week is taken over by fun, foolishness, and community bonding that for many Emory students is their fondest memory of their college years.

Florida State U: In 1962, FSU professor Dean Coyle Moore challenged the football team to beat heavily favored Georgia and bring back sod from their rival's Sanford Stadium field. Team captain Gene McDowell, who led the Seminoles to victory in that game, followed through and presented Moore with a chunk of sod, which the professor then buried at the FSU practice field to commemorate the win. Thus was born Sod Cemetery and the tradition of sod stealing that continues to this day. FSU purloins turf "only" from sod games, defined as those away matches where the Seminoles are underdogs.

Fordham U (NY): Midnight Breakfast marks the beginning of each semester's final exam period. To help prepare students for a long night of studying, the administration and faculty (including the university president) prepare and serve a full breakfast buffet.

Georgetown U (DC): Ever since the film "The Exorcist" was shot in part on the campus, Halloween has been a major holiday at Georgetown. The film is shown after dark on Halloween, either outside on Copley lawn or in Gaston Hall. The film ends around midnight, the hour at which Georgetown students gather in the cemetery on campus for the Healy Howl and ho(ooooo)wl at the moon. A less-sanctioned tradition requires that students have their photo taken as they sit in the lap of the statue of Georgetown founder John Carroll located at the campus entrance. This requires a boost from friends to get you into the lap and take your picture (selfies don't cut it) and stealth plus speed to evade the campus security patrols intent on squelching a caper they believe to be dangerous to students and harmful to the statue's longevity.

Georgia Institute of Technology: In 1927 Georgia Tech mistakenly sent two enrollment forms to William Edgar Smith, an incoming student. Smith used the extra enrollment form to enroll the fictitious George P. Burdell. Throughout his matriculation at Georgia Tech, Smith signed up Burdell for the same classes as himself and with the help of friends turned in extra copies of homework assignments. Burdell received a Bachelor of Science degree in Mechanical Engineering and later attained a Master's Degree in Mechanical Engineering. The hoax has been perpetuated ever since, with Burdell enrolled at Georgia Tech on several more occasions and serving in almost every war since WWII. Burdell lives on at Georgia Tech through a Facebook page, calls paging him at football games, and his signature appearing on sign-up sheets around campus. Introduced to incoming students as one of Georgia Tech's most illustrious alumni, Burdell is celebrated on his birthday every year, a campus holiday that fittingly, falls on April 1.

Georgia, U of: The arch between the campus and downtown Athens represents a source of peril to UGA students, who are warned that if they walk it before they complete their studies they will fail to graduate. For four years or longer, students trudge around the arch until graduation day, at which time they stand proudly under it to have their photo taken in cap and gown.

Gonzaga U (WA): Incoming Zags are greeted by a gym filled to the rafters with current students who cheer for them as they enter. Gonzaga also matches prospective students with current students who have similar interests for tours and communication.

Hollins U (VA): On Tinker Day, a surprise day in October, students, and staff dress in a crazy array of costumes and climb Tinker Mountain together. They are rewarded with a picnic of fried chicken and Tinker Cake.

Hope C (MI): The Pull, an annual tug-of-war held in September, features two teams consisting of eight "pullers" and 18 "moralers" (who cheer on pullers when they start to fade). The longest Pull lasted for three hours and 51 minutes, and the shortest was history in only two minutes and 40 seconds. Sports Illustrated crowned the Pull the "mother of all tug-of-wars."

Idaho, U of: In the 1920s, the university president required that students, staff, and faculty say hello to one another when meeting on campus. Every day, he followed his own rule and greeted everyone he passed with a "Hello" as he made his way up the walk across the Administration Lawn. This longstanding tradition continues on Hello Walk, which gives visitors a very favorable impression of the friendliness of the campus. The Found Money Fund of Idaho (FMFI) began in 1981 with three pennies and evolved into a repository for any money that Idaho faculty, students, alumni, and supporters found and were willing to donate to the university. Money can be dropped off or mailed in. The money is invested in the University of Idaho Trust, and interest from the endowment will become available for use in 2089, the year of the university's bicentennial. As of 2008, the fund was worth more than $200,000, and its value is expected to be several billion dollars by 2089.

Indiana U: Modeled on the Indy 500, the Little 500 takes place in April and is the largest collegiate bike race in the country. Four-person teams compete against each other; the men's race is 200 laps, and the women's race is 100 laps. More than 25,000 people come out to cheer on the participants, and proceeds go toward raising scholarship money for students. The Little 500 was memorialized in the 1979 coming-of-age film "Breaking Away."

Jackson State U (FL): The JSU marching band, known as the Sonic Boom of the South, has made halftime appearances at NFL games and Motown's 30th Anniversary television special and is famous for their eye-catching choreography that bring audiences to their feet.

John Muir C (CA): Pumpkin Drop is an annual tradition at John Muir College, one of six undergraduate colleges at UC San Diego. Picture one (or more) gigantic hollowed-out pumpkins filled with candy. On a countdown, the pumpkins are dropped from the tallest building on campus, and a mad scramble for the sweets ensues. At one Pumpkin Drop, a nearly 400-pound candy-stuffed pumpkin splattered more than 100 feet. Pie anyone?

Juniata C (PA): The second Wednesday of fall semester is the date for Storming the Arch, an optional rite-of-passage for Juniata freshmen that was established in the late 1940s. First-year students gather to charge Cloisters Arch intent on making it to the other side. The arch, however, is staunchly defended by sophomores, juniors, and seniors determined to thwart the first years. Despite decades of strategies ranging from the brawny to the byzantine, it is reported that no freshman class has successfully passed through the gauntlet.

Kenyon C (OH): Singing is a tradition at Kenyon, and students participate both coming and going. Every matriculation week since 1956, freshman have lent their voices to First Year Sing, submitting to the good-natured catcalls and boos of the upper classes as they mangle their attempts at Kenyon's school songs. Four years later at Senior Sing, the laughter is laced with tears as outgoing seniors perform the same songs in front of friends and families at graduation.

Lawrence U (WI): On the last weekend in January, Lawrence conducts the Great Midwest Trivia Contest, which is broadcast over the university's radio station. This extraordinary challenge—open to teams from on campus and off—runs throughout Trivia Weekend for 50 straight hours from Friday to Sunday. The event has been called The World's Longest-Running Trivia Contest because each year a question from a previous year begins the new competition.

Le Moyne C: Every year Le Moyne students eagerly await the arrival of Dolphy Day, a surprise holiday from classes that is kept secret until the last minute. Fireworks (or other clamorous activities) are set off in the wee hours of the morning to begin the celebration, and for the rest of the day, students party and feast on barbecue. Although the Le Moyne mascot is a dolphin, school officials deny there is any link between that icon and this annual day off from classes. Rather, Dolphy Day traces its name to its origin in 1971, when Le Moyne students skipped class to bask outside on a beautiful spring day and listen to (among other songs) "The Eric Dolphy Memorial Barbecue," an instrumental by Frank Zappa and the Mothers of Invention that commemorates jazz saxophonist Eric Dolphy.

Loyola Marymount U (LA): At the bluff end of the residence hall path is a large round sundial-like place on the ground. In the middle of a sundial, a person can speak and be heard clearly from many yards away, almost as if talking through a megaphone. The spot overlooks a valley with many houses, so the weird acoustics may be caused by voices bouncing off the buildings below.

Macalester C (MN): Nothing relieves the stress of preparing for finals like a little puppy love, which is the reason behind Macalester Dog Days. On the Saturday before exams, professors, neighbors, and community members bring their dogs to campus so students can get some free furry hugs and therapy. In a longer tradition, the flag of the United Nations has waved above the campus since 1950, when then college president Charles J. Turck raised it as a symbol of Macalester's commitment to international harmony.

Mary Baldwin C (VA): First celebrated in 1942 at this women's college, Apple Day in its early incarnation consisted of traveling to a local orchard for a morning of picking and gleaning apples. Afterwards the young women enjoyed a picnic lunch and skits by each class. College staff then cooked with the collected apples throughout the semester. Today Apple Day remains as popular as ever but has incorporated a strong community service focus. Apples are gathered from local orchards and donated to food banks in the Washington, D.C. area. For the past several years, students have traveled to Woodbine Farm Market, located in Strasburg, Virginia, to glean apples. The record for donated apples was set in 2011 when the college donated 10,000 pounds of gleaned apples. Afterwards students return to campus and enjoy the Apple Day Carnival and the Apple Eve dodge ball game and dance. Because it was a sophomore class that held the first Apple Day, the honor of planning and carrying out this Mary Baldwin tradition is bestowed on second-year students.

Maryland, U of, College Park: The university's mascot is the Diamondback terrapin, and a bronze replica, named Testudo, holds pride of place on the College Park campus. The statue's remarkably shiny nose is the result of students rubbing Testudo's beak for good luck.

Massachusetts Institute of Technology: At midnight on or around Halloween, MIT holds its annual Pumpkin Drop. Some years a dozen pumpkins and other years more than 100 pumpkins plummet from the top of Green Building—the tallest building in Cambridge—and are obliterated upon impact in the courtyard. The process is accompanied by yells and cheers from crowds of spectators and badly filmed by iPhones held aloft.

Menlo C (CA): For a quarter of a century, the Menlo College Hawaii Club has hosted the Annual Lu'au, with authentic Hawaiian food, music, and dances performed by club members.

Meredith C (NC): The Cornhuskin' tradition celebrated at this women's college was inspired by the original Cornhusking Bee, which was started in 1945 to honor the first-year students and was held the day before Halloween. Today Cornhuskin' occurs during the first week in November and has expanded into a series of spirited competitions between classes, spawning good-natured rivalry between even-year and odd-year classes. The four classes are judged on such activities as cornhusking (naturally), apple-bobbing, can art, class attendance, and sweatshirt design. The fun continues throughout the week with a Big Sis/Lil' Sis Bonfire, a Scavenger Hunt, the President's Raid, Hall Raids, and the Cornhuskin' Parade, which draws spectators from the community.

Middlebury C (VT): For those seniors who graduate midyear, Middlebury hosts a celebratory weekend featuring the Ski-Down Procession, in which graduates ride the chairlift or hike up the on-campus ski slope and then ski down in cap and gown.

Mississippi Valley State U: MVSU sports teams are the Delta Devils and the Devilettes. The school Fight Song is "The Devil's Gun," which includes the line, "We are looking down the barrel of the devil's gun."

Mt. Holyoke C (MA): Mountain Day is one of the oldest traditions at this women's college in South Hadley, with the first celebration taking place one year after the Mount Holyoke was founded in 1837. This tradition is not scheduled; students only learn that it's Mountain Day when the college bell rings early one autumn morning. Participants hike to the top of Mount Holyoke in Skinner State Park, where photographs are taken, songs are sung (the college song is a popular choice), ice cream is enjoyed, and fun rules. Climbing the college's namesake peak fosters camaraderie and builds bonds that last a lifetime, so much so that even as after they graduate, some alumnae get together to reconnect and celebrate Mountain Day.

Murray State U (KY): In the middle of Murray State's campus stands a tree decorated with more than 50 pairs of mismatched shoes. Although the origins of the Shoe Tree are lost to history, elaborate traditions have evolved around the unusual campus landmark. It is said that college sweethearts who fall in love and marry must return to Murray State and nail two shoes (one from each partner) to the tree. The shoes are often marked with the couple's anniversary date, and sometimes couples return to campus after starting a family in order to nail baby shoes to the tree.

North Carolina State U: The mantra of the Krispy Kreme Challenge—"2,400 calories, 12 doughnuts, 5 miles, 1 hour"—neatly summarizes this test of physical fitness and gastrointestinal fortitude. Participants travel 2.5 miles to the designated Krispy Kreme location, scarf down a dozen doughnuts, and then run 2.5 miles back to campus. What

Steven R. Antonoff

started as a challenge among ten friends has transformed into a nationally publicized charity race and the number one tradition to take part in before graduating from NC State.

Northwestern U (IL): The Rock, originally a gift from the class of 1902, is one of Northwestern's best-known landmarks. In the 1940s a tradition of painting this massive chuck of quartzite was launched, and The Rock became a canvas for student art and much more. Tradition holds that students must guard The Rock for 24 hours before they can paint it with their messages, which have included protest slogans, jokes, student group advertisements, birthday wishes, and marriage proposals. Northwestern students also take their Wildcat mascot seriously and at sporting events will growl and claw when opponents have the ball. Another fairly wild tradition is Primal Scream, which takes place three times a year on Sunday night before finals week and encourages students to howl their frustration and/or agony as they prepare for the oncoming barrage of tests. Much happier is Mayfest, a month-long celebration that culminates in Armadillo Day. Dillo Day, as it is affectionately called, began in 1972 when Northwestern students from Texas decided to hold a party in honor of one of the Lone Star State's iconic animals. Every year Dillo Day brings an impressive array of bands to campus for an all-day music fest and party.

Oberlin C (OH): Oberlin established a Black History Month on campus several years before such a month was officially recognized nationally. Since 1967, the program has hosted a series of events featuring prominent political speakers, writers, musicians, and artists of African descent. In 1977, to commemorate Oberlin as a stop on the Underground Railroad, a student created an environmental sculpture that has since been preserved as a permanent structure on campus.

Occidental C (CA): On their birthdays, students are treated to a Birthday Dunk as their fellow students ceremoniously toss them in the college's Gilman Memorial Fountain. "Treat" may not be the apt word, given that the fountain reportedly is full of green slime.

Ohio U, Athens: Halloween is a very big deal in and around the university, where it is celebrated with an annual Block Party in Uptown Athens that draws an estimated 10,000 to 30,000 costumed party-goers.

Oregon, U of: Before football games, the Oregon U team is led into Autzen Stadium by a duck mascot riding on the back of a Harley Davidson.

Pacific, U of the: A boulder in front of Khouri Hall (placed there by engineering students) is known as The Rock and is repainted nearly every night (sometimes multiple times in one night) by different campus groups to celebrate/advertise Greek Life, clubs, athletic teams, and other campus activities and by individuals to protest, complain, or proclaim their love.

Pennsylvania State U, University Park: Penn State's colors were originally pink and black, but when the pink faded in the sun, students voted to change school colors to blue and white. For special home football games, students all don white shirts to create a huge sea of white and "white out" the stands. Every February brings THON weekend, a 46-hour dance marathon (no sitting and no sleeping allowed) to raise funds for the Four Diamonds Fund to fight pediatric cancer. Since its first dance marathon in 1977, THON has raised more than $114 million for the cause. Penn State also has a student-run philanthropy dedicated to helping children and their families that are impacted by cancer.

Pennsylvania, U of: Back in the days before Prohibition, Penn students attending a home football game warbled the song "Drink a Highball," and upon singing the line "Here's a toast to dear old Penn," would raise an alcoholic toast. With alcohol prohibited at Franklin Field, Penn students took their cue from "Rocky Horror Picture Show," and the Toast Toss was born. Now as the words "toast to dear old Penn" are sung during the third quarter, bread rains down on the sidelines. The toast is swept up by the Toast Zamboni, a motorized turf cleaner modified by Penn engineering students. Penn's Spring Fling, a tradition since 1973, features free food, carnival games, the requisite debauchery, and musical lineups that put stadium shows to shame. Past Flings have starred such headliners as Snoop Dogg, OK Go, Flo Rida, and Kesha.

Pomona C (CA): Only in California could a college pull off Ski-Beach. In the early morning, busloads of students don parkas and gloves to bomb the slopes of Mountain High, a nearby resort. In the afternoon, they reboard the bus and head to a local beach for a cookout. Somewhere between mountain and ocean, ski paraphernalia is abandoned for swimsuits and boogie boards. Pomona students also enjoy Death by Chocolate, a pre-finals frenzy of chocolate consumption that begins with a long line of eager students outside Edmunds Ballroom, where assorted chocolate goodies await. A more serious tradition occurs at orientation when first-year students run through the gates past the inscription "Let only the eager, thoughtful, and reverent enter here." Upon graduation, the senior class streams out of the gates past an inscription that reads "They only are loyal to this College who upon departing bear their added riches in trust for mankind."

Princeton U (NJ): At the commencement ceremony, new graduates pass through the FitzRandolph Gate, the main entrance to the campus from Nassau Street, and leave what is affectionately referred to as "the orange bubble" to enter the real world. According to fairly recent tradition, undergraduates who use the gates to exit the campus before their own commencement put their chances of graduating at risk. Once they manage to graduate, Princeton alumni are among the world's most loyal, with upwards of 20,000 returning to Old Nassau every year for Reunions, when the campus is awash in a sea of orange-and-black couture.

Purdue U (IN): Since 1921, Purdue's Big Bass Drum, some 10 feet in diameter, has bolstered school spirit. The BBD, which requires two beaters and a crew of four to move its carriage, is well known throughout Indiana and has made appearances at national events, including the Indianapolis 500. Beginning in 1958, the university has held its own iconic race, the Purdue Grand Prix, a go-kart competition billed as "the Greatest Spectacle in College Racing." In addition to the main race in which current students build and race go-karts, associated competitions include the Classic (which is limited to go-karts built before 1986) and an alumni race that is held every five years. The Breakfast Club, a newer tradition that took root in the 1980s, takes place during Grand Prix and football season. Students and alumni wake early and hit the bars in pajamas, bathrobes, and other costumes. Purdue's Spring Fest showcases the lighter side of higher education with a free event for students of all ages to participate in two days of hands-on activities. In addition to demonstrations of live spaying and sheep shearing, participants can try their luck at cricket spitting, pedal tractor racing, and trivia games.

Reed C (OR): Reed students pride themselves on being unique, and the college's traditions support that claim. Each spring they celebrate the Seventh Annual Nitrogen Day to honor the under-appreciated seventh element of the periodic table with music, free food, and a haiku recital. This is followed a week or so later by Renn Fayre. Once a daylong authentic Renaissance Fair, Renn Fayre has shed almost every link to jesters, jousters, and other anachronisms and evolved into a three-day extravaganza that kicks off with seniors burning their thesis notes. In the days that follow, the Fayre offers fireworks, music, refreshment, and activities that can include everything from human chess games to naked slip-n-slides. A highlight is the Glo Opera, a concert performed in the dark and lit only by students wielding EL wire and glow sticks. For Reed's twice-annual Canyon Day, students set about planting native trees and shrubs in Reed Canyon. Another nod to environmental commitment is Reed's tradition of The Scrounge. Scroungers sit at the end of the cafeteria and are given leftover food by other students. As a result of this environmentally friendly tradition, "We have very little cafeteria waste," as one Scrounger boasted.

Regis U (CO): Finals Breakfast, a twice-annual tradition at Regis University, takes place on Tuesday night of Finals Week when students gather in the cafeteria for a hearty meal and a much-needed break from studying. The fall semester breakfast includes the ever-popular Nog OFF, an eggnog drinking competition. Snow Week, celebrated between mid-November and early December, is the Regis winter festival and includes specially designed Snow Week t-shirts for sale, snow bingo, and snow dodge ball (at night and often in freezing temperatures). Regis also helps ensure that students make the most of what the Centennial State has to offer. Best of Colorado enables first-year students to enjoy new adventures and vistas for a nominal fee while Senior Life Last Call encourages those about to graduate to seek out Colorado experiences they may have missed.

Rice U (TX): Beer Bike is an annual relay race, with each of Rice's residential colleges fielding three teams—a men's, a women's team, and a coed alumni team—for a combined bicycle race and drinking competition. Each team's chugger must chug beer (an option only for those over 21) or water before a team's biker can start a lap. Male participants chug 24 ounces and bike three laps, and females chug 12 ounces and bike two laps—all to the enthusiastic chants of spectators.

Rollins C (FL): Each spring, the college president selects the date of Fox Day, when all classes are cancelled. By long-standing tradition, Fox Day is announced by placement of the Rollins fox, a large stone statue, on the main lawn on the campus. The guessing that takes place about which date will be selected is as much a part of the Fox Day tradition as the day itself. Some students can hardly wait for this day off and have camped out on The Green in anticipation of the holiday.

Salem C (NC): In 1766, sixteen girls and women walked more than 500 miles from Bethlehem, Pennsylvania, to join a new community in Salem, North Carolina. One of these women was 16-year-old Elisabeth Oesterlein, who became the first teacher at what is now Salem College, the oldest women's college in the nation by founding date. Every year during Orientation Weekend, first-year students join in the Candlelight Walk to God's Acre to visit the grave of Elisabeth Oesterlein. They repeat the walk on Founders Day of their senior year.

Sewanee, U of the South (TN): At least two Sewanee traditions center on matters of dress. A way of life rather than a formal dress code, Sewanee style means many males show up for class in blazers and khakis while female counterparts wear skirts and heels. Academic gowns may be worn to class by faculty, members of the honor society, and the Order of the Gownsmen, i.e., the student government, which lends a certain air of Hogwarts to the campus. You'll also see a gown on representations of the Sewanee Angel. According to this unusual tradition, every time you leave campus, you can acquire your own guardian angel simply by tapping the roof of your car as you pass through the college gates. On your safe return to campus, you tap again to drop off your angel until the next outing.

Smith C (MA): Ivy Day, a major part of Smith commencement weekend, marks the day that the graduating seniors plant the class ivy. A tradition since 1884, Ivy Day has really taken root so to speak, with many campus buildings now nearly shrouded in the greenery. The tradition also encompasses the Ivy Procession, during which the seniors are preceded by junior ushers who bear on their shoulders the Ivy Chain (which is actually made of laurel leaves). Another Smith commencement tradition is Illumination Night, when the campus is aglow with light from brightly colored paper lanterns.

Southern Methodist U (TX): The Rotunda Passage marks the start and end of an SMU student's career. The new freshman class walks through the front doors of Dallas Hall and does not pass through them again until they graduate as seniors.

Spalding U (KY): More than 40 years ago, Sr. Julia Clare Fontaine, a professor at this Louisville university, overheard students griping about the rat race of finals week. So the good sister (who clearly had a sense of humor) decided to add a little fun to the campus by creating a real rat race. Thus was born the Running of the Rodents, a light-hearted parody of the Kentucky Derby in which rats speed around a tiny track for a prize of fruit-flavored cereal O's. Now a full seven-day event, Rat Week includes not only Rat Races, but also a Rat Parade, fruit ring eating contests, and formal balls that adhere to Derby style.

Stanford U (CA): Full Moon on the Quad began in the 1950s as a way to welcome freshmen to campus, with senior men and first-year women lining up to exchange a kiss with the person opposite them, whereupon the boys would give the girls a rose (no report on who kissed the male first-years). Now a more-inclusive event and less focused on kissing, Full Moon on the Quad invites all classes to join in and features music and free food. An integral part of the procession at commencement ceremonies is the Wacky Walk, a recent Stanford tradition that has become something of a competition as groups of students try to outdo each other with quirky demonstrations of their creativity. Past Wacky Walks have featured groups costumed as a giant caterpillar, choo-choo train, and bunch of bananas, as well as individual students cooking breakfast on a small grill or proposing marriage.

St. Catherine U (MN): A relatively new tradition at St. Catherine University (also known as St. Kate's), Citizen Katie Day is all about volunteering. Begun in 2004 as a way for students to get to know the Twin Cities area and each other, today students, alumnae, faculty, and staff volunteer side-by-side at nonprofit organizations throughout Minneapolis and St. Paul, while alumnae chapters across the U.S. have brought the spirit of Citizen Katie Day to their own hometowns by volunteering in local organizations.

St. Mary's C (IN): Closing the Circle/Opening the Circle is a recent school tradition that brings the college experience of St. Mary's women full circle, so to speak. First-year students assemble on Le Mans Green and form a giant circle where they are welcomed into the college community and given a chance to reflect on the challenges and excitement that lies ahead. A lighted candle, representing their connection and what they have to offer to each other, is passed from student to student. As seniors, the class gathers again on Le Mans Green for Opening the Circle, symbolizing that they are about to take what they have learned at St. Mary's out into the world.

Stephens C (MO). Crossing the Bridge is a relatively new, two-part tradition at this women's college. As newly arrived freshman, students traverse the bridge connecting the college to the community, moving from the community side to the campus side. During Reunion Weekend of their senior year, they reverse directions and walk across the bridge from the campus into the community, where Stephens College alumnae are waiting to welcome them.

Sweet Briar C (VA): In 1901 Indiana Fletcher Williams founded Sweet Briar College to commemorate her daughter Daisy. Every year since 1909, the Sweet Briar community has honored Indiana and Daisy on Founders' Day. On this day, Students and faculty follow a bagpiper to Monument Hill and the Williams family gravesite, where following a brief service, each student lays a daisy on Daisy's grave. Founders' Day also marks the first time that seniors don their graduation robes.

Taylor U (IN): The two-decades' long tradition of the Silent Night game takes place at an annual basketball competition shortly before Christmas. The gym is packed with Taylor students dressed in weird and wild costumes but utterly silent. Only after the tenth point is scored does the crowd erupt. Following the game, students reconvene at Habecker's

Hollapalooza, a campus-wide party where they can enjoy live holiday music, bake and eat Christmas cookies, and decorate gingerbread houses.

Texas Tech U: Since 1959, the university has encouraged students to "tech the halls" at the annual Carol of Lights. Following performances of classic holiday songs by combined school choirs at the Science Quadrangle, more than 25,000 red, white, and orange lights are illuminated, bathing the 13 buildings surrounding Memorial Circle in a cheery holiday glow.

Tufts U (MA): Traditions come and go, as is the case with Naked Quad Run (aka NQR) at this Boston-area university. Beginning in the 1970s, students of then all-male Tufts and all-female Jackson College chose the night before the start of winter reading period to throw caution and clothes to the wind. After the two colleges were combined, the tradition continued and grew into a mass run around campus that involved both little clothing but lots of alcohol. After briefly being sanctioned by university officials, NQR was banned in 2010 because of concerns about safety and binge drinking. Undeterred, Tufts students in December 2011 inaugurated Excessively Overdressed Quad Stroll (EOQR), characterized by outlandish outfits and again, excessive alcohol; though certainly more comfortable for participants (given the freezing temperatures), EOQR has yet to prove a lasting tradition.

Virginia Polytechnic Institute and State U: At one time, Virginia Tech required all able-bodied male students to participate in Reserve Officers Training Corps or ROTC. Although that requirement has been dropped, the corps and its cadets remain a strong presence on campus. The first big snowfall of the season is marked by the annual Cadets vs. Civilians Snowball Fight, which draws thousands of participants. The cadets used their training to launch formal strikes while the civilians rely more on numbers and brawn. Despite the combative name of the tradition, most students consider it a great way to make friends and beat the boredom of the fall/winter semester.

Virginia, U of: Nudity seems to be a part of many college traditions, but only UVA's Streaking the Lawn requires that participants kiss a statue of Homer. It is said that sometime before they graduate, students must run naked from the Rotunda down the Lawn, kiss (or slap, depending on the runner's height) the Homer statue on the buttocks, and then dash back to the Rotunda to retrieve their clothes. Hazards include stubbed toes, sprained ankles from slipping on wet grass, and possible arrest by campus police for public nudity and disorderly conduct.

Wellesley C (MA): One of Wellesley's oldest traditions is Tree Planting, which began in1879 and still uses a ceremonial shovel dating to that year. Every sophomore class plants its tree, which is identified by a stone marker engraved with the class graduation date. Thanks to this tradition, the Wellesley College campus now boasts some 8,000 trees. Any class trees that have succumbed to disease or storm are replaced.

Wisconsin, U of, Madison: A recent tradition at UW Madison, Jump Around pumps up the crowds between third and fourth quarters of home football games. As the 1992 hip hop hit "Jump Around" plays, U Madison supporters follow the song's instructions and go crazy. "Jump Around" has become such a tradition that its title is displayed on unofficial Wisconsin Badgers apparel. Many fans stay after the football games for the Fifth Quarter, which features entertainment by the Badger Band.

Wooster, C of (OH): Tradition holds that Wooster students can secure a snow day if they pack Delmar Archway (a.k.a. The Arch) with snow. Origins of this tradition are clouded in the mists of time, but one story ascribes it to an announcement by a school official who reportedly claimed that classes would be canceled only when snow was high enough to fill the arch. Wooster is also famed for its Scot Band whose tartan kilts have become an emblem of the college. The wearing of the kilts dates from the 1930s, and the Macleod tartan was chosen not for any Scottish clan association but because its plaid matched the school colors.

Yale U (CT): According to the Yale website, the statue of former university president James Dwight Woolsey is associated with a tradition in which "generations of students have rubbed the protruding foot for good luck." The tradition is also promoted by student tour guides and has been eagerly taken up high school prospects hoping to be accepted. The student newspaper reports, however, that there is no tradition of rubbing the foot among current Elis, likely because as one student commented, "It's covered in bacteria."

Famous People Who Attended Community College

Halle Berry: Cuyahoga Community C (OH)
Billy Crystal: Nassau Community C (NY)
James Dean: Santa Monica C (CA)
Walt Disney: Metropolitan Junior C (MO)
Clint Eastwood: Los Angeles City C (CA)
Morgan Freeman: Los Angeles City C (CA)
Tom Hanks: Chabot C (CA)
Teri Hatcher: De Anza C (CA)
Queen Latifah: Manhattan Community C (NY)
Jim Lehrer: Victoria C (TX)
George Lucas: Modesto Junior C (CA)
Eddie Murphy: Nassau Community C (NY)
Sarah Palin: North Idaho C and Matanuska-Susitna C (AK)
Ross Perot: Texarkana C (TX)
Nolan Ryan: Alvin Community C (TX)
Arnold Schwarzenegger: Santa Monica C (CA)
Sam Shepard: Mt. San Antonio C (CA)
Amy Tan: San Jose City C (CA)

Alma Maters of Actors

Tim Allen: Western Michigan U
Hank Azaria: Tufts U (MA)
Alec Baldwin: George Washington U (DC)
William Baldwin: New York, State U of, Binghamton
Angela Bassett: Yale U (CT)
Annette Bening: San Francisco, U of (CA)
Zach Braff: Northwestern U (IL)
Sandra Bullock: East Carolina U (NC)
Steve Carell: Denison U (OH)
Kristin Chenoweth: Oklahoma City U
George Clooney: Northern Kentucky U
Glenn Close: William & Mary, C of (VA)
Bradley Cooper: Georgetown U (DC)
Kevin Costner: California State U, Fullerton
Billy Crystal: Nassau Community C (NY)
Blythe Danner: Bard C (NY)
Geena Davis: Boston U (MA)
Dane DeHaan: North Carolina School of the Arts
David Duchovny: Princeton U (NJ)
Clint Eastwood: Los Angeles City C (CA)

Steven R. Antonoff

Tina Fey: Virginia, U of
Calista Flockhart: Rutgers U, New Brunswick (NJ)
Harrison Ford: Ripon C (WI)
Jodie Foster: Yale U (CT)
Zach Galifianakis: North Carolina State U
Scott Glenn: William & Mary, C of (VA)
Louis Gossett, Jr.: New York U
Hugh Grant: Oxford U (United Kingdom)
Tom Hanks: Chabot C (CA)
Woody Harrelson: Hanover C (IN)
Ethan Hawke: Carnegie Mellon U (PA)
Ed Helms: Oberlin C (OH)
Dustin Hoffman: Santa Monica C (CA)
Samuel L. Jackson: Morehouse C (GA)
Allison Janney: Kenyon C (OH)
Tommy Lee Jones: Harvard U (MA)
John Krasinski: Brown U (RI)
Lisa Kudrow: Vassar C (NY)
Ashton Kutcher: Iowa, U of
Bruce Lee: Washington, U of, Seattle
Julia Louis-Dreyfus: Northwestern U (IL)
Matthew McConaughey: Texas, U of
Debra Messing: Brandeis U (MA)
Paul Newman: Kenyon C (OH)
Cynthia Nixon: Barnard C (NY)
Edward Norton: Yale U (CT)
Leslie Odom, Jr.: Carnegie-Mellon U (PA)
Mary Louise Parker: North Carolina School of the Arts
David Hyde Pierce: Yale U (CT)
Brad Pitt: Missouri, U of, Columbia
Natalie Portman: Harvard U (MA)
Annie Potts: Stephens C (MO)
Spencer Pratt: Southern California, U of
Phylicia Ayers-Allen Rashad: Howard U (DC)
Robert Redford: Colorado, U of, Boulder
Adam Sandler: New York U
Fred Savage: Stanford U (CA)
Wesley Snipes: New York, State U of, Purchase
Kevin Spacey: Juilliard School (NY)
Sylvester Stallone: Miami, U of (FL)
Ben Stiller: California, U of, Los Angeles
Meryl Streep: Vassar C (NY)
Jennifer Tilly: Stephens C (MO)
Blair Underwood: Carnegie Mellon U (PA)
Kerry Washington: George Washington U (DC)
Emma Watson: Brown U (RI)
Kristen Wiig: Arizona, U of
Vanessa Williams: Syracuse U (NY)
Paula Zahn: Stephens C (MO)
Renée Zellweger: Texas, U of, Austin

Alma Maters of Authors

Bill Bryson: Durham, U of (United Kingdom)
Steve Case: Williams C (MA)
Michael Chabon: Carnegie Mellon U (PA) and Pittsburgh, U of (PA)
Ron Chernow: Yale U (CT) and Cambridge, U of (United Kingdom)
Tom Clancy: Loyola C (MD)
Mary Higgins Clark: Fordham U (NY)
Ta-Nehisi Coates: Howard U (DC)
Harlan Coben: Amherst C (MA)
Diane Mott Davidson: Stanford U (CA)
Gillian Flynn: Northwestern U (IL)
Jonathan Franzen: Swarthmore C (PA)
Neil Gaiman: none
Theodore Geisel (Dr. Seuss): Dartmouth C (NH)
Malcolm Gladwell: Toronto, U of (Canada)
Adam Grant: Michigan, U of, Ann Arbor and Harvard U (MA)
John Grisham: Mississippi State U
Heloise: Texas State U, San Marcos (formerly Southwest Texas State U)
E.L. James: Kent, U of (United Kingdom)
Dean Koontz: Shippensburg U (PA)
David McCullough: Yale U (CT)
Marissa Meyer: Stanford U (CA)
James Patterson: Manhattan C (NY)
Jodi Picoult: Princeton U (NJ)
Edgar Allen Poe: Virginia, U of
Thomas Pynchon: Cornell U (NY)
George Saunders: Colorado School of Mines
Jeffrey Toobin: Harvard C (MA)
Alice Walker: Spelman C (GA)
David Foster Wallace: Arizona, U of
Stuart Woods: Georgia, U of
Rick Yancey: Roosevelt U (IL)

Colleges That Produce Business Leaders

The College Finder researchers found that many business, labor, and commerce leaders of the past decade studied at these colleges.

Baylor U (TX)
Brigham Young U (UT)
British Columbia, U of (Canada)
Brown U (RI)
California State U, San Diego
Carroll C (MT)
Chicago, U of (IL)
Cleveland State U (OH)
Colombia U (NY)
Cornell U (NY)
Dartmouth C (NH)
Dayton, U of (OH)
Duke U (NC)
École Polytechnique (France)

FNA École Nationale d'Administration (France)
Georgia Institute of Technology
Georgia State U
Hamilton C (NY)
Harvard U (MA)
Hawaii, U of
Illinois Wesleyan U
INSEAD (France)
Johns Hopkins U (MD)
Kansas, U of
Keio U (Japan)
Kettering U (MI)
Kyoto U (Japan)
Lausanne, U of (Switzerland)

Louisiana State U
Massachusetts Institute of Technology
Michigan, U of, Ann Arbor
MINES ParisTech (France)
Minnesota, U of, Twin Cities
Missouri, U of, St. Louis
Nebraska, U of
North Carolina, U of, Chapel Hill
North Carolina, U of, Charlotte
North Dakota State U
Northwestern U (IL)
Ohio University
Pennsylvania, U of
Pittsburg State U (KS)
Princeton U (NJ)
Purdue U (IN)
Queensland, U of (Australia)

Quinnipiac C (CT)
San Francisco, U of (CA)
Seoul National U (Korea)
Southern California, U of
Stanford U (CA)
Stetson U (FL)
Texas A & M U, College Station
Texas Tech U
Texas, U of, Austin
Tokyo, U of (Japan)
Tsinghua U (China)
Tufts U (MA)
University College, Dublin (Ireland)
U.S. Air Force Academy (CO)
Western Illinois U
Yale U (CT)

Source: *College Finder* research including *Fortune Magazine*, Times Higher Education
(timeshighereducation.co.uk), TIME (time.com), and *U.S. News & World Report*

Alma Maters of News and TV Personalities

Tim Allen: Western Michigan U
Vanessa Bayer: Pennsylvania, U of
Wolf Blitzer: New York, State U of, Buffalo
Julie Bowen: Brown U (RI)
Tucker Carlson: Trinity C (CT)
Drew Carey: Kent State U (OH)
Steven Colbert: Northwestern U (IL)
Anderson Cooper: Yale U (CT)
Barbara Corcoran: St. Thomas Aquinas C (NY)
Katie Couric: Virginia, U of
Carson Cressley: Gettysburg C (PA)
Terry Crews: Western Michigan U
Peter Dinklage: Bennington C (VT)
Adam Driver: Juilliard School (NY)
Lena Dunham: Oberlin C (OH)
Jimmy Fallon: St. Rose, C of (NY)
Bryant Gumbel: Bates C (ME)
Chris Hayes: Brown U (RI)
Arianna Huffington: Cambridge, U of (United Kingdom)
Colin Jost: Harvard U (MA)
Jimmy Kimmel: Arizona State U and Nevada, U of, Las Vegas
John Krasinski: Brown U (RI)
Padma Lakshmi: Clark U (MA)
Matt Lauer: Ohio U, Athens
Norman Lear: Emerson C (MA)
Jim Lehrer: Victoria C (TX)
Jay Leno: Emerson C (MA)
Julia Louis-Dreyfus: Northwestern U (IL)
Bill Maher: Cornell U (NY)
Chris Matthews: Holy Cross, C of the (MA)
Phillip "Dr. Phil" McGraw: Tulsa U (FL)

Jim McKay: Loyola C (MD)
Kate McKinnon: Columbia U (NY)
Bobby Moynihan: Connecticut, U of
David Muir: Ithaca C (NY)
Conan O'Brien: Harvard U (MA)
Kevin O'Leary: Waterloo, U of (Canada)
Bill O'Reilly: Boston U (MA) and Marist C (NY)
Scott Pelley: Texas Tech U
Regis Philbin: Notre Dame, U of (IN)
Amy Pohler: Boston C (MA)
Mr. Rogers: Rollins C (FL)
Diane Sawyer: Louisville U (KY)
Amy Schumer: Towson U (MD)
Jerry Seinfeld: New York, City U of, Queens C
Jon Stewart: William & Mary, C of (VA)
Eric Stonestreet: Kansas State U
Cecily Strong: California Institute of the Arts
Greta Van Susteren: Wisconsin, U of, Madison
Chuck Todd: George Washington U (DC)
Daniel Tosh: Central Florida, U of
Alex Trebek: Ottawa, U of (Canada)
Barbara Walters: Sarah Lawrence C (NY)

Colleges and Universities Attended by U.S. Presidents

John Adams: Harvard U (MA)
John Quincy Adams: Leiden U (The Netherlands) and Harvard U (MA)
Chester A. Arthur: Union C (NY)
James Buchanan: Dickinson C (PA)
George H.W. Bush: Yale U (CT)
George W. Bush: Yale U (CT) and Harvard Business School (MA)
Jimmy Carter: U.S. Naval Academy (MD)
Grover Cleveland: none
Bill Clinton: Georgetown U (DC); Oxford, U of (United Kingdom); and Yale Law School
    (CT)
Calvin Coolidge: Amherst C (MA)
Dwight D. Eisenhower: U.S. Military Academy (NY)
Millard Fillmore: none
Gerald Ford: Michigan, U of, Ann Arbor, and Yale Law School (CT)
James A. Garfield: Williams C (MA)
Ulysses S. Grant: U.S. Military Academy (NY)
Warren G. Harding: Ohio Central C
Benjamin Harrison: Miami U (OH)
William Henry Harrison: Hampden-Sydney C (VA) and Pennsylvania, U of, School of
    Medicine
Rutherford B. Hayes: Kenyon C (OH) and Harvard Law School (MA)
Herbert Hoover: Stanford U (CA)
Andrew Jackson: none
Thomas Jefferson: William & Mary, C of (VA)
Andrew Johnson: none
Lyndon Johnson: Texas State U (then known as Southwest Texas State Teachers C)
John F. Kennedy: Harvard U (MA)
Abraham Lincoln: none
James Madison: Princeton U (NJ)

William McKinley: Allegheny C (PA)
James Monroe: William & Mary, C of (VA)
Richard Nixon: Whittier C (CA) and Duke U School of Law (NC)
Barack Obama: Columbia U (NY) and Harvard Law School (MA)
Franklin Pierce: Bowdoin C (ME) and Northampton Law School (MA)
James Polk: North Carolina, U of, Chapel Hill
Ronald Reagan: Eureka C (IL)
Franklin D. Roosevelt: Harvard U (MA)
Theodore Roosevelt: Harvard U (MA)
William Howard Taft: Yale U (CT) and Cincinnati, U of, College of Law
Zachary Taylor: none
Harry S. Truman: Kansas, U of, School of Law (withdrew)
Donald J. Trump: Pennsylvania, U of
John Tyler: William & Mary, C of (VA)
Martin Van Buren: none
George Washington: none
Woodrow Wilson: Princeton U (NJ) and Johns Hopkins U (MD)

Source: *College Finder* research. The institutions listed may be the undergraduate or graduate school attended. Some individuals attended, but did not graduate from, the institution listed. Schools from which an individual transferred to another institution have not been included. Although this information has been researched, this list may best be seen as an indication of the range of colleges attended by notable persons.

Alma Maters of Sports Personalities

Bill Belichick: Wesleyan U (CT)
Brandi Chastain: Santa Clara U (CA)
Roger Clemens: Texas, U of, Austin
Stephen Curry: Davidson C (NC)
Kevin Durant: Texas, U of, Austin
Mia Hamm: North Carolina, U of Chapel Hill
Grant Hill: Duke U (NC)
Brittney Griner: Baylor U (TX)
Magic Johnson: Michigan State U
Michael Jordan: North Carolina, U of, Chapel Hill
Jackie Joyner-Kersee: California, U of, Los Angeles
Lisa Leslie: Southern California, U of
Marshawn Lynch: California, U of, Berkeley
Eli Manning: Mississippi, U of
Jim McKay: Loyola C (MD)
Manny Pacquiao: Notre Dame of Dadiangas U (Philippines)
Arnold Palmer: Wake Forest U (NC)
Pete Rozelle: Compton Community C (CA)
Annika Sorenstam: Arizona, U of
Jordan Spieth: Texas, U of, Austin
Breanna Stewart: Connecticut, U of
Bubba Watson: Faulkner State Community C (AL) and Georgia, U of
J.J. Watt: Wisconsin, U of, Madison

Alma Maters of Well-Known People

Kofi Annan: Macalester C (MN)
Steve Ballmer: Harvard U (MA)
Joe Biden: Delaware, U of
Michael Bloomberg: Johns Hopkins U (MD)
Garth Brooks: Oklahoma State U
Chris Brown: Franklin & Marshall C (PA)
Warren Buffet: Nebraska, U of
Ken Burns: Hampshire C (MA)
Steve Carell: Denison U (OH)
Chris Christie: Delaware, U of
Hillary Rodham Clinton: Wellesley C (MA)
Kenneth Cole: Emory U (GA)
Tim Cook: Auburn U (AL) and Duke U (NC)
Francis Ford Coppola: California, U of, Los Angeles
Mark Cuban: Indiana U, Bloomington
Clarence Darrow: Allegheny C (PA)
William O. Douglas: Whitman C (WA)
Michael Eisner: Denison U (OH)
William Ford, Jr.: Princeton U (NJ)
Milton Friedman: Rutgers U, New Brunswick (NJ)
Rudolph Giuliani: Manhattan C (NY)
John Glenn: Muskingum U (OH)
Amy Grant: Vanderbilt U (TN)
Matt Groening: Evergreen State C (WA)
Herbie Hancock: Grinnell C (IA)
Jack Hanna: Muskingum C (OH)
John Marshall Harlan: Centre C (KY)
Enrique Iglesias: Miami, U of (FL)
Caitlin Jenner: Graceland U (IA)
James Earl Jones: Michigan, U of, Ann Arbor
Mike Judge: California, U of, San Diego
Mindy Kaling: Dartmouth C (NH)
Toby Keith: Villanova U (PA)
Francis Scott Key: St. John's C (MD)
Coretta Scott King: Antioch C (OH)
Martin Luther King, Jr.: Morehouse C (GA)
Calvin Klein: Fashion Institute of Technology (NY)
Phil Knight: Oregon, U of
Spike Lee: Indiana U, Bloomington
John Legend: Pennsylvania, U of
Monica Lewinsky: Lewis & Clark C (OR)
Rush Limbaugh: Southeast Missouri State U
George Lucas: Southern California, U of
Bill Maher: Cornell U (NY)
J. Willard Marriott: Weber State U (UT)
Thurgood Marshall: Howard U (DC)
Mitch McConnell: Kentucky, U of
W. James McNerney, Jr.: Yale U (CT)
Lin-Manuel Miranda: Wesleyan U (CT)
Moby: Connecticut, U of
Jim Morrison: California, U of, Los Angeles
John Muir: Wisconsin, U of, Madison
Willie Nelson: Baylor U (TX)

Steven R. Antonoff

Frank Ocean: Louisiana, U of, Lafayette
Sandra Day O'Connor: Stanford U (CA)
Trey Parker: Colorado, U of, Boulder
Ross Perot: Texarkana Junior C (TX)
Colin Powell: George Washington U (DC)
Condoleezza Rice: Denver, U of (CO)
Marco Rubio: Florida, U of
Bernie Sanders: New York, City U of, Brooklyn, and Chicago, U of (IL)
M. Night Shyamalan: New York U
B.F. Skinner: Hamilton C (NY)
Aaron Sorkin: Syracuse U (NY)
Kate Spade: Arizona State U
Mary Steenburgen: Hendrix C (AR)
Howard Stern: Boston U (MA)
John Paul Stevens: Northwestern U (IL)
Ben Stiller: California, U of, Los Angeles
Matt Stone: Colorado, U of, Boulder
George Straight: Southwest Texas State U
Clarence Thomas: Yale U (CT)
Christie Whitman: Wheaton C (MA)
Frank Lloyd Wright: Wisconsin, U of, Madison

Source: *College Finder* research

Largest Private Gifts to Higher Education

Starting with the highest donation of $101 million or more, the following list is organized by college, benefactor, amount of the gift (and designation, if known), and year of the donation.

- Vedanta U (India): Anil Agarwal Foundation; $1 billion endowment to establish the university; 2006
- The Broad Institute of Massachusetts Institute of Technology and Harvard U (MA): Ted Stanley; $650 million; 2014
- California Institute of Technology: Gordon and Betty Moore and the Gordon and Betty Moore Foundation; $600 million, consisting of $300 million over 5 years and $300 million over 10 years; 2001
- Olin C (MA): F.W. Olin Foundation; $460 million to establish the college; 1997
- National Taiwan U: Terry Gou; $454.5 million to establish a cancer-care clinic and conduct cancer research; 2007
- The Broad Institute of Massachusetts Institute of Technology and Harvard U (MA): Eli and Edythe L. Broad; $400 million; 2008
- Columbia U (NY): John W. Kluge; $400 million; 2007
- Harvard U (MA): John A. Paulson; $400 million; 2015
- Stanford U (CA): Philip H. Knight; $400 million; 2016
- Stanford U (CA): William and Flora Hewlett Foundation; $400 million; 2001
- Rensselaer Polytechnic Institute (NY): anonymous donor; $360 million; 2001
- Cornell U (NY): Atlantic Philanthropies; $350 million; 2011
- Harvard U (MA): Morningside Foundation (family foundation of the late T.H. Chan); $350 million; 2014
- Johns Hopkins U (MD): Michael R. Bloomberg; $350 million; 2013
- Massachusetts Institute of Technology: Patrick J. and Lore Harp McGovern; estimated at $350 million over 20 years; 2000

- Arkansas, U of, Fayetteville: Walton Family Charitable Support Foundation; $300 million; 2002
- Chicago, U of (IL): Booth Family Trust; $300 million; 2008
- Princeton U (NJ): William H. Scheide; collection of rare books and manuscripts valued at $300 million; 2015
- Emory U (GA): The Lettie Pate Evans, Joseph B. Whitehead, and Robert W. Woodruff Foundations; $295 million; 1996
- Carnegie Mellon U (PA): William S. Dietrich II; $265 million; 2011
- Emory U (GA): Robert W. Woodruff Foundation; $261.5 million; 2006
- Jacobs U (Germany): Jacobs Foundation; $254 million (200 million euros); 2006
- Colorado, U of: William T. Coleman III and Claudia Coleman; $250 million; 2001
- Cornell U (NY) Weill Medical C: Sanford I. and Joan Weill; $250 million; 2007
- New York U: Sir Harold Acton; a 57-acre Italian estate, a collection of Renaissance art, and at least $25 million in cash for a total estimated value of at least $250 million and perhaps as much as $500 million; 1994
- Yale U (CT): Charles B. Johnson; $250 million; 2013
- Texas, U of, Austin: John A. (Jack) Jackson; $232 million; 2002
- Pennsylvania, U of: Raymond G. and Ruth Perelman; $225 million; 2011
- Kansas State U Foundation, Oklahoma State U Foundation, and Oklahoma, U of, Foundation: Dolese Bros. Company; $210 million, divided evenly among the three recipient institutions; 2013
- Ave Maria U (FL): Thomas S. Monaghan; $200 million to establish the university; 2002
- Baylor U (TX): anonymous donor; estimated $200 million; 2010
- California, U of, Los Angeles, David Geffen School of Medicine: David Geffen; $200 million; 2002
- California, U of, Los Angeles: Lincy Foundation; $200 million; 2011
- Claremont McKenna C (CA): Robert A. Day; $200 million; 2007
- Columbia U (NY): Dawn M. Greene and the Jerome L. Greene Foundation; $200 million; 2006
- Columbia U (NY): Mortimer B. Zuckerman; $200 million; 2012
- Michigan, U of, Ann Arbor: Stephen M. Ross; $200 million; 2013
- New York U: Leon Levy Foundation; $200 million to create an institute on the ancient world; 2006
- Southern California, U of: David and Dana Dornsife; $200 million; 2011
- Southern California, U of: Lawrence J. Ellison; $200 million; 2016
- California, U of, San Francisco: Weill Family Foundation and Joan and Sanford I. Weill; $185 million; 2016
- Vanderbilt U (TN): Ingram Charitable Fund; $178 million; 1998
- Southern California, U of: George Lucas Family Foundation; $175 million to establish a new film school; 2006
- Oklahoma State U: T. Boone Pickens; $165 million; 2006
- Stanford U (CA): John Arrillaga; $151 million; 2013
- California, U of, San Francisco: anonymous donor; $150 million; 2007
- Harvard U (MA): Kenneth Griffin; $150 million; 2014
- Johns Hopkins U (MD): Sidney Kimmel; $150 million; 2001
- New York U: Julius Silver; $150 million; 2002
- New York, State U of, Stony Brook: Simons Foundation; $150 million; 2011
- Southern California, U of: W.M. Keck Foundation; $150 million; 2011
- Texas, U of, M.D. Anderson Cancer Center: Khalifa Bin Zayed al-Nahyan Foundation; $150 million; 2011
- Yale U (CT): Stephen A. Schwarzman; $150 million; 2015

Steven R. Antonoff

- Polytechnic Institute of New York U: Donald and Mildred Topp Othmer; $144.2 million; 1998
- Lesley U (MA): Trusts created by Frank C. Doble; $136 million; 2008
- Tufts U (MA): Trusts created by Frank C. Doble; $136 million; 2008
- Cornell U (NY) and Technion Institute of Technology (Israel): Irwin Mark Jacobs and Joan Klein Jacobs; $133 million for Cornell-Technion campus in New York City; 2013
- DePauw U (IN): Ruth Clark and Philip Forbes Holton; $128 million; 1997
- Harvard U (MA): Hansjörg Wyss; $125 million; 2008
- Harvard U (MA): Hansjörg Wyss; $125 million; 2013
- Louisiana State U, Baton Rouge: Claude B. (Doc) Pennington; $125 million; 1981
- Nebraska, U of, Lincoln: Mildred Topp Othmer; $125 million; 1998
- Pittsburgh, U of (PA): William S. Dietrich II; $125 million; 2011
- Utah, U of: Jon M. Huntsman; $125 million; 2000
- LaGrange C (GA) and Mercer U (GA): Remer H. and Emily Fisher Crum; $123 million; 2000
- Oxford, U of, Rhodes Trust (United Kingdom): John H. and Marcy McCall MacBain; $120 million; 2013
- Pennsylvania, U of: Walter H. Annenberg; $120 million; 1993
- Southern California, U of: Walter H. Annenberg; $120 million; 1993
- Massachusetts Institute of Technology: Samuel Tak Lee; $118 million; 2015
- Nanyang Technological U (Singapore): Lee Foundation; $117 million; 2011
- Oxford, U of (United Kingdom): Leonard Blavatnik; $117 million; 2010
- Oxford, U of (United Kingdom): Michael Moritz and Harriet Heyman; $116 million; 2012
- Furman U (SC): Estate of John D. Hollingsworth Jr.; $115 million; 2001
- California, U of, Berkeley: William and Flora Hewlett Foundation; $113 million; 2007
- Southern California, U of: Alfred E. Mann; $112.5 million; 1998
- California, U of, San Diego: Irwin M. and Joan Jacobs; $110 million; 2003
- Michigan, U of, Ann Arbor: Charles T. Mungor; $110 million; 2013
- Southern California, U of: John and Julie Mork; $110 million; 2011
- Southern California, U of: W.M. Keck Foundation; $110 million; 1999
- Thomas Jefferson U (PA): Sidney Kimmel Foundation; $110 million; 2014
- Emory U (GA): Robert W. Woodruff; $105 million; 1979
- Indiana U, Bloomington: Lilly Endowment; $105 million; 2000
- New York U: Jan T. Vilcek; $105 million; 2005
- Ohio U, Athens: Osteopathic Heritage Foundations; $105 million; 2011
- Stanford U (CA): Philip H. Knight; $105 million; 2006
- Washington, U of: Bill & Melinda Gates Foundation; $105 million; 2007
- California, U of, San Francisco: Catellus Development Corporation; $101.3 million; 1999
- Northwestern U (IL): Roberta Buffett Elliott; $101 million; 2015
- Princeton U (NJ): Peter B. Lewis; $101 million; 2005

Source: *Chronicle of Higher Education,* May 2016

Colleges Where the Greatest Percentage of Alumni Contribute

These are the colleges that had the highest percentage of alumni donors with respect to the college's total alumni of record.

Wellesley C (MA): 53.44%
Williams C (MA): 50.94%
Northwestern, U of (MN): 48.83%
Amherst C (MA): 46.06%
Bowdoin C (ME): 45.27%
Holy Cross, C of the (MA): 45.20%
Davidson C (NC): 45.19%
Carleton C (MN): 43.97%
Bates C (ME): 43.52%
Colgate U (NY): 41.82%
Haverford C (PA): 41.68%
Transylvania U (KY): 40.67%
Hamilton C (NY): 40.16%
Centre C (KY): 39.30%
Spelman C (GA): 39.14%
Swarthmore C (PA): 39.07%
Washington & Lee U (VA): 38.25%
Claremont McKenna C (CA): 37.93%
Randolph-Macon C (VA): 37.63%
Pomona C (CA): 36.88%
Kenyon C (OH): 36.50%
Colby C (ME): 36.40%
Idaho, C of: 35.99%
Rhodes C (TN): 35.02%
Middlebury C (VT): 34.88%

Wesleyan U (CT): 34.28%
Whitman C (WA): 34.14%
Union C (NY): 32.74%
Lafayette C (PA): 32.24%
Wabash C (IN): 32.13%
Hampden-Sydney C (VA): 32.02%
Grinnell C (IA): 30.31%
Macalester C (MN): 30.09%
Bryn Mawr C (PA): 29.04%
Harvey Mudd C (CA): 28.88%
Vassar C (NY): 27.90%
Agnes Scott C (GA): 27.88%
Bucknell U (PA): 27.59%
Knox C (IL): 27.30%
Smith C (MA): 27.30%
South, U of the (TN): 27.27%
Juniata C (PA): 27.22%
St. Mary's C (IN): 27.06%
Mt. Holyoke C (MA): 26.65%
Hobart & William Smith C (NY): 26.58%
Dickinson C (PA): 26.41%
Lawrence U (WI): 26.28%
Trinity C (CT): 26.22%
Oberlin C (OH): 25.95%
Ripon C (WI): 25.05%

Source: 2014 Voluntary Support of Education, Council for Aid to Education. Used with permission.

Colleges Raising the Most Money From Alumni

Harvard U (MA): $392,576,000
Cornell U (NY): $298,294,137
Stanford U (CA): $271,568,402
Pennsylvania, U of: $236,576,446
Michigan, U of, Ann Arbor: $197,293,730
Yale U (CT): $164,259,416
Notre Dame, U of (IN): $163,396,281
Massachusetts Institute of Technology: $153,392,401
Chicago, U of (IL): $152,368,560
Texas A & M U, College Station: $135,593,693
Washington, U of, Seattle: $119,430,614
Columbia U (NY): $117,539,687
Princeton U (NJ): $117,317,153
Colby C (ME): $116,678,557
Texas, U of, Austin: $100,019,822
Duke U (NC): $87,251,015
Northwestern U (IL): $87,092,912
California, U of, Berkeley: $79,489,981

Pennsylvania State U, University Park: $79,016,771
Southern California, U of: $77,069,434

Source: 2014 Voluntary Support of Education, Council for Aid to Education. Used with permission.

Colleges Raising the Most Money From Alumni (on a Per Student Basis)

Deep Springs C (CA): $69,397
Colby C (ME): $64,109
Amherst C (MA): $20,934
Harvard U (MA): $18,435
Virginia Military Institute: $17,272
Stanford U (CA): $17,102
Bowdoin C (ME): $15,382
Princeton U (NJ): $14,639
Wellesley C (MA): $13,980
Cornell U (NY): $13,814
Massachusetts Institute of Technology: $13,573
Yale U (CT): $13,565
Notre Dame, U of (IN): $13,416
California Institute of Technology: $12,818
Washington & Lee U (VA): $12,214
Lafayette C (PA): $11,435
Bryn Mawr C (PA): $11,121
Chicago, U of (IL): $10,557
Dartmouth C (NH): $10,319
Vassar C (NY): $9,993

Source: 2014 Voluntary Support of Education, Council for Aid to Education. Used with permission.

Colleges Raising the Most Money From Corporations

Texas, U of, Austin: $279,010,894
Southern California, U of: $157,192,147
Northwestern U (IL): $148,901,079
Colorado, U of, Boulder: $117,653,914
Ohio State U, Columbus: $114,538,033
Stanford U (CA): $101,040,370
Harvard U (MA): $91,470,000
Indiana U, Bloomington: $85,780,176
Minnesota, U of, Twin Cities: $77,948,794
Utah, U of: $76,403,623
Cincinnati, U of (OH): $73,543,072
Massachusetts Institute of Technology: $66,199,898
Florida, U of: $64,851,301
California, U of, Berkeley: $62,744,416
Pennsylvania, U of: $62,069,534
Texas A & M U, College Station: $60,656,006
Kansas State U: $59,199,065
Duke U (NC): $58,564,550
Washington, U of, Seattle: $55,123,222
California, U of, Los Angeles: $48,558,663

Source: 2014 Voluntary Support of Education, Council for Aid to Education. Used with permission.

Colleges Raising the Most Money From Corporations (on a Per Student Basis)

Texas, U of, MD Anderson Cancer Center: $62,651
Oregon Health & Science U: $7,847
Northwestern U (IL): $6,896
Stanford U (CA): $6,363
California, U of, San Francisco: $6,041
Massachusetts Institute of Technology: $5,858
Texas, U of, Austin: $5,360
Morehouse School of Medicine (GA): $4,928
Harvard U (MA): $4,295
Southern California, U of: $3,915
Texas, U of, Southwestern Medical Center: $3,876
Duke U (NC): $3,635
Yale U (CT): $3,427
Amherst C (MA): $3,133
Ringling C of Art & Design (FL): $2,977
Central Baptist C (AR): $2,628
Pennsylvania, U of: $2,502
Wooster, C of (OH): $2,392
Kansas State U: $2,390
Utah, U of: $2,380

Source: 2014 Voluntary Support of Education, Council for Aid to Education. Used with permission.

Colleges With the Largest Endowments

Harvard U (MA): $35,556,718,000
Yale U (CT): $23,858,561,000
Stanford U (CA): $21,446,006,000
Princeton U (NJ): $20,995,517,522
Massachusetts Institute of Technology: $12,425,131,000
Texas, U of, Austin: $11,340,759,971
Texas A & M U, College Station: $10,540,226,250
Michigan, U of, Ann Arbor: $9,731,538,493
Northwestern U (IL): $9,704,003,244
Pennsylvania, U of: $9,582,335,257
Columbia U (NY): $9,223,047,000
Notre Dame, U of (IN): $8,189,096,000
Chicago, U of (IL): $7,545,544,000
Washington U (MO): $6,719,449,000
Duke U (NC): $6,234,416,254
Emory U (GA): $6,039,139,944
Cornell U (NY): $5,806,543,769
Rice U (TX): $5,528,000,000
Southern California, U of: $4,593,014,000
Dartmouth C (NH): $4,468,000,000

Source: 2014 Voluntary Support of Education, Council for Aid to Education. Used with permission.

Colleges With the Largest Endowments (on a Per Student Basis)

Texas, U of, MD Anderson Cancer Center: $4,054,891
Princeton U (NJ): $2,619,855
Texas, U of, Health Center at Tyler: $2,473,640
Princeton Theological Seminary (NJ): $2,083,029
Yale U (CT): $1,970,316
Harvard U (MA): $1,669,721
Stanford U (CA): $1,350,589
Pomona C (CA): $1,285,297
Swarthmore C (PA): $1,223,383
Amherst C (MA): $1,182,180
Massachusetts Institute of Technology: $1,099,472
Olin C (MA): $1,071,345
Grinnell C (IA): $1,063,057
Williams C (MA): $1,021,539
California Institute of Technology: $947,869
Rice U (TX): $834,037
Wellesley C (MA): $810,131
Deep Springs C (CA): $789,964
Cooper Union (NY): $761,686
Union Presbyterian Seminary (VA): $737,463

Source: 2014 Voluntary Support of Education, Council for Aid to Education. Used with permission.

Colleges Raising the Most Money From Foundations

Harvard U (MA): $374,471,000
Johns Hopkins U (MD): $289,458,554
California, U of, Los Angeles: $237,922,522
California, U of, San Francisco: $237,472,591
Columbia U (NY): $219,638,777
New York U: $202,660,285
Emory U (GA): $190,364,169
Stanford U (CA): $186,134,779
Duke U (NC): $171,783,877
Southern California, U of: $169,936,320
California, U of, Berkeley: $165,752,119
Yale U (CT): $157,865,187
Chicago, U of (IL): $154,922,133
Washington, U of, Seattle: $142,517,993
Michigan, U of, Ann Arbor: $130,667,306
Massachusetts Institute of Technology: $130,486,865
Pacific, U of the (CA): $117,215,273
Washington U (MO): $112,977,440
Texas, U of, Austin: $103,420,885
Indiana U, Bloomington: $102,339,152

Source: 2014 Voluntary Support of Education, Council for Aid to Education. Used with permission.

Colleges Raising the Most Money From Foundations (on a Per Student Basis)

Texas, U of, MD Anderson Cancer Center: $213,997
California, U of, San Francisco: $49,900
California Institute of Technology: $30,107
Texas, U of, Southwestern Medical Center: $29,092
Texas, U of, Health Center at Tyler: $26,434
Wellesley C (MA): $22,244
Pacific, U of the (CA): $18,255
Harvard U (MA): $17,585
Claremont McKenna C (CA): $17,257
Johns Hopkins U (MD): $13,572
Baylor C of Medicine (TX): $13,471
Davidson C (NC): $13,098
Yale U (CT): $13,037
Emory U (GA): $12,889
Oregon Health & Science U: $12,868
Berea C (KY): $12,836
Stanford U (CA): $11,722
Massachusetts Institute of Technology: $11,546
Chicago, U of (IL): $10,734
Duke U (NC): $10,663

Source: 2014 Voluntary Support of Education, Council for Aid to Education. Used with permission.

Colleges Raising the Most Money From Individuals Who Are Not Alumni

Stanford U (CA): $303,812,680
California, U of, San Francisco: $146,209,141
Cornell U (NY): $142,590,123
Southern California, U of: $131,686,066
New York U: $125,667,630
Hillsdale C (MI): $96,876,090
Harvard U (MA): $94,010,000
Oregon Health & Science U: $83,335,449
Pennsylvania, U of: $82,778,001
California, U of, Los Angeles: $79,908,792
Louisiana State U & Agricultural & Mechanical: $76,458,719
Johns Hopkins U (MD): $74,623,445
Texas, U of, MD Anderson Cancer Center: $63,151,681
Washington U (MO): $61,010,650
Columbia U (NY): $56,741,871
Duke U (NC): $55,572,069
Chicago, U of (IL): $51,821,316
Charleston, C of (SC): $49,399,907
Nebraska, U of, Lincoln: $49,329,915
Indiana U, Bloomington: $48,823,987

Source: 2014 Voluntary Support of Education, Council for Aid to Education. Used with permission.

Steven R. Antonoff

Colleges Raising the Most Money From Individuals Who Are Not Alumni (on a Per Student Basis)

Texas, U of, MD Anderson Cancer Center: $207,055
Hillsdale C (MI): $65,813
California, U of, San Francisco: $30,723
Oregon Health & Science U: $29,364
Texas, U of, Health Center at Tyler: $22,374
Bethany Theological Seminary (IN): $21,401
San Francisco Conservatory of Music (CA): $19,219
Stanford U (CA): $19,133
St. Meinrad Seminary & School of Theology: $18,485
Concordia Seminary (MO): $17,908
Texas, U of, Southwestern Medical Center: $16,933
Philips Theological Seminary (OK): $13,506
Anabaptist Mennonite Biblical Seminary (IN): $12,638
Union Presbyterian Seminary (VA): $12,613
Luther Seminary (MN): $10,748
Wesleyan C (GA): $9,045
Ringling C of Art & Design (FL): $8,434
Catawba C (MO): $8,161
California Institute of Technology: $7,068
Cornell U (NY): $6,604

Source: 2014 Voluntary Support of Education, Council for Aid to Education. Used with permission.

Colleges Raising the Most Money Through Voluntary Support

Harvard U (MA): $1,155,610,000
Stanford U (CA): $928,458,429
Southern California, U of: $731,932,611
Northwestern U (IL): $616,351,194
Johns Hopkins U (MD): $614,606,146
Cornell U (NY): $546,087,720
Texas, U of, Austin: $529,391,225
Pennsylvania, U of: $483,569,483
Washington, U of, Seattle: $478,071,702
Columbia U (NY): $469,968,713
New York U: $455,718,216
California, U of, San Francisco: $444,938,223
Duke U (NC): $437,381,590
Michigan, U of, Ann Arbor: $432,596,374
Yale U (CT): $430,308,592
California, U of, Los Angeles: $430,275,827
Chicago, U of (IL): $405,350,038
California, U of Berkeley: $389,934,620
Massachusetts Institute of Technology: $375,030,964
Indiana U, Bloomington: $341,312,881

Source: 2014 Voluntary Support of Education, Council for Aid to Education. Used with permission.

Colleges Raising the Most Money Through Voluntary Support (on a Per Student Basis)

Texas, U of, MD Anderson Cancer Center: $535,041
California, U of, San Francisco: $93,494
Deep Springs C (CA): $82,862
Hillsdale C (MI): $77,620
Colby C (ME): $71,227
Stanford U (CA): $58,471
Harvard U (MA): $54,267
Oregon Health & Science U: $54,010
Texas, U of, Southwestern Medical Center: $53,888
California Institute of Technology: $51,322
Texas, U of, Health Center at Tyler: $49,458
Wellesley C (MA): $41,857
Dartmouth C (NH): $40,199
Yale U (CT): $35,536
Bethany Theological Seminary (IN): $34,444
Massachusetts Institute of Technology: $33,186
Amherst C (MA): $31,724
Princeton U (NJ): $30,064
Claremont McKenna C (CA): $29,522
Johns Hopkins U (MD): $28,818

Source: 2014 Voluntary Support of Education, Council for Aid to Education. Used with permission.

Colleges With the Highest Voluntary Support as a Percentage of Expenditures

1. Colby C (ME): 133.8%
2. Hillsdale C (MI): 127.7%
3. Deep Springs C (CA): 122.6%
4. Concordia Seminary (MO): 94.9%
5. Louisiana Tech U: 87.5%
6. Central Baptist C (AR): 83.9%
7. Harrisburg Area Community C, Harrisburg (PA): 80.0%
8. Emory & Henry C (VA): 76.0%
9. Bethany Theological Seminary (IN): 74.8%
10. Virginia Military Institute: 72.3%
11. Zane State C (OH): 65.9%
12. St. Meinrad Seminary & School of Theology (IN): 65.2%
13. Philips Theological Seminary (OK): 54.7%
14. Spring Hill C (AL): 54.5%
15. Anabaptist Mennonite Biblical (IN): 54.2%
16. Wesleyan C (GA): 53.4%
17. Lorain County Community C (OH): 52.6%
18. Luther Seminary (MN): 49.2%
19. U.S. Military Academy (NY): 46.4%
20. Judson C (AL): 45.8%

Source: 2014 Voluntary Support of Education, Council for Aid to Education. Used with permission.

CHAPTER NINE
RESOURCES

The Experts' Choice: Best College Planning Guidebooks

1. *Fiske Guide to Colleges* by Edward Fiske
2. *The College Finder* by Steven Antonoff
3. *Colleges That Change Lives* by Loren Pope
4. *College Handbook* by The College Board
5. *Rugg's Recommendations on the Colleges* by Frederick Rugg
6. *Admission Matters: What Students and Parents Need to Know About Getting Into College* by Sally P. Springer, Joyce Vining Morgan, and Jon Reider
7. *The Insider's Guide to Colleges* by the staff of the *Yale Daily News*
8. *College Match* by Steven Antonoff
9. *The Best Colleges* by The Princeton Review
10. *Profiles of American Colleges* by Barron's College Division
11. *College Admission: From Application to Acceptance, Step by Step* by Robin Mamlet and Christine VanDeVelde
12. *Book of Majors* by The College Board
13. *College Admissions Data Sourcebooks* by Wintergreen Orchard House
14. *The College Solution: A Guide for Everyone Looking for the Right School at the Right Price* by Lynn O'Shaughnessy
15. *Cool Colleges: For the Hyper-Intelligent, Self-Directed, Late Blooming, and Just Plain Different* by Donald Asher

The Experts' Choice: Top College Planning Resources

1. The College Board: *collegeboard.org*
2. College Navigator: *nces.ed.gov/collegenavigator*
3. COLLEGEdata: *collegedata.com*
4. CollegeXpress: *collegexpress.com*
5. UNIGO: *unigo.com*
6. Niche: *colleges.niche.com*
7. Naviance: *naviance.com*
8. Cappex: *cappex.com*
9. College Confidential: *collegeconfidential.com*
10. Peterson's College Information: *petersons.com*
11. YOUniversityTV: *youniversitytv.com*
12. *Colleges That Change Lives* by Loren Pope
13. *The Best Colleges* by The Princeton Review
14. *U.S News & World Report*: *colleges.usnews.rankingsandreviews.com/best-colleges*

The Experts' Choice: Best Nonfinancial College Planning Websites

1. The College Board: *collegeboard.org*
2. College Navigator: *nces.ed.gov/collegenavigator*
3. COLLEGEdata: *collegedata.com*
4. UNIGO: *unigo.com*
5. Cappex: *cappex.com*
6. Niche: *colleges.niche.com*
7. Guided Path: *guidedpath.net*
8. CollegeXpress: *collegexpress.com*
9. Peterson's College Information: *petersons.com*
10. *U.S. News & World Report*: *colleges.usnews.rankingsandreviews.com/best-colleges*

The Experts' Choice: Best College List Books

Experts were asked to identify books most helpful to students in creating a list of colleges in which to apply.

1. *The College Finder* by Steven Antonoff
2. *Fiske Guide to Colleges* by Edward Fiske
3. *Rugg's Recommendations on the Colleges* by Frederick Rugg
4. *Book of Majors* by The College Board
5. *College That Change Lives* by Loren Pope
6. *The Best Colleges* by The Princeton Review
7. *Creative Colleges: A Guide for Student Actors, Artists, Dancers, Musicians and Writers* by Elaina Loveland
8. *Find the Perfect College for You: 82 Exceptional Schools That Fit Your Personality and Learning Style* by Rosalind P. Marie and C. Claire Law
9. *The Insider's Guide to Colleges* by the staff of the *Yale Daily News*

The Experts' Choice: The Top Eight College Review Guidebooks

1. *Fiske Guide to Colleges* by Edward Fiske
2. *The Best Colleges* by The Princeton Review
3. *The Insider's Guide to Colleges* by the staff of the *Yale Daily News*
4. *Colleges That Change Lives* by Loren Pope
5. *The College Finder* by Steven Antonoff
6. *America's Best Colleges for B Students: A College Guide for Students Without Straight A's* by Tamra B. Orr
7. *Profiles of American Colleges 2016* by Barron's College Division
8. *The Hidden Ivies, 2nd Edition: 50 Top Colleges—From Amherst to Williams—That Rival the Ivy League* by Howard Greene

The Experts' Choice: Best Factual Databases

1. The College Board: *collegeboard.org*
2. Individual college websites
3. Naviance: *naviance.com*
4. *College Admissions Data Sourcebooks* by Wintergreen Orchard House
5. COLLEGEdata: *collegedata.com*
6. College Navigator: *nces.ed.gov/collegenavigator*
7. *Fiske Guide to Colleges* by Edward Fiske
8. Common Data Set for individual colleges
9. NCES: *nces.ed.gov*
10. *The College Finder* by Steven Antonoff
11. *Four-Year Colleges* by Peterson's
12. *Rugg's Recommendations on the Colleges* by Frederick Rugg
13. *U.S. News & World Report: colleges.usnews.rankingsandreviews.com/best-colleges*

The Experts' Choice: Best Financial Aid Websites

1. Finaid: *finaid.org*
2. FastWeb: *fastweb.com*
3. The College Solution: *thecollegesolution.com*
4. The College Board: *collegeboard.org*
5. FAFSA: *fafsa.ed.gov*
6. Federal Student Aid: *studentaid.ed.gov*
7. COLLEGEdata: *collegedata.com*
8. Edvisors: *edvisors.com*
9. New York State HESC: *hesc.ny.gov*
10. Cappex: *cappex.com*
11. *Forbes*—America's Top Colleges: *forbes.com/top-colleges*
12. Mapping Your Future: *mappingyourfuture.org*
13. College Navigator: *nces.ed.gov/collegenavigator*
14. UNIGO: *unigo.com*

146, 147, 149, 152, 154, 167, 170, 171,
174, 175,178, 179, 180, 183, 192, 194,
199, 200, 201, 207, 219, 220, 223, 226,
227, 230, 232, 250, 251, 252, 254, 255,
257, 258, 260, 261, 262, 272, 274, 287,
291, 294, 299, 300, 301, 307, 308, 313,
315, 320, 324, 331, 340, 346, 354, 355,
366, 368, 397, 402, 410, 422, 423, 426,
427, 428, 429, 430, 431, 432, 434, 435
Creighton U, 3, 16, 36, 85, 86, 93, 95, 104,
121, 133, 135, 136, 152, 169, 192, 231,
245, 256, 271, 277, 330, 335, 350, 372
Cuesta C, 306
Culver-Stockton C, 255, 275, 276, 372
Cumberland U, 129, 275
Cumberlands, U of the, 35, 274, 275
Curry C, 9, 63, 64, 65, 68, 236, 291, 372

D

Dakota Wesleyan U, 51, 276, 372
Dallas, U of, 7, 36, 37, 39, 42, 43, 114, 154,
156, 159, 167, 182, 190, 238, 284, 372
Dartmouth C, 3, 4, 7, 8, 11, 12, 45, 49, 50,
55, 57, 60, 62, 73, 81, 89, 90, 103, 104,
111, 114, 118, 120, 136, 138, 141, 143,
146, 147, 154, 167, 170, 175, 179, 180,
185, 187, 188, 189, 190, 213, 219, 230,
242, 255, 256, 260, 262, 272, 287, 291,
294, 300, 307, 311, 315, 331, 333, 340,
346, 355, 363, 366, 393, 398, 402, 405,
410, 422, 426, 431, 432, 436
Davenport U, 130, 275, 306
Davidson C, 3, 4, 5, 6, 8, 12, 13, 14, 23, 43,
53, 55, 60, 66, 82, 94, 114, 121, 126, 141,
146, 147, 152, 167, 172, 173, 175, 178,
181, 192, 210, 214, 215, 237, 271, 287,
315, 327, 331, 332, 333, 336, 338, 347,
355, 363, 364, 365, 367, 368, 369, 370,
405, 410, 425, 430, 434
Davis & Ekins C, 308
Davis C, 46, 277
Dawson Community C, 304
Dayton, U of, 16, 36, 85, 95, 126, 128, 133,
225, 237, 271, 291, 297, 303, 335, 336,
350, 369, 372, 375, 385, 422
Daytona State C, 130, 205, 315
De Anza C, 19, 203, 298, 420
Defiance C, 9, 66, 274, 372
Delaware State U, 20, 22, 80, 130, 265, 266,
283
Delaware Valley U, 113, 162, 291, 294, 297
Delaware, U of, 49, 52, 67, 77, 90, 100, 108,
118, 125, 132, 133, 135, 139, 141, 150,
151, 155, 167, 208, 221, 246, 264, 287,
291, 296, 303, 306, 307, 319, 320, 327,
330, 332, 335, 346, 349, 350, 354, 366,
368, 369, 393, 395, 426
Delta State U, 80, 279, 282, 296, 307, 319,
395
Denison U, 3, 12, 14, 16, 73, 77, 118, 126,
138, 143, 167, 172, 174, 175, 192, 212,

214, 215, 219, 221, 222, 238, 256, 260,
291, 315, 333, 335, 336, 349, 350, 351,
352, 355, 365, 368, 370, 372, 420, 426
Denver, U of, 51, 55, 58, 63, 64, 65, 66, 71,
79, 85, 89, 104, 106, 107, 111, 126, 127,
128, 129, 137, 138, 139, 154, 167, 179,
187, 189, 190, 238, 271, 272, 284, 287,
299, 300, 303, 311, 335, 336, 337, 350,
351, 352, 354, 366, 367, 368, 372, 427
DePaul U, 36, 39, 64, 65, 68, 71, 73, 79, 85,
86, 88, 89, 92, 95, 104, 111, 125, 128,
137, 139, 143, 187, 237, 259, 260, 271,
287, 350, 351
DePauw U, 4, 14, 16, 51, 104, 118, 125, 167,
172, 175, 178, 189, 192, 212, 214, 215,
221, 222, 240, 255, 256, 257, 281, 283,
287, 330, 335, 338, 349, 354, 369, 370,
372, 375, 429
DeSales U, 36, 37, 66, 122, 130, 132, 133,
144, 212, 246, 291, 308, 330
Dickinson C, 3, 4, 16, 47, 48, 51, 55, 62, 66,
104, 114, 117, 118, 121, 137, 138, 139,
148, 154, 155, 167, 172, 174, 175, 178,
189, 192, 211, 214, 215, 225, 239, 260,
291, 313, 315, 347, 350, 352, 368, 369,
370, 372, 424, 430
Dickinson State U, 130, 179, 305
Dine C, 17, 305
Dixie State U, 33, 34, 52, 130, 314
Doane C, 172, 275, 276, 327
Dodge City Community C, 27, 304
Dordt C, 40, 42, 276, 372
Dowling C, 72, 80, 178, 282, 312
Drew U, 51, 64, 114, 118, 122, 124, 138,
143, 166, 167, 215, 244, 291, 335, 350,
351, 352, 368, 369, 372, 375, 383, 394,
399
Drexel U, 33, 47, 48, 49, 50, 52, 64, 66, 74,
79, 83, 85, 86, 88, 99, 100, 103, 106, 107,
108, 111, 115, 121, 122, 124, 125, 128,
129, 131, 132, 133, 135, 145, 178, 179,
180, 187, 200, 202, 225, 246, 254, 266,
279, 285, 287, 289, 291, 300, 315, 341,
350, 351, 372,395
Drury U, 148, 261, 281, 282, 382
Dublin City U, 298
Dublin Institute of Technology, 298
Dubuque, U of, 53, 80, 111, 274
Duke U, 3, 4, 7, 8, 9, 14, 16, 19, 43, 44, 48,
49, 50, 51, 55, 60, 61, 82, 90, 94, 96, 99,
104, 106, 110, 114, 118, 121, 123, 126,
129, 131, 133, 138, 139, 140, 141, 143,
146, 147, 149, 152, 166, 167, 170, 171,
175, 180, 183, 184, 190, 192, 194, 199,
200, 207, 208, 219, 220, 221, 226, 227,
230, 237, 247, 256, 257, 263, 271, 276,
279, 280, 282, 287, 290, 291, 300, 301,
303, 308, 311, 315, 317, 318, 333, 340,
346, 355, 363, 364, 365, 366, 367, 368,
375, 394, 398, 399, 405, 411, 422, 425,
426, 430, 431, 432, 433, 434, 435

Steven R. Antonoff

164, 167, 208, 242, 272, 273, 276, 280,
287, 292, 294, 304, 307, 318, 319, 332,
335, 398, 426
Kenyon C, 4, 5, 7, 12, 16, 34, 57, 60, 62, 71,
76, 104, 114, 141, 144, 152, 167, 172,
178, 180, 182, 192, 212, 214, 215, 219,
220, 221, 222, 223, 230, 238, 292, 315,
340, 347, 354, 362, 365, 367, 368, 369,
371, 373, 400, 413, 421, 424, 430
Keuka C, 58, 250, 292, 309, 373
King U, 41, 78, 287, 290, 373
Kutztown U, 86, 164, 283, 292, 306, 314

L

La Salle U, 36, 37, 246, 271, 330
La Verne, U of, 25, 27, 85, 86, 186, 241, 280,
321, 327
Lafayette C, 13, 23, 99, 100, 102, 103, 105,
114, 120, 136, 139, 141, 167, 212, 214,
215, 239, 273, 292, 303, 309, 315, 333,
347, 365, 371, 373, 430, 431
Lake Erie C, 94, 274, 292, 294
Lake Forest C, 53, 65, 86, 114, 143, 167,
210, 214, 215, 224, 237, 292, 298, 337,
352, 380, 394, 400
Lake Superior State U, 17, 18, 78, 130, 299
Lakehead U, 292, 309
Lamar Community C, 305
Lander U, 292
Laramie County Community C, 292, 305
Lassen C, 306
Lawrence Technological U, 19, 59, 103, 225,
275, 287
Le Moyne C, 36, 292, 337, 373, 413
Lebanon Valley C (PA), 51, 66, 68, 120, 125,
127, 133, 178, 281, 292, 373
Lees-McRae C, 53, 78, 287, 289
Lehigh U, 3, 4, 8, 56, 60, 85, 86, 89, 99, 102,
103, 120, 122, 125, 141, 167, 178, 192,
208, 212, 219, 239, 246, 254, 255, 256,
257, 273, 287, 290, 292, 309, 315, 324,
347, 365, 367, 368, 375
Lemoyne-Owen C, 281
Lenoir-Rhyne U, 51, 296
Lewis U, 36, 37, 38, 40, 72, 124, 210, 260,
314, 320, 373
Liberty U, 6, 16, 80, 86, 177, 178, 221, 248,
254, 281, 287, 292, 296, 298, 301, 303,
354
Life U, 306
Limerick, U of, 298
Limestone C, 63, 64, 66, 274, 320
Lincoln Memorial U, 130, 146, 208, 281, 329,
395
Lindenwood U, 78, 287, 289, 303, 306, 307,
316, 319, 320, 323, 336
Lindsey Wilson C, 51, 275, 287, 289, 338
Linfield C, 78, 186, 189, 247, 280, 297, 335,
351, 352, 369, 385
Linn-Benton Community C, 207, 292
Lock Haven U, 78, 130, 135, 271, 302, 314

Long Beach State U, 322
Long Island U, C.W. Post, 64, 292
Longwood U, 67, 78, 126, 164, 272, 292,
294, 327, 371
Louisiana State U, 63, 74, 75, 78, 94, 110,
116, 120, 126, 130, 133, 134, 146, 150,
155, 162, 164, 167, 192, 208, 226, 227,
244, 258, 273, 276, 279, 287, 292, 295,
297, 306, 316, 318, 319, 323, 365, 400,
423, 429, 434
Louisiana Tech U, 80, 110, 116, 187, 272,
282, 287, 319, 436
Louisiana, U of, Baton Rouge, 307, 319
Louisiana, U of, Lafayette, 80, 89, 111, 116,
287, 322, 323, 427
Louisiana, U of, Monroe, 187, 254, 296, 322,
332
Louisville, U of, 10, 61, 94, 95, 116, 122, 124,
128, 164, 171, 208, 242, 263, 271, 276,
280, 282, 287, 290, 292, 295, 301, 316,
373
Loyola Marymount U, 27, 29, 36, 57, 67, 84,
86, 88, 93, 95, 98, 109, 111, 124, 126,
142, 143, 224, 241, 309, 322, 335, 350,
351, 373, 405, 413
Loyola U (IL), 36, 38, 71, 111, 118, 122, 138,
142, 154, 167, 237, 260, 320, 335, 337,
352, 353, 373
Loyola U (LA), 36, 86, 90, 111, 125, 128,
130, 144, 172, 244, 302, 335, 337, 373
Loyola U (MD), 3, 36, 56, 86, 95, 128, 138,
167, 190, 192, 211, 273, 279, 300, 312,
351, 373
Lycoming C, 51, 56, 105, 166, 292, 297, 354
Lynchburg C, 64, 68, 78, 134, 156, 248, 292,
313, 338, 370
Lynn U, 9, 48, 63, 64, 65, 66, 67, 68, 107,
201, 242, 279, 312, 313, 314, 352, 353,
373
Lyon C, 53, 255, 275

M

Macalester C, 4, 5, 10, 23, 54, 61, 62, 76,
105, 112, 114, 117, 123, 136, 137, 145,
152, 167, 172, 173, 174, 178, 180, 182,
184, 185, 189, 192, 210, 211, 214, 215,
243, 313, 331, 333, 338, 340, 347, 354,
363, 364, 365, 368, 371, 373, 413, 426,
430
Macaulay Honors C, 302
Madison Area Technical C, 206, 309
Maine, U of, 61, 78, 79, 80, 83, 105, 106,
110, 122, 124, 127, 130, 150, 155, 164,
167, 216, 221, 247, 280, 283, 292, 294,
299, 307, 309, 319, 327, 330, 353, 371,
373, 397
Manchester U, 56, 78, 281, 373
Marian U, 36, 37, 39, 109, 275, 276, 287,
289, 329
Marietta C, 78, 167, 280

Steven R. Antonoff

Steven R. Antonoff

Steven R. Antonoff

Steven R. Antonoff

Index

Western Carolina U, 79, 116, 135, 151, 209, 237, 239, 258, 284, 289, 294, 396
Western Illinois U, 56, 79, 294, 329, 396, 423
Western Kentucky U, 66, 93, 107, 118, 120, 135, 165, 172, 209, 259, 272, 282, 294, 296
Western Michigan U, 72, 79, 80, 81, 93, 97, 105, 116, 127, 151, 169, 202, 232, 273, 294, 303, 310, 328, 420, 423
Western New England U, 67, 86, 107, 149, 261, 303, 355, 374
Western Oklahoma State C, 304
Western Ontario, U of, 120, 294, 315
Western State Colorado U, 165, 231, 277, 374
Western State U, 263, 289, 290, 310, 354
Western Texas C, 29, 306
Western U, 41, 48, 50, 81, 94, 135, 146, 176, 197, 251, 295
Westfield State U, 56, 165, 294, 329
Westminster C, 12, 54, 65, 67, 81, 123, 128, 166, 201, 248, 250, 253, 255, 310, 328, 330, 332, 333, 336, 339, 374, 383
Wharton County Junior C, 306
Whatcom Community C, 299
Wheaton C (IL), 6, 7, 16, 41, 42, 43, 54, 120, 132, 175, 191, 214, 220, 237, 297, 312, 313, 328, 330, 336, 349, 352, 354, 370, 374, 395
Wheaton C (MA), 16, 59, 82, 105, 120, 139, 143, 145, 161, 169, 172, 173, 213, 214, 215, 236, 294, 317, 333, 336, 366, 368, 370, 371, 395, 401, 427
Wheeling Jesuit U, 37, 79, 135, 307
Whitman C, 4, 7, 13, 16, 56, 67, 105, 112, 114, 127, 137, 143, 145, 157, 169, 172, 173, 175, 181, 183, 189, 193, 214, 215, 230, 255, 256, 277, 283, 289, 310, 336, 347, 354, 364, 367, 368, 369, 370, 371, 374, 388, 395, 396, 426, 430
Whittier C, 29, 54, 57, 67, 149, 166, 214, 215, 241, 249, 322, 337, 352, 353, 368, 370, 374, 396, 406, 425
Wichita State U, 79, 93, 97, 135, 165, 279, 396
Widener U, 9, 68, 107, 123, 132, 135, 246, 297, 338
Willamette U, 15, 52, 57, 105, 127, 145, 154, 169, 174, 178, 193, 215, 225, 247, 289, 336, 337, 351, 352, 355, 370, 374, 385
William & Mary, C of, 3, 6, 13, 53, 89, 96, 114, 120, 123, 127, 136, 139, 140, 153, 169, 171, 174, 175, 180, 190, 193, 209, 219, 220, 223, 245, 248, 258, 277, 286, 289, 290, 294, 303, 317, 320, 328, 330, 342, 347, 356, 364, 365, 374, 375, 393, 420, 421, 424, 425
William Paterson U, 29, 98, 124, 127, 128, 136, 165, 280, 294
William Penn U, 54, 274, 275, 276
William Peterson U, 281
William Woods U, 59, 166, 250, 275, 276

Williams C, 7, 8, 11, 12, 14, 23, 49, 50, 57, 60, 95, 104, 112, 114, 120, 127, 139, 141, 145, 146, 147, 152, 169, 171, 172, 173, 175, 180, 181, 182, 183, 184, 185, 186, 193, 213, 214, 215, 219, 224, 226, 230, 234, 264, 281, 289, 294, 312, 315, 320, 331, 333, 340, 346, 356, 364, 366, 367, 395, 422, 424, 430, 433
Wilmington C, 54, 61, 237, 283, 294
Wilson C, 54, 58, 105, 169, 186, 294, 295, 339
Winona State U, 53, 96, 107, 281
Winston-Salem State U, 21, 22, 135, 296, 329, 371
Wisconsin, U of, Eau Claire, 11, 61, 79, 132, 165, 170, 172, 258, 281, 283, 289, 294, 299, 328
Wisconsin, U of, Green Bay, 62, 165, 286, 328
Wisconsin, U of, La Crosse, 62, 135, 165, 174, 278, 294, 297, 310, 323, 329, 374
Wisconsin, U of, Madison, 3, 4, 8, 11, 14, 16, 48, 49, 50, 61, 62, 63, 77, 79, 82, 84, 90, 93, 96, 100, 101, 102, 103, 105, 107, 110, 112, 114, 116, 117, 118, 120, 121, 132, 135, 136, 137, 139, 140, 143, 146, 149, 151, 155, 169, 171, 173, 174, 175, 179, 189, 193, 208, 209, 220, 221, 224, 225, 226, 227, 231, 243, 251, 258, 259, 262, 263, 264, 272, 277, 280, 285, 286, 289, 294, 295, 298, 299, 300, 301, 303, 307, 310, 311, 316, 319, 320, 321, 323, 324, 328, 330, 339, 346, 347, 349, 365, 367, 397, 401, 406, 419, 424, 425, 426, 427
Wisconsin, U of, Milwaukee, 16, 57, 61, 62, 93, 135, 136, 137, 157, 169, 243, 255, 294, 301
Wisconsin, U of, Oshkosh, 79, 127, 132, 165, 261, 280, 283, 303, 321
Wisconsin, U of, Parkside, 314
Wisconsin, U of, Platteville, 62, 165, 267, 281, 289, 294, 320
Wisconsin, U of, River Falls, 9, 57, 163, 165, 265, 266, 294, 299, 305, 310, 355
Wisconsin, U of, Stevens Point, 79, 93, 110, 116, 143, 174, 280, 281, 283, 286, 299, 328
Wisconsin, U of, Stout, 9, 17, 86, 111, 116, 165, 298, 355
Wisconsin, U of, Superior, 140, 165, 216, 265, 266, 299
Wisconsin, U of, Whitewater, 62, 140, 165, 280, 281, 283, 289, 297, 301, 321, 323, 389
Wittenberg U, 51, 96, 105, 114, 145, 169, 238, 281, 297, 321, 349, 352, 370, 374, 395
Wofford C, 4, 6, 52, 60, 89, 105, 169, 186, 222, 237, 239, 255, 256, 294, 330, 336, 338, 369, 371, 374
Wooster, C of, 3, 13, 16, 54, 62, 63, 64, 73, 82, 105, 112, 114, 121, 127, 128, 141,

The College Finder   465

Steven R. Antonoff

Steven R. Antonoff

Steven R. Antonoff

NOTES